Gardens & landscapes in historic building conservation

This book is part of a series on historic building conservation:

Understanding Historic Building Conservation

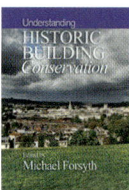

Edited by Michael Forsyth
9781405111720 hardback
9781118781593 paperback

Structures & Construction in Historic Building Conservation

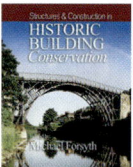

Edited by Michael Forsyth
9781405111713 hardback
9781118916223 paperback

Materials & Skills for Historic Building Conservation

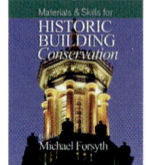

Edited by Michael Forsyth
9781405111706 hardback
9781118440575 paperback

Interior Finishes & Fittings for Historic Building Conservation

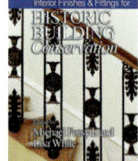

Edited by Michael Forsyth & Lisa White
9781405190220

Other books of interest:

Managing Built Heritage: the role of cultural significance
Derek Worthing & Stephen Bond
9781405119788

Conservation and Sustainability in Historic Cities
Dennis Rodwell
9781405126564

Building Pathology
Second Edition
David Watt
9781405161039

Architectural Conservation
Aylin Orbaşli
9780632040254

Urban Heritage Management: best practice from UNESCO sites worldwide
Francesco Bandarin & Ron Oers
9780470655740

Gardens & landscapes in historic building conservation

Edited by
Marion Harney
Department of Architecture & Civil Engineering
University of Bath

WILEY Blackwell

This edition first published 2014
© 2014 by John Wiley & Sons Ltd

Registered office:
John Wiley & Sons, Ltd, The Atrium, Southern Gate, Chichester,
West Sussex, PO19 8SQ, UK

Editorial offices:
9600 Garsington Road, Oxford, OX4 2DQ, UK
The Atrium, Southern Gate, Chichester, West Sussex, PO19 8SQ, UK
2121 State Avenue, Ames, Iowa 50014-8300, USA

For details of our global editorial offices, for customer services and for information about how to apply for permission to reuse the copyright material in this book please see our website at www.wiley.com/wiley-blackwell.

The right of the author to be identified as the author of this work has been asserted in accordance with the UK Copyright, Designs and Patents Act 1988.

All rights reserved. No part of this publication may be reproduced, stored in a retrieval system, or transmitted, in any form or by any means, electronic, mechanical, photocopying, recording or otherwise, except as permitted by the UK Copyright, Designs and Patents Act 1988, without the prior permission of the publisher.

Designations used by companies to distinguish their products are often claimed as trademarks. All brand names and product names used in this book are trade names, service marks, trademarks or registered trademarks of their respective owners. The publisher is not associated with any product or vendor mentioned in this book. This publication is designed to provide accurate and authoritative information in regard to the subject matter covered. It is sold on the understanding that the publisher is not engaged in rendering professional services. If professional advice or other expert assistance is required, the services of a competent professional should be sought.

Library of Congress Cataloging-in-Publication Data

Gardens & landscapes in historic building conservation / edited by Marion Harney.
  pages cm
Includes bibliographical references and index.
  ISBN 978-1-118-50814-5 (cloth)
 1. Historic gardens–Conservation and restoration. 2. Historic buildings–Conservation and restoration. I. Harney, Marion, editor of compilation. II. Title: Gardens and landscapes in historic building conservation.
  SB451.G365 2014
  712–dc23
                 2013046061

A catalogue record for this book is available from the British Library.

Wiley also publishes its books in a variety of electronic formats. Some content that appears in print may not be available in electronic books.

Cover image: Astroturf used in the long garden at Cliveden allows the visitor to experience this green enclosure as originally designed. Reproduced by permission of the National Trust: NTPL 974008
Cover design by Workhaus

Set in 9/11 pt AvenirLTStd-Roman by Toppan Best-set Premedia Limited
Printed and bound in Singapore by Markono Print Media Pte Ltd

[1 2014]

Contents

Contributors	vii
Introduction Marion Harney	xv

Part I: History and Theory

1	What is it about gardens that you want to conserve? John Dixon Hunt	1
2	The National Trust approach to garden conservation Mike Calnan	9
3	The nature of gardens and their significance John Sales	23
4	Some *Olla Podrida* from the diary of a garden historian Richard Wheeler	31
5	On design and process William Martin Wood	47
6	Evolution of principles for the conservation of gardens and designed landscapes David Jacques	55
7	Conservation of garden buildings Michael Forsyth	67
8	'Perished Perches': historic garden furniture Lisa White	79
9	The history and the future of public parks David Lambert	91
10	The history and aesthetic development of the cemetery and related conservation issues Jonathan Lovie	101

Part II: Survey and Assessment

11	Researching historic parks and gardens David Lambert	117
12	Defining significance and developing a conservation philosophy Sarah Couch	129
13	Science and craft in understanding historic gardens and their management Peter Thoday	141
14	Garden archaeology Brian Dix	149
15	Conservation arboriculture: the natural art of tree management in historic landscapes Neville Fay	153
16	The use of aerial photographs for conservation and research Helen Winton	163

Part III: Conservation and Management

17	Values in heritage management: conservation plans and beyond Kim Auston	173
18	Developing a conservation management plan Sarah Couch	181
19	Public parks and their conservation Hazel Conway	193
20	Conserving historic parks and gardens in a changing climate Jenifer White	207

21	Conserving the grey? Management of vegetation without an end-point in culturally important landscapes *James Hitchmough*	219
22	'Plants are fashioned by cultivation, man by education' *Robert Mattock*	227
23	Costing and contracts for historic gardens and landscapes *Nigel Thorne*	239
24	Constraints and working on site: some practical and contractual problems *Mike Ibbotson*	247

Part IV: The Legislative Framework

25	Designed landscapes and national designation *Fridy Duterloo-Morgan*	255
26	Conservation legislation in the UK *Colin Johns*	261
27	Historic parks and gardens: the planning system and other conservation tools *Jonathan Lovie*	271
28	The role of the Heritage Lottery Fund in the conservation of historic gardens and designed landscapes *Drew Bennellick*	283
29	Legal protection for structures, trees and wildlife *Charles Mynors*	291
30	Easy access to historic landscapes *Heather J.L. Smith*	301
31	The international context – the European Landscape Convention *Adrian Phillips*	309
32	Cultural landscapes and the World Heritage Convention *Susan Denyer*	321
33	Why should there be any international law relating to monuments and cultural landscapes? *Malcolm Forster*	331

Part V: Conservation in Action: Case Studies

34	'. . . with great art, cost, and diligens . . .' – the reconstruction of the Elizabethan Garden at Kenilworth Castle *Brian Dix*	339
35	Paradise restored – a case study exploring the restoration of three of Hestercombe's period gardens *Philip White*	345
36	Strawberry Hill, Twickenham *Marion Harney*	357
37	Stourhead – the conservation and management of a 'Living work of art' *Alan Power*	371
38	Hackfall, Yorkshire *Patrick James*	377
39	Yorkshire Sculpture Park, Wakefield *Patrick James*	385
40	The Roof Gardens, Kensington, London *Lynne Bridge*	393
41	Lowther Castle & Gardens *Dominic Cole*	405
42	Monticello *Marion Harney*	413
43	The Gardens of the Alhambra *Farhat A. Hussain*	421
44	Central Park, New York City *Michael Forsyth*	431

Index	435

Contributors

Kim Auston

Kim Auston is a landscape architect with more than 20 years' experience of working in historic landscapes. He lectures and writes on the subject and has undertaken on-the-ground restoration projects. Formerly in private practice, for the past ten years he has been English Heritage's parks and gardens specialist for the West of England. In this role he comments on planning applications affecting registered parks and gardens, advises the Heritage Lottery Fund and Natural England on grant aid, and acts as an advocate for designed landscapes within English Heritage.

Drew Bennellick

Drew Bennellick is Head of Landscape and Natural Heritage UK, for the Heritage Lottery Fund. He joined the HLF in April 2009 and sits within the Strategic and Business Development Department alongside similar posts relating to museums/archives, the built environment, and participation and learning. Drew is the Programme Director for the Parks for People and Landscape Partnerships targeted grant programmes, and is responsible for providing expert advice to the HLF Board and regional/country teams on the designed landscape and natural heritage sectors. Drew studied at Heriot Watt University in Edinburgh and is a chartered landscape architect with experience of both private and public sectors. Before HLF he was Deputy Director of English Heritage's London Region dealing with regional policy development and building partnerships with key organisations.

Lynne Bridge

Lynne Bridge is a landscape and garden designer with an international background in the corporate branding industry. A landscape design degree and MSc in the Conservation of Historic Gardens and Cultural Landscapes from the University of Bath provide credentials to run her own practice based in Bath. She currently has clients in London and Edinburgh for whom she hand-renders her own designs and plans for their private historic landscapes and gardens, negotiates planning, installs and project manages a wide range of craftsmen and contractors. Lynne is also undertaking PhD research into the architectural and landscape practices of Lancelot 'Capability' Brown.

Mike Calnan

Mike Calnan is the National Trust Head of Gardens. Joining the National Trust in 1984, initially as a Gardens Adviser, he was appointment Head of Gardens (1999), heading up the NT's professional garden community. Mike has since led the organisation's approach to garden conservation in a changing climate, set up a national centre for managing the Trust's major plant collections and developed the NT Garden Academy training programme. In overseeing the NT's 200 gardens, he encourages the close involvement of head gardeners in conservation planning and in expressing their creative talent, to ensure each garden retains its individuality.

Dominic Cole

Dominic Cole is a qualified landscape architect and Chartered Member of the Landscape Institute with some 30 years' experience. He is the designer of the Eden Project in Cornwall and was recognised for this through the Landscape Institute Peter Youngman Award 2006 and being granted Fellowship of the Institute of Horticulture. He is Chairman of the Garden History Society and Chairman of the National Trust Gardens Advisory Panel.

Hazel Conway

Dr Hazel Conway, an urban landscape historian, was formerly a technical journalist and lecturer in architectural and landscape history. She was a consultant on Crystal Palace Park, the National Maritime Museum and Greenwich Park and a number of West London parks. Her books include *Public Parks*, 1996; *People's Parks*, 1991; *Public Prospects*, 1993, with David Lambert and *Understanding Architecture*, 2005, with Rowan Roenisch. She was a member of the Urban Parks Panel of the HLF and gained her PhD for her study of Victorian parks.

Sarah Couch

Sarah Couch (MA RIBA AAGradDiplCons (gardens) HortCert (RHS)) is qualified in architecture, the conservation of historic landscapes and horticulture and specialises in historic landscape conservation. She has wide experience of working on landscape conservation projects and has written several conservation management plans (CMPs). She also lectures on landscape conservation and writing CMPs, and is a visiting lecturer on the MSc in Conservation of Historic Gardens and Cultural Landscapes, University of Bath and the MSc in Sustainable Heritage at University College London. She has worked as a Conservation Officer for the Garden History Society and has undertaken work for English Heritage and the National Trust.

Susan Denyer

Susan Denyer, FSA, is World Heritage Adviser, ICOMOS (International Council on Monuments and Sites which advises UNESCO) and Secretary-General, ICOMOS-UK. She is involved in the evaluation and state of conservation of World Heritage properties and has undertaken international missions for ICOMOS in Europe, Central Asia and the Middle East. She is an occasional lecturer at the Universities of Bath and York, and at the Architectural Association. She previously worked for the National Trust, in museums, and as lecturer, including six years in East and West Africa, and was formerly Chair of BASIN, an international network for low-cost housing. She has published widely on cultural landscapes.

Brian Dix

Brian Dix was Chief Archaeologist and head of Northamptonshire Archaeology before leaving in 1997 to specialise in the archaeology of historic parks and gardens. He has worked extensively throughout mainland Europe in addition to undertaking projects at Hampton Court Palace and Kensington Gardens, among major British sites. He contributes analysis and assessments to aid interpretation and protection, as well as carrying out detailed investigation and recording for reconstruction schemes. He lectures widely and was course tutor on the former Landscape and Garden Conservation course at the Architectural Association Graduate School, London.

John Dixon Hunt

John Dixon Hunt is Emeritus Professor of the History and Theory of Landscape at the University of Pennsylvania, the author (most recently) of *A World of Gardens* (Reaktion, 2012), and a member of the editorial board of the new preservation journal, *Change Over Time*, published by the University of Pennsylvania Press.

Fridy Duterloo-Morgan

Fridy Duterloo-Morgan was born and educated in the Netherlands where she completed her Art History and Classical Archaeology Degree at the University of Nijmegen. In 1992 she received an Erasmus scholarship to study at the Dutch Institute of Art History in Florence, where she was able to research an Italian Baroque garden for her Dutch MA dissertation. In 1993 she won a Dutch VSB Bank scholarship and was able to do her MA in Landscape Conservation at the Institute of Advanced Architectural Studies, part of the University of York, where she developed her interest in post-war landscape design and theory. Subsequently she worked freelance as a garden historian and research assistant, before joining English Heritage in 1996 where she currently works as a Designation Adviser advising the Secretary of State on the inclusion of heritage assets on the National Heritage List for England.

Neville Fay

Neville Fay (MA (Hons), MICFor, MArborA, FLS, FRGS, FRSA) is an Institute of Chartered Foresters chartered arboriculturist and principal consultant at Treework Environmental Practice. A past chairman of the Ancient Tree Forum, he is founder of the charity Tree Aid and chaired the National Tree Safety Group drafting subcommittee. In 2009 he was honoured with the Arboricultural Association's Award for Services to Arboriculture. A Fellow of the Linnean Society, he lectures internationally and writes on conservation arboriculture, tree management and public safety. He co-authored 'The Specialist Survey Method', the national standard for surveying veteran trees.

Malcolm Forster

Malcolm Forster was formerly a partner in the international commercial law firm Freshfields Bruckhaus Deringer, and remains a consultant with the firm. He has also acted as a Visiting Professor of International Law at University College, London and is a Visiting Fellow at the British Institute of International and Comparative Law. He has acted as a specialist consultant on legal matters for a wide range of international organisations.

Michael Forsyth

A chartered architect, Michael Forsyth graduated at the University of Liverpool and was awarded the Rome Scholarship in Architecture and the degree of Doctor of Philosophy. He now directs the University of Bath's postgraduate Conservation of Historic Buildings course. His books include *Buildings for Music: The Architect, the Musician, and the Listener from the Seventeenth Century to the Present Day* (MIT Press and Cambridge University Press, 1985), *Bath: Pevsner Architectural Guides* (Yale University Press, 2003) and, with Ahmet Ertug, *Palaces of Music: Opera houses of Europe* and *Domes: a journey through European architectural history* (Ertug & Kocabiyik, 2010 and 2011).

Marion Harney

Dr Marion Harney is Director of Studies for the Conservation of Historic Gardens and Cultural Landscapes, University of Bath. She devised the postgraduate degree course and was appointed Director of Studies in 2007. In 2013 Marion Harney became a Trustee of the Garden History Society, the statutory consultee for all registered landscapes in the UK, and has recently been elected as Chair of the society's Joint Conservation Committee. She is also a member of the Bath World Heritage Site Steering Group and is Chair of the Green Setting of Bath Interim Partnership Board. Recent books include *Place-Making for the Imagination: Horace Walpole and Strawberry Hill*, Ashgate (2013).

James Hitchmough

James Hitchmough is Professor of Horticultural Ecology in the Department of Landscape, University of Sheffield. Much of his research centres on understanding how to create and manage designed vegetation for urban places that has nature-like form and behaviour. In doing this he has become increasingly interested in how we conceptualise vegetation as a precursor to trying to make decisions on what to do to it as maintenance or management, and how this is particularly challenging when human cues to structure and form are absent. James Hitchmough is also involved in a large number of major design projects in practice. In conjunction with his colleague Professor Nigel Dunnett he was responsible for much of the design and implementation of the ecological vegetation that formed the skin of the London Olympic Park, and continues to be involved in shaping its development into the longer term.

Farhat Hussain

Farhat A. Hussain was born in the English Midlands and gained ten Masters degrees at the universities of London, Exeter, Cambridge, Edinburgh, Manchester, Durham, Warwick, York and Bath. He is an archaeologist, historian and historic landscape conservationist with a particular interest in Moorish landscapes and links between cultures and civilisations in history. He is a consultant and adviser in the Gulf States and an author of several books on history and heritage subjects.

Mike Ibbotson

After studying landscape architecture at Sheffield University, Mike Ibbotson joined Colvin and Moggridge Landscape Architects in 1988, becoming a Director in 1999. He has a wealth of practical experience through commissions ranging from sensitive heritage sites to industrial development. Work has been divided between private owners, public bodies and commercial and industrial companies, and has included design within the central London Royal Parks, the Royal Horticultural Society Garden Wisley, English Heritage gardens and the Historic Royal Palaces.

David Jacques

Dr David Jacques was the first Inspector of Historic Parks and Gardens at English Heritage between 1987 and 1993, during which time he devised the criteria for assessing the historical interest of parks and gardens and also principles of treatment which underlay the awarding of grant assistance. More recently he has updated the latter in writing: *Conservation Principles, Policies and Guidance for Historic Parks, Gardens and Designed Landscapes*, to be published by English Heritage. He has sat on the Gardens Advisory Committee of Historic Royal Palaces since 1994 and been a trustee of the Chiswick House and Grounds Trust since 2005.

Patrick James

Patrick James was educated at the University of London and the Architectural Association. He co-wrote a centenary history of the National Trust, *From Acorn to Oak Tree*, with Dame Jennifer Jenkins before working as a policy adviser at the Heritage Lottery Fund. In 1998 he set up the Landscape Agency, a landscape architectural practice based in York which he still runs.

Colin Johns

Colin Johns is an architect, town planner and a member of the Institute of Historic Building Conservation. Following an early career in architectural practices in Devon and London he became a planning officer at the City of London Corporation and later Head of Design and Conservation at Wiltshire County Council. Since 1997 he has worked as an independent architect and planner in Bradford on Avon, specialising in building and area conservation and in community action. A founder Trustee and former Chairman of the United Kingdom Association of Preservation Trusts, he has been involved in building preservation trust activity for over 25 years, much of which as architect to the Wiltshire Historic Buildings Trust. From 1999 to 2003 he was part-time Co-Director for the University of Bristol Diploma & MA course in Architectural Conservation and is currently a visiting lecturer in conservation legislation and practice at the Universities of Bath and Plymouth.

David Lambert

David Lambert is Director of the Parks Agency, a consultancy specialising in public parks. He has been an adviser to three parliamentary inquiries, and currently serves on a number of panels including the National Trust, English Heritage, the World Monuments Fund and Historic Royal Palaces. Formerly Conservation Officer for the Garden History Society, he has held research fellowships at the University of York and De Montfort University, Leicestershire. He is the author of several books including *Parks and Gardens: a researcher's guide to sources for designed landscapes* (2006). His latest publications include *Jubilee-ation: a history of jubilee celebrations in public parks* for English Heritage (2012) and 'Wentworth Castle in the Welfare State: the road to a public landscape', in *Wentworth Castle and Georgian Political Gardening* (ed.) Patrick Eyres (2012).

Jonathan Lovie

Since 1994 Jonathan Lovie, BA (Hons), MPhil, has developed a consultancy undertaking historic landscape research and conservation management plans for a variety of private clients and public bodies, including several commissions for National Trust properties in the South West of England. Between 1998 and 2004, Jonathan was retained by English Heritage as a Consultant Register Inspector, with particular responsibility for upgrading the Register of Parks and Gardens of Special Historic Interest in the South West. Since 2004, he has been employed on a part-time basis by the Garden History Society as its Principal Conservation Officer and Policy Adviser in England. He has been a member of the Council of the National Trust since 2011.

Robert Mattock

Robert Mattock's academic career at the University of Bath in designed and cultural landscapes, and in plant sciences, has enabled him to pursue his interests in the restoration and conservation of historic rose gardens and in the construction of contemporary rose gardens throughout Europe. Originally a specialist plantsman and Victorian retail rose nurseryman, Robert has developed his family's Oxford-based rose growing concern into a niche operation such that now his specialist rose nursery grows an extensive range of historic varieties, often rare and as large specimens, mostly for his own projects. Robert is a popular speaker internationally and has published variously on *The Silk Road Hybrids*, *Alfred Parsons*, *Horticultural Apprenticeships* and *Rose Replant Disorder*.

Charles Mynors

Dr Charles Mynors (FRTPI FRICS IHBC) is in practice as a barrister in the temple, London. He is the chancellor of the diocese of Worcester; a visiting professor in the planning department at Oxford Brookes university; and a member of the advisory panel of the prince's regeneration trust and of the legal advisory commission of the general synod. He is author of the leading books on the law as it relates to listed buildings; trees and forestry; and outdoor advertising.

Adrian Phillips

Adrian Phillips CBE worked for the UK government, UNEP and IUCN before becoming the Director General of the Cheltenham-based Countryside Commission (1981–1992). He then held a professorial post at Cardiff University and has written numerous articles on conservation and landscape. Between 1994 and 2000, he was chair of the IUCN World Commission on Protected Areas. He has been closely involved in the development and implementation of the World Heritage Convention and the European Landscape Convention. In recent years he has served on the boards of a number of UK NGOs, including RSPB, CPRE and the National Trust.

Alan Power

Alan Power is currently Head Gardener for the National Trust at Stourhead, overseeing the management of the garden and wider landscape on one of the most beautiful estates in the country. His interest in horticulture and gardening goes back to his childhood when he gardened under the direction of his mother, eventually gardening professionally for a local company. After studying horticulture at Writtle College and Arboriculture at Merrist Wood his first historic gardens environment role was at Marks Hall, Essex; and later at Stourhead where he was Gardener/Arborist and then Assistant Head Gardener. Following this he was appointed Head Gardener at Mount Stewart, Northern Ireland but always with Stourhead close to his heart, eventually returning as Head Gardener in 2003. For five years he was a Gardens Adviser to the South West Region of the National Trust.

John Sales

John Sales VMH, F.Inst.Hort (RHS), Gardens Consultant is a Vice President of both the Royal Horticultural Society and the Garden History Society. For 25 years he was Head of Gardens and Parks for the National Trust and is now an independent part-time consultant, dealing with aspects of historic garden and park conservation, renewal and design, often through the Landscape Agency.

Heather J.L. Smith

Heather Smith is the Access & Equality Specialist for the National Trust for England, Wales and Northern Ireland. She has worked at the National Trust for ten years, holding positions responsible for advising on access for disabled people as employees, volunteers, visitors and supporters across the National Trust's diverse portfolio of historic houses, gardens and parkland, holiday cottage accommodation, coastal areas and more. Her role also includes participation on the Trust's Diversity Working Group, integrating equality and diversity into the National Trust's strategy and planning. Heather Smith has published a range of articles on accessibility and the historic environment and recently collaborated with Hannah Goodwin from the Museum of Fine Arts, Boston, and Barry Ginley from the Victoria & Albert Museum, London, on a chapter for *Museums, Equality and Social Justice*, published in April 2012 by Routledge.

Peter Thoday

Peter Thoday is a Senior Lecturer at the University of Bath, Director and horticultural consultant to the Eden Project, Director of the Sensory Trust and Principal of Thoday Associates, a landscape consultancy specialising in the refurbishment and subsequent management of historic gardens. A sometime president of the Institute of Horticulture, Peter Thoday is also the author of *Two Blades of Grass: The Story of Cultivation* (2007) and *Cultivar, The Story of Man-made Plants* (2013).

Nigel Thorne

Nigel Thorne (MSc FRSA Intl.ASLA MIHort FLI PPLI) is a chartered landscape architect (a Fellow of the Landscape Institute) specialising in landscape management. He practises as an independent landscape consultant concentrating on contract administration and project implementation but also works part-time for a variety of award-winning landscape architectural practices based in London and across the UK. Having served the Landscape Institute (UK) in a variety of elected posts, he played an instrumental role in how the LI approached its work in higher education, careers promotion and professional practice examinations. He was elected president of the IFLA Europe (originally the European Federation for Landscape Architecture) at the beginning of 2010 and will complete his second term in office at the end of 2013. He is also Vice-president (Europe) of the International Federation of Landscape Architects. He works and teaches both nationally and internationally and regularly gives talks, seminars and lectures in order to promote the work of the profession around the world.

Richard Wheeler

Richard Wheeler has worked for the National Trust for the last 35 years and is now the Trust's National Specialist in Garden History. He joined the Trust in 1977 as a Chartered Surveyor in North Wales working on the restorations at Erddig, Chirk and Plas yn Rhiw, and since then has held a succession of managerial and professional roles in various parts of the country. In his current role he is available to give curatorial and historical advice on some 98 Grade I and Grade II* gardens on the English Heritage Register of Parks and Gardens of Special Historic Interest in England, and similar statutory designations for Wales and Northern Ireland. He lectures and writes regularly, mainly on the iconography of eighteenth-century gardens and their understanding and restoration. Apart from his work with the National Trust, he is a Council Member of the Garden History Society and a Trustee of the Georgian Group.

Jenifer White

Jenifer White is English Heritage's Senior Landscape Adviser working on historic parks and garden conservation issues. The 1987 Great Storm and the huge number of damaged historic parks and gardens proved to be a springboard for her to develop her interests in historic designed landscapes flowing from studies and research in historical ecology. The Great Storm landscape rehabilitation grant programme experience has underpinned an interest in managing and adapting to change and conservation planning. Jenifer's first degree is in botany and she went on to study for a MSc in landscape ecology, design and maintenance under Tom Wright at Wye College. She is also a chartered member of the Landscape Institute.

Lisa White

Lisa White MA FRSA FSA was the Director of the Attingham Summer School for the Study of Historic Houses and Collections from 2004–2011. She has taught history of art at the universities of Bristol, Bath, and Buckingham and has lectured widely across the UK and the United States. She is currently Chairman of the Arts Advisory Panel of the National Trust. Publications include *The Pictorial Dictionary of Eighteenth Century British Furniture Design* (Antique Collectors' Club), 1990, and *Interior Finishes and Fittings for Historic Building Conservation* (with Dr Michael Forsyth), 2012.

Philip White

Philip White graduated in biology and was a farmer and wildlife conservationist before rediscovering Hestercombe's lost landscape garden in 1992. He personally financed the early restoration work which started in 1995 and in 1997, for the first time in 125 years, opened the garden to the public. In 2003 he was appointed as the first Chief Executive of the Hestercombe Gardens Trust. Named *Country Life* magazine's 'Gardener of the Year' in 1997, he received an MBE in 2013 for 'services to historic garden restoration'.

Helen Winton

Manager of the Aerial Investigation and Mapping team at English Heritage, Helen Winton has over 20 years experience of archaeological aerial survey and research and has worked on numerous projects covering diverse periods, themes and locations in England. She is responsible, with colleagues, for the design and provision of aerial photograph training including thematic courses on conservation, military landscapes, and parks and gardens.

William Martin 'Min' Wood

Min Wood, LLB, MPhil, PGDip, is a place maker and garden writer with extensive experience of gardening and landscape management. He has farmed in Surrey, Hampshire and Wiltshire. Called to the Bar in 1972, he practised mainly in planning and environment law. In 2001 and 2002 he took on Spring Wood, part of the Grade I gardens of Hackwood House, Hampshire, when they had become separated from Hackwood House. He has made a study of the Picturesque as it applies to made landscapes. He has coined the term 'Naturesque' to describe those landscapes which have come about from a process of engagement with nature.

Introduction

Traditions of husbandry, garden making and landscape design have always held a poignant place in the English psyche and garden visiting historically, as now, was an important cultural pursuit. The English Landscape tradition has been described as our greatest contribution to the arts and the cultural, historic and social importance of historic parks and gardens has exerted great influence in other cultures too. Many of our perceptions of landscape stem from eighteenth-century theory and practice. These landscapes continue to make a significant contribution to our culture and heritage and it is recognised that they must be recorded and protected. Great Britain has an established framework of conservation legislation and campaigns for the protection of the historic environment have in the main been successful because communities generally feel that they have a personal stake in these cherished landscapes.

A place may be significant for many different reasons and not simply for historic value, and sometimes these may conflict. The values we place on landscapes are subjective and qualified and we often naively believe that the values we hold as individuals are universally shared by others. In truth, it is difficult to identify consensus in what is valued and by whom. Let us take a hypothetical public park and analyse diverse groups that have a vested interest in conservation. Architectural and landscape historians may value the park because of the significance of its listed buildings and the designed landscape because of its association with its renowned, if hypothetical, Victorian park designer and the fact that the site was donated by a local altruistic benefactor and for these reasons it is included on English Heritage's Register of Parks and Gardens of Special Historic Interest in England. These conservation interests, however, have to compete with the different views and values that others place on the park. Those interested in nature conservation find significant value attached to the rare ferns and lichens that colonise the park and, rather than seeing it restored, they believe it should be given Site of Special Scientific Interest (SSSI) status and managed for its wildlife and biodiversity value. Others wish to conserve the environment for five different species of bat which inhabit the site and insist on priority over other conservation considerations. Meanwhile, significant elements of the designed landscape were lost to provide local social daily amenities, children's playgrounds, picnic areas, events spaces, sports facilities and provision for dogs, all at the behest of divergent interest groups who attach valid significance to the place. As this hypothetical case study demonstrates, these may cause conflicts between conservation and user groups and a balance must be drawn that respects the range of values inherent in most historic places.

In response to these dilemmas, English Heritage has condensed the numerous values outlined above to produce a set of Conservation Principles in an attempt to explain and codify the values that underpin the significance of a place. These have been distilled into an essential shortlist of four: evidential, historical, aesthetic and communal. Evidential value is defined as 'the potential of a place to yield evidence about past human activity'; historical value as 'the ways in which past people, events and aspects of life can be connected through a place to the present'; aesthetic value 'derives from the ways in which people draw sensory and intellectual stimulation from a place'; and communal value is 'the meanings of a place for the people who relate to it'. The National Trust takes a similar approach to English Heritage, talking about meanings and values: scientific and technical, aesthetic and spiritual. These frameworks represent a positive initiative to structure an analysis of key values so that a rationale and policy for proposed works for protection and conservation can be formulated.

Value and significance is based on an understanding of the site, derived not just from research and surveys, but from consultation and a wider dialogue with those to whom a place matters. The key values attributed to a site then lead to the formulation of a Statement of Significance in which consideration will be given to its threats and vulnerabilities but also to opportunities to conserve and enhance its significance and maintain those values.

The cooperation of all heritage sector bodies with an interest in historic landscapes is vital if we are to realise our core objective of conserving and protecting them for future generations to enjoy. Yet, conventional education and vocational skills training for landscape architects and other professions destined to conserve and protect these precious heritage assets provides little or no guidance on key aspects of conservation practice and we must educate and inform those interested and involved in protecting the historic environment if we are to retain these places into the future. We also need to harness the power of local communities and the various bodies involved in conservation to see how they might work more effectively towards the key objectives: to promote sector-wide collaboration, to ensure the coordination of scarce resources, to ensure that issues are clearly identified and that the necessary skills are in place to be able to continue with the work of conserving and protecting the parks, gardens and landscapes that we cherish.

This will require engagement with capacity-building initiatives to ensure that the right skills exist and that the right tools and advice are available to those engaged in looking after our landscapes, through activities such as training and the development of advice and guidelines.

The Burra Charter formulated by the International Council on Monuments and Sites (ICOMOS, 1999) provides a definition of conservation-related terms: the general term *conservation* means all the processes of looking after a place so as to retain its cultural significance; *maintenance* means the continuous protective care of the fabric and setting of a place, and is to be distinguished from repair; *repair* involves *restoration* or *reconstruction*; *restoration* means returning the existing fabric of a place to a known earlier state by removing accretions or by reassembling existing components without the introduction of new material; *reconstruction* means returning a place to a known earlier state and is distinguished from restoration by the introduction of new material into the fabric.

However, in the conservation of gardens and landscapes, unlike built features, some intervention will always be necessary as planting will need to be renewed, following evidence wherever possible, even within a project described as *conservation* or *restoration* rather than *reconstruction* (English Heritage, 2007).[1] Where there is no site evidence, *conjectural detailing* – details derived from an understanding of history and cultural context, rather than direct site evidence, may be justified, but it is vital that this is made clear in the way the work is presented (Jacques, 1995).[2] Often it is not clear whether work carried out falls into the categories of re-creation or conjectural creation, rather than conservation and repair. However, generally speaking in the UK, the re-creation of lost features is treated with caution and there needs to be a consistent conservation philosophy in place to justify this level of intervention.[3] And, unlike a building, a garden can rarely be restored to a particular moment in time as most will have gone through various phases and iterations. In these cases we need to ask ourselves if we can restore them with any degree of authenticity and does it matter, and if it does, to whom does it matter?

The determination of significance of a historic garden or landscape is key to understanding and this lies at the heart of any Conservation Management Plan (CMP) as all discussions regarding its conservation rely on identifying significance and value. This underpins and informs the complex management and decision-making process and supports the policy aims, objectives and conservation philosophy to be agreed for the site – what makes it distinctive, special, rare, influential or unique is at the core of understanding and it is this significance and its interpretation that will guide its conservation. Views as to who values the place and why, together with issues and constraints, are all site-specific and all help to form a vision statement and determine the conservation approach to be taken.

Care and maintenance of heritage assets have widely been delivered both by private owners, trusts and voluntary organisations, and there remains a wider public interest in heritage protection and conservation which can be traced back to the late nineteenth century. A key figure in the conservation movement, John Ruskin (1819–1899) inspired William Morris (1834–1896) to form the influential Society for the Protection of Ancient Buildings (SPAB) in 1878 and these figures were to foreshadow future conservation legislation. The legal protection of historic buildings saw its beginnings with the Ancient Monuments Act of 1882 and the Garden City Movement (1898), initiated by Sir Ebenezer Howard (1850–1928) was 'intended to provide a framework for planned and self-contained communities surrounded by Green Belts containing proportionate areas of dwelling, industry and agriculture'.[4] The later Town and Country Planning Act of 1944 empowered the Minister of Town and Country Planning to prepare lists of buildings of special architectural or historic interest for the guidance of local authorities. However, it was not until the Town and Country Planning Act of 1947 that the protection of the countryside became an integral part of the planning system alongside a more effective system for the conservation of historic monuments and buildings. Octavia Hill (1838–1912) co-founded the National Trust in 1894, which grew out of the work of the Kyrie Society's Open Spaces Committee founded in 1877 by her sister and social reformer Miranda (1836–1910) to 'bring beauty home to the people'. Sir John Lubbock (1834–1913), Member of Parliament for Maidstone, purchased Avebury and Silbury Hill in 1871 to protect them from development and this aspiration of preserving and protecting sites for the long term was the basis for the foundation of the National Trust. The aim of the National Trust Act of 1907 was 'to promote the permanent preservation, for the benefit of the nation, of lands and tenements (including buildings) of beauty or natural interest'.

However, while there is much to be celebrated, some areas of the historic environment remain under threat and despite the existence of such organisations as English Heritage, Historic Scotland, Cadw, National Trust, the Garden History Society, the Heritage Lottery Fund, Association of Gardens Trusts and County Gardens Trusts, we must not be complacent in believing that English Heritage's compilation of the Register of Historic Parks and Gardens of Special Historic Interest in England, which has hopefully captured most of the significant sites, will prevent further loss and damage to important landscapes. The present impetus towards loosening the limits and constraints on planning, various conflicting conservation interests and the economic pressure to develop, all pose further serious threats to the heritage of gardens and landscapes.

Clearly, a situation where important historic parks, gardens and landscapes are at risk is unacceptable. As well as educating professionals, we must actively encourage and engage the help of members of the community if we are to meet the challenges of providing an appropriate level of protection to sites under threat, registered or otherwise. Not being designated can be cited as a rationale for their destruction, where often the reason they are not registered is simply that they are not known, lost, neglected or merely under-researched.

The Garden History Society was founded in 1965, but it was only with the establishment of English Heritage in the National Heritage Act (1983) that the first Register of Parks and Gardens was compiled. English Heritage has powers to produce and maintain the register, and the designation of sites must be taken into account by planning authorities in formulating planning policy and, perhaps more importantly, when determining planning applications.[5] The initial work on the 46 county volumes was completed in 1988 and included nearly 1300 sites. A Register Review Programme was carried out (1993–2000) which consisted of individual county-based surveys which identified sites that would merit further consideration for inclusion. Further additions have been made and the current total is approximately 1,617 registered sites and English Heritage has now also published *Selection Guides for Designed Landscapes*, which are subdivided into four categories: Landscapes of Remembrance, Institutional Landscapes, Rural Landscapes and Urban

Landscapes.[6] As with listed buildings, the selected sites were graded at I, II* or II; sites registered at Grade I are of exceptional interest in a national context; Grade II* of particular importance and of more than special interest; Grade II are of special interest, warranting every effort to preserve them.

The Register is an important tool for enhancing understanding, appreciation and protection, and to help inform decisions on repair, management and/or development proposals but nationally designated historic designed landscapes do not enjoy any statutory protection arising from the fact of their designation.[7] While parks and gardens may have been given the status of 'designated heritage assets' as defined in the National Planning Policy Framework (NPPF, 2012), the entry of a park or garden onto the register does not, of itself, confer any need for special consent to be obtained but its inclusion remains a material consideration in the planning process.[8] In Wales, Cadw maintains a similar register of historic landscapes, parks and gardens on a non-statutory basis.[9]

NPPF includes an environmental role in the planning system which states that it should contribute to protecting and enhancing our natural, built and historic environment, and Section 11, on conserving and enhancing the natural environment, emphasises that great weight should be given to conserving landscape and scenic beauty in National Parks, the Broads and Areas of Outstanding Natural Beauty, which have the highest status of protection in relation to landscape and scenic beauty. The conservation of wildlife and cultural heritage are important considerations in all these areas.[10]

Many significant gardens and landscapes form the setting of historic listed buildings such as country houses, and the law protecting a building extends to any 'object or structure' that is within its curtilage. This affords the greatest degree of protection available for the landscape. Numerous historic parks and gardens of significance are located within a conservation area, defined as 'an area of special architectural or historic interest, the character or appearance of which it is desirable to preserve or enhance'; this is undoubtedly the most beneficial local designation, and arguably the designation (national or local) which offers the greatest protection to designed landscapes. Many private gardens and landscapes are located in conservation areas and so, as the planning authority must pay special attention to preserving or enhancing the character of the area, they too are given a greater degree of protection.

In the past, different types of landscapes have been valued at different times and by diverse groups of people or interested parties and the interpretation of landscapes and recognition of their significance has an important role to play in attracting a wider audience. Engaging different groups leads to greater economic benefit which generates funding for their conservation. English Heritage's publication *Sustaining the Historic Environment* (1997) identified the potential of sustainability as a means of encouraging conservation and giving it mainstream status through public involvement in heritage activities which are valued by local communities but which are not necessarily of national significance.[11]

The notion of who values these heritage assets and why is constantly evolving and in this respect the Heritage Lottery Fund (HLF) has been inspiring and innovative, offering grants to applicants who demonstrate the historic interest of a site, whether it is registered or not. This has meant that local sites, valued by the community and of benefit to the public, have attracted funding and been restored and conserved. The re-evaluation of local heritage assets has in some cases led to the Local Authority compiling a 'Local List' or 'Heritage Audit', often with the help of local amenity societies such as the County Garden Trusts.

HLF's flagship Parks for People programme has helped to influence the perception of heritage value to include the environment where people live, work and play as well as the more 'elitist' country house and historic garden or landscape park. Parks and gardens are only one area of HLF investment, though it is estimated that over £750 million has been awarded to gardens and public parks, including almost every significant historic public park in the UK and many designed landscapes such as gardens, cemeteries, seaside promenades, squares and post-war landscapes. HLF's investment has been the saviour of public parks and it has an ongoing allocated commitment of £20–30 million a year to support the sustainable restoration and regeneration of public parks as well as funding staff costs. They championed their role by encouraging the projects that provide education, job creation and skills training and encouraging the arts; their approach has led to a growing recognition among many local authorities and developers that new parks or urban green space should be part of new urban planning and development. As a result of the HLF initiative there has been a democratisation of heritage and it provides an excellent model for other enterprises to concentrate on the public benefits of social inclusion and access and regeneration rather than just conservation and repair. The late twentieth century saw a series of conservation pressures threatening historic cemeteries and in response HLF is now extending its grant-giving remit to cover historic cemeteries which suffer from a litany of related conservation issues including abandonment, planting, memorials laid down and unsafe ones surrounded by disfiguring safety notices or completely removed. Grant aid schemes available from HLF embrace the concept of sustainable heritage and include funding for long-term staff and maintenance costs.

All landscapes are unique and most have experienced some sort of alteration or addition in their lifetime. Typically replanting and maintenance are ongoing processes, combined with less frequent major renovations or modifications to update their style. Most landscapes that are lost or forgotten have undergone cycles of neglect or abandonment and the first task, before doing anything, will always be to carry out a thorough site survey and assessment, backed up by archival and desktop research.

Before undertaking any conservation work it is crucial to understand the site and its creators in order to identify its significance and values. This relies on undertaking research to ascertain what is important about the site, and this should be combined with repeated on-the-ground surveys to evaluate what is significant about the place. Any work undertaken subsequently will be designed to restore, preserve, conserve and/or enhance that significance and should respect its history and the values inherent in the site. Most large sites will require a Conservation Management Plan (CMP) but best practice indicates that the minimum requirement for every historic place would be a Statement of Significance or Spirit of Place Statement to define its significance, determine conservation aims and guide works. The process of compiling the CMP will reveal its significance and values and this will aid the team of specialists in assessing what ideally needs to be done, what practically can be done and by whom. A Spirit of Place statement capturing its tangible and intangible qualities would certainly have been beneficial to the understanding and interpretation of the site at Strawberry Hill, Twickenham which is the subject of a Conservation in Action case study (chapter 36) as this type of statement focuses the conservation efforts on restoring particular qualities rather than just replacing what we know was there.

The conservation specialist involved in major historic conservation projects will likely work with a range of consultants to apply specialist skills, techniques and methodologies. These may include a landscape architect, garden designer, archaeologist, horticulturalist, property manager, construction contractors, and head gardener. The specialist methodologies available to help reveal and inform understanding will include desktop research, but it must be emphasised that there is no substitute for repeatedly walking the site, constantly weighing the findings of documentary research against evidence on the ground. It is from this interplay that the best attainable picture will emerge and this will determine the main resources and areas for further investigation through maps, plans, digital and archival resources and libraries.

A comprehensive site survey is a powerful interpretation tool which will supply evidence of the process of its evolution, whether designed or as a result of accidents of setting or local topography. Layout, content, buildings and structures including seats and other garden furniture all influence the philosophical approach to conservation that will be adopted. This survey may be supported by other specialist surveying and assessment techniques as required, including aerial survey which can provide a comprehensive synthesis of archaeological information to assist with research, planning and the protection of the historic environment and aid the process of conservation and management. Brian Dix (chapter 14) affirms that archaeological investigation methods and applications on the ground enable good conservation management and practice by revealing the nature of related remains and provide a valuable check on the accuracy of historical views and contemporary records. These form the basis for accurate reconstruction particularly where the renewal of original building material is required. Other specialist surveys that might be required include conservation arboriculture which helps us to understand how trees function in the landscape and enhance our appreciation of them. Ecology, geology, hydrology, movement and user surveys, consultations and oral history all aid the process of defining significance and developing a conservation philosophy and determining policies for future management and maintenance.

However, research, analysis and surveys cannot reveal everything that we need to know and some garden conservation or restoration will inevitably be conjectural but this must always be underpinned by the knowledge we do possess. The restoration of a garden can never be truly authentic; it will always be a reworking and reinterpretation of history but these 'evocations' must be based on the application of well-thought-out conservation principles. On some sites the creation of a period garden which did not previously exist may be an acceptable solution to provide an appropriate context for a historic house and help inform the visitor. New, contemporary design can also be considered a suitable response in a historic landscape but only where no archaeological evidence is destroyed in the process of its creation. When working in a historic landscape it is important to ensure that the professionals involved have a working knowledge of the design principles pertaining to that particular place and where new design is contemplated it should only be undertaken by qualified, experienced professionals. To name but few examples, the National Trust has created Winter Gardens at Dunham Massey, Cheshire and Mottisfont Abbey, Hampshire as well as introducing creative new designs by talented gardeners at Bodnant Garden in Wales and at the Grade I, Tudor, Packwood House in Warwickshire. New design has also been introduced into the 'Capability' Brown landscape at Heveningham Hall, Suffolk by Kim Wilkie and at Brown's own birthplace, Kirkharle, Northumberland.

National Trust membership has risen exponentially year-on-year and interest in visiting historic gardens and landscapes has never been greater. As foremost custodians of heritage places the National Trust has conserved and enhanced in perpetuity over 200 gardens and 100 landscapes. Over 50% of managed National Trust landscapes are registered as nationally significant and internationally recognised. As enlightened owners the Trust commits to protecting, restoring, enhancing and managing the gardens and landscapes in their care. With a commercial remit, however, specific criteria for acquisition pertain, with historical significance a primary consideration, closely followed by aesthetic, archaeological, botanical or biological significance and the likely public benefit of access. Potential to generate income is also a material consideration as restoration, maintenance and staffing are costly.

Every National Trust garden is unique and significant in terms of history, cultural context, aesthetics or botanical interest, and all require skilled gardeners and conservation specialists. An average of 80% of these gardens contain areas of planting and the National Trust is in the vanguard of addressing the horticultural skills shortage in the UK, continually putting resources into developing the skills and expertise of its gardens' curatorial staff, especially with an eye to skills training for the future.

The National Trust contributes significantly to plant conservation and compiles an inventory of significant plants in its gardens, working closely with other plant conservation bodies to promote recording, analysis and the conservation of species and cultivated plants in Great Britain. This makes available to conservation specialists, garden designers, horticulturalists and gardeners authentic species and planting styles, creating a 'living museum' at its Plant Conservation Centre in Devon. Plant health has also become a major concern, with the impact of climate change particularly affecting many native species. This presents many challenges for conservationists to maintain the available range and diversity of plant species and the National Trust's Plant Propagation Centre, also in Devon, undertakes the emergency propagation of significant plants affected by disease to ensure the survival of threatened species and supply disease-free replacements. But more research needs to be done in this essential area if we are to conserve and manage our historic landscapes into the future.

The pendulum continues to swing and landscapes are valued in their own right aside from 'stately home' visiting, to the extent that ever increasing visitor numbers threaten designed landscape. There remains a tension between keeping places vital and alive and conserving vulnerable historic fabric, though, as referred to above, gardens and landscape require a different conservation philosophy to a building – their history may be of equal importance but the nature of a garden is its ephemeral quality – it constantly changes.

We cannot and do not need to preserve everything in the natural historic environment and resistance to change is both untenable and undesirable. It is right to pose the question asked by John Dixon Hunt in chapter 1: 'what is it about gardens that you want to preserve?'. He argues that resistance to any change or adaptation prevents new design from taking place and inhibits creativity and contends that we need to take a more creative approach to conservation. We must address the philosophical issues associated with preserving particular sites by identifying the aspects of the landscape or constituent elements that require conservation. Design intention must be heeded but changes in function must also be a consideration. This must take place within an understanding of gardens' cultural context and how they have evolved over time with a succession of owners who may have created and added their own layers of historical significance.

How we visit and interpret a historic garden or landscape is an important consideration in conservation as our perception often lies in our initial impression. This begins with the approach and entry and whether we are given a planned route or sequence in which we are to experience the site. For example at Stowe, Buckinghamshire, until the recent restoration of the New Inn, which was the original entrance and traditional approach for the eighteenth-century visitor to the garden, visitors arrived at the opposite end of the chronological sequence to that which the garden was intended to be viewed and this had a considerable negative impact on how the landscape was experienced and interpreted.

Most original landowners selected the precise site on which to build their house and lay out their garden because of its wider context, setting and topography and these relative significances are often crucial to understanding the garden. If these factors are compromised by inappropriate development, this affects the presentation and aesthetic value of the site and our response to it, as we no longer experience the garden as the designer originally intended. Changes in activity too, inevitably alter places that were in most cases private originally. When they are transferred into the public domain this changes the historic perspective and different approaches need to be implemented to avoid destroying the design intention (where there was one) and objectives of the original owner.

Seventy per cent of top National Trust attractions are gardens with 16 million visitors each year. This has a significant impact on each site and poses challenges for access. In some cases modern technological interventions such as 'Astro Turf' have been used or new hard-surface paths installed to reduce wear and tear or to allow disabled access, though these can have a detrimental impact on the historic fabric and can change the character of a place if not sensitively designed. To mitigate the effects and to help historic environment organisations to find a practical balance between conservation and access, English Heritage, the Heritage Lottery Fund and the National Trust worked together to produce an overarching publication: *Easy Access to Historic Landscapes* (2005), re-published in 2013.[12] The National Trust have also developed a *Conservation for Access Toolkit* to calculate the carrying capacity and resources needed to increase access to their properties while maintaining the historic integrity of the site without affecting presentation and conservation standards.[13] Gardens open to the public rely on sensitively placed signage, car parking, restaurants, shops, plant sales areas and seats. Heritage bodies, including the National Trust and English Heritage, no longer advocate converting historic kitchen gardens into car parks, although the installation of brightly coloured plastic children's play equipment remains a dilemma. The exemplary restoration of the gardens and landscape at Wrest Park, Bedfordshire by the English Heritage team led by John Watkins, Head of Gardens and Landscape, provides sensitively designed and sustainable play equipment that blends sympathetically with its surroundings. The viability of visitor numbers to a site open to the public relies on the economic benefits brought by thoughtfully designed and integrated visitor centres and facilities.

Stewardship – temporary custodianship – is an appropriate concept for protecting and enhancing the historic environment at the core of conservation philosophy for conservation bodies and practitioners alike. Places are not static; John Sales emphasises that gardens are processes, not merely objects to admire (chapter 3). They are ephemeral by nature; processes of growth, cultivation, development, decay and renewal, continually changing and evolving, and require a different philosophical approach to that applied to buildings which are subject to repair, adaptation, preservation, maintenance and possible replacement. If gardens are to survive the best practice is to manage their changing nature by producing plans for their conservation that help those responsible for their stewardship in the decision-making process and are able to assist in solving the curatorial and conservation dilemmas that arise, especially in deciding priority, while respecting significance and sense of place.

Significance sets apart the most important buildings and landscapes and identifies the core of conservation work to help promote and protect the site. A well-written statement of significance is fundamental for every historic asset to identify and prioritise values and issues. Early provision of a statement of significance for all nationally and locally designated landscapes will improve public and professional access to the understanding of gardens and landscapes and has the potential to attract funding for conservation and maintenance.

English Heritage compiles *Heritage Counts* each year and monitors challenges faced by historic landscapes across the regions.[14] This information, in conjunction with that gathered by organisations including the Garden History Society and the County Gardens Trusts can guide local decisions by setting site-specific issues into a wider context. Active members of local communities and other individuals become involved and take responsibility for the management of their local historic assets. Working together to ensure strong measures and a robust system of protection minimises change, damage or irreversible loss of important sites and landscapes.

The identification of locally and regionally significant sites through partnership and collaboration helps ensure timely intervention and protection of the historic environment by engagement with key conservation activities. Research and information gathering on landscapes at risk (particularly where significant landscapes have been overlooked or are poorly understood), provides views on the values of heritage assets, identifying how such assets might best be protected and affords an input into planning and local lists which inform the decision-making processes that are part of the planning system.

With the recognition that there is little spare financial capacity in the historic environment sector the joint strengths of the collective bodies may help to persuade government to take a more proactive role and give clear policy guidance on the importance of the historic environment. Enhanced coordination of activity and joint working is particularly important in times of public spending cutbacks and engagement by local communities in the protection of historic gardens, parks and landscapes is essential to consider how public interest can best be stimulated and engaged with directly. Local and regional knowledge and intervention is vital when changes to the historic environment are being considered, to ensure high-quality outcomes and to minimise irreversible loss to the historic environment.

The heritage sector, amenities bodies and academics researching, interpreting, identifying, assessing and recording the historic environment have achieved much but there is more to be done. Large areas of the country have poor, even basic identification of recorded heritage and there is a risk of losing nationally significant landscapes and assets before even knowing what is at risk. Enhanced levels of engagement will be mutually beneficial to organisations and institutions interested in the conservation and protection of the historic environment. In the longer term, it is envisaged that focusing resources and research on the most threatened parts of the historic environment will help to increase understanding and appreciation of historic landscapes and protect their significance. Heritage bodies and professionals must seek to play to the strengths of our organisations and provide a basis for creating new dialogues, new partnerships and new collaborations where real, tangible protection outcomes are likely to be realised.

References

English Heritage (2007) *The Management & Maintenance of Historic Parks, Gardens & Landscapes*, (eds J. Watkins and T. Wright). Frances Lincoln, London.

Jacques, D. (1995) 'The Treatment of Historic Parks and Gardens', *Journal of Architectural Conservation*, 2, July 1995.1.

Endnotes

1. English Heritage (2007) The Management & Maintenance of Historic Parks, Gardens & Landscapes, (eds J. Watkins and T. Wright), Frances Lincoln, London.
2. Jacques (1995) 'The Treatment of Historic Parks and Gardens', *Journal of Architectural Conservation*, 2, July 1995.
3. Couch, chapter 12, 'Defining significance and developing a conservation philosophy'.
4. Johns, chapter 26, 'Conservation legislation in the UK'.
5. Mynors, chapter 29, 'Legal protection for structures, trees, and wildlife'.
6. These guides are available to download from the English Heritage website at http://www.english-heritage.org.uk/caring/listing/criteria-for-protection/pag-criteria/
7. Duterloo-Morgan, chapter 25, 'Designed landscapes and national designation'.
8. Available to download at https://www.gov.uk/government/uploads/system/uploads/attachment_data/file/6077/2116950.pdf
9. Mynors, chapter 29, 'Legal protection for structures, trees, and wildlife'.
10. Johns, chapter 26, 'Conservation legislation in the UK'.
11. This English Heritage Technical paper by Graham Fairclough is available from English Heritage.
12. Available to download at http://www.english-heritage.org.uk/publications/easy-access-historic-landscapes/
13. Assessing Conservation State in the National Trust by Katy Lithgow, Head Conservator the National Trust (2011) available at: http://www.bl.uk/blpac/pdf/impactlithgow.pdf
14. Produced annually by English Heritage on behalf of the Historic Environment Forum (HEF) and available to download at: http://hc.english-heritage.org.uk/

1 What is it about gardens that you want to conserve?[1]

John Dixon Hunt

Emeritus Professor of the History and Theory of Landscape,
University of Pennsylvania, Philadelphia, PA, USA

Gardens are complex things however we look at them, and I suspect that for conservation/preservation they pose very complicated issues, often far less resolvable than, say, in painting or building conservation.[2] So, first, it seems worthwhile asking, what exactly are the constituent elements of a garden that may have to be conserved, or rather, what aspects of a garden do we have to keep in mind when we undertake conservation/preservation? (This awkward collocation is necessary to distinguish between the different usages of the term in the UK and USA.)

There are many types, and it repays distinguishing between them: as in linguistics, there are different *registers* of gardens, and, while these may overlap on specific sites, their different uses originally determined very different spaces and treatment to which, as historians, we must pay attention. It is not simply the designers' intentions that we must heed, but how those designs were used, and perhaps changed over time. So garden sites have undergone alterations – beyond the usual changes that influence how we see them – notably in usage and visitation[3]; the formal aspects of Stowe have obviously changed during and since the eighteenth century, but beyond those there is the decisive change of function when a country mansion became a school and students used its spaces for a golf course, and again when the school grounds were taken over by the National Trust. Equally, the Bliss mansion of Dumbarton Oaks in Washington DC, while it may have occasionally been used as a forum for international events, changed fundamentally when it ceased to be a private residence and collection, and became a research institute for Harvard University that admitted visitors and scholars at certain times.

Types of gardens are best considered in terms of the cultural conditions in which they were created and established. My own attempt to register this range and variety of cultural garden forms has been explored in a book, *The World of Gardens* (London, 2012), where a series of gardens emerging from different cultures are discussed. Every garden has its own forms and can usually be seen as having been created in a given cultural style, dependent upon the period when it was laid out; similarities between different gardens may well seem identical, but on closer inspection respond to local and cultural influences. An Arts and Crafts garden, such as Hestercombe in Somerset, is not a Renaissance 'formal' garden and needs to be understood in terms of how Gertrude Jekyll (1843–1932) and Edwin Lutyens (1869–1944) envisaged its forms and uses. A good exercise to sharpen your cultural diagnostic sense is to look at recreations of earlier elements (or wholes) and identify the fresh colouring

Figure 1.1 Courances, Essonne, France (author's own).

that even the most accomplished recreations betray: for instance, the later remodelling of the water parterre at the Villa Lante in Bagnaia; the parterres at Vaux le Vicomte as we see them now; the work throughout France and elsewhere, as at Blenheim, Oxfordshire, of the Duchêne family.⁴ Then there is the reformulation of Courances (Figure 1.1) by Ernst de Ganay (1880–1963), a doyen of French garden history who employed Achille Duchêne to re-make a stunning landscape; it is truly nostalgic of traditional seventeenth-century French gardens, but its 'modern' spirit is also a subtle element throughout.

Gardens also evolve over time, with different owners who bring to their land and its management a succession of ideas and formal demands. Consulting the maps of Stowe gardens, Buckingham (Figures 1.2 and 1.4) from the early eighteenth century to the present day can make this very clear, even if we may not discern the reasons for the changes.

This complicates completely, not just what we may call the Viollet-le-Duc (1814–1879) approach (attempting to return a building to one earlier, coherent moment in its history), but any attempt to see the site in question as having a succession of phases and interventions: how do you restore a *longue durée*? And what happens when an artefact – crucial to some site – disappears or gets so weathered that it is indecipherable? Statues once lost to Stowe's Ancient Virtue have luckily been found and restored to their place inside the Temple, but do we replace other items with simply 'similar' items? One of the earliest items in Ian Hamilton Finlay's (1925–2006) Little Sparta, Dunsyre, a wooden sundial, shaped like a gravestone, carved with the words 'Evening will come They will sew the Blue Sail' is now – aptly – much weathered and barely readable; do we replace it with a newly carved piece and put the first one in a 'museum'?⁵

Plants – I am no expert here. Bio-historians and historians like Mark Laird have increased our knowledge of plants and their uses. And the commercial research and development of plants make choices both harder and easier – more types to substitute, yet thereby perhaps losing the claim of 'authenticity'. Is even a fairly recent garden like William Robinson's (1838–1935) Gravetye Manor, West Sussex 'authentic'? Does it have to be? Can it not be allowed to develop with plantings that, while not the same, create comparable effects? If so, how do we nevertheless record it and demonstrate it for visitors?

I have always been fascinated by how we circulate and move through gardens, how and in what sequence, even, we respond to their different elements.⁶ Some designers such as Humphry Repton (1752–1818) were particularly concerned with how, and at what point, to bring people into a site, and then to lead them through it. One significant and unavoidable issue today is car parks for gardens of the National Trust – how do we bring people from

Figure 1.2 Stowe in 1777. Compare this with the 1739 view of the whole estate in Figure 1.4.

them into the garden, and what is the threshold at which we enter and know we are in a garden – a momentous event in experiencing most gardens? How is it different from what might have been an older approach? How does this approach and 'entry' determine how we visit a site? But it is not just car parks, but the usual plethora of amenities – toilets, tearooms, picnic areas, and spaces for kids – that have to be inserted into gardens and parks that once were private enclaves. Creative, new work can often sit well and excitingly alongside old (more of that in a moment). One specific problem I encounter is that sites open to the public tend to tell visitors how to negotiate their spaces, by providing plans, or narratives that require specific routes directing visitors in a precise, predetermined pattern. But a great many gardens impose this single interpretation when there could be alternatives.

No site is independent of its context. The views from William Kent's (1685–1748) garden at Rousham, Oxfordshire, over the water meadows and the far hillside with its eye-catcher are crucial to the garden itself and have been threatened – mercifully so far unsuccessfully – by unsightly farm buildings on that horizon. Gardens and landscapes like those at Chiswick House and Strawberry Hill, London (the former in good shape, the latter to date less attended to than its wonderful building) are compromised by their neighbouring context: there is little we can do about that, but it does effectively manipulate our responses and presentational possibilities in relation to what was originally intended or hoped for.

This is why I was much taken with the ideas put forward by some Italian humanists in the later sixteenth century about what they termed the third nature.[7] In order to comprehend exactly what a garden was, they saw it as a formal extension of both the secondary world

Figure 1.3 Frontispiece for l'Abbé de Vallemont, *Curiositez de la nature et de l'art* (Paris, 1705) (author's own).

of some cultural landscape (towns, agriculture) and the 'wild' parts that were then untouched beyond. This idea is clearly visible in so many seventeenth-century engravings of estates, with the house and its ordered garden laid out around it, followed by orchards and less controlled spaces, all set within a less tended, if not wild, terrain. Each element of that large landscape – garden, usually productive context and broader context – is defined by the others. This idea of the three natures is diagrammed (it is hardly a sophisticated view) by l'Abbé de Vallemont in the frontispiece to his *Curiositez de la nature et de l'art* (Paris, 1705) (Figure 1.3).

Here, the immediate garden follows from the ploughed field, and its fountain is aligned on the natural spring that emerges from the far hillside. In charge, so to speak, of this evolution of terrain are, in front, the nymphs of nature and science, and, on the far hillside, what are evidently Apollo and the Muses who make clear and eloquent what we see in the world around us, the gradations of human control over the land.

A few years later the gardens at Stowe were created out of a larger landscape of woods and fields (Figure 1.4).

Generally, today, we are shown only the garden as a small part of a much larger engraving (the garden was big enough – not a site that can quickly be explored; but it is diminished if seen as but part of the larger whole). And coming to the gardens *proprement dits* through the woodland and agrarian landscape, we would have better appreciated its scale, its artistry and its difference from the estate as a whole.

A crucial aspect of gardens is that they change and that visitors see and respond to them differently at different times. I took up this issue, as best I could, in *The Afterlife of Gardens* (2004). Yet it still seems to be a theme more honoured in the breach than the observation: landscape architects themselves have started to think how a park or landscape will look and

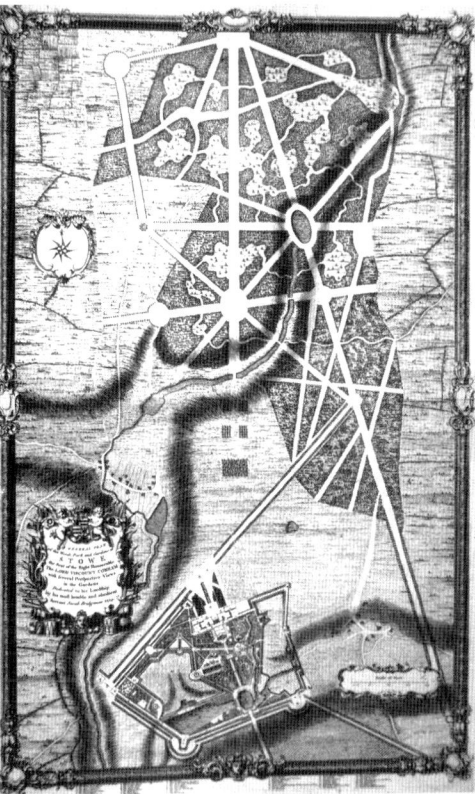

Figure 1.4 Stowe, General plan, issued by Sarah Bridgeman in *Views of Stowe* (1739). The garden is presented as the 'small' element at the bottom of the estate map (author's own).

be used 20 or 50 years hence in terms of its materials and usage, a spectacular example being, for instance, the Fresh Kills Landfill site, a landfill covering 2,200 acres (890 ha) in the New York City borough of Staten Island in the United States. But those who work to 'restore' especially famous gardens, grapple, whether they like it or not, with issues of 'authenticity'. What was authentic for Stowe in 1740 differs from how it was in 1820, and today we see and respond to things differently than people at those two dates, not least because of its immediate surrounding landscape and therefore how we visit it. So is it *our* authenticity that matters, or, say, Jacques Rigaud's, when he drew the Stowe landscape in the late 1730s? Examples are many: the restoration of the Cascade in the gardens at Chiswick (Figure 1.5) seems very different to any sketched by William Kent – our own concept of the picturesque has perhaps intervened and intruded.

Physical restorations modify how we see a place, whether it is in fact authentic now or before. A wholly different approach would be not to touch a building or site but to propose new forms, colours and more sensitive interpretations through computer simulations, where different solutions could be envisaged, either before or even in the place of actual reconstructions.

A huge resource for preservationists and conservators are the visual and verbal descriptions of specific sites (if you're lucky) and anyhow of gardens and landscapes more generally. But useful as these are, they are not objective, so we should guard against any positivistic urge! Rather, we should ask what the writer or the artist was saying, and what assumptions they were relying on in themselves or in their audience. It is crucial to immerse oneself as much

Figure 1.5 The restored Cascade at Chiswick (author's own).

as possible in the *mentalité* of a particular locality or historical period – especially if you wish to put back the items that provoked or satisfied it.[8]

One issue is not to rely upon latter-day terms to describe landscapes and gardens: avoid certain labels like 'formal' and 'informal' (terms not used as far as I can find out about landscape before the nineteenth century). Also 'baroque', 'rococo' or 'picturesque' are modern terms which – with the picturesque especially – we have debased and made banal and so are useless when we try and describe how gardens were in the early seventeenth century or to around 1800.[9] This tendency is made acute when we read – as we do often – histories of garden and landscape art, where these terms seem to do service that, in fact, historical analysis should attempt without reliance on essentially non-gardenist terms. Historians like to imply that things get better and better: Brown improved upon Kent, both upon Le Notre or any Dutch gardener. This proleptic narrative is exacerbated in England, where the ideology of the 'natural' or 'English' garden triumphs over all, leaving nineteenth-century history in some disarray! The hold of Horace Walpole's (1717–1797) Whiggish narrative is gripping, good for patriotism but not useful for garden historians of whatever nationality.

Remember, too, that garden history is an international field of study. Plant importations, the ease of travel to make sketches in other countries, and the circulation of plans, engravings and books have made gardens, for all their 'rootedness', wonderful examples of international cultural exchange. Yet, as garden forms and styles are transposed across national boundaries they also, intriguingly, may sport much more local colouring than we sometimes allow: the gardens of Massey's Court, Llanerch, Denbighshire in the seventeenth century were an almost nostalgic reminiscence of its owner's Italian journey, but surely tinged as much by local sensibilities and tastes (not to mention the exigencies of the local topography and its portrayal by an indigenous and somewhat naive artist[10]). Its bland transformation into a sub-Brownian expanse of water and grass in the next century gave it a more ordinary air. In each of its two phases, local misunderstandings of both Italianate garden art and of 'natural' landscape are as potent as their appeal to originals!

My last point is more deliberately confrontational. Compared with Europe, with its longer tradition and establishment of gardens, the United States has fewer sites that solicit that concern, and also (I suggest) a much more vigorous profession of landscape architects making things new than in Great Britain. Where are the new British works and designers that we can look to in Europe – Carlo Scarpa, Peter Latz, Paolo Burgi? Ian Hamilton Finlay's Stockwood Park, Bedfordshire, seems an awkward anomaly. Thus, it seems to me, the UK is more concerned to devote as much energy (if not more) to recovering an old and maybe abandoned garden, and in consequence displays a less vigorous and cutting-edge profession of designers to make new ones. So my title is meant as a challenge, in the face of a strongly atavistic attitude in the UK and its heritage-driven perspective. The British Garden History Society, for example, is both stronger and more influential than any named landscape architect and it devotes much of its energies to thoughtfully assessing garden preservation through Great Britain. There is, somehow, a preference (I put it crudely) to 'restore' any Capability Brown (1716–1783) landscape or dreary Victorian walled garden than to design a new one; plants are privileged over design; conservation over interpretation or new adaptations. The thinking that Niall Hobhouse is devoting to re-envisaging the gardens and landscape of the eighteenth-century Hadspen House in Somerset is a rare approach in British thinking about the land.[11] If century after century had not been so endlessly inventive in Britain, there would be no gardens and landscape work available for conservation! So I do not mean drop courses in preservation – but have a much more nuanced and creative idea of what garden and landscape conservation could mean.

Endnotes

1. This is a reworking of the notes from which I delivered a talk for historical conservation students at the University of Bath; I have amplified the text, but with fewer images (as many items cited are anyhow well enough known).
2. In this regard questions of adaptation in gardens need to be thought of differently than in architecture: see my 'Notes on Adaptation in Gardens', in *Change over Time*, Fall 2012, issue on 'Adaptation', pp. 188–200.
3. Tom Williamson is particularly useful in discriminating, not only different uses in gardens and estates, but in registering how different styles of layout (rather than a uniform mode) could be seen at the same period. Edward Harwood, Tom Williamson, Michael Leslie and John Dixon Hunt, 'Whither garden history?', *Studies in the History of Gardens and Designed Landscapes*, 27 (2007), especially pp. 97–103.
4. Various authors, *Le Style Duchêne. Henri & Achille Duchêne Architectes Paysagistes 1841–1947* (Paris, 1998); on Blenheim, pp. 32 ff.
5. John Dixon Hunt, *Nature Over Again. The garden art of Ian Hamilton Finlay* (London, 2008), p. 92, where it is also illustrated.
6. John Dixon Hunt, 'Lordship of the Feet. Toward a poetics of movement in the garden', *Landscape Design and the Experience of Motion*, in Michel Conan (ed.), Dumbarton Oaks Colloquium publication XXIV (2003), pp. 187–213.
7. Dixon Hunt, *Greater Perfections. The practice of garden theory* (London, 2000), chapter 3 'The Idea of a Garden and the Three Natures', pp. 32–75.
8. I have tried to argue how little professional landscape architects bother with this full and proper study of *mentalité* in my essay 'The politics of the past in the present. The importance of history in writing about contemporary landscape architecture', *Die Gartenkunst,* forthcoming.
9. See John Dixon Hunt, *The Picturesque Garden in Europe*, Thames & Hudson, NY (2002), and the essay, 'John Ruskin, Claude Lorrain, Robert Smithson, Christopher Tunnard, Nikolaus Pevsner, and Yve-Alain Bois walked into a bar . . .', *The Hopkins Review* (new series), Vol. 2 (2012).
10. This wonderful painting is held at the Center for British Art, Yale University; the later version is illustrated in my *Garden and Grove. The Italian Renaissance Garden in the English Imagination 1600–1750* (London, 1986), fig. 113.
11. Not much of this work is yet in the public domain; but see 'A Modernist Arcadia', *Country Life* (14 May 2008), '100 Things One Can do with the Countryside', *OASE #83, Journal for Architecture/ Tijdschrift voor architectuur,* and 'Cedric Price Disappears', *AA Files*, 50 (April 2004).

2 The National Trust approach to garden conservation

Mike Calnan
Head of Gardens, National Trust, England, UK

Why conserve gardens?

Gardening appeals on many levels. Perhaps most significantly, it brings us closer to nature and to the rhythm of the seasons. For many, gardening has offered endless opportunities for personal expression, sometimes on a scale few other activities can match. In all cultures and at all times, gardens have reflected changes in fashions and man's changing outlook on the world and, indeed, changes in the way we have seen ourselves. Historic gardens, like any inheritance from the past, can enrich our lives and we seem to be inextricably drawn to such places; seeing them in need of attention, we are propelled to care for them.

The National Trust and gardens

For over 70 years the National Trust has been acquiring gardens of international and national importance and some of more local significance for the benefit and enjoyment of present and future generations. Gardens remain central to the Trust's cause as they have from the outset, for it was the garden at Sayes Court in Deptford, London, the magnificent and celebrated creation of the seventeenth-century diarist John Evelyn (1620–1706) which first inspired the creation of the National Trust.

Sayes Court defined much that the National Trust stands for today. The garden was of exceptional importance, the historical associations were fascinating, and it was a valuable open space in the heart of London Docklands. In 1884, Octavia Hill (1838–1912) was approached with the suggestion that Sayes Court garden should become publicly owned and the adjacent Hall turned into a museum. At the time there was no organisation with the necessary legal powers to acquire the property and secure its permanent preservation. Octavia Hill's proposed name for such a new organisation was 'the Commons and Gardens Trust', although co-founder Robert Hunter's suggestion of the 'National Trust' was finally adopted and the organisation officially launched in 1895. Unfortunately, it took ten years to reach the point where the Trust could be properly constituted, by which time the opportunity to acquire Sayes Court had unfortunately passed.

'The 1921 National Trust Act' passed by Parliament 26 years after the Trust was founded, enabled the charity to hold land and property and declare it inalienable; a legal designation protecting properties from being sold or disposed of by the National Trust without Parliamentary approval. Thousands of properties, including over 200 gardens and 100 landscape parks, now come under this legal designation. In such cases, the Trust has irreversibly committed itself to their long-term care on behalf of the nation.

Historically significant gardens

Over 50% of the Trust's gardens can be considered historically significant, and are included on the English Heritage Register of Parks and Gardens of Special Historic Interest in England as being of national importance. Some are rare examples of the formal layouts that were fashionable in the seventeenth and early eighteenth century (Tredegar House, Newport; Ham House, Richmond-upon-Thames; Hanbury Hall, Worcestershire) whilst others are examples of High Victorian traditional style (Waddesdon Manor, Buckinghamshire) or engineering triumphs (Cragside, Northumberland) and eclectic taste (Biddulph Grange, Staffordshire). Gardens are also significant for their role in introducing or breeding new plant introductions (Tregwainton, Penzance; Killerton, Broadclyst and Glendurgan, Cornwall; Bodnant, Wales; Sheffield Park, Sussex or Rowallane and Mount Stewart in Northern Ireland, to name but a few), and yet more are examples of twentieth-century owners' obsessions with flower gardening (Barrington Court, Somerset; Hidcote Manor, Gloucestershire and Sissinghurst Castle garden, Kent). Modernist gardens are represented by The Homewood in Surrey.

Some gardens are of international significance, such as the magnificent early eighteenth-century 'green landscape' garden at Studley Royal, Yorkshire which, combined with the medieval ruins of the Cistercian Fountains Abbey, constitutes a World Heritage Site – a designation which puts it alongside such celebrated monuments as Stonehenge, Wiltshire, the Great Pyramid complex at Giza, Egypt and the city of Venice, Italy.

Inclusion on English Heritage's Register of Parks and Gardens may be thought to offer protection for the gardens concerned and, where such gardens are still in private hands, offer an alternative to Trust ownership. But this protection only comes as a consequence of a local authority planning decision in relation to a development application where there may be an impact on a registered site. Such planning decisions, however, impart no obligation on the owner to undertake a full restoration, to maintain an important plant collection or significant period planting style, let alone appropriate presentation standards. These more ephemeral aspects of historic gardens have generally survived despite the planning system, not because of it, and only then for the reason that enlightened owners exist who see the value of committing resources to their protection, restoration, the creation of planting effects and their ongoing maintenance. The National Trust is one such enlightened owner among the hundreds who are responsible for historic gardens in the UK.

A roll call of artistic genius

Each garden in the Trust's portfolio is unique and significant either historically, culturally, aesthetically, or botanically and together they reflect almost every example of garden fashion since Elizabethan times and the works of creative owners, designers or gardeners. The list of garden designers associated with our gardens reads like a roll call of artistic genius spanning many centuries: Sir John Vanbrugh (1664–1726), Charles Bridgeman (1690–1738), George London (1640?–1714), Henry Wise (1653–1738), William Kent (1685–1748), Lancelot 'Capability' Brown (1716–1783), Humphry Repton (1752–1818), Thomas Mawson (1861–1933), J. C. Loudon (1783–1843), Gertrude Jekyll (1843–1932) and Geoffrey Jellicoe (1900–1996), and more recently Julian and Isabel Bannerman, to name but a few.

A longstanding tradition in British gardens is their creation by a gifted owner and their head gardener, rather than a designer. Hidcote Manor garden, the creation of Lawrence

Johnston (1871–1958) or Sissinghurst, the brainchild of Vita Sackville-West (1892–1962) and her husband Harold Nicolson (1886–1968) are two well-known examples. More often than not gardens can represent many centuries of development due to the generations of the same family who, possibly with a designer, but more often a talented head gardener, have worked and reworked their garden. Such gardens owe as much to political stability as they do to the families that created them.

The National Trust has taken on gardens in varying conditions, from completely derelict sites such as Westbury Court Garden, Gloucestershire; Erddig, Wrexham and more recently the Upper Walled Garden at Quarry Bank Mill, Cheshire. Many were in serious need of specific repair and some rarer examples in excellent order, for example Woolbeding, Sussex; West Green House, Hampshire and Dyfryn, South Wales. They have also come in all shapes and sizes, from vast, 4,000-hectare (10,000-acre) designed landscapes, such as Stourhead, Wiltshire and Stowe, Buckinghamshire to small town gardens, as at Carlyle's House, London and the diminutive walled garden designed by Edwin Lutyens (1869–1944) and Gertrude Jekyll (1843–1932) at Lindisfarne, Northumberland.

National Trust Acquisition criteria

When considering a prospective acquisition, the Trust has always wished to ensure that all alternative options have been exhausted and that it is genuinely the option of last resort. Remaining in the ownership of a family that has cared for and developed it over centuries is often considered the best option for a garden, provided the funds to maintain it are available.

The prime consideration for any acquisition by the Trust is a garden's historical significance. Existing or proposed UNESCO World Heritage Site designations will be consulted, as will English Heritage's Register of Parks and Gardens, and in Wales, Cadw (there is no similar register in Northern Ireland). English Heritage grades gardens I, II or II*, depending on historical importance, rarity value and the quality of landscaping. Acquisition will also be dependent, registered or not, on a garden's historical associations, aesthetic qualities, archaeological, architectural, botanical or biological significance and the likely public benefit and the impact of access.

Taking on a garden and declaring it inalienable will commit the organisation to maintaining it in perpetuity – that is, forever, and all that implies, so the Trust is, rightly, highly selective. Many properties in the early years of the Trust came with an endowment sufficient to cover the cost of maintenance; however, due to inflation, the original sums soon proved inadequate in a number of important instances. Establishing a secure financial future, either from an endowment or via income generation has become critical for the long-term sustainability of the property – and the Trust. Likewise, there are limits to growth for any organisation and the Trust does not seek to overstretch itself financially or in any other way, no matter how significant and worthy an acquisition may be. It will therefore remain cautious of committing itself to another new property until all criteria which determine its 'merit' and financial viability have been considered.

Inclusion on the EH Register of Parks and Gardens indicates whether grant aid is likely to be available for essential repairs, whether from English Heritage, the Heritage Lottery Fund or other funding sources. Such financial considerations are paramount, especially today, and careful thought is given to restoration and ongoing maintenance and staffing costs.

Income generation opportunities are especially important if the acquisition is to be financially self-sufficient (as far as it can be). The potential for income generated through entrance tickets, shop, restaurant, plant sales and event income streams are all important considerations. A garden which scores highly in all these areas has at least a chance of being considered by the National Trust. However, access limitations, for example where a vital car park cannot be provided due to the physical nature of the site, or where the NT's presence

Figure 2.1 Plants generally make up 80% of the content of gardens. Garden conservation therefore must include the systematic care of plant collections and combinations which determine a garden's significance, character and period style. A view of 'Acers' at Top Bridge on the Top Lake at Sheffield Park Gardens, East Sussex. (Reproduced by permission of the National Trust: NTPL 67648.)

and likelihood of attracting thousands of visitors who might have a detrimental impact on the garden or its vicinity, could go against its acquisition by the Trust.

Plants and their significance

Plants contribute so much to the character or content of a garden. As a general rule, they make up over 80% of the content of an average garden and more in gardens where there has been a tradition for plant collecting. Plants can be used architecturally to provide structure (e.g. formal lawns, hedging, topiary), compositions (e.g. flower borders, rose gardens, shrubberies), specimens (ornamental trees or shrubs, see Figure 2.1) or as produce (orchards, kitchen and herb gardens). It should therefore come as no surprise to realise that most garden conservation is concerned with plant conservation. The care of plants and gardening in general constitutes a large element of the day-to-day conservation of a garden.

The incremental actions of the gardener are what keep a garden in a particular state and their skills determine how faithfully a garden can be conserved to represent particular periods, styles or influences. The National Trust puts great store in developing the knowledge and skills of its garden staff to enable them to apply their horticultural knowledge as conservators of gardens. Those with a deep knowledge of the history and horticultural context of their garden are the garden's curator, a title which better describes their role and its status.

Curiously, the conservation of gardens as a discipline has often been dominated by interest in their design, layout and man-made features. For many years English Heritage's Register of Parks and Gardens did not generally recognise the significance of plants in gardens; its main focus being archaeological, historic or design features and associations.

In the absence of any national grading for plant collections, the Trust is working on drawing up an inventory of the significant plants in its gardens. It works closely with plant conservation bodies, such as Plant Heritage, the Royal Horticultural Society and Royal Botanic Gardens Kew. Plant Heritage has recently recognised 'historic' collections, which will enable first introduction collections by famous plant hunters such as David Douglas

(1799–1834) or Robert Fortune (1812–1880) to be recognised as significant. The aim of the UK's plant conservation organisations is to promote the recording, analysis and conservation of species and cultivated plants growing in Britain. This activity has enabled the National Trust to recreate authentic planting styles using plants, more often than not, propagated from the originals, thereby offering the public a living museum of authentic design, fashions and plants covering the last 500 years.

There are some 300,000 types of cultivated plants in circulation in the UK, including species originally collected from the wild and those that are the result of breeding and selection programmes. The National Trust has one of the largest such collections in single private ownership anywhere, simply because it owns so many gardens, and this holding brings with it serious responsibilities. To this purpose the Trust has invested in its own Plant Conservation Centre dedicated to helping property staff care for their historic plants and collections.

Conservation approaches

It is probably true to say that there are as many views on how to care for heritage gardens as there are those interested in the subject. The Trust's own philosophy, as set out in this chapter, has evolved slowly, based on growing experience accumulated over 70 years across many types of gardens and sites. In essence, the Trust's aim has been to conserve what has been deemed significant about each garden, whether its design, character, content, special features, ambience or traditions. In doing so, the Trust's sights are set far into the future and it cannot allow itself to be influenced unduly by short-term fashionable opinion. Should this be the case, many fine Victorian garden features could have been altered or lost in decades past when most things Victorian were viewed with disdain.

The Trust's approach to the management of each garden has been, and will always be, determined by its significance(s), condition (and therefore cost of restoration or repair), and the ongoing financial costs, all of which in turn could determine a range of conservation options.

Development of National Trust conservation policy and practice

It is fair to say that for much of its history the Trust was 'out on its own' in the field of garden conservation, formulating policy and practice as much as emulating what had been established by others. This situation arose quite simply because there was not much else to follow in the early years, and because the range and quality of the Trust's gardens placed it in a unique position. Its approach to conservation is now well established and applied to almost all gardens in its care.

The Trust's approach to any major new property (and many that we have had for a long time) is to undertake research with the aim of developing a Conservation Management Plan. This will bring together evidence from various sources – archaeology, plant and land surveys, cross-referenced with analysis of archival and other forms of research and a thorough analysis of the garden's historical and landscape context.

A smaller less complex garden may only warrant a 'Conservation Statement' consisting of a few pages setting out significance and conservation aims. A 'Statement of Significance', defining what makes the garden special, is then written. Significance may be dependent on a garden's history or historical associations, or connection with a particular owner or designer. Its design, character, content (statuary, garden buildings, plant or wildlife), special features, qualities or traditions are also considered, as are the motivation of the original creator and the context in which they operated.

'Spirit of Place'   Gardens can have an effect on individuals, and this effect plays as much a part in determining their significance as any physical quality. These subtle but significant ingredients are aptly summed up in the term 'spirit of the place', a quality arising from the combined effect of a garden's design, layout, aesthetics, history and atmosphere. Some gardens have a more powerful effect than others. A 'Spirit of Place' statement defines these qualities and supplements the 'Statement of Significance'. It can be a short document, a few pages at most, which will aim to define the essential character or special qualities of a site. These could be tangible or intangible but their protection will be the focus of all conservation efforts that follow.

Conservation – management influences

Factors which reveal a site's history can equally present a barrier to their restoration. Archaeology is important in understanding the fragments of the past and a garden's story through its remains. Roman structures at The Weir, Herefordshire and remains of medieval ridge and furrow field systems which account for the undulating character of the area of garden known as Westonbirt at Hidcote Manor all add to their history and significance and our considerations when managing those gardens. At Stourhead, underwater archaeologists' surveys show us the form of the original valley from which the main lake was created and aerial infrared photography has revealed a long-lost former drive. Such evidence can assist our understanding of a garden's evolution, layout or content, and influence its ongoing conservation. But archaeology can also impose restrictions, preventing replacement planting on top of newly discovered remains, such as the medieval villages in the park at Llanachaeron, Pembrokeshire where parkland trees once existed, even though the trees were deemed historic plantings.

Wildlife interest can also add to a site's significance. Wildlife significance can pre-date the layout of a garden or park or be the result of later management, or lack of it. More often than not, the nature conservation value of a site of some antiquity has survived as a result of its continuous management as a garden or landscape, not despite the garden's existence. The biological significance of the wildlife content of any gardens will of course influence aims for its long-term conservation. For example, a vast conurbation of ant hills at Petworth Park, West Sussex now prevent the return of the smooth lawns that formed part of Capability Brown's vast 700-acre park. Many of the Trust's oldest parks, such as Dinefwr, Carmarthenshire; Dunham Massey, Greater Manchester and Knole, Kent contain ancient trees of more than four or five hundred years of age. Their historical and biological significance is considerable – for example, rare beetles inhabiting dead wood can provide evidence of a continuity of tree cover on sites dating back to the last Ice Age, 10,000 years ago. SSSI designation of ancient trees in parts of the garden at Powis Castle, Wales, likewise is an important aspect of what makes the place special. Thirty-five out of 80 NT parks have SSSI designations and this exerts an influence over how the designed historic layout is managed.

Evidence

In addition to the physical constraints to authentic restoration there can, despite the best efforts of researchers, surveyors and garden historians, be a lack of information, knowledge or understanding of a site. This is certainly the case with a number of Trust gardens and, curiously, it applies to one of the most written about and visited gardens in the land – Stowe, the birthplace of the English Landscape Style.

Stowe has an unrivalled collection of three-quarters of a million archive documents, 60,000 of which have been transcribed to reveal much about the construction of the vast house, the 10,000 acre designed landscape and parks, the 400-acre garden and its 36 temples and monuments. Bills for the eighteenth and nineteenth centuries record every piece of stone, the quarries they came from, and haulage costs. There are even bills for the overnight accommodation of the wagon driver who collected the stone and his assistant (and accounts of what they paid the chambermaid!).

There are bills from stone masons, bills for the laying out of paths and construction (by hand) of the 11 lakes, bills for bells and collars for the sheep that grazed within the garden and for plants from a wealth of nurseries such as Lee and Kennedy, John Williamson and James Veitch, spanning the period 1730–1921. The accounts even record the fortnightly tasks and wages for every gardener for 150 years, with those from 1741–51 being in the hand of Lancelot Brown himself, who was Clerk of Works at the time.

Other gardens rarely have anything like the same volume of archival information. But, despite such a wealth of information, it only adds up to a mere 5–10% of that needed by the National Trust to recreate the planted elements of the landscape. Archaeological investigations and archives have helped with the restoration of buildings, the reinstatement of statues and former paths, but apart from the fragmentary descriptions of planting details by some visitors (frustratingly too few recorded their observations compared to the hundreds, if not thousands, who must have visited over the decades), there was and remains little to go on in terms of recreating planting details. So, in the general absence of sufficient evidence, restorations such as that at Stowe are only able to go so far. Practically every planting decision in such circumstances has to rely on conjecture, underpinned with knowledge of how gardens might have been planted in their day.

Restoration

Restoration is an activity which understandably attracts a great deal of attention and is often cited as the reason people want to develop a career in historic gardens. Human ingenuity in restoring vast landscapes back to what they were can seem miraculous; the process brings delight and seeing images of the 'before' and 'after' never ceases to inspire. Involvement in a restoration project can be one of the most rewarding jobs in anyone's career. Restoration is effectively a reworking and reinterpretation of history. We should not delude ourselves that a restored garden is a historically 'authentic' one, especially if some of what survived has been altered or even removed in the restoration process. Where a garden relies on a high percentage of ephemeral plants for its overall effect which cannot be maintained in position indefinitely, such restorations should perhaps more accurately be called 'evocations'. Despite the inherent limitations of restoration as an approach, it can still represent the most effective way of recreating a garden layout or example of period style.

Choosing the period or moment to which a garden should be restored presents a number of philosophical dilemmas. Stowe for example never stopped changing, being continually developed to reflect the new ideas, fashions and whims of successive owners, designers and head gardeners over 150 years. The choices the Trust faced here were to restore the earlier eighteenth-century Charles Bridgeman (1690–1738) and later William Kent (1685–1748) additions and style of planting of the period, or the mid-eighteenth-century Brownian landscape style or the later 'picturesque' influence? Choosing any one moment in time would have involved sweeping away evidence of later developments or have diluted the consequence of over 150 years of evolution. This palimpsest or tapestry of overlays can be far more significant and informative than a garden, artificially taken back to one moment in time, will ever be. The solution to this dilemma was simple. Research revealed that some areas of the garden matured at different times to others, and this has conveniently guided the National Trust's approach over the last 25 years.

An alternative approach is where a series of overlays complement each other. Blickling Hall, Norfolk for example comprises four main layers representing seventeenth-, eighteenth-, nineteenth- and twentieth-century 'overlays' by different owners and their designers or gardeners. The objective here is to conserve this series of accretions as they are responsible for the garden's sense of timelessness, richness and significance. For example, the influence of twentieth-century plantsman Norah Lindsey (1873–1948) sits comfortably within the site of the formal nineteenth-century parterre she reworked. This sits at the climax of a formal woodland scheme first laid out in the seventeenth century and reworked in the nineteenth century which, in turn, is surrounded by the eighteenth-century Brownian park. If you know what you are looking at, touring a garden of many layers can be a journey through time.

Re-creation

Where a period garden is deliberately created, when no such garden ever existed, we talk in terms of 're-creation'. In certain circumstances this may be an acceptable way forward, providing an historic house with an appropriate setting it never had. This is the approach the Trust has applied at a number of gardens such as Moseley Old Hall, Wolverhampton, where a garden has been created of the type Charles II might have seen when he hid there after the Battle of Worcester in 1651. At Washington Old Hall, the home of George Washington's family in Tyne and Wear, the Trust has established a 'period style' garden in a yard of the former farmhouse, even though a garden never existed there. This development was considered appropriate in providing an enhanced setting for the house and additional benefit for visitors by interpreting the property and expanding the appeal of the site. Other examples include the Tudor-style herb garden at Buckland Abbey, Devon and Tudor vegetable garden at nearby Trerice, Cornwall with its recreated 'Great Squirt' wooden barrel early watering device.

In some instances there can be an argument for recreating a garden from early records despite it having existed for a short time, where the family took a deliberate decision centuries ago to sweep it away. Recreation could be justified in these situations on the grounds of maintaining an example of a specific and rare style. This is certainly the case with the Privy Garden at Hampton Court, Middlesex.

At the Trust's Hanbury Hall, Worcestershire (see Figure 2.2), the formal early eighteenth-century layout of London and Wise and other influences has been recreated principally using the 1732 birds-eye drawing by James Daugherty, and limited archival and archaeological evidence. Hanbury now represents a significant recreation of an early formal garden and planting style which were almost entirely swept away later in the eighteenth century in a frenzy for landscape gardening amongst British landowners. Figure 2.3 shows

Figure 2.2 Hanbury Hall parterre, based on a birds-eye view by the surveyor James Dougherty. This scheme as shown in a 1731–1733 garden survey was confirmed by archaeology in the 1990s when the garden was restored with financial assistance from the European Union. In addition to the large sunken parterre complete with bed of florist's flowers, the former fruit garden, pavilions, specimen shrub walks, hedged *allee*, grove, bowling green and other early eighteenth-century features have been restored with plants typical of the period. (Reproduced by permission of the National Trust: NTPL 121362.)

Figure 2.3 The Wilderness as recreated in 2000 based on further investigations and contextual research. Low hornbeam hedges enclose 'quarters' populated with thorns and maples for shade and flowering shrubs for scent under planted or 'enamelled' with wild flowers. The central enclosure is furnished with sentinel *Juniperus virginiana* in terracotta pots. Careful, regular pruning is required to keep everything in scale. (Reproduced by permission of the National Trust: NTPL 121340.)

the National Trust's Wilderness as recreated in 2000 based on extensive investigations and contextual research.

Flower garden conservation

A flower garden, especially from the twentieth century, presents a particular challenge for garden conservators. Such gardens generally rely heavily on a high proportion of herbaceous perennials for their effect. Maintaining the style of a flower garden's creator or creators after they have departed comes down to careful study of what makes the garden significant. A deep knowledge of the plant material used is required to establish trends and preferences, style and the contextual influences prevalent at the time of its creation.

Sissinghurst (Figure 2.4) is an interesting case in point. It was created between 1930 and 1962 by Vita Sackville-West experimenting with planting associations within the formal framework created by her husband Harold Nicolson. Many visitors past and present believe they are looking at Vita's original plantings. However, the sophistication seen today was the achievement of her two Waterperry-trained head gardeners who took her style to new heights over a 30-year period from the 1960s following Vita and Harold's deaths. The Trust's solution and policy, using a music analogy, is to seek to maintain this virtuoso horticultural performance in perpetuity. The challenge is to interpret the 'original score' conceived by Vita. If this means that individuals bring something of their own to the garden then that is both inevitable and desirable. As in other arts, if artistic talent is to be given the stage on which to interpret and perform 'classics' from the past they must be allowed a degree of creative freedom.

Plant health impacts on conservation
Plant health has become a cause for concern and one of the most significant challenges in being able to pursue conservation objectives. In less than a decade, *Phytopthora ramorum* and *kernoviae*, acute oak decline, chestnut leaf miner and bleeding canker and now 'ash die back' have all posed immense threats to our

Figure 2.4 While many owners commissioned or created significant gardens, the recreation and maintenance of horticultural features such as these impressive borders at Sissinghurst can only be achieved by qualified, professional gardeners. Conserving skills is an important aspect of garden conservation. (Reproduced by permission of the National Trust: NTPL 160368.)

countryside, historic landscapes and gardens and their plants. More threats are on the horizon as our environment is subject to change.

Phytopthoras brought in on flood waters have resulted in the loss of sections of the yew hedging at Westbury Court Garden, leading to replanting dilemmas. One or two gardens are known to have a high percentage on plants infected by *Phytopthoras*, which shows up in leaf blemishes and poor growth characteristics. Many fine specimen trees and shrubs have been lost from gardens and major plant collections in the last ten years, but sometimes new opportunities open up. We may have lived with the impact of elm disease, but chestnut bleeding canker has more recently triggered the felling of all the historic horse chestnut avenues at Barrington House, Somerset. These are to be replaced by *Liriodendron tulipifera* (tulip tree), for which there was already a precedent in the form of a short section of a surviving avenue elsewhere on the estate. In other instances, clearance of diseased plants has opened up former historic views and vistas as at Arlington Court, Devon.

The National Trust Plant Propagation Centre (PPC) in Devon exists to undertake emergency propagation in the face of such diseases and other natural threats. Its remit is to propagate significant plants, to ensure the survival of threatened specimens and the supply of disease-free replacements. The Trust has embarked on a ten-year programme to draw up an inventory for all plants in its gardens and to date has amassed records for 350,000 plants in 80 of its 200 gardens. Such work needs to be recognised as an inseparable component of the conservation of historic gardens.

Access and conservation

Seven out of the National Trust's top ten visitor attractions are gardens, with some, such as Studley Royal, Yorkshire; Wakehurst Place, West Sussex and Polesden Lacey, Surrey regularly attracting over 300,000 people annually. Overall 16 million people visit National Trust gardens each year. Access on such a scale brings many challenges, especially as many properties are moving towards year-round opening. Hidcote and Sissinghurst alone each spend thousands of pounds annually on replacing worn-out turf, and an equal amount on protect-

Figure 2.5 Heavy visitor traffic poses a great challenge for popular gardens open to the public. Astro Turf used in the long garden at Cliveden allows the visitor to experience this green enclosure as originally designed. (Reproduced by permission of the National Trust: NTPL 974008.)

ing sensitive areas from further damage. Sports turf technology has also been used at Hidcote to create all-weather visitor traffic resilient lawns.

Cliveden, Buckinghamshire recently introduced 'Astro Turf' in the Long Garden to replace the narrow central path which had become permanently worn due to constant visitor traffic (Figure 2.5). In other instances, the Trust has had to replace grass with hard paths which can change the character of a garden if not sensitively done. Former grass paths at Sissinghurst have been replaced in parts by more durable brick paths or stone paving and feel in keeping as good quality traditional materials have been used. In some gardens, restricting assess is the only option – timed tickets are occasionally required to ensure that the garden is not overwhelmed by the number of people who wish to see it.

The National Trust has developed a 'Conservation for Access' toolkit to help its property staff calculate their garden's carrying capacity and the resources needed to increase year-round access while maintaining presentation and conservation standards. Other influences on how a garden is conserved include the provision of signage, car parks, restaurants, shops, plant sales areas and seats. These features are unavoidable due to public demand, but need to be positioned sensitively. They inevitably have an impact on the site, its ambience and ongoing maintenance.

Financial implications

It is important to remember that major gardens open to the public owe their existence to the people who come to visit them. Without visitors, the National Trust would struggle to find the £11 million a year it spends on maintaining its gardens each year.

Ensuring gardens remain open and appealing is down to the number and skills of our garden staff who are responsible for translating theory into practice, and it is their skills and expertise that the Trust relies on. In reality, once wholesale restoration is over, much of the day-to-day care of historic gardens is the responsibility of professional gardeners. They in turn can be advised by a wide range of experts and practices including archaeology, nature conservation, architectural, and gardens specialists. The Trust employs four full-time Gardens Consultants and a Garden Historian who along with local Curators help properties determine the right conservation approach.

Head gardeners must, to an extent, be all-rounders, skilled horticulturalists, and equally skilled in caring for plants, record-keeping, managing staff, volunteers and budgets. They are a precious commodity and, sadly, the 90 we employ amongst our 500 permanent garden staff are not enough. With the endowment required for a single gardener post set at £1.9 million (the figure required to ensure that the necessary recurrent income is available whilst the capital sum is retained in perpetuity), increasing the number of gardeners is a formidable task. However, creative and varied ways are being used to help fund additional gardening posts, through the use of income, investments and, potentially, sponsorship.

The National Trust relies heavily on its 5,000 garden volunteers who enable it to take on new areas which otherwise it could not afford to do. They do not replace permanent staff, but supplement them. At Wimpole Hall, Cambridgeshire the extensive walled kitchen garden is maintained by a team of 50 volunteers managed by one member of staff. The Trust would simply not be able to take on this area and show it to the public if it had to employ that many people.

In order to conserve gardens, you have to conserve the skills of the professional gardener. The National Trust Gardens Academy, generously supported by the National Gardens Scheme, offers a one-year Foundation Certificate and an advanced two-year National Trust Diploma in Heritage Gardening. These develop the skills the organisation needs to restore, maintain and enhance gardens and present them to the highest standards. This internal 'supply line' has become even more critical at a time when such skills are becoming increasingly rare.

Staffing levels

By historical standards, current staffing levels are low in most gardens. In the eighteenth century gardens like Stowe were maintained by 30 full-time gardeners, supplemented by 30 labourers and temporary help from estate families and farm workers after the summer harvest. Today, the vast majority of the grounds are maintained by 11 full-time gardeners, aided by up to five long-term volunteers and a number of part-time local volunteers. Baron Ferdinand de Rothschild (1839–1898), owner of Waddesdon Manor, Buckinghamshire, employed over 80 gardeners in the late nineteenth century (raising a staggering 150,000 annuals for its bedding schemes); today the number is 14. Maintaining similar standards to those of the past is only possible due to labour-saving maintenance techniques and equipment. Labour costs account for up to 70% of the cost of running a garden and are a significant factor in determining what can be done and what is and what is not restored or conserved.

Continual development/Innovation

Commercial pressures on gardens are now immense. Despite gardens being the Trust's most popular destination for repeat visitors we constantly have to think of new ways of attracting visitors who require a more interactive and personal experience and these can be fulfilled readily in the sensual and tactile surroundings of a garden. It is inevitable that individual, small-scale innovations will be part of this process of maintaining visitor appeal. In some circumstances larger developments are an acceptable and desirable aspect of interpretation; adding new features or refreshing old ones (in keeping with the overall conservation aims and spirit of place). These keep a garden fresh, vibrant and pleasing to visitors, maintaining the essential flow of income needed for upkeep.

New features, for example winter interest and winter gardens, have been developed to appeal to visitors year-round and offer something new to see.

This has positive implications, as seen in the creativity found in the winter garden at Anglesey Abbey, Cambridge and Dunham Massey (Figure 2.6) and most recently Mottisfont Abbey, Hampshire which have changed visitors' perceptions of gardens in winter. At other properties, such as Bodnant, Conwy and Packwood House, Solihull, talented head gardeners have had the freedom to develop imaginative new designs and features for which there is

Figure 2.6 A section of the new Winter Garden at Dunham Massey. Although no precedent exists, the winter garden has been created to provide interest at a time when there would be little else to attract visitors. Gardens cannot survive without income, so such developments are occasionally necessary to the financial sustainability of a property. (Reproduced by permission of the National Trust: NTPL 950057.)

sometimes no historic precedent. At Felbrigg Hall, Norfolk, and Overbeck's, Devon, advantage has been taken of the particular climate in these gardens to take full benefit for plants which flourish in dry or temperate locations. At Cliveden, the traditional bedding in the vast parterre invented by Head Gardener John Fleming in the 1850s has been returned to the grandeur of its heyday but with the advantage of a great wealth of modern plants to choose from.

When considering a garden's significance, we should not lose sight of the tradition of innovation, experimentation and development which characterised so many great gardens. But this tradition, even 'significance' of a garden is often overlooked when a too-rigid definition of conservation is applied. 'Stewardship' is perhaps a better term, within which conservation sits as one of the tools in the management toolkit. Stewardship is an ethical approach to long-term responsible planning and the management of a place. It offers an appropriate response to the inevitability of change and desirability of development and it may become the only realistic approach as our environment changes.

Conclusion

Flexibility is a key consideration in conserving gardens and is the only realistic response to the inevitable forces of change. Despite short-term commercial and visitor pressures on gardens, the job of those responsible for a garden's conservation remains, in the long run, to fully understand what is significant about each garden, whether historically, botanically, artistically or otherwise. They must ensure that a garden's important qualities, traditions and content and the garden as a whole is passed on successfully from our generation to the next. Long may gardeners have the skills to maintain the great gardens of the past, to bring us pleasure and reveal how we once gardened.

3 The nature of gardens and their significance

John Sales

Gardens Consultant and Vice President of Royal Horticultural Society and Garden History Society, Gloucestershire, UK

Introduction

Gardens are not merely objects to admire, they are processes to experience. Obviously they incorporate both but are determined principally by the complex web of processes that are inherent in their creation and sustainability. Inanimate objects and fabric, important in a garden's structure and ornament, need to be maintained and repaired, but garden conservation in the longer term is overwhelmingly concerned with establishing and sustaining processes of growth, cultivation, development, decay and renewal, with an ideal in mind. The National Trust's Stourhead gardens (Figure 3.1) provide an excellent example of gardens whose structural beauty is perfectly complemented by skilled planting. At every level gardens are shaped by their management, and above all by the quality of their gardening. However good their structure, without consistent and considered horticultural and arboricultural intervention they soon become mere skeletons of their intended glory. The proper care of gardens demands a variety of skills, sound judgement, good timing and long-term persistence.

Defining gardens

Gardens (including designed landscape parks) are places arranged and managed for effect, enjoyment and production, incorporating site, land form, plants, animals, water, usually buildings and other artefacts. Unlike other art forms they involve all the senses – sound, smell, taste, touch – as well as vision and that indefinable sense of place that can arise in a variety of ways, including conscious design. It is perfectly possible quickly to assemble many of these components and design them so as to produce the semblance of a garden in various stages of 'maturity', depending on how much money is spent. But this will not be the real thing until the essential processes of growth and development have been established and the plants have had time to adjust to one another and form a community, to be constantly adjusted by the gardener. Skipping a few years like this is understandable in an age of impatience but it misses much of the point of gardens and gardening, which is to enjoy the creative pleasure of semi-natural processes from birth to death. Indicative of the former approach is the make-over industry – all drama and instant gratification – and those

---

Gardens & Landscapes in Historic Building Conservation, First Edition. Edited by Marion Harney.
© 2014 John Wiley & Sons, Ltd. Published 2014 by John Wiley & Sons, Ltd.

Figure 3.1 Stourhead. Gardens consist of an inorganic framework of land form, buildings and water and an ever-changing population of plants, which can be structural as well as ornamental or productive (author's own).

miraculous flower show gardens which in truth consist of static tableaux. They are admirable, but as close to real gardens as waxworks are to real people or film sets to real life. I exaggerate of course.

Gardens incorporate the living and the dead, the dynamic and the inert – a stark contrast which gives gardens their unique fascination. Buildings, structures, sculptures, even water and land form are subject to change by weathering, deterioration, modification and addition. These incorporate within them much of the garden's 'memory', i.e. evidence of its history and use. For their survival they need to be maintained and repaired, even 'preserved', but quite obviously they are incapable of spontaneous development, although they may be host to plant and animal life. They are not dynamic.

A garden's organic elements, dead and alive, comprise an always unique ecosystem of plants, birds, animals (including microorganisms of all kinds) and people, sustained by being managed with particular purposes in mind – production, design, ornament, interest, education, recreation, etc. In many ways this community of plants and animals will have a life of its own, affected furthermore by unpredictable events. Garden management consists essentially of endeavouring to stimulate, predict and control change and to react positively to unplanned and accidental events, including pests and diseases, storm damage, vandalism and so forth – always guiding events towards a known ideal. Effective management involves constant critical review and consequent adjustment.

Approach to conservation

Site To a great extent real gardens and designed landscapes are controlled and determined by the environment in which they are made. Site, surroundings, soil conditions and climate always play a large part, positively or negatively, in the garden's making and development. Indeed, choice of site may have been an overriding consideration – to take advantage of views, borrowed landscape, favourable microclimate, fertile lime-free soil and so on. But advantage in one respect often leads to disadvantage in another, e.g. views and shelter are largely incompatible; characterful sites of historic significance impose restrictions. Once a garden is sited and established we have limited control over these factors. Our job is to make the best of the situation in relation to the purposes of the place. Our conservation response can only be to modify and ameliorate as necessary, for example by providing shelter, irrigation and manuring and by choice of plants and position, while exploiting to the full advantages such as views, aspect, sun, shade and microclimate.

Buildings With the built elements we have much more control, given sufficient funding and the necessary expertise. All gardens have a more-or-less fixed structure of land form and buildings, including terraces, steps, walls and other structures; probably also waterworks in the form of lakes, ponds, canals, streams and fountains. With the necessary resources these features can be repaired or restored to a precise blueprint and held, if desired, relatively unchanged, barring accident, for long periods. Almost anything is possible. The philosophy for the conservation of historic buildings and artefacts is now firmly established – maintain and repair 'as much as is necessary and as little as possible'. The conservation response for these azoic elements in any significant garden or designed landscape must be to maintain, preserve, repair, adapt and possibly to replace.

Plants The crucial component of gardens and designed landscapes comprises the living things they contain – plants of all kinds (including trees and lesser organisms) (Figure 3.2), animals, birds and people. The possibility of control over these dynamic and interacting elements varies. It cannot, and should not, be complete and needs to be guided by a site-specific conservation philosophy; also forward planning, anticipation and flexibility. People and plants are, to a degree, inherently unpredictable so the conservation response should consist of close management. Plants and plant communities need to be consistently

Figure 3.2 Hidcote. Plants are the crucial element of gardens and they need to be consistently managed, manipulated and renewed in pursuit of a unique ideal (author's own).

manipulated, trained, controlled, regenerated and renewed in relation to other living organisms and to the garden's fixed architectural components. Continuous change from plant growth, development, interaction, decay and renewal is, in the last analysis, what people most enjoy about gardens.

Management   The management of historic gardens and landscapes is not a precise art that can be programmed into a prescriptive schedule of routine procedures. It should involve not only routine upkeep but also cycles of development and renewal based upon the pursuit of clear ideals, anticipation of change and judgements of timing and priority. The importance of consistency can hardly be overstated because change, whether natural or forced, is inevitable and constantly needs to be managed and directed towards clear objectives. Hence the need for a well-written and comprehensive conservation plan to guide every decision, including unexpected dilemmas arising from extremes of weather, change of use, opening to visitors, adaptations to take account of changing resources and so forth, as well as the more predictable changes arising from plant growth, development, maturity and senescence. As well as ideals, this plan should set out opportunities and constraints as we see them at present, so as to inform our successors. The best test of any conservation plan is to assess the extent to which it helps the manager in decision-making and in solving the dilemmas that arise in managing the place, especially in deciding priority.

Change   Not that change, day-to-day, season-to-season and year-to-year, should be a matter for regret. Much of the pleasure of gardening and of visiting gardens, whether 'historic' or not, is derived from experiencing change and development. In gardens, every repeated task, every routine event, every regular footfall has a cumulative effect. Style, quality and timing of regular operations like pruning, training, cultivation, propagation and replanting obviously have a continuous, as well as an immediate effect. But so too do routine jobs like grass mowing – height, frequency and direction of cut, choice of machine and disposal of cut material all have a profound long-term effect, as well as an immediate impact. Much the same applies to hedge cutting, which over time contributes greatly to the garden's sense of place. To write these down as mere 'maintenance' operations undermines their value as the most crucial part of the garden's conservation. True 'maintenance' in gardens refers entirely to dealing with inanimate objects like paths, buildings, machinery and ornament.

Upkeep   The terms 'maintenance' and 'repair' are relevant as far as fabricated objects and mechanical processes are concerned but make little sense when applied to organic processes and living organisms which have to be propagated, cultivated and sustained. To attempt to cram all of horticulture and garden conservation into such inadequate terms as maintenance and repair is to deny the reality of plant growth and development on which the very planet depends. Similarly there is widespread misuse of the term 'architecture' in relation to gardens in place of 'structure', which includes plants as well as fabricated objects. In almost all gardens, trees, hedges, topiary and shrubs contribute importantly to their structure as well as to their decoration, function and shelter. 'Architecture' applies to the built elements, entirely fabricated or formed by earth-moving; always inert except in the case of moving water. Perhaps the most obvious illustration of this misconception applies to trees and shrubs, which are bound to grow and die. In architectural terms their dead stumps would be 'part of the historic fabric' which would be conserved by 'repair', i.e. 'restraining the process of decay', thereby rendering the essential processes of renewal impossible in formal gardens and inviting the spread of soil-borne diseases. For reasons of nature conservation, where this is a significant value in the garden, some dead stumps and dead wood may well be retained but surely not to be 'repaired' or 'maintained'.

Art and design   The making and subsequent care of gardens is a widely accessible art form at which the British have excelled for centuries. Fine art has been traditionally defined primarily in relation to fixed objects – mythical, representative and more recently abstract, in paintings and sculpture. In modern times these certainties have been undermined by deliberately ephemeral art forms – artistic concepts and installations that cross barriers that were previously seen as immutable, thereby converging ever more closely with garden making and development. Garden and landscape art has been similarly associated primarily with the design and construction of new gardens; sometimes with the conscious redesign and adaptation of existing places. For practical reasons of site preparation, initial construction, cost estimation and design illustration it is usually necessary to produce a series of drawings, which may be art works in their own right but are principally a means of communication, not an end in themselves. And it is perfectly possible, even desirable, to set out the concept and develop the design directly in response to the site. This is in fact how many, if not most, of our greatest gardens were made, sometimes within a lifetime or less and sometimes over several generations, even centuries. Eighteenth-century landscapes like Studley Royal, Yorkshire; Stourhead, Wiltshire and Painshill Park, Surrey were laid out piecemeal according to an evolving concept and innovative twentieth-century gardens like Hidcote, Gloucestershire; Sissinghurst, Kent; Mount Stewart, Newtownards and Bodnant, Wales were developed and planted either without a masterplan or as gradual overlays transforming an earlier layout.

Garden making is undoubtedly an important art form but it can be expressed in a variety of ways, sometimes beginning as a comparatively finite design developed on paper or by computer or, more often, by starting with an outline concept to be worked out directly on the ground by trial and error over a period, responding to the site and to changing ideals. In practice, the paper plan almost invariably needs to be adjusted from the beginning in the light of reality and developed cumulatively over time as plants mature and accidents of nature and nurture take their toll. There is no end to this, and the quality of the initial design can be judged accurately by the resilience of its concept in the face of constant change. As at Powis Castle, mid-Wales (Figure 3.3), it is the simplest and most robust designs that survive to be enriched by generations of careful upkeep and detailed change.

Along with this is the phenomenon of the artist/plantsman designing with plants – trees, shrubs, herbaceous plants, annuals and alpines – day-to-day, month-to-month and year-to-year, interacting with site, climate, diseases, pests and the people who use the place. Plants need to be rearranged and controlled with change anticipated; provoked and manipulated in search of an ideal, never completely achieved, at any rate for long. It is the cumulative impact of this series of actions, decisions and judgements, large and small, incorporating

Figure 3.3 Powis Castle. Thanks to a simple and robust design the terraces at Powis have survived for three centuries, to be developed and enriched by successive owners, including the National Trust. The yew 'twmps' are powerful sculptural forms created by successive generations of gardeners (author's own).

the special skills and techniques of the place that constitutes a particular garden style, i.e. the artistry of gardening. Although an ephemeral art form it is nevertheless real and at its best analogous to the works of other artists/craftsmen. But gardening at this level is also comparable in some ways to the performing arts like music, drama, opera and especially ballet, plants being constantly choreographed to take account of change.

This expertise and artistry, a combination of plantsmanship, aesthetic sensitivity and foresight at the highest level is not common and is much underrated even by garden and landscape designers. It is not the same as putting plants together prettily or even meaningfully for a flower show or other event. Gardening, like the performing arts and even cooking, can be practised at any level from habitual routine to high art. As with other arts and crafts it is learned by working alongside expert practitioners, subject to their criticism and example.

Staffing It almost goes without saying that the most important single factor in the conservation of gardens, apart from their protection, is the calibre, sufficiency and continuity of its staff, including their management. Funding needs to be continuous and adequate to employ a core of skilled gardeners with sound judgement and a developed observational aptitude. Basic horticultural training is helpful but not sufficient and, as with volunteers, semi-skilled gardeners need constant supervision if the highest standards are to be maintained. To ensure continuity every significant garden should be involved in a training scheme internally to provide for the future; also to add to the pool of skilled gardens nationally. As with plants, the flow of fresh people through the garden contributes different approaches and invigorates the garden. Above all the garden needs to be led dynamically by someone who understands the values of those who made and developed it; their style and ideals. This person needs also to possess qualities of imagination, foresight and creativity as well as knowledge of the plants and skills relevant to the place.

Gardens of any significance are rarely made by a single genius operating alone but almost invariably by two or more people working closely together, contributing different talents and developing the necessary creative tension. This may be husband and wife, designer and client, architect and artist/plantsman, landscape architect and landowner/manager and so on. Similarly, the management of gardens of historic significance cannot be left to individuals without the critical appraisal of an informed outsider or someone else capable of interpreting a long-term conservation plan with consistency and imagination. In the absence of an interested and expert owner this is an important role for a consultant able to bring a fresh eye and breadth of experience to help make informed judgements affecting inevitable change, decay and renewal. It is also vital in order to help protect gardens from being exploited for inappropriate purposes or being unduly commercialised.

Significance The wealth, density and diversity of gardens that continue to survive in Britain and prosper for our enjoyment are unmatched anywhere else in the world. Historically, this can be attributed in part to continuity of ownership and management arising from the stability of our national institutions. While this has facilitated their survival, the reason why gardens survive through changing circumstances is because they are loved and cherished by their owners. Garden conservation was not invented by the National Trust when it acquired Hidcote in 1948, by the Garden History Society when it was formed in 1965 or even by English Heritage when it was established in 1983, although all three organisations have influenced the rescue and protection of many important places at critical times. Great gardens are created and cared for principally as a means of meeting people's recreational desires and providing for their creative needs, and most of them are still privately owned. A long-term conservation plan, set out to provide firm guidance in essentials, along with flexibility to allow for enrichment and adaptation is highly desirable for the proper survival of any important garden and vital for those that have lost the thread of continuous private ownership.

Long-term conservation policy and priority should be based on a carefully considered statement of the significant values and characteristics of the garden. The significance of a garden should refer to its origin, contents and creators and to what makes the place unique – history, design, planting, style of upkeep, buildings, special characteristics and traditions. But significance is not confined to objects and design or entirely to history; it incorporates subjective elements such as social, educational, recreational, cultural, symbolic, spiritual and aesthetic values as well as significant architectural, horticultural, biological and environmental elements. Furthermore, it is likely to involve processes of development, production and decay; also systems of upkeep and renewal and skills vital to the place. Nor should less tangible qualities be omitted from consideration – character, ethos, meaning and potential. The fact that they may be difficult to define or evaluate does not render subjective values less significant.

A valid statement of significance cannot be formulated as a paper exercise arising entirely from commissioned reports of specialists, although these will be important considerations. Views on significance should be canvassed widely and assembled from the joint contributions of those who know the garden best, for example former owners, staff, local people and those who may have managed or cared for it for some time, if possible consulting its makers, either directly or through any recorded accounts. It is valuable also to consult non-expert visitors as well as specialists in any narrow fields of significance.

Priority   It is comparatively easy to compile a raw list of significant values and characteristics relating to any site, historic or otherwise. On the other hand it is far more difficult to analyse these qualities and values and group them in order of their relative importance in conserving the fundamentals of the place. As it is neither possible nor desirable to attempt to preserve everything, it is essential to establish a widely agreed order of precedence, especially where resources are limited or where major adaptation is envisaged. Difficult choices are inevitable in management and value judgements are frequently necessary, for example where there is conflict between nature conservation and the renewal of historic features. This hierarchy of values will be guided by statutory designations but should not be ruled by legislation covering wildlife habitat, archaeology and so forth which may be incidental rather than central to the real meaning and significance of the garden.

Evaluation   A full, and as far as possible, objective evaluation of significance is the essential foundation of a valid conservation plan, setting out the relative value of each element one to another and to gardens generally. Clearly age, rarity, designer, former owner, site and so on may be important but qualities like aesthetic value, continuity, integrity, public benefit and educational potential should not be ignored. In assessing and agreeing the importance of these relative values, it is effective to involve someone who possesses a broad perspective of gardens in order to make valid comparisons. Such a consultant should be able to understand the defining characteristics of the garden and act as convenor in the inevitably delicate negotiations leading to an agreement as to the order of precedence of significant values.

Principles of management   The ultimate purpose of a statement of significance is to facilitate long-term management, including adaptation, repair and renewal. This is best achieved by using such a statement to formulate principles of management and conservation. These principles would need to take into account current realities such as planning legislation, changed surroundings, different ownerships, and adaptations to different uses, reduced resources and so forth. They should arise logically from the statement of significance, stating clearly the policies and assumptions governing all management decisions – management priority, planting style, standard of upkeep, nature conservation, etc., as well as policies governing restoration, renewal, adaptation, access, education, repair, interpretation, fund raising, staffing, training and other matters of general concern.

4 Some *Olla Podrida* from the diary of a garden historian[1]

Richard Wheeler
National Specialist in Garden History, National Trust, UK

Diary entry March 2011 – Crom Castle

To Ireland and the spectacular landscape of Crom. It is some years since I trespassed across the border from the South, one December when all was closed, and explored this magical and deserted landscape around the shores of Lough Erne. On this rather more considered occasion I met up with colleagues Jim Chestnutt and the wonderful Frances Bailey – and we had lunch with the Earl of Erne in Crom Castle itself, which the family continue to own.

The designed landscape at Crom (Figure 4.1) is really one of the best, and were there to be the same grading system here, as in the England and Wales Gardens and Parks Registers, it would certainly qualify for Grade 1 status. It is the most spectacular place and of the utmost significance in the history of designed landscapes. There are striking parallels with Scotney Castle, Tunbridge Wells where the architect Anthony Salvin (1799–1881) was working with William Sawrey Gilpin (1762–1843) in designing a new house and garden for the Hussey family, and using the ruins of the old Castle as the primary eye-catcher.

Here at Crom, Gilpin is working with Salvin's contemporary, Edward Blore (1787–1879) who followed the same idea with his new castle looking down the hillside, from quite formal terracing, onto the old house. In 1839 both Salvin and Blore were founder members, with the art critic John Ruskin (1819–1900), of the Oxford Society for the Study of Gothic Architecture, so the link is well made. In addition, Crom is unique in its use of the water. The inter-relationship of the Lough, the land and the buildings is inspired. The water provides both subject and frame for the views from the land, and in turn, the perspective from the water provides a looking glass view of that same landscape. So the elements of the landscape can be described thus (and noting detractions from the ideal):

The house and immediate gardens

Here, whilst the house is as spectacular as *it* should be, the gardens are a well maintained shadow of what *they* should be. I am not clear from when the planting schemes in the gardens date, but if they were anything like Scotney, then they would be contemporary with the house itself. I well understand that the house and gardens are only open for corporate

Figure 4.1 Ruins of the old Castle at Crom as the primary eye-catcher (author's own).

events and weddings, but it would be very exciting to have a long-term aim of working with the family to put back at least an outline of the magnificence that was there in the past.

The site of the old house

This is a magical place, and, like Scotney, intended to be both seen in the distance and to be visited as a romantic ruin. Both its original intent and its Gilpinesque qualities do need to be thought through, understood, maintained and enhanced. First, its original intent: this was a place that linked the land and the water, so we have both Land-gate and Water-gate. This latter, following the lowering of the water-levels in the Lough, is now stranded and set back from the water, just as are the walls of the garden. It would be wonderful if one of the primary aims of landscape conservation here should be to maintain that link with the water, either by a clear bank, or reeds rather than scrub.

We did not go into the old garden on this visit, and I do not know how much investigatory and archive work has been done on this part of the property. However, it would be very worthwhile to consider some 'Hodgson Burnett' gardening work within the garden walls, gently to enhance this immensely evocative place, so that the visitor can feel the bones of what was there before the fire.[2]

The water and the eye-catchers

No building at Crom, whether functional or ornamental, is wasted. All are meant to be seen, and are mostly placed facing the water, and are approached by water. Their very existence, style and position is the essence of Crom. Sadly, since the lowering of the lough, the strand that was left between land and water has, over the years, scrubbed-up, thus destroying much of the landscape intent of the place. A lot of good work has been done by the Trust in managing this intrusion, whilst maintaining the nature conservation interest. In addition, a lot of the views have become narrow slots through the vegetation, rather than panoramic and natural views through the stems of scattered trees.

This balance is critical in the management of Crom, and it would be really worthwhile to have a new set of policies agreed between the advisers in historic landscape and those for nature conservation. These policies would then back up any application for further clearance and enable the management of this extraordinary landscape to move forward in a coherent manner.

The walled garden

This is a wonderful addition to the estate and worthy of preservation in its own right. I understand the financial constraints in further development and restoration, but I hope that a way might be found to prevent deterioration of the physical structures. I would very much like to look at this again on my next visit.

Diary entry September 2011 – A visit to Castle Drogo on the edge of Dartmoor

> The Castle itself is currently the subject of a huge restoration programme to sort out the longstanding problem of a leaking roof, the responsibility for which appears to rest with the late Sir Edwin Lutyens (1869–1944). The Head Gardener, John Rippin has just moved down from Hidcote – from Cotswolds to Dartmoor, and is rapidly finding his feet with a garden that appears to be taken straight from *Abelard et Heloise* – a 'Paradise in the Wild'.

It was very good to meet colleague Simon Larkin for the first time and to catch up with John Rippin post-Hidcote.

I have known Drogo since the late 1970s when visiting with Dick Merrick and David Bett, then respectively National Trust Regional Agent and Land Agent. Their enthusiasm for the garden at Drogo then was impressive, and is reflected in Jonathan Lovie's discovery of National Trust garden adviser Paul Miles' more considered and professional view at the time.[3] This understanding of the garden and its conceptual relationship to the castle was extraordinary and immensely perceptive of the National Trust team at a time when the place was barely 50 years old. And it is the more extraordinary that it was the very lack of the Gertrude Jekyll (1843–1932), Edwin Lutyens (1869–1944) partnership, in this case, that makes it special. So no Surrey Arts and Crafts here, but a modern (but not modernist) garden to accompany a modern castle – complete with an electrified portcullis. So Lutyens' partner here, after the client Julius Drewe (1856–1931) rejected Jekyll, was the almost unknown Kent garden designer George Dillistone (1877–1957), only previously noted for a few books on the design of small suburban Home Counties villa gardens. But what an impact he made. His planting schemes for Drogo rank with the very best and what he achieved at Drogo is at once both discreet and spectacular (Figure 4.2).

Unusually for a twentieth-century garden, the records for Drogo are encyclopaedic. So there are not only all Lutyens' proposals and working plans for the house and garden structure, but all the Dillistone planting plans as well. It would be really good if there might be the possibility of publishing these plans in the same way as has been done for Wimpole, perhaps in two companion volumes for Castle and Garden. It would be equally good if we were able to work on some analysis of Dillistone's plans to enable an understanding of his use of sentinel plants, colour, texture and seasonal chronology.

We spent the morning with the plans and the afternoon in the gardens, but I hope that you will not mind if I conflate the discussions in this short memorandum?

- The Setting of Drogo is all important. The whole conceit of the place with its barely credible links between family and site, whilst undoubtedly greeted with wry smiles by local society, is the very essence of its *genius loci*. So Drogo de Teigne and Drewsteignton were ideal material for amateur family genealogy to resettle the Drewes in their ancestral home. And a baronial castle was an essential attribute to this construct, spectacularly realised by Lutyens on what is just the most ideal site imaginable. Early

Figure 4.2 Drogo: A modern (but not modernist) garden to accompany a modern castle (author's own).

photographs show just how good the site was, and Julius Drewe's admonition to Lutyens that planting by the drive should be limited to gorse, bracken and heather, accentuates his own critical understanding of the place. To a certain extent this setting and approach has been lost by lack of grazing on the hillsides and an intense mowing regime on the drive-sides. The drive now has more the appearance of the Long Walk at Windsor from that Castle to the Copper Horse – I am sure that this was never the intention for Drogo.

- The foot of the castle walls are now close cropped grass. Would it not be better to fence off these areas for a year or so, so that we then have the paths going through the bracken, rather than there being what appears as a mown plinth around the building?
- The terrace between the Castle and the lower gate into the garden is of huge importance, and works as the hinge between the two. Its design is brilliant. With the yew hedge continuing the wall above the ramparts of the castle, it provides a viewing platform not just for the landscape of the valley but also for the 1940s rhododendrons and wild garden. Then, rather than having a rather boring and simple path with wide grass verges on each side, it is designed as a green *allée*, with the path tight to the hedge on the lower side. I do hope that the temporary building might go soon – it quite successfully spoils this whole concept of the connection between castle and garden.
- The *enfilade* of Rose Garden, scented garden, shrub garden and tennis lawn is the *pièce de resistance* of the whole composition and a work of art comparable with any within the house. The opportunity to analyse and understand Dillistone's planting schemes is especially exciting. If we get this right, then I really think that we should try to get the garden re-graded to Grade I on the English Heritage Register of Historic Parks and Gardens of special historic interest in England.
- The Bunty House and the Luncheon House are again an opportunity for engaging with children.[4] I see no reason why the Bunty House garden could not be extended to include vegetables, and perhaps the Luncheon House to be furnished with appropriate, useable and expendable inter-war children's furniture, with an enclosed garden outside, again with appropriate period play equipment. Glendurgan, Cornwall is a fine example of how a place becomes more special by offering an experience for children of being at one with it, rather than yet another off-the-peg adventure playground.

I do hope that these thoughts are of some help – the garden at Drogo is a hidden pearl that needs to be more widely known and appreciated. *RWW, September 2011*

Diary entry: February 2012 Stourhead – a classical Elysium set in a picturesque landscape

Visiting Head Gardener, Alan Power, at Stourhead is ever a treat. Over the years we have argued our way around the garden with huge enjoyment. On this occasion we were looking at Stourhead within its wider landscape. Equally designed, but more expansive, the intent was for it to be seen on horseback, or by chaise.

For a dank February day, with the last of the snow just vanishing in the mud, Stourhead was looking wonderful. The work that has been done over the last year, and that being tackled now, raises Stourhead to a new plateau of excitement and discovery. Alan and his team should receive the highest commendation for the quality and quantity of work that has been done.

Alan and I began the day by looking at eighteenth-century descriptions by garden visitors of the time, and it was quite clear that they saw Stourhead as much more than the confines of the present gardens and house. Richard Fenton (1746–1821), staying at the Spread Eagle in the early nineteenth century, took as much time and trouble to walk along the terrace to Alfred's Tower and then down through the woods to the Convent, and back past Tucking Mill to the inn.

It does seem that a lot of the pressure on the garden could be eased by further restoration of the other parts of the registered landscape and encouraging visitors to explore further afield. They already use Six Wells Bottom for the walk up to St Peter's Pump. With these thoughts in mind, we then did a comprehensive tour of the gardens and the following points arose:

The village of Stourton was intended by Henry Hoare II (1705–1785) to become an integral part of the landscape and this was accentuated by Colt Hoare (1758–1838) with the building of the village hall and the fret balustrades added to the church and the Spread Eagle Inn. All this was seen both from the gardens on the lake side of the house and also from the now disused walk from the entrance gates (and the National Trust car park), along an informal terrace to the Temple of Apollo. The Nicholson images express the intent behind this walk with engaging clarity.

The designed landscape includes not just village and church, but the entire paddock (on both sides of the road) up to Colt Hoare's Gothic entrance gates. It would be really good to restore this scene as the first view that the visitor has on leaving the car park or reception building and begins his descent into the valley. The road is already a sunken way, so needs no quasi hedge on each side to screen it. However, the lower car park would have to be properly screened with laurel and the terrace cleared and rough mowed with a new fence of appropriate style against the paddock.

The churchyard is now divided from the rest of the landscape, which is unfortunate. I hope that the beech hedge has a limited life and we might revert to the existing park rails hiding inside it – or ideally the ha-ha described by John Claudius Loudon (1783–1843) in 1833[5]:

. . . the church and churchyard are pleasingly situated on a sloping bank and the churchyard is one of the best kept which are to be seen in England. Roses and other flowering shrubs are planted against the church; cypresses and other trees are sprinkled amongst the graves and the grass kept as smooth as any lawn . . . the fence is a sunk wall with its perpendicular side towards the church, so that at a short distance there appears to be no fence at all, and the whole seems a component part of the pleasure ground. We have seldom seen anything so well managed . . .[6]

Perhaps the ha-ha is still there but buried beneath hedge and fence?
The reunion of the Bristol Cross with the village is a delight.

Turner's Paddock   We walked up to the clump below the garden (Top Wood) and saw how the extension to the lake to the south-west works as well from this angle, as it fails close to. The paths across the meadow from the lower lake are a really important part of the place and it would be good to mow these out at irregular intervals if only to show people how to find the best views. This part of Stourhead is that which most reflects the move towards the picturesque in the later eighteenth century, and this is apparent in a number of Francis Nicholson's (1753–1844) views. I wonder if we should be thinking of all this area in the context of this rather different understanding of the place?

Following this theme, we rejoined the main garden at the Iron Bridge and looked at the interface between woods and garden from there to the pinetum. The plantations on the hillside to the west of the lake are now reaching the stage where they can be thinned out to select the best trees, and to release the historic trees as well. I am sure that the intent was no hard edge between garden and wood; that the wood comes down to envelop and hide the Grotto, and to leave open the areas on either side, with the grass fingering up between the trees. In addition, there are traces of a higher walk on this side of the lake – not as clear-cut as that on the eastern side but extant nonetheless. The more that the garden itself sits within a picturesque landscape the more the surprise in finding it, and the more relevant becomes the inscription on the Temple of Flora – '. . . *Procul O procul este profane* . . .' (. . . *get ye gone all ye who are unhallowed* . . .).

With these thoughts in mind I then accompanied National Trust Warden, Kim Portnell around the wider – picturesque landscape.

Six Wells Bottom   Probably the most evocative part of Stourhead, the valley from the Diana Basin to St Peter's Pump is sheer loveliness. It would not be gilding the lily though, if we were to open up the Sunny Hanging to grazing, so that there were free-growing trees with a browsing line beneath. The marginalia in the Bodleian's copy of the Stourhead guide describes St Peter's Pump as 'by much the pleasantest part of the grounds and forms a pleasing view from the Terrace'.[7] The little hanging valley that leads from St Peter's Pump to Alfred's Tower, past the remains of the farmstead is now heavily wooded. I wonder if this was more sparsely furnished in the eighteenth century to give a lighter and more naturalistic feel to the path?

Whilst it would be wonderful to remove entirely the fences around Sunny Hanging, the remaining plantations – mainly the Shady Hanging – would be better expressed in the landscape if they were enclosed by a more historic fence than the present barbed wire and sheep netting. The Hawkwell Field fence at Stowe, Buckinghamshire provides an example, or the deer fence at Charlecote Park, Warwick. Expensive, but a good long-term aim.

The Terrace itself was considered in the eighteenth century to be one of the finest things at Stourhead: '. . . dressed like a racecourse . . . one of the most striking and pleasing of all improvements affording a charming place for air and exercise any time of the year'[8] . . . and '. . . the surface of this noble Terrace is as fine and level as if it were mowed . . . and so clean, that it would not soil a lady's silk shoe, in short . . . there is nothing to rival it in the kingdom . . .'.

It would be a huge improvement if the Terrace were to be treated as the piece of design that it is, and the tenant either enjoined to look after it as described in the past, or for the National Trust to do so instead. What is required is first, more light, secondly, chain harrowing and rolling annually, and thirdly, grazing with sheep rather than cattle.

The management of the plantations on the wooded ridge above the Shady Hanging is exemplary. The clearing of the castle mounds is an obvious success and I wondered if with more public access to this area, thought should now be given to the layers of design that exist here? On the 1st edition of the 1 inch to the mile Ordnance Survey plans the ridge tops are shown only with a scatter of trees, that succeeding generations of the Hoare family with their enthusiasm for forestry have filled in with mixed and coniferous plantations leaving a fine avenue or riding down the spine of the plantation. Could there perhaps be a small

Figure 4.3 The convent at Stourhead (author's own).

working party to think through just how this area should be treated in the future? I would be very happy to help.

The circuit up to Alfred's Tower from Turner's Paddock to meet the Terrace is a part of the place where the public can easily be confused as to where they should be going – if at all. Again, it would be really good to work with the Hoare family to reorder the original route and make it sensibly available to the public. (I am sure that I shall be told that a child of four could find which way to go – but I get lost every time . . .)

The Convent   The lease here is obviously in good and enthusiastic hands. The temptation is to work again with the Hoare family, to open up a view from the front of the building down into the vale. This is quite right but must be done with caution. All the descriptions are of the building in a sequestered place and surrounded by gloomy firs. I am sure that there should be filtered views both in and out, but the trees are hugely important as well (Figure 4.3).

The lower lake and the cascade   This lake performs two functions. First, it provides a continuation of the water when seen from the upper path from the house towards the site of the Chinese Bridge, and indeed from the Chinese Bridge itself were it still there. The similar bridge at Wotton, Buckinghamshire, provides just such oblique perspective views over the whole of the waters there. Secondly, it forms an integral part of the picturesque scene below the dam. Further work is needed to explore how this part of Stourhead was presented, where the paths were, if any, and where were the viewpoints from which to see the Cascade. This latter structure was inspired by, and copies quite slavishly, that built by Coplestone Warre Bampfylde (1720–1791) at Hestercombe, Somerset, and sets the *picturesque* tone for the whole of this area.

Finally – where does all this leave us? A huge landscape of spectacular merit, surrounding the honeypot of the garden in the middle. And whilst the two parts were designed for the same audience, they were for very pragmatic reasons constructed in very different ways. The garden was intended to be viewed on foot, dry shod, and quite suitable for the dress of both sexes. The wider landscape however was, and is, so extensive that only the young and hardy would attempt it on foot – Fenton on his barrister's tour did, but everyone else would tour by chaise or on horseback. And most importantly what part did people play in the scene itself? All the pictures of Stourhead in the eighteenth century are populated with visitors, gardeners or farm-workers. So how should the present-day visitor see this wider landscape? At present most drive to Alfred's Tower, some hardy walkers do the terrace from the Tower Road end, and a few venture into the woods around the Convent. Any modern vehicles, even bicycles, would strike a jarring note in this secret and unspoiled landscape. Is there a case for chaise rides as at Osborne House, Isle of Wight or Arlington Court, Barnstaple? Food for thought . . .

Diary entry from March 2012 – Sissinghurst

We have been struggling for some time with a Conservation Plan for one of the greatest twentieth-century gardens in England – Sissinghurst Castle, Kent. We are avoiding the siren calls for '. . . allowing the garden to develop with new designs . . .'. In our view, Vita Sackville-West (1892–1962) was one of the great gardeners of the twentieth century, and however she may be viewed by professional horticulturalists, her work has stood the test of time, and is still hugely influential. It would be travesty to consign her ideas, and the fashions of her time to the dustbin of garden history. But having said that, even amongst the aficionados of Sissinghurst there is dissension. On the one hand we have romantics led by the ghost of Vita, and on the other, the horticulturalists led by that unsurpassable team of (the late) Pam Schwerd (1931–2009) and Sibylle Kreutzberger. How can this Gordian knot be undone? Or should it?

Here is the final introduction to the conservation plan:

'This *magnum opus* on the history and significance of Sissinghurst Garden written by Historic Environment Consultants Philip Masters and Sarah Rutherford will provide invaluable source material for all future decisions on the trajectory of this the most evocative and most famous of all twentieth-century flower gardens in England; appropriately situated in Kent, the Garden of England.'

Taken with this encyclopaedia of Sissinghurst one needs to remember that gardens speak to the emotions as well as the senses. If any garden can be said to be an affair of the heart as well as the mind, then Sissinghurst is it. And this state of constructive tension has been a part of the place since its inception – Vita with her emotional approach to the history and grain of the place, and Harold with sensible and brilliant solutions to its challenges. So, on the one hand you have: '. . . it was Sleeping Beauty's garden: but a garden crying out for rescue . . .' (RHS journal 1953) and:

. . . we agreed on . . . the main principle of the garden: a combination of long axial walks, running north and south, east and west, usually with terminal points such as a statue or an archway, or a pair of sentinel poplars, and the more intimate surprise of small geometric gardens opening off them rather as the rooms of an enormous house would open off the arterial corridors . . .

At the commencement of this work, Vita's grandson Adam commented to me in the same '*La belle au bois dormant*' vein:

Sissinghurst was Vita's dream of Knole . . . with her awakening in the Tower after three or four centuries – to find the ruined remains of the great house and all its courts overrun by a garden whose dreamlike quality perpetuated a sense of unreality in the place . . .

So the influence of Knole and the Tudor is huge. Between the wars the eighteenth century and its pompous classicism was rated far below the Tudor and truly ancient places. So Sissinghurst remained as a series of quasi rooms that sat within the old courtyards of the great house – unlike Hidcote, Gloucestershire where Lawrence Johnston (1871–1958) very quickly broke the bounds of the old manor garden and expanded into the surrounding closes.

So we have a philosophy of Englishness in the form of the Tudor: Anne Scott-James (1913–2009) put it succinctly:

Englishness was one of the qualities they most wanted to achieve at Sissinghurst; hence the Tudor idea of linked enclosures, the English lawns and hedges, the use of native yews and hornbeams, the many smaller indigenous plants like primroses and violets . . .[9]

James Lees Milne (1908–1997) also comments on the unfashionable taste of the Nicolsons for the Tudor continuing when the cognoscenti had abandoned the style for more classical or modernist delights. So it was the idea of the timelessness of the weald and buildings growing out of the land, the materials being of the land and at one with the land. And the medieval surviving through all the vicissitudes of the intervening centuries. Not a Pre-Raphaelite re-creation, but something that has been there for centuries, like a dismasted ship under jury-rig battling through the storms and finally reaching harbour.

> . . . a tumble of roses and honeysuckle figs and vines . . . must be romantically treated. . .' and similarly: '. . .In the overflowing clematis, figs, vines and wisteria, in the rejection of violent colour or anything too tame or orderly, one discovers her romanticism. Wild flowers must be allowed to invade the garden; if plants stray over a path, they must not be cut back, the visitor must duck; rhododendrons must be banished in favour of their tenderer cousin, the azalea; roses must not electrify, but seduce; and when a season has produced its best, that part of the garden must be allowed to lie fallow for another year, since there is a cycle in nature which must not be disguised. It is eternally renewable, like a play with acts and scenes: there can be a change of cast, but the script remains the same. Permanence and mutation are the secrets of this garden . . .

So here is one of the guardian spirits of Sissinghurst; the idea of the Briar Rose – an abandoned Knole with Vita asleep there for 400 years and waking up to find most of the buildings gone and replaced by a garden dream – overblown and luxuriant growth amongst the ruins of the courtyards (Figure 4.4).

And the planting style is one part of this – but as important is the actual management of the planting: restraint in pruning, allowing plants to grow beyond their horticultural perfection, allowing them to invade the paths etc. In common garden understanding, one is ready to find the ideas of form and function with the owner, and the interpretation of these ideas into colour and plantsmanship by the head gardener. This all gets into a constructive muddle at Sissinghurst. Vita is heavily involved with plants and planting. Is she a good horticulturalist?

Figure 4.4 Sissinghurst: 'In the overflowing clematis, figs, vines and wisteria, in the rejection of violent colour or anything too tame or orderly, one discovers her romanticism' (author's own).

It seems that history gives her quite an easy ride, whilst the expert horticulturalist has reservations. And how much at Sissinghurst is her, and how much her gardeners? The mid-twentieth century was noted for its amateur gardeners and she is probably the best known. How does she compare with the others?

The muddle continues with Pam and Sybille. Here we have two very good and strong-willed gardeners, taking on the garden in the last two years of Vita's life. By this time the balance of wills between patron and gardener was inevitably on the side of the latter, and much of Pam and Sybille's work was their own with the friendly acquiescence of Vita, rather than the more robust relationship with John Vass, the previous Head Gardener. How significant is the work of Pam and Sybille – and indeed their successors, Sarah and Lex? And the tension continues with Vita's son Nigel. His passion was for tidying the place up and putting a sharp edge to the whole composition.

So here is the other guardian spirit of Sissinghurst – brilliant horticulture, tidiness and precision. Is Sissinghurst a precise and pure work of art like a Vermeer painting or is it in the school of the Impressionists? Anne Scott James comes to our aid again:

> . . . has all this restoring and tidying spoiled the garden? It has certainly changed it, for the garden has lost some of its mystery. Sissinghurst was full of flaws, but just as the flaws of a hand-thrown pot have a charm which a smooth machine-made pot can never equal, so were the imperfections of Sissinghurst utterly delightful. They were part of its intensely personal character . . .

There it is. The state of constructive tension between Harold's geometry and Vita's romanticism gets translated into Nigel's precision and Pam and Sybille's wonderful plantsmanship. And even now the garden swings one way towards romanticism and the other towards great horticulture: It is part of the place and should always remain so.

Diary entry November 2012, Nostell Priory, Yorkshire

> The garden at Nostell Priory in Yorkshire is one of the hidden treasures of the North. It was given to the Trust in 1953 by Rowland Winn, 3rd Lord St Oswald (1893–1957), together with only a small area of the garden. In 2006 the Trust was able to buy the remainder of the gardens and park. Elation was, however, short-lived, and in 2010 the rhododendrons, the glory of the place, were hit by *phytophthera* and had to be removed and destroyed in their entirety. Three visits with head gardener Paul Dibb, Mark Lamey, gardens consultant for the north, and Roger Carr-Whitworth the curator are leading to a visit by the Trust's Gardens Panel in April 2013.

This is my report for that panel meeting:

I visited Nostell in 2012 at a time when the garden had just undergone the devastating results of a major *Phytophthera* outbreak that had led to the necessary removal of all the rhododendron collection. This work of clearance and burning up of all the infected plant material had left a garden denuded of its former spectacular clothing, but leaving the outlines of the eighteenth-century layout clear for us to now see and understand.

These thoughts and comments are very much a reaction to this uncovered landscape, and will need to be corrected and rationalised in the light of further archival research.

The Nostell that we now see was built by the architect James Paine (1717–1789) for Sir Rowland Winn (1706–1765), supposedly one of the Wynnes of Gwydir in North Wales. This new house was placed on the high ground above the great hall of the old priory that was subsequently demolished. Robert Adam (1728–1792) then built one of the proposed flanking wings and the new stable block.

Two significant plans of the gardens and grounds of Nostell survive; one by Stephen Switzer (1682–1745) that appears to be more proposal than commissioned work, and the other an estate plan by the head gardener Mr Perfect. These plans show in broad terms the idea of turning the old Priory ponds into a new river, with the main road crossing on a great classical bridge, concealing the dam between the Upper and Middle Lakes. There is no archival evidence that I have seen which tells us who designed this landscape of lakes and woodland, with its secret gardens around the Menagerie and possibly around the ruin below the Middle Lake dam, but it is a piece of work that fits the genre of the time with spectacular success.

Thoughts on the design and its possible intent

It appears that the designer of the landscape at Nostell followed the precepts of Virgil in his *Aeneid* and consulted the *genius loci* in all his work. He obviously had an appreciation of the Gothic origins of the place with its medieval priory and preceding hermits' cell of St Oswald, exemplified in the Gothic Arch and Menagerie Garden, the Menagerie itself, the Druids' Bridge, and the Ruin shown on the Victorian OS plans just below the Middle Lake Cascade, itself a representation of the Gothick in its rude and un-crafted nature (Figure 4.5).

(Mark Newman tells me that this was the remains of a medieval mill, perhaps added to with stonework from the demolished Priory.) The steps down to the ruin and the bridge were probably swept away with the twentieth-century reworking of the dam to comply with brutalist engineering legislation, but in all probability were rough and irregular. The setting of the ruin itself with its rough worked cascades and rockwork would have completed the illusion of the ascetic life of the hermit. And this eremitical life is confirmed in accounts of the community living at Nostell prior to its translation into a proper priory under the patronage of the king.

> a settlement of hermits hidden in the woods at a chapel dedicated to St Oswald, king and martyr, in a place called 'le Nostell' . . .[10]

So the ruin with the adjacent Druids' bridge effectively recreated this early ecclesiastic landscape and worked very much better than a broken relic of the priory itself. Perhaps architectural fragments of the Great Hall were recycled to form the ruin, with its wild rockwork and cascades around it. (The ruin is inspired by one of William Kent's (1685–1748) drawings for Edmund Spenser's (1552–1599) *Faerie Queene* (1751 edition).) And the dam itself then becomes one side of a rocky ravine running down past the ruin, to the Druids' bridge – a complete garden composition in itself, perhaps clad with ferns to accentuate its supposed ancient origins.

Figure 4.5 Nostell Priory: Its secret garden tucked away in the old quarry behind shrubberies and a Gothicky doorway without a door (author's own).

The route to this wild landscape led through the first of Nostell's Pleasure Ground shrubberies, now cleared of rhododendrons and obvious in their intent. The path leads from the west front of the house, takes the visitor into this small seven-acre garden and leads through to the ruin and lake dam on the one hand and through to the lower lake boathouse on the other. On the upper side of the path was an eighteenth-century shrubbery, latterly given over to rhododendrons and azaleas, now removed after the outbreak of *phytophthera*.

The palette of plants used in the 1760s included plain and variegated hollies, yew, viburnums, philadelphus, lilacs, laburnums, thorns, privets, roses, honeysuckles, snowberry and so on. These might have been planted as a ranked shrubbery, smallest at the front, largest at the back, but with bastions of the larger specimens coming to the front as well. All would have been planted in a random pattern of individual specimens, not grouped, and at about 3 foot spacing (in actuality they would have been planted at 18 inches spacing and thinned after a year). On the lower side of the path there would have been open grove – trees with no understorey and limbed up as high as possible to allow views through to the water. The shrubbery was bounded by a rabbit-proof iron-paling fence, now only extant on the house side. Beyond the path down to the cascade it continued to separate the shrubberies from the deer park that used to run down through the trees to the water's edge from here to the boathouse at the end of the lake.

Between these treats of the pleasure ground and the rockwork on the house side of the lake, and the Ladies' Flower Garden around the Menagerie, is a rather long and boring walk over the dam and around the lakeside. This should not be a surprise, since the correct way to the Flower Garden is by boat from a landing stage below the house to another amongst the terraces on the other shore leading to a series of grass paths between more shrubs and two gravel paths that take the visitor through to the Gothick Menagerie itself as tea house and shelter, with its secret garden tucked away in the old quarry behind shrubberies and a Gothick doorway without a door. Relics of a more masculine past are still to be seen in the remains of the animal cages, the animals themselves now turned to stone, and the cockpit, now sadly filled with water.

This secret garden was the usual ladies' retreat of the time; flowers, flowering shrubs, lawns, seats and tea house, hidden away so as not to interrupt the flowing nature of the landscape garden itself. The secret garden is inspired by the most famous of these eighteenth-century ladies' flower gardens: Nuneham Courtenay, Oxfordshire, the home of Lord Harcourt (1714–1777). His sister, Lady Elizabeth Lee (1739–1811) devised a similar garden at Hartwell House, Buckinghamshire, which will be the subject of restoration very soon. The planting plans for the latter are in the Bodleian Library and have been recreated in the walled gardens at Painshill, Surrey.

The shrubberies that divide the lakeside terraces and the garden are probably later in concept than those on the house side of the lake, and were to become the rhododendretum (if there is such a word), with colour spilling down the bank into the lake so that the terracing was forgotten in a chaotic cloud of colourful exuberance. It seems unlikely that this result was ever foreseen and what was intended was a series of managed studs of hybrid rhododendrons interposed with other flowering shrubs in a carefully orchestrated rainbow of horticultural restraint.

Well, there it is. An extraordinary opportunity to recreate a landscape and garden full of meaning, colour, excitement and history – a paradise for the eleven hermits hidden away in their cell in 'the woods of Nostell . . .'. And the next steps I would suggest would be a properly conducted programme of research and a conservation statement to lead us into the restoration of this fabulous landscape.

But – there is always the opportunity to get on with the obvious! The pleasure ground wood and its shrubberies are crying out to be replanted, the deer park opened up to run down to the water again, a boat (chain ferry?) on the lake, clearing the paths amongst the rocks and so on. *RWW, November 2012.*

Diary entry March 2013 – Attingham Park, Shropshire

Attingham has long been in my heart as the last stopping point on my way to Betws y Coed, where I had my first appointment in the NT in December 1977. Attingham was the Regional Office for the old East Midlands Region under the ebullient direction of Gerard Noel. But, as an NT property, it was on minimum maintenance. The house was let, and the gardens, to a large part, given over to modern plantations.

Since that time the whole place has reawakened – the house is open, the walled garden is being restored, and the Mile Walk is now the subject of plans to turn it into the splendid thing it once was.

The Mile Walk Working with the grain of the place Attingham's Mile Walk follows the design of pleasure ground begun at Stowe, Buckinghamshire, with a shrubbery and wilderness walk around an area of meadow, or *ferme ornée*. This construct by Charles Bridgeman (1690–1738) was perhaps the first attempt to follow the precept of Joseph Addison (1672–1719) to turn a whole estate into a garden:

> if the natural embroidery of the meadows were helpt and improved by some small additions of Art and the several rows of hedges set off by trees and flowers, that the soil was capable of receiving, a man might make a pretty landskip of his own possessions . . .

The formality of this arrangement was softened by Earl Temple and his Head Gardener, Richard Woodward, in the 1750s, and the design was then followed in a large number of other gardens, notably Croome, Worcestershire by Lancelot Brown, (1716–1783) and Osterley Park, Hounslow and Kedleston Hall, Derbyshire by Robert Adam (1728–1792). At all three of these gardens it can be seen that the shrubbery walk leads to the water, and there is then the opportunity to return to the house by boat.

And so it is at Attingham (Figure 4.6). The walk leads from the east side of the house, westwards towards the kitchen garden, protected by a narrow shrubbery from the working

Figure 4.6 Attingham, the Cupola (author's own).

areas to the rear of the house and stables. Humphry Repton (1752–1818) shows slot views out into the meadow, but it seems that the flanking shrubbery on this side was never planted, and one saw through the stems of the trees into the grassland beyond. From thence it meanders through the Garden Plantation, screening the path from the kitchen gardens, and then along a woodland walk, again screened from the Home Farm paddocks, but with views out over the meadow, to the Wrekin – the *leitmotif* of Attingham.

The furthest extremity of the walk is now a Memorial Garden for the Berwick's land agent, Gordon Miller. And the return to the house presents the alternatives of a boat down the River Tern, or a riverside walk, with scattered clumps of shrubbery providing a backdrop for the views over the deer park and the Wrekin. (One wonders whether juxtaposition of river and Wrekin was a pretence by Thomas Leggett and Repton to cast the Tern in role of the Severn, to remind the visitor of the ancient myth that the Wrekin was made by two giants digging a trench that became the river Severn, and the hill the spoil from their labours?) Finally, and for lack of the usual accompaniment of classical garden buildings and eye-catchers, the path aligns itself on the clock-tower – Attingham's answer to the rotundas at Stowe, Hagley, Worcestershire, Petworth, Sussex, etcetera . . .

So what about the detail?

The Stables Shrubbery   The intention of this planting was to screen the working areas of Attingham but to allow views out over the deer paddock. So, to the south of the path a ranked shrubbery probably with holly and yew at the back to hide the stables drive, and smaller shrubs at the front to provide a floriferous extravaganza to start the walk on its way. The path was set back from the railing fence, with high pruned trees to allow a clear view of the paddock through the stems – and grass (with wild flowers) beneath. Plants used would be those purchased by Leggett in the bills from Williamson's nurseries in the 1770s. In passing, one should note that the stables were designed to be seen only from the south – hence the stone facing on that side. The Moses Griffith (1749–1819) painting exemplifies this intent; with the stables' front shining through to the west of Rookery Wood. And the shrubbery ran round to the Kitchen Gardens, screening the land to the west (now used for car parking), but with open views to the east.

The Garden Plantation   The succession of plans for the Mile Walk show the Garden Plantation waxing and waning like the moon – sometimes meeting the trees by the riverside and dividing the meadows, and at other times leaving a clear gap between.

The Repton plan shows the woodland pinching into the meadows, whilst the nineteenth-century estate plan shows the meadows separately fenced and with two roundels of deciduous and coniferous trees. The answer must be that you were supposed to see through from one meadow to the next, and the trees were fenced off when young, and opened up for grazing once they were of a size. Major replanting was carried out in the 1980/90s and this is now due for heavy thinning to the best trees. I would suggest that this should be the time for opening up the wood to grazing, becoming woody park – or in other terms, wood pasture. This thinning should be heaviest in the middle to allow views through as proposed by Repton.

The Miller Memorial Garden   From the Garden Plantation to the top of the woods the path runs close to the meadow fence allowing views out over the deer park to the Wrekin. On the north-east side however, the shrubbery continues, screening the Home Farm paddocks. It is likely that once past the Walled Gardens the shrubberies will be less floristic and more of a woodland walk. The Memorial Garden itself, with its framework of honey-locust trees and rhododendrons, is a delightful addition to the walk, and just needs a light touch to make it the elegant composition that was intended. All the historic plans of Attingham show a further meadow tucked in amongst the trees to the north of the Memorial Garden. It would be good to reinstate this woodland glade – probably covered in bluebells – as a charming end point to the walk.

And was the inlet off the river a landing stage for a boat? It does seem too convenient not to be so. But if there is no boat there – then there is the riverside walk, set down nearer the water, so with few views back into the meadows, but a continually changing view of the river and deer park beyond.

It appears that shrubs and trees were all as singletons growing in grass, and the fence enclosing most of the trees inside the meadow, so leaving the cattle to do the mowing. It would be very good to move the fence back to its original line and to thin the young trees to get good open grown specimens. And as one nears the house again, with its open grove of Lebanon cedars, the path opens up onto the higher part of the meadow giving a view through to the clock tower, as mentioned earlier in this note.

The Cedar Grove   In the 1790s and 1800s groves of cedars like this at Attingham were the rage – that at Osterley Park, Isleworth is perhaps the finest. One is bound to say that the Attingham trees are nearing the end of their useful life and a lot of money could be spent on tree surgery to keep them going beyond the time that they are things of beauty. Sooner or later a decision will have to be made to take out all the mature trees and start again. This would have the added advantage of making it possible to reinstate the fine lawn down to the river.

Addendum – The Walled Gardens and their surrounds

Leggett's walled gardens are of considerable interest for the resemblance they bear to those at Wimpole, Cambridgeshire, designed by his erstwhile employer, William Emes (1729/30–1803). Both have, or had, an outer wall to contain the slips, and both have a functional entrance and a polite entrance. Furthermore, the whole ensemble is screened from the surrounding landscape.

The Plantation   To the south of the kitchen gardens, the woodland sweeps round to screen the functional area. This has now been clear felled apart from the Robinia avenue. This could be replanted as an extension of the Garden Plantation, with a mixture of native broadleaves (including sweet chestnut), and perhaps an understorey of hazel. As at Wimpole, there is a path leading to the Home Farm and perhaps an ornamental dairy as well.

A large part of the outer wall at Attingham has either been removed or was never completed. The same thing has happened at Wimpole and the missing sections have been replaced with a paling fence, replicating what was there before the outer wall was built in the 1870s. The outer parts of the gardens at Attingham could easily be treated in the same way, thus redefining and rabbit-proofing the slips at Attingham, and enabling them to be cultivated – perhaps for soft fruits?

The Bee House and a thought that will undoubtedly fall upon deaf ears.

Bees and orchards are the archetypal symbiosis – pollination in return for honey. And the hives were usually placed so that the bees flew against the prevailing wind (usually southwesterly) to get to the pollen, and then they had the wind behind them when they returned to the hive fully laden. So the original site of the bee house on the northern side of the orchard fulfils this act of kindness to bees quite nicely.

The Polite entrance   The nineteenth-century plans show not the southern central entrance as recommended by Repton, but a sinuous path leading to the area south of the frame-yard – perhaps taken as the ladies' flower garden, the essential adjunct to any landscape garden that banished flowers from the vicinity of the house. And this approach takes one through the corner of the slips with a small shrubbery to conceal the functional area of the slips with its nut walk to the south-west.

The Gardeners' entrance A broad walk along the north wall of the gardens taking one past the bothy, for all the garden boys, and the back-sheds containing boilers, potting sheds, tool sheds and perhaps mushroom houses, then round the corner into the western slips and into the walled garden via the double doors.

So there is Attingham. On the one hand, a short, discrete and floriferous walk from the house to the ladies' garden; a longer walk to be done once or twice a week around the Mile Walk, perhaps returning by boat if the weather permits and on the other, the functional side of Attingham with hidden routes from stables to house and separate entrances for family and servants to the walled gardens. These facets of the place are both equally valid and the very fact of their separation lends a heavy dose of reality to the benign Downton Abbey view that these great houses were just one big happy family . . .

> **Diary entry 2013.** New projects, research and advice are streaming in from over the horizon. After years of negotiation, the golf course at Stowe is at last to be moved from the heart of the landscape, and we are working on a proper understanding of Bridgeman's garden as naturalised by Earl Temple and his hugely under-rated head gardener, Richard Woodward. Kingston Lacy in Dorset is at the stage where we can begin to think about the whole Victorian ensemble of Henrietta Bankes's garden, Dyffryn in South Wales has just been taken on by the NT. Studley Royal, Yorkshire and Seaton Delaval, Northumberland, are calling from the North, as is Godolphin from the far tip of Cornwall.

Luckily the law has changed and I am not now due for retirement for many years . . .

Endnotes

1. *Olla Podrida*: from the Spanish *Rotten pot* but understood in the eighteenth century to be the scraps boiled up to make soup, then strained off and eaten by the lower servants. It was commonly described as 'only just edible and barely nutritious'.
2. Frances Hodgson Burnett (1849–1924), author of the *Secret Garden*, lived at Great Maytham Hall, Kent 1898–1907. The children's book was inspired by the neglected old walled garden she found there.
3. Jonathan Lovie is Principal Conservation Officer for the Garden History Society.
4. The Bunty House is a children's cottage in the style of the Queen's 'Little House' at Royal Lodge.
5. The beech hedge is to be removed in the winter of 2013.
6. Republished by John Sales in 1990 as: *John Claudius Loudon In Search of English Gardens*.
7. Unpublished work by Oliver Cox, University College, Oxford.
8. Sir John Parnell (*c.*1720–1782).
9. Anne Scott-James, *Sissinghurst – The Making of a Garden*, Michael Joseph, 1974.
10. 'The foundation of Nostell Priory 1109–1153', Judith A. Frost, 2007. This paper includes the probably fictitious story of the founding of the Priory contained in *De gestis et Actibus Priorum Sancti Oswaldi de Nostel a prima fundatione usque ad dominum Robertum de Qwyxlay* composed in the fifteenth century. This story may well have been the inspiration for the gothic landscape of Nostell in the eighteenth century.

5 On design and process

William Martin Wood
Place maker and garden writer, UK

In words lie traps for the unwary. This is particularly so in the fields of garden and landscape restoration. Take the phrase 'designed landscape'. The *Oxford English Dictionary* defines the word 'design' in this way:

1. A plan or scheme conceived in the mind and intended for subsequent execution; the preliminary conception of an idea that is to be carried into effect by action; a project.

And

6. A preliminary drawing or sketch; a plan, outline, or model produced to show the look or function of a building, machine, or other object before it is made or built.[1]

Other meanings are given which relate to aims and objectives, but the minds of most people leap to the definitions above when the words design or designed are used.

The phrase 'designed landscape' is not to be found in legislation in the United Kingdom until Section 11 of the Historic Environment (Amendment) (Scotland) Act 2011. There is no corresponding definition in legislation relating to England and Wales but it appeared in an internal English Heritage document, The Register Manual 2001. The National Heritage Act 1983 had done no more than empower English Heritage to keep a *register of gardens and other land* situated in England and appearing to them to be of special historic interest.[2]

This loose phrasing placed English Heritage in the unenviable position of having to construct a rational framework for exercising their discretion to include land in the Register. These criteria, which are generally uncontroversial, are kept under review and are posted on the English Heritage webpage 'Parks and Gardens Designation Criteria'; the phrase 'designed landscape' makes a brief appearance there without a definition being attempted.[3] The Scottish legislation does, however, grapple with that task, and provides that 'references to gardens and designed landscapes are to grounds which have been laid out for artistic effect and, in appropriate cases, include references to any buildings, land, or water on, adjacent, or contiguous to such grounds'.[4]

Although it is quite widely used by landscape consultants and Natural England, government in England and Wales has generally fought shy of using the term 'designed landscape'. It did not appear in Planning Policy Guidance 15 and does not appear in the National Planning Policy Framework (2012). The phrase is used in Planning Policy Statement 5 but only by way

Gardens & Landscapes in Historic Building Conservation, First Edition. Edited by Marion Harney.
© 2014 John Wiley & Sons, Ltd. Published 2014 by John Wiley & Sons, Ltd.

of a reference to the Landscape Design Trust's publication *Parks and Gardens: A Researcher's Guide to Documentary Sources for Designed Landscapes* (2006).

Although American usage of language does not provide the keys to unlock British administrative materials, it can help toward an understanding of general perceptions in the English-speaking world about what a 'designed landscape' might mean.

To the American Society of Landscape Architects a designed landscape is:

> A site that might appear to be natural but has elements and features that were planned and specified by a landscape architect. Designed landscapes include Central Park in New York to the siting of buildings.[5]

The Cultural Landscape Foundation in the United States offers this view:

> A Designed Landscape is a cultural landscape that was consciously designed or laid out by a landscape architect, master gardener, architect or horticulturist according to design principles or an amateur gardener working in a recognized style or tradition.[6]

Both of these definitions reinforce the notion that strictly speaking, and to the lay person, a designed landscape is one which has been the subject of change for artistic effect through the imposition of a pre-conceived plan; and that is the sense in which it is used in the following paragraphs.

The European Landscape Convention, which the United Kingdom ratified in 2006, defines a landscape as 'An area, as perceived by people, whose character is the result of the action and interaction of natural and/or human factors'. As this amounts to everywhere, and Natural England has adopted the convention objective 'that all landscapes matter', it is necessary for there to be a tighter category than 'other land' for the purposes of heritage protection.[7] Otherwise, government control over property would be extended to an unrealistic degree, and, where funding is provided, encourage conservation to an unaffordable extent.

Nothing can be more dangerous when dealing with a heritage landscape than to try to judge it against what is expected from particular genres. This is an inevitable temptation once attention is focused on whether or not a particular place has the characteristics of a designed landscape. The term 'genre' is simply the French for 'a kind' which has been incorporated into English. In French, appropriately, because men are especially keen to classify things into boxes, it is a male word. The search for whether a landscape is of this kind or that kind generally blinds the would-be conservator to the real significance of what it actually is. Both people and places are infinitely variable and conservation should look at the actual interaction between the two and not attempt to interpret a landscape by reference to some generalised template drawn from elsewhere, unless there is a specific reference in primary materials justifying such a link. Beyond that, these possible connections are best left to be pored over and disputed by academics and commentators until a firm consensus emerges.

It is understandable that broad-brush terms are used when public policy is being made; terms with fuzzy edges allow for flexibility in their application. This can be helpful to an administrator. By using the widest possible meaning of 'designed' it is possible to include almost any landscape which has been subject of an intention to create an artistic effect and English Heritage has been anxious to make a clear push for understanding that the Register is intended to embrace contrived landscapes which extend beyond the narrow confines of gardens and parks in the immediate vicinity of the house for which they have been made. However, problems arise when too narrow an interpretation of the term is used to define the character of a particular landscape. A landscape can be improved for aesthetic purposes without ever being subject to a preconceived plan. The improvement of landscape in that way has been succinctly described by Richard Payne Knight (1750–1824), who worked on his landscape at Downton on the Rock, Herefordshire in precisely this way. After discussing the improvement of relatively flat landscapes he moves from the particular to the general:

> The late Mr Southgate's farm near Weybridge, though in many parts too finely dressed, is, both in design and execution, far preferable to any of the works of Kent or Brown; and is proof of what may

be done in this humble style: but in this, as in every other, picture-esque effects can only be obtained by watching accidents, and profiting by circumstances during a long period of time. The line of a walk, the position of a seat, or limits of an inclosure, must often depend upon the accidental growth of a tree, and we must always make things, which we can command, conform to those we cannot.[8]

And later on he refines this when countering Humphry Repton's (1752–1818) criticism that he was advocating improvement by neglect and accident:[9]

> by carefully collecting and cherishing the accidental beauties of wild nature; by judiciously arranging them, and skilfully combining them with each other, and the embellishment of art; I cannot but think that the landscape gardener might produce complete and faultless compositions in nature, which would be as much superior to the imitations of them by art, as the acting of a Garrick or a Siddons is to the best representation of it in a portrait. Those indeed who think only of making *fine places*, in order to gratify their own vanity, or profit by the vanity of others, may call this mode of proceeding *a new system of improving by neglect and accident*; yet those who have tried it know, that, though to preserve the appearance of neglect and accident be one of its objects, it is not by leaving everything to neglect and accident, that even that is to be obtained. *Profiting by accident*, is very different from *leaving everything to accident*; and *improving by neglect*, very different from *neglecting*.

Thomas Hearne (1744–1817), who had the advantage of having painted in the Teme Gorge at Downton and seeing for himself the kind of effects achieved there, drew two plates of 'Contrasting Landscapes' as illustrations for Knight's poem *The Landscape* (1794). They are two of the most reproduced images in books about garden history but are usually put forward as a demonstration of contrasting aesthetic preferences. Of greater importance perhaps, is the way that they reveal the difference between process and design. In each case the bridge and the architecture of the house may be said to have been designed and in each case the major trees are seen in the same positions. The scene in the first plate (Figure 5.1) could only come about as a result of natural accident in that particular landscape, allowing the stream to take its natural course and the trees to express their natural character, while leaving the underbrush and fallen branches alone where they contribute to the desired effect.

On the other hand the scene in the second plate could, given appropriate topography and the availability of water, be imposed on this or any other landscape by design, allowing time for any newly planted trees to grow.

Figure 5.1 Illustration for *The Landscape*, a poem by Richard Payne Knight; 'An undressed scene', Thomas Hearne, 1794. (© Trustees of the British Museum.)

Figure 5.2 Illustration for *The Landscape*, a poem by Richard Payne Knight; 'A scene dressed in the modern style', Thomas Hearne, 1794. (© Trustees of the British Museum.)

Taking the second plate (Figure 5.2) as a hypothetical example of an important landscape by a noted designer, its significance as a heritage asset would be apparent from the original design and conservation efforts are likely to be focused as nearly as possible on the restoration or recreation of the landscape as it was first laid out. In the case of landscapes based on natural accident, it is the process carried on by particular owners which is significant, either because of the way in which they undertook them, such as the tunnels for visual and acoustic effects at Downton and Hafod, Wales or because of the character they gave to the landscape such as at Foxley, Herefordshire; Boconnoc, Cornwall; Hawkstone, Shropshire and Hackfall, Yorkshire. In the latter case, provided the character of the landscape and the required effects are conserved, it is of no consequence if a river has altered its course, the tree cover has changed or has been changed, and seats and viewpoints have been adjusted to take account of this. For example at Durlston, near Swanage, Dorset, the major landslip below Sunnyvale will not affect the character of George Burt's (1816–1894) landscape significantly, provided that the original path network is adjusted to take account of this and makes the most of other natural incidents in its place. At Hackfall, the path network and the functioning of features such as the Alum Spring has been adapted to take account of nature conservation interests that have arisen in the years when the landscape was untended.

Another good example of the way in which a landscape can be exploited through a process of change is dealt with by Watkins and Cowell in *Uvedale Price (1747–1829): Decoding the Picturesque* (2012) and includes the description by the botanist Benjamin Stillingfleet (1702–1771), of the way in which his friend Robert Price (1653–1733) set out paths at Foxley in the early eighteenth century: 'He first walked over the whole ground, following, as well as he could, the gentlest and most gradual ascent all the way and pacing it to the top of the hill'. Then using simple trigonometry 'he made the path rise regularly, and, in some places, where the height did not bear a great proportion to the length of the walk, insensibly; so that you go to the top of a high and steep hill without any labour and without knowing that you were not on plain ground'.[10]

There is no better illustration of the difference between process and design than the origin of Île de Peupliers at Ermenonville, France, the temporary resting place of Jean-Jacques Rousseau (1712–1778). This island was not designed to be a memorial to that great philosopher and botanist. It had been known as the Île de Cygnes, a haunt for lovers, within the landscape improved by René Louis de Girardin (1735–1808) according to the principles he had drawn from the account given of Julie's garden in Rousseau's *La Nouvelle Héloïse* (1761). When he died in 1778, after a day botanising at Ermenonville, Rousseau was buried in that happy place. Not being Catholic, he could not be laid to rest in the village cemetery. This was not an action led by design, albeit later marked by a cenotaph which was designed by the French painter Hubert Robert (1733–1808).

However, the set of lake, island, trees and memorial became an iconic symbol of death and remembrance to those making landscapes at the end of the long eighteenth century. Elizabeth Barlow Rogers has commented 'This much-copied garden feature illustrates the elegiac character of Romanticism and also reminds us of Rousseau's fundamental importance to the history of landscape design'.[11] The most celebrated copy is perhaps that at Wörlitz, Germany and there are other important examples in Berlin's Tiergarten and Helena Radziwill's Arkadia in Poland. Clearly these are designed features which remind us of Rousseau but they have none of the atmosphere that envelops the visitor at that adventitious burial plot at Ermenonville, even if Rousseau's body was, in 1794, removed to the Panthéon in Paris.

The task of the restorer of a designed landscape is relatively straightforward, technical difficulty apart; it is simply to follow the plan as nearly as possible. In some cases planting plans also become available, such as those followed to such good effect by Rosamund Wallinger in the Gertrude Jeykll (1843–1932) designed gardens at The Manor House, Upton Grey, Hampshire.[12] Difficulties arise when designs have been overlaid by later work and then, as in the case of the recreation of the Privy Garden at Hampton Court, the decision to pick a particular period as a reference point has to be justified. In that case, the approach adopted has been explained in *The Story of the Privy Garden at Hampton Court*[13] and is summarised in Section 3.5 of *The Management and Maintenance of Historic Parks, Gardens and Landscapes*.[14] In the same section the challenge presented by replacing the declining avenues at the Palace is discussed.[15] Clearly, these needed to be on their planned alignments, as do any restored Brownian clumps in the landscapes where he worked, if the coherence of the designed landscape is to be retained.

In *Led by the Land* (2012), Kim Wilkie has described how a detailed landscape design by Lancelot Brown (1716–1783) for the wet meadows at Heveningham Hall in Suffolk has been given effect more than 200 years after it was carefully drawn.[16] The natural features in the landscape have been swept away to create parkland which might have been created in 1783, the year of Brown's death. Wilkie points out that this was not a restoration but rather a new insertion into a historic landscape. A similar insertion of an early design by Brown is taking place at Kirkharle, Northumbria, his birthplace, albeit contending with, and adapting to, changes in the landscape framework which have taken place since they were conceived.[17] The lesson from both is that a good design from any period can, constraints apart, be imposed on a landscape at any time.

The challenge facing anyone in charge of a landscape improved by a process is, in one way, more onerous. They must be able to defend decisions to relocate paths and seats, replant trees and shrubs, prune or fell them to reveal new views and make other changes to take advantage of natural accidents, including those brought about by invasive species or plant diseases. In doing this, a clear and courageous sense of purpose is required, echoing, as far as is possible the approach of those who have created the landscape. Almost by definition, landscapes arrived at through process are the work of owners; they have no constraints of time, no need to draw plans, make specifications or deliver a particular effect contracted for at a particular price. They can take up or lay down the task of improvement as they please. In the case of William Beckford (1760–1844) in the grounds of the Old Abbey at Fonthill Gifford, Wiltshire, his work there took place between 1795 and 1822, only 27 years or so. At Boconnoc in Cornwall a process of improvement has extended, intermittently from about 1761 to the present day and has remained in the hands of the Pitt, Grenville and Fortescue families. In neither place was a landscape architect or designer employed.

Large corporate organisations find it difficult to manage landscapes of this kind effectively, unless the local manager is given real freedom to exercise aesthetic judgement. A committee may sit to determine which plan of a designed landscape should be followed but cannot directly supervise the hour-by-hour creative judgements demanded in places formed and necessarily maintained through a process. Similarly, bodies supervising grant aid for landscape conservation and enhancement, for example the agri-environment Stewardship Schemes and Heritage Lottery Funding, need to develop tools to deal with the unpredictable nature of work programmes for these, which should not be based on desktop studies and prescriptive specifications. Above all, there should be an understanding that old surveys of such landscapes give only a snapshot of a process rather than amounting to confirmation of a pre-existing design which should be slavishly followed.

As in our own gardens, even where there has been an element of structural design in the process of planting, dividing and rearranging plants may be left to the day and may not be specified in the original plans. So it is with some of the great eighteenth-century landscapes. Those two frustrated visionaries, Stephen Switzer (1682–1745) and Charles Bridgeman (1690–1738), working under the eye of the vendors of continental pastiche designs London & Wise at the Brompton Nursery, both drew stylised, sinuous paths within the overall Baroque geometry of their plans. In the case of Switzer, the best example is his drawing of the hypothetical 'Manor of Paston' which is little more than a trade sampler. Bridgeman's plan for Hackwood Park, near Basingstoke (Figure 5.3) can be compared with the Estate Survey of 1725 for the Duke of Bolton.

Although there are some significant differences between the two the garden was, broadly speaking, laid out in the way designed by Bridgeman.

Bridgeman's plan shows a diagrammatic representation of an informal sinuous path network threading itself between the formal avenues.

The Estate Survey of 1725 shows that these paths were, in due course, expressed on the ground not as appears in the plan, but, evidently, in a way not dissimilar from the process described by Payne Knight nearly two centuries later. In 2001 the author had the opportunity of mowing-out on the ground the smaller paths shown on the 1725 Estate Plan, some sinuous and some rectilinear, with the help of the gardeners, Mr and Mrs Mansbridge. Some of these appeared, on a plan view, to have no particular purpose or offer any aesthetic advantage. On the ground, it was another story. They provided the contrasting experiences of walking among wild flowers with intermittent oblique views down the avenues with their closely mown lawns between the laurel hedges of the designed geometry. These little paths swiftly became the preferred means of enjoying the garden. Figure 5.4 shows a sketch of Spring Wood by Yasmin Barhum made after the paths had been recreated.

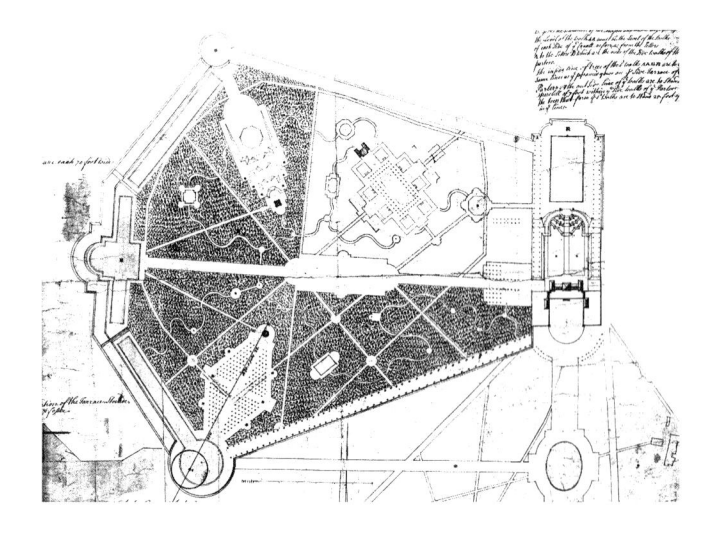

Figure 5.3 Hackwood. Plan by Bridgeman (attrib.). (© The Bodleian Libraries MSGD A4 fo34; see also Peter Willis, *Charles Bridgeman and the English Landscape Garden*, 2nd edn. 2002, plate 201a.)

Figure 5.4 Sketch of Spring Wood, Hackwood Park by Yasmin Barhum, 2001.

However, good as they were, it also became clear that the paths could and, perhaps should, be adapted to take account of changes that had occurred over 275 years.

At Hawkstone Park, Shropshire, there is the opportunity to see the two approaches to improvement side-by-side. On the low ground there is the landscape designed by William Emes (1729–1803) with the contrived 'Hawk River'. On the great mass of the rocks above that, paths thread through the natural features and old mineral workings where opportunity allows and experiences are offered. Even the invasive *rhododendron ponticum* is now, by popular demand, exploited, shedding a mauve haze over the rocks as the blossom falls. The conservation measures appropriate for those two components in what is now a fragmented landscape would be very different.

Land managers should avoid, wherever possible, being drawn into interpreting landscapes by references to genre rather than looking at the best evidence of the design or process through which a particular place has come to have heritage significance. The last thing any of us should want is a country in which myriad landscapes made by a diverse group of people are melted down and recast as a number of limited representative 'kinds'. The homogenisation of landscape style can be an unfortunate side-effect of the best intentioned conservation measures, particularly when they are led by desk-top exercises. Once the character of a landscape is altered in that way it can be difficult for it to be retrieved by later generations.

Endnotes

1. http://www.oed.com.ezp1.bath.ac.uk/view/Entry/50840?rskey=dq03bS&result=1#eid Accessed 25/11/2013.
2. The National Heritage Act 1983, Schedule 4 (amending Section 8 of the Historic Buildings and Ancient Monuments Act 1953).
3. http://www.english-heritage.org.uk/caring/listing/criteria-for-protection/pag-criteria Accessed 25/11/2013.
4. The Historic Environment (Amendment) (Scotland) Act 2011, Section 11.
5. http://www.asla.org/nonmembers/publicrelations/glossary.htm Accessed 25/11/2013.
6. http://tclf.org/content/designed-landscape Accessed 25/11/2013.
7. http://www.naturalengland.org.uk/ourwork/landscape/importance/default.aspx Accessed 25/11/2013.
8. Malcolm Andrews, *The Picturesque: Sources and Documents*, 3 vols, Sussex: (1994). vol. II pp. 185–6. Reproducing Payne Knight's own note 27 to *The Landscape: A Didactic Poem* (1794). In this passage Knight talks of design in terms of intention.

9. The letter to Uvedale Price 1 July 1794 reproduced in Humphry Repton, *Sketches and Hints on Landscape Gardening*, Commaissance Et Memoires, Paris ed. (1795).
10. Charles Watkins and Ben Cowell, *Uvedale Price, 1747–1829: Decoding the Picturesque*, Boydell & Brewer (2012), especially pp. 19 and 20, and William Coxe, *Literary Life and Select Works of Benjamin Stillingfleet, Several of Which Have Never before Been Published*, London (1811), vol. I. p. 174 fn. 2.
11. Elizabeth Barlow Rogers, *Landscape Design: A Cultural and Architectural History*, New York: Harry N. Abrams Inc. (2001), p. 263.
12. Rosamund Wallinger, *Gertrude Jekyll's Lost Garden,* Garden Art Press (2000).
13. Mavis Batey and Jan Woudstra, *The Story of the Privy Garden at Hampton Court*, London: Barn Elms, (1995).
14. John Watkins and Tom Wright, *The Management & Maintenance of Historic Parks, Gardens & Landscapes* London: Frances Lincoln (2007), p. 273.
15. Ibid. p. 275.
16. Kim Wilkie, *Led by the Land: Landscapes by Kim Wilkie*, London: Frances Lincoln (2012). pp.73–76
17. http://www.kirkharlecourtyard.net/lake.php. Accessed 25/11/2013.

6 Evolution of principles for the conservation of gardens and designed landscapes

David Jacques
Trustee of the Chiswick House and Grounds Trust, London, UK

Older approaches to conservation

Preservation, restoration, reconstruction, renewal, conservation, upkeep . . . there are many variations on the theme of retaining or recovering the qualities of parks and gardens. Prior to the late 1980s the prevailing approach was historicist till the landscape architectural profession adopted Modernist attitudes.[1]

Historicist

From early in the nineteenth century until well into the twentieth an interest in the picturesque qualities of historic gardens spawned large numbers of historicist designs and re-creations.

The intention of such work was to give a 'period' feel either to old gardens that had lost their former detail, or to new gardens designed to suit the style of some historical period. Often it stemmed from a desire to match the garden to the house as architectural fashion went through a succession of revivalist styles. Although some architects were interested in authentic architectural detail in gateways, steps and garden buildings, this was seldom slavishly adopted in new work. Indeed, the experienced eye is generally capable of detecting such re-creations because they were seldom accurate in detail.

Some authentic topiary gardens survived from the early eighteenth century, though almost always severely grown out so that the design intentions were lost, and there were many new topiary gardens, sometimes fooling twentieth-century visitors as to their age. Such misconceptions were rarely discouraged by the garden owners.

Modernist

In Modernist art circles across Europe there was a common belief that great art had a connection to universal laws, and was of timeless quality. This justified restoration of gardens to rediscover or reveal the higher artistic qualities with which places were imbued.

Gardens & Landscapes in Historic Building Conservation, First Edition. Edited by Marion Harney.
© 2014 John Wiley & Sons, Ltd. Published 2014 by John Wiley & Sons, Ltd.

The psyche of each period was thought to reveal itself through the work of that period, but it needed geniuses, in touch with the collective subconscious and with the laws of the cosmos, to produce the seminal statements of the time. Much of the architectural and garden history of the mid-twentieth century was devoted to discovering the identity of these geniuses and the nature of their genius.

Restoration in many European countries became the architect's interpretation of how the artistic message might be revealed. It was acceptable to employ modern or non-authentic materials and techniques in order to give the general form and appearance. Archaeology and research were seldom deemed necessary, and if historic plans did exist they were treated merely as background information for the architect. Sometimes the architect chose to depart radically from such information, and in the process, much archaeological evidence was destroyed.

In line with the belief in the enduring validity of great truths, international charters were written as if they were being inscribed in stone. In this spirit the International Council on Monuments and Sites (ICOMOS) produced its Florence Charter of 1982 on the preservation of historic gardens. Its preamble revealed the importance to the authors that gardens should be recognised as works of genius alongside architectural masterpieces. The historic garden was characterised as 'an architectural composition whose constituents are primarily vegetal', and it was a great concern to the authors that an historic garden could be 'considered as a monument' (this term having specific legal implications in France and several other European countries).

Restoration by charter – *The desire for accuracy*

The conservation movement strengthened in many countries during the 1970s and 1980s. Part of this movement was a rejection of the vague objectives, often incompetently and destructively implemented, of Modernist attitudes. The new mood was to want to know precisely what historic gardens looked like in their heyday, and to undertake restorations accordingly. They were often promoted as museum pieces for the benefit of the public, and indeed very many examples in Europe and North America were carried out by curators seeking to recover the settings of their houses and palaces.

Historical accuracy was vital in order to achieve these objectives. In England the initial step in the late 1960s had consisted of making new gardens at small manor houses using pattern books of knots and parterres. The notations of materials in the patterns may not always have been interpreted correctly, but this approach was popular with the public.

The next step in the 1980s was to use plans and/or views of the place in question. A seemingly useful guideline was to restore to the last significant date. But even using historic plans did not guarantee accuracy. For example, some plans are no more than design proposals, and were unreliable as to what had been there. Sometimes places had undergone previous historicist restoration, particularly common in the nineteenth century, and so the historic elements were often not of the period they purported to be. Misinterpretation of the evidence of course undermined the whole point of presenting a garden in its 'original design'.

The public purse

Whilst restoration had been undertaken by private individuals or bodies with their own money, there was little call to question the philosophy and principles underlying it, but that had to change when public money was to be allocated to support such proposals. Although public money has been given in some counties towards the upkeep of properties designated as 'monuments' for some time, and the eligible works might include aspects of their gardens, probably the first purpose-made system of grants of public money for parks and gardens was that for the repair of storm damage in England, starting in 1988. Since then English Heritage, the Countryside Commission (now part of English Nature) and the Heritage Lottery Fund have operated grant schemes, and all have needed criteria and principles for allocation of the money. At much the same time professionals in the USA and Canada were likewise formulating principles to be adopted by Government agencies.

The criteria determine whether, or what aspect, of a park or garden is eligible. They included the importance of the park or garden, the status of owner, whether other finances were available, convincing proposals and management plan and so forth. Should a place and its owner be eligible, principles were sought to determine whether the proposals were worthy of support.

The actual principles are discussed below, but it is also important to understand the background to their formulation. First, the general belief in absolutes, as supposedly enshrined in ICOMOS charters, was not yet seriously challenged. Although the trust in design professionals to reveal designs of genius had given way to militant conservation, the belief in charters, or rigid prescriptions for good practice, remained. This normative approach derived in part from a desire to establish historic gardens as a serious topic, something not always appreciated by architectural colleagues. The Florence Charter actually contained many excellent axioms for the practice of conservation, but its preamble showed how anxious its authors were to define what they saw as the unchanging truths of conservation. Amongst these was the then common assumption that value was something inherent in an object, humans being merely its observers.

Older principles for the treatment of historic gardens, and detailed guidance on preparing schemes, were drawn up by this author in the late 1980s when he was the Inspector of Historic Parks and Gardens at English Heritage.[2] Looked at in retrospect, they have the form of sets of rules, not dissimilar to the way that international charters were drawn up. However, another reason, besides the desire to form a family of charters, was that there were very few landscape architects with the skills and experience necessary for restoration work. The immediate context was replanting after the Great Storm of 1987. The paucity of skills at the time suggested that guidance, as explicit as possible, would enable the many landscape architects offering their services to appreciate what was expected of them, especially as regards the management planning process.

Restoration principles in the 1980s

The central concern within the principles was preserving the non-renewable information embodied in the authentic fabric. This was a familiar tenet from architectural conservation, though some adjustments in emphasis were desirable in order to allow gardens and their plants to meet the same criteria. One was the distinction between the 'permanent' structure of walls, paths and architecturally conceived planting like avenues and hedges on the one hand, and the impermanent elements, say those with a life of under 40 years, like shrubs, herbaceous borders and flowerbeds.

Once garden conservation had been allied to architectural conservation, it could share many of the same characteristics. A terminology that enabled forms of treatment to be distinguished was essential (even though it might differ slightly between different countries). The worth of each approach was assessed against principles laid down in the charters.[3]

Conservation-friendly forms of restoration were seen as:

- Upkeep and periodic renewal, treatments that maintained the fabric as designed
- Repair, necessary when some of the fabric had failed through decay, but where the design could be saved through the introduction of sections of replacement fabric; a repair would then be 'accurate'
- Restoration (in the usual sense of the word) when the garden or landscape as a whole had suffered an extended period of lack of appropriate maintenance, resulting in elements

being eroded, obscured or partially removed, and its continuance as a coherent design requiring often extensive capital works.

Less benign forms of treatment, which neglected the primacy of authentic fabric, were:

- Reconstruction, often to a layer that may be more congenial, but which has disappeared
- Restoration-in-spirit, whereby a landscape architect has sought to recover the 'feel' of a landscape, but without close attention to the evidence from its actual or archaeological fabric
- Period-style gardens, being re-designs or new designs of garden areas that seek to give the impression of an older garden, often as the setting of a nearby building.

The ideal of authentic fabric maintained into the far distant future was the objective in an architectural context, and shared in parks and gardens. The vision for them tended to be the unchanging landscape of their last great manifestation.

Aids to accuracy: garden archaeology and conjectural detailing

Accuracy in restoration was promoted through increasing technical sophistication. The first historical survey of a garden was that by the National Trust for Osterley Park, Hounslow, in 1979, and they became numerous and highly skilled in the 1980s. Combined with research in the archives and on visual sources, they offered the prospect of detailed examinations of their histories and surviving fabric. Often such work comprised volume I of management plans.

Initially it had been thought that the chief contribution from archaeology would be in detecting the marks of relict gardens on the ground, say in dry weather or in light snow. Although there are several 'non-destructive' techniques, the desire for accuracy often necessitated excavation, in some cases giving spectacular results from the early 1980s. It was amply demonstrated that the layout of beds, paths, steps and statues could be recovered archaeologically with great precision. The best known case in England was the Privy Garden at Hampton Court (Figures 6.1 and 6.2).

Over the period up till 1995 sufficient experience was thus accumulated for some conclusions on the techniques and uses of garden archaeology to be feasible.[4]

Very often in restoration the outlines of a design are clear, but the detail closer to the eye is damaged, missing or dead, without sufficient record of its previous existence. If the theme of restoration is to recover a design, it can hardly achieve aesthetic coherence without some conjectural replacement. Examples include path edging and the precise species and positions of planting. Research into such contemporary details often exists, or could be researched, and give a plausible representation of the whole. Mark Laird and others have developed conjectural planting as a specialist skill much to the benefit of the public's appreciation of historic designs.

Conservation thinking today

Philosophical background

Conservation being an aspect of modern culture, the assumptions behind it move on. One of the lessons of the last quarter century is that conservation principles cannot be seen as set in stone for all time – they are just our best thoughts at the present time. This is because they are a reflection of the passions and preoccupations of each succeeding generation, and also the onward march of knowledge and skills. This is well illustrated in the way that conservation thinking on parks and gardens has varied over time.

Figure 6.1 Hampton Court Privy Garden excavation, 1994: this was perhaps the most thorough excavation in Britain, revealing the layout of beds with great precision. (© Crown Copyright, Historic Royal Palaces, Photograph Cliff Birtchnell.)

Figure 6.2 Hampton Court Privy Garden replanting: research by Jan Woudstra into the methods of planting the *plates bandes* preceded the replanting.

The general belief in absolutes has given way to a greater acknowledgement of relativity, for example to accommodate non-Western concepts of conservation. Value is now seen not as something inherent in objects, but as a complex and potentially variable set of qualities derived from people's culture, expectations and preferences, so that a wider range of bodies and individuals could contribute to decisions. There is a new willingness to engage a wider range of bodies and communities in deciding upon aims and priorities.

The primary values recognised by English Heritage in historic gardens are still art-historical, with rarity and condition being additional factors, but the aesthetic dimension to significance has become more complex. As expressions of taste over the centuries, and with their range of possible associations, landscapes can have many qualities. In addition, there are the 'natural' qualities relating to geology, ecology and biodiversity, and the benefits of physical and intellectual public access.[5]

The focus on the great monuments as proof of genius has thus been matched by an interest in the vernacular and the cultural landscape as informing us as much, or even more, about the history of mankind. In 1992 UNESCO's World Heritage Committee accepted a redefinition of cultural qualities to include landscapes of a vernacular nature (e.g. rice terraces), and with associations (e.g. holy mountains).

The benefit of experience

Conservation remains primarily the business of protecting what is seen as valuable from the past, and promoting historical understanding. It is still useful to have a terminology that reduces needless confusion in debates. It is also helpful to have a robust rationale about the aim of repairs and restoration. Critics delighted in saying that restoration is about recovering a lost past, which had some validity when historicist gardens were being made, or even when the best advice was to restore to the last significant date. The counter-argument was often that conservation is for future generations. However that is still not compelling, because we cannot possibly know what future generations will have wanted from us. Advice now tends to see conservation as putting into good order those landscape components which we ourselves decide should be taken forward into the future.

As explained above, the desire for accuracy generally sought to recover a design when it was at a high point. Strategies of conjectural planting were devised to overcome the obvious exceptions, such as cyclical replanting. Several factors have led to a reconsideration of the single-moment end-point. One was taking the conservation approach to its logical conclusion; that is, respecting the landscape as received by our generation, warts and all. All overlays of a garden thus came to be of interest as part of the 'document'. Another factor is that virtual reality, although still in its infancy, has great potential for helping the public imagine a garden in the various phases of its existence, lessening the curator's perceived need for a literal representation of a single phase in a garden's history via reconstruction.

Actual projects are often more problematic than the early guidance foresaw. In real life, the opportunities for a full-blown purist restoration like the Privy Garden at Hampton Court, Richmond upon Thames are rare (and even then concessions had to be made to contemporary issues). Practical experience has shown that circumstances can vary markedly – mixed philosophies of restoration accompanied by new design in urban parks, the demands of integrated presentation of house and garden, and conundrums over what to do with previous restoration now judged to be substandard are amongst the situations when there can be no 'correct' solution. Chiswick House and Garden in London (Figure 6.3) is an example of a property where a mixed philosophy solution was applied.

On the other hand the way that Government assures its ends is through explaining to owners and persuading public bodies, rather than by inflexible prescriptions. Guidance that recognises the possibility of debate and alternative outcomes is more appropriate now that

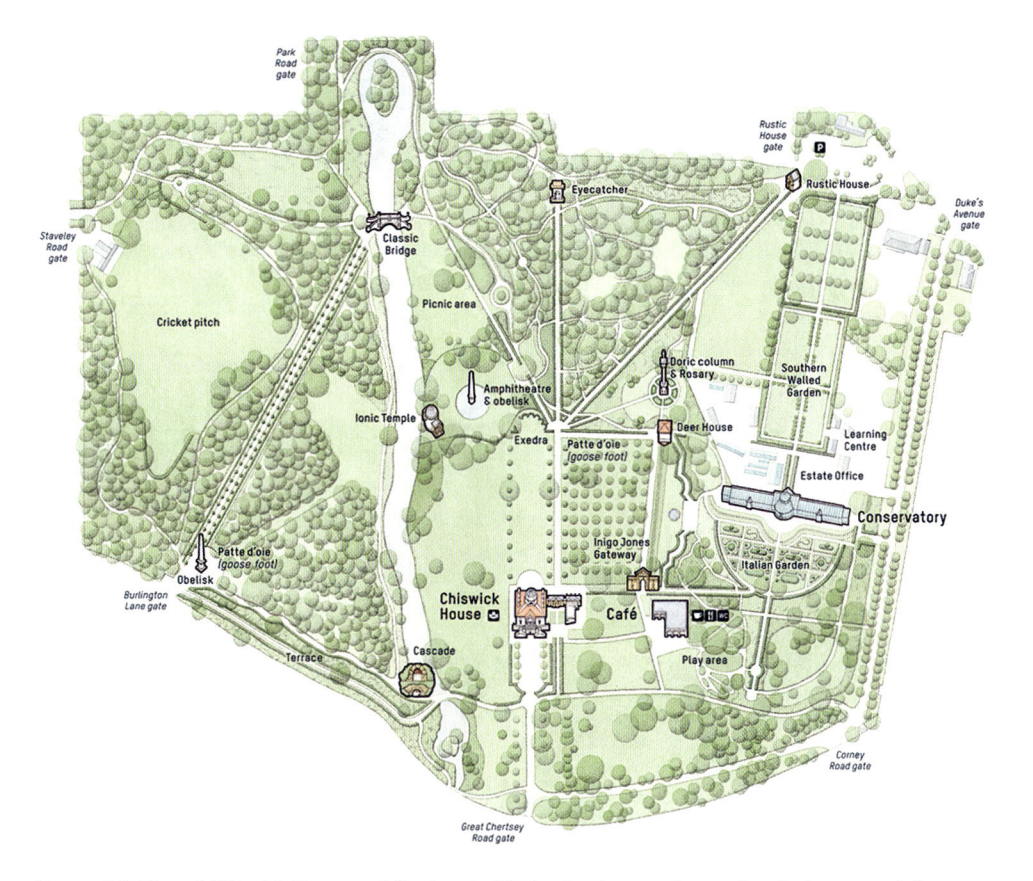

Figure 6.3 Map of Chiswick House and Gardens in 2012: a landscape of several periods was partially reconstructed close to the villa when most of it was demolished in the 1950s; this presented problems for a conservation approach, and it was judged better to complete the reconstruction, whilst pursuing conventional restoration, with an element of nature conservation, in areas away from the house; the restoration of the late 2000s, which included a brand new café, required judgement and design to achieve a mixed philosophy solution. (Courtesy of Chiswick House and Gardens Trust.)

the understanding of historic gardens issues has much increased amongst professionals and officials.

Acceptance of change

The inclusion of gardens amongst the categories of cultural landscape in the early 1990s offered an alternative to the architectural way of thinking. Cultural landscapes include National Parks which, especially in the British context, accept change of various forms as long as the essential qualities are protected. Although landscape managers had been well aware that each landscape has its own dynamic, and requires active management to protect aesthetic and other qualities, these points had barely entered into the conservation of landscapes protected for their historic interest.

For this reason there had been misgivings about conservation amongst garden owners, the largest of which is the National Trust, and the gulf of understanding between English Heritage and ecologists was deep. Each party was driven by its own ideology, and statesmanship was in short supply. However, progressive forces within the Countryside

Agency (now part of English Nature) attempted to convince all sides that conservationists of various hues had more to gain from mutual understanding and collaboration. The integrated approach, i.e. taking all values (historical, archaeological, ecological, scenic, access, etc.) into account simultaneously was best handled through a management plan.

In this spirit, proposals for garden restoration sought to improve public access and ecological diversity as well as reveal an historic design. In public parks from the late 1990s, Heritage Lottery Fund support often resulted in new work where this gave significant gains to, say, accessibility or facilities for the public, as long as they did not seriously erode the qualities that made the park historically significant.

The National Trust's philosophy is to allow each garden to evolve through changes in staff and fresh gardening approaches. In practice this seldom needs to conflict with a conservation approach. This is because the long-term elements of a garden – topography, views, structures, structural planting – can be viewed as suitable for the conservation approach, whilst everyone accepts that those shorter-term elements which represent horticultural excellence are best judged by different standards. The gardens that have retained their reputation over many decades, especially those with a significant amount of structures, have generally done so by a well-judged combination of both approaches.

New work and adaptation

New work introduces a contemporary overlay into a landscape, and can consist of full redesign in part or whole. Adaptation is work intended to change the function or appearance of a place, usually in order to meet modern requirements. It consists of elements of new work in an otherwise historic design.

Contemporary design in historic landscape often seems unnecessarily problematic. After all, all valued landscape design was once an intervention in an historic landscape. There are, though, dangers with new work and adaptation which might include, for example, the removal of historic fabric, the alteration of the manner and sequence of the visitor experience, or the added confusion to the understanding of the fabric.

At the same time, new design that pretends it has no linkage to its context will probably be poor design, displaying incongruities that emphasise that it has no place in that landscape. The blank sheet of paper, or nowadays blank screen, is very rarely presented to the designer; most schemes are adaptations of the existing for some new purpose, and these will nearly always encounter some constraint from planning policies or existing objects like trees. In real life most projects have a mix of new design and conservation in varying proportions. One would hope that designers will aspire to a quality of design and execution which may be valued both now and in the future.

Conservation is thus not the enemy of contemporary designers – bad new design leading to degradation and loss of meaning is the real enemy, and is the enemy of conservation too. Protected landscapes are a tiny proportion of the country. Elsewhere new work should be adding to the cultural value of the landscape. Hence there could be more unity between designers and conservationists, around the theme of quality.

Restoration in the 2010s

Grand projects like the restorations of the Privy Garden at Hampton Court and the Tudor Garden at Kenilworth Castle, Warwickshire, are becoming fewer, as money is scarcer and perhaps the appetite weakens. There are, though, numerous other less high-profile projects afoot, thanks in particular to the Heritage Lottery Fund.

Garden archaeology and conjectural detailing still have their place (Figure 6.4).

Archaeologists, conscious of their ethos of trying non-destructive techniques before attempting excavation, propose a role in survey work and analysis to reveal and assess

Figure 6.4 Conjectural detailing: the 'Italian garden' at Chiswick House is a well-documented early reintroduction of the formal garden; it had a semicircular border and roses and mop-headed robinias, which became a yew hedge in the 1950s, giving a false impression of its design; using an historical plan which specified the plants, this conjectural replanting has allowed the garden to recover its colour and scale. (Artist: Liz Pepperell. Courtesy of English Heritage.)

Figure 6.5 The Kenilworth garden fountain foundations in 2004: a case when a carefully targeted excavation was successful in locating the central feature of this garden, allowing the main lines of the geometry to be reconstructed.

physical remains as an input to understanding the design and design intentions. This leads to carefully chosen targeted excavations, in particular in the recovery of architectural structures, boundaries, statue bases and paths which may need simply to be exposed after a period of neglect, and deep excavation of lost features is nowadays less common. The Kenilworth Castle garden restoration in 2004 (Figures 6.5 and 6.6) provides an example of a case when a carefully targeted excavation was successful in locating the central feature of this garden (the fountain), allowing the main lines of the geometry to be reconstructed.

Figure 6.6 The Tudor Garden at Kenilworth Castle in 2009: a detailed description from 1575 filled in several of the details, and English Heritage decided to proceed with reconstruction to provide a rare image of elite gardens of that period; along the way much valuable research was commissioned. Although reconstruction is not a generally favoured approach today, there were reasons for Kenilworth being a special case, and the discussion of restoration objectives in the accompanying publication was honest, transparent and inclusive.

This appears to coincide with newer judgements over which aspect of a project should command most attention. A quarter of a century ago the desire for accuracy focused the project team's minds on the collection of data, whereas now there is increased concern for the process, including setting the sometimes complex set of objectives, rationalising the work to be undertaken, and the documentation.

The tests for good practice are not simply whether the proposals approximate a form of restoration approved of in a charter, but whether they have clear and coherent objectives, whether they are likely to lead to specific benefits in the conservation of fabric and/or design, and whether the discussion of the objectives and consequences has been honest, transparent and inclusive.

Reliance is placed on experience and judgement rather than on a rule book approach.

As an example, the checklist of points to consider when conjectural detailing is proposed will include whether the detail can be shown to be reasonably predictable; the details in question are not a major proportion of the whole; conjectural detailing is not employed as a substitute for careful recording, archaeological techniques and analysis; and the conjectural status of the details is made clear in the site archive and in information provided to visitors.

Change is inherent to parks and gardens, and has been so in the past, so successive minor alterations can result in an almost imperceptible departure from the design. This can be through annual tree growth blocking vistas, or a succession of minor decisions by those responsible for maintenance. Recording of what took place and the rationale behind decisions is thus increasingly recognised as vital to future management. An initial survey will provide a baseline against which those making decisions in the future can assess success or failure of the tactics chosen in the past or the objectives of care since.

Every project is a candidate for a site archive, a collection of all technical information generated by the project, including photography, survey work, committee papers and minutes, research reports, archaeological reports, design drawings, and monitoring reports. A policy for a site archive from the start of a project will be beneficial.

Summary

In a nutshell, the conservation approach today has moved some way towards:

- Human values, rather than universal principles
- Acceptance of change; and attention to its dynamics
- Collaboration between professions to raise the overall quality of a place
- Exercise of judgement, rather than reliance on fixed prescriptions
- Yardsticks to include informed decisions, clarity of purpose, consistency over time and honesty in presentation.

References/Further reading

ICOMOS UK (2004) 'Cultural Qualities in Cultural Landscapes', available from ICOMOS UK.

Jacques, D. (1995) 'The Treatment of Historic Parks and Gardens', *Journal of Architectural Conservation*, 2, July 1995.

Jacques, D. (ed.) (1997) 'The Techniques and Uses of Garden Archaeology', *Journal of Garden History*, 17/1.

Jacques, D. (2005) 'Post-war English attitudes in restoration work', in Conan, M., Rojo, J.T. & Zangheri, L. (eds) *Histories of garden conservation: Case-studies and critical debates*, Florence, Leo S. Olschki.

Watkins, J. and Wright, T. (eds) (2007) *The Management and Maintenance of Historic Parks, Gardens and Landscapes*, London, Frances Lincoln.

Endnotes

1. Jacques, 2005, pp. 409–16.
2. Watkins & Wright, 2007, p. 28.
3. Jacques, 1995, pp. 21–35.
4. Jacques, 1997.
5. ICOMOS UK, 2004.

7 Conservation of garden buildings

Michael Forsyth
Director, postgraduate Conservation of Historic Buildings programme at the University of Bath, Bath, UK

Introduction

Through case studies of significant but contrasting garden buildings at Stowe, Buckinghamshire and at Croome Park, Worcestershire – both National Trust properties, this chapter considers a range of philosophical approaches that might be applied in different situations for their repair. The options usually fall approximately into one of the degrees of intervention in the spectrum described by Feilden:[1]

- prevention of deterioration (or indirect conservation), inspections and maintenance
- preservation, involving repairs to keep the heritage asset in its existing state
- consolidation (or direct conservation), involving structural strengthening or the addition of other supportive materials, preferably using like-for-like materials and techniques, but sometimes using modern techniques which should be reversible
- restoration, the object of which is to revive the original concept or legibility of the building involving the replacement of missing or decayed parts but strictly based on documentary evidence
- rehabilitation, which includes modernisation and possibly adaptive re-use, though this option is usually outside the scope of options for garden buildings
- reproduction, often copying existing details to replace missing or decayed parts
- reconstruction, using new materials.

The chapter will not detail the subject as a building type as there is a substantial existing literature. Suffice it to say that garden buildings actually embrace a range of building types, some originally functional – though few retain their function – while others serve as ornamental features punctuating the landscape, providing vistas and terminating axes. English Heritage's Buildings at Risk Register has included eye-catchers, pavilions, temples, rotundas, gatehouses, belvederes, conservatories, orangeries, gazebos, seats, summerhouses, banquet halls, boathouses, towers, hermitages, mock castles, grottos and follies. To this can be added garden ornaments and structures such as statues, obelisks, urns, arches and ice houses. These heritage assets are prominent on the Register because, for the owners of country houses that survived to recent times, the conservation of small garden buildings took low priority in the maintenance of the house and wider estate. And the plight of those garden buildings associated with country houses that no longer exist is usually worse. 750 major

Gardens & Landscapes in Historic Building Conservation, First Edition. Edited by Marion Harney.
© 2014 John Wiley & Sons, Ltd. Published 2014 by John Wiley & Sons, Ltd.

country houses were demolished in the period 1945–73 and matters got worse with the socialist government's wealth tax imposed in April 1974 when the top rate of tax increased from 90 pence in the pound to 98 pence. The tide only began to turn in the mid-1970s. In 1974 Marcus Binney put on an exhibition at the Victoria and Albert Museum called 'The Destruction of the Country House' with grim pictures of decaying and crumbling houses and the same year he set up the campaigning organisation SAVE. 1975 was European Architectural Heritage Year and then in 1976 the Labour government abandoned the wealth tax with a new Finance Act because of the flood of country houses coming on to the market. Historic houses had received a measure of increased protection with the Historic Buildings and Monuments Act 1953 but in 1954 the Historic Buildings Council identified garden buildings as being in even greater danger than the country houses at the heart of their estates – 'the garden buildings which have played so prominent a part in the history of English architecture'.[2]

The essential starting point in planning the conservation philosophy for repair or restoration work to any historic asset is to understand its significance. This is developed through the conservation plan, a combination of a desktop study that reveals the structure's history, architectural qualities and position within its genre, and an in situ condition survey.[3] Conservation planning originated in Australia in response to *The Australia ICOMOS Charter for the Conservation of Places of Cultural Significance*, known as the Burra Charter after the mining town of that name. The concept of understanding the significance of a site was central to this document of 1979, and the conservation plan was later adopted in the United Kingdom by the Heritage Lottery fund to ensure that funded heritage assets were not harmed as a result, and by English Heritage and Historic Scotland to better understand their own properties.

The desktop study

To understand a heritage asset and its significance the desktop research will normally involve consulting a combination of primary and secondary sources. Primary sources may include original documents, deeds, drawings, maps, sales particulars, building control records, newspapers, engravings and prints, and photographs (and the building itself of course is the principal primary source). Secondary sources are those that interpret the primary, including books, listing schedules and anecdotal evidence. For researching garden buildings there are numerous types of maps and plans:

- Ordnance survey maps. Highly accurate six-inch maps were published from the mid-nineteenth century
- Tithe maps record landowners and the amounts payable by tenants in tithes to ecclesiastical parishes
- Manorial maps. From the sixteenth century onwards manorial lords commissioned surveyors and cartographers to plot their properties with particular regard to boundaries
- Estate maps and plans. These were produced by prominent landowners, both private and institutional and sometimes include detailed site plans of specific garden buildings.

These materials may be found in family records, local archives, and county and city record offices, libraries (local, university and national) and in national archives.[4] These are principally the English Heritage Archive (formerly National Monuments Record), Swindon, the equivalent collections for Scotland and Wales, the National Archives at Kew, Richmond, Surrey, and London's British Library, British Museum, the Royal Institute of British Architects Library, the Courtauld Institute, the Victoria and Albert Museum, and the Bodleian Library, Oxford.

Stowe, Buckinghamshire

When the National Trust acquired the gardens at Stowe in 1989 the concept of the conservation plan was little known in the United Kingdom. However, the appointed lead practice of Peter Inskip + Peter Jenkins Architects had significant experience of conservation planning through colleagues' experience in Australia and conservation plans for both the gardens and individual buildings formed the basis for determining the philosophical approach to each structure. There are 37 significant garden structures at Stowe, 32 of which are designated. The investigation into the significance of the garden buildings within their context, and an overall planned programme of works, replaced previous haphazard schemes of repair. Nearly all the buildings at Stowe have undergone change during their lifetime, either to the condition of their fabric or architectural change, and the overriding philosophical question in any conservation programme is how far to 'wind the clock back'. What kind of balance is to be struck between restoring the original architect's intentions and respecting the subsequent history of the building? The concluding general intention at Stowe was to restore the garden buildings to the point of their highest cultural significance, the late eighteenth century, provided that this is backed up by evidence.

Stowe underwent substantial evolution from formal Baroque to its immensely influential informal English landscape garden with classical buildings and Whig-political iconographic significance. Its history and iconography is chronicled elsewhere and only a brief summary here of the relevant parts of the garden provides context.

Sir Richard Temple (1634–97), 3rd Baronet, in the 1680s rebuilt an earlier Tudor house and laid out a conventional geometrically ordered garden with three formal terraces, one above the other, stepping down the slope with low retaining walls and orchards to the south, their central axis aligned on Buckingham parish church three miles to the south. His son and successor General Sir Richard Temple (1675–1749), later Viscount Cobham, leading Whig Member of Parliament and friend of English playwright and poet William Congreve (1670–1729), and the poets Alexander Pope (1699–1744) and James Thomson (1700–48), transformed and enlarged the garden to the west on a completely new scale from 1713 to designs by Charles Bridgeman (1690–1738). This was remodelled and made more naturalistic in the 1740s and 1750s by William Kent (1685–1748) and Lancelot 'Capability' Brown (1716–83). Bridgeman's setting of straight paths, hedges, statuary and moulded earthworks all disappeared though Bridgeman's enclosing ha-ha and straight avenues survive, together with the Rotunda and pair of Lake Pavilions framing the avenue beyond – both by Sir John Vanbrugh (1664–1726). The latter buildings were later moved further apart by the Italian Turin-trained architect Giovanni Battista Borra (1713–70). Other works are by William Kent, an architect with a very important place in the history of English landscape gardening. It was Kent who led the revolt against the formal gardening of the seventeenth century and who first realised the essayist Joseph Addison's (1672–1719) vision of 'a whole estate thrown into a kind of garden by frequent plantations'. As Horace Walpole (1717–97) saw it, Kent was the man who 'leaped the fence and saw that all Nature was a Garden'.[5]

The loosening of symmetry began when Cobham created a new western approach to the park following the line of an ancient Roman road, and following Vanbrugh's death in 1726 he consulted James Gibbs (1682–1754). Gibbs' first design was for the Boycott Pavilions flanking this route, originally crowned with stone pyramidal roofs but provided in 1758 with domes and cupolas by Borra.

The evolving informality of the late 1730s and early 1740s in the Bridgeman garden was largely under the direction of 'Capability' Brown, head gardener from 1741 until he set up on his own with his first commission at Croome Park in 1751. His most significant creation was the Grecian Valley, which formed a model for his own landscape designs in later life. Begun in 1746 this was conceived as an English Vale of Tempe, the belts of trees along the sides of the valley hiding shady walks ornamented with statuary.[6] The Valley is presided over by the large 'Grecian Building' completed in 1762 and renamed Temple of Concord and Victory in triumphant celebration of the ending of the Seven Years' War due to Pitt's masterly parliamentary leadership. The many changes to the garden that were made over time are revealed by comparison of editions of the guide book by Seeley of Stowe published for visitors in 1744, the first for any English garden, revised and re-issued in 1838.

In 1922 the estate became Stowe School and buildings were added east and west of the house by Clough Williams-Ellis (1883–1978). In 1989 the school handed over the gardens and its buildings to the National Trust as a condition of an anonymous benefaction and since 1989 some of the more important parts of the designed landscape beyond have been reunited with Stowe. At the end of 1995 the most important elements, the Home Farm and the major part of the fallow deer park were bought with the assistance of the Heritage Lottery Fund. Finally, in 2012 the New Inn, constructed on the edge of the garden for visitors in 1717, was restored with additions as the National Trust's new visitor centre.

The following case studies will consider contrasting approaches to the repair of four of the buildings associated with the garden, the Temple of Concord and Victory, the Temple of Friendship, the Chinese House and the New Inn, together with the significant reinstatement of Lord Cobham's original intended route to the gardens. These works, together with other buildings at Stowe, were undertaken in the context of the early conservation plan of 1990 that considered the entire site in three parts: the house, the gardens, and the park and wider landscape, the second part dividing the gardens into 'character areas' according to how they had developed: the Western Garden, the Elysian Fields, the Hawkwell Field and the Grecian Valley.

Temple of Concord and Victory

The temple (Figure 7.1) is the centrepiece dominating 'Capability' Brown's Grecian Valley and is connected visually with the Wolfe Obelisk and the Cobham Monument.[7] The first mention of the severely neo-classical temple was in 1747, towards the end of Lord Cobham's life. Of his architects only Gibbs was by then still alive, but the design of this key building in the garden is likely to have been much inspired by Sir Richard Temple himself who probably saw it as a symbol of ancient Greece, the first of his symbols of political liberty. The second, symbolising Rome, was embodied in the Temple of Ancient Virtue, while the Thanet Walk and the Saxon Deities represented the Saxons, the Gothic Temple the middle ages and the Temple of British Worthies the Renaissance.

Cobham's nephew Richard Grenville-Temple (1711–79), just back from his grand tour, is thought to have assisted in the design of both the Grecian Valley and the temple, which is partly based on the Roman Maison Carrée at Nîmes which he had visited on his tour. Said to be the richest subject in England, he succeeded his uncle and his mother as Earl Temple

Figure 7.1 The severely neo-classical Temple of Concord and Victory, Stowe, is partly based on the Roman Maison Carrée at Nîmes. It dominates Capability Brown's Grecian Valley and is connected visually with the Wolfe Obelisk and the Cobham Monument.

in 1752. His brothers were also leading politicians and his sister married William Pitt (1708–88), Earl of Chatham, 'the greatest statesman of the age'.

Borra accompanied Richard Wood to Palmyra and Baalbec in 1751 and wrote up and engraved their finds for publication thereafter. He was producing drawings for the temple in 1752, his brief to render it more archaeologically correct. He moved the front wall of the cella backwards to create a pronaos, gave the cella an archaeologically appropriate ceiling and blocked its side windows.

Lord Temple's last phase in finding the temple a new symbolic role began with the repositioning in the pediment of Scheemakers' reliefs of 'The Four Quarters of the World bringing their Various Products to Britannia', which were carved for one side of the Palladian Bridge. In 1763 a 'Victory' by James Lovell celebrating the end of the Seven Years' War was placed at the apex of the east pediment, accompanied by lead figures by Van Nost on the other pediment and at the four corners of the building. A series of 14 terracotta medallions was installed in the cella, some based on James 'Athenian' Stuart's designs for victory medals. Initially known as the Grecian Temple (despite the Roman model) the temple was renamed Concord and Victory.

In 1927–29 the Scottish architect Sir Robert Lorimer (1864–1929) built the Basilican Chapel for the new school on the site of Vanbrugh's Temple of Bacchus west of the house, and incorporated in the interior 16 columns removed from the back and sides of the Temple of Concord and Victory. The columns of the Temple were replaced with supporting brickwork so that the building took on the mutilated appearance of a brick box.

This was the first major project to be undertaken in the new programme of consolidation and restoration of the garden buildings at Stowe. The starting point was to understand the building, and a report of 1992 drew together the archaeology, history and landscape context. This was followed by analysis of materials and structure, and a record was made of the building in its current condition before work finally began in 1995. The brickwork was removed and replacement columns were restored, carved in Stoke Ground stone and lifted into position with shears, as in ancient times, then fluted in situ. As a partial reconstruction of a classical temple the project was unique in modern times. The restoration work, involving rebuilding rather than repair, represents the extreme end of Feilden's spectrum of conservation options.

Temple of Friendship

The visit of the Prince of Wales in 1737 was celebrated by the building of Gibbs' Temple of Friendship (Figure 7.2) on Bridgeman's south-east bastion in Hawkwell Field, placed at a distance but aligned with the Queen's Temple at the far end of Hawkwell Field. The temple has a Tuscan portico and is flanked by two loggias to east and west. The building contained a banqueting room decorated with murals and lined with busts of Cobham and his 'patriot' friends, including the Prince, and as such this garden structure had a definite function. Its considerable attic storey was added in the 1770s in place of Gibbs' original cupola, presumably to raise its profile within the landscape. The building was gutted by fire in 1843 and proposals shortly afterwards to rebuild the temple were never carried out, so it decayed into a classical ruin. Unlike the Temple of Concord and Victory the decision here was to conserve-as-found with consolidation, retaining the building as a romantic Roman ruin.

The Chinese House

The conservation programme at Stowe includes ongoing reinstatement work, mainly of original and reproduction sculpture. The reinstatement of the original Chinese House at Stowe was perhaps the least satisfactory of the conservation projects. There was a vogue for Chinese summerhouses in the eighteenth century and Stowe's tiny Chinese House,

Figure 7.2 Stowe's Temple of Friendship was built to commemorate a visit by the Prince of Wales in 1737. As it contained a banqueting room it was conceived as a functional structure. Gibbs' original had a cupola that was replaced in the 1770s by the attic storey visible in the picture. The building burnt down in 1843 and was not rebuilt, being left as a romantic ruin.

possibly by Kent, was the earliest in England, extant by 1738. It originally stood on stilts in a former pond in the Elysian Fields north-east of its present location. More robust than many 'Chinese' contemporaries elsewhere, which were not built to have a long life, it has diagonally latticed windows, projecting eaves, a simplified pagoda roof, and is constructed of wood and painted on canvas both inside and out with *chinoiserie*, all characteristically elegant, amusing and brightly painted. It has an odd, peripatetic history having been removed already in the late 1740s, presumably having sat uncomfortably within the context of classical Stowe, and moved to Wotton, Buckinghamshire, the nearby seat of the Grenvilles where it remained for 200 years. It was then removed to Harristown in Ireland before being acquired by the National Trust and re-erected at Stowe, though now somewhat isolated in the Pheasantry of the Lamport Gardens.

The New Inn

Stowe was famously open to tourists in the eighteenth century, and was one of Britain's earliest tourist attractions as a theme park of its time. In 1717 Lord Cobham built the 'New Inn' as purpose-built lodgings for visitors arriving by coach to his new emerging landscape garden and it formed the original entrance for visitors through the adjacent Bell Gate. In 2005 the National Trust acquired the long-derelict building and Cowper Griffith Architects restored it with additions as a new visitor centre which opened in 2012 with funding by the Heritage Lottery Fund and other donations. For the first time in 150 years visitors now experience arrival at the gardens the way its Georgian designers intended through the reinstated Bell Gate, from where three recreated pathways representing the choices to be made between, 'Vice, Virtue and Liberty' can straightaway be explored.

The reconstruction of the New Inn was based on research with historic photographs, drawings and documents, and clay tiles, bricks and timbers were salvaged and reused in the building. The historic rooms were furnished with original Georgian furniture wherever possible and visitors can now experience eighteenth-century life, with open fires in the parlour rooms, ale sampling in the old tap room on special days and the working kitchen and laundry room.

A series of newly built visitor facilities were created around the inn on the original footprint of an adjacent farm and stable block. These include a conference facility, an 85-seat café, a shop with plant sales, estate offices and interpretation for learning about the gardens and the experience of the eighteenth-century visitor. The new buildings are constructed of timber; the outbuildings behind the inn have green oak frames with oak cladding finishes and the main space, the café, has a triangulated roof structure built of larch cut from the National Trust's nearby Ashridge forest. It was designed as a memory of a fallen timber threshing barn that stood on the site.

Croome Park

The case studies at Croome Park, near High Green, Worcestershire are of three outer eye-catchers. The land occupied by Croome Park is situated in undulating countryside between the rivers Severn and Avon in a natural hollow between two ridges. The land, marshy before the mid-eighteenth century, formed part of the estate of Lord Coventry.[8] The present mansion house and landscape, Croome Court and Croome Park, were created from 1751–52 by George Coventry, 6th Earl of Coventry (1722–1809), and both designed by 'Capability' Brown following his work with Lord Cobham's gardening staff at Stowe, Buckinghamshire under William Kent. Both were his first freelance landscape and major architectural commissions, the latter carried out with the assistance of Sanderson Miller (1716–80). The severe Neo-Palladian house is influenced by Wilton House in Wiltshire by Inigo Jones (1573–1652) with corner towers and pyramidal roofs, and the landscaped park has characteristic Brownian rolling grassland, clumps of trees and planting, and an extensive artificial meandering 'Croome Lake' presenting the illusion of a river. Several temples and follies, architectural features in the landscape, were designed by Robert Adam (1728–92) and, later, James Wyatt (1746–1813), including the Park Seat built 1770–72 and the Temple Greenhouse, an orangery completed in 1763, both by Robert Adam. Croome Church, St Mary Magdalene built in 1763 by Brown forms a prominent architectural feature. Croome Park was purchased by the National Trust in 1996, and a conservation programme was put in place for Croome Court and the Park in collaboration with Natural England's Countryside Stewardship Scheme.

Three outliers, the case studies discussed below, were previously owned by the Society of Merchant Venturers of Bristol who had acquired them in 1996 and only purchased later by the National Trust in 2007. They are Dunstall Castle located to the south of the park, Pirton Castle to the north and the Panorama to the west. Each required a different philosophical approach to their conservation based on individual architectural character and construction and, importantly, visual purpose in the landscape. Dunstall Castle underwent restoration work replacing lost masonry fabric, Pirton Castle was 'conserved as found' and Panorama was carefully repaired and alterations were reversed as a unified architectural gem.[9] All were repaired over several years by the architect John C. Goom.

In preparing for the works the following information was inspected from the National Trust, Croome Estate, County Council records and the (former) National Monuments Record:

- Croome Court Historic Landscape Survey, Camilla Beresford (Oct 1996)
- National Trust Conservation Plan (1998)
- National Trust Statement of Objectives –Management Plan (1999)
- The Dunstall Castle Condition Report (Nov 1999)
- Croome Estate Archive Ancient Monument Repairs
- The Panorama Tower Condition Report (Nov 1999)
- Gifford & Partners, The Panorama Tower Structural Report
- Rowan Technologies Ltd, Panorama Tower – Corroding Metal Cramps (Feb 2000)
- Rodney Melville & Partners, Fabric Report Panorama (Jan 2000)
- Photographic Record, Croome D'Abitot

- English Heritage National Monument Record – Panorama
- Dr Jackie Underhill, Feasibility Study: Ecology At Croome Park (March 2006)
- National Trust Files May-July (2000)
- Rodney Melville & Partners, Fabric Report, Dunstall Castle (Jan 2000)
- Worcestershire County Council Record Office, Worcestershire, Outer Eye-catchers, Croome Park – Dunstall Castle Ref: 262A1
- Frank Haywood & Associates, Current Structural Condition Report (January 2007)
- Dunstall Castle, Croome by Mike Cousins (article in *Follies* Magazine Spring 2007)
- Gordon, Catherine: *The Coventrys of Croome* Phillimore & Co Ltd, (2000)
- Information from the National Monuments Record including Listing Description.

Ecological investigation

A significant component of the on-the-ground survey of a historic building within a landscape setting is to obtain an assessment of the designated historic asset's value in the context of local wildlife within the framework of current legislation. At Croome, the species most likely to be present on the estate were bats, birds and great crested newts, all of which receive statutory protection under the Wildlife and Countryside Act 1981 (as amended), while badgers also receive protection under the Protection of Badgers Act, 1992. The report also identified whether a licence was required ahead of any building works should great crested newts be found present in nearby ponds, as well as any necessary arrangements to capture and remove animals prior to damaging activities.

Dunstall Castle

Dunstall Castle (Figure 7.3) is an eye-catcher designed by Robert Adam and built between 1765 and 1771 by John Newman, the mason employed by the Earl of Coventry for most of

Figure 7.3 Dunstall Castle, Croome Park, is an eye-catcher designed by Robert Adam and built between 1765 and 1771 by John Newman, the mason employed by the Earl of Coventry for most of the building work at Croome. It has been restored to look as originally intended. (Reproduced by permission of Micah Fowler.)

the building work at Croome at the extreme south end of the designed landscape beyond the end of the Croome Lake.[10] It was intended to be seen from the Court as well as from Panorama and two further garden features, the Temple Greenhouse and Park Seat.[11] Although Adam refers in a letter to Lord Coventry to 'a drawing of the Ruin for a Visto',[12] the building is more a sham castle with overtones of a fragmented abbey. Further letters refer to poles marking out the footprint of the building and to construction activity from November 1766 into summer of 1768.[13] As built the castle was apparently not sufficiently visible, for a new drawing was produced by October 1766 proposing to raise it by four feet at a cost of £20.[14] An invoice from Newman of January 1771 for this, or perhaps other works, refers to 'altering the centre tower at ye castle, taking off ye top and widening it and raising it digging stone and carrying up'.[15]

The castle has three towers: a tall central circular tower, a smaller circular one to the east linked by a screen, originally crenellated, with a tall double-arched opening, creating a 'scenic' sense of depth, and a yet smaller square tower to the west linked by a crenellated screen wall with a tall Gothic 'abbey' window opening with remains of tracery. The central tower contains a spiral stair with a doorway raised curiously 1.8 m (6 feet) above ground level; its sole purpose is thought to provide access to mount a lantern or torch at the top to be visible from the court at night. All three towers have blind windows and string courses. Two small lean-to structures, perhaps estate-workers' dwellings, were built into the rear, now demolished. A rather crude preliminary builder's pencil drawing and a finished watercolour by E.F. and T.F. Burney of 1784 illustrate the building, the latter with crenellations, an additional turret superstructure to the central tower and tracery to the 'abbey' window on the west wall.[16] The structure is built of local grey lias limestone except for the tracery inserts and repairs that have used yellow Jurassic limestone.

The crenellations and the tracery to the abbey window and the lower part of the wall and, most notably because of its intended visibility from the park, much of the central turret had all been lost through decay or demolition.

Much of the upper structure required stabilising or reconstruction, with deep pointing required to repair structural cracks and removal of earlier dense cement pointing with replacement in lime mortar. Putlock holes (square recesses for receiving timbers to support scaffolding) have been left exposed. However, the philosophy behind the repair was not only to stabilise the structure and minimise future decay, but also to rebuild the central tower to its original height in materials that match the existing so that, with tree clearance in the park, the castle is once again visible as originally intended. It was also decided to reinstate the crenellations to return its appearance as a castle, while retaining its now ruined character. The approach here was therefore one of restoration – rebuilding missing features – rather than conserve as found in order to reinstate Dunstall Castle's original purpose as an eye-catcher visible from the park.

Pirton Castle

Grade II-listed Pirton Castle,[17] designed by James Wyatt in 1797, is situated along the crest of a ridge 2.5 kilometres north-west of Croome Court in Pirton Park, an independent park also owned by the Earls of Coventry. Originally a medieval deer park, it was landscaped by 'Capability' Brown in the 1760s as a satellite to the main park around Croome Court itself. A watercolour signed by James Wyatt dated 1801 accurately depicts the structure as built.[18]

Its main purpose was as an eye-catcher to be viewed against a backdrop of cedars of Lebanon[19] from Croome Park and visible from Croome Church, Croome Court, Park Seat and Panorama.[20] But Pirton Castle was also a belvedere, situated on the Ten-Mile Ride through Croome Park and provides a vantage point for viewing the entire estate. It was built as a ruin and comprises a length of curtain wall built of ashlar in oolitic limestone backed by rubble lias limestone, with a tall circular turret set asymmetrically with slit windows, originally containing a stone spiral staircase and viewing platform accessed through a door at the rear. Both wall and tower were crenellated but the crenellations and the top part of the tower have now disappeared, though they appear to have been intact in the later nineteenth century.[21]

Pirton Castle is the only built structure connected with Croome Park that was specifically designed to be seen as a ruin, and the philosophy of repair here, unlike at Dunstall Castle where the restoration of missing structure was undertaken, was to conserve as found. The loss of structure at Pirton Castle was not considered to detract from its character as a ruin or to diminish its character as a distant eye-catcher. It was not here proposed to reinstate the internal staircase and viewing platform as its original purpose as a belvedere was secondary to its principal purpose and the original Ten-Mile Ride by carriage no longer applies. Conservation work was therefore confined to removal of invasive ivy growth, dismantling and re-bedding of all the upper stonework with the use of stainless steel pins and cramps as necessary. The rubble work to the rear required a limited amount of repointing work but remarkably little work was required to the ashlar except for repointing a wide movement crack and gaps where vegetation has been removed. However, the reinstatement of the crenellations may be considered in the next five-to-ten years.

Panorama

The third eye-catcher is the Panorama (Figure 7.4), a Grade-I listed structure designed by James Wyatt prominently situated in a commanding position on an elevated ridge to the

Figure 7.4 The Panorama, Croome Park, has a commanding position on an elevated ridge to the south-west of the park. As its name suggests, the Grade I listed structure designed by James Wyatt provides expansive views over the park and further afield. It became very run down when the park fell into disuse in the twentieth century, suffering water damage and vandalism. Repairs in the 1950s used inappropriate materials, for example replacing the timber structure of the viewing balcony with a reinforced concrete slab. The philosophy of repair here was to reverse and repair the alterations and decay, and reinstate all lost elements including the lead roof and lead downpipes. The latter have been subject to multiple thefts and at the time of writing the replacement material is under review.

south-west of the park. It provides views over the park and the park buildings including Pirton Castle, Dunstall Castle and the Church, the Court itself, and splendid far-reaching views of the Malvern Hills, Bredon Hill to the south-east and Abberley Ridge to the north. Commissioned by the 6th Earl of Coventry it is situated on a site not purchased until 1773; construction started around 1805 and was completed by about 1811. The Panorama is similar to a (third) design of 1766 by Robert Adam for 'a pavilion between the woods',[22] in turn influenced by Donato Bramante's perfectly proportioned Tempietto in the courtyard of the Church of San Pietro in Montorio, Rome of around 1501. The completed design was illustrated by Wyatt in a watercolour dated 1801.[23] The M5 motorway unfortunately now separates the Panorama from the rest of the park.

The Panorama is circular and of two storeys clad with very finely jointed ashlar. The ground storey sits on a plinth of three steps and is divided into four porticoes *in antis*, each with a pair of slender Tuscan columns supporting a continuous entablature surmounted by a balustrade gallery. The porticos are separated by four piers each with a round-headed niche and blind panel above. The rear of the porticos is semi-circular, one of which contains the entrance doorway. The upper storey is a shallow-domed recessed drum with four windows, originally with sashes corresponding to the porticoes below, with a viewing balcony around the perimeter. Internally a helical stone staircase rising centrally in a circular stairwell ascends to an upper chamber with a domed plaster ceiling with a frieze of swags.

As the park fell into disuse during the twentieth century the Panorama became neglected, disfigured with graffiti and damaged by vandals and water ingress. In 1954 the Ministry of Works offered a grant for repairs and these were carried out in 1956–58, but replacing materials inappropriately. Notably, the timber structure of the viewing balcony was replaced with a reinforced concrete slab, the window frames were replaced in metal and the roof dome was clad in bituminous felt. Since that time the vandalism and decay continued.

The Panorama, unlike Pirton Castle and Dunstall Castle, is a complete and unified architectural design, standing out in contrast from its landscape setting as a distinctive eye-catcher within the park and intended as a 360-degree viewing platform over the park and the surrounding countryside. The philosophy of repair here was to reverse and repair the alterations and decay, and reinstate all lost elements including the lead roof and lead downpipes. The latter have been subject to multiple thefts and at the time of writing the replacement material is under review.

Endnotes

1. Feilden, B., *Conservation of Historic Buildings*, Oxford, 1994, pp. 8ff.
2. Cornforth, J., 'Efforts in Arcadia', in *Georgian Arcadia: Architecture for the Park and Garden* (1987).
3. Forsyth, M. (ed.), *Understanding Historic Building Conservation*, chapter. 14 'Preparing the Conservation Plan', p. 156.
4. The archives of some prominent family estates are now in North American institutions. For example, when the Stowe estate was dispersed in the 1920s, the family papers, almost intact from 1749 until 1923, were acquired by Henry Huntington, the American railroad magnate and anglophile collector, who bequeathed them to the Huntington Library in California. Those of Wotton, Buckinghamshire, an estate now in private hands but owned in the eighteenth century by the same family as Stowe, are also in the Huntington and the archives of Strawberry Hill are now with the Lewis Walpole Library, part of Yale University.
5. Harney, M., *Place-making for the Imagination: Horace Walpole and Strawberry Hill*, Ashgate, Garnham, Surrey, 2013.
6. Tempe: a beautiful and romantic scenic valley in the north of Thessaly, Greece.
7. Haslam, Richard, 'Concord Restored and Victory Assured', *Country Life*, 21.8.1997.
8. Gordon, Catherine, *The Coventrys of Croome*, Stroud (2000).
9. Croome Park Conservation Plan held at the National Trust's Estate Office contains detailed histories and descriptions of these structures.
10. Building estimate by John Newman, 19 November 1765.
11. Conservation Plan, View Lines, Appendix VI.

12. County Record Office Box 24 yellow F68 dated 19 September 1765.
13. Box 14 yellow F58/7a dated 16 November 1765.
14. County Record Office Box 24 yellow F64.
15. County Record Office Box 14 yellow F58 dated 5 January 1771.
16. Croome Estate Archives.
17. As named on the Estate Plan of 1894 at the Worcestershire Record Office.
18. Held at the Croome Estate Office.
19. According to the description of Pirton Park in the English Heritage Register of Parks and Gardens of Special Historic Interest in England it is believed that the cedars were planted in the 1760s.
20. National Trust Conservation Plan, View lines, Appendix VI. Conservation Plan held at National Trust's Estate Office.
21. Vignette on the Estate Plan (262A3/S5).
22. Sir John Soane's Museum (Vol. 19 p. 145 + Vol. 44 pp. 104–106).
23. Croome Estate Archive.

8 'Perished Perches': historic garden furniture

Lisa White
Chairman of the Arts Advisory Panel, National Trust, Gloucestershire, UK

'I think there are as many kinds of gardens as poetry. Your makers of parterres and flower gardens are epigrammatists and sonneteers in this art: contrivers of bowers and grottoes, treillages and cascades are romantic writers.'[1]

As with gardens and poetry, craftsmen and designers have needed to produce a range of garden furniture for every situation. However, the ravages of time, weather, constant repair, changing fashions, vandalism and the introduction of more durable materials in the nineteenth century have meant that very, very little original garden furniture survives from before 1800. Even now, a trip to any architectural antiques yard will reveal the extent of loss. Much use needs to be made of contemporary descriptions and designs to fill the gaps. Careful, thorough research can rediscover an extraordinarily rich and imaginative range of furniture that once filled our historic gardens, and can inspire the creations of equally lively examples today: we don't have to stick to the ubiquitous Edwin Lutyens (1869–1944) bench or cast-iron seat.

Whether for late seventeenth-century formal parterres, or for the arranged circuit or 'route through nature' of the eighteenth-century picturesque garden, resting points were included, to offer sunlight or shade, the chance to admire a view, take tea or other refreshments, to explore the charms of any number and variety of ornamental buildings, in order to experience the full range of romantic sensibility, as Thomas Whately (1726–72) described at Claremont in Surrey in 1779: 'a place wherein to tarry with secure delight, and saunter with perpetual amusement'.[2]

Chairs, benches, stools and tables were provided for the garden in almost as great a variety as they were for a house, and were given the same amount of attention in their design, destination, purpose and finish. The most common items were, inevitably, seats – well described by John James (1673–1746) in 1712:

> Seats, or Benches, besides the Conveniency they constantly afford in great Gardens, where you can scarce ever have too many, there is such a need for them in walking, look very well also in a Garden, when set in certain Places they are destin'd to, as in the Niches or Sinkings that face principal Walks or Vista's, and in the Halls and Galleries of Groves; they are made either of Marble, Free-Stone or Wood, which last are the most common, and of these there are two kinds, the seats with backs to them, which are the handsomest, and are usually remov'd in Winter, and the plain benches which are fix'd to their place in the Ground.[3]

Gardens & Landscapes in Historic Building Conservation, First Edition. Edited by Marion Harney.
© 2014 John Wiley & Sons, Ltd. Published 2014 by John Wiley & Sons, Ltd.

Figure 8.1 Daniel Marot (1661–1752) Design for a Garden Seat, Nouveaux Fauteuils (1703), Pl.25 (author's own).

Many views of early eighteenth-century gardens depict seats of the types described by James. Formal, stone seats created focal points at the ends of terraces and walks; lighter wooden seats were made for side-walks, niches and arbours. The first category, of formal seats, appear in illustrations of Baroque gardens of the late seventeenth and early eighteenth centuries such as those by Johannes Kip (1653–1722), and in the published designs of Daniel Marot (1661–1752), architect and designer to William III and Mary II.[4] Kip's views of gardens, published in *Britannia Illustrata* (1707), show a significant number of wooden seats placed in formal, walled gardens, usually of a similar, frontal design. Daniel Marot's engraved patterns illustrate more elaborate seats with scrolling backs, placed against or below tall structures of treillage (Figure 8.1).

Some of these seats have been recreated at Het Loo, William III's country house outside Appeldorn, in Holland, as part of the major reconstruction of the historic garden there (Figure 8.2).

The number of formal seats that have survived from before 1700 are extremely limited, but those that have been preserved give clear ideas of their design and scale. At Ham House, Surrey, two formal oak seats were provided for the loggias of the house in 1676 and are still in situ. At Boughton House, Northamptonshire, two more fine seats from the loggia beneath the State Apartment are now preserved in the unfinished pavilion of the house. They owe their survival to common factors: the high quality of their materials and construction, careful maintenance by ducal households over succeeding centuries, and the fact that both these great Baroque houses underwent little subsequent major alteration.

Thomas Chippendale (1718–79) published designs for such formal seats in the 3rd edition of *The Gentleman and Cabinet-Maker's Director* (1762), Plate 24, where he specified that they 'may be placed in walks or at the ends of Avenues' (Figure 8.3).

Figure 8.2 Reconstruction of Treillage and seat, Het Loo Palace gardens, 2008 (author's own).

Figure 8.3 Thomas Chippendale, Designs for Garden Seats, *The Gentleman and Cabinet-Maker's Director*, 3rd edn, 1762, Plate XXIV (author's own).

Early designs by Sir John Soane (1753–1837) in 1778 show similarly formal seats in a restrained neo-classical style.[5] Stone seats in the classical style still survive in some great gardens, including the splendid 'Whispering Seat' at Wilton House, Wiltshire, designed by Sir Richard Westmacott (1755–1806) in the early years of the nineteenth century.

There is a close relationship between these formal garden seats and those for country house halls, which may indeed have been placed outside during fine weather. These were usually made either in oak or other plain wood, sometimes in pine and painted in stone colours, and often decorated with a family's heraldic crest. Good examples are those at Houghton Hall, Norfolk. It is probable that more such seats once complemented those made for an interior, and were intended for loggias and porticoes, but have not survived.

A further link between hall and garden exists in the use of Windsor chairs for both locations.

These light, simple, vernacular chairs and settees, made of beech in the Buckinghamshire woodlands from the late seventeenth century, were the most ubiquitous and democratic type of seat furniture, providing essential service in offices, university common rooms and libraries, surgeries, farmhouses, schoolrooms, church vestries, family pews, shops, inns, ships' cabins, even the better class of prison cell – and gardens (Figure 8.4).[6] They were stored indoors in passages and hallways, or in garden buildings, ready to be carried outside

Figure 8.4 Anon, portrait of Captain Charles William Le-Geyt Esq, in a Windsor chair, c.1770. Mezzotint. Private Collection (author's own).

on fine days. At West Wycombe Park, Buckinghamshire, a fine set still stand under the portico. In the inventory of goods at Alexander Pope's (1688–1744) villa at Twickenham, taken after his death in 1744, there were two Windsor armchairs in the garden, along with ten other wooden chairs, and six Windsor armchairs in the hall. In the 1760 inventory taken at Holkham Hall, Norfolk, six compass-backed Windsor armchairs stood in the portico.

In many eighteenth-century conversation pieces, particularly those by Arthur Devis (1712–87) and Francis Hayman (1708–76), elegant couples and families are depicted in their gardens or parkland seated on such chairs, just visible behind voluminous skirts. The chairs and their extended settee versions were usually painted white or green, the latter being a 'common colour' achieved in a mix of white lead, linseed oil, ochre and black.

A variation on the Windsor chair was another fairly simple type of chair with turned spindles in the back panel, plain wooden or caned seats and runners connecting front and rear legs at ground level. Taken outside and placed on a lawn, these 'skis' prevented the feet of the chair from sinking into the grass. Survivors are often to be found in the halls or passages of the 'rustic' level of country houses.

The term 'Windsor Seat' should not be confused with 'Windsor Chair'. The former term was used by Daniel Defoe (1660–1731) to describe a 'small seat, fit for one, or but two at the most, with a high back, and cover for the head, which turns so easily, the whole being fix'd on a pin of iron, or brass, of strength sufficient, that the persons who sit in it, may turn it from the wind, . . . and enjoy a compleat calm' on the North Terrace at Windsor Castle in 1724. Defoe stated that the seat was invented by Elizabeth I (1533–1603).[7] Another example is recorded by Stephen Switzer (1682–1745) at Dyrham Park, Gloucestershire, in 1718, and just visible in Kip's engraving of Blathwayt's great garden, published in 1712 in Sir Robert Atkyns' *The Ancient and Present State of Gloucestershire*. High up on the warren was a seat 'call'd a Windsor Seat, which is so contriv'd as to turn round any way, either to take advantage of the prospect, or to avoid the inconveniencies of Wind, the Sun, etc.'.[8]

A trade card of the chair-makers Lockington, Foulger, now in the British Museum, of c.1773, also shows one of these wind-breaking 'Windsor Seats', though to date no early examples appear to have survived.

Switzer's account of the garden at Dyrham in 1718 included many more descriptions of different, and ingenious, garden seats. At the end of the terrace to the north-east of the house were 'large arch'd Seats on which are painted Motto's suitable to their situation', and the square garden at the centre of the Wilderness had,

> four Seats at the Corners, and a Seat round an aspiring Fir Tree in the Centre, from which your Prospect terminates in a large old Church at a very great Distance. I never did in my whole life see so agreeable a Place for the Sublimest Studies, as this is in Summer, and here are small Desks erected in Seats for that purpose.[9]

At The Leasowes, Halesowen, between 1743 and 1763 William Shenstone (1714–63) dedicated seats and urns to his friends, to John Milton (1608–74) and to ideas such as 'Contemplation'.[10] At St Giles' House, Dorset, Richard Pococke (1704–65) noted in 1754 that the garden buildings had glazed hanging bookcases containing the works of Virgil, Ovid, Shakespeare and Milton 'as further aides for sublime contemplation in the right spot'.[11]

Below the cascade at Dyrham, again according to Switzer, were two large clipped thorns 'encompassed with seats'; the trunks of the thorns were entwined with green painted lead pipes which 'appear more like ivory on rough bark' and spouted small jets of water at the turn of a stop cock 'as natural as if it rained' – a variation on the surprise 'spouting' brass tree at Chatsworth of 1695, described by Celia Fiennes (1662–1741).[12]

Apart from such exotic creations, gardens and parks of the eighteenth century were replete with many simple wooden chairs and benches with slatted seats, regularly refreshed with white or green oil-based paint and sometimes referred to in inventories and other descriptions as 'Forest Chairs'. Dating them is difficult, as they hardly changed stylistically in a hundred years, and were usually made by estate joiners. Some were built around tree trunks to afford fine views from a shaded place: Josiah Wedgwood's (1730–95) family were depicted by George Stubbs (1724–1806) seated on such an example in about 1780.[13]

Vernacular rush-seated chairs with ladder backs, often made of local elm or painted beech, were also used in the garden or even in fishing punts. As with Windsor chairs, they were stored inside garden buildings or the main house during winter months. They can sometimes be found recorded in inventories and it is important to check the date at which a probate inventory was taken to ascertain whether such items might also have been intended for garden use. At Dyrham Park in November 1710, the inventory lists a silk hammock – intended for use outside in the summer?[14]

Many eighteenth-century conversation pieces show furniture made for the house being used in the garden during summer months, especially for tea-parties or other refreshment *en plein air*. Johann Zoffany (1733–1810) depicted David and Maria Garrick taking tea with friends on the lawn outside the Temple to Shakespeare at Hampton, beside the Thames, in 1762, using a neat mahogany Pembroke table and chairs made from Shakespeare's mulberry tree at Stratford on Avon, which were usually kept in the temple itself.[15]

Taking tea in the garden during the summer months became increasingly popular in the eighteenth century, and the development of tea-houses and pavilions for the purpose inspired the creation of furniture in oriental styles. Furniture pattern-books of the 1750s and 1760s include dozens of designs for such chairs, often more fanciful and exotic than those intended for more formal areas of a country house, apart from Chinoiserie bedchambers (Figure 8.5).[16]

In 1762 Thomas Chippendale published designs for chairs 'after the Chinese manner, and are very proper for a Lady's Dressing Room, especially if it is hung with India paper. They will likewise suit Chinese Temples. They have commonly cane-bottoms (seats), with loose cushions'.[17] Such chairs were made of beech and painted either white, or in a variety of colours, and had no fixed upholstery, to avoid damp or saturation. Because of their ephemeral nature, virtually none survive, although versions made for interior use, such as those for the Chinese Bedchamber at Badminton House of circa 1752, made by William Linnell (c.1703–63), give an idea of their delectable quality.[18] Gothic, Indian or other exotic styles were often jumbled together to create seats to go under 'Umbrello's', 'being one of the most agreeable decorations yet known', thatched canopies, canvas tents, floral bowers and romantic arbours.[19]

White paint was in constant use for garden furniture in the middle years of the eighteenth century, allowing the delicate lattice work of chair-backs, gates, trellises, paling and fences

Figure 8.5 Charles Over, Design for a Garden Seat, 'in the Chinese Taste, of small Expence, Genteel and Durable', *Ornamental Furniture in the Gothic, Chinese and Modern Taste*, 1758, Plate 6 (author's own).

to stand out against the dark foliage of yew hedges, as illustrated in the charming views of Gloucestershire Rococo gardens by Thomas Robins (1716–70).[20]

Combinations of white and green, and shaded green, seem to have become more popular in the 1760s. Plates 31 and 32 of Robert Manwaring's *Cabinet and Chair-Maker's Real Friend and Companion* (1765), were 'in the Gothic Taste: they will look very genteel painted white intermixed with green'. A set of chairs decorated in this way, but repainted at a later date, with cane backs and seats, were made for the garden buildings at Osterley Park, Middlesex, in 1775.[21] Other white and green examples were provided for David Garrick's (1717–79) celebration of Shakespeare's bicentenary at Stratford upon Avon in 1769, and by Thomas Chippendale for Garrick's villa at Hampton, Middlesex. Such colour schemes may have been influenced by the popularity of Jean-Jacques Rousseau's (1712–78) essay *Emile, or, On Education*, published in 1762, where the author described the ideal of simple, rural life in a little white house with green shutters.[22]

Also included amongst the designs for garden furniture published in this period were a very few for grotto seats: after all, grottos were not places in which to linger. However Thomas Chippendale published one in 1762, with a shell back and fish-shaped legs.[23] More famous at the time was the shell seat at Strawberry Hill, designed for Horace Walpole (1717–97) by Richard Bentley (1708–82) and carved by Robinson in 1754.[24] A reproduction of the seat was made, in laminated oak, for the restored house and gardens in 2010.

The Strawberry Hill accounts also mention payment for a green garden bench in 1754, and it is certainly the case that plain green painted garden seats were popular throughout the middle of the eighteenth century. They appear in famous portraits *en plein air*, including Francis Hayman's (1708–76) of Mr and Mrs George Rogers of *c*.1748–50, where Mrs Hayman, daughter of the proprietor of Vauxhall Gardens, Jonathan Tyers (1702–67), sits on a green painted settee with an interlaced scrolling back – an outdoor version of a fashionable indoor type, the latter often made in walnut or mahogany.[25] Perhaps the most well-known of these seats is the scrolling, green-painted settee seen below and behind the voluminous skirts of Mrs Robert Andrews in Gainsborough's portrait of her and her husband against a Suffolk landscape, painted in 1748–9.[26] The shape of the settee was probably inspired by designs for Rococo garden seats published by the designer and engraver Matthias Darly (fl 1756–79) in the early 1750s.[27]

As the taste for increasing naturalism in gardens developed in the second half of the eighteenth century, the sleek green surfaces of oil-painted garden seats were increasingly sought to complement the 'camouflaged' fences admired by owners and visitors, and praised at length in William Mason's (1724–97) poem, *The English Garden*, published in l786:

> Let those, who weekly, from the City's smoke,
> Crowd to each neighb'ring hamlet, there to hold
> Their dusty Sabbath, tip with gold and red
> The milk-white palisades, that Gothic now
> And yet now Chinese, now neither, and yet both,
> Chequer their trim domain. Thy Sylvan scene
> Would fade, indignant at the tawdry glare.

After describing the mixing of paints, Mason continued,

> These with fluent oil
> Attempered, on thy lengthening rail shall spread
> That sober olive-green which Nature wears
> Ev'n on her vernal bosom . . .
> The paint is spread; the barrier pales retire,
> Snatch'd, as by magic, from the gazer's view.[28]

A short step from 'natural' green was to naturalism altogether. In the 1750s Matthias Darly and Edwards published designs for 'Chinese' chairs and a table which derived from oriental

Figure 8.6 Robert Manwaring, Rural Chairs for Summer Houses, *The Cabinet and Chair-Maker's Real Friend and Companion*, 1765, Plate 26 (author's own).

examples seen on Chinese export porcelain.[29] These were created from the natural shapes of willow, and may even have been rooted in the soil in order to create new growth and shapes each year – a highly picturesque idea. Other versions were intended to use natural branches or twigs. Thomas Chippendale incorporated twigs into designs for garden seats in 1762, although these were probably meant to be carved from solid timber.[30] In 1766 Robert Manwaring (Figure 8.6) published two plates of designs for 'Rural Chairs for Summer Houses',

> which may be made with the limbs of yew or apple trees, as Nature produces them; but the stuff should be very dry, and well-season'd; after the Bark is peeled clean off, chuse for your pitches the nearest pieces you can match for the shape of the Back, Fore Feet and Elbows . . .[31]

These most rustic of chairs were ideal for hermitages, hermits' cells and retreats in the Picturesque garden. Because of their natural fragility, very few examples survive, but the Hermitage at Badminton, Gloucestershire, designed by Thomas Wright (1711–86) in 1747, still has its attached rustic seat at one end of the building; one of the 'cresting' rails has the inscription 'Here lovers linger, here the weary rest' in brass nails. William Wrighte's *Grotesque Architecture* of 1767 includes a design for 'A Hermit's Cell, with Rustic Seat attached', to be made 'partly of large stones and trunks of trees, set round with ivy and lined with rushes etc. The roof should be covered with thatch, and the floor paved with small pebble stones or cockle shells. The seats attached are intended to be composed of large, irregular stones, roots of trees, etc.'.[32]

By the 1790s the natural look for garden furniture dominated in all areas except where a formal architectural seat was still required. *Ideas for Rustic Furniture*, published by I. and J. Taylor from 1790 to 1797, contains many designs for 'twig' furniture of every description: chairs, settees, tables, even mirror and picture frames, for the ideal garden building. In 1804 Edmund Bartell condemned the use of colour on garden trelliswork, railing, gates or bridges still 'generally painted white or green, which . . . is foreign to every principle of harmony; and although everything that is slovenly offends and ought to be avoided, we ought equally to avoid a *dressed appearance*, which would destroy the connexion that should ever subsist between the house and the grounds'.[33]

The natural colours of wood and stone for seats were also praised in Richard Payne Knight's (1750–1824) poem, *The Landscape*, published in 1794:

> The cover'd seat, that shelters from the storm,
> May oft a feature in the landscape form;
> Whether compos'd of native stumps and roots,
> It spreads the creeper's rich fantastic shoots,
> Or, rais'd with stones, irregularly pil'd,
> It seems some cavern, desolate and wild;
> But still of dress and ornament beware;
> And hide each formal trace of art with care;
> Let clust'ring ivy o'er its sides be spread,
> And moss and weeds grow scatter'd o'er its head.[34]

After 1800 Britain's Industrial Revolution had an immense impact on the production of iron garden furniture. Wrought iron seats survive from around that time, including two small armchairs of Gothic design (now in the Victoria and Albert Museum and Temple Newsam House, Leeds).[35] Analysis revealed that one of the chairs had been painted 35 times, indicating a long period of use in a garden. Between 1800 and c.1830 many simple versions, using flat iron strips riveted together, and sometimes with wheels at one end for easier removal, replaced the wooden examples that had featured in earlier gardens. During the 1850s and 1860s, bent round iron rods were used to create simple garden seats in a curvaceous neo-Rococo style.

The rapid development of large-scale production of cast iron for railways in Britain, Europe and the United States also gave impetus to the mass manufacture of cast-iron furniture, often in the prevailing, fashionable Gothic style.

A bench cast by James Yates in Rotherham, Yorkshire, in the 1830s became a standardised pattern across Europe and America, available in almost any length by the addition of its repetitive components, and accompanied by matching tables (Figure 8.7). Protected by patents and manufactured in huge quantities in Britain, these designs are recorded in detail in the Designs Office portfolios now held at the Public Record office in Kew.[36] Factories making garden furniture were located in all the major areas of the iron industry, the most notable being the Coalbrookdale Company, Shropshire, the Effingham Works in Rotherham, Yorkshire, and the Carron Company in Falkirk, Scotland. One hundred and sixty one different designs for garden benches were registered. Among the most popular were naturalistic patterns of branches and twigs, echoing the earlier designs for wooden structures, ferns, and lattice work with twining stems. Almost indestructible, these garden seats found their way into every corner of the British Empire, and were replicated in many other countries:

Figure 8.7 Cast-iron garden seat, 1854, manufactured by Yates, Haywood & Co, Rotherham, 1854 (author's own).

they have survived in greater quantities than any other form of garden furniture.[37] One of the wittiest commentaries on the advantages of cast-iron furniture was published in Anthony Trollope's (1815–82) novel, *Orley Farm*, in 1862, when the fashion for such furniture was at its height.[38]

> You see, sir (said Mr Kantwise), that new ideas are coming in every day, and wood, sir, is altogether going out, – altogether going out as regards furniture. In another twenty years, sir, there won't be such a thing as a wooden table in the country, unless with some poor person that can't afford to refurnish. Believe me, sir, iron's the thing now-a-days.

The result of such mass-production was the obliteration of vernacular or even regional styles, and hundreds of earlier wooden seats were removed and condemned to the bonfire.

As a reaction to the universality of cast-iron seats, leading designers of the twentieth century created new designs in timber for gardens designed in the revived styles of the seventeenth and eighteenth centuries, where formal, focal points were needed, especially in garden 'rooms'. Amongst the most famous of these, and still in production to this day, is Sir Edwin Lutyens' bench with its strong architectural emphasis and bold, sweeping top rail, first made in 1913. Constructed in oak, natural exposure to the elements allows the seat to bleach and blend with surrounding brick or stone walls and with natural foliage. Many other wooden garden seats of good design (Figure 8.8) are now made for new or historic gardens and provide an optimistic counterpoint to the vast supply of hideous plastic or cheap imported teak and other tropical hardwood garden furniture which blight even some of the finest gardens in Britain.

Where antique examples of garden furniture survive – and they are indeed rare – careful conservation of wooden and metal components can be carried out professionally, although very often their poor condition may require a considerable amount of replacement, especially of wooden seats which have been exposed to the elements for a long time. Even after conservation, such pieces may not be suitable for an outside location or for use, and are better brought under cover and preserved for as long as possible. Cast-iron examples can be cleaned, repainted and re-seated, and may still have a long and useful life. However, reproduction of historic designs may prove a better alternative to conservation, and could re-introduce the novelty and variety that once existed in a garden. Careful scrutiny of historic documents and images may identify many seats which have been lost from a property over the years. Consulting historic published designs may provide inspiration for creating new

Figure 8.8 Wooden garden bench, late twentieth century, Kelmarsh Hall, Northamptonshire (author's own).

pieces, and Windsor chairs, still in production today, can re-establish the idea of social use in a simple, economic manner.

Endnotes

1. Addison, J., *The Spectator*, 6 September (1712).
2. Whately, T., *Observations on Modern Gardening, and Laying-Out of Pleasure-Grounds, Parks, Farms, Ridings &c*, London (1801), p 29.
3. D'Argenville, A-J Dezallier, *Theory and practice of Gardening*, Paris (1709), translated by John James, London (1712).
4. Marot, D., *Oeuvres du Sr. Daniel Marot*, The Hague (1703), Amsterdam (1713).
5. Soane, J., *Designs in Architecture* (1778), Plate 1.
6. Evans, N.G., *The Windsor Chair* (1996).
7. Defoe, D., *A Tour throughout the Whole Island of Great Britain* (1724–6), Vol. 1, p. 303.
8. Switzer, S., 'Ichnographia Rustica', Vol. III (1718), (1742), (ed.) Dixon Hunt, J. & Willis, P. *The Genius of The Place, The English Landscape Garden, 1620–1820*, (1993), pp. 158–162.
9. Ibid.
10. Pococke, R., *Travels through England*, 24 September 1756.
11. Pococke, op.cit, 6 October 1754.
12. Morris, C. (ed.) *The Illustrated Journeys of Celia Fiennes, 1685–c.1712* (1982), p. 105.
13. The Wedgwood Museum, Stoke-on-Trent, Staffordshire.
14. Walton, Karin-M., 'An Inventory of 1710 from Dyrham Park', *Furniture History*, Vol. XXII (1986), p. 67.
15. Yale Centre for British Art/Royal Academy of Arts: Johann Zoffany RA: *Society Observed*, Postle, M. (ed.) (2011), pp. 102–3.
16. White, E., *Pictorial Dictionary of British Eighteenth-Century Furniture design: The Printed Sources* (1990), pp. 129–146.
17. Chippendale, T., *The Gentleman and Cabinet-Maker's Director*, 3rd edn (1762), Pl. XXVI.
18. Victoria and Albert Museum, W.33–1990.
19. Over, C., *Ornamental Architecture in the Gothic, Chinese and Modern Taste* (1758), pl. 8.
20. Harris, J., *Gardens of Delight, The Rococo and English Landscape of Thomas Robins the Elder* (1978).
21. National Trust, Osterley Park, Inv. No 771745.3. Tomlin, M. 'The 1782 Inventory of Osterley Park', *Furniture History*, XXII, (1986), pp. 126–127.
22. Rousseau, J–J., *Emile, or, On Education* (1762), Book IV, translated, Bloom, A. (1979), p. 351.
23. Chippendale, T. op cit, Pl. XXIV.
24. Lewis Walpole Library, Yale, Inv Nos 49.3582, 49.3678.
25. Yale Centre for British Art, B.1976.7.36.
26. National Gallery, London, 6301.
27. Darly, M., 'A Second Book of Chairs' (1751), republished in Manwaring, R., *The Chair-Maker's Guide* (1766), Plates 41–44.
28. Mason, W., *The English Garden* (1777), Book II.
29. Edwards and Darly, *A new Book of Chinese Designs* (1754), Plates 66, 86, 117.
30. Chippendale, T., op cit, Plate XXIV.
31. Manwaring, R., *The Cabinet and Chair-Maker's Real Friend and Companion* (1763), Plates 26, 27.
32. Wrighte, W., *Grotesque Architecture* (1767), Plate 4.
33. Bartell, E., *Hints for Picturesque Improvements in ornamented Cottages, and their Scenery*, London (1804), p. 25.
34. Knight, R.P., *The Landscape, A Didactic Poem* (1786).
35. Victoria and Albert Museum, London, W.11–1977.
36. Kew, Public Record Office, BT 42, 43, 44, 50, 51.
37. Himmelheber, G., *Cast Iron Furniture* (1996), plates 83–226.
38. Trollope, A., *Orley Farm* (1862), Vol. I, pp. 46–48.

9 The history and the future of public parks

David Lambert
Director of the Parks Agency, Gloucestershire, UK

The roots of the public park can be traced back to the urban commons and town moors which survived from medieval times, the commercial pleasure grounds of the eighteenth century, botanic gardens which were in varying degrees accessible to the public for a fee, and the communal but private gardens of Georgian residential development. But the Victorian park movement springs principally from the report of the House of Commons Select Committee report on Public Walks, published in 1833.[1]

This inquiry was held in response to growing awareness of the issues surrounding the unplanned growth of industrial towns and cities, pressed on corporations and government largely by non-conformists and liberals. For the first time, it examined the extent of public open space in major towns, drew attention to its loss, and recommended action to ensure that future provision was appropriate. It presented a rational but impassioned case for the benefits of public open space, arguing that access to such space was not only a moral issue but also a practical one in terms of reducing drunkenness, encouraging family bonds, and preventing disease, which led to discontent, 'which led in turn to attacks upon the government'. At a time when for example the 1819 Peterloo Massacre was still casting a shadow in legislators' minds, this was a powerful argument of enlightened self-interest.

The report was generally, although not unreservedly, welcomed, but legislation to support the creation of parks did not follow until the late 1840s. However, it did herald some important local initiatives such as the adaptation of Primrose Hill to public open space in 1842 and the construction of Victoria Park in east London in the early 1840s. It may also have encouraged the young Queen Victoria's decision to open the grounds of Hampton Court to the public in 1838. Elsewhere, Derby Arboretum (Figure 9.1) was opened in 1840 on 4.5 hectares of land, donated by the textile manufacturer Joseph Strutt (1765–1844) and designed by J.C. Loudon (1783–1843).

However, the general public were admitted free to the Arboretum on Sundays and Wednesdays and it was not fully opened until 1882, and Derby Town Council was not allowed at this time to use the rates either to acquire or maintain parks. In 1842, Joseph Paxton's (1803–65) Prince's Park in Liverpool was constructed, and although important in terms of design, this was essentially laid out as a communal garden for the adjacent new middle-class housing development, only becoming a public park in 1908 when it was taken over by the Corporation of Liverpool.

Gardens & Landscapes in Historic Building Conservation, First Edition. Edited by Marion Harney.
© 2014 John Wiley & Sons, Ltd. Published 2014 by John Wiley & Sons, Ltd.

Figure 9.1 Derby Arboretum, c.1904 (author's own).

The first truly public parks were laid out in Manchester and Salford in 1846: Philips Park and Queen's Park, Manchester and Peel Park, Salford. These were paid for by public subscription on land owned by the local authority and were fully and freely open to all members of the public. Designed by Joshua Major (1786–1866), they constituted an entirely new type of landscape, in which both managers and users found themselves having to negotiate new codes of behaviour. Early records, such as the day book of the park keeper at Philips Park, show the difficulties that ensued; whether children picking flowers or rowdy gangs of youths, and the measures hastily introduced such as bylaws, staff uniforms, signage, fencing and seating.[2]

In 1847 Paxton was chosen to design the new park at Birkenhead on the south bank of the Mersey. The park was designed as the centrepiece of a highly ambitious, largely unrealised attempt to create a new commercial and residential centre to rival Liverpool. It is instructive to observe that the Birkenhead Commissioners saw the park as integral to the development of such a centre, but also that they built it first. Little expense was spared and the result was a layout, features and planting of rich and subtle sophistication. It served as an exemplar to other designers, such as Frederick Law Olmsted (1822–1903) who applied many of its principles to Central Park in New York (1858).

During the nineteenth century all the greatest landscape designers were involved in public parks. Apart from Loudon and Paxton, these included James Pennethorne (1801–71) who designed Victoria Park (1842–6) after working on Regent's Park (1809–32) with John Nash (1752–1835); Edward Kemp (1817–91), John Gibson (1817–92) and Edward Milner (1819–94), who had all been trained by Paxton and went on to significant careers of their own, and Joshua Major and William Barron (1805–1891) each with a background in private estates. The major figure in landscape design in the late nineteenth century and early twentieth century, Thomas Mawson (1861–1933), was also closely involved in public as well as private landscapes. A number of public parks also had rockeries and grottoes designed by the firm of James Pulham & Son whose works also graced some of the greatest private estates, including Sandringham, Norfolk; Waddesdon, Buckinghamshire and Buckingham Palace, London. Design theory was widely discussed in the new horticultural journals, and by the end of the century thousands of parks had been created. It can be confidently argued that in terms of design theory, expenditure and acreage, Victorian parks are directly comparable to the English landscape gardens of the eighteenth century.

In fact it is clear that in design terms there was a continuum from the private gardens of the eighteenth century. Park designers adopted the use of Humphry Repton's (1752–1818)

Figure 9.2 Crystal Palace, from a lithograph by James Harding, 1854 (author's own).

Picturesque principles, and later the language of formal garden design from the private sector. Paxton's great gardens for the relocated Crystal Palace (1854) (Figure 9.2) were essentially a private garden written on a vast scale.

But public parks were also augmented by a pedagogical theme quite lacking in a private landscape. Public parks had a strong element of moral and intellectual improvement running through them, whether Christian, as in the homilies around People's Park in Halifax (1857), or scientific, as in the replicas of dinosaurs and geological strata at the Crystal Palace, London.

They were also designed to promulgate virtuous behaviour in their users. Sometimes this was explicit, as in the inscriptions on the drinking-fountain in People's Park – 'Thank God for water' and 'Water is best' – and in other cases, such encouragement was embodied in the bylaws, which frequently required decent dress and forbad vicious pastimes such as smoking, swearing or gambling in the park. There was a strong Christian belief that exposure to beautifully maintained walks, trees and floral displays, to examples of good lives embodied in statues and their inscriptions, and above all to other people also engaged in such enjoyment, would have a beneficial effect on the morals of the working class.

While this kind of underpinning can be seen at worst as heavy-handed paternalism, in some cases the creation of a park was a more overt form of social control. Many parks were made from previously unimproved open spaces which had become, over centuries, places for informal recreation. For example, Battersea Fields was 'notorious' for a carnivalesque mixture of side shows, horse-racing, peddlers, stalls and booths set up on Sunday afternoons. The Act which enabled its conversion to Battersea Park in 1846 wiped out this tradition and replaced it with a more ordered landscape controlled by strictly enforced bylaws. During the Bristol riots in the 1830s, the Chartist movement and the reform movement, Brandon Hill, an open space just outside the city was a favoured location for political meetings and rallies. In 1840 the Corporation began a programme of improvements, comprising new gravel walks and planting, which included new bylaws, and it is clear that this was part of a strategy to suppress working-class organisation.[3]

Similarly, while it is true that a good number of parks, like Derby Arboretum or People's Park, Halifax, were founded after a gift of land from the landowner, many more emerged out of a mixture of donations, deals and sales, generally of land which had little agricultural or development value. As in Birkenhead, parks were frequently associated with a development project, in a deal whereby a corporation was 'given' land on which it would create and maintain a park while the landowner reaped the benefits of the adjoining land's residential development value. Parks were often laid out on what was, at the time, the urban fringe – the site available for Central Park in New York was half a mile beyond the city's boundary – or on other marginal land such as former industrial sites; e.g., St Matthias Park in Bristol created in 1886 on an old burial site and a tannery yard, and Avenham Park (1860s) beside the river Ribble in Preston, on land subject to flooding. Hedgemead Park in Bath (1889) was only made into a park after a half-completed residential development had been destroyed in a land-slip; St Andrew's Park, Bristol (1895) on an area of old quarries; Victoria Park in London on an area of burial grounds and brick pits. After the 1881 Open Space Act, many small parks were made out of closed burial grounds handed over to the local corporation.

Park design developed rapidly from its roots in the landscape garden. These new landscapes were required to accommodate a wide range of activities and a large number of people in such a manner that they did not impinge on each other. At Derby Arboretum, Loudon used linear mounds to display plants and also to screen from each other paths which were in close proximity. This device prevented the whole of what was a modest area from being apprehended in any one view, and so increased the illusion of the park's extent.

Space needed to be allocated for a wide variety of sports such as tennis, bowls, archery and cricket (football, which was widely considered to be uncouth, had to wait until the late nineteenth century). Children's play areas or 'gymnasia' had to be accommodated, generally segregated in the early days of parks, while a lake for boating was highly desirable. Parks needed to accommodate areas for formal events such as parades or tattoos, often focused on a bandstand; sheltered walks and promenades and as wide a range as possible of horticultural display areas, whether woodland, shrubberies or beds (Figure 9.3). Accommodation was generally located in lodges by the entrances, but space was also needed for a gardeners' yard for storage and for raising plants which often required a

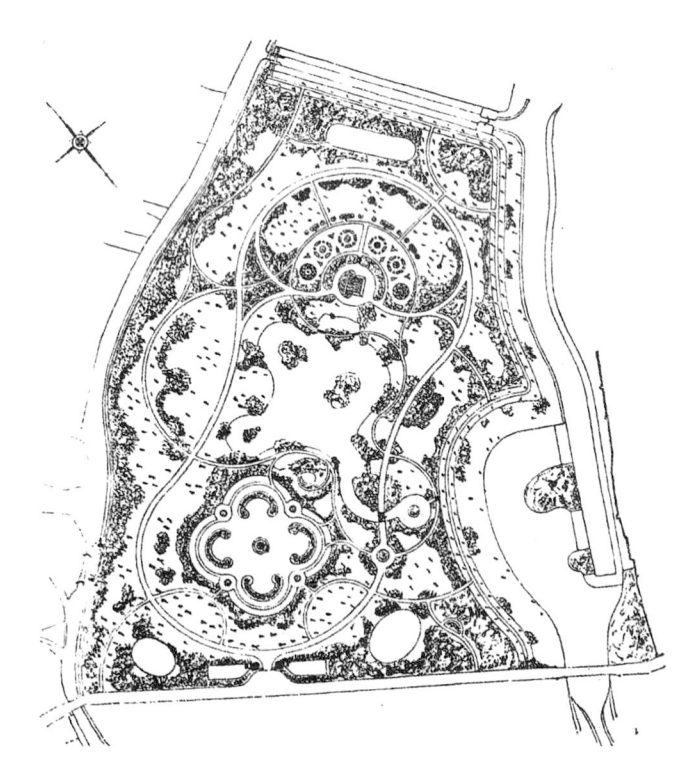

Figure 9.3 Abbey Park, Leicester, a plan reproduced in *The Gardeners' Chronicle*, 1880. The design, by William Barron, included provision for archery, tennis, cricket and bowling, all within an ornamental framework very similar to that of a high Victorian pleasure ground (author's own).

glasshouse. All this had to be fitted into a strictly limited area, and separated without reducing a park's sense of spaciousness; that is, with the minimum of internal boundaries.

Although numerically more parks were designed by the local surveyor or nurseryman, the design language and solutions established by Loudon, Paxton and others such as Edouard André (1840–1911), who designed Sefton Park Liverpool in 1867, became widely current.

Once built, parks rapidly became a favoured locus for a range of commemorative sculpture and memorials. Much of this was explicit in promoting a paternalistic notion of virtuous behaviour, whether commemorating the royal family, military victories, industrial or commercial achievements, or lives spent in worthy public office. These objects played their part in 'naturalising', in the French philosopher Roland Barthes' (1915–80) sense of the word, the Victorian world order and in the attempt to marginalise behaviour considered disorderly. The chosen ideals were literally spelt out for the crowd as, for example, on the Victoria statue in Bitts Park, Carlisle: 'Commerce, Education, Science and Art'. Statues of the queen were erected across the country in a way not dissimilar to those of Stalin in the Soviet Union; the cannon brought back from the Crimea as trophies of war were again distributed throughout the land and generally found a home in the local park.

But that is only half the story, and a detailed examination of memorialisation in public parks shows a much more heterodox range of lives and events. Many statues commemorate local heroes, such as the Corn Law Rhymer, Ebenezer Elliott (1781–1849), whose statue stands in Weston Park, Sheffield, or the four dialect poets commemorated in Broadfield Park, Rochdale, or local events, such as the poignant white marble figure in Roker Park, Sunderland erected in memory of the 183 children who died in the Victoria Hall fire in 1884. Almost equally tragic is the memorial in East Park, Southampton, to the engineers who went down with the *Titanic* (Figure 9.4).[4]

By the 1880s most towns and cities had established at least one public park. The second phase of the park movement saw a still larger number of parks being built, often more cheaply, in outer areas or suburbs as towns continued to grow. Numerically, more parks were built after 1885 than before. All Bristol's municipal parks date from the 1890s; in Glasgow, half of the city's parks were laid out after 1925. Most of the parks in this second wave were designed by the borough surveyor or nurseryman, and often to less ambitious standards. Although public parks had always been associated with the provision of space for sports, after World War I, the emphasis on recreation changed. It became more youth-oriented, more active and less genteel and deferential. The provision of recreation grounds and dedicated playgrounds with a less ornamental character grew rapidly, encouraged after 1936 by the King George V Playing Fields programme. The grandeur of the high Victorian design

Figure 9.4 The memorial to the engineers of the *Titanic*, East Park, Southampton (author's own).

language was replaced by the more modest style of the Arts and Crafts movement: in London, the LCC parks superintendent, Colonel J.J. Sexby, was responsible for a number of 'old English gardens' with rose beds, pergolas and crazy paving paths.

Park-making did not continue in any significant way after World War II.[5] Rather, landscape designers and local authorities became involved in a much broader idea of landscape design than discrete parks. Hal Moggridge described the new idea as 'landscape design through the planning process, something completely different from gardens, which can be described as landscape without boundaries'.[6] This found its canvas in such opportunities as the new towns, in which designers such as Sylvia Crowe (1901–97) and Geoffrey Jellicoe (1900–96) worked to integrate landscape with the whole fabric of the development rather than just in set pieces; the idea, as Crowe said of Frederick Gibberd's (1908–84) masterplan for Harlow, Essex (1947) of open space and landscape flowing between compact housing areas, 'a lovely, very humanised landscape'.[7]

In the 1960s a positive reaction against traditional parks became apparent. The removal of boundary railings, so often blamed entirely on the war effort in the forties, actually took another leap onward in the sixties, when railings were removed as part of a democratic wish to open up parks to the streets. Worse still, the notion of 'the garden-free park' became current: flowerbeds and horticulture were seen as getting in the way of the demand for leisure pursuits. This culminated in the Bains Report of 1972 which introduced the idea of parks as part of leisure services, a change which signalled the end of the specialist parks department.[8]

Whatever the noble motives, the removal of railings and the introduction of ubiquitous 'Keep off the Grass' signs, and the loss of parks departments heralded a spiral of decline which gathered pace during the 1970s and was accelerated after 1988 by the Local Government Act which introduced the now-infamous notion of Compulsory Competitive Tendering, which forced local authorities to tender maintenance services on the open market. Experienced staff from gardeners to managers left the profession in droves, and quality was driven down in the search for the cheapest price. Poor maintenance compounded the effect of budget cuts to turn parks into no-go areas, and by the early 1990s, the public park had become one of the icons of inner-city decay and dereliction (Figure 9.5).

It has been calculated that between 1980 and 2000 there was an accumulated underspend on parks across the country of £1.3 billion; by 2000 annual revenue expenditure was on average £126 million less than it had been in 1980. In the same period, 58% of park bandstands had been demolished along with 70% of park greenhouses, and over a quarter

Figure 9.5 Cheetham Hill Park, Manchester in 1993, showing the dereliction typical of parks in the early 1990s (author's own).

Figure 9.6 The opening of the restored bandstand at Handsworth Park, Birmingham, 2006. (Photo courtesy of Hilary Taylor Landscape Associates.)

of basic facilities such as shelters, public lavatories and cafés had been closed or knocked down.⁹

In 1992, the GMB Union wrote a report entitled *Grounds for Concern* which highlighted the cuts to parks budgets and the loss of skilled staff. In 1993, the Garden History Society and the Victorian Society published *Public Prospects: historic urban parks under threat*. This drew attention to the undervalued historic importance of urban parks and to the crisis in which they had become engulfed. Then in 1995, Comedia and Demos, two think-tanks, published *Park Life: urban parks and social renewal*, which for the first time gathered some data on the staggering number of people who still used parks despite their condition, and made the case for their vital role in urban society.

Despite these clarion calls, the future looked bleak until in 1995 the newly formed Heritage Lottery Fund, stung by popular criticism about its grants to elite culture, began casting round for a more democratic kind of heritage to sponsor and announced a programme of grants to regenerate public parks and gardens, set up with an initial £50 million (Figure 9.6). In its 1996 Annual Review the HLF pronounced, 'Nothing is more important than the restoration of parks, public gardens and open spaces in towns and cities'. This heralded an unimaginable fount of capital which to date has resulted in £600 million allocated to parks.

By way of comparison, at the time English Heritage's annual budget for grants to registered historic parks and gardens totalled £200,000.

Not only was the programme an unprecedented endorsement of the heritage value of public parks, but the HLF broke the mould in two vital ways. First, it dispensed with national lists as the key criterion for judging heritage merit: until this date, all conservation grants were judged against the status of a site in terms of whether it was registered, listed or scheduled. Instead, it invited applicants to research and demonstrate that historic interest. At a stroke this counteracted the woeful under-representation of parks on the English Heritage Register of Historic Parks and Gardens of Special Historic Interest in England.

Secondly, the HLF offered grants not just for repairs to historic fabric but for new build. This included new features which would contribute to the aim of regenerating – that is, repopulating public parks. It recognised that unless people were drawn back into parks, any amount of repairs would still leave them vulnerable to decline. So it invested in public lavatories, cafés, new feature gardens, play areas, and new park pavilions offering staff accommodation, meeting rooms and exhibition spaces for community use. In addition, it dismissed the criticism of conservation purists and supported the painstaking reconstructions of vanished features, such as cast-iron bandstands, benches and drinking fountains.

The HLF has taken to heart the principles of New York's Central Park Conservancy in viewing a successful park project as a three-legged stool, comprising capital repairs, maintenance and programming. The latter incorporates all forms of activities and events, volunteering, education, outreach and partnerships. The introduction of the latter again distinguishes its approach from any previous grant-aid scheme.

Despite being strictly a capital programme, it has also succeeded in using its one-off grants to ensure longer-term benefits. From the start, it offered grants to support new three- or five-year staff posts, such as park managers, wardens and gardeners, as well as community outreach and education officers charged with re-engaging the community in the park through events and activities. It also required applicants to sign up to a ten-year enhanced management and maintenance agreement, enshrined in a Management and Maintenance Plan, which committed them to an increased revenue budget over that period.

The HLF continues to budget some £20–30 million annually towards urban parks projects and the sheer weight of the cash value which the HLF has placed on urban parks has prompted a wide reconsideration of the other kinds of value they embody. English Heritage has added a substantial number to the Register of Parks and Gardens in recognition that it under-estimated their historic importance. The value of beautiful parks in terms of economic development and attracting inward investment has been extensively researched and recognised. The role of parks in sustainable urban drainage, of their trees in reducing the effects of global warming and their plants in encouraging biodiversity has been widely championed. Their contribution to public health – which the Victorians understood and we forgot – has in the last ten years been rediscovered. The importance of well-maintained and secure public open space to social cohesion has been rediscovered. The HLF has championed their role in education, in job creation, in skills training and in the arts.

In the wake of the HLF's pioneering programme, a raft of central initiatives followed. In 1999, a House of Commons Select Committee held an inquiry into Town and Country Parks, which represented the first major discussion of their condition and their importance since 1833. This led to a substantial debate and new policies in the Urban White Paper of 2000 and to Government support for the *Public Parks Assessment*, researched by the Urban Parks Forum, now GreenSpace, which gathered from local authorities damning evidence of parks' decline, published in the same year. In 2001 the Government set up a Government Green Space Task Force which reported in 2002 and resulted in a Government policy paper on public open space, *Living Places: Cleaner, Safer, Greener*, later that year. In 2003, the Commission for Architecture and the Built Environment was ordered to set up CABE Space, charged with acting as a champion for urban parks, which it did until abolished in 2010, after publishing a wide range of research and policy papers. At a local level too, the national attention resulted in greater recognition of the importance of parks enshrined in new Green Space Strategies. Perhaps more importantly it encouraged a surge of activity from community groups, and many hundreds of Friends groups were set up during this period.

It could be argued too that the HLF is responsible, in part, for the growing recognition among local authorities and developers that new parks, or urban green space, should be part of new urban development planning. The Thames Gateway Parklands, for example, is intended to afford a 'landscape framework' for the whole area and its planned 160,000 new dwellings. What this means in practice is 'a working landscape that has many functions including renewable energy production, local food enterprises and water management systems'.[10] The landscape architect and masterplanner John Hopkins said, 'It's not fluffy little bits of park we're talking about here, it's a whole environmental infrastructure, and the Thames Gateway green structure plans are by far the most advanced in the UK'.[11]

This vision of the city as 'total landscape' is much to be admired and has much in common with the vision of practitioners like Gibberd and Jellicoe which lay behind the post-war New Towns. However, the New Towns were enabled by primary legislation and central government investment, neither of which underpins the Thames Gateway 'aspirations'. But it could be countered that 'fluffy little parks', in the sense of discrete, high-maintenance public open space, is precisely what goes missing in this approach, and that what emerges is a diluted environmentalism, spread thin and 'multifunctional'.

The Olympic Park is of course the most prominent of contemporary standard-bearers; a great new park laid out as the centrepiece of not only the games but a major new urban development. There is no doubting the central place of the park in the plans both for the games and for the legacy, and the park is now in 'transition', with its games infrastructure being removed before it is re-opened as a public park in 2014.

The park's masterplan was driven by a 'habitat creation/restoration ecology approach', and remediation and re-naturalisation of the heavily polluted land was an enormous achievement.[12] This approach was modified by the introduction of decorative elements based on a 'meadow aesthetic'. The north park comprises 'designed versions of native UK habitats', and the south a global range of perennials lavishly and randomly planted within a formal structure of clipped evergreen hedges.[13]

The new park landscape in the north of the site is one of smoothly sculpted mounds and groups and swathes of native trees, shrubs and flowers, through which winding paths gently rise and fall above the rejuvenated river; its features include reed beds and wetland habitats, sustainable drainage systems in the form of swales or ditches, log piles for invertebrates and nesting areas for birds and bats.

Quite what will be handed over, and to whom, remains unclear but it is likely to be a fairly simple landscape of grass, water, trees and paths; a landscape of restrained good taste and worthy environmental credentials, but lacking in the exuberance of its nineteenth-century forebears.

New parks are welcome but they are a distraction. The real issue is not new parks but what to do with old parks, the existing infrastructure of public open spaces. And here, as ever, the bottom line is local authority resources. Despite the wave of popular and political support, most revenue budgets continued to decline even during the recent 'renaissance'. Despite the huge sums invested by the HLF it has still only addressed a relatively small proportion of the national stock and most parks have not benefited from a major refurbishment. Maintenance of public parks is not a statutory requirement, and in the relentless annual search for savings, parks budgets remain vulnerable. Despite the headline projects for premier parks, and the hopes of a 'trickle-down effect', the majority of local authority parks continue to struggle.

At present, the coalition government's austerity policies are threatening to undo much of what has been achieved since 1996. Parks services have to find enormous savings, some having to cut as much as 50% of annual expenditure. This is affecting not only maintenance regimes, but front-line staff and managers. Cuts have been introduced hastily with little understanding of their long-term impact or indeed long-term costs. Some councils, such as Liverpool City Council and Haringey in London, have considered 'zero-maintenance' in selected parks; the Isle of Wight Council has put Ventnor Botanic Garden, visited by around 270,000 each year, on the market in an attempt to save £300,000 per annum. Many councils are looking at the feasibility of transferring parks to trusts, charities, community groups or private–public partnerships. Parks are in the front-line of the local public services which are being attacked by central government.

It is little short of shocking to look back over the era heralded by that visionary Select Committee report of 1833. Given how rapidly the resources and morale of local councils are now being destroyed, it is hard to take comfort in the thought that this may just be another turn of the wheel of fortune for parks. Perhaps instead we are seeing the end of 180 years of consensus on the public realm; on the importance of access not only to good quality parks and gardens, but to *public* parks and gardens; on a vision of a society which shares these things.

Endnotes

1. Much of the history here is taken from Hazel Conway, *People's Parks: the design and development of Victorian parks in Britain*, Cambridge: Cambridge University Press (1990), passim, which remains the authoritative account of the subject. Hazel Conway also wrote a useful summary history in *Public Parks*, Princes Risborough: Shire Books (1996).
2. Ruff, Allan A., *The Biography of Philips Park, Manchester, 1846–1996*, School of Planning and Landscape, University of Manchester, Occasional Paper 56 (2000).
3. See David Lambert, 'Rituals of Transgression in Public Parks in Britain, 1846 to the Present', in Michel Conan (ed.), *Performance and Appropriation: Profane Rituals in Gardens and Landscapes*, Washington DC: Harvard University Press (2007).
4. The subject of sculpture in Victorian parks is addressed in more detail in 'The Meaning and Re-Meaning of Sculpture in Victorian Parks', in Patrick Eyres and Fiona Russell (ed.), *Sculpture and the Garden*, Aldershot: Ashgate Publishing (2006), passim.
5. Hazel Conway, 'Everyday Landscapes: public parks from 1930–2000', *Garden History*, 28:1, 2000.
6. 'Gardens and Landscapes 1930–2000', paper delivered at the Garden History Society and Twentieth Century Society conference, 'Landscape and Garden in Britain 1930–2000', 1998.
7. Geoffrey Collens and Wendy Powell (ed.), *Sylvia Crowe*, Landscape Design Trust, 1999, p. 54.
8. Conway 2000, op cit., pp. 130–31.
9. Heritage Lottery Fund and Urban Parks Forum, *Public Parks Assessment*, 2000.
10. CABE, 'Thames Gateway Parklands', www.cabe.org.uk/default.aspx?contentitemid=1606
11. John Hopkins, quoted in *Green Places* 15, May 2005, 19.
12. http://www.gardenvisit.com/blog/2012/08/23/wildflower-meadows-in-londons-2012-queen-elizabeth-olympic-park
13. http://www.nigeldunnett.info/Londonolympicpark/styled-2/2012gardens.html

10 The history and aesthetic development of the cemetery and related conservation issues

Jonathan Lovie
Conservation and landscape consultant, Devon, UK

The cemetery is principally, but not exclusively, a phenomenon of nineteenth-century English landscape design. Rather surprisingly, given the widespread interest in social history and genealogy, this 'type' of historic designed landscape has only been recognised as being of 'special historic interest' in relatively recent times. The original edition of the English Heritage Register of Parks and Gardens of Special Historic Interest in England published in the mid-1980s contained a mere handful of the most obvious and best known cemetery landscapes; today, as a result of a thematic designation programme in the early years of this century and subsequent spot-designation, the total of nationally designated cemeteries and related commemorative designed landscapes has risen to over 100.

Cemetery, burial ground, graveyard or churchyard?

Before considering the development of the English cemetery, it is important to clarify exactly the type of site under consideration. Obviously, a cemetery is a place in which deceased human bodies are interred; however, there are other types of site, such as burial grounds, graveyards and churchyards which fulfil a similar function, but which cannot properly be described as cemeteries.

A cemetery is, above all, a consciously designed commemorative landscape in which human bodies are buried. Its function, both practical and commemorative, finds expression in the aesthetic of the landscape design. In most cases burial grounds and other places of interment do not demonstrate this combination of practical and aesthetic intent: in such places practical considerations tend to predominate.

A cemetery differs from a churchyard in that cemeteries are not physically associated with a place of regular worship (although they may be associated with a particular parish or religious community). A cemetery may contain chapels or other religious structures, but these are places designed for the recital of the funeral office prior to interment rather than for any other form of worship.

Legalisation of cremation in England in 1885 gradually led to the emergence of a new form of commemorative designed landscape, the garden of remembrance. While the historic and aesthetic development of this landscape type remains to be fully investigated, it is important to note that some of the principal examples have been identified by English Heritage and included on the Register of Parks and Gardens. These include Golders Green Crematorium, London (1902) and the Gardens of Remembrance at Stoke Poges, Buckinghamshire (1934–37), both of which are designated at Grade 1.

The social and aesthetic context for the earliest English cemeteries

Accounts of the development of the cemetery in nineteenth-century England have tended to view this phenomenon from a twentieth-century perspective, ignoring, perhaps, some of the powerful influences which helped to shape the character of the cemeteries which began to be developed in the 1820s and 1830s.

These accounts have concentrated on the one hand on the reaction against the appalling state of squalor into which many parochial churchyards and burial grounds had fallen in the early nineteenth century and the consequent dangers to public health;[1] and on the other, have stressed the perceived influence of Pere-Lachaise Cemetery, Paris (opened 1804) on the promoters of early English cemeteries.[2] Squalor and concern for public health were undoubtedly strong motivating factors behind burial reform throughout the nineteenth century and, indeed, many of the same horrific images were adduced by promoters of cremation in the late nineteenth century; but while the general influence of the Parisian cemetery may have been in the minds of cemetery designers in the early nineteenth century, its direct influence, apart from at Glasgow Necropolis (1832), is harder to discern.[3]

The traditional account tends to omit the influence of previous attempts at burial reform both at home and abroad;[4] the prevailing aesthetic mood of the late eighteenth and early nineteenth century, particularly in relation to landscape design; the contemporary understanding of commemoration, especially in the light of a predominantly 'classical' education; and the interests of religion, and particularly sectarian interests opposed to the Established Church.[5] All of these factors, to a greater or lesser degree, combined to influence the proprietors of any new early nineteenth-century cemetery: but above all, early cemeteries, founded as joint-stock companies, had to have commercial appeal in order to succeed.

The market at which the proprietors of the early nineteenth-century commercial cemeteries aimed was wealthy, middle or upper class, and generally well educated. Such a person might well contrast the romantic and specifically English image of the peaceful churchyard – 'those rugged elms, that yew-tree's shade, Where heaves the turf in many a mouldering heap' – popularised by Thomas Gray's *Elegy written in a Country Churchyard* (c.1742–50) with the foetid reality of the churchyard down the road where turf was replaced by noxious slime and the sexton had to test the ground with an iron bar before beginning a new grave,[6] or where a crossing sweeper could offer to uncover the latest interment with his broom.[7]

Present reality contrasted equally forcefully with the remains of classical antiquity, well known to the educated late Georgian either through personal experience on the Grand Tour, or through images such as Piranesi's *Vedute di Roma* (begun 1747) and *Antichita di Roma* (1756).[8] These images showed not only the ancient Romans' concern for decent extra-mural burial, but also the highly picturesque, in some cases sublime, state to which these monuments of the greatest classical civilisation had been reduced through time and decay.

The sublime and commercial cemetery in early nineteenth-century England

A promoter of one of the earliest English cemeteries, dating perhaps from around 1820, would have been faced with two distinct aesthetic choices: whether to opt for an Arcadian 'garden' cemetery along the precedent set by Pere-Lachaise Cemetery in Paris; or whether to aim to create a sepulchral landscape that would appeal to the taste of those versed in the theories of the Picturesque and Sublime.

In part this aesthetic choice would be determined by the kind of site that was available: as commercial enterprises, these early cemeteries had always to strike a balance between the initial cost of laying out the site and the need to attract a suitably moneyed clientele. Thus, when Thomas Drummond (1764–1852), a former Unitarian minister laid out The Rosary Cemetery, Norwich (opened 1821), he made use of a former market garden and appears to have retained some existing specimen trees in his design which, combining winding drives with terraced burial plots, clearly owed its inspiration to the Arcadian landscape of Pere-Lachaise.

However, when the promoters of the highly successful St James' Cemetery, Liverpool sought in 1825 to establish a cemetery for the use of the Anglican community in the town, they acquired a former quarry adjoining a fashionable quarter and the existing eighteenth-century promenade known as St James' Walk (now the site of Liverpool's Anglican Cathedral). A disused stone quarry obviously possessed considerable potential as a sublime landscape; and at the same time it was marginal land of little alternative commercial value. The company commissioned the Liverpool architect John Foster (1787–1846) to design the architectural elements of the scheme including a neo-classical chapel, a rock-hewn tunnel leading from the chapel into the bowl of the quarry, and a monumental series of ramped catacombs which doubled as access for horse-drawn hearses into the lower parts of the cemetery.[9] The landscape was laid out by John Shepherd (c.1764–1836), Curator of the Liverpool Botanic Garden (Figure 10.1).

The design of the cemetery clearly shows the influence both of classical antiquity and eighteenth-century picturesque depictions of its remains: the tunnel entrance owes something to Piranesi's early architectural fantasies; while the great arcaded ramps appear to have been inspired by the monumental terraced remains of the Temple of Fortuna Primigania at Praeneste (modern Palestrina) outside Rome. Intriguingly, when William Huskisson, MP (1770–1830) was buried in the cemetery in 1830 following his demise at the

Figure 10.1 St James' Cemetery, Liverpool, opened as a joint-stock cemetery in 1829. Its sublime landscape planted by John Shepherd, and its neo-classical structures designed by John Foster shown in this nearly contemporary engraving, were intended to appeal to the wealthy citizens of the expanding town of Liverpool (author's own).

inauguration of the Liverpool and Manchester Railway, he was commemorated by a classical rotunda aligned axially on the centre of the ramped approach: the terraces of the classical Temple of Fortuna were surmounted by a rotunda. The sublime effect was completed by Shepherd's planting which combined trees framing the craggy surrounding rocks with lawns and groups of ornamental shrubs in the bowl of the quarry.

The economic attraction of utilising a site which had been, and in part was to remain, in use as a quarry was spotted by a group of non-conformists in Birmingham who opened Key Hill Cemetery on the edge of the area known as the Jewellery Quarter in 1835. The first cemetery to be created in the town, Key Hill had a neo-classical chapel (demolished 1966) designed by the local architect Charles Edge (c.1801–67), who was also responsible for the monumental Greek revival gate piers and gates and the original ranges of catacombs which still survive. The area around the chapel was laid out in a relatively formal style with straight tree-lined walks; while to the north there was a more informally designed area with monuments arranged against a background of ornamental trees and shrubs. Terraced catacombs were cut into the quarry face behind the burial areas, and these terraces doubled as public walks with a small observatory being added to the cemetery's attractions.[10] As sand extraction ceased in a particular area, so more ground could be released for burials, thus helping to off-set the initial cost of £12,000 incurred in setting up the cemetery. By 1839, John Claudius Loudon (1783–1843), visiting the cemetery, particularly praised the ornamental planting which had been undertaken by the local nursery of John Pope and Sons of Handsworth.[11]

Although both the aesthetic and social context in which cemeteries were formed changed in the 1840s and 1850s, the picturesque, and occasionally sublime potential of previously quarried sites was not overlooked. Cemeteries continued to be created in former quarries at Coventry (London Road Cemetery, 1845); Birmingham (Warstone Lane Cemetery, 1848) and Nottingham (Church Cemetery, 1848); and elsewhere sites with dramatic natural topography or sweeping views, such as the Abbey Cemetery, Bath (1843); Lansdown Cemetery, Bath (1848); Welford Road Cemetery, Leicester (1849) and Undercliffe Cemetery, Bradford (1854) were chosen for new cemeteries. The intrinsic drama of a cemetery landscape, whether expressed through the sublime grandeur of crags and rocky enclosures, or panoramic views across the community in which the interred had passed their lives, contributed to the overall drama associated with the Victorian way of death; which in turn was the method adopted by that society to deal with the ever-present and visible reality of mortality.

The early commercial cemeteries of the Metropolis

The first cemetery serving London was established at Kensal Green by the General Cemetery Company in 1832 as the result of a protracted campaign in the press to highlight the deficiency of existing burial arrangements in the capital. Many vested interests had to be overcome, and significant capital raised to acquire and lay out a suitable site.

All Souls' Cemetery, Kensal Green was provided with a landscape which combined formal grandeur with more picturesque intimacy:[12] a grand formal avenue leads from the monumental neo-classical entrance in one direction to the equally imposing Doric revival Anglican Chapel and catacombs; and in the other direction to the smaller Ionic Dissenters' Chapel and catacombs. Subsidiary drives and walks followed a more serpentine plan, while groups of ornamental trees and shrubs served to break up the level site and allow the creation of bosky settings for the wide range of monuments which the Company allowed to be erected. The cemetery was firmly aimed at a middle and upper class clientele to whom the neo-classical architectural style and the landscape reminiscent of contemporary gentlemen's villas and pleasure grounds was suitably reassuring; and at the same time there were references to classical antiquity for those who cared for such things: the Anglican Chapel recalls Nicholas Revett's (1720–1804) church of St Lawrence, Ayot St Lawrence (1778–9), which was itself derived from the Temple of Apollo at Delos, and the Dissenters' Chapel incorporated elements inspired by the Choragic Monument of Thrasyllus in Athens. Meanwhile, the principal avenue leading to the portico of the Anglican Chapel, with its array of monuments set against a backdrop of evergreen Ilex oak, might remind the educated and well-travelled visitor of the Via Appia or even the Via Sacra, Rome, itself. Kensal Green secured its social position with the burial of the Duke of Sussex (d. 1843) and Princess Sophia (d. 1848), both children of King George III.[13]

By 1839 the value of the original shares in the General Cemetery Company had doubled in value. Not surprisingly, many were tempted by the prospect of riches to be made from attempting to address the burial crisis in the capital. The first of these ventures was the South Metropolitan Cemetery at West Norwood, Lambeth (1837), followed quickly by the formation of the London Cemetery Company which went on to establish St James' Cemetery, Highgate (1839) and All Saints' Cemetery, Nunhead (1840). Meanwhile, a further company was formed in 1839 to create a cemetery catering largely for non-conformists at Abney Park, Stoke Newington (opened 1840), and further burial space was created to serve East London by the City of London and Tower Hamlets Cemetery Company, which opened Tower Hamlets Cemetery in 1841.

Additional cemetery provision for West London was made by the West of London and Westminster Cemetery Company, which opened Brompton Cemetery in 1840. Brompton marks a turning point in the provision of burial space by joint-stock companies. In contrast to earlier ventures, initial subscriptions were slow and the Company was hampered by generous provisions in its Bill of Incorporation to compensate parochial clergy from whose parishes the interred bodies originated. These factors, together with the cost of the magnificent set of Italianate buildings designed for the cemetery by Benjamin Baud (1807–85) and the generous provision of catacombs, which once sold and occupied became a significant wasting asset, meant that Brompton Cemetery was, unlike its predecessors, a financial disaster. The Company was wound up in 1854 and the cemetery passed, per force, into public ownership.

The early metropolitan cemeteries differ from their provincial counterparts in that they owe a much clearer debt of inspiration to Pere-Lachaise in Paris. The London cemeteries were laid out in a landscape style reminiscent of contemporary pleasure grounds, with a similar palette of planting. While Kensal Green Cemetery conformed to the pattern first established at St James' Cemetery, Liverpool (1829) of building in a neo-classical style and repeated at other provincial cemeteries such as the General Cemetery, Newcastle (1834); Key Hill, Birmingham (1835); Nottingham General Cemetery (1837) and Gravesend Cemetery (1841), other early metropolitan cemeteries used a variety of architectural styles and other novel features to differentiate themselves from one another and to attract suitably affluent patrons. Thus, at Highgate Cemetery, catacombs were designed in the Egyptian style, and at Abney Park Cemetery the entrances lodges and gates were similarly designed by William Hosking (1800–61) in the Egyptian taste, complete with a hieroglyphic inscription provided by Joseph Bonomi the Younger (1796–1878). In complete contrast, Hosking's chapel at Abney Park is an eclectic and eccentric essay in Gothic; while, as an additional attraction, the grounds were planted by George Loddiges' Hackney nursery as an arboretum comprising 2,500 varieties of trees and shrubs and a rosarium comprising 1,029 varieties. At West Norwood, by contrast, Sir William Tite (1798–1873) adopted a consistently Perpendicular Gothic style for the chapels, entrance and railings. Even the catacombs surviving beneath the site of the Anglican Chapel include several Tudor-Gothic enclosures for particularly wealthy patrons, recalling chantry chapels in a late medieval cathedral.

The transition from private to public burial provision

The joint-stock companies' quest for novelty and need to promote custom gradually led to a backlash against the *laissez-faire* approach to the provision of burial space which prevailed during the first half of the nineteenth century. Several factors combined to encourage a change in public opinion: during the 1830s and 1840s London and many provincial towns and cities were wracked by epidemics of serious diseases such as cholera and typhoid. While the exact mechanism of infection was not properly understood, the link between overcrowded burial grounds and contaminated water was not hard to make.

In 1842 Edwin Chadwick (1800–90), Secretary to the Poor Law Board, published his comprehensive *Report on the Sanitary Condition of the Labouring Classes of Great Britain*; this was followed in 1843 by a supplementary report, *On the Results of a Special Inquiry into the Practice of Interment in Towns*. In the same year, John Loudon (1783–1843) published his characteristically encyclopaedic study of the planning and management of cemeteries, *On the Laying Out, Planting and Management of Cemeteries*. At the same time propagandists such as George Walker (1807–84) continued to highlight the shocking conditions which prevailed in many existing places of burial in publications such as *Gatherings from Grave-Yards* (1839), *The Graveyards of London* (1841) and *Interment and Disinterment* (1843) as well as professional journals such as *The Lancet* and *The Builder*. A more hygienic and essentially utilitarian approach to burial appeared to be required in order to secure the health of society as a whole.

At the same time the spiritual character of the country was changing: a mood of greater seriousness began to prevail, replacing what came to be seen as the frivolity of the Regency. As early as 1837, A.W.N. Pugin (1812–52) published a caricature of an 'Entrance for a New Cemetery' for all denominations: the gates are a confection of Egyptian and classical elements and symbols, while within the cemetery a neo-classical chapel and monuments can be seen. Pugin's purpose is clear: to highlight the incongruity of the commercial cemetery with its gin-palace gimmicks as the final resting place for the 'true Christian'. For both the Roman Catholic convert Pugin and the devout Anglican, as well as the earnest evangelical, the only appropriate aesthetic style for a Christian country and particularly for such an important function as a place of burial, was Gothic in its various forms.

The result of these changes in mood was a realisation that while the commercial cemetery might go some way towards addressing the burial crisis faced by the relatively affluent, it did nothing to address the problem faced by the poor, and thus contributed to the vicious spiral of infection and morbidity which ultimately threatened the social and moral fabric of society.

While ultimately the solution to this problem was seen to be the provision of public cemeteries funded through a local rate, some joint-stock companies sought to address the burial crisis through a variety of means. John Loudon himself provided designs for three cemeteries in 1843, the last year of his life.[14] Of these, that for Histon Road Cemetery, Cambridge owned by the Cambridge General Cemetery Company was particularly influential. The design was published by Loudon, and shows a regular layout with a centrally placed chapel at the junction of carriage drives which divide the site into quarters. It is a practical plan which maximises the use of ground while not compromising hygienic considerations. Planting was integral to the design with clipped evergreens interspersing monuments along the principal drives, cedars marking the corners of the carriage turn and a surrounding hedge of holly. Loudon's approach to cemetery planting was as influential as his practical and hygienic approach to design: in a critique of the existing planting at Norwood Cemetery published in his 1843 book, Loudon describes the prevailing style as that of the 'pleasure grounds'. His alternative 'cemetery' style of planting made much more use of evergreens, partly for their symbolic value in suggesting eternal life, and partly for hygienic reasons to avoid damp, rotting leaves which could harbour disease and inhibit rapid decomposition, as well as giving an unfortunate impression to visitors.

An alternative commercial approach was adopted by the London Necropolis and National Mausoleum Company which opened the monumental Brookwood Cemetery or Woking Necropolis on a tract of Surrey heathland in 1852. The largest cemetery in England, Brookwood aspired to address, once and for all, London's burial crisis. This was to be achieved by means of the Company's private rail service, linking a private station in

Westminster Bridge Road to the cemetery where both coffins and mourners disembarked for burial services in one of the chapels designed by Sir William Tite and burial in the extensive consecrated or un-consecrated sections. Sections of the consecrated area were set aside for the exclusive use of various City of London parishes such as St Alban, Holborn, whose historic burial grounds were full; contracts were also negotiated with various London Poor Law Unions for the burial of their dead, thus ensuring that the Company made some attempt to deal with burial across the social spectrum. Despite the grandeur of the concept and the lavish planting of the cemetery which offered Londoners a permanent resting place in 'rural tranquillity', the development of cemeteries by vestries and other civil authorities in London following burial reforms enacted in the early 1850s meant that many preferred to bury their dead closer to home. Visionary Brookwood thus failed to secure the future it might reasonably have hoped for, and its decline was accelerated by the destruction of the funeral train and private station during World War II. It remains a privately operated cemetery today, and is a remarkable monument to the Victorian integration of utility and aesthetics.

Brookwood did, however, have an enduring legacy overseas. In Australia the Government of New South Wales acquired land for a cemetery in 1862 which opened as Rookwood Cemetery in 1868. This was closely modelled on Brookwood, with a rail link to the cemetery from a splendid private 'Despatching Station' in Sydney, the stonework of which is decorated with various symbols of mortality and resurrection. At home, the Corporation of Birmingham proposed a cemetery at Knowle in the Warwickshire countryside to be linked to the town by train, but this scheme fell victim to political infighting in 1859. Provision for train-borne funerals was made in the design of the City of London Cemetery at Little Ilford, Essex (1856); however, the platforms at the cemetery appear not to have been constructed. For a brief period between 1861 and 1863, a rail service operated to the Great Northern Cemetery at Colney Hatch out of King's Cross Station. This appears to have been intended for the use of poorer families rather than the social cross section which patronised Brookwood.

Municipal or 'Burial Board' cemeteries

During the 1830s and 1840s events, usually in the form of epidemic disease, had forced some municipal authorities to provide cemeteries for the burial of their dead. Exeter appears to have been among the earliest, if not the first, municipal authority to lay out a new cemetery in response to particularly severe cholera outbreaks in 1832. St Bartholomew's Cemetery was laid out by the City's Improvement Commissioners in 1836–7 to the design of Thomas Whitaker, their Surveyor. The cemetery landscape was relatively simple, but its structures, including a range of catacombs set into the medieval city wall, and monumental gates and granite gate piers were all conceived in the Egyptian style, significantly pre-dating its use at Highgate (1839) and Abney Park (1840). Elsewhere, Becket Street Cemetery, Leeds was opened by the Town Council in 1845, and in the same year the Corporation at Coventry commissioned no less a figure than Joseph Paxton (1803–65), Head Gardener to the 6th Duke of Devonshire to lay out a new cemetery for the town. The site included a former quarried area above which Paxton dramatically placed the Norman revival Anglican Chapel. A neo-classical chapel at the opposite end of the cemetery was provided for non-conformists, and the whole site was lavishly planted with a wide range of ornamental trees and shrubs reflecting both Paxton's horticultural interests and the Corporation's desire to display its wealth and taste through the design of its new cemetery. In order to ensure that the cemetery continued to develop in accordance with his original vision, Paxton installed one of his under-gardeners from Chatsworth, Richard Ashwell, as its first superintendent.[15]

Prior to the enactment of the 'Burial Acts' of 1852 and 1853 which gave the Privy Council and the Secretary of State powers to close existing burial grounds and graveyards where they were injurious to public health, and empowered parishes and other municipal authorities to set up Burial Boards which could raise a rate from inhabitants in order to form new, inter-denominational cemeteries, municipally provided cemeteries were exceptional. A further consolidatory Amendment Act was passed in 1857.

Following the passage of the various Burial Acts, the number of cemeteries formed in England increased dramatically, with many municipal authorities taking advantage of the new provisions to create municipal cemeteries in the 1850s and 1860s. To date little work appears to have been undertaken to differentiate between these sites: some have been added to the Register of Parks and Gardens as designed landscapes of national significance, but there are undoubtedly nationally significant examples, in some cases of greater significance than those already designated, which have been missed.

Many Burial Board cemeteries are essentially utilitarian in character and can never have offered much of an aesthetic of commemoration or consolation to the bereaved. Others, however, stand out for the way in which hard landscaping, planting and buildings are integrated into a successful aesthetic entity which gives opportunities for restful reflection and hopeful consolation. Some may be quite simple but powerful; others more complex. But each successful cemetery design combines planting, structures and underlying structural design in an overall aesthetic vision.

Burial Board cemeteries were established by a wide range of communities. Some, such as South Petherton, Somerset (1867) were very small rural communities; others such as Trowbridge, Wiltshire (1855) or Shipston on Stour, Warwickshire (1865) were small market towns. Spas and seaside resorts as well as industrial and manufacturing towns in the Midlands and North all quickly established public cemeteries under the Burial Acts' provisions. The early Burial Board cemeteries tended to make use of a wide range of conifers and evergreen shrubs, often within a relatively formal framework; only towards the end of the nineteenth century, with the formation of cemeteries such as Manchester Southern (1879) or the work of designers such as H.E. Milner (1819–84) at Hartshill Cemetery, Stoke on Trent (1882) was there a return to a more naturalistic, pleasure ground style of planting. Horticultural effects such as floral bedding and topiary also re-emerged as features of the cemetery landscape in the 1870s, having been proscribed as unsuitable by Loudon in 1843.

Some architects and designers developed a specialism in providing designs for laying out Burial Board cemeteries. In the north and east of England, for instance, the York architect J.P. Pritchett (1789–1868) designed cemeteries for a significant number of Burial Boards, including Boston (1854); Tottenham (1855); Sudbury (1855); St Andrew's, Newcastle upon Tyne (1855); Saffron Walden (1855); Darlington (1856); Scarborough (1856); Mansfield (1857); and Weaste Cemetery, Salford (1857); his practice continued to provide designs for cemeteries into the 1890s.[16] Similarly, the Cheltenham architect W.H. Knight provided designs not only for the chapels, lodges and gates at Bouncer's Lane Cemetery, Cheltenham (1864), but also for the cemeteries at Hereford (1858); Great Malvern (1861) and Shipston on Stour (1865). In common with the vast majority of designs for Burial Board cemeteries, these architects tended to produce Gothic structures which accorded with prevailing sensibilities. Separate chapels for the use of Anglicans and Dissenters were usually provided in order to conform to the requirements of Anglican Canon Law. Sometimes two physically separate structures were built, providing the focal point to the consecrated and un-consecrated sections of the site as at Great Torrington, Devon (1854), Trowbridge[17] (1855) or Falmouth (1857); but in other cases the chapels would be built parallel to each other or at right angles with a linking *porte-cochère* which was frequently surmounted by a tower and spire. W.H. Knight's chapels at Bouncer's Lane Cemetery are a very fine example of this genre, which he repeated on a much smaller scale for the more rural cemetery at Shipston on Stour a year later.

Such a pragmatic and economic solution to providing accommodation for Anglican and non-conformist funerals was not acceptable to all Church of England prelates. Henry Philpotts (1778–1869), the High Church Bishop of Exeter, insisted that Canon Law required consecrated and un-consecrated ground to be separated by a physical barrier such as a wall or fence. The refusal of several Burial Boards in his diocese (which in the mid-nineteenth century included Cornwall) to accede to his wishes in this matter led to lengthy delays in securing consecration for the Anglican section of, among others, the cemeteries at Great Torrington and Falmouth. The remains of the wall which was erected to divide St Bartholomew's Cemetery in Exeter are still visible today. The 1857 Burial Act sought to clarify this issue and stated that suitable markers of stone or iron were sufficient to meet the legal requirements of the Church of England. Usually these 'divisional markers' are small, relatively insignificant features, but at Rochdale Cemetery (1855), under the direction of local geologists James Horsfall and Robert Law, the markers comprise 27 short stone pillars, each different and inscribed with its name, and placed in geological sequence. This appears to be a unique survival of the didactic objectives which Loudon had suggested could be expressed through cemetery design, planting and ornamentation (1843).

Burial Board cemeteries offered municipal authorities the opportunity to express civic pride through the quality of cemetery design and ornamentation; and also an opportunity to express, through the cemetery design, a unique sense of place. At Bournemouth the Burial Board instructed the town architect, Christopher Crabbe Creeke (1820–86), to design a cemetery for the resort which opened in 1878. Placed in a prominent position on the principal road leading out of the town, the cemetery entrance and chapel spire form an important visual incident in Crabbe's townscape. This was further emphasised c.1890 when the principal cemetery drive leading to the chapel was planted with an avenue of alternate monkey puzzles and golden hollies (Figure 10.2).

Clearly, as at resorts such as Bath, Cheltenham and Weston super Mare, the cemetery was seen by the municipal authorities as an expression of civic pride and an important amenity of the town – not least for visitors for whom the sea air or mineral waters failed to prove entirely restorative. As late as 1909 the Urban District Council of Handsworth commissioned a cemetery scheme from the notable Birmingham Arts and Craft architect

Figure 10.2 Wimborne Road Cemetery, Bournemouth, is a relatively late example of a 'Burial Board' cemetery which opened in 1878. The chapel with its spire, designed by Christopher Crabbe Creeke (1820–86), forms a focal point in the townscape, while the avenue of monkey puzzles and golden hollies, planted c.1900, is a testament to municipal pride in its cemetery (author's own).

Figure 10.3 The monumental entrance lodge designed by Henry Clutton (1819–93) for Plymouth Road Cemetery, Tavistock, Devon, donated to the parish by the Duke of Bedford in 1881 is built in Dartmoor granite and is clearly modelled on a medieval tithe barn. It was intended to recall the town's origins at the gates of Tavistock Abbey, the estates of which were acquired by the Duke's ancestors at the time of the Reformation (author's own).

W.H. Bidlake (1861–1938). The surviving chapel (modelled, apparently, on Albi Cathedral, France), entrance lodge, entrance gates and a monumental stone flight of steps attest to the money that Handsworth was prepared to lavish upon its cemetery, not least to cement its position as one of the more desirable and affluent suburbs of Birmingham. However, before the cemetery could be completed, Handsworth was subsumed into an expanded City of Birmingham and the mundane landscape and planting fails to live up to Bidlake's original intent.

The link between a cemetery and the community which it served could also be expressed through its design. At Poole Cemetery (1854), for example, Christopher Crabbe Creeke ensured that there were views from within the cemetery to Poole Harbour, to which the town owed much of its prosperity; similarly at Teignmouth, Devon (1855) the designer of the cemetery ensured that a view of the sea was framed by the *porte-cochère* linking the chapels. At Plymouth Road Cemetery, Tavistock (1882), also in Devon (Figure 10.3), the sense of place is more subtly expressed: here Henry Clutton (1819–93), architect to the Duke of Bedford, who provided the site for the cemetery, executed the buildings in local Dartmoor granite and designed the entrance lodge and office to resemble a medieval tithe barn, a discreet reference to the medieval Tavistock Abbey which the Duke's ancestors had acquired after its Dissolution. This relatively late Burial Board cemetery is a particularly fine unregistered example of the genre, which has a rare but not unique 'heart' or 'tear-drop' pattern of drives which nicely expresses the Victorians' interest in symbolism in relation to death and commemoration.[18]

Twentieth-century changes in cemetery aesthetics

The legalisation of cremation in England in 1885 and the gradual rise in cremation as the usual form of committal marked the successful culmination of a long campaign waged by figures such as William Robinson (1838–1935), proprietor of *The Garden* and author of *God's Acre Beautiful, or The Cemeteries of the Future* (1880) which advocated a return to the aesthetic of a classically inspired Elysium for both cemeteries and the new commemorative landscapes which cremation would require. This aesthetic was to become almost normative for twentieth-century Gardens of Remembrance attached to English crematoria, many of which were designed by Edward White (1873–1952), Principal of the landscape practice Milner, Son and White, and along with Robinson, an early advocate of cremation.

Part of the appeal of cremation as a form of committal in the early twentieth century seems to have been the equality of both service and memorialisation which it offered. This equality in the face of death is similarly seen in the development of the aesthetic for the military cemeteries created by the Imperial War Graves Commission following the First World War. The simple, dignified design for headstones adopted by the Commission, in the face of stiff opposition from, among others, a group of Bishops' wives, provided not only a uniform and equal form of commemoration for men of all ranks and services, but also avoided distinction on the grounds of religion or denomination. This was a truly radical break with nineteenth-century memorialisation, where the emphasis had been on individuality and, very often, conspicuous display of wealth, status and faith. Similarly, the design of the Commission's cemeteries, on which it was advised by the foremost architects of the day including Edwin Lutyens (1869–1944), Herbert Baker (1862–1946) and Reginald Blomfield (1856–1942), did not differentiate on grounds of class or rank but provided a dignified, formal layout with buildings often of outstanding quality, and planting which Gertrude Jekyll (1843–1932) advised should reflect the flowers of the cottage and suburban gardens which the men might have known at home. The war cemeteries of both World Wars, but particularly those of World War I, are arguably the finest achievement of English commemorative landscape design. Most are located in Continental Europe, but some notable examples, such as the Military Cemetery at Brookwood, Surrey or the cemetery associated with the Royal Victoria Hospital, Gosport can be seen this side of the Channel. All are admirably maintained by the Commonwealth War Graves Commission.

While it was possible for the War Graves Commission to impose a uniform approach to memorialisation in its cemeteries, the powerful aesthetic which it achieved did not find general favour in the post-war period. At Saffron Hill Cemetery, Leicester (1929), Thomas (1861–1933) and Edward Prentice Mawson (1885–1954) took inspiration from contemporary American 'lawn' cemeteries, which aimed for a simple dignity of design in which memorials, while not necessarily uniform, were small and subservient to the overall landscape scheme. Such an approach did not find favour in Leicester where, according to the Cemeteries Committee Minutes, the ratepayers would not accept such regulation of their memorials. The result is a fine cemetery layout in the Beaux Arts tradition, with a good Romanesque revival chapel and Georgian-style lodges and wrought-iron gates; compromised by a discordant collection of individual monuments. This is typical of the vast majority of mid- and late twentieth-century English cemeteries, where economy, utility and banality have combined to create landscapes devoid of comfort or inspiration. While crematoria Gardens of Remembrance have attracted the skills of leading landscape designers, by and large cemeteries have continued to be laid out by engineers to a debased late nineteenth-century pattern. A notable exception to this generalisation would be the late twentieth-century cemetery at Poundbury, Dorset with buildings and structures designed by Paul Scott of Dorchester. The central baldacchino, recalling those of early churches, forms the focal point of the design and is inscribed with various sentences, including that from Revelation 21:1 'And I saw a new heaven and a new earth'; perhaps an appropriate point of departure for any aspiring cemetery designer.

Conservation issues affecting cemeteries

The latter part of the twentieth century saw a series of conservation pressures threatening historic cemetery landscapes. In many places cemeteries have become 'no go' areas, places which are best avoided: partly because of a general aversion to confront obvious signs of

Figure 10.4 Anti-social behaviour associated with cemeteries takes a variety of forms, of which camping among the gravestones is probably relatively benign. However, the perception that anti-social behaviour may be encountered in a cemetery helps to fuel a downward spiral of abandonment, decay and neglect (author's own).

human mortality; and partly because of a self-fulfilling perception that these are the haunt of the socially undesirable or those with anti-social characteristics. The less frequented by 'normal' citizens cemeteries become, the more inevitable it is that they are claimed by the 'abnormal', fuelling a downward cycle of decay, damage and neglect (Figure 10.4). In times of public sector austerity, 'no go' areas are not a high priority for funding, and 'cost effective' (which is to say cheap) management techniques can inflict serious damage on the historic fabric of such sites.

One approach to eradicating 'anti-social' behaviour has been to remove the vegetation within cemeteries to diminish 'cover'. While overgrown trees and shrubbery might benefit from sensitive and appropriate management, wholesale clearance is clearly inappropriate and damaging: it should be evident from the analysis of the cemetery landscape aesthetic above that planting is an integral element of that aesthetic, providing the visual framework within which monuments should be appreciated and heightening the visual and sensual experience of the landscape. Removal, or even insensitive management, of vegetation forming part of the original layout of the cemetery, significantly diminishes its historic and aesthetic integrity as well as its commemorative and reflective function.

If managing vegetation within cemeteries poses a significant problem for cash-strapped local authorities, monuments create even greater problems in this 'health and safety' conscious age. In both municipal and commercial cemeteries, the right to erect a monument over a grave entailed the payment of a fee, often intended to be applied to an endowment fund to cover future maintenance. In few, if any cases, have such funds proved adequate – or even survived to the present. Crumbling Victorian monuments obviously can pose a danger to the foolhardy or intrepid; and few descendants of those commemorated are willing to fund costly repairs, even if the local authority has the will or resources to attempt to track them down. The result, visible in far too many cemeteries, are rows of headstones and – ironically – particularly crosses (which appear intrinsically unstable) laid down on the ground, or disfigured by statutory 'safety' notices resembling parking tickets (Figure 10.5). Over-zealous laying down, or even worse removal, of monuments again has a significantly adverse impact on the historic significance and integrity of the cemetery landscape; while removal of monuments to ease mowing or other maintenance is entirely unjustifiable. Issues

Figure 10.5 A major monument in the Abbey Cemetery, Bath (1843), roped off after failing a safety test. Monuments, whether significant works of art in their own right, or simple headstones, play an integral role in the cemetery landscape aesthetic, and their loss through 'laying down' or demolition is significantly detrimental to the integrity of the landscape design. Relatively unusually for a provincial cemetery, this and several other monuments in the Abbey Cemetery are now listed in their own right. This monument has now been repaired and the visually intrusive barrier removed (author's own).

of monument safety and testing, as well as other management issues affecting cemeteries, are discussed in English Heritage's valuable publications *Paradise Preserved* (2007) and *Caring for Historic Graveyard and Cemetery Monuments* (2011).[19]

Clearly the most effective management tool for cemeteries, as with any other publicly accessible designed landscape, is to ensure that they are well visited and appreciated. A recent survey of cemeteries in Manchester considered to be potentially 'At Risk' showed that those which remained in use for burials, or which contained a working crematorium, were in a significantly better condition than those which were closed and therefore little frequented.[20] Despite being apparently 'full', many cemeteries in fact contain significant reserves of unused space, usually in older graves which were never filled to their maximum potential. It is a tricky and emotive subject, but in some instances, most notably at the City of London Cemetery, this potential is being realised through imaginative initiatives such as the Heritage Grave Scheme which enables people to purchase vacant grave space and, at the same time, to conserve the historic monument on the grave.[21] Apart from assisting with the sensitive conservation of the cemetery landscape and its integral structures, schemes such as this help to address the acute shortage of burial space which again threatens London and other metropolitan areas without resorting to the extensive cemetery clearance and reuse which has sometimes been advocated.

Cemeteries, whether nationally designated or not, are a hugely valuable aspect of our national heritage, commemorating past generations of prominent and ordinary citizens alike, and allowing an insight into the attitudes of our ancestors to both life and death. Those cemeteries which are included on the English Heritage Register of Parks and Gardens, and no doubt some others which have not yet been designated, are the most significant examples of this landscape type and an important record of social and aesthetic history. All deserve careful management and conservation. Two factors above all others are vital to this process: the formation of a conservation management plan, identifying the distinctive features of the landscape, its strengths and challenges; and flowing from this process, the thoughtful promotion of the cemetery landscape to the local community as a place of which they can be proud and in which they can take a direct interest, whether that is genealogical, recreational, historic, restorative or, dare one suggest, spiritual.

Endnotes

1. Prior to the Reformation in England, the parochial charnel crypt or bone house would have been a familiar feature of many churches or churchyards. Thence bones disturbed in the digging of fresh graves, or removed as part of a more concerted clearance in order to make additional burial space, would be taken for storage. The famous epitaph on William Shakespeare's tomb in Holy Trinity Church, Stratford upon Avon is best understood when it is recalled that the parish possessed a large charnel house and crypt (only demolished in the late nineteenth century): *Good Friend for Jesu's sake forbear to dig the dust enclosed here. Blest be the man that spares these stones, And curst be he that moves my bones.* Following the Reformation, with the rise of a greater emphasis upon the individual, removal of bones to a communal repository gradually became unacceptable, thus exacerbating the pressure placed by a growing population on space in churchyards which remained unchanged since the medieval period.
2. For example, J. Stevens Curl, *A Celebration of Death* (rev. edition 1993), p. 157: 'Most burial reformers took Pere-Lachaise as their model . . .'.
3. J. Strang, *Necropolis Glasguensis with Observations on Ancient and Modern Tombs and Sepulture* (1831).
4. Burial grounds had been formed to provide additional space for interments since the early seventeenth century in cities such as Exeter where existing parochial churchyards had become full (Bartholomew Yard, Exeter, consecrated 1637); the more famous Bunhill Fields, London, was established as a burial ground for dissenters (i.e. non-Anglicans) in 1663. Abroad, burial grounds were established at Rome (Protestant or non-Catholic Cemetery, Porta S Paulo, *c*.1700) for non-Catholic members of the exiled Stuart Court, while in India the East India Company provided for the burial of its deceased Servants at Calcutta (South Park Street Cemetery, 1767).
5. In addition to burial grounds such as Bunhill Fields which catered for non-Anglicans, burial grounds were also created specifically for Jewish congregations, such as Plymouth (1744), Exeter (1757), Canterbury (1760) and Falmouth (1789–90).
6. As reported at St Aldate's, Oxford in 1843 (see *Victoria History of the County of Oxfordshire*, IV (1979), p. 364), and Talland, parish church of West Looe, Cornwall as late as 1874 (see W. Robinson, *God's Acre Beautiful* (1880), pp. 90–91 quoting *The Times*, 1874).
7. Charles Dickens, *Bleak House* (1852–3). The model for the burial ground described was that of St Mary le Strand, Russell Court, Catherine Street.
8. The entire second and third volumes of *Antichita Romane* were devoted to views of remains of sepulchral monuments to be found in Rome and its environs. In 1757 Piranesi was made an honorary member of the Society of Antiquarians in London.
9. According to the architectural historian Sir Howard Colvin (1919–2007), John Foster designed the neoclassical entrance and chapel for the Liverpool or Low Hill Necropolis, a burial ground for dissenters which opened in 1825 – see H. Colvin, *A Biographical Dictionary of British Architects 1600–1840* (1995), p. 375.
10. C. Brooks, *Mortal Remains* (1989), p.124.
11. *Gardener's Magazine* (1839), p.456.
12. The initial landscape design has been attributed to John Griffith (1796–1888), Chairman of the General Cemetery Company, probably in association with the Hon Thomas Liddell who is stated to have drawn up a scheme 'under the eye of' John Nash – see J. Stevens Curl (1993), pp. 218–19. The final scheme appears to have been the work of Richard Forrest, former Head Gardener at Syon House, Middlesex – see *The Gardener's Chronicle* (1848).
13. Prince George, Duke of Cambridge, Commander in Chief of the British Army and grandson of King George III, was also buried at Kensal Green in 1904.
14. Loudon provided designs for the Abbey Cemetery, Bath which was laid out on land provided by the Rector of Bath; Cambridge General Cemetery (Histon Road Cemetery); and Southampton General Cemetery which was established by the town council. Of these, only the design for Cambridge was implemented as provided by Loudon.

15. Interestingly Ashwell went on to provide the design for Witton Cemetery, Birmingham in 1861 and the landscape design for the Warwickshire County Lunatic Asylum at Hatton in 1846–52. At Birkenhead Park Paxton installed another Chatsworth gardener, Edward Kemp, as superintendent. Kemp went on to design cemeteries at Anfield, Liverpool (1860) and Birkenhead Cemetery (1863). Ashwell and Kemp were not alone in starting their career as a cemetery designer as a superintendent: William Gay was appointed superintendent of Hamilton and Medland's Welford Road Cemetery, Leicester when it opened in 1849 and subsequently went on to design Undercliffe Cemetery, Bradford (1854) and Philips Park Cemetery, Manchester (1866).
16. Pritchett had trained in the office of James Medland, whose son, also James Medland, was a Gloucester architect who, in partnership with J.R. Hamilton, designed Warstone Lane Cemetery, Birmingham (1848), Welford Road Cemetery, Leicester (1848) and Ford Park Cemetery, Plymouth (1848).
17. Designed by C.E. Davis of Bath, who was also responsible for Weston super Mare Cemetery (1855) and Lyncombe Cemetery, Bath (1859).
18. At Preston, Lancashire (1855) the cemetery drives and paths form an even more unusual 'butterfly' design; the butterfly, emerging from its chrysalis, was seen as a symbol of resurrection and life after death.
19. Both publications are available online at www.english-heritage.org.uk/publications.
20. Unpublished survey undertaken in 2011 for English Heritage by Jonathan Lovie and Dr Sarah Rutherford.
21. See www.cityoflondon.gov.uk/thingstodo/green-spaces/cemetery-and-crematorium/conservation-and-heritage/Pages/Grave-reuse.aspx

11 Researching historic parks and gardens

David Lambert
Director of the Parks Agency, Gloucestershire, UK

At the heart of conservation planning for historic places lies understanding. And at the heart of understanding a place lies research into its historical development; how did it come to look the way it does; what changes has it gone through – designed or accidental, since it was first created. Without that basic research, informed decisions about future management and about conservation or change cannot be made, nor can the significance of the place or its component parts be properly assessed.

The conservation management plan (CMP) is becoming increasingly cumbersome, but this core material, which might once have been called a historic landscape survey, remains vitally important. Whether in the body of the plan or in an appendix, the survey will bring together all available documentary evidence for the past appearance of the site, and explain the present appearance and condition of each area or feature in the light of that evidence.

It is not possible to present a one-size-fits-all template for historical research. Every place is different and the historical resources available vary enormously from site to site. The one principle which remains constant, however, is that documentary research gives only a partial picture; it must be weighed continually against field evidence, evidence that can only be gleaned from walking the site repeatedly. The landscape needs to be read with the help of documents and documents need to be read with the help of detailed knowledge of the ground. It is in this interplay that a true picture – true but inevitably only ever partial – emerges. This chapter describes some techniques for documentary research but it should never be forgotten that the fieldwork is of equal importance.

For the purposes of this chapter, 'documentary' will be taken to encompass both primary manuscript material and secondary printed material. It will look at the range of documents and sources for research. With the continuing rapid growth of online resources for historical research, it cannot possibly remain an up-to-date guide but it can set out the main areas of investigation, wherever the sources in future can be accessed.

Storage and reference system

Research generates a large variety of material which needs to be organised into a research archive, not only for immediate use, but for the future. In some cases, the research archive will form part of the project to be handed over with a report, but in all events, it needs to be organised in a form that can be revisited in the future.

Most material will be collected or recorded in digital form. Digital copying services are available at virtually all repositories, most of which will also allow the use of private digital cameras. Notes taken in repositories can be made directly onto a laptop or tablet; where they are written longhand they will need to be typed up and stored digitally. Decisions on how to organise this material are a matter of personal choice, but separating material into different folders (e.g. Notes) and sub-folders (for example notes from a visit to a particular repository) is very helpful. Jpeg files need to be renamed to make clear the material they represent. It need hardly be mentioned how important it is to keep an accurate record of repository call-up references and shelf-marks, publishing details and so on.

In some cases, especially with Ordnance Survey or other scale maps, it can be helpful to obtain hard copies from the research archive, as this has the benefit of preserving, approximately, their original scale. Details can then be digitised for use in a report or to make digital overlays using software such as Adobe Illustrator. It is often good value to buy full-size copy sheets of historic OS maps from the Ordnance Survey's appointed agents, such as Blackwell's.

In general hard copies should always be made or obtained in addition to digital versions. This is partly for practical reasons; for example, a folder of maps or images is often easier to use than separate digital files, although tablets and hand-held GPS kit have made it easier to work outside with digital maps. And it is also probably a better bet for future historians given the rapid obsolescence of digital operating systems.

First steps

The first step is to agree and define the study area; this may be a property boundary for a single site, or an administrative boundary for a wider survey of several sites. In the case of the former, changes in ownership may have, over time, resulted in fragmentation of a once larger estate, and it may well be necessary to extend research over a larger area than just the individual property.

Preliminary research used to be termed a 'desktop survey', but with online resources growing exponentially, an enormous amount of primary and secondary material can now be gathered from that desk and the line which defines it has become blurred.

An up-to-date base map at the largest scale appropriate to the site is essential at an early stage. These can be obtained from clients, local authorities or commercial operators such as Stanfords. Where a site is large, you will need a smaller-scale map for the whole site and larger-scale maps for individual areas within the site. You will need this base-plan on your first site visit to record field observations, and it will provide the base for other analytical plans such as maps of character areas, features, historic planting, views, etc. Provided you are happy to avail yourself of US military technology, you can also familiarise yourself with a site or sites using Google Earth; its history tool can also be useful in providing aerial photography from the 1940s onwards, and Google Streetview can also be very helpful at least around the entrances and boundaries of a site.

There are a number of search aids which can be consulted for tracking down the whereabouts of relevant documentary material and preparing a shopping list for further investigation. The National Archives at Kew has a database comprising the catalogues of many hundreds of individual archives, including county record offices, many museums, university and other collections, to which more are added each year. Its Access to Archives web-page (known as A2A, available at www.nationalarchives.gov.uk/a2a) allows visitors to search by key words or phrases, using place, personal or business names, identifying the location of relevant material and providing a summary description of individual items.

In addition, each record office or other repository will have its own website with additional search aids and online resources, which should be checked in addition to A2A. Many record offices, for example, have initiated digital imaging projects, making available online their collection of topographical images (for example the London Borough of Lambeth's Landmark collection at http://landmark.lambeth.gov.uk, or the Etched on Devon's Memory collection of engravings http://www.devon.gov.uk/localstudies/100134/2.html), while others have integrated these projects in their online search engines.

Not all repositories are fully indexed on A2A. For example, it is worthwhile checking separately what is held by the British Library (BL) (http://catalogue.bl.uk) which, in addition to its unparalleled collection of even the most obscure printed material, holds a huge range of manuscript documents, maps and illustrations. The BL in addition holds the original drawings made by the Ordnance Survey (OSDs) which, although digitised, are currently only available in the map room, although some local record offices have good hard copies.

Other potentially useful repositories currently not included on A2A but with online catalogues are the Royal Horticultural Society library (http://www.lindleylibrary.org.uk/uhtbin/cgisirsi.exe/x/0/0/49), the Victoria and Albert Museum (https://backup.micromediauk.net/vam) and the library of the Royal Institute of British Architects (RIBA) (http://www.architecture.com/LibraryDrawingsAndPhotographs/DrawingsAndArchives/ArchivesCollection.aspx). The RHS library contains some important manuscripts but also a wide range of horticultural publications, and provides easy access to a wide range of nineteenth-century periodicals. The Victoria and Albert Museum (V&A) has the largest collection of topographical prints and drawings in the UK. The RIBA holds a number of architects' collections and thousands of individual drawings, now held at the V&A, although its library and its biographical reference files remain at its headquarters in Portland Place, London.

It is always worth consulting the National Monuments Record (NMR), now part of the English Heritage Archives, at Swindon. The NMR holds one of the largest collections of aerial photographs, both oblique and vertical, in the country (the other is held by Cambridge University Library), and an inquiry will give a list of those holdings (http://www.english-heritage.org.uk/forms/updated-versions/archive-originals/nmr-enquiry). A visit however allows the researcher access to the NMR's 'red boxes', which, organised by parish name, contain miscellaneous photographs, mainly of listed buildings but also occasionally of archival items such as estate maps, copies of articles or pages from guide books, etc. Contents of the red boxes are generally not included in response to an inquiry.

Three invaluable reference books can also give helpful leads. Howard Colvin's *Biographical Dictionary of British Architects, 1600–1840* (3rd edition, New Haven and London: Yale University Press, 1995) includes references to primary sources, while Ray Desmond's *A Bibliography of British Gardens* (Winchester: St Paul's Bibliographies, 1984, reprinted as *A Bibliography of British and Irish Gardens*, 1996) gives a bibliography of secondary sources for a huge range of individual sites. Thirdly, the *Victoria County History*, which is now available through British History Online at http://www.british-history.ac.uk often contains in its references both primary and secondary material which can be followed up. The British History Online website also provides access to early Ordnance Survey maps; although not of high quality, they can be useful at this initial stage. Where Desmond notes that a place has been the subject of an article in *Country Life* magazine, inquiries should be made to its Picture Library, which can supply copies of original photographs, and which also often has additional photographs not used in the article.

A good deal of background statutory material can also be collected at this initial stage. Descriptions of, for example listed buildings, registered gardens and scheduled ancient monuments, is available online from the English Heritage Archives site (http://www.englishheritagearchives.org.uk) and also from the Heritage Gateway site (http://www.heritagegateway.org.uk/gateway); a search of the latter by place name will also bring up locally held material in record offices and the Historic Environment Records maintained by the local authority. The UK Parks and Gardens Database (http://www.parksandgardens.ac.uk) contains a range of material including extracts from the English Heritage Register and County Gardens Trusts' (CGTs) survey material.

It may also be worth contacting the local CGTs direct. Many of these voluntary groups have assembled survey material as part of their core activities, while others have indexed material in their local record offices; and not all that material has yet been entered on the UK Parks and Gardens Database. Contact details are available from the umbrella organisation, the Association of Gardens Trusts (http://www.gardenstrusts.org.uk).

Finally it is always worth simply 'googling' place or personal names, as this can yield some surprising leads. There are many more online resources but these will generally be helpful at a later stage in the research once key dates and names have emerged: *The Dictionary of National Biography*, the *Times* and the Manchester *Guardian* for example are all fully available via local libraries and searchable online. Where appropriate, http://www.thepeerage.com gives excellent summaries of often complicated biographies and family trees.

Repositories

Even if an initial desktop search suggests that the county, city or borough record office does not have material specifically relating to a site or sites, it will hold material which is relevant.

A phone call in advance is often required (see the record office website for opening hours and booking arrangements) and always a good idea. It may well be necessary to book a map table. A phone call also allows you to check on individual rules about digital photography. The usual shopping list of non-specific documents would include early editions of all Ordnance Survey maps, other printed county or town maps, tithe maps, illustrative material and sale particulars for private sites, and council papers for public parks.

It is also worth ascertaining from the website whether the record office also contains the county or city reference and local history library – many of these have been amalgamated in recent years, for example the Surrey History Centre or the Wiltshire and Swindon History Centre.

Most record office staff are quite interested in inquiries which are not about genealogy, but it always helps to be as specific as possible. Staff are generally happy to steer a researcher towards relevant search aids, principally the indexes and catalogues, but also other guides such as a hand-list of tithe and enclosure maps or quarter-sessions records, or the key map for identifying relevant OS sheets.

The principal guides to the material in a record office are catalogues. These are systematically arranged descriptions of collections of material, for example a family collection, business or council collection. Within the catalogue, the descriptions will work their way through various sub-groups of papers, so for example an estate or family collection will deal in turn with manorial papers, deeds, estate papers, maps and plans, personal papers, papers relating to key activities of individuals, and a miscellaneous collection which might include anything from printed ephemera to photo albums.

Making sense of the catalogues is generally helped by indexes. The extent of these has traditionally varied according to the resources of the individual record office, but digitisation has helped considerably. Nevertheless, most record offices will have indexes by personal and place name, and will also have indexes of maps and plans, sale particulars, and sometimes illustrative material.

Once material has been identified either by a word-search in an online catalogue, or by an index, it is sensible then to read the relevant catalogue description, which will often give more information. Only then should material be ordered.

Maps and plans

Despite its militaristic origins in the defence preparations during the Napoleonic Wars, the Ordnance Survey mapping is one of the glories of British history. The original surveyors'

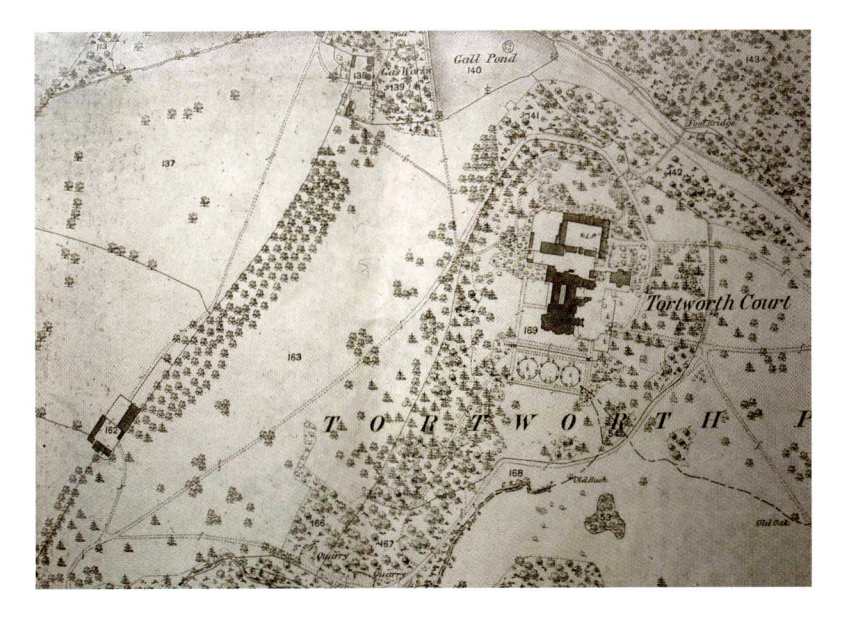

Figure 11.1 Tortworth Court, Gloucestershire, from the 1879 25-inch Ordnance Survey.

drawings (OSDs) are held in the British Library and are an extremely useful source. Although drawn for the first edition 1 inch: 1 mile maps, they were drawn at 2 inch scale which means they have more detail, and they date generally from several years prior to the 1 inch when it was eventually published. Although isolated surveys were made in Kent in the 1780s, the decision to survey the whole country was taken in 1795 and was largely complete by 1815. The printed 1 inch maps appeared between 1801 and 1844, but publication was delayed towards the end as the demand for larger-scale maps increased.

Although the 1 inch is an invaluable record, the most useful OS maps are those at a larger scale. The 25-inch survey began in 1854 and was completed in 1893 (Figure 11.1). The 6-inch set was a scaled-down version of this and 6-inch maps were generally published shortly after each 25-inch map. In addition, between 1855 and 1895 the OS surveyed some 400 large towns at a scale of 1:500 or 10 foot:1 mile; 58 towns, chiefly in Yorkshire and Lancashire, were surveyed slightly earlier; 1843–66. After the first edition of any given sheet, revisions were published about every ten to fifteen years until the 1930s, and after World War II the OS began to issue large-scale maps under its National Grid programme.

Although containing the same information, both 6 inch and 25 inch are useful, depending on the size of the study area. The 6 inch has an additional advantage, in the convention it employs to indicate parkland in grey stippling. The 25 inch is of course more legible, while its coloured form has the advantage not only of picking out buildings and water in blue, but roads in a yellow-brown tint. The latter can be particularly helpful in, for example, identifying principal routes around a landscape park.

Record offices generally have a good collection of OS maps, though rarely a complete one. Copies of all editions of 1 inch, 6 inch and 25 inch should be obtained, preferably, as mentioned above, in the form of photocopies to ensure comparability of scale and to help in making overlays. The best guide to the history of the OS and to its mapping conventions is J.B. Harley, *Ordnance Survey Maps: Descriptive Manual*, 1979, of which most record offices have a copy.

The OS was not the first large-scale map available for sale. Christopher Saxton had produced his 34 county maps between 1574 and 1579 and they heralded two centuries of commercial map-making. In the mid- to late eighteenth century, cartographers such as John Rocque, Thomas Jefferys, Isaac Taylor and in the early nineteenth century the brothers C.

Figure 11.2 Detail from parish tithe map for Madresfield parish, Worcestershire, showing Madresfield Court, 1841. (Diocese of Worcester and Worcestershire Record Office, s760 BA 1572/434. Reproduced with permission.)

& J. Greenwood were publishing large-scale maps of counties, cities and radial maps around cities and towns. Record offices will almost certainly have copies of these maps. They will also have many other county or city maps, and generally a map index; many early county maps are at too small a scale to do more than indicate whether a park or property was in existence at a given date, but the larger-scale maps will provide a good deal of useful information.

At a still larger scale almost every parish was surveyed between the end of the eighteenth century and the 1840s either for an enclosure or tithe award. Enclosure maps were prepared to accompany private acts to enclose common land in the parish. Although the first enclosures date from Tudor times, a large number were undertaken, as readers of the poet John Clare (1793–1864) will know, in the early nineteenth century. Where a parish was enclosed, the map is accompanied by a book detailing ownership, acreage and land use. The Record Office will have a hand-list to enclosure maps and awards as it will to tithe maps and awards. Tithe maps (Figure 11.2) were prepared after the Tithe Commutation Acts of 1836–60 and the majority date from the early 1840s. They were prepared at a large scale and annotated with key numbers on every parcel of land down to cottage plots. These numbers refer to the tithe award or apportionment, which gives details of the landowner, occupier (where different), acreage, land use, and the parcel's name. Many parishes had already been enclosed by the early to mid-nineteenth century, and in general, if an enclosure had recently taken place, no tithe award took place, as tithes would have been commuted at the time of the enclosure.

Sketch maps of road diversions, often associated with important changes to a designed landscape, can be found accompanying road orders in the Quarter Sessions Records. These are rarely indexed and can only be searched once key dates have been identified.

In the wake of the Public Health Act of 1848, some towns and cities, such as Warwick and Coventry, commissioned maps from the Ordnance Survey to assist in the laying of sewers, water pipes and drains. These are at a large scale and can be extremely helpful.

Many estates commissioned hand-drawn maps at key points in their history, whether a change of ownership, or before or after some major change. Estate maps in record offices are often highly finished presentation copies. They can be located either via a map index or via the maps and plans section of the catalogue of the relevant collection.

Plans were also prepared for public parks, either as proposals put before the councillors as working records, and where they survive they will be in the collections of the local authority. Public parks were often made out of pre-existing parks or gardens which will need to be researched; similarly, the previous land use will often have affected the way a park is laid out (whether reclaimed industrial land in which spoil was landscaped or agricultural land with hedgerows or other features).

Private estate papers

In the case of the larger, privately owned parks, estate records were a fundamental part of their smooth running, and they were maintained for many decades by staff whose livelihood depended on careful record-keeping. Where a collection is largely intact, it will contain numerous volumes of accounts, work-journals and letter books, and bundles of receipts, bills and correspondence. These records can contain particularly useful information about the timing and detail of work to a property (Figure 11.3).

More often there are phases of good record-keeping interspersed with periods from which little survives.

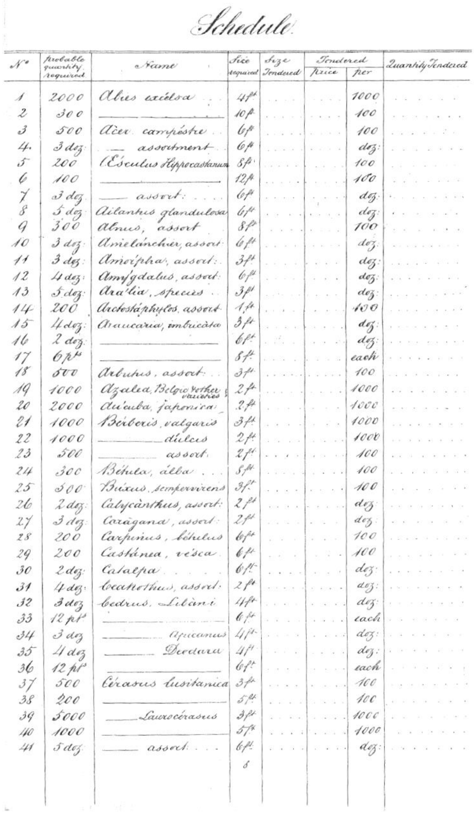

Schedule

Nº	probable quantity required	Name	Size required	Size Tendered	Tendered Price	Tendered per	Quantity Tendered
1	2000	Abies excélsa	4ft			1000	
2	300	———	10ft			100	
3	500	Acer campéstre	6ft			100	
4.	3 doz:	— assortment	6ft			doz:	
5	200	Æsculus Hippocastanum	8ft			100	
6	100	———	12ft			100	
7	3 doz	— assort:	6ft			doz:	
8	5 doz:	Ailantus glandulosa	6ft			doz:	
9	300	Alnus, assort	8ft			100	
10	3 doz:	Amelánchier, assort:	6ft			doz:	
11	3 doz:	Amorpha, assort:	3ft			doz:	
12	4 doz:	Amygdalus, assort:	6ft			doz:	
13	5 doz:	Ara'lia, species	3ft			doz:	
14	200	Arctostáphylos, assort	1ft			100	
15	4 doz:	Araucaria, imbricata	3ft			doz:	
16	2 doz:	———	6ft			doz:	
17	6 pts	———	8ft			each	
18	500	Arbutus, assort:	3ft			100	
19	1000	Azalea, Belgic & other varieties	2ft			1000	
20	2000	Au'cuba, japonica	2ft			1000	
21	1000	Bérberis, vulgaris	3ft			1000	
22	1000	——— dúlcis	2ft			1000	
23	500	——— assort.	2ft			100	
24	300	Bétula, álba	8ft			100	
25	500	Buxus, sempervirens	3ft			100	
26	2 doz:	Calycánthus, assort:	2ft			doz:	
27	3 doz:	Caragana, assort:	2ft			doz:	
28	200	Carpinus, bétulus	6ft			100	
29	200	Castánea, vesca	6ft			100	
30	2 doz:	Catalpa	6ft			doz:	
31	4 doz:	Ceanothus, assort:	2ft			doz:	
32	3 doz	Cedrus, Libàni	4ft			doz:	
33	12 pts	———	6ft			each	
34	3 doz	——— Africanus	4ft			doz:	
35	4 doz	——— Deodara	4ft			doz:	
36	12 pts	———	6ft			each	
37	500	Cérasus lusitanica	3ft			100	
38	200	———	5ft			100	
39	5000	——— Laurocérasus	3ft			1000	
40	1000	———	5ft			1000	
41	5 doz:	——— assort:	6ft			doz:	
			8				

Figure 11.3 First page of the 'Specification of Trees and Shrubs to be supplied to the City of London Cemetery now being formed at Little Ilford', 1856. (City of London Cemetery Papers, Box 2 (601 D, E.))

An estate collection may also contain copies of deeds, although the originals were also often deposited with solicitors. While they are key elements in piecing together the history of a site through changes in ownership, acquisitions of additional land, or sales of other parts, deeds can be challenging to understand. The best guide to making sense of them is N.W. Alcock's *Old Title Deeds* (2nd edition, Phillimore: Chichester, 2001). Where deeds are in solicitors' collections, the place-name index or search can usually locate them.

Manorial papers, where an estate owner was also lord of the manor, may also be included in an estate collection and can include useful surveys and terriers recording tenancies and boundaries.

Depending on the nature of the owner, a collection may also contain a large amount of personal correspondence and accounts; in addition it may often also contain items such as photograph albums, sketchbooks and notebooks with material relevant to the landscape history. Where a collection is directly linked to the study site, it is simplest just to work through the catalogue. Cataloguing has improved greatly over the years, and many archivists have written summaries of each individual letter and bill in often voluminous collections. Earlier cataloguers may just have noted a 'bdl. misc.', leaving the researcher to decide whether to investigate.

The most spectacular of items generally kept in estate collections are estate maps (Figure 11.4). Maps were usually prepared at a time of change, either of ownership or when development was proposed. Maps are usually surveys but they are sometimes proposals, and sometimes a survey is annotated with proposals. They were generally prepared by a professional land surveyor and are often quite highly finished. As a map of a relatively small area, they are usually at a large scale which makes them particularly useful.

Some estate collections stored in record offices remain the property of the owners, whose permission is required to access the papers. And many larger estates retain their archive collections on the property, some in conditions worthy of a record office with a dedicated archivist, such as Chatsworth, Derbyshire or Badminton, Gloucestershire; some in a cellar or a cupboard in an estate office.

Figure 11.4 Gobions, Hertfordshire, estate plan c.1735. (Gloucestershire Archives D1245 /FF.75. Reproduced with permission.)

Other material

In the case of more obscure properties, research often focuses on putting together the line of various owners. In identifying who was occupying a property at a given time, a number of sources can be of assistance, including poor law rate books, highway rate books, and land tax returns, along with the postal directories which were published from the late eighteenth century onwards with increasing frequency and detail, culminating in Kelly's *Directories* in the early twentieth century.

Record offices contain a range of illustrative material, principally photographs, prints and drawings. Many of these are scattered through a number of collections and will have been indexed. In some places, a collection will comprise the work of a local topographer, such as the beautifully illustrated travel diaries of the Reverend John Swete (1752–1821) compiled 1789–1800, and deposited in the Devon Record Office in 1959. It is always worth asking whether a record office has a local topographical collection. In addition, many record offices also have copies of relevant photographs by national figures such as Francis Frith (1822–98), although these are also now accessible online (http://www.francisfrith.com).

Most record offices have amassed large numbers of sale catalogues (Figure 11.5). Generally these will be the subject of a specific index, as they can be scattered throughout different collections, particularly solicitors' papers. Sale catalogues were first printed in the eighteenth century and in the nineteenth century gradually increased in detail and sophistication, especially for the more prestigious properties.

By the early twentieth century, many sales catalogues contained not only annotated maps and extensive descriptions, but also photographs.

Local authority records

Local authorities regularly deposit their archives in their local record office. Essentially, these comprise the minute-books of the various Council committees; that is, the record of decisions made and the reports of the various Council employees to those committees, on which those decisions were based. The history of public parks is such that very often there was no Parks committee at the initial stage, and decisions were made either by the full Council, by

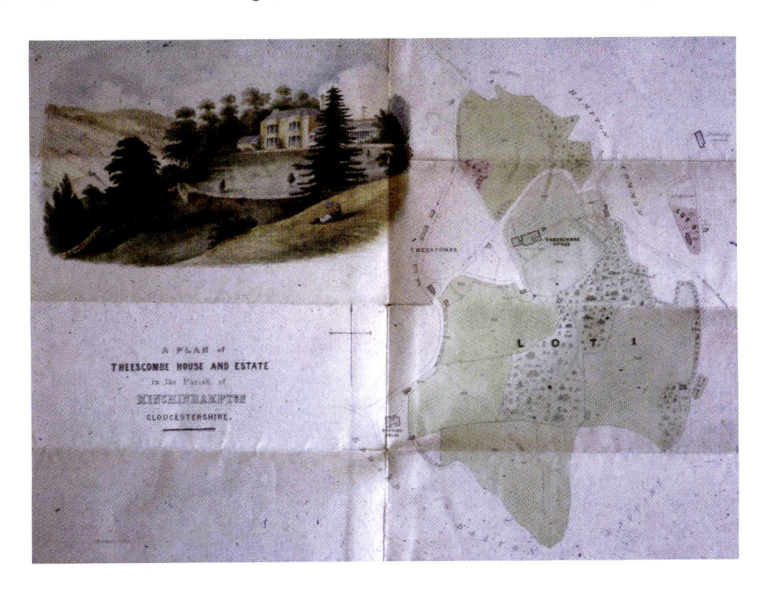

Figure 11.5 Theescombe, later known as Amberley Court, Gloucestershire, sale catalogue 1851. (Gloucestershire Record Office D1388 Box 91. Reproduced with permission.)

a Treasury or Finance committee, or in many cases by a Sanitary committee, the development of parks being initially a public health issue. Parks committees tended to be established subsequently. Committee minutes will record quite detailed decisions about a park, from the initial proposal, through every stage of expenditure, the opening and subsequent management issues. Reports will record proposals, tenders, costings, contractual matters, and later bulletins from parks' superintendents about a wide range of subjects from vandalism to park events.

A helpful complement to these two sources is provided by local newspapers. The Council papers will provide key dates, which can then be checked in the local press. The development of a park was both highly newsworthy and also often controversial so that the letters pages are often full of debate about a project.

Library

This brings us on to the local reference or local history library which will hold copies of the local newspapers, some going back as far as the eighteenth century. Local history libraries are dedicated to collecting the widest possible range of documentary material relating to their particular geographical area. While this is generally printed material it may well also include original documents, such as Bristol City Library's wonderful collection of some 3,000 pen and ink drawings by Samuel Loxton (1857–92), prepared for the *Bristol Observer* and the *Bristol Evening News* (later *Post*) (1888–1922) (Figure 11.6).

The printed material will include often sumptuous histories of the county or city. These were a niche market throughout much of the eighteenth and nineteenth centuries. Gloucestershire, for example, was the subject of Robert Atkyns' *Present and Ancient State of Glostershire* (1712), Samuel Rudder's *A New History Gloucestershire* (1779) and Thomas Dudley Fosbrooke's *History of Gloucestershire* (1803). Every county and large city was the subject of at least one such history and library staff will give you a steer if you do not have an author's name.

But those histories were thoroughly trumped in 1899 when the *Victoria County History* (VCH) series was established. This set out to provide encyclopaedic accounts of every county in England, parish by parish. It is based on fantastically detailed research in the public records

Figure 11.6 St Agnes Park, Bristol, drawn by the local artist Samuel Loxton, *c.*1910.

office, augmented by equally detailed research in the county archives and elsewhere. The volumes are still being produced, each one more painstaking than the last, but as the marvellous detail increases, so the pace of publication slows.

Almost as extraordinary are the Royal Commission on Historical Monuments' county surveys (again, incomplete), and in particular its monumental *Survey of London*. Like the *VCH*, the *Survey of London* is ongoing and also like the *VCH*, is available online via the British History Online website mentioned earlier.

The local history collection really comes into its own at a slightly lower level of local history publications, providing histories of parishes, towns or cities. This is still a relatively thriving market today, with publishers such as Tempus and Phillimore producing high-quality books by local historians. But parish histories have been in production since the nineteenth century and only a search of the library catalogue, usually indexed by place-name, will reveal the full range of titles available.

Such a search will also bring up the rich vein of local topographical and guidebooks, which begin roughly at the time when the Napoleonic Wars curtailed European travel and turned tourists' attention to the beauties of the British Isles, and continues up to the present. Guidebooks from the 1960s can be surprisingly helpful about places which have changed significantly. In the eighteenth and early nineteenth centuries there was even a vogue for topographical poetry, most of it execrable but still useful, whereby a local poet would eulogise local beauty spots in the hope of drumming up patronage from the local landowners. Again, this will probably be found via a place-name search.

Local history libraries will make a point of collecting topographical images for their location and will probably have holdings of photographs, prints and drawings. Among the most useful sources for public parks are postcards. Produced in extraordinary numbers from the late 1890s and the first decade of the twentieth century, but continuing to be popular into the 1980s, many are of public parks and their features, which were particularly photogenic subjects. There are also two other useful sources for postcards: the RHS has a collection of some 5,000 although they are not yet indexed online, while the English Heritage Archives contain the wonderful collection of the late Dr Nigel Temple (1926–2003) which can be searched specifically (http://viewfinder.english-heritage.org.uk/intro.aspx).

Finally, it is worth pointing out the transactions of local archaeological societies and field clubs. Many of these began publishing annual reports with papers on antiquarian and topographical subjects in the nineteenth century, and a good number are still going strong. Searching these volumes can be arduous where they are indexed annually or only at intervals, but they can contain relevant material.

Copyright libraries and publications available online

There are six copyright libraries in the British Isles, which contain copies of every book published: the British Library, the National Library of Scotland in Edinburgh, the National Library of Wales in Aberystwyth, Trinity College Dublin, Cambridge University Library and the Bodleian Library, Oxford. Access to a copyright library remains invaluable, not only because they have copies of all published works, but because they are also major repositories of manuscript material – the NLW in Aberystwyth, for example, has the second-largest collection of topographical sketchbooks in the UK, while the Bodleian has the extraordinary archive of the nineteenth-century topographer and antiquarian Richard Gough (1735–1809). However, on the matter of access to obscure publications, it is worth mentioning that millions of useful books are now available online through sites such as Google books, the Internet Archive (http://archive.org/details/texts) or the Biodiversity Heritage Library (http://www.biodiversitylibrary.org/). Similarly, most modern journal articles are available online through sites such as Jstor (http://www.jstor.org), although at present the latter is only accessible to researchers at accredited institutions. Other key reference works such as the *Dictionary of National Biography* are also now available online through county libraries.

In this short chapter, as in a single lecture, it is impossible to do justice to the range of sources for documentary research. The subject is explored at greater length in *Parks and Gardens: a researcher's guide* (Landscape Design Trust, 2006) by David Lambert, Peter Goodchild and Judith Roberts, copies of which can still occasionally be found on the internet, and in some reference libraries.

# 12 Defining significance and developing a conservation philosophy

Sarah Couch

Historic landscape consultant and visiting lecturer on the MSc in Conservation of Historic Gardens and Cultural Landscapes, University of Bath, and the MSc in Sustainable Heritage at University College, Oxfordshire, UK

The determination of *significance* is the core of an assessment of a historic asset and is central to the conservation management plan (CMP), as all decisions should flow from an understanding of the significance and values attached to the site. In turn, *significance* underpins the conservation philosophy adopted for a site.

Whatever the length of a CMP or historic landscape analysis, an assessment of significance is an essential component: it is the most challenging but also the most rewarding part of the process. Very often the determination of significance can provide new inspiration for owners and managers, motivation to users and stakeholders and unlock funding opportunities. More than any other part of historic landscape analysis, the assessment of significance requires knowledge and judgement.

There is no universal way of defining significance, although some guidelines are described below. Within this framework, experience shows that each site needs an individual response: this is indeed the essence, as significance marks out what is distinctive, special or unique about a place, on many levels.

The crucial parts of historic landscape analysis or writing a CMP are to (1) define significance and (2) define the approach to conserving that significance – including a conservation philosophy.

Considering first the overall conservation approach or philosophy, it is clear from visiting historic sites that there is a great range of approaches and levels of intervention. How does one decide to strip away later layers and recreate a lost garden, as at Hampton Court's Privy Garden, Surrey or maintain a garden substantially as an archaeological site, as at Lyvedon New Bield, Northamptonshire (1605)? Why was the Elizabethan garden at Kenilworth Castle, Warwickshire recreated, largely on the basis of a letter? Why are so many of our great Victorian cemeteries managed as nature reserves rather than designed landscapes? Why are some features repaired as if they are new and others preserved as near ruins? Apart from financial constraints, much of the answer lies in the overall conservation approach adopted and, in turn, this derives from the evidence and its interpretation in assessing the significance of the site.

Landscapes are multi-layered, living heritage, so conservation decisions are complex. By comparison, in some ways, the conservation of buildings and structures is relatively straightforward. The manifesto of the Society for the Protection of Ancient Buildings (SPAB) was written by William Morris (1834–96) and other founder members and issued as early

Gardens & Landscapes in Historic Building Conservation, First Edition. Edited by Marion Harney.
© 2014 John Wiley & Sons, Ltd. Published 2014 by John Wiley & Sons, Ltd.

as 1877, enshrining principles of 'repair not restore'; that is, repair without reproduction of missing elements. However, this approach cannot be applied directly to all parts of a landscape where, by its nature, planting material will have changed and need renewal; indeed, its richness derives from its many layers.

In developing a conservation approach, it is important to define terms, as words such as 'restoration' are often used very loosely. Landscapes are complex and dynamic, reflecting periods of change. Even if there are no modern interventions, all landscapes will change and grow; therefore the concept of fixing the design at a certain point in the past is rarely feasible or appropriate. The Burra Charter provides definition of terms: *conservation* means all the processes of looking after a place so as to retain its cultural significance, i.e. it is the general term; *maintenance* means the continuous protective care of the fabric and setting of a place, and is to be distinguished from repair; *repair* involves *restoration* or *reconstruction*; *restoration* means returning the existing fabric of a place to a known earlier state by removing accretions or by reassembling existing components without the introduction of new material; *reconstruction* means returning a place to a known earlier state and is distinguished from restoration by the introduction of new material into the fabric (ICOMOS, 1999). However, unlike built features, some intervention will always be necessary as planting will need to be renewed, following evidence wherever possible, even within a project described as *conservation* or *restoration* rather than *reconstruction* (English Heritage, 2007). Where there is no site evidence, *conjectural detailing* – details derived from an understanding of the time rather than direct site evidence, may be justified, but it is important that this is made clear in the way the work is presented (Jacques, 1995). Often it is not clear that work carried out is really a recreation or conjectural creation, rather than conservation and repair. In general, in the UK, recreation of lost features is treated with caution and needs a consistent philosophy to justify this level of intervention.

In developing a conservation philosophy, one needs to consider whether to go beyond simple *maintenance* and some replanting, to removal of later work as part of *restoration* or even *reconstruction* incorporating new fabric or recreating lost features. Again, planting is an area that will fall outside normal definitions, as not only will planting need to be renewed, but usually later vegetation, for example self-seeded trees, will need to be removed. The conservation philosophy can be incorporated in an agreed project description or vision statement and this will be discussed in the examples below.

Significance

The conservation philosophy and approach derives largely from an understanding of the *significance* of a place: why it is distinctive, rare, influential or unique; what are its special qualities and values; which elements contribute most to those values; who values the place and why. Defining significance is central to a CMP and will include evaluation of historic landscape layers and a large range of historic, aesthetic and social (or communal) values and associations.

The determination of the significance of historic assets is based on professional judgement against four broad values:

Types of significance defined in English Heritage *Conservation Principles*:

- Evidential value: the potential of the physical remains to yield evidence of past human activity. This might take into account date; rarity; state of preservation; diversity/complexity; contribution to published priorities; supporting documentation; collective value and comparative potential
- Aesthetic value: this derives from the ways in which people draw sensory and intellectual stimulation from the heritage asset, taking into account what other people have said or written

- Historical value: the ways in which past people, events and aspects of life can be connected through the heritage asset to the present, such a connection often being illustrative or associative
- Communal value: this derives from the meanings of a heritage asset for the people who know about it, or for whom it figures in their collective experience or memory; communal values are closely bound up with historical, particularly associative, and aesthetic values, along with educational, social or economic values.

The inclusion of communal (or social and spiritual) value was an important addition, as these aspects have not always been assessed in the past. These values can be further defined or refined to apply to a landscape and can be used later in the CMP to structure sections covering issues and policies.

If the site has designation in the planning system, this will form a natural starting point; for example the English Heritage Register of Parks and Gardens of Special Historic Interest in England or Inventory entries. Background information or 'reasons for designation', which are not part of the published description, can be requested. Registration criteria take account of age, survival, influence (and rarity), association with designers or other significant people or events or group value; more recent sites need to be more intact and of greater importance than older sites. The fact that a site is protected means it has national significance, but a CMP needs to go further in defining significance in detail. As no one person has expertise in all areas, it is useful to gain other experts' opinions if at all possible and attempt to gain some consensus, especially for unusual sites or sites that have not previously been assessed.

The assessment of significance needs to be as broad and imaginative as possible and look outside of the site itself. The assessment will draw on evidence from specialist surveys and analysis, if available, for example archaeological survey, arboricultural survey, condition survey of landscape, buildings, and structures, ecological surveys, hydrology, geology, movement surveys, user surveys, consultation and oral history. This also means understanding the context and relative significance in the site. Comparison within its historical, aesthetic and social context will reveal whether it is typical of a type of design or the work of a certain designer; whether it is unusual, or an influential example; whether it is rare and why. This applies to all aspects, not only architectural and landscape design – for example, whether significant social or sporting events occurred here, or whether it contains rare species or rare archaeological remains, or whether there is exceptional evidence which can be used as an educational resource. The process aims to balance evidential, aesthetic, historical and communal values. Landscapes often have complex overlapping values which do not fit neatly into categories. One helpful technique is to develop themes of significance beyond the categories of evidential, aesthetic and so forth as these themes can help lead to a conservation approach, as discussed in the examples below.

Often there is pressure to define levels of significance or give scores; for example, for use in a Heritage Impact Assessment or Environmental Impact Assessment. However, this should be approached with some caution, as it can become rigid; the interrelationships of a landscape as a whole are of primary interest.

If used, levels of significance should be defined, for example as:

- Very high: Grade I sites and buildings, Scheduled Ancient Monuments; sites/features of international significance
- High: Grade II* sites and buildings; sites/features of national importance
- Medium: Grade II sites; sites/features of regional importance
- Low: Sites/features of local importance, local listed buildings and landscapes
- Negligible: Sites/features with no significant value
- Negative: Negative or intrusive features, which detract from the value of a site, such as impact on views.

The assessment will include the overall significance of the site as well as the significance of individual elements, and their contribution to the value of the place, as well as the impact of negative or lost features. In addition to aiding understanding and providing information for interpretation and engagement, the assessment of significance can also be used to justify levels of heritage protection, contribute to planning guidance, support planning applications and provide a sound basis for assessment of the impact of any interventions, using Heritage Impact Assessment or Environmental Impact Assessment.

Examples of significance and conservation philosophy

All of the following examples are projects supported by the Heritage Lottery Fund.

Pitzhanger Manor and Walpole Park in Ealing

This was the country villa of John Soane (1753–1837), the influential architect of the Bank of England (Couch, 2011). He purchased the estate of 28 acres in 1800 and set about rebuilding all but the south wing of the house and redesigning the grounds as a country idyll and architectural showcase. Soane hoped to inspire his sons and cultured visitors in the pursuit of architecture. He intended to impress, not only with the house, built in his own idiosyncratic architectural style with its stripped classical detail, radical colour schemes and inventive use of space and light, but also with his artificial Roman ruins. Soane had an unusually active involvement in the design and use of the gardens and park, developed with the advice of John Haverfield (1744–1820) of Kew, who frequently worked with Soane. The resulting landscape was a miniature landscape park suited to a Regency country villa, with lawns, shrubberies, exotic trees, flower garden, kitchen garden, a serpentine lake with rustic bridge and arbour above, an ornamental shrubbery walk and a great number of classical fragments, all set within a small park (Figure 12.1).

Soane sold the estate in 1811 and the park went through relatively minor changes during the rest of the nineteenth century. In 1901 it became a public park and various additions and adaptations were made for public recreational use. Gradually the area around the Manor House took on the character of a municipal park and it became visually isolated from the

Figure 12.1 Pitzhanger Manor, birds-eye view, showing the dramatic diagonal entrance and the Manor House in its landscape with artificial ruins, shrubberies, serpentine lake and park. (By courtesy of the Trustees of Sir John Soane's Museum; Vol. 90 Plate 1.)

rest of the park. The park is included in the English Heritage Register of Parks and Gardens at Grade II and lies within the Ealing Green Conservation Area.

To understand the site and its significance better, site-specific and contextual research was carried out on several topics. The extensive archive of documents and drawings at the Soane Museum, London was studied for the many references to the design and building of Pitzhanger Manor itself in Soane's and Mrs Soane's notebooks, accounts and Soane's office drawings. Research here also explored wider issues – references to Soane's contacts with Haverfield and the sites where they worked together; parallels with design features at those sites; other Soane villa designs and the relationship between house and garden and the extent of attention to the landscape; Soane's views on landscape design and contact with other designers such as Repton; Soane's garden at the Chelsea Hospital, where he was Clerk of Works from 1807; comparative design of features at other sites such as bridges, gates, conservatories, kitchen gardens, trellis work decoration and so on.

Further work was conducted on the relatively little known career of John Haverfield, tracing drawings, documents, locating rare Haverfield sites and visiting these where possible. In addition, contextual research was carried out on relevant areas such as the development of the Regency period villa and its landscape, the design of mixed flowering shrubberies in the period and the picturesque in landscape design.

Significance   This work concluded that the greatest significance derives from the site's rarity and associations with two main areas of significance related to the park's association with the pre-eminent architect Sir John Soane and to its intensive public use since it became a public park in 1901. The analysis of significance was grouped under the four broad areas defined in Conservation Principles and according to themes, as follows:

- Historical value: visual and associative
- Association with Soane
- The park forms the setting of the Grade I listed Pitzhanger Manor House, which is regarded as an architectural treasure. The whole is a unified design of house and grounds, which adds to its heritage value
- It is probably the only surviving landscape closely associated with Soane and with his direct input. The landscape at his home at Lincoln's Inn Fields, London, was restricted to courtyards and his garden at the Chelsea Hospital was destroyed. There is arguably more physical and documentary evidence about this garden than any other Soane garden
- The extent of drawn and written information relating to the grounds is very rare in the Soane archive, if not unique. In his practice Soane designed numerous villas, but the villa landscapes were barely illustrated, or perhaps only visible in glimpses from windows. Numerous Soane office drawings exist but it seems that the landscape design was usually given over to other landscape designers
- The gardens contain important architectural artefacts associated with Soane, including a Rustic Bridge (Grade II*), Portland stone bench (listed Grade II); Entrance Archway (Grade I) and Lodge (Grade II). The use of classical antiquities is an important forerunner of the celebrated display at Lincoln's Inn Fields. The designations at Grade I and II* indicate the exceptional national, arguably international, significance of the manor and related structures within the park
- Representative design: the design illustrates Soane's fascination with the interplay of inside and outside of a building; indeed, the landscape was apparently designed to be seen from the innovative, raised greenhouse-gallery, where one could appreciate 'a succession of beautiful effects, particularly when seen by moonlight, or when illuminated, and the lawn enriched with company enjoying the delights of cheerful society'. The garden was also brought into the house via the use of trellis and the inside-outside spaces of the courtyard and the ruins; a major design feature
- Group value: Pitzhanger Manor and Walpole Park are important parts of a larger group of Soane sites in London including the Dulwich Picture Gallery and the Soane Mausoleum

at St Pancras old churchyard, as well as the Soane Museum. There are very close links with the Soane Museum at Lincoln's Inn Fields; much of Soane's collection of art and statuary, now at the Museum, was originally displayed at Pitzhanger Manor and many elements, including the use of ruins and antiquities, were a rehearsal for Lincoln's Inn Fields.

Example of Villa design

- The Villa landscape is relatively little studied and its rarity is not fully understood but research indicates that it was a rare survival of a Regency villa in its landscape, which is largely intact
- It is an important and early example of the trend towards relatively small villas near the capital, set in a miniature landscape park, with all the elements of a much larger country estate including serpentine lake, flower garden near the house, use of exotics and walled kitchen garden.

Regency landscape   It is a relatively rare example of a Regency landscape: Brighton pavilion is the only major Regency garden recently conserved. There seem to be few direct surviving comparisons, although the exceptional design of Pitzhanger suggests comparison with sites such as the Deepdene, Surrey and Brighton Royal Pavilion rather than more modest villas (Batey, 1995; Hinze, 1996).

Connection with Haverfield

- It is a very rare and characteristic example of the work of the well-regarded landscape designer John Haverfield the Younger
- The association with Haverfield is of greater significance than previously understood; this is one of only two or three known surviving landscapes by Haverfield – a designer who enjoyed greater stature than previously known.

Social connections

- In Soane's time the house welcomed visitors of great artistic, social and intellectual standing, including frequent guests such as, the artist J.M.W. Turner (1775–1851), the antiquarian John Britton (1771–1857), the Flaxmans (John, sculptor, 1755–1826), the painter Prince Hoare (1755–1834), the architects James Wyatt (1746–1813), and George Dance the younger (1741–1825), the painter Henry Tresham (c.1751–1814), the English landscape painter Sir Augustus Wall Callcott (1779–1844) and the gothic novelist Matthew 'Monk' Lewis (1775–1818). (Darley, 1999)
- The association with past owners and visitors is significant: particularly the Gurnells, Soanes and Percevals; the Perceval sisters were daughters of Spencer Perceval (1762–1812), the only British Prime Minister to be assassinated who was famously shot in the House of Commons on 11 May 1812
- The park is associated with significant events of the public park period and Borough Surveyor Charles Jones' (1830–1913) major role in its establishment and design is of great local interest.

Aesthetic (& design) value

The site has exceptional design significance

- Pitzhanger Manor: the manor itself has international and national significance
- Quality of design and composition: this is a complete integrated design of a Villa and its landscape, and one of the best examples of Soane's interest in the creation of a progression of theatrical spaces linking the garden and house united by carefully controlled views
- Influence of design: Soane's influence as an architect is widely acknowledged; Pitzhanger was a precursor and testing ground for many ideas seen at parts of Lincoln's Inn Fields

and elsewhere; Pitzhanger was the original home of much of the collection now on display in the Soane Museum
- Innovative design: Here Soane experimented with his pioneering use of classical ideas in house and landscape, reinterpreting the Roman idea of bringing the outside into the building, via garden courtyard and conservatory, developing his characteristic play of views and light with use of large areas of plain and coloured glass
- Representative design: The villa demonstrates many of the principles of the late eighteenth-century/early nineteenth-century landscape, incorporating qualities of picturesque and sublime design within the limitations of the site, enhanced by Soane's use of artificial ruins and rustic bridge to create an Arcadian landscape, as well as typical Regency use of flowers and flowering shrubberies
- Aesthetic or architectural interest: structural planting in terms of tree layout and shrub belts within the park remain and provide much of the site's character. The avenues define the quality of the wider public park and the variety of trees is much valued
- Public park: The wider park displays features typical of a public park design of the early twentieth century, notably the redesigned boating and skating pond and Water Garden.

In addition, *Evidential value* and *Community value* were assessed in detail. To summarise briefly: *Evidential value* includes the value of archaeology, exceptional records and evidence of design, documentary evidence as a source of evidence or knowledge, evidence from trees and several layers of history. *Social or community value* includes connections with life in Ealing, the establishment of the park and the debate over its future, the campaign to save the kitchen garden, significant events held here, World War II uses, and recent activities and events including the establishment of a Friends' group.

Conservation philosophy This assessment led to the conservation approach for the project. An important aspect in shaping the approach was the conclusion that not only was the park the setting for an exceptional building but also that Soane had been closely involved with the design and day-to-day care of the garden, making it unique in his extensive body of work. It also became clear that there were very few Haverfield designs remaining and that he held high status as a designer in his lifetime. Therefore, the decision was taken that the main areas of landscape extending from the house held the highest design significance and that the Regency character and holistic design should guide the approach here. This would mean reopening views, removing some of the later adaptations and planting of the public park period and, to some extent, recreating the Soane period design. This would include replanting mixed shrubbery beds with plants of the Regency period, work to conserve structural tree planting, repairing the main part of the former serpentine, repairing structures and replacing lost features on the Soane adapted bridge – all based on research from original documents. However, in the wider park, which does not provide an immediate setting to the Manor House, the approach is different. In Soane's day the wider park was used for grazing and was not laid out as an ornamental area until the early twentieth century. The area also accommodates most of the much-loved park events and facilities. Therefore, in these areas, the philosophy is to conserve these features created in the early–mid twentieth century and to reinforce this public park character.

This led to an adopted vision statement:

> Walpole Park will become Ealing's premier heritage park. This much loved park will be restored to reveal its Regency landscape and will provide new opportunities for learning, volunteering and activities in the park. The project will reunite Walpole Park with Pitzhanger Manor and provide it with a unified design, which celebrates the national significance of Sir John Soane's legacy.

Wicksteed Park, Kettering, Northamptonshire

By contrast, Wicksteed Park is a site where the highest significance is not related to design but to social aspects and influence. Wicksteed Park is an unusual combination of a public country park and paying attraction which has survived substantially intact since its opening in 1921. When the engineer Charles Wicksteed (1847–1931) bought the land in Barton Seagrave in 1914, his original intention was to build a model garden suburb to provide workers' housing with large gardens in a park setting, much as was done by philanthropic industrialists at Port Sunlight, Merseyside; Cadbury's Bournville, Birmingham; Saltaire, Yorkshire; New Lanark, Scotland or Rowntree's New Earswick at York. However, after the First World War, local authorities took on the responsibility of housing and Wicksteed concentrated on creating a public park unlike others. From the start he provided experimental play equipment and he was passionate about providing opportunities for all to play with minimal supervision on all days of the week, in contrast to the limited and tightly controlled play opportunities elsewhere.

Initially the park had much the character of a country park, and the attractive valley landscape was beautified by the excavation of a large recreation lake, providing opportunities for swimming, paddling and boating: it incorporated early features of the outdoor swimming and lido movement of the 1930s. There were soon a pavilion, terrace and enclosed rose garden, as well as a range of formal recreational facilities, such as tennis courts, as many other parks of the period provided. The success of improvised play equipment led Wicksteed to design and install more and more equipment in the free playground, using the park as both a testing ground and showcase for his ideas. A significant addition was the erection of the first water chute in 1927, which still provides an exciting experience, and a cycle track in 1930. Steam, and then the new diesel railways, were a particular passion and it is fitting that his last work at Wicksteed was the planning and construction of the diesel railway circuit in the park which opened just after his death in 1931. From the 1930s and into the 1950s it flourished as a rural park with a range of traditional outdoor family activities and a few rides integrated into the landscape. During the mid–late twentieth century its dominant character became one of an amusement park in a rural setting.

Significance An analysis of its history and context has revealed many layers or themes of significance, including its role as a setting for an eighteenth-century designed landscape; its place as a park made by an industrialist and philanthropist; its place in public park and recreation ground design; its place in theme park and pleasure garden design; its place in the history of healthy outdoor recreation and swimming; its place as a celebration of engineering and invention; the founder's influence on the local area and its importance to Kettering and region and its natural or scientific interest. The park's intensive public use, and memories associated with it since its foundation, are also highly significant.

It was a representative but unexceptional example of public park design of the period. However, without doubt, its greatest significance relates to its unique role in the development of children's play in parks; to Charles Wicksteed's ethos of adventurous recreation; to his international influence on the provision for play and the importance of the park to the local and regional community (Figure 12.2).

In the early twentieth century, provision of play equipment was very limited and opportunities for play strictly controlled; boys and girls were segregated and supervised and play on Sundays was prohibited. In many cases, children's play had not been incorporated into new public pleasure grounds, and the popular solution was often a dedicated recreation ground elsewhere (Groves, 2010). Wicksteed found that the emphasis was on formal recreation and that parks were full of prohibitions. He gave a damning report of play equipment in municipal parks in the early twentieth century:

> I went on a tour all-round the country to find what playthings were made for the children. The result was that I found very little was made, used or new, except the old-fashioned swing, a few broken down, dangerous giant slides and an exceedingly clumsy and dangerous bumper see-saw. It appeared that no one had devoted themselves to the bringing out and development of a variety of really good playthings (Wicksteed, 1928).

He saw the possibility of child-centred play which he felt was more important than a beautifully laid out park. By 1938 Wicksteed's had supplied 4,000 playgrounds, and by 1967 the company claimed to have supplied 10,000 at home and overseas (including Kuwait,

Figure 12.2 The recreational lake and train at Wicksteed Park. (Photo courtesy of the Wicksteed Trust.)

Figure 12.3 View of the newly completed Alexandra Road Park in 1979. (Photo courtesy of Janet Jack).

Jamaica and South Africa). 'Thus the history of children's play equipment in public parks is virtually synonymous with that of Wicksteed's development' (Groves, 2010).

Conservation philosophy   This led to a conservation philosophy which reflected the founder's ethos and approach to adventurous play as the most distinctive feature of the park, and this is contained in the vision statement:

> Our vision is to celebrate the unique contribution of Charles Wicksteed and lead the way in adventurous, educational and imaginative play in an outstanding heritage parkland setting thereby making future generations healthier and happier for another 100 years.

Alexandra Road, Camden, London

Finally, Alexandra Road Park (Figure 12.3) is an unusual example of a later twentieth-century public park within a housing estate. The estate was designed from 1968 by the architect

Neave Brown and, later, the detailed landscape design and all of the planting were developed by a landscape architect through BDP. Construction began in 1973 and the landscape was constructed from 1978–80.

To both designers, the project was, and is, one of their most significant works. It is a rare challenge to value such a recent project.

While the building's II* listed curving, stepped terraces have attained iconic status and are much studied and visited, the landscape has received less attention. However, the landscape and architecture were conceived as one design and the whole surface of building and site is treated as a garden.

Research included the context of twentieth-century and post-war housing in Europe and the UK; housing in London; the major contribution made by Camden's architecture department and the approach to play in the period. Various experts were also consulted about their views on the significance of the landscape design.

Significance

The conclusion was that the whole landscape at Alexandra Road, as an intrinsic part of the overall design, is of international significance. It has been described as 'the most significant landscape of its type in the UK' and 'a unique concept in the international context'. It is an outstanding example of modernist design in which the II* listed buildings and landscape are an integrated whole. The whole surface of the site is treated as a sculpted landscape, which relies on strong geometric design defined by diagonal paths and sculpted into complex levels, very dense planting and a consistent approach to detailing. There is an unusual variety of open and closed, private and communal, sheltered spaces designed to create intimacy, a sense of mystery, to encourage adventurous play or to evoke a sense of country in a dense urban setting. Its rich design is a key example of the mid-twentieth-century approach to design, social inclusion and play. The concept of the design is unique in the international context; it has been extremely influential and is a major subject of study.

In this case, individual elements were not given separate significance as the entire site is an integrated whole, a unique sculpted landscape; buildings and landscape are one design. Therefore, in this case, all areas are equally significant. However, themes of significance were developed reflecting the areas of research: its modernist integration of landscape and architectural design; its place in housing and public park design; the role of the landscape architect and approach to planting; its approach to children's play; and as a source of knowledge and natural or scientific interest. It is considered to be amongst the most important housing schemes in Camden, which was the leading borough for social housing in the later twentieth century. Finally, and not least, it is of great social value to its community. It is notable that significance is affected by loss of play features, lack of maintenance and some detractors.

Conservation philosophy   The approach adopted was to repair the original design following original drawings, paying particular attention to the architectural and hard landscape detailing and planting which were a part of the design palette and typical of their period; to replace lost play elements inspired by the original intentions and bespoke designs but not replicating detail in all cases (for example where off-the-peg equipment had been removed), also to make some interventions to improve accessibility and connections. The adopted aim was:

> To repair conserve and restore the landscape as originally conceived as an integrated, consistently detailed modernist design, to replace lost features consistent with the design ethos of the park, improve management, to generate appreciation by a wide range of local residents and visitors and revitalise the park as the focus of community activity.

These examples illustrate the importance of research in defining significance, which is a prerequisite for developing a conservation philosophy. Significance is central to the conservation management planning process and should not be overlooked, however limited the overall scope of the project.

References/Further reading

Batey, M. (1995) *Regency Gardens*, Shire, Princes Risborough.
Couch, S. (2011) *Walpole Park Conservation Management Plan*, London Borough of Ealing.
Couch, S. (2012) *Wicksteed Park Conservation Management Plan*, the Wicksteed Trust.
Couch, S. (2012) *Alexandra Road Park Conservation Management Plan*, London Borough of Camden.
Darley, G. (1999) *John Soane an Accidental Romantic*, Yale University Press, New Haven & London.
English Heritage (2007) *The Management & Maintenance of Historic Parks, Gardens & Landscapes*, (eds J. Watkins and T. Wright). Frances Lincoln, London.
Groves, L. (2010) *The History of Children's Play Provision in Public Parks* (draft report). English Heritage, London.
Hinze, V. (1996) 'The Re-creation of John Nash's Regency Gardens at the Royal Pavilion, Brighton', *Garden History*, Volume 24, no 1.
ICOMOS (1999) *The Burra Charter – the Australia ICOMOS Charter for Places of Cultural Significance*.
Wicksteed, C. (1928) *A Plea for Children's Recreation after School Hours and after School Age*.

13 Science and craft in understanding historic gardens and their management

Peter Thoday
Principal of Thoday Associates, Wiltshire, UK

Introduction

John Sales, former Head of Gardens and Parks for the National Trust, often remarked that gardening is a process, and indeed, like all other forms of cultivation, it is. And hence the garden is the site in which this process, or craft, takes place. Garden and gardening, place and process are inevitably linked: change one and you change the other. As a consequence, over the thousands of years that humans have gardened, these interactions have changed each other. At times changes to the garden, driven by fashion and aesthetics, have required changes to the craft, yet on other occasions it has been our better understanding of plant husbandry that has changed the appearance of the garden. But there is one further pressing consideration which helps determine the management of a garden: gardens change not only through time but also as a consequence of their purpose. Different aims and objectives call for the use of different craft skills.

Recognising a garden's objectives and the changing role from private to public

Many of our best-preserved historic gardens, set within the grounds of private properties, are now open to the public. This change of activity brings inevitable consequences, with pressures to inform and entertain a visitor clientele unimagined by the garden's earlier designers and uncatered for by earlier managers. What once went on behind closed doors to provide produce and beauty for a single household and its guests is now open to the curious scrutiny of a mass audience. From the cabbage patch to the potting shed to the compost heap, all are listed in the guidebook and may be judged for their quality and period correctness. Most enthusiastic garden owners enjoy instigating change. It is only after their death that the site becomes set in its period and becomes a 'historic garden' – a designation that often stultifies its design, its flora and its methods of cultivation. Such an attempt to perpetuate the past is contentious; however, the title of this chapter assumes a desire to maintain the continuation of at least some old practices.

Some once-private gardens were designed as showpieces by which the owners communicated their ideas and interests and even their social standing. Others were places where such ideas and interests were pursued away from public view. Gardens of both types are now open to the public; however, their curatorship requires contrasting approaches. Show gardens tend to have followed the best professional practice of their time, whereas those made and maintained exclusively for the interests or indeed the curiosity of their owners may be rich in quirks and fancies – features that require their own form of husbandry, in some cases at variance with perceived best practice.

A garden, whether historic or contemporary, should be managed to achieve both its design intent – (if it had one) – and the objectives of the owner. Designs and objectives vary not only from garden to garden but also over time in the same garden. Although the design will form the template in which the craft of gardening takes place, its maintenance and the cultivation of its plants should reflect its perceived function. From this comes a demand for specific skills and equipment. At its simplest a private garden may contain little other than collections of plants grown to satisfy the interests of the grower or owner. Take for example the garden of a late-nineteenth-century sweet pea enthusiast: his horticultural interest went public on the show bench, not within the serried ranks of his plants, let alone through the winter landscape of excavated trenches. Again, Charles Darwin's (1809–82) garden at Down House, Kent was not a showpiece; it was both the site of his experiments and a place for contemplation and exercise. At times an owner's passion and expertise leaves behind issues that challenge future managers: should we struggle to reflect the skill and overriding enthusiasm of Harold Hillier (1905–85) as a collector of trees, or thin out his arboretum for the sake of producing fewer but better specimens?

Dangers in intellectualising the process of gardening

This chapter is not about design except inasmuch as it impinges on plant cultivation. While the creation and analysis of garden and landscape design has become an aesthetic and intellectual pursuit, it falls to the horticulturist to succeed in the technical skills required to grow the plants. In this respect it is not unknown for there to be conflict when a design requires a plant to be located where the biotic and abiotic conditions within a garden are unsatisfactory. In the past such questions were resolved by observation and trial and error, whereas nowadays the approach is perhaps more cerebral, via a knowledge of plant science. One very common example comes as a direct consequence of a garden maturing. As trees grow they shade and dry out beds that were once in the open, so preventing the success of their original selection of herbaceous subjects. No amount of craft skill will resolve the situation, which becomes a stark choice: the tree or the flowerbed.

There is a danger of being too academic when considering the management and maintenance of a garden. There is a risk of seeing it more in the context of the social history of the site than in the realities of the many tasks of its husbandry programme. Gardening has always been a down-to-earth occupation. Even the best of those remarkable individuals, the nineteenth-century head gardeners, had crop failures, and while some specialised and excelled in some areas, they may have had only very mediocre results in others, as tales from the recipient cooks have let slip. A garden whose records show it to have had both large vineries and herbaceous borders may well not have been famous for the quality of both, or at least not at the same time. Indeed the replacement of one head gardener by another may have reversed the relative emphasis placed on each feature and as a consequence their reputation.

The literature as a source of information on past practices of gardening

Across Europe gardening has a long and rich literature, well established by the late sixteenth century. As might be expected, authors have approached the subject from different angles. Some conveyed to their readers that, although not designers, they were both knowledgeable and capable should the opportunity arise. In contrast, and of great value to this chapter, are the many authors who focus on husbandry practices of their time. Here a word of warning: many of the authors were or had been head gardeners, nurserymen or owners with many years of practical experience. Their writings can exhibit a mix of tradition, contemporary best practice and individualism, and not infrequently all in the same chapter. So when discussing tree transplanting John Lindley (1789–1865), in *Theory of Horticulture: or an attempt to explain the principal operations of gardening upon Physiological principles* of 1840 wisely compared and contrasted the opinion of several authors: an approach that reminds us of the need to consult widely when trying to understand old husbandry instructions. A further point is that in turning to the old literature to learn about craft skills, today's historic garden managers face the frustration that most of the best-known gardening books from before 1900 were written for professional gardeners or their employers and, as a result, they rarely describe the basic tasks that an under-gardener or garden labourer carried out; such tasks and the skills they required were regarded as common knowledge.

The place of science in managing historic gardens

One has only to read Theophrastus in *De Causis Plantarum* written around 300 BC to realise that a cultivated plant's response to various husbandry practices such as transplanting, pruning and even the damage caused by hoes has been noted for millennia. In fact there is indeed little difference between Theophrastus' musings and the didactic warnings found in the writings of a Victorian head gardener. Both will have written on the basis of astute observation and both knew what a plant's reaction would be to a gardener's actions, be they skilled or unskilled.

Need we know more? It is only in the last hundred years that the biology that lies behind the plant's response has been understood. This brings us to one of the central questions of this chapter: how many of the operations that were so effective in producing excellent results were done by rote, albeit with a clear understanding of cause and effect, action and reaction between gardener and plant, and how many were understood at a deeper level in terms of what we now know as plant science? Clearly this depends to a great extent on the date of our garden. This chapter is not the place for a detailed analysis of what was understood when; it is worth remembering, however, that plant cultivation became enmeshed in the scientific revolution of the eighteenth century but suffered from the piecemeal nature of our understanding of what became the natural sciences, particularly owing to the late arrival of plant physiology and genetics. Hence it took a long while for separate nuggets of comprehension to become what some have described as a joined-up understanding of the plant sciences. Nevertheless, we have excellent records of some of the early investigations thanks to books such as Stephen Hales' (1677–1761) *Vegetable Staticks* of 1727. Gardening books written around the same time demonstrate the great interest of horticulturalists in those discoveries and their possible application to plant cultivation. Philip Miller's (1691–1771) great work, the *Gardener's Dictionary* (3rd edition, 1737), although dedicated to Sir Hans Sloane (1660–1753) is written for a head gardener readership, its many articles addressing scientific issues of the day – such as the six pages given to a discussion on the properties of air. This approach was continued and developed in Peter Lawson's *The Agriculturist's Manual* of 1836, John Lindley's *The Theory of Horticulture* of 1840 and Robert Thompson's *The Gardener's Assistant* of 1859 – the last with, for example, its analysis of the composition of the ash of the potato and its possible link to fertiliser application.

Reading this succession of British writers and others from continental Europe makes clear that it was recognised that science might provide the way to a deeper understanding of husbandry and perhaps in so doing influence the nature and timing of its techniques. These writings prove the enthusiasm of their authors but they tell us little of just how much the typical head gardener was persuaded to 'think scientifically' or the extent to which the garden was managed through the conscious application of science. Behind such issues lie deeper questions that are almost sacrilege to pose in today's science-based culture: what is the value of today's science in managing historic gardens? And to what extent does such knowledge improve the husbandry of a historic garden over that learnt by experience and practised by rote?

To these questions I am a biased respondent. As a child of my age I have no choice but to think scientifically about horticultural matters. To me some understanding of the plant sciences brings the ability to predict and hence anticipate plant behaviour in a way that was not possible in a pre-scientific age. Thanks to the applied research of the last century there is a wealth of information on the commercial cultivation of crop plants, vegetables, fruits and most of the important florist's flowers, much of which has the potential to be of use in the garden. Our current understanding of the interaction of plant physiology, anatomy and morphology is directly applicable and, for example, allows the anticipation of a plant's response to the removal of roots, shoots and leaves, albeit with variations in detail from species to species.

In contrast, the understanding of soil pH is of more indirect application. Historically soil was described as sour or sweet but not of course acid or alkaline. That level of the understanding of a garden's soil is certainly helpful, as is the fact that there is a neutral zone between these two conditions. It must also be helpful to know that the vast majority of garden soils fall in the mid range and that whereas this region is more or less satisfactory for most plants there are some that do not grow successfully at one end of the scale or the other. Following this level of understanding, practical gardeners will want to know how to influence a soil's pH.

So far so good, but it is also helpful to know that the pH scale runs from one to 14 but is logarithmic, let alone the deeper science that starts with the understanding that the scale is named from the potential of hydrogen and based on the logarithm of the reciprocal of the hydrogen-ion concentration in gram atoms per litre. All this is prerequisite to a real understanding of the physical chemistry of solutions that explain how pH influences a plant through its effect on the nutrients within the soil. In practice even the basic science, the calculation of both the amount and form of lime to use to correct acidity, will take place in a laboratory 'off site' and arrive as an instruction, just as the dilution rates for pesticides do.

To a considerable extent the need for a deep knowledge of the cultivation of a 'crop' depended on its importance in the overall running of the garden. Most old productive gardens grew culinary herbs, or more correctly they virtually grew themselves. I would guess that few old gardeners were deeply concerned over their nutrition, pests or supplementary lighting illumination. Yet there is today a company that produces some 14 million pots *per annum* of the same herbs destined for retail sale. Not surprisingly its management has these very subjects high on its list of considerations.

Understanding problems may allow one to take remedial actions or at the very least plan alternative strategies to counter the loss of a particular plant. For example, if in a productive kitchen garden based on a Victorian walled garden onions are dying from white rot, then a knowledge of plant pathology will tell those in charge that the soil will continue to harbour the pathogen responsible for several years, allowing them to avoid this crop and thereby the disappointment of a succession of failures. Today the greatest benefit to a grower facing a problem often comes not from botany but from knowledge of chemistry, pedology, entomology, mycology or nematology. To this list I would add taxonomy. Some will no doubt find this surprising, but I have found knowledge of plant relationships valuable when faced with a poorly chronicled subject, and response to factors as disparate as regrowth following pruning to required soil conditions can often be estimated by comparison with a better-known relative. Alongside plant pathology and entomology, the scientific developments in plant propagation, based on our greater understanding of plant physiology, must surely be in the first rank of aids to historic garden management. Knowledge of these fields applies across the whole range of vegetative propagation techniques. In grafting there is the selection of rootstocks, the elimination of virus and fungus pathogens from infected stock, and advanced methods of micro-graftage. The relative ease of propagation by cuttings, including the use of micropropagation techniques, has made once-rare cultivars available, and in such numbers that they can be used in the way designers used them when they and the gardens were in their heyday. It is sometimes said that there is no such thing as a rare plant, only those that are infrequently propagated; certainly the story of some once-popular plants' decline and then rise from obscurity to renewed popularity supports this, as in the case of chocolate cosmos (*Cosmos atrosanguineus*) and Malmaison carnations. The evidence of the impact of propagation technology on the availability of a rare plant is brought up to date by the remarkable story of the Wollemi pine (*Wollemia nobilis*), a species that has gone from discovery in Australia to being commonplace around the world in 25 years. In fact, the remarkable developments in vegetative propagation tend to overshadow the advances in a combination of genetics and seed physiology that have given us the opportunity to grow hundreds of cultivars of annual and biennial flowers and vegetables that many thought lost only a few decades ago.

One group of plants whose availability and cost has changed dramatically, thanks to advances in our understanding of reproductive biology, are certain sections of the Orchidaceae. Who would have thought just 25 years ago that a small orchid house, similar to the many built within nineteenth-century walled gardens, could be stocked for less than £1,000, and that with flowering specimens! Of course at that price they would not be those most beloved of orchid collectors past and present, but they would delight the general visitor and create an (almost) period-correct feature.

When cultivating a historic garden there is a great difference between following an 'old way' of doing a meaningful task and perpetuating an old and baseless practice that, thanks to our greater understanding, can now be transferred from the work schedule to the history section in the guidebook.

Craft skills

What is a skill? Is making a hole large enough to spread the roots of a transplant or distributing bedding plants evenly over a flowerbed a skill or common sense? Clearly they are things that gardeners should know but which in themselves are neither difficult nor require practice to achieve. Such basic practices are fundamentally different from an activity such as raking, where the novice needs not only to know that a level, even surface of similar-sized soil particles is required but also to acquire the dexterity, the skill, to produce it. For much of the time gardeners working in a period garden should be practising craft skills in the same way that a farrier, a wicker basket-maker or stone mason still uses time-honoured techniques. Such activities should not be self-conscious period performances but simply day-to-day routines done as and when required with the tender loving care, the TLC, of good husbandry. It is surely these skills, embedded within routine tasks, that are the most important for the gardening staff to master – skills of basic good practice that may need to be modified or supplemented in specific cases to respect either the husbandry or the design history of a specific garden. Moreover, there should be no excuse that most visitors will be oblivious of any poor performance.

Gardening in the past was a manual occupation. Woven into the chore of maintaining a neat and tidy garden, a large number of operations each required manual dexterity and hand–eye coordination. New recruits, probably arriving as garden boys at around the age of 14, would learn from the experienced men they worked alongside – how to dig, hoe and rake and, if today's most frequent inabilities are anything to go by, to water and train wall shrubs. Some of these skills are simple tricks of the trade and take only minutes to learn, while others require hours of practice, but almost all need guidance from a mentor; hence if no one on the staff knows the technique the skill chain is broken. Maintaining this continuum is difficult, but what should be done when the old way is period-correct but wrong? We now recognise that some of the almost universally followed approaches to tasks were misguided, as for example the ramming of soil in repotting. Should a faulty method be corrected at the risk of abandoning a craft?

Senior garden staff in the past were blessed with labourers whose dexterity and basic skills in tillage and plant handling contributed hugely to the overall appearance and smooth running of the garden. There was a skill base practised throughout the garden and across the seasons without which the majority of the operations that make up the craft of traditional gardening are frustrated. And there is today little reason for pessimists to predict the irrevocable loss of these straightforward craft skills, just as there are people today who can make a flint arrowhead as well as any Neolithic hunter and someone on television demonstrates making fire by friction or spark most weeks. Some simple skills have been so 'elevated' by today's media that the single quick stab and push of a dibber to complete the transplanting of a brassica becomes rich in mystique.

Learning the old skills of horticulture and agriculture is made more difficult because many of them are evident for only one part of the annual life cycle of the plants upon which they are practised. Anyone wishing to learn the skills required to make fine furniture can both practise and study examples of finished works the year round, but many horticultural techniques have left no trace come the end of the season – take for example the making and use of hay bands to blanch celery, the 'stopping' of chrysanthemums or the building of a potato clamp. In the past, craft skills were found across the whole hierarchy of a garden's staff. Few garden historians would doubt the intelligence and knowledge of many of the old head gardeners and indeed their writings speak for them. However, while they did the thinking and planning it was the large staff they directed who carried out the manual work using craft skills based on the use of hand tools. The humblest labourer would have been expected to dig to leave an area level and even, so requiring the minimum of work to produce the tilth needed for a seed bed. Surely, you may say, digging requires no skill. Not so – as evidenced by Battle-of-the-Somme-like results of the efforts of a group of self-sufficiency motivated academics!

Today the ideal remains, as in the past, the appointment of dextrous new recruits who first become proficient in the handling of tools before progressing to master their application in specific husbandry tasks. Sadly, however, there are many historic gardens now bereft of such people.

Period correctness

Few would argue against the proposition that a historic garden has the potential to be living history, but opinions differ widely on how far such a site should attempt to re-enact the past. At one extreme there are well-produced living-history projects where the garden layout, the crops, the equipment and even the costume of the volunteer workers are in period. At the other extreme lie many British walled gardens with their internal layouts completely changed but which remain regarded as historic gardens. Concern for period correctness depends on the perceived role and presentation of the garden. Of course, gardens open to the public may stage period events, from wassailing the apple trees to collecting seaweed after a storm. These are often unashamedly photo-opportunities to advertise the garden as a visitor attraction.

Turning from both lifestyle reproductions and design alterations, we shall focus at this point on period-correct horticulture, its plants and their cultivation. At its most basic the growing of period-correct plants in historic gardens is concerned with dates of introduction. If a species had not been introduced to the region when a garden celebrated its heyday then it must surely be out of place and out of time – for example, the growing of New World species in Moorish gardens in Andalusía, where the last Arab rulers left in the very year that Columbus made his momentous discovery. In some cases, the date of introduction of a particularly striking cultivar is as critical as the choice of a species. One well-documented example is the fastigiate Irish yew *Taxus baccata* 'Fastigiata', which arrived around 1760 when it was collected from Lord Enniskillen's estate at Florence Court, County Fermanagh. However, in many cases we may adopt a less rigid approach to a cultivar's period correctness.

Many would argue that with run-of-the-mill flowers and vegetables what matters is the effect produced rather than the genome used to achieve it. For example, it may be period-correct to edge a bed of zonal pelargoniums in a late Victorian garden with a variegated type, but must that be 'Flower of Spring'? Overall, morphology can be important to 'period ambience' and vegetables and flowers from cabbages to forget-me-nots have changed their shape and size over the years, so that today's cultivars may not look much like the early photographs, let alone much earlier illustrations such as those in Gerard's *Herbal* (1597). The disappearance of many old cultivars places a natural limitation on this pursuit of genetic purity and in some cases there are simply none left from which to choose.

Having considered the selection of plants, let us turn to their husbandry, their cultivation, and the selection and use of the tools involved. Several books from the eighteenth century carry illustrations of the tools of their time, for example *Le Jardinière Solitaire* (1704), but the picture most often reproduced is a slightly earlier sketch drawn by John Evelyn (1620–1706) in 1676. Period tools have a role as part of a historical enactment but there are many craft skills in which the tool, correctly used, is fundamental to the successful completion of the task. In this respect gardening is no different from furniture-making or bookbinding – tool and task go together. Cutting a boundary hedge with a powered trimmer does not produce the same results as using a slashing hook, and rotovation is most definitely not the same as digging with a fork or spade. In contrast, some operations such as the grafting of fruit trees, while still governed by a changeless biology, now use much-improved tools and materials. As a result such tasks look different but in their present guise produce far better results. We have drawings and instructions from the sixteenth century, but it would not be wise to depend on them to produce top-quality grafted trees for wall or orchard.

Period correctness can be as much, or more, about the appearance of the specimen as about its genetics. Tree transplants provide two good examples, both involving the demand for instant gardening. In the first instance, which occurs only too often, when an old natural-form tree must be replaced by a crafted street-tree nursery transplant with a ramrod-straight branchless trunk is planted 'for quick results'. The second example concerns walled-trained espaliers, which are best trained *in situ* yet are on offer at many garden centres as half-formed mock-ups. The spacing and patterning of plants have strong period resonance; both have varied over time, everywhere from the herbaceous border to the apple orchard and in the distance between rows of vegetables.

Perhaps the most critical period-correct skill is training and pruning. These activities are closely linked, but to simplify matters let us reduce training to the tying-in of stems and put all other aspects of the craft within pruning. The correct positioning and the consequent tying-in of stems is fundamental to the shaping of the specimens that became iconic symbols of their period. These range from the fan-trained wall fruits in the productive walled garden to the umbrellas of ramblers in the rose garden. Training by tying-in selected shoots while nailing and tagging wall-trained subjects requires knowledge of the likely response and subsequent growth of the shoots. Traditional training required the plant to be securely but gently held, a craft that produced its own knots, in a range of materials from tar string to fillis and bass, and required both dexterity and skill. Many pot-plants had specific forms of training or support that were considered to best display their beauty. These ranged from maypole tying of Schizanthus to cane-through-the-bulb for hyacinths. In the Edwardian herbaceous border methods of support varied to suit the species. Michaelmas daisies were supported by growing them through brushwood, delphinium flower spikes were individually tied to canes, and dahlia stakes were of standard dimensions.

Pruning may or may not be linked to training; it embraces every form of plant surgery, requiring many and diverse tasks and skills. In some cases the cuts are superficial, as when a fruit tree is ringed to induce fruiting, or shoots in the nursery are notched to control bud break. The more dramatic removal of organs can be directed to all parts of the plant, and includes disbudding flower heads to induce larger individual flowers or fruits, removing roots to control growth, de-leafing tomatoes and the many forms of pruning stems of all positions, sizes and ages. An important form of pruning that affects the appearance of historic gardens is that applied to ornamental shrubs. This ranges from the clipping of formal hedges which, in the hands of a craftsperson, controls both form and size, to the appearance and flowering and fruiting potential of decorative specimens. To see just how poorly this craft is often understood today we might compare, for example, the traditional skill demonstrated in the gardens of the National Trust with the uniform, short-back-and-sides-fits-all approach of many local authorities.

Managing with a skills shortage   Labour costs have always been, and remain, the single most expensive item in maintaining a garden. In earlier times that cost was easily managed by most owners; now it is not, with the result that most historic gardens carry a greatly reduced staff. Among the large staff of yesteryear, a chargehand or foreman responsible for a section of the garden – perhaps the fruit, the rock garden or the orchid collection – carried out the most demanding and complex tasks. But though craft skills were in the past found among all ranks of gardener, this is no longer the case. Today, there are many gardens where the majority of those on the payroll are unskilled in even the most basic of husbandry activities and it is said that such workers do not aspire to become gardeners and so lack the incentive to learn. In contrast, gardening still recruits a small number of keen and committed new entrants willing to learn their craft; these include many of those seeking a rewarding second career. Thanks to them the number of skilled gardeners just about keeps pace with those reaching retirement.

Avoidance of the need for skills   How then should today's managers deploy the reduced labour force? Naturally, skilled staff should be both respected and rewarded and given the time to carry out key tasks. For more than a century maintaining high standards of upkeep in a large garden has depended on replacing traditional craftsmanship with new materials, tools and methods. Examples are the use of tying guns rather than hand-tied raffia to support cordon sweet peas, pollen vibrators replacing the rabbit's tail, hosepipes rather than watering cans, chainsaws rather than crosscuts, and powered lawnmowers. In many cases the results are as good if not better, but among today's equipment some items such as hedge trimmers produce a noticeably different finish. Some, faced with managerial and financial worries, might argue that nevertheless if the garden retains its ambiance then all that is lost is the very esoteric pleasure of knowing that the work was achieved by traditional means.

The avoidance of skilled operations is more difficult. Not supporting sweet peas and not mowing lawns each produce very noticeable results! Many of the great gardens in Britain have reduced the size of their staff without dropping their standards by reducing the area or number of some features such as bedding designs and rock gardens. Such blanks in the design can be seen as preferable to their replacement with a completely new feature, in the same way that a blank area of ancient mural is preferable to conjectural painting of a new image. The essential consideration is that this reduction should save enough money for the remaining features to be skilfully maintained.

14 Garden archaeology

Brian Dix
Consultant in the archaeology of historic parks and gardens, Gwynedd, UK

Archaeological studies both above and below ground are an important means to trace the evolution and development of many historic gardens and related landscapes. The techniques of careful field observation and analysis, together with other scientific investigation and recording show what survives of earlier gardens as well as increasing our understanding of their former appearance. The results provide a valuable check upon the accuracy of historical views and contemporary records such as maps and written descriptions. By demonstrating the nature of related remains, future repairs and other schemes for improvement can take proper account of their significance and fragility, enabling good conservation management and practice. The archaeological excavation of historical garden layouts also forms the basis for accurate reconstruction, especially where the renewal of original building materials adds to authenticity.

The scope of archaeological fieldwork therefore ranges from the recognition and examination of visible field remains to sub-surface exploration, involving complete or total area excavation in addition to more selective investigation, which might target a specific aspect as an aid to reconstruction, or be solely for academic interest. Systematic analysis can distinguish separate phases of site development and thereby identify different trends or changing fashions and the contexts for them. The detail provided by archaeology indicates what individual features may have looked like and how they were constructed. It also shows how they were connected with each other, not only in original layout and composition, but topographically too. Analytical fieldwork involving the recognition of all relict features, including veteran trees and other vegetation, provides an important insight into the significance of former planting and sight lines. At the same time, the demonstration of earlier patterns of land use extends our knowledge of garden and parkland design by showing how existing features may have influenced later development, in some instances providing special meaning as well as a sense of identity.

Most archaeological surveys combine several techniques, involving remote-sensing applications such as aerial reconnaissance and geophysical investigation in addition to field observation. Together, they help to identify abandoned sites or to discover the lost details of those that still exist. Yet, whilst the earthworks of terraces and dried-up water features seem often to have outlasted the changes of attitude that have occurred since such rigid structures and their symmetrical layouts were originally fashionable, perhaps, at most, only one in five English formal gardens of that kind now survive with tangible remains. Examples of other sites are similarly limited, although they are found of various dates, stretching from classical antiquity and earlier times, and continuing through the medieval period up to the present. In addition to having once provided the setting for royal and other magnate residences, they extend to the lost features of modern public parks and other amenities. They include surviving town and cottage gardens as well as the remains of the elaborate layouts, kitchen gardens and parkland around country houses.

As seen today, therefore, the landscape is the product of centuries of development in which the broad processes of remodelling can often be traced, showing the present appearance to be made up of several layers. The identification of patterns of spatial and chronological variation and the recognition of how features may interrelate are an essential prerequisite for understanding the motives and perceptions of past owners and garden designers. Archaeology is a powerful tool to discover such details in addition to demonstrating the nature of change. The features associated with past water management, woodland planting, parkland and farm use, for example, all form part of local landscape development and character. Together with other vestiges of earlier land use and exploitation, they reflect aspects of social and economic history as well as influencing present ecology.

Typical elements of rigid landscape design can be traced from the Middle Ages onwards and previous layouts and their planting may be preserved within parkland and other development. Earthworks such as terraces, other banks and scarps, individual scoops and hollows may all denote former garden features, which might sometimes also be indicated by different grasses and other changes of vegetation. The historic core of many gardens still survives beneath modern lawns and with the evidence of abandoned carriage drives, circuit-rides and other designed routes helps to build a picture of how the landscape may have been manipulated to impress or even overawe the visitor. Although some places have been completely built-over, the lines of modern streets sometimes perpetuate earlier access arrangements or previous tree avenues.

The potential for survival of former garden and park layouts can be determined by establishing when the basic structure of the site was laid out and what were the significant phases of development, indicating the form that each took and showing what remains of them. Such an assessment of the value of the archaeological and historical resource should underpin related conservation policies and the site management plans based upon them.

Most forms of investigation involve at least some of the following methods, which are appropriate to all types of site from the large-scale and well documented to the small and obscure, where earthworks may constitute the only evidence.

Desk-based studies

The study of the primary archival sources for the history of any place, including pertinent maps, allows the individual stages of landscape development to be charted and sometimes closely dated. Relevant information from aerial photographs should also be checked, including any data available from airborne laser scanning (LiDAR) which is particularly suitable for recording features in wooded areas. Depending upon conditions, minute differences of surviving relief can be emphasised by shadow or lingering frost and surface-water, so bringing new understanding to features that are vague or obscure to the observer on the ground. Similarly, aerial reconnaissance can reveal sites where the original topography has been destroyed and the only evidence is formed by soil or crop-marks. Differences in vegetation and susceptibility to parching in dry weather can also help to characterise previous planting arrangements. All such information should be transcribed at a uniform scale onto a modern cartographic base. The sequence of development can then be reconstructed in a series of landscape regression maps to show the changing character at different times, and thereby help to define the intrinsic qualities of the site. The details can also be compiled into a GIS database for use as a management tool.

Field archaeology

Fieldwork, involving site inspection to check for visible remains, should be the next step. The banks and ditches of former raised walks and moats may represent early garden features, with lesser scarps and other depressions marking the lines of walls and sunken paths. Previous flowerbeds can also be identified. All remains should be accurately measured by a full metric survey to produce a plan which shows their overall context, spatial relationship and relative heights. This should be augmented by a detailed earthwork survey to be undertaken of slopes and other visible archaeological remains, noting the extent and nature of any degradation.

The topographical survey should be linked to analysis of access routes, boundaries and other built features of the gardens or parkland. It should also incorporate the identification and recording of historic trees, with appropriate sampling by coring and slicing of dead specimens for dendrochronology and growth analysis. In addition to noting the occurrence of trees and other flora possibly associated with historical planting, the more general character of the vegetation and tree canopy should be assessed. The species, form and branch structure of surviving trees and bushes can give evidence of past function and use, for example as pollards, pleached alignments, or clipped topiary. Dates for planting or changes in pruning can be estimated and methods of cultivation might be suggested by the examination of knots and root structures. Variations in surface vegetation denoting previous garden divisions and evidence for former tree-sites should also be mapped, particularly where shallow depressions of rotted root material have encouraged nettles and thistles to grow along the lines of lost avenues.

Geophysical survey

A further tool of non-destructive investigation is geophysical prospecting, either to augment other forms of survey or to search across lawns or even ploughed-out sites, where occasional parchmarks and soilmarks may be the only indication of lost features. In favourable conditions both electrical earth resistance measurement surveys and magnetometry have proved useful. The resistivity technique is particularly suitable for locating high-resistance features such as the compacted surfaces of earlier paths as well as buried masonry and drains. Higher water content in the soil creates low-resistance locations, often to be found in flowerbeds, tree holes and the sediments filling garden canals and ponds. Magnetometry, which measures the contrast between the magnetic properties of buried features and those of the surrounding soil, is frequently used to add further detail. The technique is particularly sensitive to ferrous materials and can aid the identification of iron objects, like the buried posts of a former pergola, or distinguish between different types of drain. Flowerbeds have also been detected in suitable conditions, possibly where past manuring has organically enriched the soil within them. A sampling interval of 1 m x 1 m is normally sufficient for the detection of most historic garden features, and a variety of data-treatment procedures can be used to enhance significant anomalies and present the results in graphic form. Depending upon the nature of soil conditions the results can achieve extraordinary detail but the effect is sometimes confusing, especially where a garden has been remodelled several times with the result that later features have become superimposed.

Excavation

Archaeological excavation and allied studies, such as soil chemistry and biological analysis, might be undertaken in order to increase understanding of the site as well as in relation to specific design proposals. The scope ranges from the comprehensive to the selective, targeting particular aspects either for the academic interest of the historical information alone or for assessing the veracity of a reconstruction. The investigation may be used to gather detailed information concerning site history and development, defining the appearance at specific times, as well as to test the degree of survival of the buried layout to ensure that significant features are not lost or obscured during routine maintenance or repair.

Sampling strategies might therefore range from uncovering an entire formal layout in readiness for accurate reconstruction to the examination of the salient points and key features of the grounds. The excavation of paths, for example, can provide evidence of the material used for their construction, together with details of their former dimensions, previous cross-section and original arrangement, as well as indicating their vulnerability to damage.

In addition to such information, detailed archaeological excavation can show how the ground was prepared for staking-out and creating the original design. Traces of plants associated with former garden features may be preserved in old pond-silts and other soil. They can include seeds, pollen and phytoliths (mineral particles formed within plant tissue), as well as macrofossils such as leaves, stems, wood and roots. With the remains of molluscs, insects and vertebrates, such botanical information can improve knowledge of the former environment and supplement historical planting records. Related studies of the soil itself may show the extent and nature of deliberate enrichment or other improvement, further indicating the original gardening practice. However, whilst the nature of individual flowerbeds may suggest what types of plant they once contained – for example those with shallow roots or requiring a greater depth of soil to grow in – sampling does not often show where specific plants grew previously. The reconstruction of planting arrangements therefore relies mainly upon other evidence and remains largely conjectural.

The location of planting beds and former parterre design are generally best recovered by open area excavation. In Britain, several fairly intact garden plans dating from the seventeenth century onwards have been investigated for the purpose of reconstruction. They include town house and other small gardens in addition to those laid out for royalty and the aristocracy. Whilst the excavation of King William III's Privy Garden at Hampton Court Palace is best known, similar large-scale work has been carried out in other places such as at Audley End, Essex and Witley Court, Worcestershire. Such investigations serve not simply to guide the future repair and reconstruction of garden features but also permit a better understanding of the history and sociology of garden design.

Further reading

General

>Currie, C. (2005) *Garden Archaeology*, Council for British Archaeology Practical Handbooks in Archaeology No. 17, York.
>Dix, B. (1999) 'Of Cabbages – and Kings: Garden Archaeology in Action', in *Old and New Worlds. Historical/Post Medieval Archaeology Papers from the Societies' joint conferences at Williamsburg and London 1997 to mark thirty years of work and achievement* (eds G. Egan & R.L. Michael), pp. 369–77, Oxbow Books, Oxford.
>Jacques, D. (ed.) (1997) 'The Techniques and Uses of Garden Archaeology', *Journal of Garden History*, 17.1, 1–99.
>Malek, A-A. (ed.) (2013) *Sourcebook for Garden Archaeology: Methods, Techniques, Interpretations and Field Examples*, Peter Lang AG, Bern.
>Taylor, C. (1983) *The Archaeology of Gardens*, Shire Publications, Princes Risborough.

Excavation and reconstruction

>Dix, B. (2011) 'Barbarous in its magnificence: The archaeological investigation and restoration of W.A. Nesfield's parterre design for the East Garden at Witley Court, Worcestershire', *Garden History*, 39.1, 51–63.
>Thurley, S. (ed.) (1995) 'The King's Privy Garden at Hampton Court Palace 1689–1995', *Apollo Magazine*, London.

15 Conservation arboriculture: the natural art of tree management in historic landscapes

Neville Fay

Institute of Chartered Foresters chartered arboriculturist and principal consultant at Treework Environmental Practice, Bristol, UK

Introduction

'These splendid remnants of decaying grandeur' . . . (Gilpin, 1791)

Conservation arboriculture, informed by the natural sciences, also draws from cultural traditions. In order to improve our understanding of trees and how they function in the landscape, we are wise to consider the humanities and arts for their contribution to an enhanced appreciation of trees. Here we find aspects of what might constitute the 'arboricultural imagination', the development of a faculty that paradoxically 'observes' invisible qualities both temporal and spatial, within and beneath the tree.

Fifteen years ago I was asked to carry out a conventional arboricultural assessment of an ancient population of English oak trees in a thousand-acre historic parkland. This led to a salutary lesson. Intervention was intended to improve the light reaching important old trees and to manage their stability. A small, though significant number of veteran trees declined as a result of my intervening too intensely (Figure 15.1). Strangely I owe a debt of gratitude to those trees, which suffered despite my good intentions.

The experience led to an unexpected dialogue between tree specialists, those with responsibility for the broader landscape and other specialists involved with the communities of colonising organisms (invertebrate, lichen, fungal, etc.) associated with decaying woody habitats. These conversations illuminated the rich interrelationship between trees and wildlife as a complex ecosystem. They also contributed to the emergence of a non-governmental organisation, the Ancient Tree Forum (ATF), a 'knowledge community' formed to further awareness, science and good conservation practice for ancient trees. The ATF collaboration has always punched above its weight, influencing national policy, publishing standards for veteran tree surveying (Fay and de Berker, 1997) and guidance on specific knowledge and good management (Read, 2000; Lonsdale, 2013).

Tree time and human time

I had been taught that trees have a natural life cycle: they set seed, grow old and die.
However, from those early multi-disciplinary discussions the arboricultural paradigm began to shift from the planning, planting and maintaining of trees in safe and amenable

Gardens & Landscapes in Historic Building Conservation, First Edition. Edited by Marion Harney.
© 2014 John Wiley & Sons, Ltd. Published 2014 by John Wiley & Sons, Ltd.

Figure 15.1 Ancient English oak population in historic deer park; some trees are over 500 years old. Intervention was intended to maintain structure and increase light, but too rapid intervention runs a risk of causing stress and decline.

condition, to considering trees *as* ecosystems operating *within* a mosaic of ecosystems. Instead, I learned that trees are a fundamental intimate and largely hidden life-support system, a mother to dependent wildlife. Britain's ancient trees support 2,000 invertebrate species needing dead and decaying woody habitat for some stage of their life cycle (Alexander, 2012). When we risk the loss of an old treasured tree we also threaten the species in and around it.

This discourse continues today and is consciousness-changing.

Perhaps the greatest influence on arboriculture in the second half of the twentieth century came from the life's work of Dr Alex Shigo (1930–2006), widely venerated as founding father of modern arboriculture. His *New Tree Biology* (Shigo, 1986) enriched the concept of 'compartmentalization of decay in trees' (CODIT) and brought respect for the way trees had evolved a special capacity to grow around decay, leading to a more technical approach to pruning that attempted to respect the natural boundaries established in the branching pattern of trees (target pruning). Modern conventional arboriculture approaches are crucially different from traditional and vernacular approaches such as with pollard cutting, in that the latter does not respect natural branch attachment boundaries, often cutting between nodes. While I had grown up professionally with the modern convention, eventually everything was forced to turn on its head when I met the irrefutable evidence presented by my colleagues in all the other fields working with, and prizing, decay in trees. This led to observing the way trees evolved to shed branches naturally and whether there was a role for artificially mimicking these processes of damage, ageing and decay.

I had been taught about pests and diseases and the need to protect trees from biological harm – fundamentally important after the devastation and attrition of our tree populations from Dutch elm disease and more recent threats. But now the perspective focused on health and biodiversity, what might constitute a functioning above- and below-ground ecosystem, and about what might tip the balance towards disease.

Given favourable circumstances, trees, through their vegetative capacity, could theoretically live forever. Ancient trees are by definition natural survivors, living for hundreds and even thousands of years, immersed and infused with microorganisms. So the question arises – what creates the grounds for pathogenicity or a spiral of decline? Practitioners and managers need a conceptual framework that draws on an understanding of natural processes as a basis for developing mature tree management strategies and enhancing ancient tree longevity.

Sometimes the modern world has to re-invent things before we can believe in their veracity, things which in times past had been taken for granted. For over a century modern agriculture added industrial fertilisers and pesticides to the soil to increase agricultural productivity; the organic movement then emerged to explain an alternative, as if this was something new – before the chemical processing of fossil fuels, the organic approach was taken for granted to the extent that the system did not even warrant a name.

Travel and the comments of travellers open our eyes to things we may take for granted. Washington Irving (1783–1859), the nineteenth-century American author (renowned for *The Legend of Sleepy Hollow*) was moved, while visiting England, by the trees of Sherwood Forest. He described 'mighty trunks of veteran oaks, the patriarchs of Sherwood Forest . . . shattered, hollow and moss grown . . . noble and picturesque in their decay . . . ruins of their ancient grandeur' (Irving, 1835). Had the Ancient Tree Forum existed when Irving visited Sherwood, he would, without doubt, have been a member. His lyrical observations should not be lightly dismissed. They show arboricultural *and* ecological imagination; awareness that mighty trunks reflect age, that shattered broken branches decay, hollowness suggests veteran qualities, and that the colonising epiphytes associated with moss all point to the trees' ancientness. Irving, even 175 years ago, clearly found the trees of Sherwood remarkable for their antiquity (Figure 15.2a and b). In perceiving 'veteran' and 'ancient' through the perspective of decay and age, he presaged qualities that we have come to understand in terms of habitat.

The poet John Dryden (1631–1700) touched on how tree time compares with human time, describing the oak as patriarch of trees with 'shoots rising up and spreads by slow degrees' (Dryden, 1700).

> Three centuries he grows
> And three he stays supreme in state
> And in three more decays

Figure 15.2 a, b Ancient trees still surviving at Sherwood Forest; the ancient tree on the left is the iconic 1,000-year-old Major Oak. The tree on the right, though much smaller, is probably similar in age, and rejuvenating. Washington Irving may have been inspired by these trees when visiting Sherwood.

Figure 15.3 This ancient tree in Savernake Forest was just reaching its mature phase after six human generations.

So Dryden had an arboricultural imagination, perceiving the English oak as having a natural longevity greater than 13 human lifespans, of 900 plus years. He understood natural ageing; inherently recognising that oak is in what we would call in arboricultural terms the *developmental phase* (300 years), the *mature phase* (300–600 years), and finally the prolonged *ancient phase*.

Getting a sense of time is a difficult trick and yet vital to the arboricultural imagination. The brevity of our human lifespan compared to that of trees allows us but a mere glimpse of its developmental processes, let alone its evolutionary time (Figure 15.3). Yet such knowledge is necessary to support the arborist in making everyday management decisions. The life cycle is key to understanding the ageing process, and moreover, what is meant by 'veteran' and 'ancient'.

An *ancient tree* is one that is old for its species. The term 'ancient' describes an *age class*, a life stage where the chronological age of the individual is considered in light of the species' life cycle and typical life expectancy. A *veteran tree* has decaying woody (saproxylic) habitat derived from wounding and the ageing process, through which the tree becomes host to wildlife. In this sense a veteran might be thought of as a 'battle scarred survivor', who, having been through the wars, has tales of experiences and wounding. The physiological effects of damage, shading, drought and storms initiate veteran habitat and can occur 'pre-maturely' in a non-ancient tree. Whereas all ancient trees are veterans, not all veterans are ancient.

We think of an *ancient* as having the wisdom of the ancestors. So it is with ancient trees: being true survivors, they communicate their physiological encounters with history through their form and body language (morphology). The skills necessary to interpret their form are needed if we are to understand how to enhance their longevity and help today's trees become tomorrow's ancients.

A crucial stage of the ageing process is when the crown of a fully mature tree begins to *retrench* (when nutrient and water supply lines from root to crown periphery start to reduce). This is naturally prompted when the roots are unable to finance new peripheral extension, due to the canopy having developed to its maximum potential in its growing conditions. *Crown retrenchment* defines the onset of the ancient phase – often the longest phase (Fay, 2002). Observing crown retrenchment gives a pointer to ways the arborist can mimic a natural process in the service of conservation management of heritage trees (Figure 15.4a–c).

Figure 15.4 a–c Natural crown retrenchment; trees naturally retrench their crowns, entering the ancient phase.

There is no model for how one can trade in rot. Modern conventional arboriculture concerns itself largely with how trees and people coexist and has been inevitably influenced by utilitarian models with a somewhat narrow aesthetic range. This has led to trees being assessed for their retention suitability, often considered in terms of their 'safe useful life expectancy'. In this sense arboriculture has also been influenced by forestry, in that, at the stage when a tree begins to decay, it declines in commercial value.

The human lifespan is so short by comparison. It is not surprising therefore that we have come to focus on functionality and amenity rather than values associated with the tree's potential lifespan, and where we do this we inevitably cut short the ageing process, removing trees at highest mature 'use value', before their veteran qualities begin to flourish.

It is our human lot that we seldom witness the long-term effects of our actions. Developing the faculty to comprehend tree time, imagining how a tree will respond to influences, requires close observation of natural processes to appreciate that when we intervene (as with pruning), growth responses occur slowly and seldom how we would have imagined. The Arthur Clough Oak is the subject of a rare, 100-year photographic record sequence of a tree (Figure 15.5) that illustrates the rejuvenation responses and the long-term 'self-pruning' and shaping in the tree's interactions with the environment. I would venture few tree specialists on the planet would have foreseen this response.

1910   **1920s**   **c: 1950**   **1981**   **2009**

Figure 15.5 A hundred years of ageing: 'The Arthur Clough Oak', at Boars Hill near Oxford, offers a rare example of a sequential photographic record of a tree over a century. The sequence demonstrates our limitations in being able to foresee the natural tree's response over 'tree time'. (Photo courtesy of Philip Stewart.)

Necessity – mother of arboricultural invention

In Europe 'vernacular arboriculture' has taken place for millennia.

Hæggström (1994), who searched for pollards in art, notes that art historians have not known what to look for and in this sense, have not 'seen' the pollards, featured in visual representations of cultural landscapes. Yet, from ancient times, works of art reveal the shaping of the landscape by man and beast, with beautiful pollard depictions dating from as long ago as 1,500 BCE (before the common era). Over these 3,500 years of European history a remarkable record in pottery fragments, carvings and paintings shows human connections with pollard trees dating from ancient Greece, through medieval and Renaissance periods and beyond (Hæggström, 1994).

Damaging chance events to branches from storms, fire and flood, and from grazing and gnawing animals created and stimulated new growth in trees (Green, 2000); a lesson that our early ancestors learned and mimicked.

Cultural management of trees, their cultivation and care, is an ancient art that has been subject to changing fashions as man's connection to his environment has changed. It predates agricultural cultivation, and, as that environment changed, so too did man's relationship to changing landscapes.

Living off the produce from trees (nuts, fruit, etc.) is natural for birds and animals, including man. Coppicing (cutting near the ground), pollarding (cutting above grazing height) and orchard cultivation have been used to produce woody, foliar and fruit crops. Pollarding created a system where it was possible to combine cutting of trees for produce within a landscape with grazing animals, landscapes characterised by parkland-like settings with grassland and scrub and mostly open grown trees (Rackham, 1990; Vera, 2000). As humans became skilled in pollarding, they, together with the grazing animals, helped shape the European landscape.

The cyclical removal of pollard stems (poles) from the trunk (or 'boll') creates cutting-wounds that promote decay and hollowing. This also, curiously, may serve to extend the life of the tree, by reducing and managing the size of the crown and its water and nutrient demands: the decay processes that alter the state of the wood also serve to generate a range of habitats for colonising organisms that dynamically change over time.

In mainland Europe, the influence of the Enlightenment lent a sense of sophistication to the way pollarding and hard-pruning were used, as a means of man controlling nature, reflecting aesthetic and pragmatic approaches to managing trees in alleyways, boulevards and squares; methods that included pleaching, 'curtain pruning' and topiary (Clair-Maczulajtys et al, 1999).

In Britain, since Georgian times and the period of Romantic landscape design, municipal trees began to be managed by pruning as urban pollards to control their scale and form, while in the wider landscape traditional pollard management gradually began to go out of fashion – to the extent of eventually being thought unsightly, unnatural and even damaging to the tree (Petit and Watkins, 2003).

This strong legacy from the pollard tradition, which had sustained local economies throughout Europe, did not persist in any significant degree into the New World. Without being able to see pollards as common features in rural and urban landscapes, there is little opportunity to observe the pollard tree's response in terms of the ageing process and to develop appreciation for its form and the aesthetics of decay.

Ancient pollards teach us that decay has little to do with disease and often much to do with longevity. The oldest trees in European landscapes, particularly in lowland Britain, many in old growth savannah-type wood-pasture, have been lost or harmed through wars as well as 'civilising' influences associated with landscape design, ornamental gardening, intensive modern agriculture and new development and, in recent years, from 'tidiness' and efficient, mechanised working.

Britain has also lost many ancient trees in recent decades, when no longer considered 'safe' or 'useful' – this has raised passionate discourse between tree people, nature conservationists and owners, increasing the momentum of conservation arboriculture. Neither have tree professionals escaped a modernising tendency to prefer a safer, more sanitised environment, free from the risks of ageing trees. Tree managers have played their part in cleansing environments of dead wood, impoverishing biodiversity and unwittingly deconstructing the younger generation's experience of living processes – all suggesting a responsibility to reassess arboricultural principles; to review assumptions that in some instances may be considered unchallengeable.

This failure to comprehend our own relatively short-lived existence, compared to that of trees, pushes us in the direction of mechanistic, ingenious intervention rather than patient observation.

On the other hand, by drawing on our long tradition of living and working with trees, taking the best from the conventional and combining this with the vernacular, we take a step towards reconciling the difference between tree time and human time and lay a foundation for conservation arboriculture.

Dead wood – hidden life

> 'Life and death are one thread, two faces of the same sinew'. Lao Tzu

Despite 300 million years of co-evolution between trees and fungi (and the late arrival of man on the scene) the view that 'dead wood removal is good for the health of the tree' (Shigo, 1989), as a scientifically valid and intuitively self-evident principle, has in large measure driven arboricultural practice based on an assumption that dead and decaying wood are food sources for 'invasive' harmful fungi.

Inspired by Shigo's dictum (1989) that 'education starts when you doubt something', I felt confident to question more deeply some of the tenets of modern arboriculture. Having had the privilege of visiting old-growth landscapes and wood pasture systems, and seeing a great many ancient trees, I became curious about how thousand-year-old trees survive with copious amounts of dead, decaying and advanced-rotting wood. The view that dead wood is harmful is challenged by mycologists exploring tree–fungi interrelationships, fungal colonisation, nutrient recycling and decomposition (Cooke and Rayner, 1984; Rayner and Boddy, 1988).

Despite there being fairly wide acceptance of mutualistic associations between fungi and tree roots (mycorrhizas) that confer co-evolved health and survival benefits, there was little knowledge about the complex array of fungi residing for the most part benignly within living tissue (endophytes). Evidence of these endophytic fungi, functioning as latent organisms within live tissue, has challenged accepted wisdom and practice about decaying wood and fungi (Rayner, 1993), and led to reconsideration of the current model of fungi as inherently invasive, potentially pathogenic organisms against which the tree had evolved defences (Shigo, 1989).

A model was needed which would take a more sophisticated account of fundamental relationships between the tree, fungi, water and air. Conservation arboriculture, influenced by the many ecological contributions from those interested in the myriad organisms which colonise the tree and its soil, reminds us that the huge bulk of living space in and around the root system and soil particles teems with life, and itself constitutes 'the tree'.

So, fungi, water, air. How are we to consider their interrelationships in this revised model? The whole system is predicated on the essential role of water in the life of the tree and microorganisms, and without understanding this, we are led to regard fungi already present in the tree as inherently hostile. Our ancestors supported the tree in its long life's journey by pollarding, thus 'managing' the water transportation distances. While this benefited them, the hidden world of fungi, insects and other organisms also quietly flourished, as passengers on the journey through time.

The tree is 'a fountain of the forest' (Rayner, 1998). It moves water from the soil to the clouds. Not only is energy expended to transfer a column of water great vertical distances, but a strategy is needed to keep it intact in its passage through the vessels of the tree, maintaining 'pipe integrity' while being lifted to the furthest leaves before evaporating (evapotranspiration). We have only a theory to satisfactorily describe this mystery, *the cohesion-tension theory*, which requires the exclusion of air for the hydraulic system to work.

It is surprising that fungi can live in this vessel water. These endophytic fungi are quiescent in hydrated vessels, circumstances that prevail for many years. When, as a consequence of bark damage, pruning and wounding, sapwood hydration is significantly reduced and air is introduced, the cohesion between the water molecules is disrupted, causing the chain of vessel-borne water to 'snap' (air embolism). Under these circumstances microscopic endophytes come to flourish and forage, benefiting from available oxygen, changing their lifestyle, eventually expressing their presence when they emerge as fruiting bodies on exposed wood.

It appears that tree-related fungi are capable of different modes of behaviour and that their macroscopic (visible to us) expression, such as fruiting bodies, is influenced by the tree's hydrology. If we bear in mind this 'hydrodynamic' model of the tree and its fungal communities we may come to different conclusions about what the tree has evolved to defend itself against. Rather than the tree marshalling its defences against fungi, both fungi and trees, being mutually 'plumbed' together, need to manage water and exclude air.

Rayner shows that, once freed from dormancy, fungi are greedy for territory, and highly antagonistic to other fungal communities. Given that endophytes compete strongly between one another and against opportunistic colonisation from other outside fungi, there is a case for characterising the relationship between endophytes and the tree as an immune system.

So, conservation arboriculture has suddenly become far more complex. We see that dead wood is not dead but decaying, it contains hidden life. We can only guess at what we change in the ecosystem when we intervene with trees and their landscape or when we remove dead wood.

Integrating vernacular, modern and conservation arboriculture

Thus, veteran trees are important in their own right as iconic features of natural heritage, due to their age, history and place in the landscape. But it is their veteran qualities, their *wounds* and *decaying wood*, which endow them with intrinsic value as host to colonising organisms.

The tree is clearly a far more complex organism than can be understood by an over-simplified biological model. Exploring the tree as an ecosystem and observing through the lens of co-evolution contribute to an integrated approach to management. The internal topography of an ageing woody structure, infused with a network of fungal hyphae, progressively hosting communities of invertebrates and other organisms, expresses the web of life that is the ancient tree.

Conservation arboriculture therefore engages our stewardship of this ecosystem spun over time. We hold this delicate web in trust for the future. In so doing, we walk in the footsteps of others who, before modern science helped define the complexity, saw these same connections, so well expressed in the words of the Reverend Johns:

> Though but a hollow shell, blasted above, and worm-eaten below . . . it is a monument of the past more eloquent than buildings the most time-hallowed; or, save one, than books of the most remote antiquity. It is now a living tree, and it was the same thirty generations back (Johns, 1882).

Acknowledgements

This chapter develops further ideas first presented to the International Society of Arboriculture 87th Annual Conference, Parramatta, Australia, July 2011 (http://www.isa-arbor.com/). I would like to acknowledge a debt of gratitude to Nigel de Berker for discussing these ideas with me and Chrissie Gray, who has helped me with the many revisions. Also to my colleagues at Treework Environmental Practice (http:// www.treeworks.co.uk) and Ancient Tree Forum (http://www.woodland-trust.org.uk/ancient-tree-forum), who have given me the opportunity to experience ancient trees. Thanks also to Philip Stewart for assisting with the compilation of the images of the 'Arthur Clough Oak' in Figure 15.5. Further acknowledgements are to Paul Lack for the 1981 photograph; Philip Stewart for providing the 2009 photograph; Oxford City Library for the photograph taken by Henry Taunt in 1910. The 1920s photograph is anonymous, from *Country Life*, and for which there remains no current record. The 1950s photograph is anonymous, and acknowledgement is due to the *Quarterly Journal of Forestry*, for which there is no current traceable record.

Further reading

Alexander, K.N.A. (2012) *What do saproxylic (wood-decay) beetles really want? Conservation should be based on practical observation rather than unstable theory*, Trees beyond the wood conference proceedings, September 2012.

Clair-Maczulajtys, D., Le Disquet, I. and Bory, G. (1999) 'Pruning trees: changes in the tree physiology and other effects on tree health', *Proc. Int. Symp*, On Urban Tree Health. *ActaHorticulturae*, 496, 317–324.

Cooke, R.C. and Rayner, A.D.M. (1984) *Ecology of Saprotrophic Fungi*, Longman, London.

Dryden, J. (1700) 'Palamon and Arcite', in *Fables, Ancient and Modern*, Book 3, Vol. I.

Fay, N. and de Berker, N. (1997) *The Specialist Survey Method*, Veteran Trees Initiative, Natural England, Peterborough.

Fay, N. (2002) 'Environmental Arboriculture, Tree Ecology & Veteran Tree Management', *The Arboricultural Journal*, 26 (3), 213–238.

Green, E.E. (2000) 'Coppicing Like a Beaver', *British Wildlife*, 11 (4), 239–241.

Gilpin, W. (1791) *Remarks on Forest Scenery and Other Woodland Views*, Vol. I, Smith, Elder & Co, London.

Hæggström, C-A. (1994) 'Pollards in Art', *Botanical Journal of Scotland*, 46, 682–687.

Irving, W. (1835) *Abbotsford and Newstead Abbey*, John Murray, London.

Johns, Rev. C.A. (1882) *The Forest Trees of Britain*, SPCK, London.

Petit, S. and Watkins, C. (2003) 'Pollarding Trees: Changing Attitudes to a Traditional Land Management Practice in Britain 1600–1900', *Rural History* 14 (2), 157–176, Cambridge University Press.

Rackham, O. (1990) *Trees and woodland in the British landscape*, Dent & Sons Ltd, London.

Rayner, A.D.M. and Boddy, L. (1988) *Fungal Decomposition of Wood – Its Biology and Ecology*, Wiley, Chichester.

Rayner, A.D.M. (1993) 'New Avenues for Understanding Processes of Tree Decay', *The Arboricultural Journal* 17 (2), 171–189.

Rayner, A.D.M. (1998) 'Fountains of the forest: the interconnectedness between trees and fungi', *Mycol. Res.* 102, 1441–1449.

Read, H. (ed.) (2000) *Veteran trees: A guide to good management*, Natural England, Peterborough.

Shigo, A.L. (1986) *A New Tree Biology*, Shigo and Trees Associates, Durham, New Hampshire.

Shigo, A. (1989) *A New Tree Biology*, Shigo and Trees Associates, Durham, New Hampshire.

Vera, F.W.M. (2000) *Grazing Ecology and Forest History*, CABI, Oxford.

16 The use of aerial photographs for conservation and research

Helen Winton
Manager of the Aerial Investigation and Mapping team, English Heritage, London, UK

Aerial survey is a broad term, used to describe various activities related to the recording of sites and landscapes from the air; this includes taking photographs, interpretation, description, and mapping using new and historic photographs. The use of aerial photographs is long established in archaeological survey and newer technologies, such as LiDAR (airborne laser scanning) and multi-spectral data gathering are adding to the toolkit of the aerial photograph interpreter. Archaeological aerial survey provides a better understanding of past landscapes to inform research and conservation.

The use of aerial photographs in the study of historic parks and gardens is an integral part of a process involving multiple sources and methods, which are explored elsewhere in this publication (see also Taigel and Williamson, 1993; Taylor, 1998). This chapter explores the main applications of aerial photographs when used in conjunction with these other techniques.

Aerial photographs illustrate extensive designed landscapes such as parks associated with grand houses, municipal urban parks, or the settings of hospitals, housing estates or military complexes. The focus might be on individual elements, such as ornamental buildings, planting schemes, landscaping, or a wide view demonstrating the interplay between different components of a design. The aerial view, although distanced from the usual, or intended, experience of the landscape or garden, provides an overview perhaps similar to the designer's concept exemplified by the eighteenth-century views of Kip and Knyff.

Ways of seeing the evidence

A key use of aerial photographs in the study of the historic environment is the discovery of buried archaeological features which are impossible, or very difficult, to see from the ground. The layout of these buried features is revealed as patterns in crops or in the plough soil, called cropmarks and soilmarks. Discovery is not limited to buried features – the different perspective and wide-ranging geographical scope of aerial survey can reveal previously unnoticed earthworks or structures. The aerial view can therefore reveal 'lost' garden or vestigial design features. There may also be remnants of earlier land use linked to the story of a park, such as deserted medieval villages and ridge and furrow cultivation, or from a completely separate phase, for example prehistoric settlement. As well as recording archaeological

Gardens & Landscapes in Historic Building Conservation, First Edition. Edited by Marion Harney.
© 2014 John Wiley & Sons, Ltd. Published 2014 by John Wiley & Sons, Ltd.

features, the aerial perspective captures many aspects of gardens and designed landscapes including topographical subtleties and botanical features.

A combination of the right ground conditions and suitable weather are required for recording the historic environment from the air. These conditions change throughout the year and different types of features, cropmarks over different geological types, earthworks, or buildings, will be photographed in different conditions (Grady, 2007). Existing knowledge, research frameworks, heritage protection priorities and other strategies also influence observer-led aerial reconnaissance programmes.

Cropmarks are differences in the colour and height of a crop and features in and below the plough-soil cause these variations in growth. Cropmarks can show at all stages of the growth of a plant and sometimes only for a very short period. This might be while the plant is germinating (September/October or February/March) and/or ripening (May to July). Cereal crops like wheat and barley can produce particularly good cropmarks due to their relative density and deep roots within a small area. Cropmarks also show in flax or linseed, sugar beet, oil seed rape, maize, borage, peas and beans, and even potato crops. Grass and pasture fields may also show colour differences and in the height of summer lack of moisture can cause parching (these are sometimes known as parchmarks). The terms 'negative' and 'positive' are sometime used with the term cropmark – negative cropmarks occur where crop growth is stunted by lack of moisture over walls, roads and compacted surfaces. Positive cropmarks occur where crop growth is enhanced by extra moisture over cut-features such as ditches, pits, palisade trenches and robbed walls.

At Wrest Park in Bedfordshire (Figure 16.1), the English Heritage aerial reconnaissance team recorded, in 1994, parchmarks of buried remains of the previous house and associated gardens showing in the lawns of the present house.

The buried foundations of the former house and forecourt, corresponding to the locations marked on eighteenth-century plans, were seen as lighter marks in the grass. Elements of

Figure 16.1 Wrest Park, Bedfordshire. Parchmarks reveal the location of buried remains of the former house (foreground), former paths (middle) and tree boles (either side of the bushes below the ornamental beds). (15165/05 29 July 1994 © Crown copyright.)

the gardens associated with the former house were also recorded as negative cropmarks, for example diagonal paths and small circular statue plinths. Other garden features showed as positive cropmarks, for example dark circular marks indicate the sites of tree boles from the ornamental planting depicted on a panorama of the gardens dating from the 1830s (Alexander and Small, forthcoming).

Soilmarks are differences in the colour and tone of soil due to archaeological features in the plough-soil. The effect of ploughing drags these deposits up and away from their buried position, creating a zigzag effect as the farmer works backwards and forwards across the field. These features can be the remains of a wall or bank (usually lighter), or the contents of a ditch (usually darker). Settlements can show as large dark areas of debris-rich soil. Industrial activity may leave distinctive areas of coloured or patterned soil.

Features which survive at the ground surface include 'earthworks' such as banks, mounds and spoil heaps and cut features such as ditches, pits and quarries. They are revealed by contrasts in highlight and shadow and are best photographed in low sunlight, which enhances the shadows. A light dusting of snow can make the contrasting highlights and shadows of the earthworks more pronounced. They are also discernable by contrasts of texture and colour. Ditches may be more easily visible when they contain standing water or unmelted snow.

Other features on the ground surface, such as exposed stone-built features like walls, foundations, and ruined buildings, are revealed by contrasts of highlight and shadow. Differences in colour, tone and texture may also distinguish them from the surrounding surface; for example, stone foundations contrasting with surrounding grass, bare rock or sand. Stonework often appears light in tone, but may look dark against snow cover. Turf-covered walls may have a lumpy texture or some exposed stones may be visible, but when grassed over these essentially become earthworks.

Earthworks photographed at Risby Hall (Figure 16.2) in the Hull Valley in East Yorkshire represent a rare survival of an eighteenth-century garden.

The low winter sun highlights the earthworks and the aerial view illustrates the general layout of the gardens. A depression marks the site of the cellars of a late seventeenth-century house which burnt down twice in the late eighteenth century. The remains of the gardens associated with the house include several terraces, avenues and ornamental ponds (Evans, forthcoming). These correspond to those illustrated on an early eighteenth-century print which shows a terraced walk overlooking a parterre, garden statues, pavilions and water features (Neave and Waterson, 1988).

Figure 16.2 Risby Park, East Yorkshire. Earthworks of the seventeenth-century house, garden terraces and water features. The ponds in the mid-background appear to have been altered recently. (28224/25 19 October 2011 © English Heritage.)

The skills of the air photo interpreter are aided by studying the form (morphology) of sites and their landscape context. For example, using aerial photographs the garden specialist will recognise the form, pattern and context of buried paths, parterres, statue plinths or arrangements of tree boles, which perhaps formed an avenue or a quincunx. However, to understand the nature of the pre-garden landscape, and to avoid possible misinterpretation of earlier or later features, a basic knowledge of other archaeological site types is required, for example prehistoric settlement or burials, or World War II features. Similarly an understanding of the soils, geology and modern land use, twentieth-century farming practices in particular, are required to interpret potentially confusing non-archaeological features seen on aerial photographs. The key reference for understanding the range and types of archaeological and non-archaeological features visible from the air is David Wilson's publication *Air Photo Interpretation for Archaeologists* (1986 and 2000).

Sources

Aerial photographs held in national and local archives are a huge resource for studying archaeological sites and landscapes. These should be supplemented by other information derived from historic maps, soil and geology maps, analytical earthwork surveys, geophysical surveys, excavations, documentary evidence and other research.

Aerial photographs are often categorised as 'obliques' or 'verticals'. Oblique photographs are usually taken with a hand-held camera through the open window of a plane. Any kind of light aircraft can be used, preferably high-winged for maximum visibility. The photographs are taken at an oblique angle to the ground but vertical or near-vertical shots are common. The aircraft can be easily manoeuvred and a number of views taken from different angles. This maximises the visibility of the archaeology and provides sufficient control to correlate the features on the photo with a map. These are a deliberate and focused record of historic and archaeological sites or landscapes.

Vertical photographs are taken using one or more fixed cameras pointing straight down at the ground, usually within a modified plane. They fly on prescribed courses to provide blanket coverage of large areas. This kind of survey was usually made for topographical mapping and so may not have been taken in ideal conditions for recording archaeological features.

One of the biggest national collections of aerial photography is held at the English Heritage Archive and this is an essential source. Cambridge University holds a less extensive but very high quality national collection of aerial photographs of mainly archaeological and geological subjects. The English Heritage collection has vertical aerial photographs taken at regular intervals from the 1940s to the present. These sorties usually covered large areas of land, and sometimes provide almost blanket cover of the country, in 1946 for example. The oblique aerial photograph collections include some 1940s military photos but mainly comprise photographs of archaeological sites taken from the 1960s onwards.

Early pioneers in the applications of archaeological aerial photography include Major G.W. Allen and O.G.S. Crawford, who took and collected archaeologically focused aerial photography mainly in the 1920s and 1930s. Some of their photographs are in the UK national collections but the main archive is curated by the Ashmolean Museum, Oxford. The Aerofilms Collection has major holdings from before World War II. Aerofilms pioneered commercial aerial photography and covered a wide range of subjects including some historic and archaeological sites. Part of this unique collection is being developed by the English Heritage Archive, Swindon into an online resource – see britainfromabove.org.uk.

Equivalent national collections exist in Wales and Scotland. The Scottish collections include The Aerial Reconnaissance Archive (TARA), which includes results of World War II allied and German aerial reconnaissance in Europe and RAF aerial photography around the world up to the 1990s. Local Historic Environment Records (or Sites and Monuments Records) will normally be able to advise on the availability of local collections, which usually comprise a limited range of vertical photographs and some specialist oblique photographs.

Some websites, such as Google Earth and Bing, now offer seamless aerial photographic cover, often free of charge, subject to terms and conditions. These provide relatively up-to-date colour photographs and sometimes offer photographs taken at intervals since about 2000. The drawback is that these photo mosaics cannot be viewed stereoscopically and the resolution, while mostly good, can be variable in more remote areas.

Historic aerial photographs and landscape change

Historic aerial photographs provide a fantastic record of landscape change through the twentieth century. They record many unrecognised earthwork and cropmark sites because much of the vertical collection has not been examined for archaeological purposes. The historic collections capture 'lost' sites which may have been ploughed level, due to the expansion of arable in the post-war period, or been covered by urban expansion and other developments. Pre- World War II photographs will sometimes reveal planting schemes in urban parks and country estates maintained from an earlier era. Many post-war aerial photographs, taken at intervals during a period of major change, show the decline of large country houses, their gardens and parks, urban parks and green spaces. However, they also record the development of large twentieth-century designed landscapes such as the peri-urban university campus in the mid–late twentieth century, for example at the Universities of Bath or York, or the major post-war housing developments, including 'garden cities'.

The historic aerial photographs also provide an important contemporary or near-contemporary record of structures relating to World War II. These include military defensive structures, airfields, camps, hospitals, civil defence and training areas. World War II saw many changes in urban parks and at the large country houses and their surrounding parkland. The Dig for Victory campaign caused the conversion of many urban parks to allotments. Open spaces, often parks, were used for air raid shelters and other civil defence structures such as emergency water supply tanks, barrage balloon moorings and anti-aircraft batteries. The country houses and their grounds were used for military storage, training, and camps, including prisoner of war camps.

Newer technology

Most of the easily available satellite imagery has poorer resolution than conventional aircraft-flown data and is not commonly used in the UK. On satellite images, features smaller than 5m (or 1–2m on the best available quality) are usually not discernible, and even larger features can appear pixelated and difficult to identify. Satellite imagery has proved extremely useful to archaeologists working in remote or dangerous terrain, or regions where mapping is not available. Satellite and other airborne surveys often include multi-spectral data that can provide an overview of environmental and land use information, which is useful for setting sites in their landscape context and in assessing potential threats. The use of multi-spectral data is well appreciated for vegetation studies, but for archaeological purposes it is still developing and has had limited application.

Airborne LiDAR (Light Detection and Ranging) uses a pulsed laser beam to create a precise digital elevation model (DEM) of the ground and the features upon it. This DEM can be used to view the landscape form and is an excellent tool for the identification and mapping of archaeological earthworks. A particular benefit of LiDAR is that when the laser beam can reach the ground between leaves and other vegetation, such as a tree canopy or understorey, it is possible to record features that are not easily seen from the air. However, this is not possible if the tree canopy or other vegetation is too dense so there are no gaps through which the light can pass to the ground. A key reference for this is the English Heritage publication *The Light Fantastic – Using airborne lidar in archaeological survey* by Simon Crutchley and Peter Crow.

Archaeological mapping and landscape analysis

As well as taking and collecting aerial photographs in the 1920s and 1930s, individuals such as Major G.W. Allen and O.G.S. Crawford realised the importance of interpreting and collating the information on the photographs to produce an archaeological map of sites seen from the air (Crawford and Keiller, 1928; Allen, 1934). This was a move from the usual site-based approach of excavating archaeologists to an appreciation of extensive archaeological landscapes. However, relatively little similar work was carried out until the 1960s when publications began to present archaeological landscapes known from aerial photographs in the form of interpreted maps and descriptions (e.g. Royal Commission on the Historical Monuments of England (RCHME), 1960; Benson and Miles, 1974; Riley, 1980; Palmer, 1984; Stoertz, 1997).

Many photographs are required to build up a picture of an archaeological site or landscape. Features in adjacent fields may only show as cropmarks in different years, or all the elements of a feature in one field may not always appear as cropmarks at the same time. The same is true, to a lesser extent, for earthworks and structures, as the lighting conditions, i.e. the position of the sun, can highlight details of a site, or render it nearly invisible from the air. The historic aerial photographs may serendipitously record cropmarks or earthworks or features lost to the plough or other development.

The best way to collate and understand the archaeological information on aerial photographs is to map the information accurately and to provide interpretations of the sites and landscapes. This mapping provides information for research and further work using different techniques. The mapping also provides essential information on the extent and nature of archaeological sites to inform the planning process.

Both oblique and vertical photographs provide a means of mapping archaeological features to produce a scaled plan. To create a scaled map or plan of archaeological features, an Ordnance Survey map base is usually used as a background. The accuracy of mapping varies according to the base map and the method applied.

Mapping from aerial photographs is most effective when all archaeological features are included, not just those of specific relevance to the researcher. Therefore, features will be recorded with a date ranging from the period with the earliest known construction of monuments, the Neolithic, through to near the present, including the twentieth century. To be of use to researchers and planners the descriptions of the sites must include an interpretation suggesting a date, function and the condition of the remains such as cropmark, earthwork, and levelled earthwork. This provides information on a period of interest and allows an assessment of how this phase may have been influenced by earlier features. Assessment and mapping identifies why and where there may be gaps in the aerial photograph evidence due to more recent features.

The interpretation and mapping should record a reference to the original sources, including all relevant aerial photographs providing an essential starting point for future updates or re-evaluation of the site or landscape. Finally, a synthesis and overview is required to place individual elements into a landscape narrative; often this is illustrated with a series of phased coloured plans highlighting the relevant areas on the mapped evidence.

English Heritage fund and carry out aerial photograph mapping projects under the banner of the National Mapping Programme (NMP) – this is a national standard aimed at providing the quality of mapped and interpretive data required for consistent value judgements on the nature and extent of the archaeological resource visible on aerial photographs. This comprehensive synthesis of the archaeological information is intended to assist research, planning and protection of the historic environment. This standard developed over more than 20 years and early projects did not normally include garden features. The remit of NMP now covers all features from the Neolithic period up to the twentieth century and includes assessment and mapping of historic parks and gardens. Therefore, the survey results and reports often include sections on gardens, for example in the North Gloucestershire Cotswolds (Stoertz, 2012).

Conservation and heritage management

As well as providing a tool for research and understanding of the historic environment, aerial photographs and air photo interpretation and mapping have a role to play in the conservation of sites and landscapes. This is particularly true of those with heritage designations, such as scheduled monuments, registered parks and gardens, or wider designations such as a World Heritage Site (WHS), National Park, or Area of Outstanding Natural Beauty (AONB).

RCHME's *A Matter Of Time* (1960) used aerial photographs by J.K. St Joseph and others, not just to demonstrate the value of aerial photography for discovering sites, but also to highlight the threats to them from agriculture, quarrying and post-war development.

In the early 1980s there was a growing realisation that understanding the nature, extent and significance of aerial evidence is a fundamental requirement for the conservation and management of archaeological sites. English Heritage's Monuments Protection Programme (MPP) recognised this, and in 1993 the Institute of Field Archaeologists (IFA) published a technical paper to encourage proper use of aerial photographs for archaeological survey and evaluation, in particular as a response to the implementation of Planning Policy Guidance 16 (PPG16) (Palmer and Cox, 1993). Aerial photographs are now listed in the IFA's standard and guidance for desk-based assessments (2011) as an essential source.

Aerial photographs provide a snapshot or record of historic parks and gardens for the English Heritage register, illustrating the details and setting of the buildings and parkland features. Many parks are smaller now than they were at their peak and the registered area may be only part of the original extent of the park. An aerial view sometimes allows you to see 'lost' areas of the park – fossilised in the surrounding field pattern. These may also provide an important element of the 'setting' for the surviving core area (English Heritage, 2012).

An aerial photograph taken of New Hall in Essex (Figure 16.3) illustrates the landscape changes around the park.

The avenue of trees, which extends south-east from the park, was cut across by the Great Eastern Railway in 1844 and then in the late twentieth century by construction of the A12

Figure 16.3 New Hall, Essex. A photograph taken for the English Heritage Register of Parks and Gardens illustrates the landscape changes through the nineteenth and twentieth centuries. (21739/20 21 August 2001 © English Heritage.)

and a service area. The former hedgerows and small fields marked on the nineteenth-century maps have mostly been amalgamated into larger arable fields. The final change to this landscape is captured in progress on the left of the photograph with development of housing in the 2000s advancing towards the park and its old lodge.

Historic aerial photographs can also provide a retrospective 'timeline' to illustrate particular conservation issues such as the long-term effects of woodland management or grazing regimes on the preservation and presentation of archaeological sites, including parks and gardens.

Aerial reconnaissance assists with monitoring of monuments and helps identify major issues such as damage from animals, ploughing or other events. Because of the extensive geographical reach of the light aircraft, aerial photography can be used as the first stage to rapidly assess monument condition in areas with extremely high numbers of scheduled sites, or sites in difficult to access or remote areas. Extreme close-ups taken from the air, as opposed to the usual more general view, can be used to identify issues and to prioritise ground-based visits.

Mapping derived from aerial photographs has a role to play in the contexts above but is also fundamental in the understanding, research and conservation of sites and landscapes with no statutory protection. The mapping provides the baseline knowledge and understanding that allows the appropriate level of protection in the context of landscape change. The interpretation and mapping provide a framework for the application of different methods, such as documentary research, analytical field survey or geophysical survey, to address thematic, chronological and physical gaps in knowledge.

Provision of training and easily accessible resources, including aerial imagery, is the key to encouraging professionals, amateurs and community groups to use aerial photographs. Raising awareness of the potential of aerial survey as a tool for research leads to better conservation and heritage management.

More generally, and equally importantly, aerial photographs and air photo mapping can have a significant role in communicating and illustrating issues in archaeological conservation, for sites and landscapes; for example in leaflets for farmers and land managers – see the *Farming the Historic Landscape* series of leaflets which includes one covering historic parks and gardens (English Heritage, 2005).

Acknowledgements

This chapter is based on the work of the English Heritage Aerial Investigation team with particular thanks to Cathy Stoertz, Fiona Small, Damian Grady, Pete Horne and Yvonne Boutwood.

Further reading

Alexander, M. and Small, F. (Forthcoming) *Wrest Park Understanding the Landscape*, English Heritage Research Report.
Benson, D. and Miles, D. (1974) *The Upper Thames Valley: an archaeological survey of the river gravels*. Oxford; Oxford Archaeological Unit.
English Heritage (2005) *Farming the Historic Landscape*, Online document: http://www.english-heritage.org.uk/publications/farming-the-historic-landscape-historic-parkland/
English Heritage (2012) *The Setting of Heritage Assets*, Online document: http://www.english-heritage.org.uk/publications/setting-heritage-assets/
Evans, S. (Forthcoming) *Chalk Lowlands and the Hull Valley NMP*, English Heritage Research Report.
Grady, D. (2007) 'Cropmarks on Clay, Getting the Timing right', in Mills and Palmer, *Populating Clay Landscapes*, Tempus, Stroud.
Institute for Archaeologists (2011) *Standard and Guidance for historic environment desk-based assessment*, Online document: http://www.archaeologists.net/codes/ifa
Neave and Waterson (1988) *Lost Houses of East Yorkshire*, Georgian Society for East Yorkshire.

Palmer, R. (1984) *Danebury, an Iron Age Hillfort in Hampshire: an aerial photographic interpretation of its environs*, RCHME Supplementary Series Vol. 6, London.

Palmer, R. and Cox, C. (1993) *Use of Aerial Photography in Archaeological Evaluation*, Institute of Field Archaeologists Technical Paper No. 12, Birmingham.

RCHME (1960) *A Matter of Time: an archaeological survey of the river gravels of England*, RCHME, London.

Stoertz, C. (1997) *Ancient Landscapes of the Yorkshire Wolds: aerial photographic transcription and analysis*, RCHME, Swindon.

Stoertz, C. (2012) *The North Cotswolds: A Highlight Report for the National Mapping Programme*, English Heritage Research Report 17/2012 http://www.english-heritage.org.uk/professional/research/landscapes-and-areas/national-mapping-programme/north-gloucestershire-cotswolds-nmp/

Taylor, C.C. (1998) *Parks and Gardens of Britain: a landscape History from the Air*, Edinburgh University Press, Edinburgh.

Taigel, A. and Williamson, T. (1993) *Parks and Gardens*, Batsford, London.

Wilson, D.R. (2000) *Air Photo Interpretation for Archaeologists* (2nd edition), Tempus, Stroud (1st edition 1986, out of print).

17 Values in heritage management: conservation plans and beyond

Kim Auston
Regional Landscape Architect, Western Territory, English Heritage, Bristol, UK

Introduction

Today it seems that every quango, every grant-giving body and every cultural organisation requires owners and managers of historic places to have a conservation management plan in place. But what exactly is a conservation management plan and why do these bodies think having one is such a good idea? The doyenne of the conservation plan in Britain, Kate Clark, wrote that, 'at its very simplest, a Conservation Plan is a document which states why a place is significant and what policies there are to ensure its significance is retained'.[1]

Among the many sets of guidance available, probably that produced by the Heritage Lottery Fund (HLF) has taken on the mantle of industry standard. It advises that 'a plan helps you care for a site by making sure you understand what matters and why BEFORE you take major decisions'. It identifies an eight-stage process that is intended to ensure that everyone involved has a stake in the plan:

1. Decide why a plan is needed and how it will be used
2. Identify stakeholders
3. Understand the site
4. Assess significance (including all the different values)
5. Explore issues, including how significance is vulnerable
6. Set policy aims and objectives
7. Implement it
8. Monitor and review the plan.[2]

There are many challenges to producing a good conservation management plan. One of the greatest challenges is how you define the values ('what matters' in HLF parlance) that underpin significance.

For example, the British are commonly assumed to be in the grip of a love affair with classical architecture, but this love cannot be taken for granted. John Henry Parker (1806–84), a don in Victorian Oxford, was less than impressed by the revival of the classical tradition in Europe:

> at a time when the Latin language was attempted to be revived as the universal language, the same pedantry was applied to architecture, and the style called *The Renaissance*, a bad imitation of the

Gardens & Landscapes in Historic Building Conservation, First Edition. Edited by Marion Harney.
© 2014 John Wiley & Sons, Ltd. Published 2014 by John Wiley & Sons, Ltd.

Roman, became almost universal, and it was not until the middle of the nineteenth century that the national styles of the different countries of modern Europe were revived.[3]

This critique was penned when the Gothic revival was at its height, but contemporaries can be no less unkind. Far from welcoming the arrival of a neo-classical fire station at Poundbury in Dorset, one wag memorably – if unkindly – described it as 'the Parthenon meets Brookside'.[4]

These two comments on classical architecture, 150 years apart, demonstrate that the value we place on such architecture is qualified. Parker, in particular, illustrates our propensity to believe that our own values – in this case the value we attach to a particular kind of architecture – reflect those of society at large. Further, the presumption is that the society in which we happen to find ourselves living is in some way 'the norm'. There is plenty of evidence however, to suggest that the value society attaches to things, particularly in the field of design, is malleable. When trying to persuade Sarah, Duchess of Marlborough (1660–1744), not to demolish Woodstock Manor at Blenheim, Oxfordshire, her architect Sir John Vanbrugh (1664–1726) wrote: 'there is perhaps no one thing, which the most Polite part of Mankind have more universally agreed in; than the Vallue they have ever set upon the Remains of distant Times'.[5] The Duchess dismissed Vanbrugh's arguments about the value of antiquity as ridiculous, thereby illustrating the truism that it is difficult to identify shared or common values even *within* a society. Perhaps a more obvious example for students of landscape of the change in the value we place on things is the lauding of Lancelot 'Capability' Brown (1716–83) in his lifetime, his excoriation after his death and his gradual rehabilitation from the second half of the twentieth century.

When even contemporaries cannot agree on what is 'valuable', how then is it possible to capture the values of a place, specifically a designed landscape, and incorporate them meaningfully into a plan for its management? Moreover, if we cannot always find shared values among ourselves, how can we presume to know what future generations will value? Difficult though it may be, it is the role of a conservation management plan to tease this value out, and that includes the values with which a place is imbued for others, which we may not necessarily share. What everyone who embarks on a conservation management plan is hoping is that it will help them 'to understand the value and significance of a place and its component elements and to propose appropriate management strategies to ensure their preservation and renewal in perpetuity'.[6] The underlying assumption is that a good conservation management plan will be both proactive in shaping the future and reactive to specific events, thereby helping owners and managers plan for, respond to and manage change in an informed and intelligent manner.

Valuable and significant . . . to whom?

Imagine a public park, designed in the high Victorian period by Robert Marnock (1800–89). Regardless of the actual quality of the design, the park is by a major Victorian park designer and has acquired significance through that association alone. Its suite of park structures, including the bandstand, the park railings, the drinking fountain and the statue of the mill owner who donated land for the park, are of architectural interest and some are listed. The drinking fountain no longer functions but has been colonised by a rare fern; the park railings are home to a type of lichen that has been recorded at only three other sites in the county. Five species of bat are known to frequent the park. One of Marnock's ponds has been levelled to provide a popular adventure play area; his original elliptical lawn defined by raised banks of shrubbery is now laid out as soccer pitches. Every year a circus raises its big top in the park and every other year the place is the venue of a mela for the substantial local population with origins in the Indian subcontinent. Marnock's grove of horse chestnuts is a popular picnicking spot with mums whose children attend a crèche in the former sports pavilion. In short, all kinds of people value this park in all kinds of ways. The people who most care about the historic design of the park, the reason why it is included on the English Heritage Register of Parks and Gardens of Special Historic Interest in England at Grade II, are a very small group indeed. In 2010 The Garden History Society has a membership of 1,500; the Victorian Society has a membership of around 3,500.[7] The number of park users exceeds 400,000.

Values as defined in English Heritage's *Conservation Principles*

Various attempts have been made to identify and codify the values that underpin the significance of a place. The best known is English Heritage's *Conservation Principles* which reduces the myriad values that a place might be imbued with to an essential shortlist of four: evidential, historical, aesthetic and communal.[8] Evidential value is defined as 'the potential of a place to yield evidence about past human activity'; historical value as 'the ways in which past people, events and aspects of life can be connected through a place to the present'; aesthetic value 'derives from the ways in which people draw sensory and intellectual stimulation from a place'; and communal value is 'the meanings of a place for the people who relate to it'. It is by no means clear that everyone working in the historic environment subscribes to this shortlist but, as with any shortlist, it has the merit of at least providing a framework around which to structure an analysis of values. David Thackray for the National Trust takes a similar approach to English Heritage, talking about meanings and values: scientific and technical, aesthetic and spiritual.[9] However, identifying the values that underpin what makes a place significant is only a start. A good conservation management plan is not just about research, investigation and survey ('understanding the site', step three in the Heritage Lottery Fund's guidance) but about how you synthesise that understanding into active management. A place may be valued for many different reasons and sometimes these values conflict.

Even the stoutest defenders of the values set out in *Conservation Principles* will admit that they cannot cover every eventuality or express every nuance. As in the example of the fictitious Robert Marnock park above, a heritage asset (a building, a park, a monument) is seldom valued for its historic interest alone. Other values, such as the value of a place to wildlife, may overlap with the heritage value of the site but they are not, inherently, the same as heritage values. Secondly, even within specific value types – especially what English Heritage calls 'communal value' – conflicting emphases may emerge, as described in relation to classical architecture, above. It is salutary for those of us working in the heritage sector to recognise that not everyone shares our awareness of, let alone our interest in, heritage. In the winter of 2009–10 a survey was carried out of users of, and the wider community around, Ashton Court Park, a former landscape park now owned by Bristol City Council, to find out what people thought about a proposal to create a new cycle route through the park. Just three respondents mentioned the issue of the potential impact on the historic landscape.

There is a risk that those involved in managing, conserving and restoring historic parks and gardens can be perceived as purists who are out of touch with the day-to-day needs and aspirations of the community they are supposed to be working for and who, we are often reminded, ultimately pay their wages. For this reason, it is worth taking to heart the words of David Thackray: 'conservation is based on understanding, derived not just from research and survey, but from consultation and wider dialogue'.[10]

Guidance on the subject

There is a great deal of advice on how to write a conservation management plan. Apart from that of the Heritage Lottery Fund, published guidance includes: *A Guide to Producing Parks and Green Spaces Management Plans*, CABE, 2004; *Preparing a Heritage Management Plan* (NE63), Natural England; *Conservation Plans, A Guide to the Preparation of Conservation Plans*, Historic Scotland, 2000; *Conservation Principles*, CADW, 2011; *Management*

Guidelines for World Cultural Heritage Sites, ICCROM/UNESCO/ICOMOS, 1993 (two of England's most outstanding designed landscapes, Blenheim and Studley Royal, Yorkshire are also World Heritage Sites). Additionally, in-house guidance has been produced by Natural England for Higher Level (Environmental) Stewardship and by the National Trust. Although the umbrella term 'conservation management plan' is widely used, a plan may go under several related titles such as conservation plan, restoration plan, parkland plan and management plan. Students are sometimes unduly exercised by this varied nomenclature but the principles and structure of any form of management plan are basically the same: understanding what you've got so that you can manage it sensibly and sustainably.

The process in a little more detail

To outsiders, confronting the plethora of advice and guidance about producing a conservation management plan can be daunting but the process of producing a conservation management plan for a designed landscape generally falls into several clearly defined phases of work.

The first stage is information gathering. This requires historic research, preferably using primary sources (the author has periodically come across misattributions first made 50 or more years ago and repeated without question ever since). It may also require specialist surveys of wildlife, hydrology and archaeology, and consultation with the users of the place. This raw data has to be analysed and synthesised so that the key values of the place begin to emerge, leading to the formulation of a Statement of Significance. Consideration has to be given to threats and vulnerabilities, and also to new opportunities such as those presented by grant aid or a change of ownership. Having begun to understand the values and significance(s) of the place, the next stage is to form an over-arching vision that expresses how the values and significance that have been identified are to be enhanced and maintained. Aims will be required for the key attributes of the place and these will be broken down into specific tasks or projects. It is basically a simple process of refinement, based on a sound initial understanding of the place and what's special about it. The process, once begun, is open-ended. Conservation plans need to be updated or they become obsolete.

The scope of CMPs and the principle of proportionality

One of the biggest concerns about conservation management plans is their cost. A plan for a 500-acre landscape park requiring a small library of surveys (trees, hydrology, archaeology, wildlife) could cost more than £50,000. On the other hand, a more focused plan might be delivered for less than half that amount. There are levels of sophistication and complexity but the guiding principle is that a conservation management plan should be no longer than it needs to be. At one end of the spectrum is the full-blown conservation management plan and at the other the conservation statement.

There is no point in producing a conservation management plan when there is, in fact, no need for one. English Heritage was perfectly satisfied that the repair of the Grade II* listed obelisk at Hagley Hall in Worcestershire (Figures 17.1 and 17.2) could proceed in advance of a restoration management plan for the whole Grade I registered landscape because the work could quite reasonably be achieved as a discrete, stand-alone project. The restoration of the obelisk was completed in January 2011 and the plan for the park nine months later.[11]

It is sometimes suggested that conservation management plans should be imposed as a condition of a planning consent. However, even if the conservation staff of a local planning authority, together with the statutory consultees, perceive a need for a conservation management plan, they must act within the guidelines set out in the National Planning Policy Framework (NPPF) 2012. The NPPF embodies the principle of proportionality. Paragraph 128 requires applicants to describe the significance of any heritage asset affected by a

Figure 17.1 The obelisk at Hagley, a grade II* listed building in a grade I registered park – before repair. Essential repairs were grant-aided by Natural England and supported by English Heritage in advance of a park-wide Conservation Management Plan. (© Nick Reading, March 2010.)

Figure 17.2 The obelisk after repair. (© Nick Reading, June 2010.)

proposed development but states that 'the level of detail should be proportionate to the assets' importance and no more than is sufficient to understand the potential impact of the proposal on their significance'.[12] It is only with the very largest developments that a conservation management plan can be argued to be proportionate.

Conservation plans in practice

There is still a widespread reluctance among owners and managers of heritage assets to commission a conservation management plan and there are instances when this reluctance

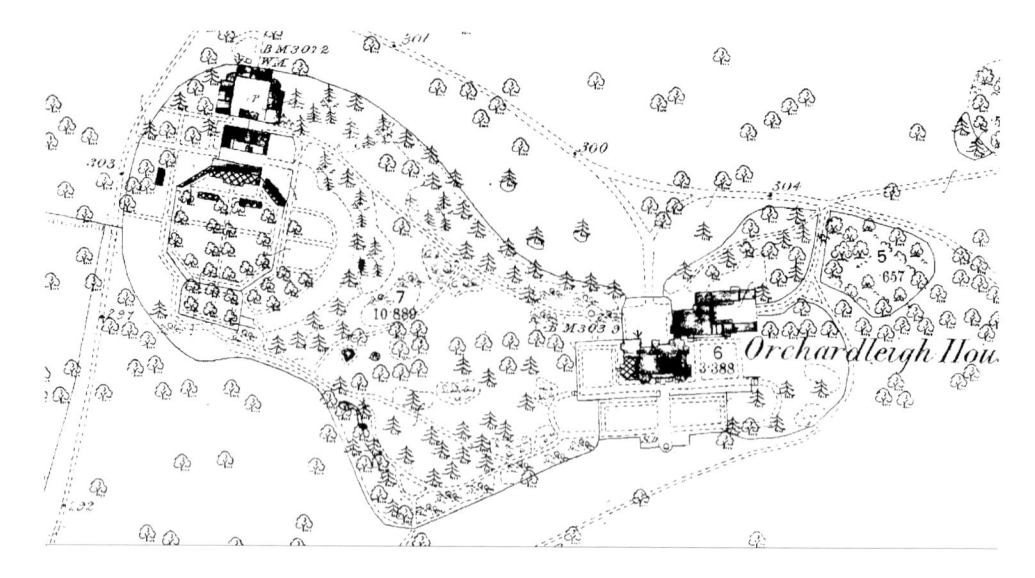

Figure 17.3 The Ordnance Survey 1st edition covering Orchardleigh, in Somerset, reproduced from the 1887 Ordnance Survey map. Many conservation plans use the OS 1st edition as the basis of their restoration proposals.

is understandable. A remarkable number of plans for the restoration of landscape parks conclude with the advice that the park should be replanted on the basis of the Ordnance Survey first edition or 'the last complete phase', which often amounts to the same thing (Figure 17.3). The argument for using the Ordnance Survey maps, published in the second half of the nineteenth century, is that they capture in unrivalled detail the moment when so many of our great landscapes – not just landscape parks but cemeteries and public parks – expressed most clearly the intentions of their designers. One cannot but have sympathy with an owner who asks if it really does require nine months, ten consultants and sub-consultants, and the expenditure of £40,000 pounds to come up with the 'vision' that a park be replanted as it was in 1887.

Given the variety of guidance available and the emphasis that is increasingly being placed on the usability of conservation management plans and the need for those who commission them to take 'ownership', it is sobering how frequently conservation management plans are laid aside and sometimes forgotten about entirely. The author recently attended a meeting where the owner, their agents and the local authority appeared to suffer collective amnesia about a conservation management plan for a registered landscape which had been produced at the local authority's request just four years earlier. This is by no means unusual.

Outside the heritage sector there is, in fact, widespread cynicism about conservation management plans: their size and cost, the staff resource required to deliver them and the fact they are often perceived as an obligation imposed by external bodies rather than something generated from within. The Heritage Lottery Fund acknowledges this problem when it states 'many people embark on writing a plan simply to secure a grant for a capital works project. Not only is this a waste of time and money, it misunderstands the purpose of a plan'.[13] The author cannot recall a single instance of an owner or manager of a park or garden initiating a conservation management plan because they thought it would be a good idea. It has always been the case that conservation management plans have been a requirement of external bodies such as the Inland Revenue (for Inheritance Tax Exemption), the Heritage Lottery Fund, Defra's/Natural England's agri-environment schemes and English Heritage (and their counterparts elsewhere in the UK). Even the consultants themselves, the people who you would have thought had most to gain from ever larger conservation management plans and more of them, are beginning to question what they are being asked to do. From a 'blissful' situation where 'we would turn up at a park, map the trees and earthworks, relate that data to the documents, get to work on planning what, if anything, was to be done, and still have time for lunch', things have seemingly changed dramatically for the worse and, 'for anyone working in the world of historic landscape today . . . the greatest change has been in the scale of the reports we have to write . . . every move over the last two centuries has been towards a more formalized document, with an ever-larger number of subjects to be covered in an ever-more prescribed manner'. And of course it's all down to 'the coming of the quangos'.[14]

Some conclusions

In view of the problems around conservation management plans – their size, their perceived lack of relevance, their cost – it might be questioned why heritage bodies continue to ask for them as a grant condition. Perhaps the answer can be found in Winston Churchill's (1874–1965) comment about democracy, that it is the worst form of government except all the others that have been tried. Conservation management plans may have their faults and they certainly have their detractors, but the best plans help everyone who is involved – owners, managers, local planning authorities, statutory consultees, grant bodies – to understand what's special about a place and why and how it should be conserved. Conservation management plans are about understanding what you've got so that you can manage it appropriately. And, as another great Englishman, Sir Francis Bacon (1561–1626), observed, knowledge is power.

Endnotes

1. 'Conservation Plans: a guide for the perplexed', *Context 57*, March 1998.
2. *Conservation Management Plans, A Guide*, Heritage Lottery Fund, 2008. The most recent guidance from the HLF, April 2012, offers separate advice for Conservation Plans and Management Plans in an attempt to reduce confusion.
3. John Henry Parker, *A Concise Glossary of Architectural Terms*, fourth edition, 1896, reprinted in paperback by Studio Editions, 1992, pp. 25–26.
4. The phrase was coined by Justin McGuirk in a piece about the new fire station at Poundbury, Dorset. It appeared in the *Guardian* on 31 March 2009.
5. *Reasons offer'd for preserving some part of the old manor*, 11 June 1709. BL Add MSS 61353, ff62–3Webb.
6. Quoted from Dyrham Park, Gloucestershire, *Conservation Plan for the Garden, Park and Wider Estate*, Teasdale Environmental Design, for the National Trust, November 2004, p. 1.
7. Personal communication from Richard Seedhouse of the Victorian Society.
8. *Conservation Principles*, English Heritage, April 2008.
9. Thackray D., 'Conservation Plans and the National Trust', Published in *Conservation Plans in Action*, Proceedings of the Oxford Conference.
10. Thackray (ibid).
11. Both the restoration of the obelisk and the subsequent parkland plan were funded with grant aid from Natural England's Higher Level Stewardship scheme.
12. The National Planning Policy Framework (2012), paragraph 128, p. 30, DCLG.
13. Heritage Lottery Fund (ibid).
14. John Phibbs, 'Conservation Management Plans for Historic Landscapes: an open letter', *Garden History*, 39:1, Summer 2011, pp. 124–126.

18 Developing a conservation management plan

Sarah Couch

Historic landscape consultant, Oxfordshire, and visiting lecturer on the MSc in Conservation of Historic Gardens and Cultural Landscapes, University of Bath, and the MSc in Sustainable Heritage at University College London, UK

The conservation management plan (CMP) has become the standard way to assess heritage assets, be they landscapes, buildings or collections, and the process is widely understood, yet methods vary and many different documents result. The challenge is to create a long-lived and practical, working document. Many sites gather an indigestible range of reports in different formats by different authors, produced to suit different projects and sources of funding (Phibbs, 2011). Not only is this wasteful but it also means that a site manager does not necessarily have ready access to clear, consistent guidance on the site's management.

To be a useful document, a CMP should be underpinned by rigorous research and analysis, tell a compelling and motivational story, but also provide succinct tools which will guide interventions and the long-term management of the landscape. The understanding and analysis sections should be able to stand alone and embody principles which are not tied too closely to a particular project, but can be used to test and inform any plans. At best, a CMP provides inspiration and new insights for managers and stakeholders and suggests a positive way forward within a reassuring, well argued and well researched framework. At worst it is yet another report produced to satisfy funding requirements, quickly obsolete and rarely consulted.

Some CMPs are very lengthy pieces of work involving a whole range of specialist surveys; others are constrained by resources and there are moves to develop a model for shortened CMPs. There are, however, some essential components for historic landscape analysis, discussed below. The process can be just as revealing as the end result and the involvement of managers and users is an essential part of the process. To be successful, 'the process must be creative, analytical, participatory and synthetic' (Clark, 2003). The focus of this work is to reach a point where the significance can be established and understood, as all decisions and interventions should be informed by, and assessed against, that significance. It is not surprising that this is also the most challenging part of the process and is discussed in detail in chapter 12 of this volume: 'Defining significance and developing a conservation philosophy'.

In the UK, a major impetus to developing a methodology was the devastation in the south of England caused by severe storms in 1987 and 1990. In response to the storms, grant schemes were developed which required an assessment of historic designed landscapes.

Conservation Plans were defined in the 1990s (Kerr, 1996) and from this grew the process of conservation management planning as we understand it today.

> A Conservation Plan is a document which sets out the significance of a site and explains how the significance will be retained in any future use, repair, alteration, development or management (Clark, 2003).

A Conservation Plan covers understanding, assessment of significance, identification of conservation issues and policies for retention of significance. A CMP takes this one step further by setting out management actions and a programme of work that follows from the conservation policies into action. While the Conservation Plan elements can be an objective, stand-alone assessment of the site which, in the absence of new evidence, should stand over time, the management aspects need to be flexible and are more likely to be tailored to a development and a planned programme of work.

In the UK, funding schemes such as those run by the Heritage Lottery Fund have developed standard guidance documents on the production of CMPs which have been required for projects that they fund. One major change over the years, partly in response to requirements of funders, and increasingly as a result of reduced maintenance funding, is the emphasis on social and community involvement, both in assessing significance, and also in delivering and managing the project. This is particularly important for public open spaces.

The level of detail in the management section of a CMP may vary: if there is also a full, costed Management and Maintenance Plan, the CMP may only set out management aims and an overview of actions but not include individual management and maintenance tasks. Indeed, the 2012 guidance from the Heritage Lottery Fund for its 'Parks for People' programme now requires a Conservation Plan, in place of a CMP, together with a Management and Maintenance Plan. In recent years, documents which cover much the same material have been produced with a range of titles such as 'Historic Landscape Survey and Management Plan', 'Restoration and Management Plan' and 'Parkland Plan', but the CMP concept provides the most consistent framework, placing significance at its core.

Before beginning a CMP, it can be useful to consider who will be using it and what it will be used for. Direct and indirect purposes may include:

- Understanding the asset
- Recording the current condition of the site, its hard and soft features
- Aiding interpretation
- Providing education materials
- Assembling an archive: physical, digital, oral history
- Improving physical and intellectual access and increasing involvement
- Contributing to planning guidance and heritage protection
- Developing conservation projects
- Reducing environmental impact
- Providing tools for long-term management and maintenance
- Supporting day-to-day work planning
- Contributing to management systems e.g. compatible links to client mapping systems
- Supporting an application for Green Flag status
- Supporting planning applications
- Supporting funding applications
- Providing the basis for Heritage Impact Assessment or Environmental Impact Assessment.

The main sections of a CMP cover understanding, significance, issues, policies, management action plan and gazetteer and it is supported by illustrations, plans, references and appendices. Within this broad structure, material can be organised and presented in a number of ways to suit resources and technical constraints. One approach which helps organise the material and make it digestible to non-specialists is to think of the CMP as a compelling story with a clear thread which runs from beginning to end. This concept is

Figure 18.1 Crystal Palace Park, South London: a view looking up the Grand Centre Walk towards the Palace site and terraces, which are now hidden behind the National Sports Centre and its raised walkway.

reinforced by the use of a summary section and summaries at the beginning of each chapter. These can be drawn together into a summary document with a few key illustrations and made more widely available than the full document: the reality is that not everyone will read the full CMP and its supporting material, but they may well need to understand the principles and be able to refer to specific information without reading an entire thesis.

To consider the contents and the process in more detail: before beginning documentary research it can be useful to visit the site, to gain a first impression. For example, visiting the very large Crystal Palace Park (Figure 18.1) in south London can be a confusing experience, as the site of the former Crystal Palace and its vast terraces is now invisible from the lower part of the park.

The park is bisected by the National Sports Centre and its raised walkway, cutting off important views and connections. At any level, this inhibits visitor orientation, but further research confirms that the main structure of the park and some of its most important features have been severely disrupted, such as the Grand Centre Walk leading up to the Palace, designed by Joseph Paxton (1803–65) in the 1850s. When a site masterplan was developed, one of the main aims was to recreate the central axis and bring it back to ground level (Couch and Latz and Partner, 2007).

Gaining understanding through research

The first section of a CMP is about understanding the site, and this covers many areas. Looking at the bigger picture, researching the wider geographical context is an informative first step. Geology and hydrology are in many senses fundamental to a site: natural characteristics may have influenced the choice of site, the development of features such as terraces, viewpoints and design features, dictated the feasibility of water features and influenced soils, vegetation and plant choice and also the educational use and value invested in the site. A pilot study on the concept of 'geodiversity' in the London area revealed close links between geology and many aspects of gardens, but also that it was a concept often largely neglected in descriptions and analysis of historic landscapes (Rutherford, Couch & Robinson, 2011). Geodiversity is defined as 'the variety of rocks, fossils, minerals, landforms, soils and natural processes, such as weathering, erosion and sedimentation, that underlie and determine the character of our natural landscape and environment' (Greater London Authority, 2011). Understanding a site's hydrology is becoming increasingly important in responding to and mitigating the effects of climate change.

Research: written material

The process and sources for documentary research are described by David Lambert in chapter 11, where he stresses the importance of thorough research and record keeping. There is no limit to the extent of research which can be undertaken, but in practice it may well be limited by financial and time constraints. Local history and archaeological societies and the County Gardens Trusts may already have researched the site and clearly this can be a valuable contribution. The files held by English Heritage Register of Parks and Gardens of Special Historic Interest in England, established in 1983, can also yield useful information. Sometimes all of the original research material is presented to the client as a resource in an appendix or stand-alone document. In any case, a list of material, organised into types of sources, should be included and it is good practice to write and update a bibliography of sources during the research, rather than leaving this task to the end. In preparing a CMP, one strategy is to organise research information into a gazetteer or appendix from the start; this will then provide the material for briefer sections within the main text as well as providing a useful source of reference material.

Understanding the history of the site extends beyond the site itself into its landscape design history, architectural, social and political context: this is an essential part of understanding significance as previously discussed. Other baseline research will cover designations and heritage protection, the Historic Environment Records (Sites and Monuments Records – largely archaeology), planning policy framework, other national and local policies e.g. relating to access and biodiversity, legislation and strategic documents, location, boundaries, ownership and so forth.

Within the main text, it can be useful to structure descriptions by historic period, relating to owners or design phases, and by character area (see below). Succinct summaries of research material are useful in a short or a full CMP. There may be a fuller description of the site's history within the main text or extensive material in appendices. Tables are one readily accessible method of presenting information and often include a chronology of events affecting the site, a chronology of changes in ownership and changes in management.

Research: map material

Map sources are an invaluable aid to understanding a landscape. Previous chapters describe the range of map sources available to the landscape researcher and explain the importance of obtaining good quality, true-to-scale, hard and digital copies. Even if there are no manuscript or estate maps and surveys, it will normally be possible to assemble the following: John Rocque (mid-eighteenth century) and other county maps, Ordnance Surveyor's Drawing (1789–1840), Enclosure and Tithe maps (mid-nineteenth century), four editions of Ordnance Survey 25-inch County series and 6-inch series; some Ordnance Survey special editions and 5 foot series of towns and aerial photographs from the 1940s and later. A modern base map at a large scale is also needed: current Ordnance Survey mapping is less useful to the landscape specialist than the County Series, as some features such as individual trees are no longer recorded, but it is, of course, an accurate base to which detail can be added. An Ordnance Survey base map can be obtained from clients, from local authorities or from commercial sources and some OS data are available free of charge from Ordnance Survey Opendata. Details of tree cover can be added with the help of Google Earth. However, for greater accuracy and when proposals need to be developed, a site-specific topographical survey which locates trees and records levels as well as hard features will be required (see below).

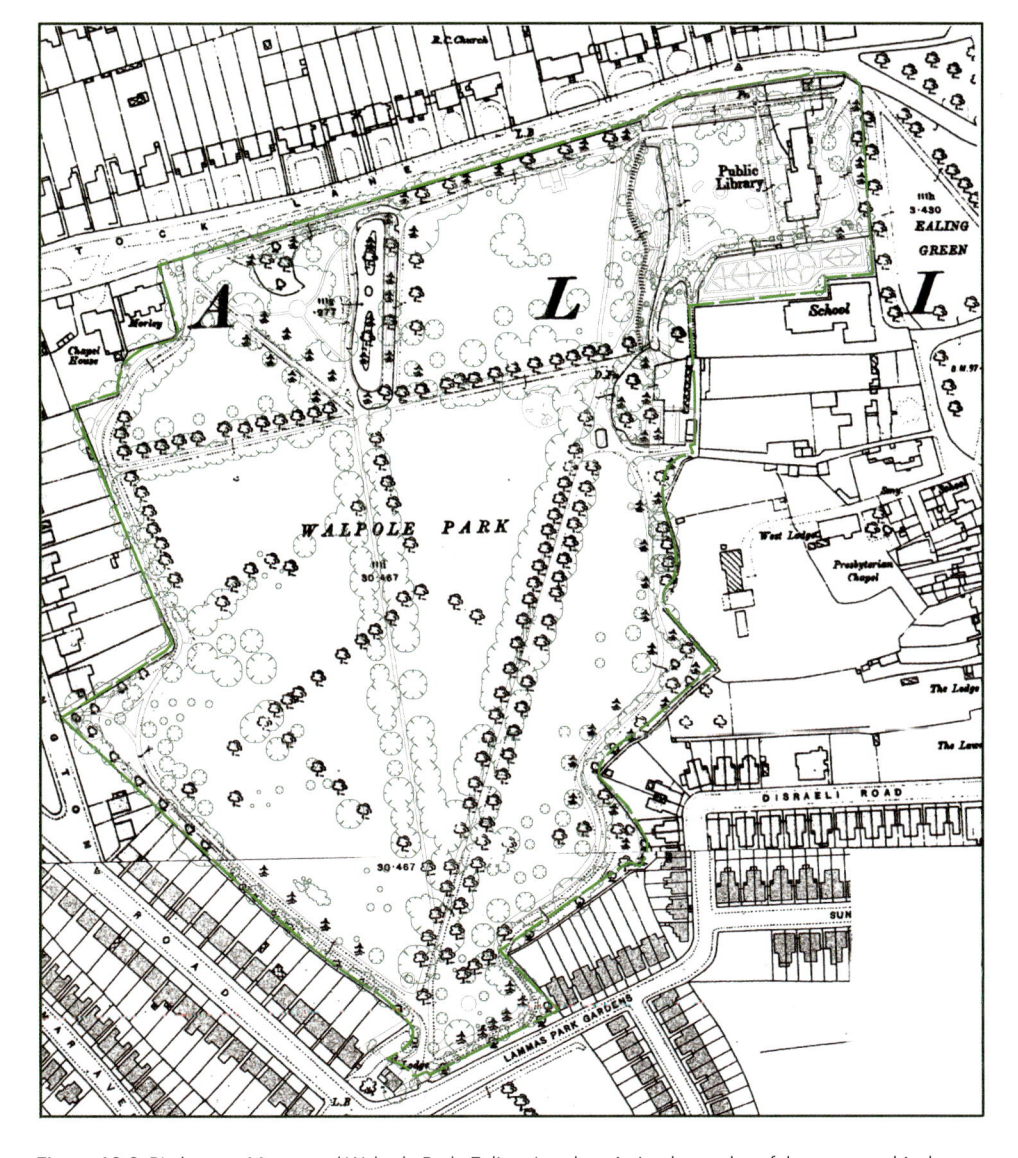

Figure 18.2 Pitzhanger Manor and Walpole Park, Ealing, London. A simple overlay of the topographical survey and 1915, 25-inch Ordnance Survey with current site boundary.

Before writing up documentary research, one of the most revealing and essential tasks is to prepare overlays or 'map regression' of all the maps collected, including current Ordnance Survey or topographical survey, starting with the most recent and working back in time. Figure 18.2 shows such an overlay.

This is best done digitally and can be completed with a range of computer programmes including Geographic Information System (GIS) and Computer Aided Design (CAD) programmes, Adobe Photoshop or Adobe Illustrator. The maps need to be adjusted to the same orientation and scale; in the case of older maps, they may need adjustment based on known fixed points to obtain a realistic fit. Transparency can be adjusted to suit the visibility required. The important point is to retain the ability to select layers and combinations of layers. Other details, such as boundaries and keys to features, can be added. This file can then be used to generate a series of maps showing the development of the site and is arguably the single most useful tool in explaining a site's development: it is a basic tool for even a short CMP. These maps can then be used to compare the site evidence with its known history.

Research: images

Documentary sources will also yield a number of illustrations: paintings, drawings, engravings, photographs, press cuttings and so forth; these also need to be catalogued and sorted into date period and by area or feature. Although it is more labour intensive, it is much more useful to the reader to include images with the relevant parts of the text. There may be more images which can be arranged in a gazetteer, to illustrate particular features. A simple but effective technique is to compare historic images with current views. Again, this is a basic technique for even a short CMP.

Gaining understanding through a site survey

The next task is to compare research findings with site evidence. Site surveys range from simply walking the site to a great number of specialist surveys. It is useful to walk the site as much as possible to interpret and compare historical research material and understand site conditions. This is a cyclical process: every visit will reveal new information, such as new views, new plants, different issues, maintenance activities and activities at different times of the day, week or year. Each visit will shed new light on documentary research and vice versa.

The base map used for site work may be Ordnance Survey or a full topographical site survey. For large sites, especially where archaeology, other features and ground modelling are obscured by vegetation, a relatively new technique, LiDAR, is a very powerful tool. LiDAR is airborne digital terrain mapping using a laser beam scanned from an aircraft to create very accurate, high-resolution digital elevation models. These 3D models can be integrated into GIS for analysis and interpretation.

A landscape historian's walkover survey will involve marking features on a base map, or sections of map if it is a large site. It is common practice to divide the site into character areas; that is, areas with a defined landscape character, for example flower garden, kitchen garden, lakes, park or parts of a park. This is a useful way to organise, collect and present material and can be used as a structure throughout the CMP. Essential tasks include recording and locating important surviving historic features from a comparison of documentary and site evidence, plotting historic and current views, lost views and intrusive views, recording the general condition of the landscape and comparing this with its history and also recording field archaeology, significant trees and areas of vegetation. Figure 18.3 shows a photo taken during a walkover survey.

Some of these surveys can only be completed in conjunction with analysis of documentary sources.

Trees form the main living structure of a landscape and merit special attention. If there is no funding for a specialist arboricultural survey, a useful minimum is to compare existing trees with historic maps and mark trees which contribute to the historic landscape character, due to their age, location, species or design, for example if they are or were part of geometric feature such as an avenue. The Ordnance Survey 25-inch County series maps are particularly useful, as individual trees were accurately located and, from the second edition, surveyed trees are shown by a special symbol. It is often possible to locate these trees on site. At least an approximate location, species and girth of trees should be recorded. In surveying features such as avenues, it is good practice to record and interpret the layout in dimensions used at the time and with an understanding of historic planting practice, preferred measurements and geometry. An assessment of tree age by girth and other

Figure 18.3 Ascott Park, Oxfordshire: this view shows several historic landscape features: field archaeology in the foreground marking the site of a possible early house and its garden; an early dovecot and avenues of the distinctive forms of common lime.

techniques allows an analysis of planting dates, which can be most informative (Couch, 1992 and 1994). Even where a full tree survey is undertaken (BS 5837:2005 'Trees in relation to construction') results need to be reviewed in the light of historic landscape and ecological significance to the site, as the BS survey looks at trees from an individual tree health viewpoint. If significant trees are causing concern, then further surveys such as Picus (ultrasound) or resistograph can be conducted to detect decay, and stress tests to assess stability. These tests may yield information which allows retention of the trees or enables special management or time for propagation. There may also be a need for specialist surveys of other vegetation, for instance where there is a collection of rhododendrons and azaleas, which are notoriously hard to identify, but may include important early introductions.

A site archaeological survey in addition to a desktop study is frequently required. Some field archaeology can be recorded from a walkover survey, although specialist surveys may be required including field archaeology survey and/or geophysical survey followed by targeted excavation of buried archaeology to test results and locate features shown on maps: overlays are very helpful in locating areas of interest.

Most CMPs also involve ecological surveys which can be carried out by the Wildlife Trusts or independent ecologists and may include general habitat surveys as well as targeted surveys of protected species such as bats, amphibians or stag beetles. Sometimes, special interest groups such as bird or bat recording groups can contribute to ecological surveys. All CMPs should also record current management arrangements and changes to management practices. Depending on the site, other specialist surveys may include condition surveys of structures, measured drawings of buildings or structures, hydrology, geology, forestry or farming surveys.

A vital part of understanding a landscape, especially those open to the public, is studying the way it is used and valued by people. Audience, access and movement surveys and various consultation and engagement activities contribute to many CMPs. The Heritage Lottery funding places great weight on extending community engagement and requires Activity Plans to be developed for the projects they fund.

People often have a great affection for and sense of ownership of their local green space; this should be reflected in the development of a CMP and will benefit any projects which follow. Activities related to a CMP can include workshops with local groups and schools, recording local knowledge and oral history, talks, guided walks, exhibitions, questionnaires and providing training material and running training workshops, for instance in historic planting or for heritage guides. Some of these may be run in parallel to the CMP, but the CMP should contain a summary of consultation activities and the main conclusions, which will inform CMP Policies and future decisions.

Gaining understanding through analysis

The task of the CMP writer is to synthesise and summarise the surveys described above so that they inform the development of the CMP. Most will be appendices to the CMP with the main points summarised in relevant sections. The presentation of the analysis of surveys will be a mixture of written and drawn work. Again, it is helpful to organise information by character areas and for each area, define what the historic designed landscape was, define changes and the current character and then, in later parts of the CMP, this will lead to policies and an overall management aim for that area, to conserve or achieve the desired character.

In addition to the map regression described above, plans can be used to represent analysis of the site. The number will reflect the scope of the survey but most will include: character areas – survival of historic features from different periods, possibly with different annotation or separate plans for each period; historic and current views, referenced to historic images and current photographs; boundaries and designations; existing trees and vegetation types, including trees by planting period; lost trees. Other plans may be made as part of the CMP or as part of a wider design project, such as: ownership and leases; management areas; services; hard landscape features; archaeology; ecology; access points and paths for pedestrians, bicycles and vehicles, public and private.

'Significance'

This understanding and analysis leads to an assessment of significance, and defining significance is the most important part of a CMP; it is discussed in detail in chapter 12 of this volume. The determination of significance is the core of the CMP, as all decisions should flow from an understanding of the significance and values attached to the site – what is important, rare and unique and to whom it is important. The determination of the significance of these assets is based on any statutory designation and professional judgement against four broad values: evidential value, historical value, aesthetic value, communal value (English Heritage, 2008). However, within this framework, areas of significance can be defined in a range of ways – for example the value of landscape design and architectural design, archaeology, ecology and scientific value, past and current use, amenity, recreation, sports or educational significance – but terms must be clearly defined. Generally, there is an assessment of overall significance which should be informed by comparison with the site's historical, aesthetic and social context; it should be as broad and imaginative as possible and it may be helpful to develop themes of significance. If the site has protection in the planning system and therefore has national significance, the reasons which support the designation will form a useful starting point, but a CMP needs to explore these reasons in more detail. This is followed by an assessment of significance of character areas and individual elements and their contribution to the importance of the site. If there is a need to give different elements a weighting, for use in Heritage Impact Assessment or Environmental Impact Assessment, then the methodology needs to be explained. However, giving levels of significance should be treated with some caution, as in many respects the landscape needs to be treated as a whole; for example in cemeteries, the whole site is invested with spiritual and emotional significance and indeed this may be greater in recently used areas than in older areas which have higher design or aesthetic significance.

Defining issues

The next section of the CMP looks at what is affecting this significance. The 'issues' section describes the general issues, vulnerabilities or risks – and opportunities which affect the significant aspects of the site, as identified and described in the significance section. These conclusions are drawn from site surveys, specialist surveys and the results of public consultation. Issues are normally general and specific: the general issues may relate to understanding and protecting the significance of the site as a whole, knowledge and skills, legal and policy constraints, governance and management issues including issues such as divided ownership, design issues, damage or loss of features, access and visitor issues (for example pressure and requirements of use, need for facilities, impact of parking and vehicle access), funding, development issues (on or off site), tree cover and tree health, wildlife issues, engagement and widening the 'audience' and site conditions such as flood risk and the effects of climate change. This section should also identify the need for further surveys or other work. Then there will be more detailed issues by character area or feature, where the current condition and use is assessed against design intentions and current needs. All these issues should be closely tied to the themes of significance. Comparison of historic and current views can vividly illustrate design and maintenance issues.

Policies

The following section of the CMP sets out policies, aims and objectives to address the issues. This is usually the final section of a Conservation Plan and sets the agenda for the management part of the CMP. The policies form a central part of the conservation planning process and their adoption will underpin the future care of the park. Relevant parties should be involved in the development of policies so that they can be adopted and implemented. Policy aims and objectives should flow from the understanding and analysis of the site, respond to the issues identified, safeguard the significant aspects of the site over the long term and increase understanding and enjoyment of the site.

A good starting point is an overall aim or 'vision statement', which has been agreed by all interested parties. It can be challenging but helpful to reach a consensus of shared aims, which set out the approach and conservation philosophy, including the extent and focus of conservation for the site; this statement will have applications outside the CMP.

As with the issues, policies, aims and objectives are usually both general and specific. It can be useful to summarise the main issues for each topic, to give continuity with the preceding section and context to the resulting policies. General, high-level policies will include the steps needed to ensure that an understanding of significance underpins the management regime and that the necessary skills are available. In the face of dwindling maintenance budgets, new forms of governance are considered more frequently, as part of the management structure. General conservation policies will include good conservation practice, recording work, updating records and use of Heritage Impact Assessment, design principles, a palette of appropriate materials or features, the use of new elements, historic layout, structures and planting, tree management, views, archaeology, ecology, sustainability, access and security and the park's use for heritage, educational or arts activities. The policies should reinforce the themes of significance identified and may be directly related to them.

General policies will be followed by more detailed aims and objectives for each character area or feature. These will need to take account of original design principles, as well as current use and conditions. For instance, to reinforce the historic designed character of parkland, the aim may be to reinforce eighteenth-century parkland character by replanting clumps of trees, following historic precedent, to define important views and to vary grassland management, possibly with traditional grazing regimes, which will improve biodiversity and visual interest; but the aims may also need to take account of current issues such as the management of veteran trees for their historic and wildlife value, planning appropriate replanting with species to deal with diseases and forecasts of climate change and planning for educational opportunities.

Management action plan

The final section puts the policies into action: as explained above, the level of detail will vary from plan to plan. The management action plan builds on the description of the historic and current landscape character, the significance, ecology and other issues and it sets out management aims to enhance, protect and sustain the significance of the area. The overall aim of this part will be to ensure that all management is informed by an understanding of the site's significance so that effort and available resources are directed towards the long-term implementation of an agreed vision.

The management action plan is best set out as a table which describes the overall design objective (referring to the analysis of character areas above) and actions needed to achieve the desired character of each area, outcomes, responsibility for carrying out the work, and a proposed timescale for implementation over different timescales. For a ten-year plan this could be short (one to three years), medium (three to five years) and long (five to ten years). There are of course cases where it is desirable to plan 50 years or 100 years ahead, for instance when preparing a tree strategy. Actions will also be divided into policy objectives relating to the whole site and those relating to the individual character areas. The table may include budget cost for items of capital work and, in some cases, a programme of detailed annual management and maintenance operations will also be scheduled, with costs. There may also be a costed training and volunteering element, which describes training and volunteering required to implement the management action plan and this may be related to a separate Activity Plan. Maintenance prescriptions may also be added if they do not appear in other documents and also specialist advice for things like the management of veteran trees or other significant trees. A business plan may well be developed alongside Management and Maintenance planning.

If there is only a summary management action plan, it would normally be developed into a full, detailed Management and Maintenance Plan, ideally by the site's managers.

Gazetteer

As mentioned earlier, it can be useful to assemble a gazetteer early in the process, although it is usually presented at the end of the document. Gazetteers can be a simple list or schedule of features or more complex databases or documents incorporating historic and modern images and plans. The simplest method is a schedule which draws together all the main information on each feature, so that it can be used as a reference document. Suggested contents would include: reference by location (character area) and number; designations; date; short history and description of designed character; significance; description of current condition; issues; relevant policies; recommendations for short-, medium- and long-term action and references. It can be cross-referenced to an image database. A schedule is most useful in presenting information succinctly and can be adapted to other purposes (such as a Heritage Impact Assessment) and updated by the site manager. If it is done well, the gazetteer will be the main point of reference for planning conservation work, as has been the case at the City of London Cemetery and Crematorium. There should also be recommendations for monitoring, reviewing and updating the CMP.

Appendices

Finally there will be a bibliography and a series of appendices of supporting information. A bibliography is often arranged by types of sources such as published items (books and periodicals), archival items, maps, illustrations and press cuttings. Some people give all sources a reference system related to the type of source. Appendices may include specialist surveys, more detailed historic research material, copies of designations, heritage impact assessment template, annotated tree schedules, additional illustrations or larger-scale plans and so forth.

Whatever the scope of the CMP, it needs to focus on its purpose of being a tool to aid understanding and manage change in an informed way. If it is succinct, readable, with a consistent and well-argued thread, it is well illustrated with plans, images and analysis, then there is a good chance it will motivate those involved to cherish the landscape's significant values.

Further reading

Clark, K. (2003) *Informed Conservation: Understanding Historic Buildings and their Landscapes for Conservation*, English Heritage, London.

Couch, S. (1992) 'The Practice of Avenue Planting in the Seventeenth and Eighteenth Centuries', *Garden History*, Vol. 20, No. 2, Autumn 1992, 173–200.

Couch, S. (1994) 'Conservation of Avenue Trees', *Arboricultural Journal*, Vol. 18, 307–320.

Couch, S. (2007) *Crystal Palace Park Conservation Management Plan*, London Development Agency; prepared in connection with Latz and Partner Masterplan, 2007.

English Heritage (2007) *The Management & Maintenance of Historic Parks, Gardens & Landscapes* (eds J. Watkins and T. Wright). Frances Lincoln, London.

English Heritage (2008) *Conservation Principles, Policies and Guidance*, English Heritage, London.

Greater London Authority (2011) *The London Plan Spatial Development Strategy for Greater London*.

Jacques, D. (1995) 'The Treatment of Historic Parks and Gardens', *Journal of Architectural Conservation*, No 2.

Kerr, J.S. (1996) *The Conservation Plan. A Guide to the Preparation of Conservation Plans for Places of European Cultural Significance*, National Trust of Australia, Sydney.

Lambert, D. Goodchild, P. and Roberts, J. (2006) *Parks and Gardens. A Researcher's Guide to Sources for Designed Landscapes*, Landscape Design Trust with English Heritage, Redhill.

Phibbs, J. (2011) 'Conservation Management Plans for Historic Landscapes: an open letter', *Garden History*, Vol. 39, No. 1, 124–126.

Rutherford, S. Couch, S. & Robinson, E. (2011) *Geodiversity in London's Designed Landscapes. A pilot study to examine geology and its influence on historic landscape design in Greater London*, Natural England & English Heritage, London.

19 Public parks and their conservation

Hazel Conway
Urban landscape historian, London, UK

The Victorian park movement took place in a period that saw massive population and urban growth. Britain was at the forefront of the industrial revolution and was the first country to 'invent' the municipal park. Before the nineteenth century towns were small, the countryside was accessible and commons and greens formed the people's playgrounds. Official recognition of the need for public parks dates from 1833 when the Select Committee on Public Walks was set up by Robert Slaney MP (1791–1862). It found that the poorest people in the largest urban centres had the greatest need for parks. Parks would refresh the air, provide contact with nature, places for exercise and recreation and generally improve people's health. They would also be an alternative focus for recreation to the public house. The Committee recommended a new park for the East End of London, Victoria Park, for there were no parks south of the river or to the east, except for Greenwich Park.

Park movement – first phase

In the first phase of the park movement, the 1830s and 1840s, parks were created mainly in the industrial centres of the north-west of England and in Glasgow. Early parks such as Derby Arboretum or the Manchester/Salford parks were located on the edges of expanding towns which subsequently encircled them. The plan of Derby Arboretum, 1840, was inward looking, with no views in or out to the wider landscape, for John Claudius Loudon (1783–1843) foresaw that the expanding town would soon surround it. The design intention was to make a small site appear larger, so the land was mounded up between adjacent footpaths so that visitors could not see each other. It featured a formal axial route and picturesque curving paths. By contrast People's Park, Halifax, 1857, designed by Edward Milner (1819–94) who was trained by Joseph Paxton (1803–65), architect and gardener, was built on a sloping site, with a terrace giving views of the moors beyond the town.

Parks were created out of a variety of sites: from the estates of mansions; ancient historic sites such as Dane John, Canterbury, built on the site of 1–2 AD Romano-British remains (laid out 1790 by Ald. John Simmons, public park formed 1836) and from the sites of ruins, such as York Museum Gardens, with St Mary's Abbey, 1088 (1844–50) designed by Sir John Murray Naysmith. They were built alongside the new railways, such as Miller Park, Preston (Milner, 1860s); on brownfield sites, quarries and spoil heaps and on the commons and greens that were the traditional people's playground and meeting place. Kennington Common, London, was the location of the Chartist rally in 1845 and became a public park in 1852; thereafter no public meetings were allowed. Manchester was the first major industrial centre to create public parks and first to hold a competition to select a designer. The instructions to competitors for the design of Philips Park, Manchester, in 1846 (Figure 19.1), stated that they should 'provide the greatest variety of rational recreations for the greatest possible number' and space 'for the promenading of large numbers of persons'. They should include a playground, archery, quoit, skittle and ball alleys, a refreshment room and lodges.

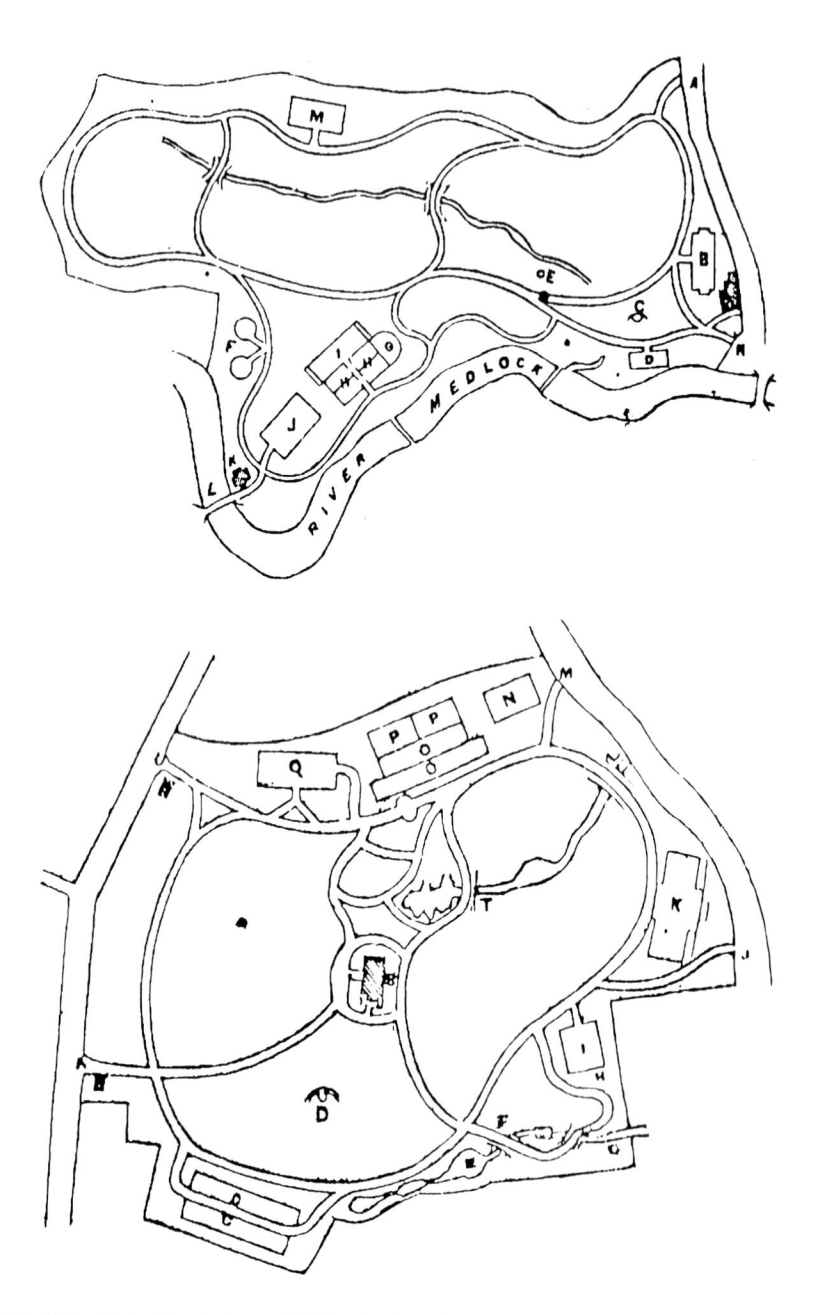

Figure 19.1 Philips Park, Manchester, c.1900 (author's own).

The budget for this was restricted and the competition was won by the landscape gardener and designer Joshua Major (1786–1866).

Birkenhead, Wirral Peninsula, was the first town to apply for an Act of Parliament to raise funds for park development and is often cited as the first public park (Paxton, 1847). For much of the nineteenth century park creation was restricted by legislation until its removal by the Public Health Act of 1875. The formation of parks thereafter increased. Further impetus to park creation came with Queen Victoria's Gold and Diamond Jubilees of 1887 and 1897. There was also added pressure to create open space in densely populated inner city areas. In London the Metropolitan Public Gardens Association (1882) sought to convert churchyards and disused burial grounds into public gardens and recreation grounds.

Influences on Public Park design

Humphry Repton (1752–1818), John Nash (1752–1835), Loudon and Paxton were influential figures on early nineteenth-century park design. Loudon's design for the Derby Arboretum, 1840 and his prolific writings were particularly significant. Victoria Park in the East End of London (Figure 19.2), recommended by the Select Committee of Public Walks, was initially laid out by the architect and planner James Pennethorne (1801–71), who had worked with Nash, and subsequently by John Gibson (1817–92), who had trained with Paxton. However, in the first phase of the park movement the most influential figure was Joseph Paxton, not only for his own work, but because of the number of park designers who trained with him. Paxton's first public park, Birkenhead Park (1847) featured varied circulation routes, lakes,

Figure 19.2 The magnificent Burdett Coutts or Victoria Fountain, Victoria Park 1862, had to be fenced off because of the risk of vandalism in the era when the park became run down and neglected (author's own).

islands, contrasting open and secluded areas and a variety of vistas. Among its many visitors was Frederick Law Olmsted (1822–1903), who subsequently designed Central Park, New York.

Paxton's best known park, Crystal Palace Park, II, Sydenham (1854–6) had huge terraces, grand fountains and cascades, central axis, and specially developed bedding plants (Crystal Palace lobelia is still available; an all-blue variety with no white centre). Among the many attractions of this park are the English landscape garden and the dinosaurs, which are Grade 1 Listed Buildings which 'inhabit' the islands in the lake. These represent the latest scientific knowledge of the time and have recently been restored. High fencing was installed around the lakes at the same time to protect them.

In 1894 the grand fountains at the centre of the park were filled in and 1895 saw the FA Cup Final ground constructed on the site of the south basin. The following year a banked cycle track and sports arena was built on the north basin. In 1911 a huge number of temporary buildings were erected for the Festival of Empire and in 1936 the Crystal Palace burnt down. During 1940–5 the central area was used as a military tank park and from 1945–50 bomb rubble was dumped on the top site where the Palace had stood. In 1964 the National Sports Centre was built on 36 acres of the north basin and a stadium on the south basin sites. Latz and Partner developed a Masterplan (1996–2009) for the restoration of the park and in December 2010 the Secretary of State granted planning permission. At the time of writing an architectural design completion has been launched for the re-creation of Paxton's Crystal Palace on the site. The restoration of Crystal Palace Park represents a central element in the regeneration of south-east London.

Battersea Park, London (1856) bordering the south bank of the Thames, was designed by John Gibson (1815–75), who trained with Paxton. Here, Gibson developed a new form of gardening using palms, bananas and other subtropical plants which previously could only be seen in the glasshouses of Kew and other botanic gardens. He also included bedding plants in raised beds. The subtropical garden in Battersea Park was widely praised in the gardening press and became very popular with both the public and with park keepers. This has now been successfully restored. Gibson's original design included planting a 1km-long Riverside Promenade, which was not executed but has been created in the current restoration together with a new river wall built of materials matching the original nineteenth-century design. In 1951, the park became the site of the Festival of Britain Pleasure Gardens with landscaping by Russell Page (1906–85). These too have been restored and a new glass block toilet and boathouse added.

Edward Milner trained with Paxton and worked with him on People's Park, Halifax (1857) – a miniature Crystal Palace Park. Milner then went on to design three parks in Preston, Buxton Pavilion Gardens (1871), Lincoln Arboretum (1872) with its formal terrace giving views over the park, the gardens of St Paul's Cathedral (1879), and many private gardens. Edward Kemp (1817–91), the landscape architect who supervised the construction of Birkenhead Park, also trained with Paxton. Kemp's reputation was such that in 1857 the New York Park Commission consulted him on the design of Central Park. He designed parks in Chester (Grosvenor Park, 1867), Southport (Hesketh Park, 1868), and Gateshead (Saltwell Park, 1877) and the Grade II Stanley Park, Liverpool (1870). Park designers also included nurserymen: William Barron (1805–91) for example designed Locke Park, Barnsley (1877) and Abbey Park, Leicester (1882) but the majority of parks were designed by borough surveyors and engineers; the unsung heroes of the park movement.

Turn of the century and inter-war period

There was no town planning in the nineteenth century so the distribution of urban open space could not be controlled; consequently the park movement was of an *ad hoc* nature. The Town Planning Act (1909) gave Local Authorities the power to plan for the future. The garden city movement stressed the importance of the relationship between town and countryside and between buildings, parks and other types of urban green space. The poor health and physique of townspeople was becoming increasingly apparent from medical reports on army recruits for the Boer War and from details of the poor physique of young people published in the Report on Physical Deterioration (1904). After World War II the impact of these reports began to be felt. Other influences on public park design in the twentieth century included the role of town planning, the garden city movement, suburban and new town development, the growth of transport, the growing emphasis on sport and an increasing awareness of ecology. As a result the concept of the public park changed from that of individual parks and recreation grounds to a much broader perception of parks in their many forms and in their relationship to the urban environment. North Evington Gardens, Leicester (1924) was built as part of the national programme of 'Homes for Heroes' after World War I by Arthur Wakerley (1862–1931), Leicester councillor and architect. The gardens which run at the end of the private gardens on either side consist of a footpath with 2.5 m-wide shrub borders which open out into circles with seats placed either side.

In the inter-war period four million houses were built on greenfield sites across the country. There was a huge expansion of the suburbs and satellite towns, and space for recreation was an integral part of suburban development. The National Playing Fields Association and the Public Health Act (1925) both promoted land for recreation. Just as Paxton was a major influence on nineteenth-century park design, Thomas Mawson (1861–1933) was the leading landscape architect of the period 1880–1933 for the number of parks he designed and the ideas he spread though his writings and lectures. He designed parks in Newport, Wales; Burslem, Wolverhampton, Rochdale, Cleethorpes and Preston. In Stanley Park, Blackpool (1926) sports were a dominant feature of the design.

Recreation and public health

The promotion of park development in the 1930s recognised the link between public health and recreation, and the King George V Memorial Fund provided funds to set up open spaces and playing fields. The Physical Training and Recreation Act (1937) enabled grants to be made for the purchase and development of land for playing fields, parks, recreation grounds and swimming pools. A National Fitness Campaign was also launched in the same year. In Abbey Park, Leicester (1882), designed by William Barron (1805–91), the new extension of the park in 1932 included the ruins of Leicester Abbey, and added further sporting facilities.

Park systems, chain parks and parkways

The new suburbs provided the opportunity for the comprehensive planning of park systems, chains and parkways. By 1935 Birmingham had provided more than 23 miles of chain parks. At Bournville land was acquired over many years. South of the Green, the original focus of the village, Bournville Park formed the start of a continuous system of parkland, following streams and valleys through the estate, with the Valley Parkway pool for model yachts laid out in the early 1930s.

The loss of railings is often associated with World War II, but from the 1930s onward there were many debates about their role. With the removal of the railings of Preston Park, Brighton, in the 1930s, the park became part of the parkway into the resort, particularly when the new rock garden (1936) was laid out on the other side of the road. By 1939 the 'wonderful improvement in the formation and lay-out of traffic islands at the junction of busy roads and roundabouts' was noted.

Post World War II

Immediately after World War II the main priorities were clearing areas of bomb damage (blight and blitz), building New Towns and confronting the legacy of redundant industrial sites. The Tyne Landscape Plan dates from 1965 and the Stoke on Trent reclamation programme from 1970. Central Forest Park, Hanley was part of a wide reclamation project, which included redundant railway lines, marshalling yards and track. Some 50 sites were created with greenways stretching from the centre of Stoke on Trent to its periphery. Westport Lake was a site of subsidence and became the largest lake in the region. It became known locally as 'Blackpool on Trent'. To stock it, tons of aquatic plants were imported from Staffordshire. In the 1960s and 70s the philosophy of clean sweep planning involved clearing derelict industrial sites, greening the city, and improving living conditions by a variety of means.

Parks in the 1970s and 80s

Public parks were well maintained until the late 1970s and the 1980s, when all local authorities' Parks Services were merged with Leisure Services. This is when parks lost their dedicated budget, but they were not included as part of the Standard Spending Assessment. With the introduction of Compulsory Competitive Tendering (CCT) parks lost their dedicated park keepers and local authorities were compelled by law to accept the lowest tender for maintenance. Between 1979–80 and 2001 a revenue deficit of £126 million per annum was identified and its impact on public parks was evident. Peripatetic maintenance gangs meant declining quality; while the lack of the visible presence of park keepers meant increasing anti-social behaviour went unchecked and in many places parks became no-go areas. This situation continued for some 20 years and it was not until the Urban Parks Programme was set up by the Heritage Lottery Fund (HLF) in 1996 that the situation slowly began to change. C.F.A. Voysey's (1857–1941) Emslie Horniman Pleasance, Kensington (1914) was the first park to be restored under this programme. This sector of the HLF's work has been by far the most popular of its initiatives and the first ten years of this and its successor programmes saw more than 250 historic parks restored. By 2012 more than £700 million funding had been delivered through the HLF and subsequently the Green Parks Initiative.

The traditional criterion for parks to attract grants was that they should be listed as either Grade 1 or 11* on the English Heritage Register of Parks and Gardens of Special Historic Interest in England. By contrast HLF grants were offered to urban parks whether or not they were registered. This meant that for the first time local and national heritage were assessed equally. By the mid-1990s the derelict state of many urban parks and gardens meant that any repair or restoration of individual features was likely to become the target of vandalism.

If people were going to want to use and be engaged with a park then restoration had to involve the whole park. Only then would the future of the park be viable. This meant not only restoring the historic features such as the gates and railings, lakes, bridges, planting, bandstands and shelters, but the introduction of new features to encourage park use such as toilets, cafés, playgrounds and visitor centres.

In 1998 a directive to the HLF from the Secretary of State demanded that its grants addressed new issues that were very different from those hitherto associated with grants for conservation. These included reducing social and economic deprivation; achieving sustainability via local involvement; providing public benefit, access and enjoyment for all ages; and social, economic and environmental regeneration. In park terms, this meant finding new uses for existing buildings and introducing new facilities. The resulting regeneration has been a major factor in achieving viability for these historic parks which restoration and repair alone could never have accomplished. Regenerated parks also have a role in the wider urban regeneration process. Parks can link communities; add value to properties; form the basis of regional spatial strategies and, from redundant industrial sites, dynamic new landscapes have been created. The parks at the centre of this process can be new or historic. People visit parks for a variety of reasons; to relax, enjoy the floral displays and greenery, listen to music, feed the ducks and play sport and they need drinking water, refreshments, shelter and toilets. In addition, park keepers need accommodation and facilities for park maintenance.

Buildings

The lodges at the entrance gates to parks displayed bylaws and signalled an environment separate from the urban surroundings, but this relationship began to change in the inter-war period. Lodge styles varied with their location; for example the lodge (1867) by John Brooke in Queen's Park, Crewe was half-timbered; in Birkenhead Park, Robertson & Hornblower designed an Italianate-style lodge (1847). Under the right-to-buy legislation of the Thatcher Government of the 1980s, many of these lodges became privately owned and fenced off so they were no longer associated with, or appeared to be part of, the park and by 2001, 22% of park lodges had gone.

The restoration of park buildings can raise many issues. In Birkenhead Park, the wooden Swiss bridge had survived since 1847. In order to protect the bridge it was isolated from the mainland in 1970. This entailed removing and dispersing large quantities of earth and subsequently the vegetation around the bridge grew and the bridge became inaccessible and began disintegrating. The bridge had been intended to provide important views of the park, but if access was allowed there was a risk of vandalism or it being burnt down, so many local people objected to its being reconnected to the mainland. Reconnection would involve either major earth-moving or the building of an additional bridge to span the gap. So what was the 'right' answer? One option was to take the bridge down, relocate it, preserve it and rebuild a replica using fireproofed materials. Another option was to re-establish the link to the mainland but fence the bridge off, so it was accessible only on special occasions. The third option was to retain the bridge, restore it, treat it with fireproofing, install CCTV and let it take its chance and this was the option chosen. In the restoration process full details were recorded so that if the worst happened it could be rebuilt to the original specification. The City Council envisaged that the restoration of the whole park with enhanced levels of staffing and maintenance would reduce the risk of arson and, so far, the bridge has survived.

Many historic parks were originally landscape parks with listed mansions and from the start local authorities faced the problem of how to use the historic building. Sometimes they became libraries, museums, art galleries, or refreshment rooms. Queen's Park, Manchester (1846) inherited Hendham Hall (1800). This was demolished in 1884 and replaced by a local authority built museum and art gallery designed by J. Allison which is now part of the City Art Galleries. Saltwell Park, Gateshead (1877) was formed from the grounds of Saltwell Towers (1862) designed by its owner, William Wailes (1808–81). The park and the mansion were acquired by the local authority in 1876 and laid out the following year by Edward Kemp. When the park went into decline, so did the mansion and in the 1970s the local authority proposed demolishing it. A local campaign successfully opposed this and in 2006 both park and mansion were restored. Saltwell Towers is now a gallery, café/restaurant and conference centre, with an education and training centre in the stables.

Gunnersbury Park, London contains two mansions, and 22 listed buildings and structures. The large mansion has fine interiors and now houses a local history museum which displays a collection of Rothschild carriages in the drawing room. The pavilion in Baxter Park, Dundee (Paxton, 1863), designed by G.F. Stokes (1827–74), Paxton's son-in-law, sits on a terrace overlooking the southern part of the park and forms a focal point in the landscape. By the mid-1990s the park had become a no-go area and the pavilion had fallen into disrepair. An HLF grant awarded in 2001 enabled restoration, including reinstating the boundary walls and railings which secured the park; glassing in the Stokes pavilion which now has a café at one end and a meeting room at the other; removing the overgrown shrubberies and reinstating the Paxton bedding layout. The new park centre, formally opened in 2007, is used by schools, health clubs and the local youth project and there is a new playground.

New buildings

Jephson Gardens, Leamington (1890s) designed by the engineer William Louis de Normanville (1843–1928) forms part of the chain of parks running through the centre of the town. In 2006 a large new £3 million lakeside pavilion was built which incorporates a temperate house, restaurant and education unit. The new visitor centre in the important, historic Birkenhead Park combines a café with a gallery and information centre, but its two-storey scale and materials seem more appropriate to an urban environment. In Avenham Park, Preston, designed by Milner (1860s) the new single-storey wood-clad pavilion by McChesney Architects (2008) seems, by contrast, to be a more sympathetic intervention.

New, well-maintained visitor centres can attract visitors back to parks. In Norfolk Heritage Park, Sheffield (1848), local people were involved in deciding what facilities were needed. The Centre in the Park is a single-storey building, with a community centre, café and nursery. It has had an important role in regenerating the park, and this in turn has led to the social regeneration of the area.

Bandstands

During the latter half of the nineteenth century many parks acquired bandstands and by the end of the century they had become *the* park icon (Figure 19.3).

Bandstands constructed of cast iron survived two world wars but without maintenance they subsequently decayed or were deliberately removed in the years that followed. Victoria Park, London, lost its bandstand but the drawings of 1865 survive and it was meticulously reconstructed by RMJM in 1991, thus restoring a missing focal point. The colour of some of them certainly ensures they command attention. Lincoln Arboretum was restored in 2004 when the bandstand and cast-iron shelter were repainted in their original colours of blue, red, gold and purple.

Figure 19.3 Crowds around the bandstand at Peel Park, Salford, Lowry, 1931 (author's own).

Palm houses and winter gardens

To survive, some park buildings had to find new uses. Palm houses and winter gardens were added to many parks towards the end of the nineteenth century but they are large buildings and expensive to run and, by 2001, 70% of public park glasshouses had gone. The palm house in Sefton Park, Liverpool (1872) was manufactured by Mackenzie and Moncur and donated by Henry Yates Thompson in 1896. It was designed to 'delight the eye, interest . . . the student and generally make life brighter'. The original planting was by James Veitch & Sons and the statue of Highland Mary (from Burns' poem) stood amid the vegetation. By the 1990s much of the glass was missing from the palm house and it was in a very sad state. With HLF and other funding it was restored and reopened to the public in 2001. The main entrance was repositioned, a new basement area with toilets and rooms available for small groups, a new interior with a capacity for 400 people and a flexible layout, including a restaurant and stage were created. It can be hired for corporate entertainment, weddings and so forth but the main emphasis is no longer on plants. To ensure security a 4-metre-high metal fence has been constructed.

Mowbray Park, Sunderland (1857) featured magnificent Winter Gardens added in 1866. These were bombed during World War II and a new temperate winter garden was built in 2002 as part of the regeneration of the park, with a café and visitor centre alongside. Kibble Palace was erected in Glasgow Botanic Gardens (1873) in an attempt to reverse the gardens' financial decline but it was not successful and it was taken over by the Corporation in 1891. By the end of the last century Kibble Palace had deteriorated badly but it has now been restored with areas for plants, concerts and other events. In view of this change of use in 2007 it was decided to re-glaze the building with Stipolyte frosted, toughened, laminated glass in order to protect the plant collections and reduce the light levels. Previously the clear glass in the fernery had been painted white to reduce the glare. Some of the original panes have been retained to form a strip from the top of the main dome to the cupola above the entrance. The derelict palm house in Tollcross Park, Glasgow (1872) has been restored and planted (2006). At the rear is a café/restaurant that also provides training for students.

Statues and monuments

Parks commemorated local and national heroes and international events, with monuments and statues including the Queen, Prince Albert, local MPs, aristocrats, entrepreneurs and benefactors. The Khyber Pass, East Park, Hull (1887) made of Pulhamite, by E.A. Peak forms part of the original layout. These statues were often paid for by public subscription linking the park to its community and promoting local and national pride. The Doulton Fountain (Figure 19.4) designed by Arthur Edward Pearce and standing 14 metres high, is the largest terracotta statue in the world; made for the International Exhibition of 1888, its subject is Queen Victoria ruling over her Empire. It was moved to Glasgow Green in 1890.

The monument survived until the mid-1980s, but thereafter became the target of vandals. In December 1997 Glasgow Green was awarded £6.6 million by the HLF and the Doulton Fountain was taken down and removed for restoration. In 2005 it was re-assembled in a new location by the People's Palace. For safety, CCTV has been installed and if anyone ventures into the pool, alarms sound and the police are called.

One of the delightful features of People's Park, Halifax (J. Paxton, E. Milner, 1857) is the terrace which overlooks the park and gives views to the moors beyond the town and is lined with classical statues on pedestals. Decay and vandalism caused them to reach such a state that they were encased in green plywood boxes. When it was proposed to restore the statues, part of the debate centred on the fact that the park now stood in the midst of a largely Asian population and it was argued that these classical figures were irrelevant because they were not part of Asian culture and that they should be replaced by features that were more relevant. Consultation with the local population, however, demonstrated

Figure 19.4 Glasgow's Doulton Fountain, photographed in 1996, comprises the tallest terracotta structure in the world (author's own).

that this was not the case. They saw the original classical statues as part of their park and they wanted them restored as they were, and this is what happened.

A pair of Dogs of Alcibiades stands in Victoria Park, London. The original second century AD Roman sculpture of a Molossian hound had been rescued from rubble in a Roman workshop and brought to Britain by Henry Jennings in 1753. For a time it was on display in the Great Court of the British Museum. The Victoria Park dogs were originally at ground level and very popular with children who loved to cuddle and climb on them. Since the restoration they have been placed on plinths and surrounded with railings. Alas, this has not protected them from vandalism.

Planting: trees and shrubs

Trees often form the main structure of a landscape, whether in glades or clumps or in avenues as at Moor Park, Preston. Particular species were chosen and in many parks individual trees predate the formation of the park. If tree and shrub planting does not refer to the original design intention of the park it can be very damaging. Peel Park, Salford (1846) for example, was designed as a series of through routes with vistas across the park which provided a sense of place. It suffered badly from the building of Salford University when much of it became part of the University car park. The final *coup de grace* came in 1973 when 'Plant a tree in 73' was the slogan and tree planting was encouraged up and down the country. In Peel Park this resulted in a forest of trees which completely obscured the original design intentions.

The serpentine shrubbery in Carr Ellison Park, Hebburn (1897) still survives from the late nineteenth century, as does the dell. The HLF application proposed taking the walls away from the dell to create an ecological area; however, the recommendation was that they were compatible. Shrubberies can be very attractive and colourful and their great advantage is that they survive the seasons (Queen's Park, Longton (1887) is an excellent example). In recent years shrubberies have been the focus of a number of contentious issues; rubbish collects under them causing cleaning difficulties and there is concern that they could shelter anti-social behaviour or be places for muggers to lurk. Indeed, Cardiff police suggested setting one park aside just for anti-social behaviour – that way the rest of the town would be safer! In 2006 the London borough of Lambeth suggested that parks should be truly inclusive of all members of society, including drunks and drug takers and dealers! However, it is not wise to photograph them using a telephoto lens as this author discovered!

Flowers

In the 1860s the influence of the Crystal Palace massed bedding schemes spread and was adopted enthusiastically by public park keepers as flowering hybrids became increasingly available.

Carpet-bedding is very labour-intensive; however, there were practical reasons for its use in the polluted atmosphere of nineteenth- and early twentieth-century parks. In many locations in Manchester pollution was so bad that trees would not grow at all and flowering shrubs lasted three years at the most before they had to be renewed. Bedding plants and carpet bedding were a practical solution as they were easier to replant than trees and shrubs. It was not until 1956 that the Clean Air Act was passed. The carpet bed in Mowbray Park, Sunderland (c.1883) was restored, c.2002. Carpet bedding and sculptural planting provided vivid displays, as demonstrated in the plan of West Park, Wolverhampton (Figure 19.5).

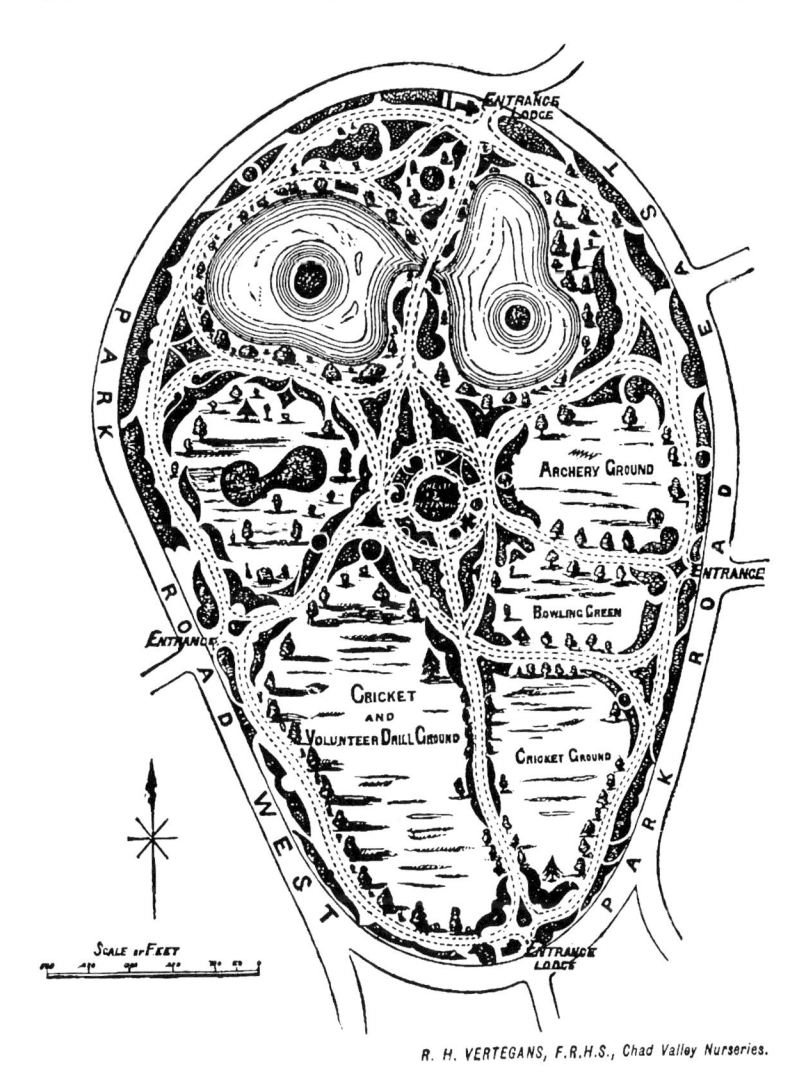

Figure 19.5 West Park, Wolverhampton, sculptural planting, 1911 George V coronation (author's own).

Figure 19.6 Pulhamite waterfall, Madeira Walk, Ramsgate, 1893 (author's own).

In Locke Park, Barnsley, the magnificent ribbon bedding was maintained until 1991. One of the main problems of restoring historic planting is the skills that are necessary and maintenance costs. A significant element of the attraction of parks was the variety of gardens that could be experienced and, as parks have been restored, some new gardens have been added where appropriate. Alpine plants and rockeries became popular, especially with James Pulham's (1793–1838) success in creating Pulhamite artificial rockwork that was so realistic it fooled geologists (Figure 19.6).

The rockwork cascade in Battersea Park was initially restored by spraying it with gunnite which had the unfortunate effect of changing its colour to pink. English Heritage has now produced recommendations for the restoration of Pulhamite. New types of garden were introduced as knowledge expanded and tastes changed and towards the end of the nineteenth century Japanese gardens and Shakespeare gardens became popular. A new garden and pavilion were added to Preston Park, Brighton in the 1930s.

Conclusion

Our public parks are physically accessible to all income groups and abilities but this does not mean that intellectual accessibility can be assumed, and this is why interpretation and community involvement are so important. The HLF stressed the importance of both the physical restoration of urban parks and their regeneration. Thus, funding has been available for repair and restoration, as well as new works such as playgrounds, toilets, cafés, visitor centres and new additions such as the Mughal Garden in Lister Park, Bradford (1998–2002). Today, every town in this country has its public parks, gardens, commons and recreation grounds, each of historic significance, and all of them are important to the historic environment of our townscapes.

Further reading

Brason, G. (1978) *The Ungreen Park: the Diary of a Keeper*, Bodley Head, London.
Brooks, C. et al (1989) *Mortal Remains: the history and present state of the Victorian and Edwardian cemetery*, Wheaton, Exeter.
Chadwick, G.F. (1966) *The Park and the Town*, Architectural Press, London.

Clayden, P. (1992) *Our Common Land: the law and history of commons and village greens*, Open Spaces Society.
Colquhoun, K. (2003) *A Thing in Disguise, the Visionary Life of Joseph Paxton*, Fourth Estate, London.
Commedia and Demos (1995) *Park Life: Urban Parks and Social Renewal*, London.
Conway, H. (1991) *People's Parks*, Cambridge University Press.
Conway, H. (1996) *Public Parks*, Shire Publications.
Conway, H. (2000) 'Everyday Landscapes: public parks from 1930–2000', *Garden History*, Vol. 28, No. 1, pp. 117–134.
Conway, H. (2005) *Understanding Architecture*, London, 2nd edn.
Conway, H. (2009–10) 'Greening the City: The Development of Tree-lined Streets and Avenues 1860–1930', *The London Gardener*, Vol. 15, 2009–10, pp. 100–111.
Conway, H. and Lambert, D. (1993) *Public Prospects: Historic Urban Parks under Threat*, Victorian Society and Garden History Society.
Gilding, R. (1997) *Historic Public Parks, Bath*, Avon Gardens Trust.
Gilmour, W. (1996) *Keep off the Grass!* (Glasgow), Ochiltree.
Green, F. (1995) *Historic Parks and Gardens of Tyne and Wear*, Tyne and Wear.
Greenhalgh, L. and Worpole, K. (1995) *Park Life: Urban Parks and Social Renewal*, London.
Harding, S. and Lambert, D. (1998) *Parks and Gardens of Avon*, Avon Gardens Trust.
Jordan, H. (1994) 'Public Parks, 1885–1914', *Garden History*, Vol. 22, No. 1, pp. 85–113.
Jordan, H. (2003) *Public Parks Review: Summary* (thematic review on public parks), English Heritage.
Lambert, D. (2000) *Historic Public Parks, Bristol*, Avon Gardens Trust.
Lambert, D. (2005) *The Park Keeper*, English Heritage.
Lambert, D., Goodchild, P. and Roberts, J. (2006) *Parks and Gardens: a researcher's guide to sources for designed landscapes*, English Heritage.
Lambert, D. and Williams, S. (Parks Agency) (2005) *Commons, Heaths and Greens in Greater London*, short report for English Heritage.
Lawley, I. (1998) *Parks for the People*, Stoke on Trent Leisure and Recreation Dept.
Layton-Jones, K. and Lee, R. (2008) *Places of Health and Amusement: Liverpool's historic parks and gardens*, English Heritage.
Loudon, J.C. (1822) *An Encyclopaedia of Gardening*, London.
Loudon, J.C. (1840) *The Derby Arboretum*, London.
Mawson, T. (1911) *Civic Art: Studies in Town Planning, Parks, Boulevards and Open Spaces*, London.
Pettigrew, W.W. (1929) *Handbook of the Manchester Parks*, Manchester.
Pettigrew, W.W. (1937) *Municipal Parks: layout, management and administration*, London.
Report of the Select Committee on Public Walks, 1833.
Ruff, A. (1996) *The Biography of Philips Park, Manchester, 1846–1996*, University of Manchester.
Sexby, J.J. (1898) *The Municipal Parks, Gardens and Open Spaces of London*, London.
Taylor, H. (1995) 'Urban Public Parks, 1840–1900: design and meaning', *Garden History*, Vol. 23, No. 2, pp. 201–221.
Town and Country Parks (1999) Environment, Transport and Regional Affairs Committee, 20th Report, Stationery Office, London, November.
Urban Parks Forum (2001) *Public Parks Assessment*, Caversham.
Watkins, J. and Wright, J. (eds) (2007) *The Management and Maintenance of Historic Parks, Garden and Landscapes*, English Heritage Handbook, London.
Woudstra, J. (ed.) (2000) *The Regeneration of Public Parks*, Landscape Trust.

20 Conserving historic parks and gardens in a changing climate

Jenifer White
Senior Landscape Advisor, English Heritage, London, UK

In conserving historic parks and gardens, we aim to sustain their significance for present and future generations. The challenge has always been to understand the dynamic nature of designed landscapes with their many features and different timescales for upkeep and periodic renewal, repair and restoration, and of course this includes the trees and shrubs that form the design which will be continually growing and maturing. Added to these challenges are now climate change impacts.

This chapter discusses some of the issues for major historic designed landscape features like trees and lakes and conservation management approaches for sites now and in the longer term.

The climate is changing

The causes of climate change, rate of change, consequences and mitigation measures continue to be debated but there is unequivocal evidence that global warming will continue over the next century. Changes in climate are already being witnessed. In the UK over the last 50 years we have seen the growing season lengthen, fewer frosts and warmer early spring temperatures, and there is some indication that extreme rainfall events have increased. Current climate change projections show that over the long term we will see increasing summer and winter temperatures, more winter rainfall and less summer rainfall, more heavy rainfall, and rising sea levels. In the short term, due to the natural variability of the UK climate, we should still expect to see some cool summers and cold winters, dry winters and wet summers which may seem to counter the long-term trends. There are also likely to be social and economic consequences for the UK arising from other climate change impacts around the world.

Climate change projections for the UK continue to be developed and they will become increasingly more detailed and regionally specific. The current UK Climate Projections (UKCP09) projections look at the 2020s, 2050s and 2080s and three different scenario levels based on high, medium and low levels of greenhouse gas emissions.[1] The purpose of the projections is to provide a consistent approach to mapping potential risks and opportunities and to develop a national adaptation programme. The impacts and risks increase with the rate of global warming and, until climate change impacts for individual areas are better

Gardens & Landscapes in Historic Building Conservation, First Edition. Edited by Marion Harney.
© 2014 John Wiley & Sons, Ltd. Published 2014 by John Wiley & Sons, Ltd.

understood, it is difficult to understand the specific conservation challenges and appropriate adaptation measures and timescales for sites. Current evidence indicates we should be planning for higher emission scenarios; even so, in the medium scenario by the 2080s the average UK summer temperature is likely to rise by 3–4°C, summer rainfall is expected to decrease by 11–27%, and sea levels are expected to rise. Even if emissions were stopped now, past emissions mean changes to the climate will continue for the next 30–40 years.

Learning from past extreme weather events and other threats

Our needs for light, shade and shelter are reflected in the design, layout and planting of gardens and parks. In hot climates cool shady vistas and pools help ameliorate temperatures and provide respite from the heat. In Mediterranean countries strong sunlight can be used to create drama out of strong shadows and playing water. In the UK, large, open spaces make the most of the sunlight, and the iconic green lawn is a product of our northern temperate climate. For centuries designers and gardeners have been manipulating sites to create favourable microclimates like walled gardens or protected environments like orangeries, conservatories, and glasshouses to grow plants and as places to enjoy.

The UK is already vulnerable to extreme weather events. Severe winters, droughts, storms and flooding (Figure 20.1) have taken their toll on parks and gardens. Although scientists cannot confirm that extreme weather events to date are associated with climate change there is evidence that heavy rainfall events and heatwaves are becoming more intense across the world. The impacts of past extreme weather events and lessons learnt could offer us insights to managing future climate change.

Floods, droughts and temperature extremes

Provisional statistics from the Met Office show that 2012 was the second wettest year in over 100 years of UK national records. The year started with droughts and threats of hosepipe bans but, from April onwards, there were heavy rains which caused widespread flooding, and serious flooding had occurred only two years before. The year 2000 was the wettest year on record by a few more millimetres, and four of the top five wettest years are all in

Figure 20.1 There was extensive flooding in North Yorkshire in September 2012. Flooding can cause physical damage and undermine plant and tree health, and historic park and garden visitor and business operations can be badly affected. (© English Heritage.)

the twenty-first century. Flood risk is predicted to increase significantly over the next century and there will also be water scarcity issues due to climate-driven changes in hydrology and supply–demand deficits. Both flooding and water shortages pose potential serious threats for historic parks and gardens. Heavy rainfall and flooding can cause a range of problems from soil erosion and the leaching of nutrients, to damage of paths and other features, especially wooden structures; pollution due to flood waters contaminated with oil, chemicals and untreated sewage and, in the longer term, the development of anaerobic conditions which will kill trees and plants by suffocating the roots. Wear and tear to lawns and grass paths can be exaggerated by waterlogging. As climate changes and the growing season extends, plants become increasingly less tolerant of waterlogging as their dormancy shortens. On light soils, increased rainfall could, of course, be beneficial.

As well as damage to historic parks, garden fabric and costs of repair, poor weather deters garden visitors. Flooding may necessitate sites, areas or paths being temporarily closed and re-opening delayed until flood damage can be sorted out. In summer 2012 many garden tourist attractions saw their visitor numbers drop significantly, representing millions of pounds of lost income; many other visitor events and shows had to be cancelled because grounds became waterlogged and those that persevered faced landscape reinstatement costs.

Although the UK's temperate climate brings frequent rain, long droughts do occur. Low rainfall is an aspect of all droughts but topography, land and water use also influence the vulnerability of areas to drought. The 1975–76 drought is remembered as severe. It had serious impacts for agriculture, forestry and nature conservation as well as water users from industry to domestic consumers. Many trees died from moisture stress, lakes dried out, and there were moor and heathland fires. There were also widespread droughts in the 1980s, and more recently a 2006 hosepipe ban affected 16 million people in England and Wales and had impacts such as fish deaths and outbreaks of poisonous blue-green algae in lakes and rivers. Summer heatwaves like 2003 could become a normal event by the 2040s and, by the 2060s, such a summer would be considered cool according to some climate change models.

Although snow and extreme cold events are likely to decrease in the longer term, the UK will still experience freezing temperatures due to climate variability and these can damage, even kill, plants and snow-melt can cause waterlogging and localised flooding. Late spring frosts can be sharp and unexpected, devastating fruit blossom and early flowering shrubs. Warmer temperatures could be deleterious for some plants like bulbs and garden effects, such as autumn colour, are triggered by cold.

Storms

The UK weather is often windy. The Great Storm in the early hours of 16 October 1987 had huge impacts for historic parks and gardens. The mid-latitude cyclone generated winds gusting up to 120 mph and felled some 15 million trees across a great swathe of southern England stretching from the Dorset coast to East Anglia. The equivalent of five years' cut timber was lost in one night. The storm has been described as 'the arboricultural equivalent of the London Blitz', with 18 people killed and an estimated £1 billion in repairs and clear-up costs. The wind-throw was exacerbated by the wet ground conditions and many historic parks and gardens were devastated. A storm of this magnitude had not been witnessed since 1703 yet, at the beginning of 1990, storms raged across the south-west damaging more historic parks and gardens and in January 2012 Scottish gardens were badly damaged by severe gales.

Pests and diseases

One of the consequences of global trading and the UK's warming climate is the increase in the spread of tree and horticultural pests and diseases. Changes in climate can also create

Figure 20.2 Upright tall English elms were once characteristic features of many historic parks, as shown in this archive photo of Clayton House, taken on an unknown date after 1945 by John Gay. (© English Heritage.)

stress for individual species or ecosystems and can lead to increased vulnerability to pathogens. Alarmingly, in the last 12 years, more than double the number of tree pathogens has occurred compared to the last hundred years. Ash dieback (*Chalara fraxinea*) fungus now threatens UK ash trees, the third most common species, and work is underway to reduce the rate of spread, develop resistance and resilience. In addition *Dothistroma* Needle Blight (affecting pines), Acute Oak Decline, *Phytophora ramorum* (affecting rhododendrons, beeches, non-native oaks and now larch) and Chestnut Blight are also rapidly spreading across England. Other forestry pests like grey squirrels, which, since their release in the late nineteenth century have advanced relentlessly, could further spread as a result of earlier springs and milder winters.

English elms were once a characteristic tree of many parks and southern lowland landscapes (Figure 20.2) but Dutch elm disease devastated the population and dramatically changed the treescape. The disease was first recorded in north-west Europe around 1910 and it had spread to the UK by the 1920s; however, by the 1940s it had died down. A second outbreak in the 1960s proved to be very destructive and by the 1990s over 25 million trees had been killed. There was great interest in trying to replicate elms in the landscape. Experimentation with alternative elms and other species was a reminder that the range of size and forms amongst any genera vary greatly and the design effect needs to be considered carefully. As the tallest British broadleaved tree and with a very distinct canopy shape, the elm was difficult to replace. New disease-resistant hybrids have now been bred and are gradually being reintroduced in planting schemes.

Planning adaptation in the historic park and garden

We need to ensure our historic parks and gardens are resilient to climate change. The legacy of landscape design is very diverse in its form, character, function, size, age, condition, and historic interest and consequently climate change impacts and adaptation needs will vary.

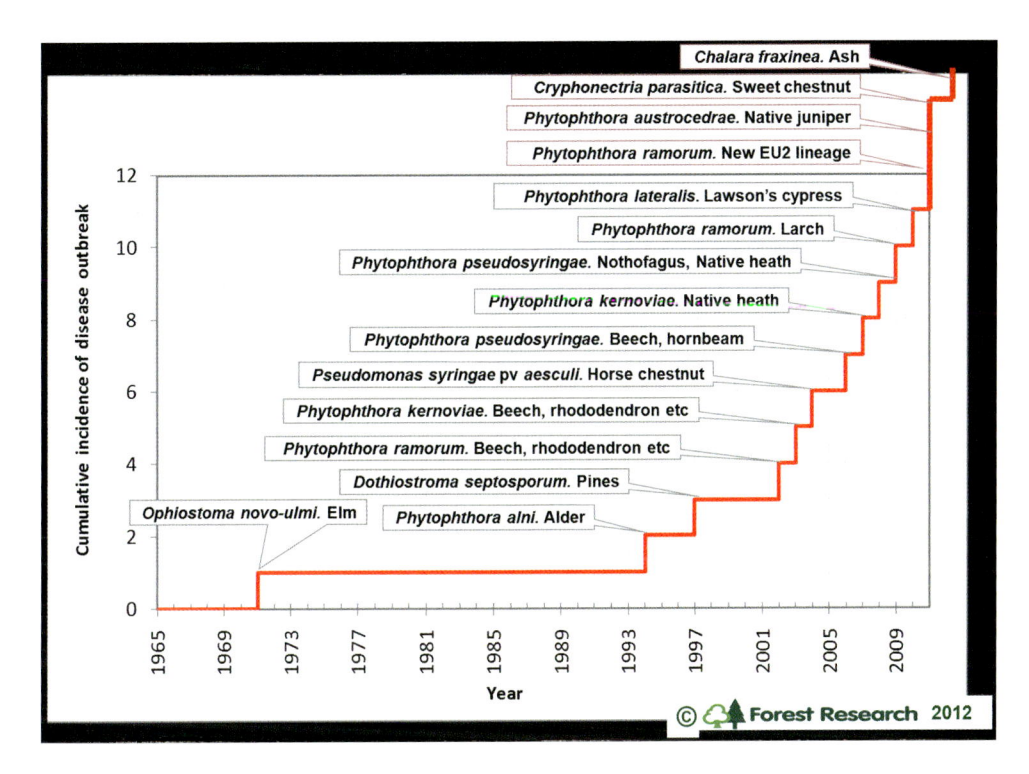

Figure 20.3 The cumulative increase in the number of tree pests and pathogens over the last 20 years has been dramatic and reflects increases in the global trading of plants. A changing climate could facilitate the spread of pests and diseases. (© Forest Research.)

Historic parkland, wood pasture and veteran trees are important wildlife habitats at an international level so conservation strategies also need to protect and extend these habitats. In planning for climate change adaptation in historic parks and gardens we not only need to consider individual climate change impacts but cumulative effects and geographical variations across the country (Figure 20.3). Historic park and garden adaptation planning needs to consider the immediate term, the 2050s, 2080s and into the twenty-second century.

The Royal Horticultural Society, National Trust and the UK Climate Impacts Programme coordinated organisations and industries involved in gardens to start thinking about the consequences for the care and management of gardens through their *Gardening in the Global Greenhouse* report (2002). The study projected both opportunities and threats for the horticultural sector. Warmer temperatures and longer growing seasons were seen as potential opportunities to diversify and grow more exotic plants in the UK but ten years on, a more holistic appreciation of the cumulative impact of wetter winters, weather variations, and sunlight, limited by our 50°N latitude, will check such aspirations. The 2002 report also looks at historic and botanic garden conservation issues. The authors highlighted the need to establish the degree of exposure of Britain's gardening heritage to climate change; to identify resources and level of investment required to maintain the integrity of gardens of greatest historical significance and establish the criteria for the management of significant plant collections on a national basis. This research has yet to be carried out.

Other land-use sectors like forestry, agriculture and nature conservation have also begun to scope and research climate change impacts which have cross-application for historic parks and gardens, and the recent *UK Climate Change Risk Assessment 2012*, for agriculture and forestry, confirms the issues outlined in the 2002 report.

Adaptation of important historic parks and gardens will be challenging. Like any other proposal for change, the significance of an individual site and conservation aims need to be well understood in order to assess impacts and sustainability. Conservation principles such as the English Heritage 2007 guidance provide a useful basis for making adaptation decisions. All adaptation has the potential to confuse the historic design and its interpretation; proposals for change should aim to retain the significance and qualities of sites and climate change adaptation will also need to be integrated with the ongoing adjustment, removal and replacement of plantings. There will be implications for garden management programmes, staffing and budgets too. Detailed documentation of adaptation approaches, monitoring and review of outcomes will allow successful strategies to be identified.

Lessons from past extreme weather events underline the importance of good landscape maintenance and management, including renewal, in developing greater resilience and conservation principles. English Heritage's 2007 guidance exists to help us through the decision-making process. Historic park and garden conservation has to be long-term in its approach and conservation action taken now such as tree planting will be evident in the 2080s and beyond when climate change will have advanced considerably. Good planting and establishment practice (including site preparation like drainage) will help ensure trees grow strong and robust.

Conservation management plans

The conservation management plan has proved to be a useful tool in developing understanding about heritage significance, vulnerabilities, sustaining values and managing change of individual sites. The storm damage in 1987 and 1990 highlighted the state of decline of many historic designed landscapes, and that good landscape restoration requires a longer timescale than disaster management which can inadvertently result in the loss of archaeology and wreck natural ecosystems. Although costly, the storm damage created opportunities to review conservation objectives and funding was focused on research and planning future management which has been further developed in current agri-environment schemes. Conservation management plans should be regularly reviewed and updated and this process could be used to track and monitor climate change related issues and to begin to identify likely longer-term adaptation strategies and resource requirements. Securing a conservation management plan for each historic park and garden would help move towards a planned, rather than reactive, approach to adaptation for our designed landscape heritage and through the plans we could collectively assess the extent of conservation challenges, management needs and successful strategies. Policy and fiscal incentives could be targeted to encourage such adaptation planning and conservation management. Current agri-environment schemes such as Environmental Stewardship are designed to secure widespread and multiple environmental benefits, including parkland conservation measures, and schemes are being reviewed with respect to providing more ecosystem regulating services such as flood alleviation, coastal protection, erosion control and water quality and climate change mitigation through land management.

Trees in a changing climate

One of the major garden and park conservation concerns is trees. The form, colour and texture of trees and their composition are important in most landscape designs. Often tree species are readily recognisable, even from a distance. Repetition of the same form, as in lines or avenues creates rhythm; single specimens can be a focus; groups of different species selected for contrasting form create interest. Blocks of woodland within the park, and the parkland plantings of specimen trees, clumps and belts have traditionally been managed as a long-term crop, subject to a cycle of thinning, felling and replanting. They have silvicultural value as well as serving an ornamental and often sporting role.

Up until the late eighteenth century a palette of predominantly native trees such as oak, lime, elm, beech and sweet chestnut were used and exotics such as cedar of Lebanon were planted as specimens. Plantations of American and other exotic trees became increasingly popular towards the end of the century with the development of Picturesque design. With the growth of plant-hunting in the nineteenth century, a far wider variety of trees were used in parks, and arboreta and pinetums were planted.

Forestry modelling research has looked at the suitability of tree species across the UK against the climate change scenarios for the 2050s and 2080s. As climate change intensifies, many characteristic parkland trees like the large spreading beeches and oaks become increasingly unsuitable in southern Britain and southern species like sweet chestnut will become more suitable. One of the more adaptable species, the ash, is now threatened by disease. Trees like sycamore and silver birch, which often dominate regenerated woodland, could become marginal or poor.

Species such as holm oak, a predominantly Mediterranean tree, are likely to be favoured by climate change and indeed holm oak is already spreading in southern England. Other non-natives like cedar of Lebanon pose interesting conservation challenges too. In their native Lebanon, the trees depend on a minimum amount of snow and rain for natural regeneration, and climate change could have a serious impact along with the spread of pests and disease. The trees are already on the International Union for Conservation of Nature's (IUCN) red list of threatened species. Nature conservation in the UK to date has placed a high priority on native trees and shrubs but definitions will inevitably change as other species become naturalised as the climate changes, so a flexible approach needs to be adopted. Non-natives such as Turkey oak, a common parkland tree, can be an alternative host for some native oak invertebrates and there are many examples of ageing, exotic, parkland trees which will be amongst our future veteran trees. Perhaps their biodiversity value has yet to be revealed, especially if fungi and invertebrates are associated with types of decay rather than host species. Conversely, some of these introduced species could also have the potential to act as hosts for diseases threatening native trees. Forestry research highlights the future vulnerability of free-standing trees and veteran trees typical of hedgerows, fields and parkland and the longevity of these trees can be protected through tree and site management. The Ancient Tree Forum provides guidance.

Some ornamental tree species like cedars, firs, and planes are now considered to have potential for use in UK forestry as new components of woodlands in climate change strategies. The species structure and flora of woodland is likely to change too as different trees begin to dominate. In high-emission scenarios, typical parkland species such as the native oaks may be increasingly difficult to establish and may be out-competed by other species. Figure 20.4 shows a table listing the changes in tree suitability for England in view of the changing conditions.

UK forestry guidance now encourages broadening the mixture of trees and ages and varying management systems and the timing of operations to increase woodland resilience to climate change, but such strategies may not be historically appropriate for tree features in parks and gardens. Further guidance on the viability and investment requirements needed for the successful planting, establishment and maturation of amenity trees in gardens, parks and streets against climate change projections would be helpful. Current research findings do show which forestry species are likely to be more difficult to establish as the climate changes and techniques for good tree establishment including selection of smaller-size stock to mulching and protection are well understood. There is some anecdotal evidence from 1987 that veteran parkland trees proved to be more storm-robust than younger plantation woodland trees, as the veterans have inherent resilience. If it becomes increasingly more challenging to establish new parkland trees at the end of the century there may be a good case to press on with new tree planting sooner to ensure best establishment chances and to improve the age diversity of parklands. The longevity of veteran and maturing trees can be nurtured through good management. Woodland management also needs to begin to

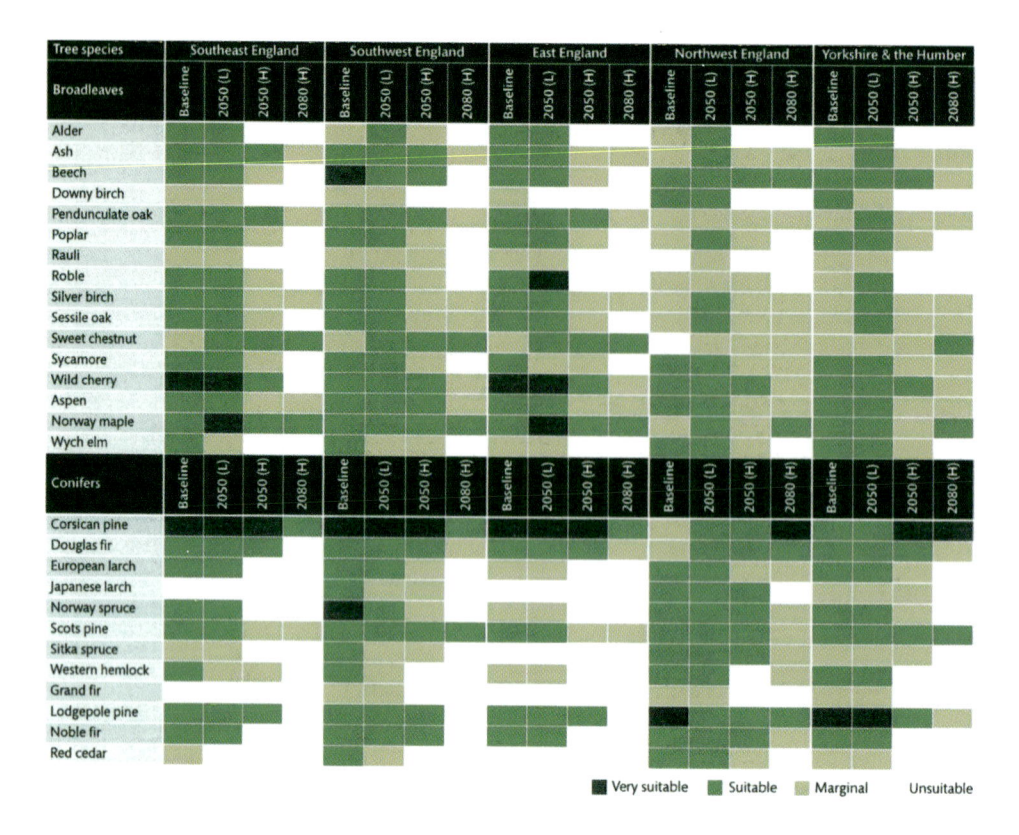

Figure 20.4 Climate change adds to the complexity of species selection and silvicultural management decisions. Forestry Commission research (2010) provides an analysis of how well tree species are matched to site conditions for forest production. Other factors like pests, pathogens, and increased carbon dioxide levels affecting tree productivity would have to be factored in too. This table shows changes in tree species suitability for England. (Source: Ray et al (2010) 'Climate Change: impacts and adaptation in England's woodlands', FCRN201 p. 7.)

address the threats of drought and increased risk of damage from pests, pathogens, wind and fire.

The lawn in a changing climate Expanses of green lawn and grassland, characteristic of many UK gardens and parks, will become increasingly difficult to maintain as temperatures increase. Brent Elliott's study of weather observations and horticultural records as evidence for climate changes shows that current average temperatures are probably similar to those in the mid-to-late eighteenth century and that the nineteenth century was cooler with later flowering times. Landscape management and use will need to adapt to keep swards in good condition in the long term.

Managing water features in a changing climate, and sea-level rise issues

Water is another important feature in many designed landscapes adding scale, perspective and interest and, of course, it is essential for plant growth. Adaptation steps are already being taken to address some climate change flood and water scarcity risks. Following a review of the series of destructive summer 2007 floods, new legislation was introduced in England and Wales to provide a more comprehensive approach. The Flood and Water

Management Act 2010, which updates the Reservoirs Act 1975, has implications for many historic parks and gardens as it increases reservoir safety regulation for lakes and chains of water bodies which pose a high risk of loss of life in the event of dam failure. The regulations reinforce the need to ensure large water bodies are well maintained. Improvements to dams and related structures may be required, which will need to be sensitively designed to complement historic design and interest. Local authorities have taken the opportunity of Heritage Lottery funding to restore public parks and improve the water quality of lakes through de-silting and better aeration. Some owners are now looking to develop their own boreholes to reduce their dependency on mains water.

In the scope of this chapter it is not possible to address heritage impacts resulting from sea-level rise. Some coastal historic garden features such as ornamental rockwork are already being eroded by increased wave action. Projects such as the Dorset Coast Forum and National Trust's scenarios of coastal change identify vulnerabilities and knowledge gaps and review management options. Shoreline Management Plans provide policy options and the importance of heritage assets is taken on board.

The climate change management experts

Horticultural and landscape professionals are trained to manage change and are exceptionally qualified to tackle climate change adaptation. Good horticultural and arboricultural practice can help abate short-term climate change impacts and, with appropriately trained staff and adequate resources, many special sites could continue to be conserved and enjoyed for several generations. Good soil cultivation, drainage and irrigation, mulching, choice of plants and plant sizes, planting and staking techniques will minimise risks from heavy rains, droughts and storms. There is a long history of gardeners' diaries and these records could provide useful insights to the past, tracking ongoing changes, and informing conservation management plans.

Mitigation, to reduce greenhouse gas sources, carbon emissions and the scale of climate change impacts, is vital and everyone – individuals, businesses, organisations and government – has a role to play. Many historic parks and gardens are actively involved in mitigation from promoting public transport options, energy saving measures, promoting local produce to recycling waste and composting. The National Trust has a campaign to involve and raise awareness amongst its 3.5 million members and 13 million visitors (including school children) in these issues. One element of the campaign is a Green Solutions Fund which has been set up to help raise money for renewable energy technology solutions for National Trust properties. Such technologies offer opportunities to provide power to remote garden buildings and other new uses.

Beyond the historic park and garden

As well as getting involved in mitigation, owners and managers will need to be aware of other strategies which could impact negatively on the historic significance of sites. Views and vistas, or their screening, are often key features in parks and gardens. They provide axes and establish the scale, structure, layout and character of the design. Focal points may lie way beyond the formal garden and park area to outlying features such as a distant church steeple or a folly. Renewable energy developments are needed as part of the UK's mitigation strategy but large structures such as wind turbines, if poorly sited, could be detrimental to the setting and views of such special places. Similarly, new woodland planting and bio-energy crops could be problematic. Current UK woodland planting targets will result in a 4% change in land cover by the 2050s and there is a good case to increase woodland creation in the UK to help abate greenhouse gas emissions. Conifer plantation and energy crops would be the most cost-effective options.

Cooling the urban environment is an increasingly high priority in urban planning and design. By 2050 the annual mean temperature in cities such as Manchester could have increased by as much as 3.6°C. We know our parks, gardens and green spaces in towns and cities have an important role in moderating the 'urban heat island' that will become even more exaggerated as global warming increases. The cooling evapotranspiration function of green spaces needs to be maximised through keeping grass and trees in good condition. Irrigation could be necessary to keep swards green and functional, rather than the current practice of banning garden watering during periods of drought. Parks will be increasingly valued as places of refuge from the heat. Similarly, street trees are important too, yet in many towns and cities the large forest species are disappearing in favour of more compact trees.

Conclusions

In *Heritage Counts 2008* the approach of the historic environment sector to climate change is defined as a six-fold statement:

- The historic environment is a finite resource and we have a responsibility to maintain it for future generations
- Changing people's behaviour is just as important as improving the energy performance of buildings in decreasing emissions
- It is possible to respond to climate change and improve the energy efficiency of older buildings without destroying their distinctive character and value
- Re-use and recycling of older buildings is sustainable
- The historic environment and patterns of development can inform and inspire us how to live in a lower energy economy
- Some parts of the historic environment will be lost as a result of climate change; and some will need to be adapted to avoid permanent damage.

We need to ensure our historic parks and gardens are also resilient to climate change and the *Heritage Counts 2008* statement is just as applicable to these heritage assets.

The interplay and cumulative impact of individual climate change effects across decades and geographical differences are multiple and complex and we are only beginning to understand the implications for historic parks and garden conservation. We also need to factor in extreme weather events and variability. We need to keep abreast of new developments in climate change science and to think about the cross-application of research from other sectors such as forestry, agriculture and nature conservation. As highlighted in *Gardening in the Global Greenhouse* (2002) we need to establish the degree of exposure of Britain's gardening heritage to climate change; to identify resources and the level of investment required to maintain the integrity of gardens of greatest historical significance.

Each historic park and garden is unique with its own values and significances and conservation interests and challenges. Important historic parks and gardens would benefit from long-term conservation management plans and all such plans should be revised to begin to consider climate change risks, likely adaptation needs, and related timespans. Conservation management plans should be used to monitor sites, track climate change effects, record climate change adaptation measures and assess and mitigate risk such as plant health. Conservation management plans should also look at mitigation measures. Periodic renewal, repair and restoration are valid adaptation strategies and conservation principles can help guide decisions about managing change. Good horticultural and arboricultural practice can help minimise risk and improve resilience (including bio-security) and should be the first adaptation strategy. Incentive schemes like grants could be helpful to encourage adaptation work.

The sector needs to ensure we have skilled personnel to ensure good maintenance and long-term stewardship. We do need to be able to anticipate change and adapt practices to

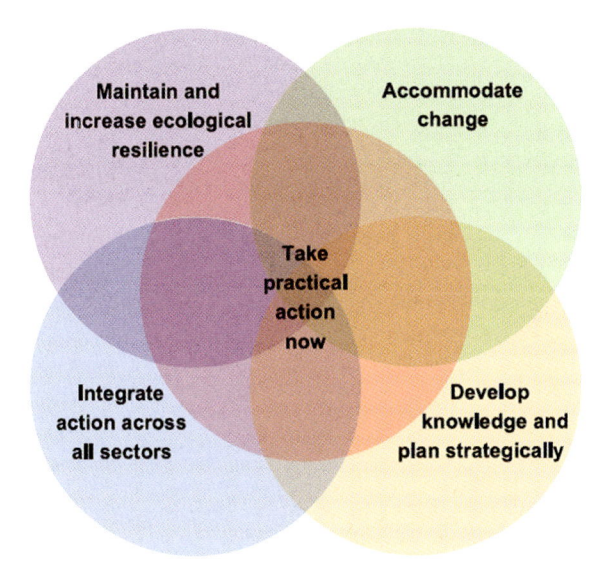

Figure 20.5 The England Biodiversity Strategy (2008) identifies five main adaptation principles to conserving biodiversity in a time of rapid climate change. The precautionary principle underpins all of these. The principles are equally applicable for historic parks and garden conservation.

deal with emerging threats. Sharing experience and new landscape management approaches will help the development of long-term adaptation strategies. It will be some time before we begin most site adaptation work so it is vital that we protect and conserve our heritage of parks and gardens and their settings and reduce harm not linked to climate change. Visitors and the wider public should be encouraged to get involved in understanding climate change impacts and future conservation strategies, and mitigation.

Historic parks and gardens have an important role in biodiversity conservation too – both globally and locally – and conservation management plans need to address species and habitat conservation. Biodiversity adaptation principles have much synergy with historic park and garden conservation needs as summarised in the *England Biodiversity Strategy* (2008) (Figure 20.5):

- Take practical action now – conserve existing biodiversity and protect areas
- Maintain and increase ecological resilience – conserve the range and diversity of habitats and species
- Accommodate change – respond to changing conservation priorities
- Integrate action across partners and sectors, and
- Develop knowledge and plan strategically.

Where climate change extremes lead to decisions to abandon historically important gardens because of natural processes like cliff erosion or sea-level rise, sites should be fully recorded before damaged or lost.

The views expressed are those of the author and not necessarily of English Heritage.

Further reading

Ancient Woodland Forum (2008) *Tree Guide no. 5; Trees and climate change*, Grantham: Woodland Trust.
Bisgrove, R. and Hadley, P. (2002) *Gardening in the Global Greenhouse. The impacts of climate change in the UK*, Oxford, UKCIP www.ukcip.org.uk
Defra, *Future Worlds images*, www.defra.gov.uk/adaptation

Defra, the Scottish Government, the Welsh Government and Department of the Environment Northern Ireland (2012) *Summary of the Key Findings from the UK Climate Change Risk Assessment 2012*, www.defra.gov.uk/environment/climate/government

Dorset Coast Forum and the National Trust, *Exploring future implications of climate change for three National Trust areas in Dorset*.

Elliott, B. (2010) 'The climate of the landscape garden, in Painshill Park: the pioneering restoration of an 18th-century landscape garden', Proceedings Painshill Park & Beyond Conference, Painshill Park 24–25 June 2010. *New Arcadian Journal* No. 67/68.

English Heritage (1997) *After the Great Storm*, London, English Heritage.

English Heritage (2008) *Conservation Principles. Policies and guidance for the sustainable management of the historic environment*, London, English Heritage.

English Heritage (2008) *Climate Change and the Historic Environment*, London, English Heritage.

English Heritage (2008) *Heritage Counts 2008* (Climate Change), London, English Heritage.

Hopkins, J.J. Allison, H.M. Walmsley, C.A., Gaywood, M. and Thurgate, G. (2007) *Conserving Biodiversity in a Changing Climate: Guidance on building capacity to adapt*, London, Defra.

Jenkins, G., Perry, M.C. and Prior, J. (2009) *The Climate of the UK and Recent Trends*, Revised edition May 2010, Exeter, Met Office Hadley Centre.

Natural England (2009), *Technical Information Note TIN053 Guidance on Dealing with Changing Distribution of Tree Species*, Peterborough, Natural England.

Ray, D., Morrison, J. and Broadmeadow, M. (2010) *Climate Change: Impacts and adaptation in England's woodlands. Forestry Commission Research Note FCRN201*, Roslin, Forestry Commission.

Read, D.J., Free-Smith, P.H., Morrison, J.I.L., Hanley, N,. West, C.C. and Snowdon, P. (eds) (2009) *Combating Climate Change – a Role for UK forests. An assessment of the potential of the UK's trees and woodlands to mitigate and adapt to climate change, The synthesis report*, Edinburgh, The Stationery Office.

Rhodda, J.C. and Marsh, T.J. (2011) *The 1975–76 Drought – a contemporary and retrospective review*, Wallingford, Centre for Ecology & Hydrology, www.ceh.ac.uk

Smithers, R.J., Cowan, C., Harley, M., Hopkins, J.J., Pontier, H. and Watts, O. (2008) *England Biodiversity Strategy. Climate Change Adaptation Principles. Conserving biodiversity in a changing climate*, London, Defra.

Taylor, L., Flatman, J., Marshall, T. and Rydin, Y. (2011) *Heritage & Climate Change: Protection at Any Cost?* London, UCL Environment Institute.

Endnote

1. Jenkins G. Perry, M.C. and Prior, J. (2009) *The Climate of the UK and Recent Trends*, Revised edition May 2010, Exeter, Met Office Hadley Centre.

21 Conserving the grey? Management of vegetation without an end-point in culturally important landscapes

James Hitchmough

Professor of Horticultural Ecology in the Department of Landscape, University of Sheffield, Sheffield, UK

Vegetation management in designed landscapes has a long history, and it seems pretty safe to assume that for most of this history it was concerned with meeting the needs of the present. For a pragmatic, problem-solving species like our own, this is a natural perspective to hold. It is therefore not surprising that inserting the evolving and often unfamiliar values of cultural heritage into this relationship between managers and the vegetation they manage should be challenging to their thought and practice. In part, this is because many of the notions underpinning the conservation and management of cultural heritage are derived from art and architecture, and historically these disciplines are focused on the making of objects that, given interventions to periodically repair them, are essentially unchanging in form and spatial volume. The typical clarity of understanding of the original spatial volume and form, and the capacity to regain this once processes of degradation and decay are halted or reversed, is fundamentally what distinguishes non-living objects from landscape vegetation. This chapter looks at how to incorporate understanding of vegetation change in time and space into the management necessary to conserve aspects of its cultural significance. Particular attention is paid to plant assemblages which may be either designed or spontaneous in origin but which pose particular management challenges due to the difficulties of knowing what the endpoint is that management seeks to achieve.

In designed vegetation, form and spatial volume of individual plants and assemblages of these plants only approaches stasis in the case of regularly mown lawns or clipped trees and shrubs. Where this is absent, even at the level of the individual plant, vegetation is subject to dramatic short- and long-term cycles of changes in form and spatial volume. In temperate climates, this is most dramatic in winter deciduous herbaceous plants. These demonstrate cycles of canopy biomass accretion over the spring to autumn period and then the disappearance of this in autumn/winter. For a given species the number of these annual cycles that constitute a plant's biological life varies hugely from 5–9 months in annuals through to over 100 or even 1,000 years. In most species we do not know what the biological lifetime is, and in any case it is relative, being much affected by the environmental conditions a plant is grown in. Biological life tends to be lengthened under very unproductive conditions that are insufficiently hostile to kill the plant (for example, dry and infertile soils) and shortened under highly productive conditions.

Gardens & Landscapes in Historic Building Conservation, First Edition. Edited by Marion Harney.
© 2014 John Wiley & Sons, Ltd. Published 2014 by John Wiley & Sons, Ltd.

As these cycles progress there is ongoing increase in width (but rarely height), as the rhizome system gradually expands. In some species this lateral expansion is so slow as to be almost unnoticeable; in others it is rapid. As herbaceous plants in managed, designed landscapes are rarely present as monocultures, these cycles are highly significant for the survival of the planted neighbours of species in both horticulturally and ecologically founded plantings.

The combination of long life and the vegetative means to expand laterally by underground or above-ground stems means that these types of herbaceous plants physically move over time, away from where they were originally planted. This creates dilemmas for conservation management, though, when this seeks to rigidly preserve original form. This movement of plants normally takes the form of a ring of new shoots creating a doughnut as the growth points move radially, ever outwards. As these ring-like structures get bigger, and potentially overlap with the rings of other individuals, it becomes increasingly unclear that the component plants are actually clones of one original individual. In grassland for example, Red fescue (*Festuca rubra*) clones have been shown to be more than 1,000 years old (Harberd, 1961). Woody plants and some trees (for example, *Tilia* species) also show the same behaviour, and clones of aspen in North America may be older than 8,000 years (Kemperman and Barnes, 1976).

Whilst moving through space over time is not particularly congruent with the conventional fabric conservation paradigm, with clone-forming plants of the type described, at least the fabric that is still present in 100 years is the same as was first planted. Authenticity is maintained in genetic, if not spatial terms. Plants that are not immortal as vegetative root:shoot systems, depend more on the process of self-seeding to continue to exist. In designed landscapes this means that the plants both move around, and are ultimately represented by generations of that species that are genetically different from the original individuals. Even in garden-type plantings these offspring are often more robust (i.e. better fitted to the site environment) because they are the result of natural selection working on that species over potentially long periods of time.

In woody plants such as trees and shrubs, in the absence of severe pruning there is no annual cycle of canopy retreat to where it was the previous spring. Instead, the phenomenon of additive growth results in an ever-expanding canopy periphery. Change in volume, height and width is much more rapid and much more obvious. Because woody plants are potentially very large, these increases in the spatial volume of their foliage canopy have profound effects on the environment of the site in terms of views, perception of space, light-shade, and soil moisture. Whilst it is usually clear what the architect intended for the dimensions and character of an extant building, this is rarely so for the designers of planting. Even where a planting designer has expressed a view on these matters, it is normal for them to under- or over-estimate (normally the latter) the ultimate size of woody plant canopies involved. These underestimates have profound impacts on both the character of the site and its ecology, which are potentially detrimental to the rest of the planting.

What would the members of the Sheffield Botanical and Horticultural Society who created the Sheffield Botanical Gardens think of the tree canopy of today? Whilst these issues can be extremely difficult to resolve in the politically charged context of cultural heritage conservation, when dealing with what are essentially individual plants, as in parkland trees, the nature of the management issues are not particularly complicated to conceptualise. This notion of conceptualisation in vegetation management and maintenance is extremely important and refers to the process by which people must first look at the landscape vegetation; understand what they are looking at in physical, character, aesthetic, cultural and ecological terms; identify a vision for changes that need to be effected through maintenance in space and time and then undertake or direct the works in order to achieve the vision.

The complexity of thinking about managing vegetation becomes more challenging as one moves away from conceptualising plants as individuals to an interacting group of individuals – what plant ecologists typically refer to as a community. In the community, whether it is based on plants in an Arts and Crafts herbaceous border or a designed woodland in a 1940s Amstelveen Heem (Home) Park (see for example Bekkers, 2003), these interactions generate more to think about, and much more ambivalence, making conceptualisation for management, 'getting one's head around it', much more challenging.

In plant communities, interactions between species and the environment generate behaviours that are different from those exhibited by individual plants of the same species. In the classic Arts and Crafts style herbaceous border, intense interactions (i.e. competition) between plants is often delayed to late summer due to the wide spacing between groups of different species. Plants that are robust and long-lived under these conditions may be non-robust and short-lived when placed closer together. Many of the divergent behaviours of individuals versus the same plants in communities are driven by relatively simple ecological factors. Plants that are taller than their neighbours capture more light and this initially gives them small competitive advantages, which then snowball, leading to the decline and ultimate extirpation of shorter species where these are not shade tolerant. These interactions are scale independent and occur in woodlands as well as garden borders.

As these competitive interactions develop, it can become very difficult to maintain some species at rational levels of management. An example of this is the widely grown herbaceous plant, *Echinacea purpurea*. Initially this species is robust in new plantings, but as the plantings develop, the increasing amount of shade from neighbouring plants increases the density of molluscs, and as *Echinacea* is a highly palatable species they are gradually eaten out, and their self-sown seedlings too (Hitchmough and Wagner, 2011). Unpalatable species benefit from this reduction in competition due to the decline of *Echinacea* and other palatable species, to potentially become over-dominant. In Britain the combination of high mollusc density and competition for light means that in the long term the species that can be maintained in herbaceous vegetation will always be restricted to the less palatable species. These processes occur everywhere, in designed landscapes and also those where human agency seems to be absent.

These immutable ecological processes raise interesting questions about how one might manage such vegetation in a more sustainable world: does one give up on species that no longer are well-fitted, even though they might be key to the site character that a conservation analysis might want to preserve or reinforce. These interactions occur across a gradient of vegetation types from the highly designed to the spontaneous. At the strongly cultural, designed vegetation end of this gradient, there are plantings such as the woodland herbaceous understorey in the Nuttery at Sissinghurst Castle.

This was originally dominated by polyanthus primula but these ceased to be viable due to various soil pathogens, and today are replaced by a naturalistic carpet of various native and non-native shade tolerant perennials. At the other end of the gradient we might place heavy metal contaminated industrial spoil colonised by spontaneous 'brown field' native and non-native urban species. In these sites, unlike the Nuttery at Sissinghurst (Figure 21.1), human agency is not very obvious, other than being intensely involved in the creation of the original site conditions. This vegetation used to be very common in the industrial conurbations of Britain, but has become less common due to national planning policy to build new houses and industry on these landscapes. As a result some of these sites should be targeted for heritage conservation as part of an industrial history that also generated very high species richness, paradoxically because of biological hostility.

Some of these spontaneous sites have become public parks, for example the Sudgelande Nature Park on the old Tempelhof railway sidings that were made redundant by the 1945 partition of Berlin, or on a much more humble level, the more or less forgotten 'Ecology Park' in Sheffield's Don Valley.

In between these extremes there are landscapes that paradoxically are designed to look as if no human agency was involved, for example suburban wet fen in the Thijsse Park in Amstelveen, Amsterdam, or a dry native meadow at the London Olympic Park (Hopkins and Neal, 2012), or woodland in the Emscher Park (Chintis, 2011) in Duisburg North, Germany. It seems very likely that the twenty-first century will produce many more landscapes based on these types of ecologically designed or conceptualised plant communities, some of which we may ascribe sufficient value to, to believe we have to conserve them.

Figure 21.1 Naturalistic herbaceous understorey planting in the 'Nuttery' at Sissinghurst Castle, Kent (author's own).

These types of landscapes raise significant issues for heritage management, and in particular what the goals of management should be. The fundamental difficulty in identifying these is that human brains appear much more comfortable with the idea of managing to conserve a product rather than what is largely process, with the product ever-changing. One of the reasons for this is that generally speaking, we are very attracted to the idea of stability in vegetation. Things that are stable can be known and understood; things that are unstable seem undesirable or potentially harmful. In human culture there is an intrinsic belief (for example; Budiansky, 1996; Pollan, 2003) in a balance of nature (i.e. stability) and that this is an intrinsic good, even though most ecological scientists will tell you that there is no balance and there never was any to be found in nature. Balance in nature is just an artefact or not looking very rigorously. Nature is all about process and has no will or informed direction of travel, but we desire to invest it with these properties. Not having a clear fixed point in vegetation (the product) that we can readily value and understand is therefore very challenging to us.

When confronted by vegetation with some of these characteristics there are a number of approaches we could take to its management. First, we could do nothing. Consciously doing nothing is a strategy in itself and very attractive from a resource consumption-sustainability perspective. In a post-industrial world in which human agency is still widely believed to be incompatible with caring for the natural world, doing nothing is likely, in these contexts, to be seen as benign, even caring. We will however ultimately be disappointed with doing nothing, unless our conservation objectives are explicitly about letting process take place irrespective of resulting appearance or function. This re-wilding tradition plays well in countries such as the USA where there is a desire to downplay the impact of aboriginal agency, but would be culturally naive even in a British National Park, let alone a city.

In the case of the contaminated derelict land example given earlier, the high levels of heavy metals combined with highly compacted and infertile soil materials, lead to very open, low vegetation that is readily invaded by wind-blown seed. Because of the abundance of light, species that can establish under these conditions do so, and as a result many species accrue, leading to high species diversity. As these species develop however they deposit leaf-litter on the site that builds a more productive soil on top of the severely unproductive, hostile starting point. This leads to the development of more biomass that generates more shade, causing the loss of shade-intolerant species and slowing down the immigration of new species. Plant biodiversity declines and the appearance of the system changes, as do the dominant plant species.

To halt this process, management is required in the form of cutting to check the development of new vegetation and to keep the site unproductive. These issues of plant succession leading to undesired futures have been discussed in the conservation literature (for example Charlesworth and Addis, 2010) in relation, for example, to the development of a new landscape in the surrounds of the Auschwitz death camp. Here, colonisation since World War II by the adjacent steppe grassland and woodland has led to new-old landscapes that are argued to be too visually benign to be compatible with the memorialisation of the horrors of this site.

Although the under-planting at the Nuttery at Sissinghurst commenced life as a designed cultural artefact, it too is subject to the spontaneous behaviour of the species planted as well as immigration from the outside. Garden management is historically focused on checking the latter, because this involves plants not meant to be there and hence easy to conceptualise for action. The immigrants are killed or removed; the 'meant to be there' are left. In many cases, however, the real challenge is how to manage the interactions between the latter species. In many designed landscapes we run the system until we feel it no longer resembles what we wanted it to be and then we 're-do' it and start the cycle again. Trying to maintain the system is desired though ongoing management is less common, but desirable from a sustainability perspective. In practice this involves asking the question: to what degree can dominance, for example of a few species over the total number planted, be allowed, and if not, how might this be changed?

Avoidance of decision-making and doing nothing results in plant communities heading in potentially very divergent directions depending on the nature of the starting point and the level of biological productivity present. At the London Olympic park for example, the ideal long-term management of the dry native meadows would involve cutting in August and removing all of the above-ground biomass from the site. This 'resets the clock' by allowing all species to once again have the same access to light as in spring, hence preventing extirpation of shorter shade-intolerant species by taller species, thereby helping to preserve both cohorts of species. Because the soils were chosen by the designers to be extremely unproductive, if cutting is ceased, loss of meadow species will be slowed down but would, ultimately, happen. The likelihood of cessation of cutting is always high in these urban sites because it is a cost that management agencies would like to defer, and secondly it may be seen as unnatural by publics who see human agency as an affront to their urbanised conceptions of nature.

If the Olympic meadows had been created on far more productive topsoil, then cessation of cutting would very rapidly lead to change, and in particular loss of plant diversity. One of the reasons the Amstelveen Heem Parks have high maintenance requirements (in some areas similar to National Trust gardens) is that they are created on polder peat, a relatively productive substrate.

What this suggests is that the key element in the conservation management of such vegetation types is to identify a stage of development at which the vegetation is to be held, and then to use management and maintenance actions to achieve this. Ecologists refer to these 'frozen in time' vegetation types as a Plagioclimax, and they are all around us. Native wildflower meadows, for example, only existed historically in Britain because of the need to cut vegetation in summer to produce winter fodder hay and then to graze the regrowth to further feed animals. A vision has to be created for each vegetation type, from which a range of maintenance inputs can then be identified and applied in space and time to achieve this.

In the case of the urban brownfield site, if the conservation vision is to preserve the essential qualities of this spontaneous vegetation at the peak of plant diversity (as opposed to the peak of total biomass, when it becomes climax oak woodland) then it will be necessary to maintain the areas in an open state through removing trees, shrubs and herbaceous plants that would close the canopy. Removed trees are likely to be longer-term community dominants associated with the climax succession, such as oak and other species. It might also be necessary to apply disturbances to the ground-level vegetation such as cutting or burning in spring to open up the ground strata to allow the processes of immigration to continue. All of this is relatively resource intensive, so it might be more attractive to identify a vision of just allowing process to take its course, in which case the derelict land will increasingly resemble an oak-dominated woodland with a short herb understorey.

Under the latter model, the key idea in management might simply be to maintain the integrity of the original approximate spatial volume of each major vegetation type, whilst allowing detailed species facility to change. Alternatively, management might only aim to maintain broad character notions; for example that a vegetation is grassy with some forbs (broadleaved flowers) present in it.

Where this does not seem appropriate, then it is necessary to engage with the idea of managing for-or-against particular plant species. This is not particularly difficult with trees as they are few per unit area and not very diverse. It is much more difficult to do this with herbaceous plants, whether these are naturally occurring or planted in designed landscapes, because they are many per unit area and their canopies are often closely intermeshed. The Nuttery under-planting at Sissinghurst Castle has already changed substantially since its replant in the early 2000s, but interventions to shape its direction of travel are daunting, both because of the work involved, and because of the problem of conceptualising just what might have to be done.

Making decisions on management at the level of individual species also raises questions about how we manage vegetation in culturally important landscapes in response to some key ideas of our time; for example sustainability, biodiversity and climate change. This is perhaps best thought of as the technical processes, and includes materials used in managing vegetation, and secondly the plants we use. If you are besieged by volunteers, as is the case in some National Trust gardens in south-east England, it is almost possible to re-institute many of the practices used in past eras. Hand weeding and endless surface cultivation could be used to create the character of a time when labour was relatively inexpensive. In many other landscapes a sense of authenticity in the landscape has to be achieved as far as possible by use of more contemporary technologies. The National Trust Manual on Sustainable Practice (Hitchmough *et al*, 2010) encourages its gardeners to compost all arisings which are then utilised in gardens as surface mulch. In many cases this is not the practice that would have been contemporary with the garden itself. These issues have, in most cases, been well resolved through compromises between pragmatism and authenticity.

Dealing with the role of vegetation in the context of sustainability, biodiversity and climate change has been much less resolved, as it deals with issues that are much more visible and high-profile. The central issue becomes to what degree is it appropriate to substitute new plants for the original species that gave the site its character, in order to meet what might broadly be defined as sustainability goals? This substitution process can operate at the level of either species or sub-specific variation. In many landscapes, plants that are deemed to be particularly important because they represent some taxonomically valuable set of genetic material, or because they are associated with a particular individual or event, assume the form of historical artefact and, as the need for replacement becomes apparent, are propagated vegetatively to preserve the exact same genetic complement in the replacement planting. This is the ultimate in authenticity, but what if, because of climate change, that particular genotype is increasingly poorly fitted to that site? This then poses the question of replacement with plants of possibly the same species but perhaps from a different genetic origin in the wild or a different horticultural cultivar that is believed likely to be more tolerant of the new climatic conditions.

Many of the plant collections maintained by organisations such as the National Trust will have to confront these issues. The establishment of pathogenic organisms such as *Phytophthora* has forced a stark re-think of how to cope with very rapidly changing environments, but the longer-term changes will be more dramatic still than this, although incrementally more subtle, particularly in terms of notions of authenticity.

It is interesting to compare how nature conservation, as opposed to heritage conservation, deals with these types of issues. In terms of plants both of these traditions are concerned with authenticity. In the case of nature conservation the idea that genes that have evolved in a place must be conserved to allow the continuation of these processes. In the case of heritage conservation and that which deals with plants, authenticity is also strongly desired – particularly within collections such as the National Council for the Conservation of Plants & Gardens (NCCPG) – but in garden and landscape settings the issue is perhaps more about how this can be perceived through appearance and character. At present there is no real strategy to deal with these issues of climate change in nature conservation, other than to wait and see. There have been discussions with government agencies about releasing genes of more continental or southern ecotypes of current UK native species into the UK biota to try to contribute to improving the adaptive fit of species that might otherwise disappear, but this is just too terrifying at present for decisions to be made.

In cultural landscapes which are largely small islands surrounded by something else, the political stakes are much lower, and unlike climate change in the landscape of the nation state as a whole, there will be opportunities as well as threats. There will also be opportunities within nature conservation; the prognosis for some species that live in Britain as outliers of their main distributions in Europe will probably improve, but few will say this. The cultivated woody plant flora of Britain has already expanded considerably in the twentieth century (see Grimshaw and Bayton, 2009) in some cases because of the warming climate as much as patterns of plant collection. These and other new plants will gradually replace some of the taxa that are currently growing in cultural heritage landscapes as the twenty-first century and climate change proceeds, in some cases changing the character of these landscapes (see also chapter 20 of this volume). This brings us full-circle back to the conflict introduced at the beginning of this chapter with the idea of cultural landscapes as fixed fabric which, through repair, is indefinitely preservable.

Perhaps the way to avoid being hoisted on our own cultural heritage petard is, where possible, to try to perceive the development and management of the vegetation of designed and other landscapes not as a fixed fabric but as a process. What becomes important is that the management decisions reflect the spirit of the process. Coming back to the Gentlemen of the Sheffield Horticultural and Botanic Society: in the 1830s they set up their garden to be at the cutting-edge of horticultural thought, and, if released from some cryogenic deep sleep, would be reading Grimshaw and Bayton's book on new 'exotic' trees, clamouring for new cold hardy *Schefflera* and hardy succulents from South Africa. They would not be celebrating the vegetation ossification we might practise on their behalf.

Decisions on how vegetation is to be managed have to be undertaken by someone, and this raises the question: how does one train people to develop the skills and understandings to make what are often complex judgements? Many of those who currently manage vegetation of the types discussed in this chapter have been trained as horticulturalists, foresters or ecologists. There are clear differences in the focus of their training; horticulturalists tend to operate at the small to medium scale, with an emphasis on whether their maintenance interventions might be seen as desirable or attractive. Forestry tends to operate at the medium to large scale, is very utilitarian and historically has much less emphasis on aesthetics. Ecology tends to operate at all scales but is most comfortable with naturally ordered vegetation that can be categorised into community types as a forma for management approach, and is largely uninterested in whether the works might be seen as attractive.

When dealing with nature-like vegetation perhaps the most inspirational approaches to training people to make judgements on the management of this vegetation in public urban landscapes have occurred in the Heem Parks of the Netherlands, and in particular those in Amstelveen (Koningen, 2004). These Heem or 'Home' parks arose in the early twentieth century from the belief that urban dwellers needed to have access to nature and that professional landscape architects would design this to look beautiful (Bekkers, 2003). These landscapes are now at maturity (whose maturity?) and are internationally important; the most polished and beautiful application of designed native nature parks in the world. The success of these parks has been based on recognising the need for ongoing insightful, responsive management. They developed this through applying craft-based ecological management techniques, learnt through a lengthy apprenticeship. This master-gardener-apprentice approach has also been discussed in Sweden by Gustavsson and Ingelög (1994). The specific approaches employed, how and why, are discussed in detail by Koningen (2004). There is probably no parallel with these approaches in Britain, or indeed elsewhere in the world, where practical training has integrated physical maintenance skills with appreciation of aesthetics, and ecological process. The emphasis was very much about making decisions on what is 'in front of' you, in a holistic context. This is the antithesis of many contemporary approaches to landscape management and maintenance in British public landscapes which are often driven by standardised specifications, which contribute to disempowering the capacity of staff to make appropriate decisions on what is 'in front of' them.

Whilst there is, with the exception of Koningen's book chapter, no explicit curriculum for the management of the Amstelveen Heem Parks, it is possible to extract key skills that maintenance and management must be able to practise:

- the capacity to visualise what the vegetation is to look like at various points in time from its initial creation
- to understand through observation in practice, the outcomes of competition and other processes on the nature and appearance of plants growing in combination with other species
- to be able to identify seedlings and adults of all of the species, both desired and undesired, that are likely to occur
- to understand how different maintenance techniques can be used to change or preserve vegetation in a desired state.

Whilst the principles practised in the Amstelveen Heem Parks are admirable and effective in practice, they are also expensive to implement in the landscape in general. Compared, for example, with British conservation management of semi-natural vegetation, they are slow and extremely mannered. The challenge is how one gets the underlying principles of this form of management into the curriculum and practice of mainstream vegetation maintenance.

References/Further reading

Bekkers, G. (2004) *The Jac P. Thijsse Park, Designed Dutch Landscape*, Architectura and Natura Press, Amsterdam.
Budiansky, S. (1995) *Nature's Keepers, The New Science of Nature Management*, Free Press, New York.
Charlesworth, A. and Addis, M. (2010) 'Memorialization and the Ecological Landscapes of Holocaust Sites: The cases of Plaszow and Auschwitz-Birkenau', *Landscape Research*, 27, 229–251.
Chintis, C. (2011) *The Emscher Park Design Guide*, Lulu.com ISBN-13: 9781257297313.
Grimshaw, J. and Bayton, R. (2009) *New Trees: Recent Introductions to Cultivation*, Kew Publishing, London.
Gustavsson, R. and Ingelög, T. (1994) *Det nya landskapet*, Skogsstyrelsen, Jönköping.
Harberd, D.J. (1961) 'Observations on population structure and longevity of *Festuca rubra* L', *New Phytologist*, 60, 184–206.
Hitchmough, J.D. Houldcroft, E. and Dunnett, N. (2010) *Environmental Standard for Parks and Gardens*, National Trust, University of Sheffield.
Hitchmough, J.D. and Wagner, M. (2011) 'Slug grazing effects on seedling and adult life stages of North American Prairie plants used in designed urban landscapes', *Urban Ecosystems*, 14, 279–302.
Hopkins, J. and Neal, P. (2012) *The Making of the Queen Elizabeth Olympic Park*, Wiley, London.
Kemperman, J. and Barnes, B.V. (1976) 'Clone size in American Aspen', *Canadian Journal of Botany*, 54, 2603–2607.
Koningen, H. (2004) 'Creative Management', in Dunnett, N. and Hitchmough, J.D. (eds) *The Dynamic Landscape, Design, Ecology and Management of Naturalistic Urban Planting*, pp. 256–292, Taylor and Francis, London.
Pollan, M. (2003) *Second Nature, A Gardener's Education*, Grove Press, New York.

22 'Plants are fashioned by cultivation, man by education'

Robert Mattock
Horticultural consultant and rose specialist, Oxfordshire, UK

Introduction

The French philosopher Jean Jacques Rousseau (1712–78), the first to define designed landscape in Julie's garden in his novel *La Nouvelle Eloise* (1761),[1] had insisted that 'Plants are fashioned by cultivation, man by education' (Rousseau, 1726).[2] He was emphatic that contrasting cultivated plants in the designed landscape with the natural world was pivotal to the art of gardening. For Rousseau, plants are the vocabulary of the designed landscape.

In comparison to the diversity of plants used in gardens over the last three centuries, current conservationists use a short list of plant varieties and species that would barely interest, let alone enthuse, the great landscape and head gardeners of the recent past. The mother plants are still available; stored in the hands of specialist nurserymen, botanical gardens, Plant Heritage, Garden Trusts and by amateur collectors. Individuals and organisations are largely responsible for housing the collections of the National Council for the Conservation of Plants (NCCPG), now Plant Heritage, which brings together the talent of botanists, horticulturalists and conservationists and the dedication of keen amateurs and a few professional gardeners.

There has been a tradition established over the last 50 years of knowledgeable amateur gardeners who often know more than experts in the field. These non-professionals are also likely to be the paying visitors who are essential to the economic viability of historic gardens and designed landscapes where repeat business is crucial. This horticulturally expert gardening public know their plants and know whether plants are correctly chosen and if they are being properly tended. If displays are not up to scratch, repeat visits are postponed and visitor income inevitably falls significantly.

There are two reasons why this rich diversity of plants is no longer cherished or used by conservationists. First, the only means of assimilating the characteristics of several tens of thousands of plants in order to identify which plants should be used is learning by rote. However, some contemporary educationalists adhere to the idea that students can get the same level of instant knowledge from internet sources. Don Tapscott (1947–), sums up this argument in *Wikinomics*:[3]

Learning by heart is 'pointless' for the Google generation. For generations of pupils, learning key historical dates, places, and names off by heart has been the bastion of academic success. But for today's youngsters, tedious rote learning is pointless because such basic facts are only a mouse click away, via Google, Wikipedia and online libraries.

However, this notion is misconceived and as Simon Carr observes, 'It is like saying you do not need to know many words if you own a dictionary'.[4] The internet is unable to make original decisions in terms of composition and design, despite its ability to accumulate extensive lists; only the ingenuity of the human mind possesses the ability to articulate plant knowledge creatively and this is only possible through acquiring an extensive learned vocabulary on which to base inspirational expression. Currently, the enormous language of landscape and garden plants is being reduced to a tabloid dialect and, if this continues, within a generation it will be text-speak.

Assuming the plant has been identified, it takes years of experience and hard graft to learn the skills of its cultivation. However, for some, because of the long hours and often harsh working conditions, this vocation is not considered to be an appealing profession. In short, we have lost the craftsman's work ethic or, as Benjamin Franklin (1706–90) wrote, 'the principle that hard work is intrinsically virtuous or worthy of reward' (Franklin, 1748) no longer pertains.

As a consequence, while the plants are still available, ineffective shortcuts, created for expediency and to avoid hard work have, for the most part, eliminated the use of the diversity of planting that once gave the much admired character to those gardens that we now think worthy of conservation. Instead, it is now deemed necessary only to learn the genus, or at best, the family, which is not much use in making the choice between a rose and a rhododendron let alone on deciding whether that rose should be *Félicité Parmentier* rather than *Félicité et Perpetue*.

For today's professional, flowers have become unfashionable because it is too much trouble to learn which is which and because they take too much effort to grow. It has been left to the amateur to collect and cultivate and, as a result, many conservationists now live in a sea of green. Iford Manor, Harold Peto's rose garden near Bath, is one example of this greening, but here painstaking efforts are being made to re-establish the rose garden (Figure 22.1).

The question is not where have all the flowers gone, but rather, where are those with cultivation skills. Indeed, what has happened to the craftsmen?

The Craftsman – 'Learning How' as well as 'Learning That'[5]

Standing in the midst of a throng of young schoolboys participating in a cricket match, I was surprised to be asked 'how do you get a new rose'? and, 'how did your late father [R.H. Mattock 1927–2002], manage to get the white into the strawberry red of the Summerfields rose (Figure 22.2)?.'

Fortunately, I was standing next to a 1950s shrub rose whose flowers were in full maturity. Carefully picking off the petals (so that insects would no longer be attracted) I sent a boy off to find another variety. I showed them how to cut off the male part of the plant (the anthers and stamens) to leave the female stigma. The boy arrived back with a flower full of pollen and we brushed its pollen on to the stigma of the other. That, I explained, is invention. Horticulturists had to decide which pollen to use, based on what they wanted to create. I explained that looking after the plant we had hybridised, the cultivation of plants, was the job of a craftsman. The craftsman takes his time, is meticulous in his attention to detail and it is his experience, not that of the inventor, that ensures the successful outcome of hybridisation: the new plant, of which he might justifiably feel proud. It is pride in his work that enables the craftsman to incentivise himself to do the best he can. It is the same pride that enables him to respect not only his own work, but that of others. Mutual respect for each other's work is a sound, practical basis for mutual respect for one another's cultures, particularly in a school full of boys from around the globe (Pring, 2012).

Figure 22.1 Iford Manor, near Bath; Harold Peto's rose garden. For many years the garden was a sea of green, but over a period of 20 or more years the informed owners of Iford Manor have found the original labels marking the old Hybrid Teas that Harold Peto planted in his rose garden from 1900–1930. A specialist nursery was commissioned to search for propagating material from the same clones which were found in (sometimes obscure) European collections. Skilled craftsmen are now propagating new plants with which to re-establish the original varieties. It can be done! (Author's own.)

Figure 22.2 Rose 'Summerfields', bred by Mattock (UK 1971) and named for the eponymous preparatory school in Oxford (author's own).

In *The Craftsman* (2008) Richard Sennet encapsulated this practical demonstration using the model *Homo faber, Animal laborans* (1958) of Hannah Arendt (1906–75). Sennet eloquently explored the reasons why contemporary culture denigrates the hands-on apprentice and the sheer hard work it took to become a craftsman.[6]

'We have lost it, the system's broke!' said John Watkins, Head of Gardens and Landscape at English Heritage. 'It's a sad fact of life that we have perilously few craftsmen-head-gardeners in the true sense of the term, let alone under-gardeners, who are equipped with the skills necessary to maintain our historic gardens and cultural landscapes.'[7]

The rise of the Victorian head gardener

Before seeking a solution conservationists might well consider the Victorian head gardener and examine how and why this craftsman rose to such prominence before his descendants allowed his cultivation skills to dwindle. Lacking the advantages of electronic communication, horticultural skills were disseminated through literature before being passed on to the illiterate.[8] From as long ago as the tenth century through to the head gardeners of the nineteenth century, horticultural development was primarily disseminated by word of mouth, from educated employers to uneducated, hands-on gardeners: the craftsmen.

A review of literature over the last ten centuries reveals a progression from plant descriptions toward ever-more exacting details of practical cultivation. The first books generally available aiming to disseminate horticultural knowledge came in the form of herbals, authored by monastics and physicians, and characterised by *Gerard's Herball* (1597).

During the Restoration there was an explosion of horticultural treatises marked by the publication by Robert Morison (1620–85) of *Historia* (1680) and *Plantarum umbelliferarum* (1672). Published in three expensive and lavishly illustrated volumes, these tomes were the domain of the rich and educated. 'Things had to change', stated Ralph Austen (c.1612–76) in his *Treatise of fruit trees* (1665). He was the first to note that botanical and horticultural books were only available to the educated and wealthy, and stated categorically that books on gardening should 'be of small bulk and price; because great volumns . . . are of too great a price for mean husband-men to buy'. This sentiment was taken to heart by John Evelyn (1620–1706) in his successful one-volume *Compleat Gardner* (1693).

The tending of plants was left to the more-or-less illiterate gardeners until the great horticulturist William Curtis (1746–99), known for his meticulous and beautifully illustrated work *Flora londoniensis* (1775–98), first produced the *Botanical Magazine* (1787) as a monthly periodical for gardeners, featuring ornamental plants complete with botanical descriptions and cultural details.

Progressing from the eighteenth to the nineteenth century, horticultural literature, including practical details of cultivation, was published at a pace matched only by the increase in literacy of head gardeners. Early Victorians gardeners had become sufficiently literate to be able to read the 'gardening press' and hence to learn a gardening vocabulary and a horticultural skills base hitherto only taught by practical demonstration and verbal communication.

Learning the skills of cultivation

The problems in horticulture are the result of changes in the way skills have been developed and applied within the socio-political context of the last hundred years. Historically, workmen aspired to become hands-on productive craftsmen rather than inventors – a small population who promoted new ideas or product. The millennia-old regime for the dissemination of horticultural skills was the apprentice–craftsman–journeyman–head gardener system (Figure 22.3).

Figure 22.3 The 'Boss', Foreman, Journeymen and Apprentices at the Mattock rose nursery during summer 1906 (author's own).

The apprentice learned his skills and work ethic over a period of five years to become a junior craftsman under the tutorial direction of the head gardener. The apprentice spent time working under the supervision and tutelage of a journeyman or senior journeyman within the different departments of the garden or nursery. Literacy was taught so that he could study in the evenings. Once skilled and considered sufficiently mature by the head gardener he would be promoted to journeyman status and sent off to work elsewhere to gain further experience, often returning to his *alma mater* carrying the respect of the experienced craftsman to pass on his newfound skills to the apprentices.

The *Gardeners' Chronicle*, later *Horticultural Week*, published a series of charts illustrating skills together with a weekly calendar of operations. The apprentice was required to keep a diary of what he did each day and would often learn or be taught from the charts. After three years of working through the garden departments an apprentice would be promoted to the position of journeyman. He would travel to work in different gardens or nurseries with a view to broadening his experience sufficient to gain a reference. This training had to be funded. The down payment to secure a position was the 'apprentice fee' levied by the head gardener. If he was fortunate, the fee was paid up-front by his family, but more often than not, the fee was deducted from the boy's wages at the rate of 1s.6d per week. Wages were low before the deduction; typically in 1850 an apprentice started on 8s. per week, rising to 11s. per week after two years. The regulations ruling the apprentice's life were harsh. Life was not, as they say, a bed of roses.

The working hours were onerous. A 60-hour week, Monday to Saturday (6.00 am to 6.00 pm) was the generally accepted norm. The 'bothy', the accommodation available for the apprentices, was not exactly homely either. This entry is taken from an anonymous diary of 1884:

> There are two beds of coarse un-planed deals. All the sheets and blankets must be provided by the lads themselves, and all bowls plates and spoons. Their food consists of milk when it can be got, and oatmeal. Beef, mutton, pork or fish or flesh of any kind they rarely taste.

At the end of his working life the under-gardener, despite his craftsman status, had little to look forward to. He was normally obliged to move out of his tied accommodation and for those fortunate enough not to fall ill or suffer disability, the workhouse or starvation on the streets was a reality.

It took ten years to achieve the rank of head gardener. He had learned his practical skills during his time as an apprentice and journeyman, and his scientific and artistic skills from evening classes and periodicals. Head gardeners' pay was also comparatively low, although being paid a salary, complete with tied accommodation, albeit on four months' notice, gave a degree of seniority that made most other trades envious. The salary for the mid-nineteenth-century head gardener amounted to some £100 per annum, compared to £36 for a journeyman and £20 for an apprentice. Nevertheless, after a rough and tough adolescence and early manhood learning the skills of the craftsman, the head gardener could expect a well-respected, albeit only tolerably well financially rewarded life, for running a team of gardeners and cultivating the huge diversity of ornamental plants that were used as a matter of course to build what are now historic gardens.

So, despite his status as a craftsman, and in common with his fellow tradesmen, the gardener's lot in the nineteenth century was not a happy one. Job security and security of housing was tenuous. Free welfare, health, education and pension-funded retirement were virtually non-existent. Britain's welfare was characterised by voluntary provision with mutual and friendly societies delivering a whole range of benefits. Living on charity was not considered an acceptable option and a change in culture was required.

The Welfare State was conceived in the early 1900s and notionally the prize was security 'from the cradle to the grave'. We have now had three generations of potential hands-on workforce and management who have been dis-incentivised to learn a craft by heart or by job experience, relying instead for their health, education and pension on the support of the Welfare State. In short, while the Welfare State has bettered the craftsman's lot enormously it has, for some, at the same time, destroyed his work and his work ethic.[9]

Is there a solution?

The problem has not gone unnoticed; indeed over the last decade there has been a proliferation of initiatives designed to attract young people into apprenticeship schemes. Great efforts have been made by the Department for Business Innovation and Skills (BIS) towards improving the levels of skills in the workplace through vocational training. Regrettably, the term 'apprenticeship' has been bastardised by extending the commonly understood definition of hands-on learning with the aim of becoming a craftsman into any workplace learning, even up to graduate and professional levels. Much thought and financial support has been given to these upper levels of 'apprenticeship' at the expense of support for the lower levels, which, of course, are where the majority of our manual workforce lie.

The *Richard Review of Apprentices in England* was commissioned by the Government and published in November 2012. Richard's brief was 'What should an apprenticeship be in the future, and how can apprenticeships meet the needs of the changing economy?'. He recommended that there should be:

- A move to employer ownership of apprenticeship and its delivery
- A focus on outcomes not content or process
- A narrowing of the definition of apprenticeships and an end to signing up existing adult workers
- New qualifications system and assessment regime to be set up via open competition, and that assessment should involve employers
- A rise in information, advice, guidance and awareness standards.

Writing in the *Guardian* in the spring of 2013, Will Hutton, while not entirely dismissing the *Richard Review*, felt that 'it had dropped into a cultural and business wasteland'. In the same piece and much in the same vein, Hutton comments on the fallout from the business entrepreneur Alan Sugar's attitude to apprenticeships:

It is the British disease in microcosm. The crisis through which we are living is more than the aftermath of a near financial collapse. The long credit boom disguised the degree to which British capitalism and society have completely lost their way. We do not have a productive business culture. Of course, apprenticeship has become devalued and degraded.

The *Richard Review* was discussed in depth at a conference organised by the Economic & Social Research Council on Skills, Knowledge and Organisational Performance (SKOPE) at Oxford University.[10] In the land-based horticultural, agricultural and construction industries in the UK today lack of skills is a serious issue. Despite its disciplined regime, the army is successful in retaining the apprentices that it trains as tradesmen, losing only 20% of its intake and those largely through drug abuse, compared with a 47% loss nationally.[11] Why then should the army not be approached to see how many of those soldiers coming to the end of their commission might take up a horticultural career instead? The Oxford conference also discussed how a de-incentivised workforce has lost its role models. Might our apprentices aspire to emulate these soldiers in the same way that young sports people seek to emulate Olympic heroes?

Would such role models inspire children? 'I don't know about that but come and look at these children's gardens', said the energetic and distinguished horticulturalist, journalist and broadcaster, Peter Seabrook at Chelsea Flower Show, 2013 (Figure 22.4).[12] Peter, together with *The Sun* newspaper and the Royal Horticultural Society supported and encouraged some 200 schools to compete for a place to build a small garden at the show, the children having honed their gardening skills in their own school gardens. The results were remarkably articulate.

The author asked several of the children, who had worked hard to grow the plants for their displays, who had most influenced them. There was absolutely no contest and no debate. Mummy, teacher and Prince Harry!

In this author's experience, attendance at master classes and workshops is poor when school leavers are introduced to the notion of work through Work Experience Schemes.

Having been taught how to work in only six weeks, the allegedly 'work-experienced' progress towards apprenticeships with stints at work and stints at college, and I have found that the level of skills taught at college are not adequate for the reality of the workplace. Why? Hands-on skills are not taught because, with perilously few exceptions, the lecturers are not horticulturally skilled themselves so are not suitably equipped to impart the essential horticultural knowledge required to maintain colour and flowers in historic gardens. The municipal 'clip and trim', regardless of the type of plant, has become the norm; the result, a sea of green hair-cuts. Master classes and workshops, where available, are enthusiastically attended by students but very rarely by lecturers. Yet it is these workshops that are so essential for teaching apprentices the very basics of their craft.

Figure 22.4 Peter Seabrook of *The Sun* supported this children's garden at Chelsea Flower Show 2013 (author's own).

Unfortunately candidates for apprenticeships are slow to come forward because of the negative public image of horticulture. The Royal Horticultural Society's survey of 2012 revealed that, according to young people, 'Horticulture is for dropouts, it's unskilled and unfulfilling'. Almost 70% of 18-year-olds questioned believe horticultural careers should only be considered by people who have 'failed academically'. Nearly 50% of under-25s think horticulture is an 'unskilled career'.[13]

The National Trust and English Heritage are front runners in promoting apprentice schemes in the heritage sector. The National Trust Academy provides vocational qualifications, refreshingly claiming 'that not all training takes place in the class-room or lecture hall'. Their Flower Shows and Gardens Open to the Public are arenas where apprentices might display mastery of their craft and it would not require a great effort in educational direction to promote winning apprentices as role models.

Following his *No Stone Unturned* report (2012), where he suggests devolving decision-making and spending controls to the country's regions, Lord Heseltine is firmly of the view that garden festivals should take a pivotal role in promoting regional regeneration.[14] Furthermore, the labour trained in growing, constructing and planting the festivals could be set to work for the community. People are living longer and in their later years are often physically unable, despite their love of colour and floral display in their front gardens, to undertake all of the work. Gardeners are going to become much in demand.[15]

Over the last three or four decades there have not been sufficient working nationals, let alone apprentices, to meet demand. This gap has largely been filled with workers from Eastern Europe. Poland, Germany and the Punjab, who retain traditional respect for the craftsman and his work ethic. There are also different combinations of on- and off-the-job learning and young people can attain high standards which enable them to gain employment for which local youngsters are not qualified.

Conclusion

Rousseau's philosophy, which introduced this chapter, remains relevant today. Plants, and by extrapolation their cultivation, are pivotal in determining designed landscapes and the propagating material is still available from mother plants that were introduced in every era of the development of these historic landscapes. The tradition of dissemination of expertise by plantsmen and gardeners through publication continues, with Haymarket's *Horticultural Week* and The Royal Horticultural Society's *The Garden* and *The Plantsman*. Ignoring the 'celebrity gardener – immediate effects brigade', television and internet sources have considerably extended accessibility to techniques once thought to be the domain of the specialist.

The problem remains the lack of craftsmen with a strong work ethic and the know-how to teach practical, manual horticultural techniques both in the workplace and at master classes and workshops. As a result, it seems that in the immediate future, we are not going to find the skilled labour force required to maintain our heritage of historic gardens. Notwithstanding the myriad schemes aimed at encouraging young people to take up apprenticeships, it will require generations of re-evaluation and re-education before enough people will be sufficiently trained to work effectively 'on the land' once again.

In the interim, we must rely on significant sectors of the population who have inherited cultures that continue to regard manual skills as both honourable and respectable, and a very satisfactory way of life. There are large numbers of people from Eastern Europe, the Punjab, Pakistan and south-west China who are superbly horticulturally gifted (Figure 22.5). What is more, their forbears have been growing 'our' garden plants for at least 1,000 years.

Using this workforce, in conjunction with encouraging gardening skills in schools and by employing apprentices at provincial garden festivals, combined, could enable us to develop the potential to save our horticultural heritage. However, time is of the essence; we have the requisite science and culture not only at our fingertips but also recorded for posterity. The immediate problem is that we are losing the old men and women who practised

Figure 22.5 Skilled Punjabi horticultural craftsmen and craftswomen planting out rare varieties of roses on an Oxfordshire nursery.

Figure 22.6a Lacking the craftsman's vocabulary, Parsons' rose garden displayed a paucity of plants in July 2006.

traditional gardening and who harbour the all-important practical and artisanal skills. The chance of imparting their knowledge and those skills essential to managing and maintaining the central role of plants and horticulture in our historic gardens and designed landscapes for the future to a new breed of gardeners will be lost with them.

It is not all gloom: there are institutions which are prepared to employ craftsmen of the highest calibre and offer apprenticeships to those aspiring gardeners. Figures 22.6a, 22.6b and 22.6c depict the restoration of Alfred Parsons' garden at Worcester College, where the work was successfully undertaken by college staff.

Figure 22.6b Restoration by Head Gardener S. Bagnall and his apprentices November 2006. Note the good craftsmanship: metal edging, double digging incorporating manure and the large specially prepared specimen roses.

The Provost's Garden, Worcester College, Oxford
A template for the reconstruction and conservation
of historic rose gardens

Figure 22.6c The restored and under-planted rose garden (Mattock 2007). The restoration and conservation of Parsons' rose garden in the Provost's Garden, Worcester College, Oxford.

Endnotes

1. Rousseau, J.J. (1761) *Julie, ou la nouvelle Héloïse*, Marc-Michel Rey. Amsterdam.
2. Rousseau, J.J. *Emile, or on Education*, (1726) J.M. Dent, London, 1914, pp.6, 80–81,126,131.
3. Tapscott, D. and Williams, A. (2008) *Wikinomics*, Atlantic Books.
4. Carr, S. (2013) Exchange of e-mails between Robert Mattock and Simon Carr 01.03.2013.
5. Pring, R. (2012) *The Life and Death of Secondary Education for All: Dream or Reality?* Routledge, pp. 72–73.
6. Sennet, R. (2008) *The Craftsman*, Penguin, London, p.6.
7. John Watkins, Head of English Heritage's Garden and Landscape Team, in discussion with the author during a lecture as part of University of Bath MSc in the Conservation of Historic Gardens and Cultural Landscapes programme in the Autumn of 2008.
8. Musgrave, T. (2007) *The Head Gardeners*, Aurum Press Ltd, p. 7.
9. The Welfare State (2013) *The Welfare State – Never Ending Reform*. http://www.bbc.co.uk/history/british/modern/field_01.shtml 08.17 23.02.13 [accessed May 2013].
10. SKOPE (2013) The Economic & Social Research Council on Skills, Knowledge and Organisational Performance; Conference, Oxford University.
11. Cirin, R. (2009) *The Benefits of Completing an Apprenticeship*, Learning Skills Council, Table 34 p. 77
12. Seabrook, P. In a conversation with Robert Mattock, May 2013.
13. Royal Horticultural Society, 2012.
14. No stone unturned: in pursuit of growth (2013) Lord Heseltine review, Department for Business, Innovation & Skills: Pdf available at: https://www.gov.uk/government/uploads/system/uploads/attachment_data/file/34648/12-1213-no-stone-unturned-in-pursuit-of-growth.pdf
15. Heseltine, Lord (May 2013) In conversation with Robert Mattock at Thenford, South Northamptonshire.

23 Costing and contracts for historic gardens and landscapes

Nigel Thorne

Vice-president of the International Federation of Landscape Architects (IFLA) and consultant landscape architect, London, UK

Introduction

The creation of any successful landscape project demands adherence to a series of fundamental principles: the understanding of the initial brief; the compilation of a design that adheres to that brief; specifications, bills of quantities and schedules of rates that determine how the project is to be implemented, the quality of materials and the standards of workmanship; the selection of an appropriately qualified and competent landscape contractor and finally, a landscape management and maintenance programme that appropriately acknowledges that all landscapes are processes, not pre-determined projects in their own right.

These fundamental principles do not change dramatically for the implementation of historic garden or landscape projects but they do command a few additional considerations. Things such as the need for a more precise and focused understanding of the historic landscape in question, which places very specific demands upon the landscape architect or garden designer and an even greater importance upon the necessarily prescriptive details within the specification. The qualitative demands of the finished product, irrespective of what these might be, must be identified with precision in order to emphasise the specific nature of the project in hand. Extreme care must be taken when determining a realistic budget for the project, and when selecting an appropriate landscape contractor due consideration must be given to the skills, knowledge and competences required to complete the works.

This chapter highlights the considerations that need to be made by clients, designers and contractors responsible for the commissioning, designing, financing, implementation and management and maintenance of historic landscape projects, irrespective of scale and location.

Costing the project

The majority of landscape projects are completed via a tripartite agreement between a client (not necessarily a single individual but possibly a group of interested parties or agents acting on behalf of the owner of the site), a designer and a contractor, who may or may not need to engage further specialist contractors to complete specific elements identified within the project.

The level of knowledge, skills and understanding of clients varies tremendously. Many may have a sound understanding of what their project demands and what their ultimate aims may be, but there are some who may be embarking upon a specialist project for the first time. The range of clients varies considerably between these two extremes.

Irrespective of the level of client knowledge, the need remains to select their project partners very carefully. There needs to be an understanding that if a client is to engage appropriately skilled, educated, knowledgeable and experienced professionals in the successful completion of the project then the cost is likely to be higher than if the project was for something other than a landscape of historic importance. In essence, this sets the scene for the duration of the commission and without this basic client acknowledgement, the success of the project will be questionable.

In a situation where client knowledge is limited it may be beneficial to employ an appropriately qualified and competent agent to act on their behalf. This establishes an additional client cost at the outset but should add a considerable return on investment by the end of the project. Without such competences an increased emphasis is placed upon the decisions of other professionals the client appoints, who, having acknowledged their limited experience, may not necessarily make the right choices.

Appointment of a competent designer is a necessary investment if the project is to be successful. Securing the skills and knowledge of a chartered landscape architect or a member of the Society of Garden Designers does not necessarily mean that consultant fees will be more expensive but it does offer the client certain 'comfort' factors in terms of professionals acting within codes of professional conduct and courses for action should they fail to deliver. The designer's specialist knowledge and skills in the realm of historic gardens will prove invaluable in the successful implementation of the project on many levels. It is important that the relationship between the client and designer is based upon mutual trust, respect and goodwill from the outset and that the relationship and integrity of the two parties remains robust throughout the commission.

Securing the services of the appropriate designer will prove to be invaluable. They are there to advise on everything from project feasibility and inception through to management and maintenance. Clients should be wary of engaging the designer for only a limited period of the project, as this can be a false economy. A competent designer's knowledge is rarely limited to the project design elements alone and they will regularly be able to advise on the appointment of other professionals (e.g. Quantity surveyors, CDM Coordinators if the Construction (Design and Management) Regulations apply, engineers, specialist landscape contractors, etc.). They also have a wide variety of practical skills that allow them to assist with tendering the project and to act as contract administrators for the implementation programme.

Selection and appointment of the contractor is equally important. The world of gardening and landscape is littered with incompetence and ignorance. Historic gardens and landscapes demand specialist skills, knowledge and competences that, perhaps, are beyond the abilities of many contractors available in today's marketplace. Thus, the process of tendering for an appropriate contractor needs to be carried out in accordance with strict selection criteria that the designer can help the client determine before the process starts. There is an approved practice code for the tendering of all contracts (the Joint Contracts Tribunal Practice Note 6) and it will be a false economy if these procedures are ignored for important conservation or restoration projects.

Whichever method of tendering is adopted, whether it is an open, selective or negotiated process (the benefits vary depending on the project under consideration), it is vitally important to consider the widest range of information in relation to the choice of contractor. Works within an historic garden context often require specialist skills, knowledge and competences for which the tendering contractors need to be prepared and appropriately resourced. The implementation works contracted for may be more costly to fulfil because of the need to meet these quite specific demands.

Checking the contractor's credentials in relation to resources available, availability to carry out the work in the necessary timeframe, a robust health and safety record, financial capability, and so forth are standard demands prior to engagement on any contract but the requirement to obtain references from previous clients and the availability to inspect work carried out on previous projects is of paramount importance in relation to historic garden operations.

Thus, even before the project begins, the client needs to understand fully the initial additional cost implications of engaging both specialist designers and contractors in order for their investment to be wisely spent. If the client is relatively inexperienced in such matters, or has experience only in less specialist areas of landscape operations then all of this information will need to be passed on by the commissioned designer and contractor in the early stages of the project in order to avoid misunderstanding and possible areas of conflict as the project progresses.

With the appointment of the designer secured, the client brief can be fully explored. With historic garden projects it is rarely a simple matter of clients' wishes, aspirations and demands being transcribed into a detailed design that can immediately be tendered for contract and thereafter implemented. The historic garden is likely be on the English Heritage Register of Historic Gardens and Landscapes of Special Historic Interest in England (1983) and governed by a statutory body that will necessarily need to be consulted depending upon the project proposals. This will again incur unavoidable costs in both fees and time. If the site contains an ancient monument or the project, due to the nature of the works, requires planning permission in whole or part, then there will be additional costs in terms of fees, time and resources.

Assuming the client's brief accords with the demands of the statutory bodies and any necessary planning permission is granted without too much delay or the need for fundamental changes, the costing exercise then needs to focus on the specific detail and build specification. This is where design expertise will prove invaluable in terms of the project outcomes.

Historic garden projects are neither unusual nor unique in terms of the two basic types of work generally required: simply categorised as hard and soft landscape. What tends to be much more specific is the precise nature of that work and the necessary quality of the finished product. The designer needs to understand the original design concept and the elements that comprised the original outcome.

With hard landscape elements there may be a need to renovate or rebuild using only original construction methods and materials. This will generally involve much higher costs due to the need (perhaps) to source the materials in the first place and then find a contractor with the particular skill-set to achieve the desired outcome. Costs may be slightly reduced if alternative materials can be used (with an acceptance of a loss of integrity from the original build) but it may still take time to source appropriate replacement materials. Cheaper still might be to rebuild a facsimile of the original feature using aesthetically sympathetic but modern materials and build methods. If renovation is not required then it may only be necessary to secure existing features in terms of their safety and potential dangers to visitors, and so on. This will be a much less expensive option and perhaps offer a more appropriate recognition of the 'process' of landscape over time.

Hard landscape features are generally more costly to renovate or recreate than soft landscape features, irrespective of whether the project involves an historic garden or not. Hard landscape features in an historic garden tend to be more expensive in terms of construction costs, resources and the demands placed upon the competences of the contractor at all stages. There are always exceptions to the rule and the practiced designer will be able to identify these on their client's behalf.

It is important when determining the finer detail of the hard landscape features to be renovated, restored or renewed to determine how the competences of the potential contractor might be identified to the satisfaction of the client and designer before the work on site is commenced. Contractors may be required to build sample products of a representative section of wall or paving for example, in order to ensure they can adhere to the specification. There should be no expectation that such exploratory work will be carried out without cost to the client but it is hoped that this will bring its own rewards when the final product is completed.

Although less expensive in general terms, soft landscape features within historic gardens may also be more costly than those within more general landscape contracts. This may be for a variety of reasons but will generally come about because of the need to preserve the integrity of the original planting design. Seed may need to be collected from what is identified as original plant stock, or cuttings taken and plants propagated from existing stock, which all demand additional resources of time, money, effort and skill. Provenance of plant stock can be of great significance and all three parties (client, designer and landscape contractor) will need to work collaboratively to achieve the desired outcome.

The designer needs to be fully conversant with the project research data. They need to understand not only how the garden has progressed and developed throughout its existence but also how it may be appropriately renovated, repaired or renewed (conservation not preservation) to make it fit for the twenty-first century. The extra over-cost for such expertise will again be justified by the end result.

Specifications compiled for historic garden projects need to be precise, concise, and uniquely site-specific. Standard specification documents will rarely suffice. The illustrative, qualitative and quantitative material supplied in the tender documents for the prospective contractors needs to be of a standard such that all parties can be in no doubt as to the aspirations of the project. Without such attention to the fine detailing there are likely to be delays and disputes as work progresses when inconsistencies arise from misinterpretations and lack of clarity within the documents. Relationships between the client, designer and contractor need to be transparent and completely honest throughout the process with each party engaging on a collaborative and cooperative basis to secure a successful outcome.

Contractual obligations

There are rare exceptions to the rule that landscape projects, whether in relation to historic garden projects or otherwise, need written contractual agreements in order to secure pre-determined success. Having identified the need for very precise consideration when pricing and budgeting for such projects, it would be foolish to think the project could be completed on purely verbal agreements between the parties involved. From the perspective of a chartered landscape architect, project completion without formal, written contractual agreements would be professionally unthinkable (as well as fundamentally contrary to the Code of Professional Conduct).

The options when selecting standard forms of contract are numerous and varied but careful consideration needs to be made when the project includes soft landscape initiatives as the majority of contract forms have been compiled to cover mostly construction implementation processes and procedures (hard landscape). Most historic garden projects will, as a matter of course, include soft landscape operations.

The most cost-effective way for a project to proceed to successful completion is for the designer to be formally engaged throughout the process. Acting as the client's agent from the outset, the designer will have a comprehensive understanding of all matters to be covered by the contractual arrangements. This will enable them to ensure that all parties fulfil their obligations in accordance with the demands agreed at the beginning.

Standard forms of contract exist for a variety of reasons. They offer all parties a high degree of certainty in terms of what each can expect if the contract proceeds as planned (and in most instances, what to expect if this is not the case). Contract forms are known as 'standard forms' offering a degree of familiarity with the 'rules' of engagement, saving time in terms of not having to re-invent the wheel on each occasion, helping to avoid confusion or misunderstanding and providing a series of tried and tested formulae for successful project completion. The majority of standard forms have been 'tested' in a court of law, which helps no end when disputes or disagreements arise.

In essence, a contractual agreement is a very simple operation; someone wants something completed to a certain standard, within a specific timeframe and for a particular cost. Someone else is prepared to complete that demand by agreeing to carry out the specifics of the project to the standards required, within the timeframe suggested and for the price of the budget quoted. This amounts to an offer, an acceptance and a 'consideration' (more frequently referred to as a fee).

Each standard form of contract will identify the parties to the agreement and who will be doing what in order for the contract to be considered acceptably fulfilled or complete; it will identify the project to be undertaken and where this will happen; it will detail the full list of contract documents that identify the illustrative, quantitative, and qualitative elements of the project; it may highlight certain specialist consultants required (e.g. a contract administrator, a quantity surveyor, etc.) and will identify the necessary witnesses to the agreement. The selection of the contract form for the project will be made on the advice of the designer in consultation with the client in order to fulfil the client's detailed brief. Things to be considered range from the contract start date (i.e. it may be necessary for the project to start before the design work is finished) to whether there is a need for a 'lump-sum' ('fixed-price') contract or even how quickly the project needs to be finished.

In all contract forms there are three key elements that will be played one against the other to determine the best selection. These comprise time (i.e. how long the contract will take to complete); cost (i.e. how much will it cost to complete the contract); and quality (i.e. the standard of workmanship and materials used to complete the contract). It is essential that the designer is able to comprehensively inform the client of the interrelationship between these three considerations, not only when selecting the contract form but also as the project progresses and the client has second thoughts about choices made at the beginning and wishes to see changes to the original agreement terms. It is rare that changes to the timing of the project have no knock-on effects to either cost or quality and vice-versa. Compromises are inevitable; it is a matter of determining, through careful discussion, elaboration and consideration what is most important when effecting the implementation process and programme.

The parties to the implementation contract are the client and the contractor. Although the client may engage the designer as the contract administrator (and by dint of this agreement be paid for their services by the client), this role is one of an impartial professional overseeing the terms of the signed contractual agreement. It is the contract administrator who identifies where each party may be failing in their duties under the contract or not complying with specific demands. It is a duty of the contract administrator to point out such responsibilities to both parties at the beginning of the agreement and ensure that they fully understand the implications of this arrangement.

The level of engagement in contract administration varies in accordance with the project under consideration. Historic garden projects demand a specific level of craftsmanship and thus careful consideration when a contract is to be let. The contractor will be selected on the basis of particular or specialist skills and it may be important for them to be engaged at an early stage, running concurrently with the design development programme. This allows the design package to evolve alongside the production work on the contract with the contractor's knowledge and skill set available for inclusion into the design production process. This form of 'Management Contract' demands efficient communication, collaboration and cooperation between all parties but can prove immensely beneficial to the final outcome. The contractor (who may or may not be the main contractor implementing the works) will be paid a separate fee for this management role.

The majority of clients entering into contractual agreements will want to secure a 'lump-sum' ('fixed-fee') arrangement. This does not mean alterations to the original price are not possible, rather that unless major changes are agreed by both parties, then the final sum paid by the client will be very close to that agreed at the beginning. The question asked most frequently by a client is usually 'How much is this all going to cost?'. Thus, a lump sum contract can be useful to set a client's mind at ease and add a degree of certainty to the process. The inclusion of a comprehensive Bill of Quantities with the lump sum contract will give all parties greater reassurance on costs involved. A Schedule of Rates will allow for some 'unknowns' to be included but these should be kept to a minimum. (A Bill of Quantities allows for the returned tender packages more readily to be assessed on cost alone, assuming all other factors remain equal.) The underlying principle of the Lump Sum Contract relates to the client having agreed to a comprehensive overall control of costs at the outset of contractual operations.

'Design and Build' contractual agreements are based upon a necessarily qualified, experienced and skilled (and appropriately resourced) contractor agreeing to take on both the design and construction elements of the contract. The design, even if not directly completed by the contractor, is under their control and not that of the client. Although this allows the client a single point of contact with the contractor effectively taking on the contract responsibility in its entirety, the elements of time and cost become of paramount importance and can often lead to a diminution of the quality of the finished product. The quality of the design is difficult to safeguard under such contractual arrangements, and in terms of historic gardens the issue of quality is generally paramount. Due consideration of the design specification is critical where a Design and Build option is selected.

Master-planned historic garden projects may be divided into specific elements that are projected for implementation over a period of years. This may comprise a series of 'mini' projects each to be let over an extended timeframe (years rather than months) as finance and circumstance allow. 'Continuity Contracts' are often considered useful where the existing contractor has performed in accordance with everything asked of them under the original contract terms and the follow-on contract covers elements of a similar nature. Thus, rather than have to complete a whole new tendering operation, negotiations can be had with the current contractor to determine the continuance of their services on a new but similar project. Negotiations would be based upon the prices, services and quality of operations completed to date but acknowledging that certain costs may well have increased due to inflation, etc.

Standard forms of contract are produced and published by a range of expert bodies from the Institute of Civil Engineers (ICE) and the government to the Joint Contracts Tribunal (JCT) and the Joint Council for Landscape Industries (JCLI). The majority of standard forms do not include specific clauses in relation to soft landscape works other than those produced by the JCLI. Thus, when selecting the form of contract for an historic garden project, serious consideration must be given as to why the JCLI Standard Form of Contract for Landscape Works might not be used. It is, of course possible to insert specific clauses into other standard contract forms but care must be taken not to undermine overall contractual integrity. Any additional clauses must be simple, clear, precise and concise in relation to the specific elements required. (Since 2005 the JCT has carried out sequential publication of a new suite of contract documents with the intention of simplifying and shortening the standard forms. This does not in anyway suggest a diminution of the effectiveness, terms of engagement or legal standing of these documents.)

Under the standard forms of contract (i.e. not 'Design and Build') the parties to the contract will be divided effectively into two teams; namely the client or design team and the contractor team. Each will comprise a number of individuals appointed under the contract to fulfil certain duties and particular roles. On the client's side there will be the client, the designer, and the contract administrator but also possibly a project manager, a quantity surveyor, a clerk of works, a CDM Coordinator (under the Construction (Design & Management) Regulations 2007) and other professional consultants (e.g. architect, engineer, planning consultant, and so forth) depending upon the size and complexity of the project.

In the contractor's team there will be a contract's manager, a site agent or foreman, a health and safety representative and possibly a range of specialist contractors to complete specific elements of the contract demands. The size and complexity of the project will determine the number and range of individual appointments necessary. Each appointment should be based upon a level of skill, knowledge, training and experience of the individual to complete their duties and tasks as determined by the contract to a level of competence that complies, in general terms, with acknowledged best practice. Each role will form a vital link in the contractual path that allows for cooperation and collaboration in all areas to ensure the project is completed on time, within budget and to the pre-agreed quality standards. It is imperative that the designer identifies (and clarifies on behalf of the client) the duties and responsibilities of each of the parties needed, as well as understanding the full implications of the terms of engagement for their own services.

An important element of every contractual agreement is a variety of certificates that must be issued as the contract progresses (the form of contract chosen will determine which these are and when they should be presented). They take the form of either Progress or Payment Certificates. The latter tend to be included when the project term is extended over months rather than just a few weeks and Progress Payment Certificates are issued to reflect either the completion of certain stages of the work or certain intervals of time (e.g. four-week periods). Their value must relate to work properly executed and any materials stored on site (and any deduction necessary for a pre-agreed retention sum) for which an invoice is submitted. The client is obliged to pay within a set timeframe. As the project nears its close a 'Penultimate Certificate of Payment' will follow the issuing of the 'Certificate of Practical Completion'. A 'Final Certificate of Payment' is compiled covering all outstanding monies to be paid after all the relevant documentation has been received from the contractor.

'Progress Certificates' are of paramount importance, not only to secure contractor payments, but more specifically as the contract nears its end. When the site is deemed by the contract administrator to be largely fit for the purpose for which it was designed (and any minor outstanding works will not hamper the day-to-day operations of the client in fulfilling the intended site function) a 'Certificate of Practical Completion' will be issued to all parties signifying a number of important changes that come into force at this stage. Thus, all parties become aware that the project has, for the best part, concluded, and the insurance liability for the site switches from the contractor back to the client. Any contractor monies held as guarantees under the contract will be returned to the contractor and 50% of any retention sum held against the progress payments can be claimed and must be paid. Any period of final measurement will also begin and the official Rectification Period will start. Every contractor will be keen to have the 'Certificate of Practical Completion' issued.

Other certificates of similar importance are the 'Certificate of Non-completion' where all parties are aware that the works have not been completed by the agreed date and, although the contractor must continue in order to complete the works, any liquidated damages claims may justifiably be submitted at this time. There is also the 'Certificate of Making Good Defects', where the contractor has to make good all defects in any aspects of the work completed to date within a specified timeframe following the issue of the Certificate of Practical Completion and the 'Final Certificate', when the project is effectively completed under the terms of the original contractual arrangement. The contract administrator needs to be aware, and to make their client aware, of the importance of each of these certificates and the significance of issuing them.

Part of the reason many contract forms are incredibly lengthy and often seem more complex than necessary is to try to avoid disputes and disagreements. All standard contract forms will have clauses covering termination on behalf of either party but also clauses relating to dispute resolution. When all parties are operating in an atmosphere of mutual trust and goodwill (to be encouraged in all circumstances) it is hoped that most misunderstandings (for that is generally what they start as) can be resolved by considered discussion. Where this fails, the first course of action should be mediation (i.e. a third-party mediator offers a process of structured negotiation and allows determination and agreement between the two parties); a voluntary, consensual process encouraged by the courts, in the hope that agreement can be reached and become binding as set out in a written document. Stepping up a level takes the dispute to adjudication. Determined by a third party adjudicator, this is used to obtain a relatively speedy, neutral outcome with the adjudicator's decision becoming binding only if the two parties agree in writing for it to be so. Adjudication is often simply seen as a swift method of 'chasing' unpaid monies within a strict timetable. The contract usually continues without delay or significant interruption.

Dispute resolution via arbitration (a private hearing, with or without qualified legal representation, presided over by a chartered arbitrator) or litigation (a public court hearing presided over by a judge) is best avoided in all instances. These are generally costly affairs that can take an inordinate amount of time, money and resources to resolve and conclude, with no guarantee that the outcome will necessarily be to the benefit of either party. In both cases the decisions of the arbitrator or the judge are legally binding on both parties (unless it can be proven that either have acted outside accepted legal procedure).

Historic garden conservation and restoration projects place very specific demands upon all parties engaged with the process. Extreme care needs to be taken to ensure the most comprehensive analysis and costing exercise is carried out at the beginning of the process before the tendering exercise is entered into. Thereafter, it is imperative that due consideration is given to the type and form of contract entered into between the client and the appropriately qualified, competent and adequately resourced contractor with the assistance of the designer who is also best placed to act as contract administrator. If the correct procedures are followed with due diligence and in line with acknowledged best practice there will be little need to worry about achieving a wholly successful outcome.

24 Constraints and working on site: some practical and contractual problems

Mike Ibbotson
Founder, Ibbotson Studios, Gloucestershire, UK

Topographic survey

It is essential to obtain a detailed digital topographical survey in advance of any significant undertaking where drawings will be the principal means of communication for guiding works on any site. Detailed topographical surveys will incorporate accurate measurement and representation of all visible features above ground and, where necessary, services and drainage below ground. It is important to give a clear specification for the survey. A checklist should be discussed with the surveyor and their knowledge will enable them to choose the most appropriate survey equipment and software to fulfil your brief, which may include specialist surveying techniques such as GPS location and laser scanning.

Commissioning a survey requires definition of the area of cover and the level of detail. The area, which may be wider than the boundary of the site, is most usefully defined by a line drawn on an Ordnance Survey plan, with the option to have a higher density of data capture identified by different coloured lines or hatches for parts of the site where more detail will be helpful. A full measured building survey with elevations may not be needed, but the specification for the topographical survey should ensure doors and threshold levels are surveyed, and it can be useful to have window positions and windowsill levels surveyed.

Accurate topographic surveys, and subsequent drawings based on them, will not precisely match historic plans and contemporary or historic aerial photographs when they are placed above or behind as overlays. Duplicated digital files of historic maps and aerial photographs can be made to 'fit' to the topographic survey by manipulating them through scaling, stretching, rotation, and other distortions, until there is good correlation between the lines of the historic documents and the topographical survey. Smaller extracts of the historic plans (related to identifiable site compartments) will require less distortion to correlate with the topographical survey than the whole historic plan.

On large landscapes it may be impractical, or too expensive, to engage a surveyor to record features across the whole area. A handheld GPS receiver may usefully record coordinates of important elements. GPS works especially well for locating features spread out over many acres, such as veteran trees within a park. The canopy size and shape of trees in parkland can be traced from vertical aerial photography overlaid on the site plans.

Gardens & Landscapes in Historic Building Conservation, First Edition. Edited by Marion Harney.
© 2014 John Wiley & Sons, Ltd. Published 2014 by John Wiley & Sons, Ltd.

Visual survey and assessment of the site

Additional information in the form of observation notes, sketches and photographs will have to be gathered to build up on the knowledge gained from the topographical survey. Photographs of objects should include a ruler or measuring tape to give approximate scale to the objects in the view. Another technique that can be useful for recording irregular features such as random coursed stone-work is to place a grid of a known dimension over the subject being photographed. Such a grid can be made from a square rigid frame with a string grid at 25 cm intervals. Objects close to the plane of the tape or grid can be scaled relatively accurately in viewed photos. Aside from verifying measurements, photos can be used to document and count elements or units of features such as steps and brick-courses. Often two or more photographs of the same object must be compared to reduce errors.

Covered and hidden items

The very character and nature of work on historic sites means that elements of fabric will often be hidden from view by overgrowth, soil or other material. If labour is available to assist, partial or full clearance of site vegetation can be really helpful. Digging trial holes into the ground to reveal the extent of necessary works before letting a contract can add a degree of certainty to what you are going to find when the works on site start in earnest. A contractor equipped to assist with advance investigations by digging trial holes or trenches may be engaged. Any cost expenditure related to uncovering hidden features at the planning and design stage is potentially returned many times over later in the project.

Well-placed trial holes can help establish the general makeup of the ground and are useful in establishing the composition and depth of materials buried under vegetation and soil. A carriage drive through an eighteenth-century deer park in Gloucestershire which had been 'lost' during the last century was recently reinstated to bring it back into use as the main access to the mansion. The line of the drive was known because an obvious scar crossed the park on exactly the route indicated by the 1st Edition Ordnance Survey map, but in advance of preparing contract schedules, a number of small pits were hand-dug at regular intervals along its whole length. This established roughly how much turf and soil lay over the remaining hidden base of the old drive, and the depth and condition of the buried stone base at different points. The tender for reinstating the carriage drive could therefore be let with reasonable certainty that the schedule of works had a fair description of the intended works including the over-burden of soil and quantum of repair required. As soon as a contractor was employed to undertake the contract works, their first task was to dig full-width trial trenches every 50 m along the 800 m drive. This information allowed further refinement of instructions and accurate measurement for the costing of works.

If archaeological investigations have been undertaken on a site, these are going to inform the preparation of production information. At Aberglasney Gardens in Carmarthenshire, archaeological excavation preceded restoration and provided detailed information enabling decisions to be made about which features were to be reinstated and how they were to be restored, as well as information about features that could not be reinstated for practical or other reasons. Investigations provided information for the repair of large derelict architectural structures such as the raised cloister walk and also some small, fascinating features, which may otherwise have been missed. In the wall around the central garden pond, the position and form of rills from hidden watercourses that fed water at points all around the pond were unearthed. These little structures were rebuilt with their unusual water chutes guiding the inflowing water on to decorative stone ledges.

Drawings

Scale drawings have varying levels of detail depending on their ultimate use. Drawings that are intended to provide the basis for landscape restoration will require extensive dimensions and annotations to record the necessary historical and conditional information, while drawings intended for more general management purposes such as maintenance, may require little more than material or plant indications and dimensions for calculating gross areas requiring treatment.

Computer aided design (CAD) drawings offer advantages of flexibility in transferring data between different drawing applications and other people you are working with. Measurement of area and length is much easier than on hand-drawn plans, especially if the drawings are prepared with forethought so that drawing entities represent the items that you need to have information on. Changing working dimensions to imperial dimensions may be appropriate when trying to tie in with existing structures whose original setting-out and component units would have been imperial dimensions. Hand-drawn plans do however still offer some advantages over CAD drawings as the very nature of their exact precision can prove to be a disadvantage; historic sites usually aren't built with electronic precision to orthogonal grids. Creation of truly useful drawings is reliant on careful observation and measurement on site. There are occasions where a well-crafted hand-drawing will be quicker to prepare than a CAD drawing and will more accurately convey the character of the desired works.

Health and safety considerations

Consideration of hazard and risk must be integrated with the site planning and design process with responsibility for eliminating hazards and reducing risks so far as is reasonably practical. Construction works are subject to the Construction (Design and Management) Regulations 2007. Clients making an appointment for a consultant or a contractor have to take steps to ensure they appoint people or companies competent for what they are required to do. Discussion related to prior experience of similar commissions and approach to handling the scope of work is a good starting point in assessing such competence prior to making appointments. Domestic clients (connected to the nature of the client, not the site) have less onerous duties under the Regulations.

The nature of arrangements to manage health and safety factors will depend on the size and type of work. Historic sites may require special efforts to incorporate protective measures in a manner sensitive to the historic fabric both during the construction phase and after completion. The effort required in reducing risks associated with a hazard is proportional to the degree of risk and there is no need to spend time or money on low-risk hazards.

Programme and sequencing works

A wide range of matters may have an impact on the timing and the sequence that works can be carried out; these include:

Legislative constraints Before works on the ground can be taken in hand, consideration should be given as to whether any statutory restrictions are in place. These may involve obtaining Planning Permission and Listed Building Consent, and consents such as Scheduled Monument or Ancient Monument, Conservation Area and Tree Protection Order permissions. Potentially, extensive consultations could take place in advance of submissions for obtaining these consents. Granted permissions may have conditions attached, which may need to be discharged prior to commencement of the work on site, and landscape works may well be subject to conditions of consents obtained for main contract building works.

Seasonal factors   Exposure to cold or wet weather in winter may restrict some operations. Problems caused by winter weather can be mitigated by arranging for working areas to be covered by temporary shelter, which is also likely to increase the speed by which work can be undertaken. If the shelter is freestanding and mobile it may be moved from section to section as work proceeds.

Planting season and availability of plants may have to be factored into the progamme. It can be time-consuming locating the right plants, especially if particular varieties, sizes or trained forms are wanted. An extra growing season or two can make a huge difference to choice and availability, particularly if suppliers can be nominated and contracted to grow and supply to exact specifications.

Public access and opening   In publicly accessible sites, seasonal opening may lead to time constraints on what can be done, where and when. It can be beneficial to give advance notice of impending works due in public places. In the Royal Parks, a notice board is erected on site advertising drawings and details of proposed works with a list of addresses and telephone numbers to enable interested people to contribute comments.

Protected species   Birds, bats, badgers, dormice, otters, water voles, reptiles and amphibians all enjoy statutory protection and historic sites seem to be the favourite haunt of various protected creatures. If there are protected species on a site, a pragmatic ecologist should be commissioned who understands the constraints and context of the site and can respond in a positive or creative way to the issues that need to be addressed. The time taken up dealing with protected species surveys, licensing arrangements and modified work requirements should not be under-estimated.

Archaeological watching brief   Works may need to be sequenced to facilitate an archaeological watching brief and this can modify the progress of works. Contractors should be advised of the detail of a watching brief at time of tendering so they can assess how works may be affected and plan accordingly.

Sourcing materials   Allow plenty of time for sourcing and obtaining materials. Order materials or features with long lead-in times before the main contractor is on board but beware that late delivery of a nominated supply is the perfect opportunity for your contractor to claim for an extension of time.

Retention of trees   During the restoration of Aberglasney Gardens, many trees were removed to facilitate its reconstruction. It is not generally difficult to determine whether self-sown sycamore and yew trees should be removed when they are growing out of derelict buildings, walls and dried up ponds. It was, however, decided that a single yew tree should be kept on the corner of the cloister wall-top for aesthetic reasons.

If a tree is to be kept, then ensure it has the space to thrive and grow; otherwise all that has been done is to leave a problem that will be bigger or more difficult to deal with at a later date. Trees are often retained, resulting in a compromised design, only later to gradually decline because construction work has damaged their roots and canopy.

Trees in Relation to Design, Demolition and Construction BS 5837:2012 provides a helpful guide for assessing a tree's value and methods to ensure long-term retention. This replaced the 2005 British Standard *Trees in Relation to Construction*, with the broader scope of the new title more accurately conveying the need to properly consider trees in the planning and design of a project. It describes current practice in relation to protection, management and planting of trees near built structures and for the protection of structures in the vicinity of trees. The Standard includes guidelines on:

- Constraints posed by existing trees
- Proximity of structures to trees – tree survey and categorisation method

- The principle of the root protection area (RPA)
- Arboricultural impact assessment
- Tree protection during demolition or construction
- Arboricultural method statement
- Barriers and ground protection
- Site monitoring
- New planting design and associated landscape operations
- Works within the RPA
- Underground and above-ground utility apparatus.

One practical measure that can sometimes be used to protect the really valuable trees or shrubs is to temporarily retain scrubby vegetation as a buffer between the important trees and the construction activity. The sacrificial vegetation is removed once all potentially damaging operations have ceased or have moved to a safe distance from the protected trees.

Choosing materials

Matters to consider when deciding what materials are suitable include:

- Aesthetic qualities and character of fabric or components
- Appropriate for site because it matches existing, or because it doesn't match but is complementary and therefore appropriate to the location
- Available in sufficient quantity
- Availability in the time frame of the contract. Some nominated materials can have a long lead-in time and may need to be ordered in advance of placing the contract with a contractor. You are exposed to a potential claim if the supplier doesn't deliver the quality or quantity of goods stipulated on time
- Fit for purpose
- Variability
- Dimensions and coordination with existing fabric.

Re-using materials reclaimed from the site offers advantages over new or imported materials, but some thought should be given to the method of salvaging the material to avoid causing damage, and for transport, storage, sorting and cleaning. A careful analysis of quantity, quality and breakage losses should precede any final determination of use.

A good-sized sample should be checked when considering using reclaimed materials from an outside source. Ideally the whole stock pile will be checked to get a better understanding of quality, consistency, dimensions and how much cleaning will be required. Ensure your contractor is advised on what condition the material will be in when it's delivered and what cleaning and preparation should be expected.

Finding materials with dimensions that coordinate exactly with existing components can be tricky. Handmade bricks are variable and when collapsed sections of a walled garden in Oxfordshire were repaired, replacement bricks from a specialist manufacturer didn't provide a good match, even though numerous measurements and samples were taken on site. After the repairs were complete it could be seen that the original bricks varied in size more than had been appreciated beforehand.

Choosing contractors

When selecting contractors to work in historic environments, significant weight should be applied to the contractor having a particular skill set and knowledge of techniques applicable to the particular work. General points to consider include:

- Trust
- Range of skills
- Flexibility
- Understanding the context as well as the specifics of the works
- Health and safety competence
- Site management
- Ability to bring on board the right subcontractors and manage them effectively
- Existing knowledge of the site
- Financial stability and ability to finance the contract works.

Options for selecting the right contractor for the job may depend upon the client organisation tender procedures. In unrestricted circumstances, there are occasions when negotiating directly with a favoured contractor, who has the correct skills and experience, will be the best way forward. Some consideration should also be given to the choice between using an all-encompassing managing contractor responsible for everything, or for employing separate specialists undertaking individual parts.

Protection

One of the first tasks of operations on site is the protection of its assets from theft or damage. Theft of ornaments is a well-known risk but an inadequately protected site can be stripped bare of its stone paving overnight.

The level and type of protection must be specified clearly and stated within the schedule of works so that the contractor properly prices to undertake what is otherwise an easy area for a contractor to cut corners and save time and money.

Gateways, railings and narrow passages vulnerable to damage from plant and vehicles should be boxed within a sturdy frame and plywood. Steps and paved surfaces are also vulnerable to damage and may also need to be boxed in.

A sufficient and robust exclusion zone must be established and maintained around retained trees for the duration of works (refer to guidelines in *Trees in Relation to Design, Demolition and Construction BS 5837:2012*).

Vegetation can suffer harm, not just from obvious physical contact, but also through damaged soil structure. It is useful to know the capabilities of the soil at the site in terms of its ability to resist damage from site works causing compaction and destruction of structure. Some soils can apparently drain well but are prone to damage from compaction whilst wet after which they become waterlogged easily and the affected area of the site will be unworkable until it thoroughly dries. Areas of topsoil should be fenced off from the works and from transport routes, and storage areas should be planned so as to avoid unnecessary compaction damage.

Temporary access routes and hard-standing areas

Surplus hard material emanating from site clearance works can be incorporated into temporary access tracks or hard-standing and should be placed on a geotextile fabric to reduce sinking into soft ground below. When site access tracks suffer heavy wear, particularly in winter, it is tempting for dumper drivers to move off rutted routes and to travel across adjacent ground. Tracks gradually get wider unless they are fenced in and properly constructed to allow for the site traffic.

Temporary tracks and hard-standing should not cross tree-root protection areas unless there is no alternative route. If root protection areas do have to be violated, then a raised mattress construction can be formed and stabilised with a three-dimensional 'Geogrid' filled with even-graded stone.

Disposal of surplus subsoil

Disposal of surplus material is a problem for many projects. There may be a hollow within the wider site that can be filled with clean uncontaminated surplus subsoil. But care is needed to consider the impact on the host site in terms of character change and ecology. Access routes to the host site may impact on tree roots. Any intention to deposit material should be assessed as part of the project planning well before a contractor has started work so that permissions can be obtained as necessary. Material dug out of the ground will bulk up approximately 20% and will therefore need a bigger hole to fit back into.

Dredging lakes and ponds can generate huge volumes of liquid silt. Generally this will be placed in bunded settling ponds to dry out so that it can be handled and spread somewhere on site. If there is adjacent space then the wet material can be spread directly onto the ground, but it is very unstable and mobile, and its transport, even over very short distances, creates a huge mess. If there isn't room to dry the silt in situ, it will have to be pooled and then removed from site. Removal of silt from Regent's Park boating lake could only be undertaken by transporting much of the silt out from central London in sealed lorries after the bulk of the water content had been allowed to drain off.

Services, utilities and drainage

New underground utilities and services should be placed in locations that aren't going to impact on the quality of the finished landscape. Large clusters of service covers and manholes, especially on sloping surfaces, are particularly difficult to handle in a manner that is sensitive to the appearance of a site. The sheer number of underground services on some sites is quite a challenge to integrate with finished surfaces without affecting the positions of proposed trees or spoiling paved areas.

Purpose-made covers and frames designed to have recessed paving do not look right in many historic settings and they are generally less appropriate than a quality cast-iron cover. Depending on the use of the site and agreement with the client, it may be possible to have service access chambers placed under paving with surface markers and accurate location plans denoting their positions. Some covers may be hidden under gravel, but with care to ensure they do not become a slip hazard and the chamber cover will need protecting to stop fines jamming the lid within its frame.

Repair

Maintaining historic character will be assured through the use of appropriate materials and techniques, especially where repairs are undertaken. The first question that should come to mind is whether a repair is actually necessary. Repointing of walls is only needed where mortar has become so loose, powdery, decayed or eroded that water has begun to penetrate joints. A recessed joint or chalky mortar does not necessarily mean that repointing is required. If mortar can't easily be raked out by hand to a depth at least twice the width of the joint then repointing is probably unnecessary. Defective pointing is usually the result of other problems such as missing or defective copings and these problems need to be dealt with prior to repointing.

Adopting a clear methodology prior to commencing repairs will make a significant contribution to the success of the work. In one example for extensive paving repairs, adopting and following a defined work procedure ensured that the brief could be fulfilled to take up the paving, clean it and re-lay it exactly. Although there was a repeating pattern through the paving, the stones were individually cut to fit and had to be put back on new bedding in the same position they were laid originally. As this work covered several garden areas with paving over 1,000 m^2 in extent, there was plenty of scope to muddle the paving.

The method adopted in this case ensured that a stone mason lifted each paving stone in turn and marked the orientation and a location number on the back of every single slab. These were then put on palettes and moved to a position where a specialist subcontractor (with a successful track record) cleaned each stone, before moving the stone back to its original position to be re-laid by the stone mason. A handful of slabs broke out of several thousand lifted, but luckily there was a stockpile on site of unused original stone slabs. It is therefore worth bearing in mind that a few spare units of materials used on sites should be left behind after works are completed.

A significant part of the character of historic structures and their individuality derive from historic or traditional forms of construction, detailing and materials. Successful and sympathetic repair, restoration and new work in historic locations is reliant upon careful advance planning and research. The correct materials should be sourced with an appropriately skilled labour force employed to undertake the works.

The practical and contractual problems associated with historic landscapes are similar to those found on any project with external work, but with an added dimension of care and sensitivity related to the context. The sequence of work through a project is generally the same, but with potentially extended phases of research, planning, consultation and obtaining consents. The works may also have to be more carefully specified to account for protection of the site, and for obtaining and working with traditional materials and construction techniques. A general purpose landscape contractor is unlikely to have the skills in-house to undertake much of the work that may be encountered at an historic site; therefore specialist subcontractors with the appropriate knowledge will need to be brought on board, adding to the contractual complexity.

25 Designed landscapes and national designation

Fridy Duterloo-Morgan

Designation Adviser, English Heritage, London, UK

Introduction

In England, the inclusion of a site on the national Register of Parks and Gardens of Special Historic Interest in England remains one of the most important tools to enhance understanding, appreciation and protection, and to help inform decisions on repair, management and/or development proposals.

In the early 1980s a much broader awareness had developed of not only the beauty and quality, but also the cultural, historic and social importance of historic parks and gardens in England, which in many cases had influenced cultures well beyond the country's own boundaries. It was felt that the rich and varied contribution parks, gardens and other designed landscapes make to heritage and culture deserved to be acknowledged through both recording and protection. Following the introduction of the National Heritage Act in 1983, English Heritage was enabled to compile the first Register of Parks and Gardens and work on the 46 county volumes began that year.[1] The last volume was completed in 1988. Ten years after the first publication of the last county volumes, the Register included nearly 1,300 sites, and by 2005 this had grown to approximately 1,500 sites. Since then, over 100 sites have been added, making a current total of approximately 1,617 registered sites. In 2011 the Register of Parks and Gardens was firmly embedded within the National Heritage List for England database where it takes pride of place next to other national designation regimes, including listing and scheduling.[2] The 25th anniversary of the Register of Parks and Gardens in 2013 seems an appropriate time to have a close look at the history of this national designation regime, how it has developed since its first publication, and to consider what the future may hold.

The first edition of the Register of Parks and Gardens

In the early 1980s, the research for the first few county volumes of the new Register was carried out mainly by the Centre for the Conservation of Parks and Gardens at York University on behalf of English Heritage. Subsequent volumes were compiled under the direction of Dr Christopher Thacker, English Heritage's first Garden Inspector. Although the work did not involve a systematic survey and the majority of parks and gardens could not be visited,

Gardens & Landscapes in Historic Building Conservation, First Edition. Edited by Marion Harney.
© 2014 John Wiley & Sons, Ltd. Published 2014 by John Wiley & Sons, Ltd.

they were selected on the basis of extensive existing knowledge which had grown significantly over the years. Substantial information was also submitted by the Garden History Society and (local) expert volunteers. The selected sites were graded at I, II* or II, in line with listed buildings. In 1987 English Heritage formally agreed selection criteria for registration, which were endorsed by an independent Gardens Committee. These were slightly updated and revised in 1993, and more recently, in 2010.[3]

The first edition of the Register did not include maps to show the extent of the designated area. During the Great Storm that took place in October 1987, a large number of registered parks and gardens were damaged. English Heritage and the Task Force Trees Unit of the Countryside Commission both generated emergency storm damage repair grant-aid programmes and, for this purpose, boundary maps were needed. The mapping process continued over the next few years, and was largely carried out under the direction of David Jacques, Gardens Inspector at English Heritage from 1987–92. At first it focused on sites damaged in the Great Storm but, eventually, maps were drawn for all sites, mainly to meet the requirements of local planning authorities who were including policies for historic parks and gardens in their statutory Development Plans. Due to the limited amount of resources, site visits could not be undertaken and the mapping was mostly a desk-based exercise.

English Heritage has a statutory duty to notify all owner(s) and occupier(s) of sites included on the Register. Unlike listed buildings, a registered park or garden cannot be registered as a local land charge and, if owners are not notified, they would not necessarily be aware of the status of their land in this respect. During the mapping programme it became apparent that in many cases registered parks were in multiple ownership, and many owners were not aware of their land being registered. As a result, between 1993 and 1996, in order to fulfil its statutory duty, English Heritage carried out a Notification Project to find and notify the owners of all registered sites. The Project showed that the majority of registered parks and gardens are indeed in split or multiple ownership.

Improving the Register 1993–2000

In the early 1990s, English Heritage embarked on two major Register programmes led by the then Head of Register of Parks and Gardens, Dr Harriet Jordan. These aimed to review and enhance the existing Register to ensure it was up to date and correct, and to improve its coverage.

The Register Review Programme (1993–2000) consisted of individual county-based surveys which identified sites that would merit further consideration for inclusion. The surveys also aimed to enhance local understanding of historic parks and gardens and included extensive consultation with local authorities, county gardens trusts and local experts. Local authorities were encouraged to compile local lists of historic parks and gardens and take the identified sites into account, whether included on the national Register or not, when formulating policies for their statutory Development Plans. Although the second phase of the Register Review Programme, to carry out individual site assessments, could not be fully completed at the time due to limited resources, the lists of potential candidates and the information gathered for these sites continues to inform current designation work.

The Register Upgrade Programme (1996–2000) aimed to update and enhance the descriptive texts of all Register entries, confirm the boundary maps, and make personal contact with owner(s) and occupier(s) of each registered site to provide an opportunity for discussion and dialogue. In 1997, as a result of this programme, the entirely paper-based Register was stored for the first time on a computer system: the English Heritage Parks and Gardens database (PaG). Unfortunately, mapping could not be included; nevertheless English Heritage was able to store the text-based entries and query them through this electronic system. Although a fairly basic system, it assisted in research and enabled a better overview of the sites to be obtained. It was also possible to generate statistical information which could give data on distribution, thereby identifying potential gaps in coverage.

During this period, specific selection criteria for different types of sites were also agreed: garden squares and cemeteries were amongst the earliest to be compiled, with those for cemeteries recently updated following the Cemetery Review Project, completed in 2010.[4] Further guidance on the selection of different types of designed landscapes for the purpose of registration is given in English Heritage's Designed Landscapes Selection Guides, published in 2013, which are discussed further below.

Heritage Protection Reform and Unified Designation

Since 2000, the Government, English Heritage and the heritage sector have been working towards a reform of national heritage protection. The existing protection regimes and the different legislation related to each of them is complex, having evolved piecemeal over the past 120 years. Following extensive consultation, it was felt the system needed to be streamlined and improved to make it more useful for those involved with the care and management of heritage assets. It would also enable those concerned to take a more a holistic approach to the management of complex sites with multiple designated heritage assets.

The Heritage Protection Reform's long-term goal is to aim for a unified national designation system which includes all of the different designation regimes. The changes to the planning legislation that are needed to fully implement this unified approach have not yet been introduced, but in anticipation of this, in 2006 English Heritage introduced the Unified Designation System (UDS). This is an internal electronic filing system, which holds all the information related to the assessment of individual sites, building(s) and/or structure(s), including all correspondence and information gathered through the designation process. The Unified Designation System is directly linked to the National Heritage List for England, where all designated assets, including registered parks and gardens, are stored. The National Heritage List for England is publicly accessible via the English Heritage website and the Heritage Gateway.[5]

Although listing and scheduling remain separate and distinct from registration, in their assessment (each has their own set of criteria), and in their status within the planning system, the UDS allows for an integrated assessment process during which owners and local authorities are notified and consulted.

Electronic application forms for designation and an explanation as to what information is needed in order for English Heritage to validate the application, can be found on the English Heritage website, which allows photos and other relevant supporting documents to be uploaded onto the system. Since it was first introduced the assessment process used by the Register of Parks and Gardens has involved owners and local authorities, and has significantly influenced the current integrated designation process. The success, rigour and transparency of the early parks and gardens programmes and the Upgrade and Review Programmes, which included extensive consultation with owner(s), local authorities, amenity societies and other external experts, helped shape the current national designation assessment processes.

Once a site has gone through the initial assessment stage and is perceived to merit consideration for designation, the current process allows English Heritage to consider all different aspects of the site in order to decide which designation regime(s) would be most appropriate to use, and most importantly, ensure that where different designation regimes are recommended, they are cross-referenced. This is especially valuable where designed landscapes, buildings and structures share the same history and form a strong unity in their layout and design and cannot be fully understood in isolation.

Larger and/or complex sites may also become (part of) a Defined Area Survey (DAS). These surveys can cover a specific geographical area or a series of heritage assets of a specific type; for example Ashton Wold in Leicestershire, where the various heritage assets of the estate were reviewed and under consideration for national designation. This resulted in the listing of a number of buildings and structures within the estate, including the inclusion of the designed landscape on the Register. Another example is the Defined Area Survey on

Arts and Crafts villas in the Cotswolds undertaken by English Heritage's Designation Team in the west. This project includes the identification of gardens and, where appropriate, these will be considered for inclusion on the Register.

A designed landscape, whether of local or national importance, may also be referred to in the history section of a List entry for a building or structure that is associated with it. Where a designed landscape contributes to the special interest of an associated listed building or structure, it may be appropriately described under the heading 'setting' in the List entry and referred to under the Reasons for Designation. Many parks or gardens incorporate archaeological sites which may or may not be associated with the landscape design, and where of sufficient interest and importance, these may also be scheduled. Although formal garden earthworks are normally eligible for scheduling, they may also be included within a registered landscape.

Revised Criteria and publication of Selection Guides

In 2010, revised selection criteria and grading definitions for the Register of Parks and Gardens were published. Similar to listing, the designation criteria are categorised in date bands that reflect the main trends in garden and landscape history and design. The older a designed landscape is, and the fewer surviving examples of its kind, the more likely it is to have special interest. The current Register criteria are as follows:

- Sites formed before 1750 where at least a proportion of the original layout is still in evidence
- Sites laid out between 1750 and 1840 where enough of the layout survives to reflect the original design
- Sites with a main phase of development post-1840 which are of special interest and relatively intact, the degree of required special interest rising as the site becomes closer in time
- Particularly careful selection is required for sites from the period after 1945
- Sites of less than 30 years old are normally only registered if they are of outstanding quality and under threat.

Further considerations which may influence selection and may exceptionally be sufficient by themselves to merit designation are:

- Sites which were influential in the development of taste, whether through reputation or reference in literature
- Sites which are early or representative examples of a style of layout or a type of site, or the work of a designer (amateur or professional) of national importance
- Sites having an association with significant persons or historic events
- Sites with a strong group value with other heritage assets.

These criteria are not mutually exclusive categories and more than one of them may be relevant to any particular site.

In terms of grading, sites registered at Grade I are of exceptional interest in a national context; at Grade II* of particular importance and of more than special interest and those registered at Grade II are of special interest, warranting every effort to preserve them. The grade of any listed building or structure within a registered site is independent of the grade of that park or garden as included on the Register. However, where they show particularly strong unity, such as expressed in their design, date and history, they may be graded at the same level.

In order to offer further insight into designation decisions made for the Register, English Heritage has published Selection Guides for Designed Landscapes, which are subdivided into four main categories: Landscapes of Remembrance, Institutional Landscapes, Rural Landscapes and Urban Landscapes.[6] Each fully illustrated guide discusses the different types of landscapes within these categories and contains a short historical overview, a consideration of specific designation issues and a list of sources for further research and reading. Importantly, the guides are cross-referenced with the relevant Listing Selection Guides to ensure consistency and full coverage, as is the case with the Selection Guide for Park and Garden Structures, which gives a short summary of buildings and structures commonly used in designed landscapes, both ornamental and functional, and explains the specific criteria that are used when considering them for listing.

Designed landscapes and the National Heritage Protection Plan

In 2011, following public consultation, English Heritage launched the National Heritage Protection Plan (NHPP), which sets out what it intends to protect – and/or help others to protect – over the next four years. The NHPP promotes the development of more focused strategies across the heritage sector and aims to provide a framework within which each organisation's efforts at protection can be articulated in relation to its partners and other participants. The programme sets out a number of measures, and those that are directly relevant to designation are the assessment and protection of significance which are linked to a number of thematic priority Activity Plans. The Activity Plans include programmes which contribute to the updating and management of the existing designation base, thus including the Register of Parks and Gardens, and focus on the strategic designation of new assets. In order to balance the high number of applications for designation against its strategic work, English Heritage must direct its increasingly limited resources to those sites that are most in need of attention. Currently they are only taking forward applications for 'spot' designation where the building or site is demonstrably under threat and worthy of consideration for inclusion on the National Heritage List for England, or where there is clear evidence of special interest.

Many of the programmes instigated under the various National Heritage Protection Action Plans incorporate the identification, assessment and protection of designed landscapes. The current Action Plan for Historic Towns and Suburbs includes a review of public parks, and that for the Later Twentieth Century Heritage incorporates identification and assessment of post-war designed landscapes. Under the Activity Plan for Sport and Entertainment Buildings and Landscapes, recreational landscapes are included, and the Action Plan for Rural Historic Buildings and their Settings incorporates the assessment of villa landscapes in the Lake District. The assessment and listing of significant monuments within cemeteries included on the Register of Parks and Gardens will form part of the Action Plan for Churchyards, Cemeteries and Burial Grounds. It is important that local authorities, national Amenity Societies, Civic Societies and other local interest groups or communities are involved in the National Heritage Protection Plan. They are encouraged to send in suggestions and ideas, and most importantly, to develop their own local Action Plans, as this can unlock opportunities for collaboration and sharing. To ensure the Action Plans within the NHPP include or focus on designed landscapes where appropriate, it is especially important that the Garden History Society, County Gardens Trusts, and owners of parks and gardens, continue to use their knowledge and expertise to positively influence the NHPP, and guide the priorities and objectives set through it.

Conclusion

Since the completion of its first publication 25 years ago, the Register of Parks and Gardens is viewed by many as a relatively robust, transparent and inclusive tool specifically designed to understand, identify and protect designed landscapes. It is one of the oldest of such designation regimes, and it is well respected by heritage organisations all over the world, having influenced and helped shape many successful parks and gardens protection mechanisms in other countries, including the Netherlands. However, as an evolving tool in an ever-changing environment, its effectiveness and purpose, as well as its coverage and scope, will need to be examined, evaluated and assessed continually, and this process will rely on the continued input and active engagement of local communities, the Garden History Society, County Gardens Trusts, and other interested amenity societies, academic experts, scholars, and owners. This is difficult in an economic climate where funding and resources are scarce or even non-existent and, in times of austerity, it is even more important that amenity societies and local trusts work together to share their expertise and limited resources.

Endnotes

1. The legislation can be found in Section 8C of the Historic Buildings and Ancient Monuments Act 1953 (inserted by section 33 of, and paragraph 10 of Schedule 4 to, the National Heritage Act 1983.
2. The NHLE is a searchable database of all nationally designated heritage assets that can be accessed via http://www.english-heritage.org.uk/professional/heritage-list-for-england
3. The revised designation criteria for inclusion on the national Register of Parks and Gardens can be accessed via http://www.english-heritage.org.uk/caring/listing/criteria-for-protection/pag-criteria/
4. See 'Paradise Preserved': Updated list of cemeteries included in English Heritage's Register of Parks and Gardens of Special Historic Interest (January 2011) and the register 'criteria', published by English Heritage (2011).
5. www.heritagegateway.org.uk. The Heritage Gateway enables researchers to cross-search over 50 resources, including: over 50% of local English Historic Environment Records (HERs), the National Heritage List for England (NHLE) and eight other national resources, including Images of England.
6. The Selection Guides for Designed Landscapes can be accessed via the following links: http://www.english-heritage.org.uk/publications/drpgsg-urban-landscapes/
http://www.english-heritage.org.uk/publications/drpgsg-rural-landscapes/
http://www.english-heritage.org.uk/publications/drpgsg-institutional-landscapes/
http://www.english-heritage.org.uk/publications/drpgsg-landscapes-remembrance/

26 Conservation legislation in the UK

Colin Johns
Architect, town planner and member of the Institute of Historic Building Conservation and visiting lecturer in conservation legislation and practice at the Universities of Bath and Plymouth, UK

Our appreciation of the English landscape is today much enhanced by the freedom we have to visit and walk in the countryside and by the planning and other controls that provide protection from intrusive development. Similarly, historic towns and cities have become destinations and grand country houses and historic parks and gardens are places to visit for a day out. A wide range of conservation and planning controls makes all this possible, but it is a process that has evolved over more than 100 years.

The ownership and control of land and buildings has long been a contentious issue, as evidenced in many parliamentary debates. The introduction of legal constraints on the rights of private property owners was strongly resisted and the same arguments are sometimes heard today. Consequently, the introduction of planning and conservation controls has been a slow process, achieved largely through the sustained efforts of individuals and organisations over many years.

The unchecked development of the Industrial Revolution in the eighteenth and nineteenth centuries and the concomitant rapid expansion of cities created conditions that would become unsanitary and unacceptable. The development process was often driven by the desire for large profits and there was scant concern for the well-being of those forced to live and work there. Although originally government intervention was concentrated on securing improvements in public health, later arguments developed around the need for development controls. The building of workers' villages by their enlightened owners at Saltaire, Yorkshire 1853; Bournville, Birmingham 1878 and Port Sunlight, Merseyside 1887, demonstrated the benefits of planned development, but it would be some time before this approach became the norm.

The Garden City Movement (1898), initiated by Sir Ebenezer Howard (1850–1928), was intended to provide a framework for planned and self-contained communities surrounded by Green Belts containing proportionate areas of dwelling, industry and agriculture. His intention was that a garden city would be self-sufficient and when it reached full population (then thought to be 32,000 people) another garden city would be developed nearby. Howard founded the Garden Cities Association, later to become the Town and Country Planning Association, which created the first garden city in Letchworth, Hertfordshire (1899). The design of Letchworth emerged from a competition in 1904 won by Raymond Unwin (1863–1940) and Barry Parker (1867–1947). Welwyn Garden City, Hertfordshire (1919) was the next such development although it did not become self-sustaining as it was situated only 20 miles from London.

The Planning Acts of the early twentieth century were intended to improve the quality of development and the amenity of those affected whilst at the same time maintaining the ability for landowners to secure financial benefit. The Housing and Town Planning Acts of 1909 introduced the concept of planning schemes which could be prepared for any land in course of development. This was to ensure proper sanitary conditions and the convenient use of land. Under the Housing and Town Planning Act of 1919 planning schemes became compulsory where the population was above 20,000. The Town and Country Planning Act of 1932 extended the concept to rural areas, but preparation of schemes was not compulsory. The Barlow Report of 1940 debated the distribution of industry and population as the basis for a future planning policy and was a significant influence on the future acceptability of a planning system.

There are strong parallels between the development of planning and the evolution of controls on historic buildings and monuments because many of the issues are interrelated. Key to understanding was the recognition that the protection of buildings and landscapes and the countryside was far too important to be left to market forces, but this was not a universally held view. As with the debates on town and country planning, questions related to the preservation of buildings and monuments were frequently focused on whether or not the state should have any jurisdiction over property in private ownership.

The beginning of a formal legal system for the protection of historic buildings can be traced back to the Ancient Monuments Act of 1882. Towards the end of the nineteenth century, Sir John Lubbock (1834–1913), MP for Maidstone, who had wide-ranging interests including archaeology and biological science and was also a trustee of the British Museum, had sought to introduce legislation to protect ancient monuments. His Bill was rejected on a number of occasions but finally became law in 1882 in a truncated and amended form. The law covered only historic monuments and it would be some time before legal controls were introduced for historic buildings.

Minor improvements were introduced with the Ancient Monuments Protection Act of 1900, the Ancient Monuments Protection Act of 1910 and the Ancient Monuments Consolidation and Amendment Act of 1913. A further Ancient Monuments Act of 1931 introduced increased powers and, during the passage of this Act, there were further representations in Parliament that buildings should be included for protection but this was rejected.

The Ancient Monuments Consolidation and Amendment Act of 1913 established the Ancient Monuments Board with Inspectors and Commissioners of Works who were required to prepare lists of monuments, the preservation of which was of national importance. The Town and Country Planning Act (1932) gave powers to local authorities to make preservation orders for buildings of special architectural or historic interest, each order to be approved by the Minister who had to consider representations from those involved. The problem was that there was no effective mechanism for identifying 'architectural or historic interest', and it was not until 1945, following the report of the Listing Advisory Committee, that a formal definition of 'architectural or historic interest' was determined. This Committee, under the direction of Sir Eric Maclagan (1879–1951), established the concept of listing buildings in categories as Grade I, II and III with brief definitions to define their selection.

The Town and Country Planning Act of 1944 was essentially concerned with post-war reconstruction but nevertheless it empowered the Minister of Town and Country Planning to prepare lists of buildings of special architectural or historic interest for the guidance of local authorities. The Minister was required to consult expert opinion, hence the establishment of the 1945 Listing Advisory Committee.

The Planning Acts of the first half of the twentieth century were limited in their effectiveness but the situation changed dramatically following World War II. In 1945 the problems facing the country were immense and it was recognised that formal structures needed to be put in place to ensure that development was undertaken on the basis of clearly identified priorities. Housing, employment, education and health were to be provided within a proper framework: the 1947 Town and Country Planning Act.

In moving the second reading of the Bill in January 1947 the then Minister of Town and Country Planning, Lewis Silkin (1889–1972), described it as the most comprehensive and far-reaching planning measure which had ever been placed before the House. He went on to say that the objectives of town and country planning were being increasingly understood and accepted. Primarily, the purpose of the Act was to secure a proper balance between the competing demands for land so that all land in the country would be used in the best interests of the whole population. He recognised that there was heavy pressure on a limited supply of land and that it was inevitable that more and more land would be brought into development.

The need for a high level of agricultural production and the safeguarding of mineral resources was also recognised. Significantly, particular mention was made of the necessity to safeguard the beauty of the countryside and coastline 'especially now that holidays with pay will enable more people to enjoy them, and because we must develop the tourist industry as a source of foreign exchange'.[1] There were many contributors to the debate during the second reading, though much of the time was spent in seeking to determine how planning controls would impact on land values. This once again highlights the conflicts that emerge involving ownership, development and profit. The Town and Country Planning Act of 1947 was nevertheless the beginning of an effective planning system of which protection of the countryside was an integral part, and where the beginnings of a proper system for the conservation of historic monuments and buildings can be seen. The 1947 Act repeated the requirement for lists of historic buildings to be provided, but this time the Minister was not simply empowered to prepare lists; it was his express duty to do so.

The three categories of listed buildings defined in 1945 were:

Grade I – buildings of such importance that their destruction should in no case be allowed.
Grade II – buildings whose preservation should be regarded as a matter of national interest and destruction or alteration should not be undertaken without compelling reasons.
Grade III – buildings of architectural or historic interest, which do not rise to the degree properly described as special. Grade III buildings were placed in the supplementary list and were not afforded legal protection.

This formed the basis of the selection system that has survived in a modified and expanded form until today.

To understand how conservation and planning legislation slowly became accepted by Parliament and the public we need to look back to the nineteenth century. This was a time of profound change, with many of the changes seen as threats to the well-being of society, the care and protection of historic buildings and the wider countryside. John Ruskin (1819–99) was a key figure and was influential in inspiring much future conservation legislation. He had been influenced by the work of the ecclesiastical restoration movement and developed a strong dislike of such activity. His description of restoration clearly sets out his view.

> The most total destruction which a building can suffer: a destruction out of which no remnants can be gathered: a destruction accompanied with false description of the thing destroyed. Do not let us deceive ourselves in this important matter; it is impossible, as impossible as to raise the dead, to restore anything that has ever been great or beautiful in architecture . . . Do not let us talk then of restoration. The thing is a lie from beginning to end.[2]

Ruskin followed up his writing and campaigning by seeking to initiate a practical approach for the preservation of buildings and this initiative led to the formation of the Society for the Protection of Ancient Buildings (SPAB) in 1878. He was joined in his endeavours by William Morris (1834–96), who became the Society's first secretary. The SPAB approach to the repair of historic buildings has over time had a profound effect on the process and it remains influential today. The architect William Weir (1865–1950) was one of many followers of SPAB philosophy and was frequently recommended by the Society as the right man for the job. He worked very closely with SPAB and undertook a wide range of commissions including Tattershall Castle (1911–14) for Lord Curzon of Kedleston (1859–1925). Weir also directed the restoration of Dartington Hall, Devon from 1931–38. Although the most visible long-term legacy of this project was saving the Great Hall, a key purpose of the original exercise was to improve local farming practices and the plight of agricultural workers.

The nineteenth century was also a time of significant social reform and Octavia Hill (1838–1912), co-founder of the National Trust (1894) was a highly influential figure, described as a conservationist, artist, social reformer, writer and teacher. She was the driving force and treasurer of the influential Kyrie Society founded in 1877 by her sister and social reformer Miranda (1836–1910). The Society was formed to 'bring beauty home to the people' and was supported by William Morris and is seen as the forerunner of today's amenity societies and the Civic Trust. The National Trust grew out of the work of the Society's Open Spaces Committee, which was also instrumental in saving or creating many of London's recreational areas that would otherwise have been built over. There is also a direct link with Henrietta Barnett (1851–1936), another social reformer, instrumental in the creation of Hampstead Garden Suburb (1904).

It is not surprising, given the activity and discussions of the mid-to-late nineteenth century, that attention should be given to the protection of the nation's monuments and buildings and the desire to obtain access to the countryside.

We owe a considerable debt to these people for the efforts they made to save buildings and countryside at a time when there was no formal framework to achieve this. In the nineteenth century and in the early part of the twentieth century there was no effective mechanism for legal protection. In recognition of this, Sir John Lubbock purchased Avebury and Silbury Hill (Figure 26.1) in 1871 to provide protection against development. It is this same process of acquisition for long-term preservation that was the basis for the foundation of the National Trust, and the objective of the National Trust Act of 1907 was 'to promote

Figure 26.1 Silbury Hill was purchased by Sir John Lubbock (later Lord Avebury) in the 1870s together with part of the Avebury Estate 'to save it from harm'. Although it is now a scheduled ancient monument and English Heritage has undertaken extensive repair, it is still owned by his descendants (author's own).

the permanent preservation, for the benefit of the nation, of lands and tenements (including buildings) of beauty or natural interest'.

Patrick Abercrombie (1879–1957), one of the pioneers of the town planning profession, was largely responsible for bringing the concept of amenity into general use. He supported the setting up of the Council for the Preservation of Rural England in 1926 and was critical of the failure of local authorities to make proper use of the Town and Country Planning legislation of the early twentieth century. Much of the legislation of the time was ignored because it was discretionary.

In *England and the Octopus* (1928), the architect Clough Williams-Ellis (1883–1978) was also highly critical of the state of planning and development and was concerned that unchecked development would have catastrophic consequences. He recognised that development was necessary but demanded that it be well designed. He concluded that the condition and appearance of rural England depended on effective local government administration and that the administration would need a proper framework in which to operate.

In conjunction with campaigns for the preservation of the countryside against inappropriate development and its amenity value there were also efforts to provide public access to areas from which they had historically been excluded. Efforts to secure legally enforceable public rights of access to the countryside had begun in Parliament in 1884 when James Bryce MP (1838–1922) first introduced a right to roam Bill. The Bill failed to gather sufficient support and was rejected each time it was reintroduced. Long before the age of mass travel, populations from the industrial cities sought recreation in the countryside, even though access was often denied. The mass trespass of Kinder Scout, Derbyshire (1932) was only the beginning, as the prosecution of some of the 400 that had taken part generated a protest by some 10,000 prepared to do the same. The later enactment of the National Parks and Access to the Countryside Act (1948) was thus seen as the positive achievement of a national aspiration.

The evolution of building conservation legislation was also influenced by a series of controversial events. These usually took the form of demolitions or demolition proposals of important structures and the public protests that followed added weight to the arguments that historic buildings needed legal protection. In 1932 there was a proposal by the Crown Estate Commissioners to demolish Carlton House Terrace, London and although this was not carried out it illustrates the attitudes of the time. The demolition of Waterloo Bridge in 1934 went ahead in spite of combined opposition from the Royal Institute of British Architects, the Town Planning Institute, SPAB, Royal Academy and others. The significance of this event was the way in which the various interest groups came together in a joint protest and this set a pattern that would continue. The 1937 demolition of Adelphi Terrace, London (1774, by the brothers Adam) brought about the formation of the Georgian Group, but it was the widespread destruction of property from wartime bombing that focused national attention on losses to the country's architecture and history. The founding of the National Buildings Record in 1941 was a direct response to this. This list of campaigners and organisations is far from complete and there are many more that should be recognised for their achievements in saving our historic buildings for future generations to enjoy. If, however, we take the 1947 Town and Country Planning Act as the starting point for the evolution of a formal historic building control system, we can trace the way in which building conservation has evolved to the system that remains in force. The Gowers Report of 1950 outlined many of the problems that would face building owners in the immediate post-war period, and a direct consequence of this report was the Historic Buildings and Ancient Monuments Act (1953) which introduced the concept of state grant funding for buildings of outstanding interest.

The formation of the Civic Trust (1957) continued the encouragement for public involvement in conservation and town amenity, and the establishment of the Victorian Society (1958) was further demonstration of how specialist groups sought to influence the future. It is worth recording that the accolades given to the restoration of St Pancras Station (2007) and the accompanying rescue of the former Midland Grand Hotel (2011), London, would not have been possible without the efforts of the Victorian Society and its great campaigner Sir John Betjeman (1906–84).

Another major destructive event that enraged public opinion was the proposal to demolish Euston Arch, London (1962). This formed part of a plan to rebuild Euston Station and, although opposition and public protest was widespread, demolition was endorsed by the government of the time. Frequently historic buildings were threatened by proposals to construct or widen roads on the basis that there was a vital need to provide more space for the ever-increasing road traffic. On the other hand, the Local Authorities Historic Buildings Act (1962) allowed those authorities that wished to, to offer grants and loans to owners for the repair of listed buildings. Further destruction towards the end of the 1960s, including a substantial part of Eldon Square, Newcastle, demonstrated the need for more effective conservation based on a willingness to incorporate new and old.

The formation of the Preservation Policy Group (1970) by the then Ministry of Housing and Local Government focused attention on the potentially positive benefits of conservation. In the 1960s there were still many who believed that excessive conservation was an impediment to progress, and the creative links between new development and conservation had yet to be forged.

The protection of individual buildings is only one aspect of an effective conservation system. This was highlighted in 1965 when the Council for British Archaeology published its list of 324 historic towns in England and Wales, 51 of which were said to be of national importance. The 1967 Civic Amenities Act, which was a Private Members Bill, introduced by Duncan Sandys (1908–87) on behalf of the Civic Trust, introduced the concept of conservation areas for the first time. The 1968 Town and Country Planning Act introduced a number of detailed requirements including the need for listed building consent and was intended to encourage conservation activity. This can best be seen in the accompanying Circular 61/68 which provided further guidance. The Circular explained in detail how local authorities should approach conservation within the overall planning system and encouraged them to do so. Further legislation followed in 1971, 1972 and the 1974 Town and Country Amenities Act provided for further expansion of the conservation movement.

Nevertheless, there were still many plans for demolition including that for the complete destruction of Covent Garden, London and its surroundings (1974). This became another *cause célèbre* and was only prevented by the listing of a number of buildings in the area. The incentive to demolish Covent Garden was the decision to move the fruit and vegetable market across the river, thereby releasing the land for 'development'. At that stage, the idea of saving historic buildings by providing them with a new use had not been properly considered. Consequently the study of how best to encourage new uses was the focus of the 1979 Montague Report, which included a series of recommendations for the retention of redundant historic buildings with an emphasis on how they could be creatively re-used. Longleat House (Figure 26.2) is an example of how the creation of an innovative Safari Park generated sufficient income to maintain the house and estate intact.

The listing process that began in the early 1950s had proceeded relatively slowly and there were many omissions from the published lists. In the 1950s travelling to remote parts of the country was more difficult than it is today and inevitably a number of interesting buildings were lost. This was not, however, restricted to the rural areas because redevelopment and new opportunities were often the guiding force behind the demolition of interesting but unlisted buildings. Buildings were not only excluded from the list because they were unknown, but changing attitudes to the quality of architecture and a continuing evolution of the definition of architectural and historic interest meant that lists needed to be regularly reviewed. Once again a single event would be influential. The demolition of the 1930s Firestone Factory on the Great West Road (1981) when it was under consideration for listing, led to the then Secretary of State for the Environment, Michael Heseltine (1933–) instigating an accelerated three-year listing resurvey.

It may be assumed from this event that conservation legislation was achieving its aim, but this was not always the case. The introduction of conservation areas was intended to

Figure 26.2 Longleat House, now listed grade I and with a grade I Registered Park and Garden. This image was taken in the late 1960s when Longleat Safari Park was established as a way of generating sufficient income to maintain the estate. It was described as an innovative idea to safeguard the heritage for all to enjoy (author's own).

encourage more effective conservation policies but the legislation proved to be relatively ineffective. Extensive changes had taken place in many conservation areas and many of these changes fell outside of planning control. It had been stated in Circular 46/73 that the 'conservation of the historic environment should be the starting point for thought about the extent of redevelopment needs; and conservation of the character of cities should be the framework for planning both the scale and pace of urban change'. But this was by no means a universally accepted process.[3] Various improvements and amendments to the legislation followed in the 1980s and the publication of further government guidance continued to promote conservation as an integral part of the planning process.

It is often felt that central government is not best placed to encourage positive conservation and this was part of the reasoning behind the 1983 National Heritage Act which established the Historic Buildings and Monuments Commission for England – later known as English Heritage. Its remit was to:

> Secure the preservation of ancient monuments and historic buildings situated in England: to promote the preservation and enhancement of the character and appearance of conservation areas situated in England, and to promote the public enjoyment of, and advance their knowledge of, ancient monuments and historic buildings situated in England – and their preservation.

English Heritage has gradually taken a wider role within the legal framework and its research and technical publications are a major source of information for building owners and professionals alike.

Gardens are a major feature of the setting of many listed buildings, and although the Garden History Society was founded in 1965 it was only when English Heritage was established that a Register of Gardens of Special Historic Interest in England was compiled. Gardens are graded as for listed buildings, i.e. I, II* and II. The purpose of the Register of Parks and Gardens is not to preserve gardens in the sense of being unaltered but to prevent harm. It has further been recognised that, for example, a pattern of private gardens within a Conservation Area might be a feature of the area that it would be desirable to preserve or enhance. Alterations to parks and gardens generally do not require statutory consent unless they involve development, in which case planning permission will be required. Where, however, work affects a registered park or garden, permission is necessary and local planning authorities are required to consult the Garden History Society, a statutory consultee.

The 1990 Planning (Listed Buildings and Conservation Areas) Act, which is the basis for current controls, sits alongside the accompanying Town and Country Planning Acts. The 1990 Act consolidated all previous legislation and was followed by Planning Policy Guidance Note 15 – Planning and the Historic Environment, published in 1994. The note not only explained government policy but included guidance on the care and repair of historic buildings and on the measures that should be taken to protect their special interest. Later changes were formulated in the 2010 Planning Policy Statement 5 – Planning for the Historic Environment.

A key feature of PPS5 was its holistic approach to the historic environment. The term 'heritage assets' used in the guidance was intended to identify the various elements of the historic environment worthy of consideration in planning matters. This guide states that a 'heritage asset' holds meaning for society over and above its functional utility.

The aim of the policies within the PPS was to ensure the conservation of these assets for the benefit of this and future generations. This was to be accomplished by requiring that change to an asset was undertaken in ways that sustain and, where appropriate, enhance its heritage significance. The PPS required all applicants to provide a level of information proportionate to the significance of the asset and the potential impact upon that significance of the proposals. For example, for a substantial demolition it would be reasonable to expect the applicant to provide detailed information on the asset as a whole and a thorough explanation of the impact. An application for a minor alteration should only require a brief explanation and focus on establishing the significance of the heritage asset.

The 2010 PPS5 was, however, short lived and soon replaced by the National Planning Policy Framework (2012). At the heart of the NPPF is a presumption in favour of sustainable development which applies to both plan-making and determining planning applications. The Framework emphasises the need for the planning system to perform a number of roles:

- an economic role – contributing to building a strong, responsive and competitive economy by ensuring that sufficient land of the right type is available in the right places and at the right time to support growth and innovation; and by identifying and coordinating development requirements, including the provision of infrastructure
- a social role – supporting strong, vibrant and healthy communities by providing the supply of housing required to meet the needs of present and future generations; and by creating a high quality built environment with accessible local services that reflect the community's needs and support its health, social and cultural well-being
- an environmental role – contributing to protecting and enhancing our natural, built and historic environment; and, as part of this, helping to improve biodiversity, use natural resources prudently, minimise waste and pollution and mitigate and adapt to climate change including moving to a low carbon economy.

The Framework makes it clear that these roles are mutually dependent and should not be undertaken in isolation.

Section 11 of the NPPF on conserving and enhancing the natural environment emphasises that great weight should be given to conserving landscape and scenic beauty in National Parks, the Broads and Areas of Outstanding Natural Beauty, which have the highest status of protection in relation to landscape and scenic beauty. The conservation of wildlife and cultural heritage are important considerations in all these areas (Figure 26.3).

In addition, Section 12 covering conserving and enhancing the historic environment advises that local planning authorities should set out in their Local Plan a positive strategy for the conservation and enjoyment of the historic environment, including heritage assets most at risk through neglect, decay or other threats. Local authorities should also recognise that heritage assets are an irreplaceable resource and seek to conserve them in a manner appropriate to their significance. In developing this strategy local planning authorities should

Figure 26.3 The National Trust's Neptune Coastline Campaign, set up in 1965, has secured the protection of, and access to, many hundreds of miles of our finest coastlines – this section is the South West Coast Path between Seaton and Sidmouth, Devon (author's own).

take into account: the desirability of sustaining and enhancing the significance of heritage assets and putting them to viable uses consistent with their conservation, recognising the wider social, cultural, economic and environmental benefits that conservation of the historic environment can bring.

Although we have come a long way from the first legal protection of a small number of historic monuments there is still an essential debate to be had around how to achieve truly sustainable development. This quotation from the foreword of the 2010 Land Use Futures report – *Making the most of land in the 21st century* by Professor John Beddington (1945–), Chief Scientific Adviser to HM Government and Head of the Government Office for Science, asserts:

> Together with our human capital, land is possibly the UK's greatest asset. It provides the basic services that we need to prosper and flourish, the environment in which we all work and live our lives, and it forms the historical and cultural bedrock of the country. It is difficult to imagine a national asset that affects us all so profoundly.[4]

This report takes a broad and over-arching view of future land use in the UK for the next 50 years. It proposes that there is a strong case for the advancement of a strategic approach to guide incremental land use changes, incentivise sustainable behaviour and unlock value from land. The report documents the hitherto haphazard approach to land use and challenges our failure to make intelligent and informed decisions. It is within this context that the appreciation and enjoyment of landscape and the countryside and the creative use of our historic environment should be assessed. We may have come a long way but there is still much to do.

Further reading

Anson, B. (1981) *I'll fight you for it! Behind the Struggle for Covent Garden 1966–74*, Cape.
Britain's Historic Buildings: A Policy for their Future Use (1979), British Tourist Authority, 'The Montague Report'.
Cullingworth, B. and Nadin, V. (2006) *Town and Country Planning in the UK*, 14th edition, Routledge.
Delafons, J. (1997) *Politics and Preservation*, E & FN Spon.
Fawcett, J. (ed.) (1974) *The Future of the Past: Attitudes to Conservation 1174–1974*, Thames and Hudson.
Godfrey, W.H. (1944) *Our Building Inheritance*, Faber and Faber.
Hunter, M. (ed.) (1996) *Preserving the Past*, Alan Sutton Publishing Ltd.
Report of the Working Party – Historic Buildings Council / British Tourist Authority.
Williams-Ellis, C. (1928) *England and The Octopus*, facsimile reprint (1996) CPRE.

Endnotes

1. Hansard Volume 432 cc 947–1075. Town and country Planning Bill, Second Reading, House of Commons debate 29 January 1947.
2. John Ruskin, *The Seven Lamps of Architecture* (1949), 'The Lamp of Memory'.
3. Conservation and Preservation – Local Government Act 1972, Department of the Environment Circular 46/73.
4. *Foresight Land Use Futures Project 2010*, Final Project Report, The Government Office for Science, London.

27 Historic parks and gardens: the planning system and other conservation tools

Jonathan Lovie
Conservation and landscape consultant, Devon, England

Unlike other nationally designated elements of the historic environment such as listed buildings or scheduled monuments and archaeology, nationally designated historic designed landscapes do not enjoy any statutory protection arising from the fact of their designation. This fact, which sometimes comes as something of a surprise, means that it is essential when trying to fight proposals for inappropriate or damaging change affecting a designed landscape, to make use of as many aspects of the planning and designation systems in tandem to avoid unnecessary damage. Similarly, when attempting to secure a degree of protection for a designed landscape it is important to understand which tools will best deliver the desired objective.

This chapter aims to set out, as succinctly as possible, the relevant aspects of the designation and planning systems and to highlight where and how these dovetail in order to provide a degree of protection for designed landscapes. It is not intended to offer a detailed analysis of the legal aspects of designation or planning; neither will extensive sections of the National Planning Policy Framework (NPPF, 2012) be quoted; instead, relevant clauses will be highlighted where appropriate.

The National Planning context for the conservation of designed landscapes

In 2012 the Government published a new core planning document, the National Planning Policy Framework (NPPF) to replace earlier Planning Policy Guidance Notes (PPGs) and Planning Policy Statements (PPSs) with a single, clearer statement of planning guidance and objectives.

The NPPF confirms the plan-led system of planning in England, with Government providing the over-arching strategic framework and local planning authorities at district and county levels drawing up local plans. Local plans are required to conform in their objectives to those of the NPPF and the central underlying principle of the planning system is to deliver 'sustainable development'.

Use of the phrase 'sustainable development' set alarm bells clanging during the consultation process on the draft NPPF. Sustainability was perceived to be a cloak for either exclusively economically driven development, or for an undue emphasis on 'green' development. In fact the final version of the NPPF makes clear that sustainability is to be

Gardens & Landscapes in Historic Building Conservation, First Edition. Edited by Marion Harney.
© 2014 John Wiley & Sons, Ltd. Published 2014 by John Wiley & Sons, Ltd.

understood in much broader terms. Following United Nations Resolution 42/187, sustainability is to be understood as 'meeting the needs of the present without compromising the ability of future generations to meet their own needs'. This understanding of sustainability clearly allows – indeed requires – a conservation-based approach to the historic environment in order to allow future generations to meet their emotional and spiritual needs, and adequately to understand their past. This philosophical approach is made very clear in Section 12 of the NPPF which deals with the historic environment, and particularly in paragraph 126:

> Local planning authorities should set out in their local plan a positive strategy for the conservation and enjoyment of the historic environment, including heritage assets most at risk through neglect, decay or other threats. In doing so, they should recognise that heritage assets are an irreplaceable resource and conserve them in a manner appropriate to their significance. In developing this strategy, local planning authorities should take into account:
>
> - The desirability of sustaining and enhancing the significance of heritage assets and putting them to viable uses consistent with their conservation
> - The wider social, cultural, economic and environmental benefits that conservation of the historic environment can bring
> - The desirability of new development making a positive contribution to local character and distinctiveness
> - Opportunities to draw on the contribution made by the historic environment to the character of a place.

The NPPF is unequivocal in its understanding that 'heritage assets are irreplaceable', and that any harm or loss requires clear and convincing justification. Great weight should be given to the conservation of heritage assets when considering the impact of proposed development (para 132):

> Substantial harm to or loss of a grade II listed building, park or garden should be exceptional. Substantial harm to or loss of designated heritage assets of the highest significance, notably scheduled monuments, protected wreck sites, battlefields, Grade I and II* listed buildings, Grade I and II* registered parks and gardens, and World Heritage Sites, should be wholly exceptional.

As part of the planning process, the NPPF places, for the first time, a two-fold requirement on both applicant and planning authority to demonstrate a clear understanding of the significance of any heritage asset affected by the development proposal:

> 128. In determining applications, local planning authorities should require an applicant to describe the significance of any heritage assets affected, including any contribution made by their setting.
>
> 129. Local planning authorities should identify and assess the particular significance of any heritage asset that may be affected by a proposal (including by development affecting the setting of a heritage asset) taking account of the available evidence and any necessary expertise.

The concept of 'significance' is key to the NPPF and its approach to the historic environment. On the one hand it is essential to understand how the particular heritage asset or designed landscape has evolved over time, its key components and wider cultural context; on the other hand it is vital to understand the way in which the various elements of the historic environment interrelate, overlap and, through this interaction, create an increased cumulative level of significance. Information, including accurate research and analysis, is essential to this process and it is here that local and national amenity societies, professionals and interested amateurs can all play an important role in ensuring that the planning system works to deliver a sustainable future (see also chapter 12 of this volume).

One objective measure of 'significance' can be found through the various national and local heritage designations, and other designations within the planning system. These are critical 'tools' in the kit of anyone wishing to use the planning system to secure the conservation of precious historic designed landscapes.

National designation for the historic environment

Since the late nineteenth century there has been recognition that certain elements of our heritage are of national importance, and merit legal protection or identification in order that they can be conserved. Starting with archaeology and monuments which were first 'scheduled' in 1882, designation has broadened out to encompass buildings of special architectural or historic interest in 1947, and more recently, in the 1980s, historic designed landscapes and historic battlefields. Each national designation varies in its scope and in the statutory controls, if any, which flow from it. Some may seem rather remote from the sphere of designed landscapes but in fact each national designation has something to offer for the conservation of designed landscapes.

Historic environment designations are an objective and agreed form of quantifying significance: designation itself indicates that a place or structure is of 'more than average' significance; where the designation is broken down into grades, it can be understood that those assets designated at Grade I or Grade II* are of exceptional national significance.

Although each element of the historic environment retains its individual form of designation, all historic designations are now brought together in the National Heritage List for England, which is available online at the English Heritage website.[1]

Listed buildings

Listed buildings comprise the largest number of nationally designated heritage assets, and are structures of 'special architectural or historic interest'. Listed buildings enjoy statutory protection and any proposal for change will require consent from the local authority's conservation officer (Grade II listed structures) or English Heritage (Grade I and II* listed structures). Proposals for change will require careful justification.

Statutory protection applies to the structure itself; objects fixed to the structure (including, for example, certain fixtures inside the building) and objects or structures lying within the curtilage of the structure prior to 1947, which might include garden walls, steps, fountains and ornaments. The setting of the listed building is therefore also protected by the designation from adverse change. This latter point is particularly important when assessing the likely impact of change on a designed landscape associated with the listed building. Some listed buildings were designed specifically to play an ornamental role in a designed landscape, such as the Dairy at Endsleigh, Devon, designed by Jeffry Wyatville (Figure 27.1).

In many cases, probably the vast majority of cases, a designed landscape will have a listed structure as its focal point. Often this will be a house or other residential structure, for which the landscape is the consciously designed setting. There is now a much greater appreciation among planners and other professionals, in part prompted by the underlying philosophy of the National Planning Policy Framework, that heritage assets do not exist in isolation, and that the historic development and significance of one asset is often intimately linked to another related asset. The cumulative significance of these assets is often greater than the significance of any one of the individual elements.

In addition to a listed focal structure, designed landscapes often contain other structures which are individually listed in their own right. These may owe their existence and design to their function in relation to the overall landscape design, and could range from relatively small structures such as garden ornaments, horticultural structures such as glasshouses or fruit rooms, to much larger landscape structures such as temples, belvederes, triumphal arches or follies. There are even examples of nineteenth-century rock gardens such as those at Endsleigh, Devon (Figure 27.2), and Pencarrow, Cornwall, which are listed structures in their own right. Each of these listed structures and its setting also enjoys its own statutory protection.

Clearly, where a designed landscape contains a number of individually listed structures in addition to a principal or focal listed structure, the combined heritage asset comprising

Figure 27.1 Jeffry Wyatville's Dairy at Endsleigh, Devon, is an early nineteenth-century listed building designed as an ornamental structure in the landscape created for the Duke of Bedford by Humphry Repton (author's own).

Figure 27.2 Listed buildings and structures can take a wide variety of forms, from country houses to rock gardens. This example is the Grade I listed early nineteenth-century rock garden in the Grade I registered landscape at Endsleigh, Devon (author's own).

designed landscape and listed structures must be considered to be of greater significance in heritage and planning terms than any of the designed assets in isolation.

Scheduled Ancient Monuments

Ancient Monuments are popularly thought of as 'ruins and remains', or 'above ground' archaeology such as standing stones or monastic ruins; however, the designation often covers 'below ground' archaeology, and, in certain cases, structures – which may also be designated as listed buildings. The earliest of the national heritage designations, scheduling, confers the highest degree of statutory protection for the structure, ruin or remain itself.

While Iron Age remains may seem totally removed from designed landscapes, scheduled monuments and ornamental landscapes coincide surprisingly often. There are relatively obvious examples of scheduled sites which include garden archaeology, such as the sixteenth-century garden at Kenilworth Castle in Warwickshire or the garden remains at Holdenby, Northamptonshire; in other cases the landscape design makes specific reference to or use of a scheduled monument as a landscape feature or eye-catcher outside the landscape. Examples of this use of scheduled monuments as a feature within a later landscape design can be found at Duncombe Park, North Yorkshire where the scheduled remains of Hemsley Castle act as an eye-catcher, and at the related Rievaulx Terrace where the ruins of the medieval Rievaulx Abbey similarly act as a focal point of the landscape design. On a much smaller scale, at Pencarrow, near Bodmin in Cornwall, Sir William Molesworth (1810–55) designed his early nineteenth-century drive to pass through what is today the scheduled earthwork known as Pencarrow Rounds in order to create a picturesque incident on the approach to the house (Figure 27.3).

The scheduled nature of any heritage asset within a designed landscape would be an important factor to be considered when any proposal for change in its vicinity was under consideration, and should be highlighted in any response to a planning application.

Figure 27.3 Sir William Molesworth's early nineteenth-century drive at Pencarrow, Cornwall, passes through Pencarrow Rounds, a set of Iron Age circular earth works. Now a scheduled ancient monument, the earthworks were appropriated by Sir William as a picturesque incident on the approach to the house, and are now, in addition to being an important archaeological survival, a key element of the design of this Grade II* registered landscape (author's own).

Registered Battlefields

Inclusion of a battlefield site on the Register of Historic Battlefields does not entail any additional statutory control over the site; however, the fact of a site's inclusion is an indication of its special historic significance in the national context and the relevant planning authorities must take this significance into account when considering any proposed change affecting that site or its setting.

Battlefields may seem even more remote from historic designed landscapes than scheduled ancient monuments. However, there are a very few examples of designed landscapes which are linked to a battlefield. Perhaps the best example is the mid-eighteenth century landscape created by Sanderson Miller (1716–80) at Radway Grange, Warwickshire which overlooks the site of and forms part of the setting for the Civil War engagement at Edge Hill. Miller was keenly aware of the association of his estate with the Battle of Edge Hill and laid out his walks on the escarpment to take advantage of the views of the battlefield and built his folly tower on the site traditionally held to be that on which the Royal standard was raised prior to the Battle.

Any proposal for change affecting the registered battlefield is therefore likely to affect the setting of the designed landscape of Radway Grange; while conversely any proposal for change affecting Radway Grange is likely to affect the setting of the Registered Battlefield.

Registered Parks and Gardens

Like the Register of Historic Battlefields, inclusion of a site on the Register of Parks and Gardens of Special Historic Interest in England does not entail any additional statutory control over the site; but its inclusion remains a material consideration in the planning process.

The Register of Parks and Gardens was first established by English Heritage in the 1980s, and now comprises over 1,600 sites. These registered landscapes include not just the greatest examples of the landscape genre such as Stowe in Buckinghamshire, Stourhead in Wiltshire, or Blenheim in Oxfordshire; but also much smaller gardens such as Hidcote in Gloucestershire or Great Dixter in Sussex. There are also examples of public parks, cemeteries and institutional landscapes associated with colleges, hospitals and asylums included on the register.

Although inclusion on the register does not of itself provide any additional statutory protection for the site or its setting, the relevant local planning authority should include in its local plan appropriate policies to safeguard registered sites and their settings (as well as other designated heritage assets) from inappropriate development which would adversely affect the special historic interest and character of the designated site. Such policies should be used to support any representation with regard to proposed development or change affecting a registered landscape.

Entries for sites included on the Register of Parks and Gardens can be found on the National Heritage List for England. Each entry is supported by a written description which sets out the special historic significance of the site or reason for its national designation; and a map which defines the extent of the area covered by the designation. Both are useful when considering proposals for change: the written description highlights those areas of significance to which the planning authority should pay particular attention when considering proposals affecting the registered landscape and the map will indicate likely pressure points such as adjacent urban development or key designed views and vistas from within the designed landscape to external objects, or conversely views into the designed landscape or structures within it from external points. Where these features form part of the original design, whether mentioned in the register text or not, they contribute to its special historic significance and should be safeguarded in the planning process.

Other useful national designations

World Heritage Sites Inscribed by the United Nations Educational, Scientific and Cultural Organisation (UNESCO) on the advice of the International Council on Monuments and Sites (ICOMOS) and its specialist advisory panels in the United Kingdom, World Heritage Sites encompass a wide variety of types of site, including both built environments which may include a number of nationally and locally significant designed landscapes, such as the Bath World Heritage Site; or they may relate to a single designed landscape in its own right, such as the Fountains Abbey and Studley Royal World Heritage Site. The NPPF affords World Heritage Sites in England the same level of protection from inappropriate change as Grade I and Grade II* listed buildings, registered parks and gardens and scheduled monuments. They should therefore be considered to be assets of the highest significance.

National Parks These nationally protected extensive areas of countryside are designated under the relevant legislation in order to protect natural beauty, wildlife and cultural heritage. Each national park functions as its own planning authority, with control over development affecting heritage assets and with local plan policies setting out development and conservation priorities. Given their extensive nature, many national parks will include designed landscapes of national and local significance. The recent South Downs National Park, for example, includes within its boundary the Grade I registered landscape at Petworth, Sussex; and the Dartmoor National Park includes the Grade II* landscape at Castle Drogo, Devon (Figure 27.4).

Areas of Outstanding Natural Beauty (AONB) AONBs are also nationally protected areas of high scenic value and quality but, unlike national parks, do not function as planning authorities. Instead, AONBs have a management board to care for them, made up of representatives from the relevant local authorities and local communities. Local plan policies specific to an AONB should seek to preserve special landscape features and natural beauty; designed landscapes can clearly make a significant positive contribution to the character of an AONB and should be expected to be a 'landscape feature' worthy of conservation and preservation from adverse change.

Figure 27.4 Castle Drogo, Devon, and its associated Grade II* registered landscape lie within the Dartmoor National Park, which functions as the relevant local planning authority (author's own).

Locally designated designed landscapes

It is tempting to assume that the Register of Parks and Gardens is a complete document recording all nationally significant designed landscapes. It is not. There are a significant number of designed landscapes which have been identified through the English Heritage Register Review Programme (early 1990s) as being of potential interest for national designation, but which have not, to date, been formally assessed. Realistically, given the present state of resources and public finances, such a comprehensive review is unlikely to happen in the near future, and additions to the register are likely to arise as the result of 'fire fighting', when a site is the subject of inappropriate development pressure.

This means, in many cases, that there may be 30 or more sites per county which are considered to be of potentially national significance, but which have not been nationally designated. In these circumstances it is particularly important that interested bodies such as County Gardens Trusts take the initiative and ensure that each local authority includes in its local plan a list of locally significant designed landscapes. The National Planning Policy Framework supports the inclusion of lists of locally designated heritage assets, including designed landscapes, in the local plan. Such sites may be ones which, ultimately, fulfil the criteria for national designation; or they may be ones which, although falling just short of the standard required for national designation, nonetheless make an important contribution to the character and distinctiveness of their locality.

When proposing sites for inclusion on local lists, it is important that robust research is available to justify designation. The English Heritage Register of Parks and Gardens offers a good model which those researching locally significant designed landscapes can follow in order to summarise their findings, as well as a format which will be familiar to planners and other professionals and which allows the significance of the landscape to be readily understood. Similarly, the extent of the area proposed for local designation should be defined on an agreed map base.

Other useful local designations

Local listing is an important way in which interested groups and individuals can become engaged in the planning system in order to conserve, and where appropriate, enhance their local environment. Other locally determined and conferred designations can also be very helpful in securing the sympathetic conservation of historic designed landscapes, while at the same time engaging the support of the community.

Tree Preservation Orders (TPOs) At first sight TPOs might seem an entirely beneficial locally imposed designation. An order can be made to protect an individual specimen tree which may make an important contribution to the character and amenity of a particular area; or a 'blanket' order may be made to protect a block of trees or woodland which similarly may make a significant contribution to the character of its wider setting. In both cases the tree or trees may form part of a designed landscape and the controls flowing from the TPO, which include the requirement for prior consent for works to the trees in question, may be helpful in securing the conservation of the designed landscape.

However, there can be problems with TPOs, especially when a blanket order is applied. It is possible, for example, that a block of scrubby woodland has developed within a designed landscape through a lack of appropriate management rather than as a part of the original design. Indeed, the existence of the trees may significantly detract from the designed intention of the landscape by blocking key views or damaging important structural elements. The imposition of a blanket TPO on the basis, all too frequently encountered, that 'every tree is intrinsically good and valuable' will obviously prevent appropriate conservation management of the designed landscape, and can lead to long-term damage and even loss of the designed landscape. An example of a deleterious effect of a blanket TPO is shown in Figure 27.5, of a road at Durlston Castle, near Swanage.

Figure 27.5 Durlston Castle, near Swanage in Dorset, is a Grade II registered landscape comprising late nineteenth-century public walks and pleasure grounds laid out along the coastline. This part of the site, the Isle of Wight Road, was intended to provide dramatic coastal and maritime views. However, imposition of a blanket TPO has inhibited the proper management of vegetation along the path, resulting in the loss of the historic designed views (author's own).

As with most locally applied designations, the effectiveness of a TPO will depend upon the resources and willingness of the local authority properly to police and manage the system.

Conservation areas   Undoubtedly the most beneficial local designation, and arguably the designation (national or local) which offers the greatest protection to designed landscapes, is Conservation area designation.

Conservation areas are designated by the local authority and comprise localities with 'special architectural or historic interest' the character of which it is desirable to conserve, and where appropriate, enhance. Within a conservation area, demolition of buildings or structural features such as garden walls cannot take place without the prior consent of the planning authority (Conservation Area Consent), and works to trees, defined for this purpose as a plant with a trunk diameter of 75mm at a height of 1m above the ground (so often encompassing larger shrubs and structural planting as well as what would normally be considered to be a 'tree') similarly require the prior approval of the planning authority. Clearly both controls can be very helpful in preventing adverse change to a designed landscape within a conservation area. But more importantly, perhaps, the very existence of a designed landscape can be the key reason for the designation of a conservation area in the first place.

Local authorities are expected periodically to review their conservation areas to ensure that their special characteristics are adequately documented and that their boundaries are correct. This gives interested bodies, such as gardens trusts, as well as individuals, the opportunity to comment and suggest amendments such as the inclusion of an adjacent, but relevant, area of designed open space within the conservation area. A review might also be a trigger for the local authority to impose an Article 4(2) Direction on all or part of a conservation area in order to remove 'permitted development rights' covering changes to windows, doors, paint colour or potentially highly detrimental changes such as paving over front gardens to provide private off-road parking.

Figure 27.6 Parade Gardens, Bath, illustrates the fact that historic environment designations tend to overlap and attain a cumulative significance. This Grade II designed landscape lies within the Bath Spa Conservation Area and the Bath World Heritage Site. It contains several listed structures and forms the setting to several further listed buildings (author's own).

The majority of conservation areas are to be found in an urban context. Here, designed landscapes such as public parks, walks or gardens can be the focal point of an historic residential development, such as a group of Regency or Victorian villas around a public garden or park. Very often the surrounding built heritage will itself be the subject of national designation or listing; while the designed landscape may be nationally or locally designated. Thus a series of local and national designations will overlap, each contributing a different level of protection and all helping to highlight the overall historic and aesthetic significance of the locality. In Bath, for example, Sydney Gardens is a Grade II registered landscape which contains several listed structures, including the Grade I listed Holburne Museum, and forms the focal open space at the heart of a very significant eighteenth-century residential development which is itself almost entirely Grade I listed. All these heritage assets lie within, and make a significant contribution to, the Bath Spa Conservation Area (Figure 27.6).

However, conservation areas can also be found in a rural context, and can also be linked to designed landscapes. An estate village such as Milton Abbas, Dorset, is a good example of a rural conservation area which adjoins the Grade II* registered landscape of Milton Abbey. The picturesque thatched cottages forming the model village are, in fact, an integral part of the aesthetic of the eighteenth-century landscape design and clearly each contributes to the significance of the other, and the conservation of each is essential to the ongoing significance of the other (Figure 27.7).

Conclusion

Conservation area designation demonstrates, perhaps better than any other, the interrelated nature of the historic environment and the way in which, inevitably, national and local designations and other conservation controls overlap. It fits particularly well with the philosophy underpinning the National Planning Policy Framework, which prompts those involved in planning decisions to take a more rounded view of the historic environment in order to deliver a more locally accountable and sustainable (in the broadest sense) and community-responsive system for the future.

Figure 27.7 The eighteenth-century 'model' village of Milton Abbas, Dorset, was designed by Lancelot 'Capability' Brown, perhaps with help from Sir William Chambers, as part of the designed landscape of Milton Abbey. The village street forms a picturesque incident in the landscape, and is a key designed view from Brown's south drive. Today most of the buildings in the village are listed, and the village is a conservation area; in addition, it forms the setting of the Grade II* registered landscape of Milton Abbey (author's own).

Endnote

1. See www.english-heritage.org.uk/professional/protection/process/national-heritage-list-for-england

28 The role of the Heritage Lottery Fund in the conservation of historic gardens and designed landscapes

Drew Bennellick
Head of Landscape and Natural Heritage UK, Heritage Lottery Fund, London, UK

It was the National Lottery Act of 1993 that established the Heritage Lottery Fund (HLF) as a body to distribute funds raised by the National Lottery for good causes. In the beginning HLF was a small organisation with around 15 staff distributing a budget of about £9 million per annum. Now it is an organisation of just over 200 staff distributing an annual budget of around £375 million across the UK. In 2012 HLF announced it had distributed over £5 billion to more than 30,000 heritage projects covering everything from museums to places of worship, from historic buildings to natural heritage, from heritage skills and training to public parks and historic gardens. Whilst parks and gardens are only one area of HLF investment, it is estimated that awards of in excess of £750 million have been made to gardens and public parks. The list of designed landscapes receiving HLF support over the years provides an impressive roll-call including virtually every significant historic public park in the UK and many of our most treasured designed landscapes such as gardens, cemeteries, seaside promenades, squares and post-war landscapes.

Perhaps one of the greatest impacts of HLF on the lives of British people has been the investment in public parks. When HLF began, in 1993, public parks were in a parlous state. Years of underinvestment, crumbling Victorian infrastructure and a lack of realisation of their wider values meant many parks were unsafe, unkempt and lacking modern facilities. A series of reports in the early 1990s including the seminal publication *Park Life: Urban Parks and Social Renewal*, published by Comedia and Demos, led HLF's Trustees to realise that investing in public parks offered a tremendous opportunity to reverse years of decline. The *Park Life* report revealed that some 40% of people were using parks regularly, so investing in these truly significant public spaces could provide an opportunity to use lottery money to provide maximum public benefit whilst turning public liabilities from the past into assets for the future.

The Urban Parks Programme/Parks for People

In 1996 HLF launched the Urban Parks Programme which still runs today under the new name Parks for People. Since the first park grants were awarded in 1997, over £640 million has been invested in public parks by HLF. In addition, the huge potential to deliver wider community benefits resulted in Big Lottery joining HLF in 2006 to distribute grants for parks

Figure 28.1 The Grade 1 listed restored Iguanodons at Crystal Palace Park, London restored as part of the restoration of the southern area of the Grade 11* park in 2002. (Reproduced by permission of the Heritage Lottery Fund.)

in England. Now over 700 public parks have benefited from significant investment which in all cases has been matched with investment from local authorities or managing trusts raised from their own resources as well as contributions of voluntary labour by local groups and increased funding to ensure that the newly restored parks are maintained.

In May 2001, to establish the need for investment in historic public parks, a study was funded by HLF, English Heritage, the Countryside Agency and the Department of Environment, Transport and the Regions. The *Public Parks Assessment*, undertaken by the Urban Parks Forum (now GreenSpace), showed that historic parks were suffering more than other recreational open spaces. Data returned from over 85% of local authorities showed that around 75% of parks had lost historic features and that 25% had lost basic facilities such as toilets and cafés. The study confirmed the need for HLF to focus on the restoration of historic public parks, the conservation of their historic features and layout, and the provision of essential facilities to make visits enjoyable and educational (see Figure 28.1).

The study also showed the need to fund the re-creation of historic features where evidence showed they had once existed and where they were considered to be fundamental to reading and understanding the landscape design. This led to HLF funding the complete re-creation of features where they formed a focal point of a park, such as the construction of a new bandstand at Roberts Park in Bradford (Figure 28.2), or the replacement of perimeter railings previously removed to help the war effort as at Russell Square in London.

Most spectacularly, HLF funding has allowed the creation of features that were part of an original design proposal but were not implemented at the time, often due to cost constraints. At Victoria Park in the London Borough of Tower Hamlets, an HLF grant has helped to enhance access around the West Lake by funding the construction of the Chinese-style Pennethorne Bridge following the original designs. This new bridge also permits access to the marvellous re-construction of the Chinese Pagoda which sat on an island in the park's West Lake from its opening in 1847 until it was pulled down in the 1950s following war damage. The new pagoda is a high-quality modern replica based on the original pagoda, which was sold to the park for £110 following its starring role in the Chinese Exhibition in Hyde Park (1841–43). The new pagoda is crucial to appreciating the design of the west end of the park, where it acts as an eye-catcher and focal point across the lake.

The investment at Victoria Park between HLF and the London Borough of Tower Hamlets totalled around £12.4 million and is one of the largest restoration schemes completed to

Figure 28.2 The new bandstand at Roberts Park. (Reproduced by permission of the Heritage Lottery Fund.)

date. An investment of this scale has inevitably led to many dramatic outcomes and added to the vast increase in knowledge and understanding of park management and restoration. Research has shown that many park restoration projects can take up to eight years to deliver, on average cost around £1.8 million and can increase annual park visits by around 15%, although significantly higher figures have also been recorded. There are now plenty of exemplary public parks across the UK, many of which annually attain a Green Flag Award, the UK quality marque for parks and green spaces and a contract requirement for many HLF investment projects. But the funding has enabled projects to go beyond simply conserving historic features and infrastructure. There has also been a rise in innovation, in community participation, in volunteering and in horticultural skills associated with the projects supported. HLF has always insisted the projects it supports must engage local people, enhance skills, broaden understanding and ultimately ensure that the investment of public lottery funding is seen as a long-term investment strategy and not simply a short-term replacement for revenue funding.

Engaging people in understanding, valuing and caring for heritage is critical to its future. *Making a lasting difference for heritage and people*, the HLF's current key strategic aim, is reflected in all the grant programmes. Grants are not simply awarded for capital conservation works but must be part of a suite of activities that show the applicant is willing to deliver a step change in the way a site is managed and maintained. Successful applicants must demonstrate that local people value their local park and are willing to take a role in its future by joining a Friends group, helping to run events, operating facilities such as cafés or regularly volunteering. The role of local park Friends groups has developed significantly since the early 1990s. It is estimated by the National Federation of Park Friends and Community Groups that over 5,000 such groups exist across the UK. The size and reach of groups varies, but many arose from the creation of local action groups which developed to raise the standards of local parks and to fight for increased investment. Research by HLF has shown that these groups have been key to driving forward improvements to parks and green spaces by ensuring maintenance standards are upheld and by acting as local pressure groups to resist future cuts to revenue funding. Many local groups have now acquired the skills to run social enterprises to operate cafés, events and sports facilities. HLF sees the resilience of these groups and the skills gained by volunteers as critical going forward in a world of increasing pressure on local authority resources for non-statutory services such as parks and where the opportunity for greater social enterprise is increasing.

Whilst aiming to deliver a step change in the way parks are managed, HLF investment has also provided an opportunity to stimulate and support innovation. Our Victorian ancestors were some of the world's greatest innovators and created many of the magnificent parks the UK has today; however, innovation has been lacking from the sector for some years. HLF investment has provided the opportunity and resources for grantees to develop and try new approaches in response to some of the threats and opportunities facing designed landscapes. Urban parks are on the frontline when it comes to our changing climate and have a significant role to play in mitigating the effects of climate change and helping our cities to adapt. Project funding has been used in many cases to provide the substantial initial investment needed to introduce micro-renewables able to provide green power for park facilities and also to provide valuable income. At Morden Hall Park in London, an HLF grant helped fund the installation of an Archimedes screw, the first hydro-electric turbine in London, which generates enough energy to power the National Trust's new onsite park visitor centre. At St James Park, in Southampton, photovoltaic panels fitted to a new pergola in the park provide power for a community-run café and meeting place as well as generating income by selling surplus power back to the National Grid. Park projects have also stimulated a rethink in land management to help reduce rainwater runoff, to increase tree cover, to improve water quality and to enhance biodiversity. At Wandle Park in the London Borough of Croydon, the River Wandle, which was for years hidden in a constricting culvert, has been unearthed to create a new wetland area. In all these projects HLF investment has allowed schemes once considered aspirational to be delivered whilst also ensuring that new works are closely aligned with conservation objectives and set out within an agreed conservation plan. Our parks have always had to adapt to changing fortunes, such as to support the population in World War II through the Dig for Victory campaign; however, the key is to ensure that the historic designed landscape is always understood and managed to reduce potential loss or damage through the introduction of new technologies or management practices.

Conservation plans at the heart of HLF approach

The conservation plan approach as advocated by English Heritage, Historic Scotland and others is at the heart of the HLF approach. As part of a two-stage application process, funding is made available through a development phase to help fund physical survey work as well as the compilation of three key documents; an activity plan, a conservation plan, and a maintenance and management plan. These documents govern the success of the project and HLF often employs expert mentors to help grantees produce quality practical documents. Since the mid-1990s the sheer number of projects funded has helped develop professional skills in producing such documents, with many landscape professionals now adept in preparing plans for HLF projects. The very best plans, however, tend to be those tightly led by the grantees themselves ensuring that the plans produced are highly relevant to the site in question and benefit from local buy-in and local knowledge. With most HLF-designed landscape projects producing conservation plans, a wealth of knowledge now exists amongst professionals within the sector. Researching the history of over 700 grant-aided designed landscapes has led to increased understanding and greater appreciation of the work of some of the lesser known landscape designers and historic landscape features. For example, research connected with the restoration of Battersea Park in London provided greater understanding of the hierarchy of paths used within historic parks, the importance

Figure 28.3 Chiswick House and Gardens. (Reproduced by permission of the Heritage Lottery Fund.)

of understanding the historic paint colour palette for all structures and features, and the way in which public park gardeners laid out subtropical gardens making use of topography and employing innovative planting techniques. The huge amount of research and investigation undertaken by the landscape profession as well as by amateurs and local history societies has led to a vast growth in knowledge about who designed our public parks, who looked after them and how they were used. This knowledge has led to new publications on historic landscape features as well as lesser-known designers; new websites such as the UK Parks and Gardens Database (PGUK); better archiving of primary records and materials and new digital media such as smartphone apps and innovative onsite interpretation such as QR codes and interactive exhibitions. Recent investment at Stowe in Buckinghamshire and Great Dixter in East Sussex have both helped to increase facilities for visitors, provide new interpretation opportunities and enhance the sites as learning environments.

Whilst the retention of conservation knowledge and skills within the landscape profession is hopefully assured through the registered landscape practices, it is the loss of skills from local authorities and in particular park maintenance teams that is now of great concern. The step change in park management HLF seeks to deliver has led to some projects re-introducing posts such as head gardeners with the express aim of raising horticultural standards by taking on more tasks locally and away from area-based general landscape maintenance contractors. At Chiswick House and Grounds in the London Borough of Hounslow (Figure 28.3), a change in management and an HLF grant of £7.8 million towards a total project cost of £11.6 million has facilitated the introduction of a Trust with responsibility for both the historic house and the gardens.

Previously managed by staff from Hounslow as part of a much broader portfolio of parks and green spaces, the gardens are now managed by a site-based head gardener focused on returning excellence to the care of the historic gardens. Wherever possible, HLF encourages projects to focus on providing training for people to acquire skills and the Parks for People programme has a particular outcome aimed at stopping the skills drain currently afflicting the horticultural sector.

Funding for training

Apprenticeships and training opportunities are positively encouraged in all HLF projects but some targeted grant programmes have been created to expressly provide funding for training. One project directly benefiting designed landscapes is the Historic and Botanic Gardens

Bursary Scheme, which is a partnership between English Heritage, the National Trust, LANTRA and the Royal Horticultural Society. HLF funding has so far allowed over 130 year-long placements to be funded, giving horticulturalists the opportunity to work in historic landscapes to gain skills such as the propagation of heritage varieties, management of veteran trees, record-keeping for plant collections and the restoration of garden features and planting schemes. Trainees are now employed across the UK in many of our best-known parks and gardens where they, in turn, can pass on their newly acquired skills.

Cemeteries, country parks, seaside promenades and urban squares

Whilst the work on regenerating the UK's public parks is probably the area most associated with HLF and where greatest impact has been made in changing the fortune of many historic landscapes, there has also been significant investment in over 200 gardens including other designed landscapes such as cemeteries, country parks, seaside promenades and urban squares. HLF grants of over £100,000 can be awarded to any site providing it is run by a not-for-profit organisation and that it allows public access. As a result, investment has been made in many historic gardens run by a multitude of trusts or other bodies such as the National Trust and English Heritage. Small independent trusts run many of our great designed landscapes such as the Painshill Park Trust Ltd in Cobham, Surrey which is responsible for the care and future of a Grade I registered garden laid out between 1738 and 1773. HLF has supported several projects at Painshill including the restoration of buildings and structures, physical access improvements and the provision of new visitor facilities. One of the most exciting recent projects is the restoration of the Crystal Grotto funded through an award of £750,000. Created around 1760 and costing just £8,000, the grotto was in a state of severe decay. As a result of the grant the grotto roof has been repaired and the elaborate timber structure, including the inverted timber cones plastered with lime and embedded with crystals, are being recreated. The works included a detailed survey of the entire grotto to inform the restoration project and to ensure that the recladding of the interior with calcite, gypsum, quartz, fluorite and other minerals is both accurate and durable. New skills will be learnt in restoring the grotto, so the project includes the appointment of two apprentices as well as guided tours for visitors during the restoration works, visits by schools and the appointment of an education and community outreach officer. By investing in activities as well as simply conservation, the project will deliver wider outcomes such as learning, volunteering and the participation of audiences not currently engaged, as well as an increase in visitor numbers and therefore greater revenue generation.

One of the greatest challenges for trusts responsible for managing historic landscapes is the need to generate income, and that challenge is never greater than for those responsible for managing an historic cemetery. In 2003 Bristol City Council acted to save the then neglected Arnos Vale Cemetery by purchasing it from the Bristol General Cemetery Company. The cemetery had opened in 1839 and was inspired by the Victorian idea of a garden cemetery designed with beauty and peace as the setting for spectacular monuments and headstones. Managed by a team of gravediggers and gardeners, the cemetery evolved into a beautiful landscape until grave space ran out and income dried up. By the late 1980s ash and sycamore seedlings had invaded many areas and bramble and knotweed hid many of the monuments. The purchase by the council in 2003 allowed the creation of the Arnos Vale Cemetery Trust, which now manages the site with a team of nine staff and a Board of Directors. An HLF grant of around £4.9 million was needed to help fund conservation of the landscape and the many listed buildings and monuments. The grant also helped to deliver educational opportunities and to develop new business approaches aimed at securing the crucial annual income needed to maintain the site in perpetuity. The restoration has been a huge success and the Trust has developed a strong brand and reputation for innovation and fundraising. The historic buildings have adopted a variety of new uses and the educational programme, including paid classes, is extensive. To further ensure a lasting legacy, HLF and the Trust are working together to secure an endowment for the site. In 2012 HLF launched a new programme called Catalyst, and Arnos Vale was one of the first 16 projects to be awarded an opportunity. The Trust has now established the Arnos Vale Endowment Fund Challenge which hopes to match every £1 raised with £1 provided by the HLF up to a ceiling of £500,000. The objective of the Catalyst grant scheme is to incentivise private and corporate giving, which has not been seen as a major income stream for designed landscapes in the past. As funding sources become more difficult to find in future, programmes such as Catalyst and the use of endowments will become more significant.

HLF's changing role

Over the years the role of HLF in conservation of the UK's parks and gardens has changed and developed. In the early days HLF's role was about understanding the scale of the issues involved, pioneering techniques needed to restore complex designed landscapes and delivering some of the largest landscape projects ever seen in the UK. As the number of projects completed grew, attention shifted to measuring and evaluating the success of investment both to ensure money was being wisely invested but also to ensure results could be gathered to demonstrate the need for continued investment. Project outcomes are varied and obviously include the conservation of historic landscapes but also an increased understanding of the value of parks and gardens by local communities, and a pool of practitioners with skills in landscape restoration, project management, management planning and community engagement. New techniques have been invented and trialled with the availability of funding which has allowed parks and gardens to continue to evolve and develop to meet modern demands and threats. Today the HLF role is to continue to invest in gardens and parks, but also to ensure its past legacy of investment is protected and sustained. It would be tragic if all the good work of the past were allowed to rapidly decay due to decreasing future revenue funding. In response, HLF is looking at how it can stimulate continued investment in parks and gardens by encouraging more private philanthropy, by stimulating innovation and by continuing to shout loud about the importance of the UK's unique collection of designed landscapes.

29 Legal protection for structures, trees and wildlife

Charles Mynors

Barrister, visiting professor in the planning department, Oxford Brookes University, member of the advisory panel of the Prince's Regeneration Trust and of the Legal Advisory Commission of the General Synod, London, UK

Introduction

There has always been a need for a mechanism to enable society to strike a balance between, on the one hand, the protection of those features of the environment that are perceived to be desirable and, on the other, the promotion and regulation of change and development that can be shown to be either desirable or necessary. Since World War II, this need has been met by the system of town and country planning – the origins of which have been explored in an earlier chapter.[1]

That chapter also drew attention to the National Planning Policy Framework (NPPF), adopted by the Government in 2012 as the core policy document underlying current planning decisions, and to its emphasis on the need for the planning system to perform an economic role, a social role, and an environmental role, noting that the third of these requires it to contribute to protecting and enhancing our natural, built and historic environment.[2] Historic gardens and designed landscapes are the result of past change and development, by public authorities or private landowners, probably perceived as being desirable rather than strictly necessary. But now, ironically, the places thus created have become an element of the environment – perhaps almost uniquely natural, built *and* historic – that merits protection and enhancement. The question is, then, how that can most effectively and appropriately be achieved either by law or policy.

The most obvious legal mechanism to achieve protection for a particular category of items is to prepare some form of register of all the valuable items in that category, and then to require consent to be obtained for the destruction or alteration of any included in the register. That is, after all, the approach adopted to protect special buildings, monuments and trees – considered later in this chapter – whereby items of particular value are selected by experts, and special consent is then needed to carry out works affecting them.

However, that approach would not really work in the case of gardens and landscapes. For one thing, although it is relatively straightforward to prepare a list of the truly outstanding gardens and landscapes, to produce a comprehensive register would be a very challenging exercise, possibly stirring up considerable local controversy. Secondly, even if such a register were to be prepared, it would be wholly unrealistic to expect consent to be obtained every time a plant in a registered garden was to be inserted or removed – or to require a new bush to be introduced to replace every one that dies or becomes diseased. And, in any

Gardens & Landscapes in Historic Building Conservation, First Edition. Edited by Marion Harney.
© 2014 John Wiley & Sons, Ltd. Published 2014 by John Wiley & Sons, Ltd.

event, the whole point – or at least one point – of a designed landscape is that it changes, both through the seasons and over the years. Perennial plants come and go; fashions in planting change. And a garden that was once special can very quickly degenerate into a wilderness without any intervention by its owner (indeed, precisely because of the lack of intervention). And all living things are subject, as buildings are not, to 'a secret and unobservable operation of nature'; in other words, they grow. The quoted phrase was used in two judgments of the High Court, in relation to trees; but it applies equally to shrubs and other plants.[3] It would therefore be difficult to know precisely what was being preserved.

Such considerations no doubt explain why the legislation providing for a register of historic parks and gardens, in the National Heritage Act 1983, is very limited in its scope.[4] English Heritage is given powers to produce and maintain a register, the existence of which can then be taken into account by planning authorities in formulating planning policy and, perhaps more importantly, when determining planning applications. Registered parks and gardens are 'designated heritage assets', as defined in the NPPF.[5] In Wales, Cadw maintains a similar register of historic landscapes, parks and gardens on an entirely non-statutory basis. But the entry of a park or garden onto the register does not, of itself, confer any need for special consent to be obtained.

Indeed, it would be possible – however undesirable it might be – for the owner of a registered park or garden to flatten it without any consent at all. Or at least it would be, if there were within it no elements in the landscape that are protected by other legislative codes. Of those, the most significant are:

- the Town and Country Planning Act 1990 ('the Planning Act'), requiring planning permission to be obtained for development
- the Ancient Monuments and Archaeological Areas Act 1979 and the Planning (Listed Buildings and Conservation Areas) Act 1990, protecting historic structures
- the Planning Act and the Town and Country Planning (Tree Preservation) Regulations 2012, protecting trees of special amenity value
- the Wildlife and Countryside Act 1981, protecting wildlife.

This chapter briefly considers each of these in turn. However, it needs to be borne in mind that none of these legislative codes was devised with the particular circumstances of historic parks and gardens in mind; and any protection that may be given by them is largely fortuitous.

Mainstream planning control

The need for planning permission

Planning permission is required for the carrying out of development – that is, the carrying out of building, engineering and other operations, and the making of a material change in the use of land.[6]

Building operations are defined as any operation carried out by a builder – including the alteration or demolition of a building. In the context of gardens and landscapes, this means that planning permission is required for the introduction of any new built structure – such as a gazebo, a flight of steps, or a retaining wall – or the alteration of an existing one – whether listed or not. Similarly, the addition of any hard landscaping – including terraces, paths and patios – might amount to an engineering operation, requiring permission. But planning permission is not normally required for soft landscaping works, including the introduction or removal of trees, shrubs or other plants.

There is a legal maxim *De minimis non curat lex* – the law takes no account of trivia – which means that minor alterations to buildings, and small-scale landscaping works (including, of course, routine horticulture) would not amount to development requiring planning permission. And no doubt a planning authority would not consider it expedient to take enforcement action if minor works were to be carried out without permission.⁷ But that cannot always be relied on, particularly since works considered to be 'minor improvements' by a landowner may be regarded as harmful innovations by others.

Further, even where a building, landscaping or other operation does technically amount to development, many such operations are permitted automatically by the Town and Country Planning (General Permitted Development) Order 1995. That applies in particular to building works within a garden that forms part of the curtilage of a dwellinghouse, the construction or alteration of gates, fences and walls, and demolition works.⁸ However, demolition is only permitted if it has been notified to the planning authority, which is then entitled to require an opportunity to approve the method of works and the details of any proposed restoration. And the permission granted by the Order for other categories of development generally do not apply within the curtilage of a listed building.

Any application for planning permission will be determined in the light of the local development plan (including any relevant neighbourhood development plan), national planning policy, and other material considerations.⁹

National planning policy for England is now largely contained in the NPPF. It has already been noted that parks and gardens included in the statutory English Heritage register are defined in the NPPF as 'designated heritage assets'. But any historic garden or designed landscape will be a 'heritage asset' if it has been identified (for example, by the local planning authority) as having a degree of significance meriting consideration in planning decisions, because of its heritage interest.¹⁰ 'Significance' in this context means the value of the heritage asset to this and future generations because of its heritage interest – which may be archaeological, architectural, artistic or historic; and may derive not only from the physical presence of the asset, but also from its setting.

It is therefore important that planning authorities and other interested bodies such as the Garden History Society ensure that all gardens and landscapes of significance, whether or not included on the statutory register, are identified in some form of inventory – with a note as to why they are significant. The requirement for planning permission to be obtained will then provide a considerable degree of protection for the existing built elements that form an important part of the character of many such places, and a safeguard to prevent the introduction of inappropriate new ones.

Similar considerations will apply to the consideration of proposals for works affecting sites included in the non-statutory registers of parks, gardens and landscapes in Scotland, Wales and Northern Ireland.

Environmental impact assessment

Under European law, it is necessary to obtain an environmental assessment for any significant project that is likely to have significant effects on the environment; and a project is defined as including the execution of construction works and other interventions in the natural surroundings and landscape.¹¹ Generally, that requirement has been transposed into UK domestic legislation by a series of regulations dealing with a wide variety of categories of project – none of which directly relate to historic gardens and designed landscapes. Where no domestic legislation applies, it is still necessary to consider whether the Directive may apply, by virtue of the legal doctrine of 'direct effect'.

The projects that may require assessment in this way are listed in the Annexes to the relevant EU Directive. And in considering whether a particular project falls within Annexe II, it is necessary to consider, amongst other things, 'the absorption capacity of the natural environment . . . having regard in particular to landscapes of historic, cultural and archaeological significance'.¹²

Major works to a garden or landscape of significance – or even its complete obliteration – might, arguably, have an environmental effect comparable to that of many of the schemes in the Annexes and therefore might well amount to a 'project' for the purposes of the

Directive. But such works do not seem to fall within any of the categories listed there and therefore cannot require an assessment under the Directive.

Historic structures

Structures protected in their own right   The value of garden buildings and structures has already been emphasised earlier in this book.[13] And they may indeed be listed in their own right. Thus the Secretary of State can list any building in England that seems to him to be of special architectural or historic interest, and that may include any 'structure or erection'. Further, in considering whether to list a building, the Secretary of State may (and in practice does) take into account not only the building itself but also 'any respect in which its exterior contributes to the architectural or historic interest of any group of buildings of which it forms part'.[14] And this would be obviously relevant in the case of a group of structures within a historic garden.

The Secretary of State, in choosing which structures to include in the list, is in practice guided by advice from English Heritage, which has issued a series of listing selection guides on different categories of buildings. In April 2011, it issued guidance on the selection of *Garden and park structures*, which makes the point that:[15]

> All designed landscapes are likely to contain buildings and other hard landscaping features such as balustraded terraces that will often make a positive contribution to the overall character of the place. Those buildings of special interest will deserve to be designated, just like the designed landscapes within which they stand, which may be included on the Register of Historic Parks and Gardens.

The guidance goes on to identify the many types of structures that may be eligible for listing, including bridges, cascades, columns, dairies, dovecots, fountains, gatehouses, gates, gazebos, glasshouses, grottoes, icehouses, kennels, obelisks, orangeries, pedestals, pyramids, screens, temples, urns, vases, walls, and waterfalls.

It is therefore not surprising that, amongst the 500,000 or so buildings that have now been listed in England, there are a very large number of structures within or associated with parks, gardens and designed landscapes.[16] Thus, as one would expect, the park at Castle Howard in North Yorkshire is included within the English Heritage register; but within it are some 50 or so structures that have been listed by the Secretary of State in their own right. And even life-size dinosaurs have been listed, at Crystal Palace Park in London (which is not itself a registered park) (see Figure 28.1).

Similar lists are maintained by the Welsh Ministers and the Scottish Ministers (advised by Cadw and Historic Scotland) and by the Northern Ireland Environment Agency; and similar legislation and guidance applies to protect buildings that have been included in such lists.[17]

Structures in the curtilage of listed buildings   Many significant gardens and landscapes form the setting of historic buildings such as country houses. Where a building is listed, the listing extends to include – as well as the actual building in the list – any 'object or structure' that is within its curtilage and has been since before 1948, and is ancillary to the building in the list.[18] In other words, when a stately home is listed, that listing will also include any pre-1948 objects in the grounds – such as structures in any of the categories noted above (boundary walls, gates, fountains, icehouses, and so forth) – regardless of whether those objects or structures might be worthy of listing in their own right.

This recognises the fact that, in many cases, a building that is worthy of listing is associated with a number of other structures that are part of an ensemble that has some value. And indeed the Secretary of State, in considering whether to list a building, may take into account 'the desirability of preserving, on the ground of its architectural or historic interest, any feature of the building consisting of a manmade object or structure . . . forming part of the land and comprised within the curtilage of the building'.[19] Thus, for example, the listing of a house has been held by the courts to include the listing of a stables block some distance from it,[20] as well as a ha-ha forming the boundary of its formal garden.[21] This does not mean that an object or structure that is part of a listed building solely by virtue of being within the curtilage of a building that is listed in its own right is imbued with interest that it otherwise does not possess; but it is subject to some protection.

So, for example, the structures – such as retaining walls, flights of steps, pergolas and glasshouses – in the gardens of Munstead Wood, the creation of Gertrude Jekyll (1843–1932) in west Surrey, are not listed in their own right. But they are within the curtilage of the house, designed by Edwin Lutyens (1869–1944) and listed Grade I. They are ancillary to the house, and have been there since long before 1948; they are accordingly protected by the listing.

Protection for listed structures

Works to a listed structure require planning permission – and, as already noted, the categories of development permitted by the General Permitted Development Order are more limited in the case of listed buildings. However, where a structure is listed in its own right, listed building consent will also be required for the carrying out of any works for its demolition or for its alteration or extension in any manner that affects its character as a building of special architectural or historic interest.[22] Where a structure is not listed in its own right but is within the curtilage of a listed building, listed building consent will be required for any works to it that affect the character of the listed building as a whole.

The removal of the statue of Silenus at Castle Howard – a listed structure – would thus require listed building consent, as that would be 'demolition' of that structure. So would the relocation of a flight of steps at Munstead Wood, even though the steps themselves are not listed, as that would alter the character of the group of buildings associated with the listed Lutyens house.

It may be imagined that such works to structures of significance will rarely be proposed. Where they are, and an application for consent is made, it will be determined on the basis of the effect of the works both on the significance of the structure itself and on that of the garden or landscape of which it forms part.[23] And the effect of the proposed works on that significance will need to be balanced against the need for the works and the benefit arising from them.[24] In practice, therefore, it will be difficult, if not impossible, to obtain either listed building consent or planning permission for works to listed structures within gardens and landscapes of significance.

It is a criminal offence to carry out works to a listed building for which listed building consent is required without that consent having first been obtained.[25]

Conservation areas

Many parks and gardens of significance are located within a conservation area, defined as 'an area of special architectural or historic interest, the character or appearance of which it is desirable to preserve or enhance'.[26] For example, in London, most of the 152 registered parks and gardens – including many of the public parks, the cemeteries, and the landscaped settings of notable public buildings – are within conservation areas. And many of those that are not registered – such as some of the garden squares and many churchyards – are the focus of their local area. And Prince's Park, Liverpool is both a registered park and a conservation area.

Where a structure is within a conservation area, it may not be demolished without the approval of the planning authority. The required approval used to be conservation area consent; it will in the future (in England at least) be planning permission.[27] Probably of greater significance is that in carrying out any function under the planning Acts in relation to land in a conservation area – including the determination of any planning application – a planning authority is to pay special attention to the desirability of preserving or enhancing the character of the area.[28] And the Court of Appeal has held that a pattern of private gardens in a conservation area might be a feature of the area that it would be desirable to preserve or enhance.[29]

Scheduled monuments

Archaeological sites and structures, and other ancient monuments, may be scheduled under the Ancient Monuments and Archaeological Areas Act 1979 – which applies throughout Great Britain. The English Heritage guidance on garden structures, noted above, observes that scheduling (as opposed to listing) has generally been the preferred designation option in the case of early designed landscapes where the remains are mainly below-ground or survive as earthworks.[30] More detailed guidance will be issued in due course.

It is necessary to obtain scheduled monument consent from the Secretary of State (or the Welsh or Scottish Ministers, as appropriate) before carrying out works to a scheduled monument, or to the land around it.[31]

Urgent repairs

Where all or part of a listed structure (or an unlisted structure in the curtilage of a listed building) is unoccupied, and is in poor condition, the planning authority is able to carry out works urgently needed for its preservation.[32] It must give advance notice of the works to the owner, who will then have to pay for them; or it can put a charge on the property, and recover the cost of the works when it next changes hands. The same power can be used in relation to an unlisted structure in a conservation area, but only with the consent of the Secretary of State.[33] A similar power exists in relation to ancient monuments in need of urgent repairs.[34]

These powers may be useful to enable relatively inexpensive works to be carried out to prevent the deterioration of decaying historic structures that are important elements in gardens and landscapes.

Where the condition of a structure (whether listed or not) or area of land is such that it is adversely affecting the amenity of the neighbourhood, it is also possible for an authority to use its powers under section 215 of the Planning Act to require the owner to carry out works to remedy the situation. If the issue of the notice does not produce the desired result, the authority can then enter the land and carry out the necessary works itself. That power too may be useful in the case of garden structures in poor repair – and indeed where a garden is falling into decay.

Protected trees

Trees and the law generally

An earlier chapter in this book has emphasised the importance of trees as crucial elements in the makeup of historic gardens and designed landscapes.[35]

Generally the law imposes no restrictions on the owners of trees, which may be lopped, topped or felled without the need for any consent to be obtained. The principal restriction is that those responsible for them must ensure that their condition does not cause anyone nearby to be in danger – it is sometimes suggested that the duty is to take such care as would be expected of a 'reasonable and prudent landowner', whatever that means.[36] But the duty to ensure safety always takes precedence over the desirability of preserving amenity.[37] In the context of a large open space, the fulfilment of this duty is likely to take the form of carrying out a risk assessment, and assessing which areas are most used, and which trees are most likely to cause problems.[38]

The felling of trees on any scale normally requires a felling licence from the Forestry Commission, but this does not apply in the case of trees growing in orchards, gardens, churchyards and public open spaces – the latter including 'land laid out as a public garden'.[39]

It should also not be forgotten that the restrictions on damaging wildlife habitat, touched upon in the last section of this chapter, will also have the by-product of protecting trees.

Tree preservation orders

Whilst very many trees are of amenity value, those of particular importance may be the subject of a tree preservation order, made by the local planning authority under the Town and Country Planning Act 1990. Orders may be made in relation to individual trees, groups of trees, trees specified by reference to an area, and woodlands. Those in the first two categories only protect trees existing at the time the order is made. The 'woodland' designation, and probably also the 'area' one, also protects trees at the specified location even if they were planted (or self-seeded) after the making of the order.[40]

Area orders are usually made to protect all of the trees on a site about to be developed; but it has been observed in the High Court that:

> Merely because more than one tree is included within an order, it does not follow that the trees must be described either as a group or as a woodland. For example, scattered trees in a parkland surrounding a listed building may not comprise a group or be fairly described as a woodland, but in such circumstances it may very well be sensible, rather than specifying each tree, to specify the parkland area within which they are located.[41]

And clearly this is not limited to land surrounding a listed building. Thus an area order may be made to protect all of the trees, of whatever species and whenever planted, in a particular garden or designed landscape. This may be of particular importance in the case of parkland containing a number of veteran and ancient trees, which may be crucial to its character and significance – notable examples are the collections of veteran oaks in Windsor Great Park in Berkshire, and at Moccas Deer Park in Herefordshire.

The procedure for making orders in England is now governed by the Town and Country Planning (Trees) Regulations 2012. These provide, in effect, that an order will in future consist merely of a schedule specifying the trees being protected, and a map. Orders made in England before 6 April 2012 – and orders of any date in the rest of the UK – will also contain details of when consent is required, and the procedure for applying for it. In relation to England, such a pre-2012 order will still be valid, but everything in it other than the details of the trees in question can be completely ignored.[42]

All orders in England, and almost all orders elsewhere, will come into effect as soon as they are made; but will only remain in effect for six months unless they are confirmed.

Works to protected trees

Where a tree is protected by a tree preservation order, consent must be obtained from the planning authority or (on appeal) from the Secretary of State to fell it, or to carry out any other works of any significance.

This requirement is subject to a number of exceptions, specified in the 2012 Regulations (in respect of orders in England) and in the order itself (outside England).[43] The principal exceptions are as follows:

- works to trees that are dead (or, in Wales, dying)
- the removal of dead branches (in England only)
- works that are urgently necessary in the interests of safety

- works necessary to abate a nuisance (that is, where a tree encroaches onto neighbouring land)[44]
- works that are necessary to comply with a statutory obligation, or to implement a planning permission, or that are carried out by statutory undertakers or other public bodies.

Where consent is required in England, it must be sought in accordance with the procedure in the Regulations; elsewhere, under the procedure set out in the order in question. Where consent is granted for felling, it will often be subject to a condition that a replacement tree is planted. It is also now possible for an authority to grant consent for multiple operations, in accordance with a management plan – for example, to authorise repeated pollarding of the trees in a particular avenue – which may be appropriate in the case of a professionally managed estate. Where consent is refused, compensation is payable by the authority for any loss incurred.

It is a criminal offence to carry out works without consent – presumably on the basis that the planting of a replacement will be at best only a very limited remedy.

Trees in conservation areas

It has already been noted that many gardens and landscapes are included in conservation areas. Where work is to be carried out to a tree in a conservation area, six weeks' notice of the works must be given to the planning authority, to enable it to have an opportunity to impose a tree preservation order – which would bring into force the protective provisions outlined above.[45]

Not surprisingly, this requirement is subject to a raft of exceptions – which are in the 2012 Regulations, and are broadly similar to those applying to the need for consent under a tree preservation order. But where notification is needed, and is not carried out, that too is a criminal offence.

Where an application for consent under a tree preservation order is sought for works to a tree in a conservation area, the application will be determined in the light of the general duty to preserve or enhance the character and appearance of the conservation area, which will of course include the significance of any open space within it.[46]

Wildlife

This chapter does not extend to nature conservation generally. Nevertheless, the provisions of the law relating to species protection should not be ignored, since historic gardens and designed landscapes, and the structures and plants within them, will often provide valuable habitat for a variety of animals and birds. It follows that the carrying out of works – either major re-landscaping projects or just routine horticulture – may have the unintended result of killing protected birds or animals (or at the very least disturbing their habitats) or destroying protected plants.

The principal legislation is contained in Part 1 of the Wildlife and Countryside Act 1981. The enforcement provisions of the 1981 Act were strengthened by the Countryside and Rights of Way Act 2000,[47] the Natural Environment and Rural Communities Act 2006 and, most recently, the Environmental Civil Sanctions (England) Order 2010. And other amendments have been introduced by a variety of Acts and Regulations. The 1981 Act applies in principle throughout Great Britain, but has been significantly amended by Acts and Regulations applying only in Scotland.[48]

Importantly, the provisions of the 1981 Act should be read in conjunction with those of the Conservation of Habitats and Species Regulations 2010, which provide somewhat stronger protection for those few species that are considered to be of international, rather than simply national importance.[49] But note that this whole area of law is subject to particularly frequent amendment, and some of it applies differently in the various parts of the UK.

In each case, the Act or the Regulations provide that it is an offence to do certain things without a licence, but that there are certain defences to a prosecution for such an offence. The most significant of these, in practice, is that a person can avoid a conviction in some cases if he or she is able to prove that the act that would otherwise be unlawful was the incidental result of a lawful operation and could not reasonably have been avoided. However, since 2007, the 'incidental result' defence no longer applies in relation to European protected species, protected as such under the 2010 Regulations.[50]

It seems that relatively few prosecutions have been mounted in practice under these provisions; but this may alter as the climate of public opinion and Government policy changes – as evidenced by the tightening-up introduced in more recent legislation. It is therefore increasingly necessary for those dealing with gardens and landscapes to be aware of the relevant provisions and, in particular, which species are currently given special protection.

These considerations should therefore be borne in mind in deciding both whether and how to carry out particular works. At one level, the decision will be simply whether a licence or other consent is required; but obtaining such authorisation may be difficult or impossible. It may therefore be necessary simply to avoid the problem – for example, by programming a project so as to leave untouched during the breeding season a branch on which there is a protected bird's nest, or felling a tree in such a way as to leave undisturbed a clump of protected wildflowers growing to one side.

Much guidance on the implementation of these provisions is available on the websites of Natural England and Natural Resources Wales (Cyfoeth Naturiol Cymru) – the latter being the body established on 1 April 2013 to absorb the role of the Countryside Council for Wales (CCW), the Forestry Commission Wales and the Environment Agency Wales.

Finally, in addition to the protection given to birds, animals and plants as such, protection is also afforded to habitats generally, by means of the wider designations considered earlier.[51]

Endnotes

1. See chapter 26 of this volume: Johns, C. 'Conservation legislation in the UK'.
2. National Planning Policy Framework (NPPF), DCLG, March 2012, para 7.
3. *Noble v Harrison* [1926] 2 KB 332; *Wringe v Cohen* [1940] 1 KB 229.
4. See chapter 25 of this volume: Morgan, F.D., 'Designed landscapes and national designation'.
5. NPPF, Annex 2.
6. Town and Country Planning Act (TCPA) 1990, s 55.
7. TCPA 1990, s 172(1) (b).
8. TCP (General Permitted Development) Order 1995, art 3, and Sched 2, Part 1; Part 2, Class A; Part 31.
9. TCPA 1990, s 70; Planning and Compulsory Purchase Act 2004, s 38.
10. NPPF, Annex 2 (Glossary).
11. Directive 85/337, *Assessment of effects of certain public and private projects on the environment*, art 1.
12. Directive 85/337, Annexe III, para 1(h).
13. See chapter 7 of this volume: Forsyth, M. 'Conservation of garden buildings'.
14. P(LBCA)A1990, s 1(3)(a).
15. http://www.english-heritage.org.uk/content/publications/publicationsNew/guidelines-standards/dlsg-garden-park-structures/garden_and_park_final.pdf
16. For details of what is included in the list, see http://list.english-heritage.org.uk/
17. See *Listed Buildings, Conservation Areas and Monuments*, Mynors, Sweet & Maxwell, 2006, s 3.5.
18. P (LBCA) A1990, s 1(5); *Debenhams PLC v Westminster CC* [1987] AC 396, HL.
19. P (LBCA) A1990, s 1(3) (b).
20. *Skerritts of Nottingham v Secretary of State* [2001] QB 59, CA.
21. *Watson-Smyth v Secretary of State* [1992] JPL 451.
22. P (LBCA) A1990, s 7.
23. P (LBCA) A1990, s 66.
24. NPPF, paras 133–135.

25. P (LBCA) A1990, s 9.
26. P (LBCA) A1990, s 69 (England and Wales). There is similar legislation in Scotland and Northern Ireland.
27. Enterprise and Regulatory Reform Bill, expected to obtain Royal assent in mid-2013.
28. P (LBCA) A 1990, s 72.
29. *Ward v Secretary of State* [1990] 1 PLR 85, CA.
30. *Garden and park structures*, English Heritage, 2011; see note xx above.
31. AMAAA 1979, ss 2, 61(9).
32. P (LBCA) A1990, s 54.
33. P (LBCA) A 1990, s 76.
34. AMAAA 1979, s 5.
35. See chapter 15, Fay, N. 'Conservation Arboriculture: the natural art of tree management in historic landscapes'.
36. *Caminer v Northern & London Investment Trust* [1951] AC 88, HL.
37. *Quinn v Scott* [1965] 1 WLR 1004.
38. *Bowen v National Trust* [2011] EWHC 1992.
39. Forestry Act 1967, s 9(2) (b); *McInerney v Portland Port Ltd* [2001] 1 PLR 104; *Rockall v DEFRA* [2008] EWHC 2408 (Admin).
40. *Palm Developments Ltd v Secretary of State* [2009] 2 P&CR 16.
41. *Robinson v East Riding of Yorkshire* [200] EWHC 63 Admin.
42. Planning Act 2008, s 193 (this will, in due course, also apply to Wales).
43. TCP (Tree Preservation) (England) Regulations 2012, reg 14.
44. *Perrin v Northampton BC* [2008] 1 WLR 1307, CA.
45. TCPA 1990, s 211.
46. P (LBCA) A 1990, s 72.
47. Countryside and Rights of Way Act 2000, ss 81(1), 103(2), Sched 12.
48. Including in particular Nature Conservation (Scotland) Act 2004, and Wildlife and Natural Environment (Scotland) Act 2011.
49. The Conservation (Natural Habitats, etc) Regulations 1994 still apply in Scotland.
50. 1994 Regulations, reg 40, 43, substituted by Conservation (Natural Habitats &c) (Amendment) Regulations 2007, reg 5; see now 2010 Regulations, regs 42, 46.
51. See chapter 26 of this volume: Johns, C. 'Conservation legislation in the UK'.

30 Easy access to historic landscapes

Heather J.L. Smith
Access & Equality Specialist, National Trust, London, UK

'No one will protect what they don't care about and no one will care about what they have never experienced.'[1]

Historic environments are valued by many people for their significance and diversity. The term 'historic landscape' covers a wide variety of spaces including country and urban parks, formal gardens, ancient monuments and commemorative sites. The nature and origin of many of these places means that they are not always easy for people who visit them, or who could potentially visit them, to get around. Improving access to historic landscapes is important to sustain and preserve them for future generations, to widen understanding of their heritage and to offer more people the opportunity of enjoying them. Creating a balance between the conservation of, and access to, historic landscapes exercises all historic environment organisations. The National Trust, with its founding principle of being 'for the benefit of the nation' cannot fail to focus on, and meet, the challenges this brings. This is not always 'easy' but it presents interesting conundrums to work through for land managers and staff responsible for the experience of visitors to maintain the integrity of the site and to provide for the needs and changing requirements of developing audiences.

'Easy access' in this chapter relates to access for disabled people. It is estimated that around a sixth of the UK population is disabled.[2] Census returns for 2011 show that one in six people is over 65.[3] The older people become, the more likely they are to experience disability.[4] The provision of 'easy access' is therefore likely to improve the experience of historic landscapes for an increasing number of people. The term 'disabled people' has developed from the social model of disability which sees people as disabled by the environment around them rather than the disability relating purely to an impairment of a person. In this context, the historic environment presents many and varied challenges, from the traditionally considered physical aspects of ground topography to intellectual barriers of inaccessible information. It is also worth noting in the context of this chapter that disabled people remain less likely to take part in leisure activity, including visiting heritage sites, than non-disabled people, and this situation has not improved in the last five years.[5] Recent studies also indicate the importance to health and well-being of access to the outdoors, particularly emphasising the potential for improvement in the physical and mental health of young people.[6] On the basis of this evidence, it would seem that the historic environment is still not seen as an inviting place for disabled people but that the potential for it to be

Gardens & Landscapes in Historic Building Conservation, First Edition. Edited by Marion Harney.
© 2014 John Wiley & Sons, Ltd. Published 2014 by John Wiley & Sons, Ltd.

beneficial is increasing.⁷ It also shows how much work historic environment organisations need to do to show that 'access for all' matters to them.

The principle of enabling access for everyone is important for the continuing success and relevance of heritage. To both protect historic landscapes and make sure access is possible for disabled people, there is a network of legislation, regulations and responsibilities to work within. The Equality Act 2010 (hereafter EA2010) replaced the Disability Discrimination Acts 1995 and 2005 but maintains the same requirements for provisions for disabled people. As with the previous legislation, the EA2010 does not impose technical standards to attain for accessibility and revolves around a 'reasonable' approach: an ultimate definition of 'reasonable' in any particular case can only be decided by a court of law but it is obviously preferable to avoid that recourse. There are some regulatory and guidance documents which itemise technical standards for designing for accessibility – the Building Regulation Approved Document Part M – Access to and Use of Buildings and British Standard 8300 – Design of buildings and their approaches to meet the needs of disabled people – Code of Practice. These mostly focus on the built environment, although some of the content is applicable to the outdoor surroundings of buildings which may well include historic landscapes. Exact implementation of the standards in these publications is not always practical when aiming to balance conservation and access; to do so could lead to the removal of a significant historical feature or a surface which is integral to the history of the site. It is possible, though, taking the specifications in these documents as a guiding principle, if they are not able to be literally applied, to create dignified high-quality solutions which are sensitive to the special interest of particular environments and the visitors.

Alongside EA 2010, there are many other pieces of legislation, principles and regulations concerning conservation. These include the process of designating landscapes to give them listed status, declaring them as Areas of Outstanding Natural Beauty, Scheduled Monuments, and Sites of Specified Scientific Interest. Such status places additional protection on the environments and is designed to make sure that any alterations are appropriate to the conservation of heritage but not to preclude alteration. A key guidance document – 'Planning Policy Guidance 15 – Planning and the Historic Environment' emphasised a flexible and pragmatic approach to achieving a balance between conservation and increased access. A careful, considered and positive approach is required to meet these requirements and keep interested parties happy.

In order to help historic environment organisations to find a practical balance between conservation and access, English Heritage, the Heritage Lottery Fund and the National Trust worked together to produce an overarching publication: *Easy Access to Historic Landscapes* (2005), re-published in 2013.⁸ It was produced to encourage understanding and good practice in making historic landscapes more accessible for all visitors. A key example of good practice is to work with experienced partners and not try to do everything alone. The publication illustrates this by relying on the lead authorship of the Sensory Trust, an organisation focused on making places more accessible, attractive and useful for everyone.⁹ The combination of technical information and practical examples make it a useful resource for land managers and disabled people alike to understand what might be possible.

Finding answers when developing this approach is not always straightforward but *Easy Access to Historic Landscapes* describes the process land managers should work through to have the best chance of finding the most appropriate answers for specific sites. Generally, it is important to maintain the integrity of the historic landscape as that is what visitors, disabled and non-disabled, come to experience and enjoy. To do this effectively, a conservation management plan should be in place. This should include a description of the historic landscape, an analysis of how the landscape has changed over time and how it is currently used, and an assessment of its significance. The conservation management plan should also include what opportunities there might be for improving access so that more people can experience and enjoy the site and increase its sustainability. Increasing access is not always about creating something new and 'alien' to the original design; with a full understanding of the history and significance of a landscape, it is sometimes possible to increase access by replacing a route or element of the site which had been changed previously. Whatever the intervention, the access improvement should be in context with the nature of the specific historic landscape. Major changes should be well designed and short-term or temporary solutions should be easily reversible. These latter options should be seen, wherever possible, as a step on the way to a design more appropriate to the style of the environment. If a clear process is followed, many skilful adjustments can be made that will not compromise the integrity of individual environments.

To assist with a full development of the opportunities to increase access, a thorough examination of what might be possible to improve the experience for disabled people, or an access audit, needs to be undertaken.[10] It is important that access audits cover the whole experience of a visit to a historic landscape, and not just focus on the traditional physical aspect of topography. The aim of the access audit should be to achieve independent access for disabled people wherever possible and to create an inclusive environment for all visitors. Another way to view the audit process is as the 'Access Chain' (Figure 30.1) which illustrates how all the elements of a visit join together to create an overall experience.

The access audit should consider the whole experience, from the information available before a visit; arrival; experience on the site, including facilities such as catering and retail, and leaving the site.

It is rarely possible to cover everything every disabled person requires from a visit to a historic landscape in one access audit; the nature of disability is too varied and requirements too specific. An audit could become an unwieldy tome which land managers approach with

The Access Chain

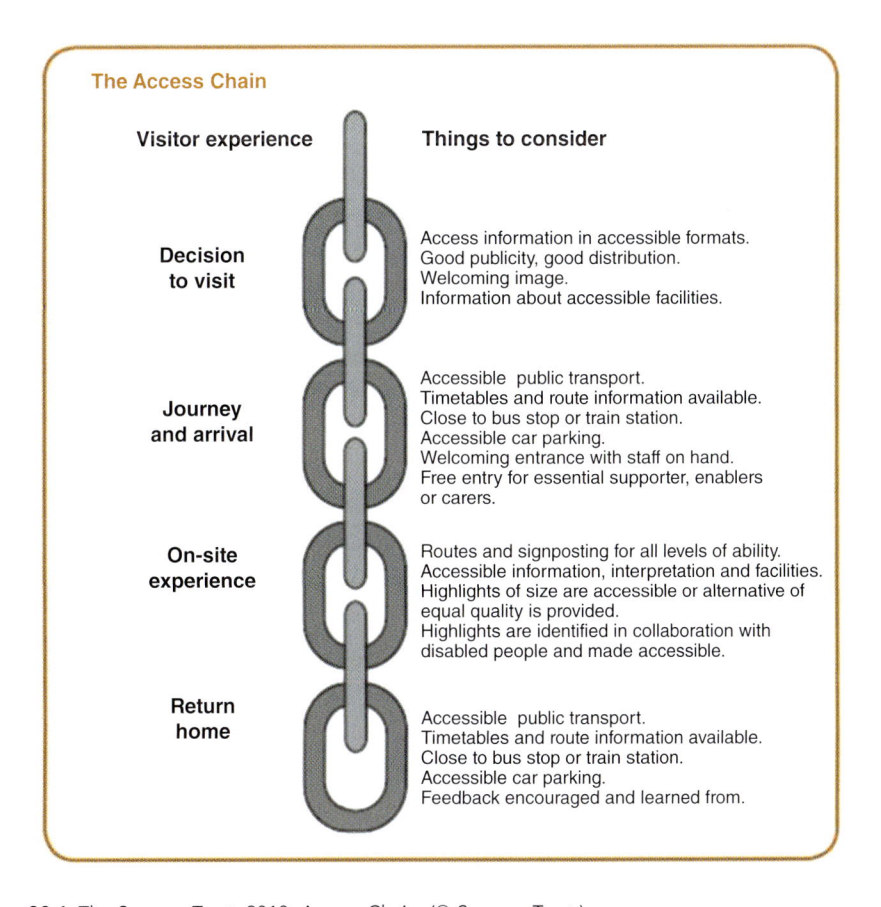

Visitor experience	Things to consider
Decision to visit	Access information in accessible formats. Good publicity, good distribution. Welcoming image. Information about accessible facilities.
Journey and arrival	Accessible public transport. Timetables and route information available. Close to bus stop or train station. Accessible car parking. Welcoming entrance with staff on hand. Free entry for essential supporter, enablers or carers.
On-site experience	Routes and signposting for all levels of ability. Accessible information, interpretation and facilities. Highlights of size are accessible or alternative of equal quality is provided. Highlights are identified in collaboration with disabled people and made accessible.
Return home	Accessible public transport. Timetables and route information available. Close to bus stop or train station. Accessible car parking. Feedback encouraged and learned from.

Figure 30.1 The Sensory Trust, 2010, Access Chain. (© Sensory Trust.)

caution rather than enthusiasm. The process needs to be ongoing and, no matter how experienced the access auditor is in both methods of improving accessibility and how to achieve this successfully and sympathetically, the involvement of different disabled people in the process of improving access to a historic landscape is crucial to success. Following a design specification built on the regulatory documents mentioned earlier is a starting point but to find a solution which best matches the needs of visitors and a specific environment itself, further dialogue and discussion is required. This process can help manage expectations of what might be possible; the true historic significance of a site is not obvious to everyone and exactly where to place access improvements which are required needs proper consideration and testing to make sure that investment and time is not wasted and the experience truly improved. The early stages of building these relationships do not always go smoothly. It takes time to get to a point of understanding and to realise the mutual benefit of this new way of working; however, experience shows that most people engage willingly and pragmatically, providing they fully understand the situation. It is rarely possible to do everything for everyone, but common sense and creativity will go a long way.

The National Trust has some relevant examples of this way of working. Disability Stockport, an umbrella organisation for groups and individuals with an interest in disability matters, began working with properties in the North West region of the National Trust in 2007 following a workshop where the group had some fairly forthright comments to make about accessibility. Property teams and regional colleagues decided to explore these comments in more detail and a longstanding working relationship began. Representatives from the group have now advised on accessibility improvements for new areas of properties being opened to the public and also enhancements to interpretation. Enable NI, an organisation which promotes inclusion for disabled people in the Southern Area of Northern Ireland, worked with Divis and the Black Mountain, one of the mountains above Belfast, to develop a new visitor centre and Changing Places, an adult changing facility – the first one at a National Trust property.

When making decisions about how to develop access improvements, it is useful to consider the following guiding principles for creating an inclusive environment: ease of use, comfort, offer of choice, safety, and embracing the diversity of the landscape.[11] Each of these principles should be applied at each stage of the access audit and below are some examples of how these could be applied in particular circumstances.

Whilst access to historic landscapes is not just about the topography, paths and routes around a site are a crucial part of the experience. In addition, the available paths and routes, and the materials they are made from, are often important elements in the historic significance of a site. Cobbles are a traditional surface used in historic landscapes which can cause difficulties of access for disabled visitors. They were a traditional surface in areas where high levels of durability were required, for example courtyards where vehicles required a firmer surface than grass to move around easily. These courtyard areas are now used by feet and narrow wheels rather than large carts, and this style of surface, particularly when affected by wear and tear, can become problematic. The conservationists' desire to keep materials and design integral to the history of a site means that the removal of cobbles or any form of alteration for accessibility purposes often causes complications. However, there are ways to balance these requirements and meet the inclusive design principles. A cobbled surface can be entirely or largely maintained and an accessible route created over or around them. Examples of this include adding a paved pathway around a cobbled yard as at National Trust properties Tatton Park, Cheshire and Ilam Park, Derbyshire, or using a temporary surface over the top of cobbles which protects them but also provides a firm surface for visitors. An example of this can be seen at Hampton Court Palace, Surrey (Figure 30.2).

These options give ease of use for visitors who prefer or require a firm or level surface, and make the process of moving round the site more comfortable. The experience is safer for more people, visitors can still use the cobbled surface and the historic surface is

Figure 30.2 Pathway across cobbles at Hampton Court Palace.

Figure 30.3 Paved pathway around a cobbled yard at National Trust property, Llanerchaeron, Ceredigion, Wales. (©National Trust Images/Arnhel de Serra.)

respected. Examples of this include adding a paved pathway around a cobbled yard as at National Trust property, Llanerchaeron, Ceredigion (Figure 30.3).

Sometimes the balance of conservation and access is challenged by the size of a site and the distance from one area to another. Although many historic environment organisations encourage visitors to arrive by public transport, the location of the site and the accessibility of transport means this is not always possible. Feasible locations for car parks and a desire to keep vehicles away from the significant areas of a site can create further difficulties. In these cases it is possible to make access easier, more comfortable and safer by providing accessible transfer vehicles to transport disabled people from the car park to the main site features. Making this provision provides choice and can, in part, help people preserve their energy for getting around the site itself. It avoids making further changes to the environment and preserves the diversity of the landscape.

Information provided about historic landscapes should also be inclusive. This includes pre-visit information which may be available on a website or in a specific property leaflet. There are specific design principles for websites which enable them to be accessible for people using assistive software. Following these principles can make websites generally easier to use for more people.[12] Websites also provide an opportunity for further virtual interpretation. The National Trust virtual tour project has been designed and tested with disabled people as members of the project team and as testers at various stages. The comments raised throughout the process made for a more accessible design and for a more reasonable approach to finding a solution. The virtual tours are also available at many properties to view during a visit.[13]

Leaflets often contain so much general information about a site that there is insufficient room left for details about accessibility, which is crucial for disabled people. The design of leaflets often causes barriers for understanding, with small type and poorly contrasting colours. There are specific principles set out by the Royal National Institute of Blind People (RNIB) for accessible design[14] and also further information from Mencap about designing for people with learning disabilities.[15] Following these principles will make documents easier to use, the process of taking in the information more comfortable and visitors will be more aware and safer on the site. Accessibility awareness can be increased by adding extra information to a website, creating a specific accessibility leaflet to be available at a site, or increasing the amount of accessibility information in an existing leaflet. Websites and paper leaflets provide choice in how to receive information but these options are unlikely to be enough to cover every disabled person's requirements and it is now expected that a short notice will be provided to indicate that alternative formats are available, including large print, Braille and an audio format.

One of the key ways to create an inclusive environment is to provide a warm welcome. When new visitors come to historic landscapes, it is important that staff and volunteers are supported appropriately with training and opportunities to learn more about how they can make the environment more welcoming for disabled people. This can range from disability awareness training, which many organisations now provide, to making sure that staff and volunteers in a variety of roles are involved in any consultation exercises with disabled people. Such opportunities should not be a 'one-off'; as with access audits, the process needs to continually evolve to make sure sites keep in step with the expectations of disabled people and examples of opportunities to improve accessibility. If possible, a practical element should be included in training so that staff and volunteers can appreciate how easy or difficult access is around their site for people with different disabilities.

Easy Access to Historic Landscapes presents further examples which illustrate that access can often be significantly enhanced through minor interventions that produce significant improvements. In addition, improving the number and location of seats available around a site; consideration of the requirements of people who are deaf and hard of hearing by including induction loops at points of conversation, for example till points, and the addition of 'Easy Read' publications which can make complex documentation easier to read for children and people with learning disabilities, all help make access to the historic environment easier without changing the environment itself.

Access to the historic environment is possible in a reasonable manner with an understanding of conservation issues. It is possible to find a way to make most environments accessible without detracting from their significant features or from the process of the visit if you work with stakeholder groups. Aside from the difficulties of the definition of 'reasonable', if clear approaches are followed which are informed by, participated in, and co-created by disabled people there is a much better chance of success and understanding. The balance between conservation and access continues to stimulate significant debate throughout historic environment organisations and provides an opportunity to task land managers with the challenge of arriving at some innovative and more accessible solutions and a more inclusive approach.

Endnotes

1. Sir David Attenborough, November 2010, Speech at the Communicate Conference.
2. Department for Works and Pensions, 2012, Family Resources Survey 2010/11. Available at http://research.dwp.gov.uk/asd/frs/2010_11/frs_2010_11_report.pdf [Accessed 26 November 2013].
3. Office for National Statistics, July 2012, 2011 Census – Key statistics for England and Wales, March 2011. Available at http://www.ons.gov.uk/ons/dcp171778_290685.pdf. [Accessed 16 December 2013].
4. Department for Works and Pensions, 2012, Family Resources Survey 2010/11. Available at http://research.dwp.gov.uk/asd/frs/2010_11/frs_2010_11_report.pdf [Accessed 26 November 2013].
5. Department for Culture, Media and Sport, June 2011, *Taking Part: the National Survey of Culture, Leisure and Sport*. Available at http://www.culture.gov.uk/images/research/Taking_Part_Y6_Release.pdf [Accessed 26 November 2013].
6. NHS Information Centre, 2009, *Health Survey for England 2008: Physical Activity and Fitness – Volume 1*. Available at www.ic.nhs.uk/pubs/hse08physicalactivity Quoted in NHS 2010 *Statistics on obesity, physical activity and diet: England 2010*, Available at www.ic.nhs.uk/webfiles/publications/opad10/Statistics_on_Obesity_Physical_Activity_and_Diet_England_2010.pdf [Accessed 10 February 2012]. See also Faber Taylor, A. et al (2001) 'Coping with ADD: The Surprising Connection to Green Play Settings', *Environment and Behaviour* 33, pp. 54–77.
7. More information available at www.heritage2health.co.uk [Accessed 26 November 2013].
8. English Heritage, Heritage Lottery Fund, National Trust and Sensory Trust, 2013, *Easy Access to Historic Landscapes*, Available at http://www.english-heritage.org.uk/publications/easy-access-historic-landscapes/ [Accessed 26 November 2013].
9. More information available at www.sensorytrust.org.uk [Accessed 26 November 2013].
10. Grant, A., 2005, *Access Audit Handbook*, Centre for Accessible Environments.
11. English Heritage et al, 2005, p. 15.
12. More information available at http://www.w3.org/WAI/intro/wcag [Accessed 26 November 2013].
13. More information available at http://virtualtours.nationaltrust.org.uk/calke-park/home.html
14. RNIB, 2011, *See it Right*, Available at http://www.rnib.org.uk/professionals/accessibleinformation/Pages/see_it_right.aspx [Accessed 26 November 2013].
15. Mencap, 2002, *Am I Making Myself Clear?*, Available at http://www.easy-read-online.co.uk/media/10609/making-myself-clear.pdf [Accessed 26 November 2013].

31 The international context – the European Landscape Convention[1]

Adrian Phillips
Professor (ret'd), Cardiff University, Cardiff, UK

A chapter about an international treaty may seem an oddity in a book about historic gardens and designed landscapes in Britain. But there are aspects of the European Landscape Convention (ELC) which could help better protect these valuable places in our own country. However, before looking at these, we should first explain the origins of the convention, what it is about and what it seeks to do, progress made in implementing it in Europe, and how the UK has responded to its requirements.

The origins of the ELC

The ELC is the first, and so far only, international agreement specifically focused on the topic of landscape. Cultural landscapes of Outstanding Universal Value are a concern of the World Heritage Convention;[2] many naturally productive wetland landscapes are protected by the Ramsar Convention on Wetlands of International Importance,[3] and several other global and regional treaties are concerned with aspects of the protection of natural systems which underpin many natural and semi-natural landscapes. But none of these agreements specifically addresses the idea of landscape as such.

It is no accident that a convention about landscape first emerged in Europe. Landscape plays a large part in the identity and culture of Europeans, and figures centrally in our shared artistic heritage. Along with food, history and language, landscape is what we think of as distinguishing one country from another. Moreover, because of the complex geography and history of Europe, and because European rural landscapes evolved slowly and are well adapted to natural conditions, they vary greatly over short distances. The result is a continent full of numerous and diverse cultural landscapes which are 'greatly cherished not only for their biodiversity, but also for their landscape beauty and the opportunities that they offer for informal outdoor recreation ... Such rich cultural landscapes, in general, do not occur in those parts of the world where human intervention is more recent'.[4] It is indeed the richness and diversity of landscape heritage that Europeans – and many visitors to Europe – most admire.

But of course the diversity and distinctiveness of the landscapes of Europe everywhere have been under increasing threat. They have been affected by large-scale changes, such as those caused by infrastructure developments, urban expansion, the Common Agricultural

Gardens & Landscapes in Historic Building Conservation, First Edition. Edited by Marion Harney.
© 2014 John Wiley & Sons, Ltd. Published 2014 by John Wiley & Sons, Ltd.

Policy (CAP) of the European Union (EU) and pollution. They have also suffered from the cumulative effects of small-scale changes, which may appear to have a local cause but which are really due to profound social and economic forces, such as the loss of skilled craftsmen to lay hedges, build and repair stone walls or thatch roofs, the intrusion of small but unsympathetic structures, and the effect of noise and light upon the previously unspoiled tranquillity of landscapes. The result is a trend that can be observed across Europe; the loss of landscape distinctiveness and diversity. The French have a good word for it: 'banalisation' – everything becoming more and more the same.

It was awareness of these destructive forces, and a concern that landscape as such was being ignored in decision-making, that led to the adoption of the ELC. This process began in the early 1990s, when two strands came together to demand action for landscapes at the international level.

One strand was a campaign to persuade the Council of Europe (CoE) to develop a rural landscape convention, an initiative that originated in the UK and France and was supported by the International Union for Conservation of Nature (IUCN) in a plan of 1994 for protected areas in Europe, and given further encouragement by the Dobříš Assessment (European Environment Agency, 1995).[5] Advocates of this course argued that the CoE had already developed international agreements in the fields of nature conservation, architectural heritage and archaeology, but needed now to respond to the threats to the rural landscape heritage of Europe. Particularly because some of these threats had a specifically European origin, for example the effects of the CAP, there was an urgent need for a Europe-wide response. However, there was agreement among the supporters that action was better taken through the CoE than the EU, both because the CoE includes nearly all the countries of Europe and because it was feared that Member States of the EU would resist the intrusion of the EU (with its instrument of choice, the EU directive) into this area of essentially national action.

The other strand arose with a desire to build on the 1993 Mediterranean Landscape Charter. This identified the kinds of actions needed to manage the threats to that region's distinctive landscapes, but it was no more than a declaration of aspiration and applied only to a part of Europe. So, in 1994, the Congress of Regional and Local Authorities, which is a constituent part of the CoE, decided to 'draw up, on the basis of the Mediterranean Landscape Charter . . . a framework convention on the management and protection of the natural and cultural landscape of Europe as a whole'.

Six years of negotiation followed, culminating in the adoption of the text of the ELC at a conference convened in Florence, Italy in October 2000 (hence it is sometimes called the 'Florence Convention').[6] During these negotiations, the UK played a significant part in sharing its expertise in landscape matters, and in the diplomatic and technical discussions that led to the agreed text.

What does the ELC do?

The central idea of the ELC is that it is concerned with landscape everywhere. It is not, therefore, like the World Heritage or Ramsar conventions, focused on a few places of great importance. This view of what the convention should be about was not easily arrived at. During negotiations some argued that the convention should identify and protect rural landscapes of European significance and thus in effect create a new tier of internationally protected sites. Initially IUCN advocated this, as did the UNESCO World Heritage Centre, which hoped that a European landscape treaty of this kind would relieve pressure for further sites in Europe to be designated as World Heritage Cultural Landscapes. However, the supporters of the more holistic view of landscape won the day.

Thus, the convention acknowledges in the preamble that 'the landscape is an important part of the quality of life for people everywhere: in urban areas and in the countryside, in degraded areas as well as in areas of high quality, in areas recognised as being of outstanding beauty as well as everyday areas'. The convention is concerned with urban and 'peri-urban' landscapes as well as rural ones; and it embraces inland and marine waters, seascapes included. In short, the ELC says *all* landscapes matter.

The preamble to the convention is democratic in its values, rejecting any rather elitist connotations that regard for landscape sometimes has. Thus, the ELC notes 'the public's wish to enjoy high quality landscapes and to play an active part in the development of landscapes'; and that 'landscape is a key element of individual and social well-being and that its protection, management and planning entail rights and responsibilities for everyone'. Importantly the convention encourages the participation of the public in landscape decisions and in this way could be seen as a challenge to the pre-eminence of landscape experts.

The convention is the product of the dawn of the twenty-first century in its references to sustainable development and its optimistic views about Europe: 'landscape . . . is a basic component of the European natural and cultural heritage, contributing to human well-being and consolidation of the European identity'. Also, 'the quality and diversity of European landscapes constitute a common resource' which require international action.

So the ELC is not about trying to pickle landscape in aspic – a Canute-like endeavour – but understanding what makes the landscape the way it is, how it has come to be, the forces working upon it and the values it has to society. The convention encourages us to manage change in the landscape rather than just resist it; and to do so by guiding change in ways that respect the underlying characteristics of a landscape, and indeed to use these as a 'medium' through which change can be made acceptable. This will be true even in heritage landscapes, where the main purpose of policy should of course be landscape protection, but achieved by managing the forces of change.

These ideas are expressed in the four aims of the ELC:

- *landscape protection*, that is, 'actions to conserve and maintain the significant or characteristic features of a landscape, justified by its heritage value' (Figure 31.1)
- *landscape management*, to 'ensure the regular upkeep of a landscape, so as to guide and harmonise changes which are brought about by social, economic and environmental processes'

Figure 31.1 The European Landscape Convention promotes landscape protection of heritage landscapes, such as this ridge and furrow field in Gloucestershire (author's own).

Figure 31.2 The European Landscape Convention promotes landscape planning or creation, such as the new landscape that is emerging in the National Forest (in this case in a former open cast area) (author's own).

- *landscape planning*, defined as 'strong forward-looking action to enhance, restore or create landscapes' (this includes the creation of new landscapes) (Figure 31.2)
- '*European co-operation on landscape issues*' (all quotations from articles 1 and 3 of the convention).

The ELC provides an important definition of landscape: *an area, as perceived by people, whose character is the result of action and interaction of natural and/or human factors.* This captures the idea of landscape as a meeting ground between people and the rest of nature, and between past and present, and embodying tangible and intangible values. Providing an agreed international definition for something as slippery as the notion of landscape is in itself a significant contribution made by those who drafted the ELC. This definition is now being widely referenced.

The treaty, though relatively easy to read, is written in 'legalese'. Scottish Natural Heritage has placed an excellent, accessible summary on its website of the ELC's principles:

Our landscape – people, from all cultures and communities, lie at the heart of efforts for landscape, as we all share an interest in, and responsibility for, its well-being.
All landscapes – the landscape is important everywhere, not just in special places and whether beautiful or degraded.
Changing landscapes – landscapes will continue to evolve in response to our needs, but this change needs to be managed.
Understanding landscapes – better awareness and understanding of our landscapes and the benefits they provide is required.
Tomorrow's landscapes – an inclusive, integrated and forward-looking approach to managing the landscapes we have inherited, and in shaping new ones, is required.

Fine words, but what are the practical implications? Countries that sign the ELC agree to:

- undertake to recognise landscapes in law, adopt policies for landscape protection, management and planning; promote participation of the public, local and regional

- authorities, and others in landscape issues; and integrate landscape into the whole range of planning and other issues that affect landscape (Article 5)
- adopt policies of awareness-raising, training and education, and landscape identification and assessment, to set landscape quality objectives, and to put landscape policies into effect (Article 6).

In short, the ELC aims to persuade governments to give more attention to landscape issues by raising the profile of landscape in decision-making and recognising its central role in our lives. Its requirements are expressed in general terms and its language is essentially hortatory. Countries that join the ELC commit to upholding its principles in domestic law and policy. But the CoE has no legal powers over Member States: 'Since its Conventions rely on agreement and consensus, enforcement of this Convention is through voluntary compliance and potentially through challenges made under domestic law'.[7] The implications of signing the convention are therefore not like adopting an EU directive; indeed, the Convention allows any country that has ratified it to withdraw without penalty.

What progress has been made with the Florence Convention since 2000?

The ELC has been enthusiastically embraced by most Council of Europe States: thus by July 2012, 37 States had signed and ratified the treaty, three had signed it only and seven had done neither.[8] The table shown in Figure 31.3 summarises the position at the time of writing.

Austria, Germany and Russia represent three important gaps in the present coverage of the ELC. From the outset of negotiations, Germany opposed a landscape convention for Europe, with its delegates arguing that they could not sign, as the responsibility for landscape lay with the regional authorities (*länder*) under the German constitution and not with the federal government. And in both Austria and Germany (and perhaps elsewhere), there remains a 'not quite comprehensible' fear that the convention is another piece of intrusive European legislation; in particular, many landowners are believed to be unenthusiastic because of their experience with the EU's habitats directive.[9] It is not clear why Russia has so far failed to sign the convention but a Russian official at the 10th anniversary of the treaty in 2010 said that the convention 'possessed enormous potential . . . and [that] the Russian Federation is on the way to get it launched'.

The convention has attracted more signatures than most CoE treaties, and the Council considers it a 'true success story'.[10] However, the convention is not 'driven' as hard from the centre as some others – for example, the World Heritage Convention – as it does not have its own secretariat or its own funds. Because of this, perhaps, three Europe-wide groupings have come into being to support the convention and work with the CoE: UNISCAPE, an alliance of universities in support of the ELC; CIVISCAPE, made up of non-governmental organisations (NGOs) working for the convention; and ENELC, representing local and regional authorities.

The ELC in the UK

The UK itself took time to sign the convention, not doing so until 21 February 2006 (nearly six years after the Florence meeting and after 27 other countries had joined). The ELC came into force in the UK on 1 March 2007. This six-year delay is surprising as UK experts played a large part in developing the treaty.[11] It is surprising too, because many of the ideas in the ELC draw upon experience in the UK and so the requirements of the convention are not unfamiliar to us. For example, the ELC encourages work on the protection of lived-in and working landscapes (Figure 31.4), countryside management, agri-environmental schemes, community engagement in landscape matters, the recovery of despoiled landscapes and landscape character assessment – all areas where the UK is experienced.

States	Signature	Ratification	Entry into force	States	Signature	Ratification	Entry into force
Bosnia and Herzegovina	9/4/2010	31/1/2012	1/5/2012	Malta	20/10/2000	-	-
Bulgaria	20/10/2000	24/11/2004	1/3/2005	Moldova	20/10/2000	14/3/2002	1/3/2004
Croatia	20/10/2000	15/1/2003	1/3/2004	Monaco	-	-	-
Cyprus	21/11/2001	21/6/2006	1/10/2006	Montenegro	8/12/2008	22/1/2009	1/5/2009
Czech Republic	28/11/2002	3/6/2004	1/10/2004	Netherlands	27/7/2005	27/7/2005	1/11/2005
Denmark	20/10/2000	20/3/2003	1/3/2004	Norway	20/10/2000	23/10/2001	1/3/2004
Estonia	-	-	-	Poland	21/12/2001	27/9/2004	1/1/2005
Finland	20/10/2000	16/12/2005	1/4/2006	Portugal	20/10/2000	29/3/2005	1/7/2005
France	20/10/2000	17/3/2006	1/7/2006	Romania	20/10/2000	7/11/2002	1/3/2004
Georgia	11/5/2010	15/9/2010	1/1/2011	Russia	-	-	-
Germany	-	-	-	San Marino	20/10/2000	26/11/2003	1/3/2004
Greece	13/12/2000	17/5/2010	1/9/2010	Serbia	21/9/2007	28/6/2011	1/10/2011
Hungary	28/9/2005	26/10/2007	1/2/2008	Slovakia	30/5/2005	9/8/2005	1/12/2005
Iceland	29/6/2012			Slovenia	7/3/2001	25/9/2003	1/3/2004
Ireland	22/3/2002	22/3/2002	1/3/2004	Spain	20/10/2000	26/11/2007	1/3/2008
Italy	20/10/2000	4/5/2006	1/9/2006	Sweden	22/2/2001	5/1/2011	1/5/2011
Latvia	29/11/2006	5/6/2007	1/10/2007	Switzerland	20/10/2000	-	-
Liechtenstein	-	-	-	The former	15/1/2003	18/11/2003	1/3/2004
				United Kingdom	21/2/2006	21/11/2006	1/3/2007
Total number of signatures not yet followed by ratifications: 3							
Total number of ratifications/accessions: 37							

Figure 31.3 ELC: Signatories and Ratifications: Status as of 25/7/2012.

Figure 31.4 The European Landscape Convention promotes landscape management for the day-to-day upkeep of landscapes, such as through training courses for stone walling in the Cotswolds Area of Outstanding Natural Beauty (AONB) (author's own).

Even so, campaign groups had to work hard to persuade the UK to sign the treaty. While there was no public consultation there were wide-ranging discussions between government departments, statutory agencies and specific sectors with an interest in the subject matter of the ELC. The sector-specific consultation was undertaken by the Institute for European Environmental Policy, which was employed by the Department for Environment, Food and Rural Affairs (Defra). The consultant's report found that 'discussions present a generally positive view of the likely impacts of ECL ratification . . . The notable exception is the view from those responsible for national planning policies, particularly in England, which is less positive'.[12] Resistance came mainly from the then Office of the Deputy Prime Minister (the planning department), which feared that the convention would be used by pressure groups to obstruct development. More generally, there may have been a sort of arrogance at work ('we are doing it anyhow') and a fear, not it seems shared by other countries, that the UK would be forced by the convention into doing things it did not want to do. To overcome this resistance, a joint lobbying group was formed by International Council on Monuments and Sites (ICOMOS) members (the heritage sector) and IUCN members (the nature conservation sector) in the UK. It held two conferences in Oxford and supported another in Cardiff, all designed to raise awareness of the convention and to make the case for signing. By the time of signature in February 2006, the ELC already had a high profile and was beginning to affect practice. To celebrate success and to launch implementation in the UK, the group held another event in London.[13]

When Ministers eventually informed Parliament of their decision to sign the ELC, they said that they recognised the value that landscape plays in the environmental, physical, psychological, economic and social well-being of the nation, that they saw no major financial implications in ratifying the convention, and that it would apply to the whole of England, Scotland, Wales and Northern Ireland – though not, at the time, to the Crown Dependencies.[14]

The Government assigned ministerial responsibility to the Secretary of State for Environment, Food and Rural Affairs, in consultation with other UK Ministers, and responsible Ministers were also identified in each of the devolved administrations, along with lead agencies (Figure 31.5).

```
┌─────────┐  ┌─────────┐  ┌─────────┐  ┌───────────────┐
│ England │  │ Scotland│  │  Wales  │  │Northern Ireland│
└────┬────┘  └────┬────┘  └────┬────┘  └───────┬───────┘
     ▼            ▼            ▼               ▼
┌──────────────────────────────────────────────────────┐
│                      DEFRA                           │
└──────────────────────────────────────────────────────┘
```

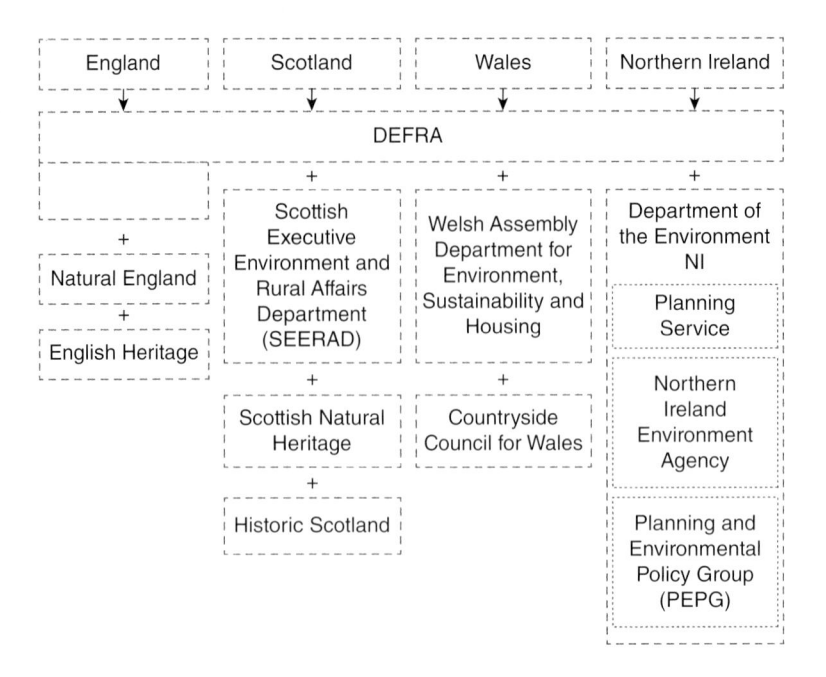

Figure 31.5 The lead responsibilities for the implementation of the ELC in the United Kingdom.

Progress since 2006 in the UK

Because of the devolved nature of implementation, it is most convenient to assess progress against countries and agencies, drawing on three assessments:[15]

England: Natural England (NE) leads the implementation of the ELC in England and works with Defra and English Heritage (see below). Since 2006, they have adopted an implementation framework to direct their work for the ELC, reviewed government policies for their compliance with ELC purposes and prepared an ELC action plan. They supported landscape character assessment work, especially through the Landscape Character Network, and in 2012 launched a new set of descriptions of national landscape character areas which brought this work up to date. NE has also published three guidance reports: *What does the ELC mean for your organisation?*, *Integrating the intent of the ELC into plans, policies and strategies*, and *Preparing an ELC Action Plan*,[16] and adopted landscape policy positions on the ELC and its own work, including *All Landscapes Matter, Protected Landscapes, Future Landscapes*.

English Heritage committed itself to the aims of the convention from the outset, adopting an action plan for its implementation. It recognised that the ELC is relevant to the view that 'the significance of place' should be at the heart of heritage conservation practice, and that the convention supports the concept of Historic Landscape Characterisation.[17] Similarly, EH believes that the ELC supports its call for historic area assessments and projects (including novel features like the Heritage Connect website, which helps local people and visitors connect with the urban landscape).

Scotland: Scottish Natural Heritage (SNH) published its own Landscape Policy Framework, ahead of the UK's signing the European Landscape Convention, but in spirit with it. In 2009, it undertook a 'gap analysis' of Scotland's performance under the convention. A report on good practice elsewhere in Europe concluded that 'The European Landscape Convention provides an unparalleled opportunity for planning, managing and protecting Scottish landscapes and for mainstreaming landscape considerations into public policy'.[18] The SNH website now states that the convention provides a framework for its landscape work in Scotland.

Wales: the Countryside Council for Wales (CCW) declares that it champions the view of landscape taken by the ELC through its work with the Welsh Assembly Government and its partners, and commits to 'embrace and help to deliver the ELC's principles'. There is, however, no CCW action plan for the ELC comparable to that drawn up by NE, nor does the ELC seem to feature as strongly in its promotional work as it does for NE and SNH.

Northern Ireland: there is as yet no reference to the convention on the website of the Council for Nature Conservation and the Countryside. However, a report was commissioned on the ELC in Northern Ireland from the University of Ulster.[19]

In summary, NE and to a degree SNH have 'driven' the convention forward in their countries, although there are some gaps, for example advice is needed on defining landscape quality objectives and the marine landscape; in Wales there has so far been less progress. In Northern Ireland there has been some progress, but only recently.

Defra convened a major landscape conference in Liverpool in November 2010 to demonstrate the UK's engagement with the principles of the ELC and celebrate landscaping achievements.[20] The conference also announced the first bi-annual UK nomination for the European Landscape Award introduced by the ELC (Article 11); this went to Durham County Council which led the partnership that restored the much-damaged Durham coastline. However, Ministers did not attend and there has been little overt political enthusiasm for the convention in recent years. 'Landscape' is not referred to in the Coalition agreement of May 2010, and one might guess that the government's overriding concern with the deficit reduction programme and removing perceived obstacles to economic growth, as well as anti-European sentiment in parts of the Conservative party, do not sit comfortably with advocacy for a European treaty on landscape. Neither the National Planning Policy Framework nor the Natural Environment White Paper (both published in 2012) refer to the ELC, and cuts in NE's budget have made it a less effective champion of the convention in England. Proposals in the review that Defra commissioned for a way to assess the implementation of the ELC have not been adopted, though, as noted above, more progress has been made in Scotland and Wales in recent years.[21] More importantly, the convention's implementation does not depend on government alone.

Regional/local level: NE's guidance on preparing an ELC Action Plan is important: it shows how public and other bodies can incorporate the aims of the convention into their own plans.[22] The convention originated in the part of the CoE in which local and regional authorities are represented, and it is to this level in particular that one looks for action to turn the generalised concepts in the treaty text into landscape-related projects on the ground.

In fact, the ELC has been taken up by a number of local authorities and protected landscape agencies (national parks and AONBs). Examples of such work include:

- A publication of case studies of good practice in relation to the ELC in England's National Parks.[23] The Peak District has prepared an ELC action plan[24]
- The National Forest Company has adopted its own ELC action plan, believing that the convention exemplifies the principles behind the development of the forest[25]
- Many local plans, etc., refer to the convention. Perhaps its most important influence has been to reinforce the importance of landscape character assessments, and their influence over land management and land use planning
- Many Landscape Partnership schemes across the UK have received grants from the Heritage Lottery Fund; these all exemplify the principles of the ELC. The evaluation of this HLF programme comments that 'Landscape Partnerships . . . contribute significantly to the UK's commitment to implementation of the European Landscape Convention . . . which sees "landscape" as multifaceted, multipurpose and multifunctional, the product of the action and interaction of humans and nature over time'.[26] The HLF has so far invested more than £100 million in this programme, supporting 69 schemes. Each partnership focuses on an area of distinct landscape character, and contains a range of programmes and projects that together address the holistic view of landscape in a way that the convention espouses.

Given the amount of local activity now underway, it is perhaps surprising that NGOs have been slow to champion the cause of the convention: the nature conservation and environment bodies have not seen its relevance to their aims, and the Campaign to Protect Rural England (CPRE) seems to regard it just as an added way to combat unwelcome development pressures rather than to espouse the cause of landscape in general (there is, for example, nothing about the ELC on the CPRE's website). However, the Campaign for the Protection of Rural Wales (CPRW) convened a conference in July 2011 'to consider how the principles of the European Landscape Convention and the stewardship of landscapes and seascapes in Wales, should be reflected in . . . Wales'.[27]

The ELC and the historic gardens and designed landscapes

From the above, one can draw this assessment of the current significance of the ELC:

- The treaty has been an international success in that it has attracted many signatories and is considered to be a global pioneer in developing an agreement around landscape
- It has helped to achieve some important conceptual advances in our understanding of landscape (e.g. what landscape is, and that all landscapes matter)
- Within the UK there has been a variable response, many examples of good practice but a rather uneven pattern of activity and a noticeable drop-off in political interest since 2010
- The potential of the convention is apparent in the way that some organisations have used it. More could do so, including the community interested in historic gardens and designed landscapes.

While the ELC does not refer directly to gardens and designed landscapes, since it takes a holistic view of landscape, it could benefit them in several ways:

- As one of its main aims is the protection of heritage landscapes, the convention is directly relevant to the needs of such areas
- With its emphasis on landscape assessment (Article 6), the convention reinforces the value of landscape characterisation work in which agencies (such as NE) and many local authorities have been, and are, engaged. Those interested in historic and designed features, and their conservation needs, should ensure that these are recognised in such assessments
- Likewise, the ELC supports the work done on Historic Landscape Characterisation, a very useful approach to identifying historic and designed landscapes of importance
- With its emphasis on public participation in landscape matters, the ELC challenges those responsible for historic gardens and designed landscapes to be more inclusive in their approach, listening more to what people see as important to them in these places, and taking the ideas of the public more into account
- The ELC's requirement to set explicit landscape quality objectives is especially relevant for historic gardens and designed landscapes. Arriving at these in consultation with the local community would be in the spirit of the ELC
- Advocates of historic gardens and designed landscapes should consider working with the national heritage agencies (English Heritage, Historic Scotland and Cadw) in schemes designed to show how the convention can work for the historic landscape heritage
- Through engagement with HLF-funded Landscape Partnerships, those interested in historic gardens and designed landscapes can work in a broader context, make new alliances and access new sources of funding
- Academics and NGOs interested in historic gardens and designed landscapes can build stronger pan-European connections through participation in the work of UNISCAPE and CIVISCAPE.

So, while the ELC brings no new powers or funding, it provides a potentially sympathetic context for work on historic gardens and designed landscapes. To get the best out of the convention, those interested in such areas should: engage more with those who are concerned with landscape at a larger scale; put the conservation of such areas into a broader geographical, cultural and social context; and seek new allies, in the UK and elsewhere in Europe.

References/Further reading

Campaign for the Protection of Rural Wales (CPRW) (2011) *Connecting landscapes through 'A Living Wales'– Proceedings of Landscape Symposium, Cardiff:* 11–12 July 2011, CPRW.

Clark, R. (2010) *Evaluation of the Landscape Partnerships programme – report to the Heritage Lottery Fund*, Centre for European Protected Area Research, University of London.

Hadden, E. and Coates, S. (2010) *For the Achievement of Valued Places for People Through Design*, Landscape Institute Northern Ireland (LINI) and Ministerial Advisory Group for Architecture and the Built Environment for Northern Ireland (MAG), pub. University of Ulster, 32 pp.

Dwyer, J., Eaton, R., Ten Brink, P. Mills, L,. Wilkinson, D. and Bate, R. (2003) *UK Participation in the Council of Europe's European Landscape Convention – a study for Defra*, Institute of European Environmental Policy, London.

English Heritage (2008) *Conservation Principles: Policies and Guidance*, English Heritage, London.

English National Parks Authorities Association (ENPAA) (2010) *England's National Parks and the European Landscape Convention*, ENPAA, London.

European Environment Agency (1995) *Europe's Environment – the Dobříš Assessment* (edited by David Stanners and Philippe Bourdeau), Office for Official Publications of the European Communities, Luxembourg.

FCO (2006) *Explanatory Memorandum on the European Landscape Convention*, Command Paper Number 6794.

Green, B. and Vos, W. (2001) *Threatened Landscapes – Conserving Cultural Landscapes*, Spon Press, London and New York.

ICOMOS (2006) *Implementing the European Landscape Convention – Outcomes of an ICOMOS-UK & IUCN UK Invited Workshop*, 28 February 2006, ICOMOS/UK London.

IUCN Commission on National Parks and Protected Areas (1994) *Parks for Life: Action for Protected Areas in Europe*, IUCN, Cambridge, UK.

Knoll, D.I. Dr (2008) *'Landscape in planning policies and governance: towards integrated spatial management'*, Paper for the Seventh Meeting of the Workshops of the Council of Europe for the implementation of the European Landscape Convention; Piestany, Slovak Republic, 24–25 April 2008 see: http://www.knollconsult.at/zt/pub/31_2008_Knoll_ELC%20Piestany_Knoll.pdf

National Forest Company (NFC) (2009) *National Forest European Landscape Convention Action Plan, 2008 13*, NFC, Donisthorpe.

Natural England (NE) (2009) prepared by Land Use Consultants: *Part 1 – What does it mean for your organisation? Part 2 – Integrating the intent of the ELC into plans, policies and strategies; Part 3 – Preparing an ELC Action Plan*, Land Use Consultants, London.

Peak District National Park (2009) *Landscape Strategy, 10: Action Plan*, Peak District National Park, Bakewell.

Phillips, A. (1992) 'Proposal for a Convention for the Conservation of the Rural Landscapes of Europe', in *Paysage et Amenagement*, 21, 1992, pp. 95–101 (in English and French).

Phillips, A. (2010) *Implementing the European Landscape Convention* – an unpublished internal report by the ICOMOS UK/IUCN UK Landscape Working Group for the Liverpool Landscape Conference.

Roe, M.H., Jones, C. and Mell, I.C. (2008) *Research to Support the Implementation of the European Landscape Convention in England Contract No.PYT02/10/1.16, Final Report*. A Study for Natural England, March 2008. http://www.naturalengland.org.uk/Images/ELC-NE-Research-March2008_tcm6-23598.pdf

Roe, M.H. Selman, P. Jones, C. Mell, I.C. and Swanwick, C. (2009) *Establishment of a baseline for, and monitoring of the impact of, the European Landscape Convention in the UK*, Research Report for Defra.

Endnotes

1. I am grateful to Dr Marion Harney and Prof. Maggie Roe (Newcastle University) for their constructive comments on earlier drafts of this chapter.
2. See chapter 32 of this volume: Denyer, S. 'Cultural landscapes and the World Heritage Convention'.

3. The convention resulted from a meeting in Ramsar, Mazandaran, Iran in 1971, and was adopted in 1975.
4. Green and Vos, pp. 139.
5. The origins can be traced to a conference in Blois, France, organised by the UK's Landscape Research Group and its French equivalent, *Paysage et Amenagement*. See Phillips 1992.
6. For convention text, see: http://conventions.coe.int/Treaty/en/Treaties/Html/176.htm
7. Roe et al (2008).
8. Signing a treaty is a statement of intent; ratification is the formal adoption by the country concerned. In the case of the ELC, the convention normally comes into force three months after ratification in the country concerned.
9. Knoll, 2008.
10. Mikko Härö, the Chair of the Steering Committee for Cultural Heritage and Landscape of the Council, speaking at the 10th anniversary celebrations in October 2010.
11. for example: the author of this chapter, who was Director General of the Countryside Commission (1981–92), led the IUCN campaign for the development of a European convention on landscape; Michael Dower, his successor at the Countryside Commission (1992–96), chaired the expert group that worked with a parallel legal group in shaping the convention; and Roger Clarke, who worked for both Adrian and Michael, chaired the group at the Council of Europe that drafted the Convention.
12. Dwyer *et al*.
13. ICOMOS (2006).
14. FCO (2006).
15. Roe *et al* (2008), Roe *et al* (2009) and Phillips (2010).
16. NE (2009).
17. EH (2008).
18. ICPL (2009).
19. Hadden, E. and Coates, S. (2010) *For the Achievement of Valued Places for People Through Design*, Landscape Institute Northern Ireland (LINI) and Ministerial Advisory Group for Architecture and the Built Environment for Northern Ireland (MAG), pub. University of Ulster, 32 pp.
20. see http://www.uklandscapeconference.org/docs
21. Roe *et al* (2009).
22. NE (2009).
23. ENPAA (2010).
24. Peak Park (2009).
25. NFC (2009).
26. Clark (2010).
27. CPRW (2011).

32 Cultural landscapes and the World Heritage Convention

Susan Denyer

World Heritage Adviser, ICOMOS (International Council on Monuments and Sites) & Secretary-General, ICOMOS-UK, London, UK

What are cultural landscapes?

Reflecting broadening views of cultural heritage, the phrase 'cultural landscape' has emerged as a heritage term over the past three decades in order to acknowledge the way landscapes reflect the interaction between people and their environment over time. The notion of cultural landscapes embraces dynamic processes as well as tangible assets and also respects change and evolution. In 1992 the World Heritage Convention became the first international legal instrument to formally identify and protect cultural landscapes as a category of heritage property; this has had a pronounced impact on the profile of what is now recognised as an important heritage concept.[1]

In one sense landscapes shaped by people have been celebrated through the medium of landscape painting in Europe since the Renaissance (14th–16th century ACE) and in China since at least the Tang Dynasty (7th–10th century ACE). In many rural societies around the world, the mores of cultural collaboration, social structures and often also belief systems were defined by the way communities ordered their landscapes for living and production. As early as 1908, the geographer Otto Schlüter formally put forward the idea of two types of landscapes: those that reflect human culture and those that might be seen to reflect nature untouched by people.[2] And Carl Sauer's classic definition of 1925 stressed the idea of culture as a force for shaping the environment around us: the 'cultural landscape is fashioned from a natural landscape by a cultural group. Culture is the agent, the natural area is the medium, the cultural landscape is the result'.[3]

Since the 1920s the concept of cultural landscape has been much debated within academia and particularly by geographers. Its adoption as a formal category in 1992 by the UNESCO World Heritage Committee has done more than anything else to mainstream its use. Importantly, it has prompted debate on ideas of the value, protection and management of cultural landscapes. Some universities now offer specialist postgraduate studies in cultural landscapes, including, for instance, the universities of Bath, UK; Naples, Italy; St-Étienne, France and Stuttgart, Germany.

It is important to underscore that purely 'natural' places where people have had no or little impact now account for a very low percentage of the world's land surface. Thus, in one sense, most landscapes can be considered as cultural landscapes – places that reflect the impact of cultural processes associated with human endeavour across space and over time.

Gardens & Landscapes in Historic Building Conservation, First Edition. Edited by Marion Harney.
© 2014 John Wiley & Sons, Ltd. Published 2014 by John Wiley & Sons, Ltd.

People are the social forces; the environment provides both opportunities and constraints, and various technical, economic, or spiritual processes link these two together.

Cultural landscapes may, for instance, reflect the gaining of food through hunter-gathering, agro-pastoralism, arable farming, or viticulture. The physical manifestations of such processes might also reflect the extraordinary efforts that had to be made in order to utilise the environment, such as large-scale irrigation projects, or the massive terracing of mountain landscapes, or the outcome of those processes – buildings created with substantial wealth generated by trade. Landscapes can also reflect very specific responses to particular conditions such as distinctive building traditions that arise from the use of scarce materials or the reaction to hostile climatic conditions.

At times the processes of interaction can be almost invisible. Landscapes with strong spiritual associations may be left virtually untouched – such as sacred groves or sacred mountains. These landscapes look natural but they are strongly imbued with cultural meaning. Cultural landscapes may also be urban areas where the processes of interaction have so completely transformed the environment that the immediate interaction with natural resources appears minimal.

Cultural landscapes can also be linked to strong cultural associations like sense of place, identity or well-being that may be unrelated to the communities that were responsible for their creation. Outsiders may imbue landscapes with ideas of beauty or harmony and may see them as manifestations of perceived noble ideas and may sometimes 'improve' them to make them look more like some visual ideal. In the past three decades cultural landscapes have also become associated with both positive and negative ideas of ecological value, mostly by technical specialists from outside the farming communities.

Whereas most landscapes around the world may be considered as cultural landscapes, some have come to be more valued than others. The strength and persistence of the interactions between people and their environment over time, or the specificity of the outcomes, have created landscapes that could be considered as outstanding or exceptional in some way or other. It is these landscapes that might be inscribed on the World Heritage List as World Heritage cultural landscapes. There is thus no difference in concept between cultural landscapes and World Heritage cultural landscapes: World Heritage cultural landscapes are seen as places that have outstanding value that gives them international importance just in the same way as some monuments, or ensembles of buildings, might be considered exceptional.

The emergence of World Heritage cultural landscapes

The complexity of articulating the landscape of the English Lake District in terms of identifying how 'culture' and 'nature' are linked turned out to be a catalyst in defining how cultural landscapes might be recognised and inscribed under the World Heritage Convention.[4]

In the 1980s the singular importance of the Lake District landscape (Figure 32.1) as a fusion between culture and nature was recognised by the UK government when it submitted two nominations to UNESCO for the area to be considered for World Heritage status. The first nomination dossier was for the Lake District as a mixed natural and cultural property while the second dossier put forward the Lake District as a cultural property only: neither of these bids was successful but they led to productive reflection on the interaction between culture and nature of such properties that has now opened the way for places to be nominated as cultural landscapes.

The Convention for the Protection of the World Cultural and Natural Heritage (1972), commonly known as the World Heritage Convention, is significant for the way it links together in a single document the concepts of nature conservation and the preservation of cultural properties. The Convention recognises the way in which people interact with nature, and the fundamental need to preserve the balance between the two. It allows for properties to be inscribed on a World Heritage List that are considered by a UNESCO World Heritage

Figure 32.1 Great Langdale, the Lake District, England.

Committee (elected by representatives of state parties that have ratified the Convention) to have 'Outstanding Universal Value' (OUV) and deserve protection for the benefit of all humanity and transmission to future generations.

In the early days of the Convention, properties had to be nominated either for their cultural or for their natural values. As early as 1984 the UNESCO World Heritage Committee had noted that in many countries there were landscapes that were not truly natural but had been modified by people and that in certain instances this interaction had created ecologically balanced, aesthetically beautiful and culturally interesting landscapes. However, it was not clear how these might be considered under the World Heritage Convention. A Task Force was set up to debate this issue. This reported to the 11th session of the Committee in 1987 that while the Convention was unique in bringing together culture and nature, which had hitherto been considered separately by the international community, it seemed desirable to make provision for sites where the two elements were harmoniously 'married' together – which seemed to be the case in certain rural landscapes. Accordingly, recommendations were made to amend the Operational Guidelines which set out the criteria and conditions under which sites might be nominated.

The same Committee discussed the first Lake District nomination and decided to leave open its decision until it had further clarified its position regarding the inscription of cultural landscapes. IUCN, the International Union for the Conservation of Nature, who evaluate natural sites, stated that they had not been able to come to a conclusion as to whether the nomination met the criteria for natural properties since there was a debate within IUCN as to whether the Lake District was truly a 'natural' site in the sense of Article 1 of the World Heritage Convention (i.e. nature not modified by man).[5] They also considered that the condition of integrity relating to the natural values was inadequate since the Lake District National Park did not have full control over agriculture and forestry activities which were of central importance in maintaining the natural beauty and character of the Lake District.

The second nomination was considered by the Committee at its 14th session in 1990. ICOMOS recommended that it should be included in the World Heritage list under cultural criteria. The Committee discussed this case in detail and, although many members showed great interest in inscribing the Lake District, no consensus could be reached. The Committee considered that it did not have sufficiently clear criteria to allow it to take a decision on this type of landscape property. The Committee therefore asked the Secretariat to develop such a criterion or criteria.

However, it was not until 1992 that a solution was found as to how such landscapes might be considered under the Convention. That year the first Earth Summit, the United Nations Conference on Environment and Development (UNCED), held in Rio de Janeiro, Brazil, paved the way for a new approach to the relationship between people and their environment being accepted by governments and civil society. This new approach provided the context within which a consensus emerged in the World Heritage Committee at its 16th session in 1992 that landscapes such as the Lake District landscape were neither purely natural nor purely cultural but rather a fusion between the two. The Committee adopted criteria for what have come to be known as 'cultural landscapes', and these have allowed many landscapes modified by people to be considered for World Heritage inscription.

World Heritage cultural landscapes are acknowledged to represent the 'combined works of nature and of man' designated in Article 1 of the World Heritage Convention. They are defined as being 'illustrative of the evolution of human society and settlement over time, under the influence of the physical constraints and/or opportunities presented by their natural environment and of successive social, economic and cultural forces, both external and internal'.[6]

Cultural landscapes are seen to be of three main types. First there are designed landscapes created intentionally that embrace garden and parkland constructed for aesthetic reasons which are often (but not always) associated with religious or other monumental buildings and ensembles. Secondly, there are organically evolved landscapes that result from an initial social, economic, administrative, and/or religious imperative and have developed into their present form by association with, and in response to, their natural environment. Such landscapes may be relict (or fossil) landscapes or be continuing landscapes which retain active social roles in contemporary society closely associated with a traditional way of life, and in which the evolutionary process is still in progress. And thirdly, associative cultural landscapes are seen to be related to powerful religious, artistic or cultural associations of natural elements.[7] These categories are not intended to be mutually exclusive and indeed many cultural landscapes exhibit a combination of more than one of these types.

The emergence of the category of cultural landscapes for World Heritage has opened up the debate on how we value cultural landscapes. Value is not inherent; it is given by society and may change over time. Sometimes there are differences between what is valued locally by people who live and work in cultural landscapes and those who articulate national or international value. What is valued internationally may not be valued by local communities and vice versa. For cultural landscapes to be inscribed on the World Heritage list, the World Heritage Committee must recognises that they have OUV. This does not mean that at the same time such places cannot have national and local values that may be associated with different attributes of the landscape: World Heritage inscription does not necessarily recognise all values related to a landscape but that does not diminish its other values. The challenge in managing World Heritage cultural landscapes is to sustain OUV as well as other attributes that convey other values in order to ensure the overall vitality and resilience of the property.

Examples of World Heritage Cultural Landscapes

By the end of the 37th session of the World Heritage Committee, held at Phnom Penh, Cambodia in 2013, 81 properties had been inscribed on the World Heritage list as cultural landscapes[8] (out of a total of 759 cultural properties), and these include four trans-boundary properties.[9]

Of these cultural landscapes, although five have been inscribed as designed landscapes and eight as relict landscapes, by far the majority of those inscribed reflect a complex fusion

Figure 32.2 Val d'Orcia, Italy.

between the various 'types' of cultural landscape and also between social and economic interactions and spiritual and/or aesthetic bonds. Below are examples that illustrate these multi-layered responses and above all the fundamental fusion between cultural and natural processes.

Val d'Orcia, Italy

A prime example of the fusion between beauty and utility is Val d'Orcia, Italy, near Siena (Figure 32.2).[10] Siena's dramatic growth as a trading state in the thirteenth and fourteenth centuries led it to expand its agricultural base outwards from the periphery of the city. The Val d'Orcia, an agricultural estate to the south of Siena, was 'colonised', together with other outlying areas such as the Maremma along the coast north of Rome. The wealth of Sienese merchants was invested in turning these landscapes into productive farmland within an innovative land tenure framework. So, far from being at the edge of the state, the valleys became a focus for display.

The Val d'Orcia is seen as representing the '*bel paesaggio*'; the ideal or prototype landscape of the early Italian Renaissance. It reflects the radical reorganisation of the existing feudal and medieval landscape in the fourteenth century. Fortified settlements adorn the hills and in the plains large elaborate farmhouses surrounded by fields look like villas in parks or gardens. Merchants supported the development of settlements, built palaces and churches and commissioned paintings that depicted the life of ordinary people in the landscape. The artists, particularly from Siena, portrayed the outcomes of the agricultural systems as images of beauty.

The agricultural landscape was radically reorganised by the merchants of Siena in the fourteenth and fifteenth centuries when they took over what had been a medieval feudal estate. The landscape was laid out deliberately to express the ideal of a beautiful and harmonious landscape and good governance as expressed in the painting of the *Effects of Good Governance in the Countryside*, one of a series of frescoes by Ambrogio Lorenzetti (1290–1348) painted 1337–39 in the Palazzo Pubblico or Town Hall in Siena.

Furthermore, it is the involvement of architects and artists in the development of the landscape that is so crucial. The ideal landscape was seen as something visual, not merely socio-economic. The area reflected a sort of mini agricultural revolution when the old feudal tenures were swept away and the farmers became key parts of the new system, and their work in creating beautiful landscape was seen as something to be celebrated by artists. The

Val d'Orcia was a reflection of the comparatively egalitarian nature of the Sienese state. Its creation is well documented in Renaissance treaties.

The landscape's distinctive aesthetics, flat chalk plains out of which rise almost conical hills, on top of which cluster fortified settlements, were widely painted by the artists of Siena and their images have come to exemplify the ideal of a Renaissance landscape that in turn influenced other artists and shaped other landscapes.

West Lake Cultural Landscape of Hangzhou, China

Such a direct relationship between artists, poets and landscape also developed into a strong cultural tradition in China from the Tang Dynasty (ACE 618–907) onwards. It reached its peak under the Song Dynasties from the eleventh to thirteenth centuries. What were seen as 'picturesque' landscapes attracted famous scholars and artists, and their ideas in turn led to the improvement of such landscapes through the additions of temples or the creation of lakes and ponds. An outstanding example is West Lake Cultural Landscape of Hangzhou (Figure 32.3), a large lake framed on three sides by mountains and on the fourth side by the City of Hangzhou, where numerous temples, pagodas, pavilions, gardens and ornamental trees overlaid the wooded and farmed landscape, and man-made islands and causeways were added to the lake.[11]

The successful fusion of these interventions with the natural hills and water of West Lake has been formally recognised since the Southern Song Dynasty (thirteenth century) in a series of ten poetically named scenic places which capture the visual and aural impact of various seasons, times of day, fleeting clouds, the sound of gentle wind, or the music of birds and bells.

These views are seen to embody perfection in terms of the way they encapsulate the fusion between people and nature. Overall the West Lake landscape is seen to have become a 'classic' example of the poetic and picturesque fusion between art and gardening that was practised by the Chinese intellectual elite. Although the wider West Lake landscape is still farmed, largely as tea plantations, these are mostly hidden from the main viewpoints around and across the lake landscape. The designed landscape has all but taken over the farmed landscape.

Figure 32.3 West Lake, Hangzhou, China.

Osun-Osogbo Sacred Grove, Nigeria

The dense forest of the Osun-Osogbo Sacred Grove, on the outskirts of Osogbo city in Western Nigeria, is one of the last remnants of primary high forest in southern Nigeria.[12] The Grove is seen as the abode of Osun, the Yoruba goddess of fertility, or the waters of life – one of the pantheon of Yoruba gods. Through the forest meanders the river Osun, and set within the forest sanctuary are shrines, sculptures and art works erected in honour of Osun and other Yoruba deities. Ritual paths lead devotees to 40 shrines and to nine specific worship points beside the river.

All Yoruba towns once had sacred groves, areas of virgin forest reserved for the worship of the gods. Unlike other Yoruba towns whose sacred groves have atrophied or disappeared, the Osogbo Grove has, over the past 40 years, been re-established as a central, living focus of the city. Shrines have been recreated, or created anew in sacred spaces, by an Austrian émigré, Suzanne Wenger, working with a group of local artists called New Sacred Art, under the patronage of the *Oba* (ruler) of Osogbo. This new art was to support and strengthen traditional religion, making manifest and tangible previously intangible aspects of the Yoruba gods, in a way that staked out the grove and acted as a powerful force against encroachment of the sacred spaces.

The revitalisation of the grove at a time when groves in other Yoruba towns were disappearing, has given the Osogbo Grove much more than local importance. It is now seen as a symbol of identity for all Yoruba people, including those of the African Diaspora, many of whom make pilgrimages to the annual festival.

Cultural Landscape of Bali Province: the *Subak* system as a manifestation of the *Tri Hita Karana* philosophy, Indonesia

The five sites of rice terraces and associated water temples on the island of Bali, Indonesia, known collectively as the 'Cultural Landscape of Bali Province: the *Subak* System as a Manifestation of the *Tri Hita Karan* Philosophy', represent the *subak* system, a unique social and religious democratic institution of self-governing associations of farmers who share responsibility for the just and efficient use of irrigation water needed to cultivate terraced paddy rice fields.[13] The success of the thousand-year-old *subak* system, based on weirs to divert water from rivers flowing from volcanic lakes through irrigation channels onto rice terraces carved out of the flanks of mountains, has created a landscape perceived to be of great beauty and one that is ecologically sustainable.

The supreme *subak* temple, Puru Ulun Danu Batur, on the rim of a volcanic crater, Lake Batur within the crater, temples and *subaks* along the Tampaksiring valley, a sacred landscape of forests, lakes, temples and *subaks* around Mount Batukaru, and the Royal temple of Pura Taman Ayun are together seen as manifestations of the Balinese philosophical principle *Tri Hita Karana* (three causes of goodness) that promotes a harmonious relationship between the realms of the spirit, the human world and nature.

A line of volcanoes dominate the landscape of Bali and have provided it with fertile soil which, combined with a wet tropical climate, make it an ideal place for crop cultivation. Water from the rivers has been channelled into canals to irrigate the land, allowing the cultivation of rice on both flat land and mountain terraces.

Rice, the water that sustains it, and *subak*, the cooperative social system that controls the water, have together shaped the landscape over the past thousand years and are an integral part of religious life. Rice is seen as the gift of god, and the *subak* system is part of temple culture. Water from springs and canals flows through the temples and out onto the rice paddy fields.

Water temples are the focus of a cooperative management of water resource by a group of *subaks*. Since the eleventh century the water temple networks have managed the ecology of rice terraces at the scale of whole watersheds. They provide a unique response to the challenge of supporting a dense population on a rugged volcanic island.

The overall *subak* system exemplifies the Balinese philosophical principle of *Tri Hita Karana* that draws together the realms of the spirit, the human world and nature. Water temple rituals promote a harmonious relationship between people and their environment through the active engagement of people with ritual concepts that emphasise dependence on the life-sustaining forces of the natural world.

In total, Bali has about 1,200 water collectives and between 50 and 400 farmers manage the water supply from one source of water. The property consists of five sites that exemplify the interconnected natural, religious, and cultural components of the traditional *subak* system; where the *subak* system is still fully functioning, farmers still grow traditional Balinese rice without the aid of fertilisers or pesticides, and the landscapes overall are seen to have sacred connotations.

Impact of the World Heritage cultural landscape category

The World Heritage category of cultural landscapes has brought the interaction between nature and culture to the forefront of conservation thinking. Specifically, it has allowed World Heritage nominations to come forward from under-represented areas of the world that do not have monumental heritage; it has given a value to time-honoured traditional processes; it has allowed an understanding of the way places created by people need to be understood and respected through an integrated, multi-faceted approach that articulates both the tangible and the intangible, and the dynamic and the static; and it has put people at the centre of protection and management.

The category of cultural landscape has also opened up certain aspects of the nature–culture duality for debate. Among the most interesting aspects are how we define 'managed nature', which has been improved by people and is no longer pristine (and to find a better name for this notion); how we value nature that has a spiritual or aesthetic value in cultural terms; and how we articulate the difference between cultural and natural beauty of landscapes. As the above examples suggest, philosophical concepts of landscape beauty have evolved in different ways in different parts of the world, while within many traditional and indigenous cultures there also exist ideas of landscape harmony which do not always make distinctions between nature and culture: nature that is seen as sacred and nature that is managed to produce food are perceived in different ways but nevertheless within an integrated overall landscape perception that often embraces aesthetic ideas. Within the World Heritage Convention, natural beauty has been defined as an inherent attribute of natural properties under criterion (vii), while cultural beauty is not specifically defined but implied within cultural criteria (i) to (vi).[14] This divide is tending to limit the possibilities for a seamless approach to acknowledging the aesthetic dimensions of some cultural landscapes.

As can be seen, within the World Heritage Convention we do not yet have wholly adequate tools for articulating fully the various relationships between culture and nature, and their value, particularly in relation to aesthetic ideas and ideals. It must be acknowledged that the process of identifying those places in the world that reflect exceptional and symbiotic interaction between people and nature still has further to go. Given that the Convention is one of the main international instruments that bring together culture and nature, it would be desirable if there could be an improved understanding of the relationship between cultural and natural beauty. To explore this area further will need much closer collaboration between environmentalists, ecological and social scientists and far fewer cultural heritage specialists.

References/Further reading

Denyer, S. 'The Lake District as a Cultural Landscape', in Walton, J.K. and Wood, J. (eds) (2013) *The Making of a Cultural Landscape: The English Lake District as Tourist Destination, 1750–2010*, Ashgate Publishing.

James, P.E. and Martin, G. (eds) (1981) *All Possible Worlds: A history of geographical ideas*, John Wiley & Sons, New York.

Mitchell, N., Rössler, M. and Tricaud, P-M. (Authors/eds) (2009) *World Heritage Cultural Landscapes: A Handbook for Conservation and Management*, UNESCO World Heritage Papers no 26.

Mitchell, N. (lead author), Leitão, L., Piotr, M. and Denyer, S. (2013) *Study on the application of Criterion (vii): Considering superlative natural phenomena and exceptional natural beauty within the World Heritage Convention*, IUCN World Heritage Study no 10.

Operational Guidelines for the Implementation of the World Heritage Convention July 2012, UNESCO.

Sauer, C. (1925) 'The Morphology of Landscape', *University of California Publications in Geography*, Vol. 2, No 2, pp. 19–53.

Endnotes

1. The Convention Concerning the Protection of the World Cultural and Natural Heritage, known as the World Heritage Convention, was adopted by the United Nations Educational, Scientific and Cultural Organisation (UNESCO) General Conference at its 17th session in Paris on 16 November 1972. The Convention came into force in 1975.
2. Quoted in James, P.E. and Martin, G. 1981, *All Possible Worlds: A history of geographical ideas*, John Wiley & Sons, New York.
3. Sauer, C. 1925, The Morphology of Landscape, *University of California Publications in Geography*, Vol. 2, No 2, pp. 19–53.
4. For more on this see Denyer, S. 'The Lake District as a Cultural Landscape', in Walton, J. K. and Wood, J. (eds), *The Making of a Cultural Landscape: The English Lake District as Tourist Destination, 1750-2010*, Ashgate Publishing (2013).
5. Under Article 1 of the World Heritage Convention, the following are considered as 'cultural heritage':
    - monuments: architectural works, works of monumental sculpture and painting, elements or structures of an archaeological nature, inscriptions, cave dwellings and combinations of features, which are of outstanding universal value from the point of view of history, art or science
    - groups of buildings: groups of separate or connected buildings which, because of their architecture, their homogeneity or their place in the landscape, are of outstanding universal value from the point of view of history, art or science
    - sites: works of man or the combined works of nature and man, and areas including archaeological sites which are of outstanding universal value from the historical, aesthetic, ethnological or anthropological point of view.
6. Paragraph 47 of the *Operational Guidelines for the Implementation of the World Heritage Convention*, July 2012.
7. These categories are set out in paragraph 10 of Annex 3 Guidelines on the inscription of specific types of properties on the World Heritage list of the *Operational Guidelines for the Implementation of the World Heritage Convention*, July 2012.
8. There are other properties which were inscribed on the World Heritage list before 1992 which might now be considered as cultural landscapes.
9. See http://whc.unesco.org/en/list/
10. See http://whc.unesco.org/en/list/1026
11. See http://whc.unesco.org/en/list/1334
12. See http://whc.unesco.org/en/list/1118
13. See http://whc.unesco.org/en/list/1194
14. For a discussion of these issues, see chapter 5, 'Aesthetic considerations in the application of cultural criteria: the application of the concept of cultural beauty', in *Study on the application of Criterion VII: Considering superlative natural phenomena and exceptional natural beauty within the World Heritage Convention*, IUCN World Heritage Study No. 10, 2013. The criteria that properties must satisfy if they are to be considered as having OUV are set out in paragraph 77 of the *Operational Guidelines for the Implementation of the World Heritage Convention*, 2012.

33 Why should there be any international law relating to monuments and cultural landscapes?

Malcolm Forster
International law consultant, London, UK

By definition, international law deals with matters which transcend natural boundaries and which therefore cannot be properly addressed by the application of national legal systems, even when the provisions of the national laws involved are broadly similar. So, international trade, navigation or other rights on the high seas, major threats to the global environment or to international peace and security are all clearly subjects in which law on the international plane has a role to play.

It is a little less easy to see how international law has much to say about the protection of monuments or cultural landscapes. These, particularly the former, are typically located within the territory of a single State and therefore, at first glance, it would seem that their protection and management would be entirely a matter for the domestic law of the host State, with little obvious scope for legitimate international involvement. There are, however, a number of ways in which the international law can be brought to bear on the question, including the following:

- The landscape in question may extend into two or more States
- The landscape may be so important and valuable that it is recognised as having a legitimate value to States other than the host State or to the global community as whole; or
- The host State has entered into binding international obligations to other States to preserve or rationally manage the landscape.

When international lawyers speak of 'international law', what do they mean?

Professionals working in the field of monument or landscape protection are familiar with a plethora of international instruments, often described as Charters, Declarations and so on, many of which are influential in determining national policy or action. Examples include the Venice Charter for the Conservation and Restoration of Monuments and Sites (1964), the Brussels Charter on Cultural Tourism, the Florence Charter on Historic Gardens (1981), and so on. For the international lawyer, however, none of these instruments *of themselves* has the character of law. This apparently rather dismissive judgment stems from a number of factors, including that:

Gardens & Landscapes in Historic Building Conservation, First Edition. Edited by Marion Harney.
© 2014 John Wiley & Sons, Ltd. Published 2014 by John Wiley & Sons, Ltd.

- There was no intention on the part of those negotiating the texts to create binding international legal relations
- The texts were not formally adopted at a diplomatic conference
- The 'national' representatives agreeing the texts were not accorded by their governments plenipotentiary powers to commit the States from which they came to binding international obligations
- The texts are not subject to the ratification process which is required for binding international treaties; or
- The wording of the instruments is often merely non-mandatory, recommendatory, precatory or otherwise indicates that binding international law obligations are *not* being created.

In effect, therefore, these instruments are regarded by international lawyers as mere statements of best practice or declarations of intent. It is not impossible that their terms (or some of them) *might in the fullness of time become international law*, but they do not enjoy that status at present.

So what is international law?

International lawyers look for their law in a curiously narrow spectrum. Conveniently, the legitimate sources of international law are listed in Article 38, Statute of the International Court of Justice. This recognises three primary sources of international law:

- Treaties
- International customary law; and
- General principles of law recognised by civilised nations.

In addition, resort may be made to two subsidiary sources:

- Decisions of international tribunals; and
- Writings of the most highly qualified publicists in international law.

It is worth considering some of these sources a little further.

Treaties   It is very tempting to think of treaties as the international equivalent of legislation, but this is a potential source of great confusion. Insofar as there is a domestic equivalent of a treaty, it is a contract rather than legislation. Why is a treaty not to be regarded as legislation? This question merits a very complex answer, but in short, the reason is that the international community is (in theory, at least) a community of equals. Each State is sovereign and, in principle, it is at liberty to do or refrain from doing anything it wishes. There is no international equivalent of a legislature which can makes rules which its subjects must obey. This pure theory of sovereignty is, of course, subject to numerous exceptions, but it remains the basic building block of international law.

A State may voluntarily agree with other States to act in a certain manner (e.g. to refrain from damaging or degrading monuments or cultural landscapes within its territory); by so doing, it of course limits its sovereign right to do so, but the acceptance of this limitation on its freedom of action is *itself* an act of sovereignty and can, if necessary, be revoked. So, the nearest domestic analogy with a treaty is the contract. Like contracts, treaties *only* bind States or other international law actors *which are party to the treaty*. With very limited exceptions (none of which apply in the field we are considering), a treaty can never impose obligations on States which have not accepted its terms by ratifying the treaty.

Ratification is a very formal process by which States acknowledge that they have agreed to assume the obligations in the treaty. It frequently, but not invariably, requires a constitutional process to be completed in the State party. As the process can take a significant time to complete, the effect is to rob the treaty of its former virtue as a means of speedily introducing new principles into international law. Therefore, a number of devices have been invented to avoid the engagement of the full formality of amendment and re-ratification, particularly the 'delegation' of powers to carry out amendments to subsidiary treaty bodies, such as an annual or biannual Conference of the Parties. While this process is rarely used to effect substantial changes to the fundamental principles enshrined in the treaty (although this does occasionally happen), it is very useful as a convenient method of, for example, updating listed or protected sites to which the treaty obligations apply.

Customary international law   Much less sclerotic, although not necessarily more flexible, is the development of customary international law. This is, in effect, what States *do*, or, perhaps, what States *say they do*. Treaties cannot cover every subject and quite significant areas of international law are largely governed by customary law, which often forms a substratum upon which 'islands' of treaty-based law are based. The importance of customary law is that, unlike treaties, its does not depend on voluntary buy-in – it binds all members of the international community, but in order to have this binding effect a customary law rule must be:

- Uniform in its content; and
- Accepted as binding by the members of the international community because they see it as having the force of law (*opinio juris*).

Avenues for protection of sites and landscapes in international law

There are several possible avenues:

The landscape (or possibly the monument) may be regarded as a resource shared by two or more States. This might occur, as we have seen, where the feature is physically situated in two or more States. That may be simply because of geographical accident or it may result from the fact that the boundary between the States is of recent date (perhaps a legacy of decolonisation) or where the internationally recognised boundaries do not reflect the ethnic or cultural integrity of populations – both not uncommon occurrences. Shared resources of this type have always necessarily been the subjects of international law. There are many examples, especially in the field of international environmental and natural resources law of shared resources managed by international law instruments; these include international watercourses, mineral resources (particularly oil and gas deposits), migratory species of animals and birds, and so forth.

The monument or landscape is of sufficient importance for its preservation or management to transcend the national interests (or shared natural interest) of the host State or States. The idea that objects within national jurisdiction may have value for other States or the international community in general has been developed most prominently in the fields of international environmental law, where it is responsible for the identification of such objects as forming part of the 'common heritage or mankind' or, more recently, as the 'common concern of humanity'. The principle has been applied to a wide range of resources and values, including migratory species and the attributes and properties represented by the biological diversity of ecosystems within national boundaries. The principle is of obvious application to monuments and sites and is part of the inspiration behind the UNESCO World Heritage Convention (see section 7 below).

The monument or landscape is protected as a 'by-product' of international instruments dealing with other matters. The relative paucity of international legal instruments specifically relating to the protection of monuments and cultural landscapes is relieved by the much larger *corpus* of international law primarily directed at other objectives, but which incidentally confer some degree of protection. For example, the conservation of certain species or groups of wildlife and, more particularly, the habitats of those species has generated a very significant body of international law. Many of these instruments have an important potential contribution to the protection of landscape. Among the most obvious instruments of this type are the Ramsar Convention on the Protection of Wetlands of International Importance and the Bern Convention on the Conservation of European Wildlife and Habitats. The Ramsar Convention has been ratified by 164 States, and sites which are designated by those States as protected wetlands cover over 200 million hectares. The Bern Convention is the principal habitat conservation treaty of the Council of Europe, although it has a small number of parties (mostly North African States) which are parties to the treaty even though they are not members of the Council of Europe. The flagship wildlife treaty is the Convention on Biological Diversity. Amongst the obligations accepted by the States Party to the Convention are the duties imposed in Article 8 to:

> develop, where necessary, guidelines for the selection, establishment and management of protected areas or areas where special measures need to be taken to conserve biological diversity;

and to:

> promote environmentally sound and sustainable development in areas adjacent to protected areas with a view to furthering protection of these areas.

At the European level, a similar effect is produced by the Council Directive 94/43/EEC on the conservation of natural habitats and of wild fauna and flora, which (despite its title) also extends to semi-natural habitats, totalling some 200 different categories of habitat types, such as specific types of forests, grasslands and so forth, which are of European importance.

International legal instruments specifically relating to monuments and protected landscapes

The principal global treaty relating to the protection of monuments and landscape is the UNESCO Convention Concerning the Protection of the World Cultural and Natural Heritage. These sites are regarded as suitable subjects for the application of international legal obligations because they are of 'outstanding universal value'. In other words, their value is such that it transcends the domestic interests of the State in which they are located, even if they are wholly situated on the territory of that State.

Cultural sites protected by the UNESCO Convention vary widely. They include architecture, works of monumental sculpture or painting, archaeological sites, inscriptions, cave dwellings and so on, including complex sites which consist of groups of buildings which are of value by virtue of their homogeneity or their place in the landscape. The Convention expressly recognises that the outstanding universal value which it demands may be derived from the grouping together of more than one building to produce a site of such value by virtue of their architecture, homogeneity or place in the landscape.

Natural sites can qualify for protection under the UNESCO Convention if they demonstrate natural features, including things such as geological or physiological formations, which are of *outstanding aesthetic or scientific value*, including sites or clearly defined areas of *outstanding value for conservation, science or natural beauty*. The Convention also extends to 'mixed sites', where a combination of nature and human influence produces sites which are of *outstanding universal value from the historical, aesthetic, ethnological or anthropological point of view*.

It can be seen that the *potential scope* of the UNESCO Convention is quite broad, but, for a candidate site within this scope, the major hurdle to inclusion on the World Heritage List is the standard of quality which must be demonstrated. In order to qualify for protection under the Convention, these sites must be shown to be of *outstanding universal value from the point of view of history, art or science*. This is an extremely demanding test, which is difficult to satisfy. While this aspect of the Convention may be frustrating to heritage professionals, it is entirely comprehensible to international lawyers, as it is only the genuinely international character of the site's value which justifies the restriction on the sovereignty of the host State. This restriction stems from the recognition by the host State in the UNESCO Convention that World Heritage Sites are places which it is the duty of the *international community as a whole* to protect and from the duty imposed by the treaty on States to cooperate to this end.

The Grenada convention – a regional model

In 1985, the Council of Europe States concluded a regional treaty, with the objective of protecting the architecture of Europe. This agreement is the Convention for the Protection of the Architectural Heritage of Europe, adopted in Grenada. It has attracted no fewer than 41 ratifications (final acceptances by States) and a further two States have signed the Convention, although they have not yet ratified it (this means that, while they are not fully bound by the obligations contained in the treaty, they may not act in such a manner as to undermine its purposes). Just as the scope of the Grenada treaty is narrower than the UNESCO Convention, so the standard required for qualification is a little more modest. What is required is that the monuments in question must be of *conspicuous* interest from an historical, artistic, social, scientific or technical perspective (rather than *outstanding* or *universal* value). Like the UNESCO Convention, the treaty recognises that this standard can be attained by groups of buildings forming a topographically distinct area and by sites displaying the interaction between nature and humanity, including sites which are only partially built upon. As the Convention only applies to the European architectural heritage, purely natural sites are not included (although, as mentioned above, they may attract protection under the Bern Convention and, more especially, under the Florence Convention, discussed below).

In respect of these buildings of conspicuous interest, the obligations of States Party are extensive. The sites must be protected; the demolition or disfigurement of the buildings must be prevented; they must not be permitted to fall into dilapidation; powers must be enacted to require the owners of the buildings to conduct repairs (or be obliged to allow the public authorities to do so in default) and to provide for compulsory purchase of the buildings in appropriate cases (although these last powers are subject to some reservations, often related to the constitutional protection of the right to property). The Convention also obliges States to prohibit the removal of such buildings, unless it is imperative to do so and, even then, there is an expectation that the building is to be re-erected on another site. There are also constructive hints in the treaty about harnessing the resources of the private sector to achieve these goals and fostering new or alternative uses of protected buildings.

Recognising people in the landscape

In the last years of the twentieth century, the view of landscape in international law underwent a gradual change, from regarding landscape as an objective value towards a recognition that landscape formed an integral part of people's lives and culture. An early straw in this wind was the Convention on the Protection of the Alpine Region. The principal purpose of the treaty is, of course, the protection and preservation of the Alpine environment, including the conservation of nature and the countryside especially for its variety, uniqueness and beauty, but the text also recognises as a protected value the social and cultural independence of local people. Furthermore, there is special recognition of the contribution to the Alpine environment of typical influences on the landscape, in particular the contributions made by traditional methods of mountain agriculture and forestry.

The most recent significant international instrument relating to landscape protection also demonstrates this anthropocentric trend. The European Landscape Convention 2000 (the Florence Convention) is another product of the Council of Europe. The Convention defines landscape as 'an area, *as perceived by people*, whose character is the result of the action and interaction of natural and human factors'. Unlike earlier treaties, the Florence Convention does not confine itself to outstanding landscapes, or even conspicuously interesting ones, but includes also everyday and degraded landscapes. Indeed, it even extends to maritime space, namely the territorial sea of the States Party (usually 12 miles in width from the mean low-water mark, in Council of Europe States). Thus, seascape and the coastal landscape as viewed from the sea is included (a fact not always as well understood as it might be).

The Florence Convention also imposes a raft of conservation duties on States Party. Thus, States must recognise landscape *in their legal systems* as an essential element of people's surroundings, an expression of diversity or shared culture or natural heritage and as the foundation of their identity (see, in particular, Article 5). The States are also obliged to monitor landscape changes and identify landscapes which require special attention. In particular, they must draw up Landscape Quality Objectives, which are forward-looking statements of the characteristics which local people want to see recognised in their surroundings. These obligations, together with the necessarily consequent public participation mechanisms, must be effectively integrated into the planning process.

What about the Charters, Declarations, etc.?

In the section above, we were rather dismissive of the effect in intentional law of the many Charters, Declarations and so on which guide heritage professionals in their tasks. Yet, it would be precipitant to regard these instruments as entirely worthless in international law. It is possible that, over time, the principles contained in these instruments may be capable of developing into customary international law (even though the parent documents in which those principles are set out may never become so). Even if the contents of the Charters appear merely to be declarations of intent or statements of agreed best practice, it may be possible to demonstrate that the principles they contain (or some of them) may form the basis of State practice, which, as explained above, is a legitimate source of international law. Although, in the interim, the Charters remain what has become known as 'soft law', repeated and consistent reference to them by States may cause them to coalesce into binding international customary law.

A prominent example of this process is provided by Principle 21 of the Stockholm Declaration on the Human Environment. This is, in formal terms, merely a paragraph in the Declaration produced by the UN Conference on the Human Environment held in 1972. The Declaration was not intended to create binding international law obligations, but this Principle (which asserts that each State has the sovereign right to pursue its own environmental policy, provided it does not harm the environment of other States or areas beyond national jurisdiction) has been repeated so frequently, like a mantra, by so many States over the intervening years that it would be a brave advocate who challenged its emergence as a rule of customary international law. Therefore, the principles contained in the Charters and so on, used by heritage professionals, may well follow the same road, provided they can be shown to be uniform in their application and that they are regarded by the States as *opinion juris*.

Monuments and landscapes may also look for protection in other areas of the international law

It is possible that some protection for monuments and landscapes may also be derived from other areas of international law. Reference has already been made to the possible contribution to be made by international environmental law, but there are other fields to be considered.

Many human rights treaties have been interpreted to extend to protect elements of people's culture, whether as part of the right to life, to family life, to religious observance and otherwise. The decisions of the several human rights tribunals and the opinions of the regional commissions (especially the outstanding Inter-American Commission on Human Rights) and of the UN Human Rights Commission itself, contain useful material for supporting the application of the treaties to cultural values in particular. Monuments and, to some degree, landscapes are often threatened most severely in zones of conflict. Heritage professionals should therefore be aware that international humanitarian law (formerly known as the law of war) offers some degree of protection. The *ius in bello* (which governs *how* armed conflicts must lawfully be waged) proceeds upon the fundamental principle of discrimination between military and non-military targets, only the former being legitimate objects of military force. In addition, that force must by proportionate to the military objective to be attained. The customary law of war has long regarded cultural and historic monuments as being non-military targets and thus immune from attack. The only exception is if the monument is itself being used for military purposes (e.g. for observation or the mounting of weapons). The importance of preserving monuments in times of conflict has recently been underlined in the 1998 Rome Statute of the International Criminal Court. This provides that 'intentionally directing attacks' against, amongst other things, historic monuments, is a war crime. Landscapes are less specifically protected, but it is a war crime intentionally to launch an attack which the perpetrator knows will cause 'widespread, long-term and severe damage to the environment'. The International Criminal Court (and also the Special Tribunals established by the United Nations to deal with the aftermath of conflict in former Yugoslavia, Rwanda, Sierra Leone, etc.) have demonstrated that individuals guilty of war crimes now face a significant prospect of prosecution for their misdeeds.

34 '... with great art, cost, and diligens...' – the reconstruction of the Elizabethan Garden at Kenilworth Castle

Brian Dix

Consultant in the archaeology of historic parks and gardens, Gwynedd, UK

At around eight o'clock in the evening of Saturday, 9 July 1575, Queen Elizabeth I (1533–1603) arrived at Kenilworth Castle in Warwickshire to begin a visit that was to last for 19 days. Her host was Robert Dudley (1532–88), 1st Earl of Leicester, who had arranged a lavish programme of pageantry and private pleasures that was designed as a message of love as well as to delight and honour the queen. Two detailed contemporary accounts of the visit survive. The first is by George Gascoigne (1535–77), who was responsible for organising the various spectacles and displays that took place during the course of the queen's stay, when the entire landscape served as the backdrop for recreation, ceremony and festivity. The second is in the form of a letter written by Robert Langham (c.1535–79/80), (often called Laneham), an official in Leicester's household. In addition to relating events of the royal visit, it includes a lengthy description of the elaborate garden that appears to have been created specially for the occasion. It provides one of the most detailed eye-witness accounts of an ornate pleasure garden of that period.

In the early twenty-first century English Heritage created a part-archaeological and – perhaps controversial but enlightening – part-conjectural reconstruction of this remarkable and theatrical garden. The garden lay on the north side of the castle between the recently refurbished Norman keep and outer curtain wall. In contrast to the very public spaces of other parts of the castle, it provided a secure and convenient private place that could appeal to the senses through a mixture of sights, scents and sounds. Langham's description portrays a *locus amoenus*, or place of joy and delight, where beauty could be enjoyed and lovers might meet. He describes a series of pretty conceits, alluding to Leicester as much as to the queen herself.

The layout comprised a high bank or terrace running along the base of the keep with a timber aviary directly opposite and arbours at each end. The area in between was divided into quarters by sand and grass walks with an obelisk at the centre of each plot which was otherwise filled with flowers, fragrant herbs and fruit trees. Such luxuriant planting emphasised the sensual quality of the garden and was clearly intended to enchant and seduce the onlooker. In the middle of all there stood a tall sculptured marble fountain with side panels decorated with amatory scenes from Ovid's *Metamorphoses*.

Although Langham's description is often quoted, there was, until recently, very little consideration of the actual size and form of the Elizabethan garden. It was generally assumed

Gardens & Landscapes in Historic Building Conservation, First Edition. Edited by Marion Harney.
© 2014 John Wiley & Sons, Ltd. Published 2014 by John Wiley & Sons, Ltd.

that it occupied the same area as the later kitchen garden and orchard that survived there until well into the twentieth century. Indeed, the garden that the Ancient Monuments Branch of the Department of the Environment laid out in 1975 to replace the last remaining trees of the orchard reproduced a formal layout which was shown filling the space on a plan of the castle first published in 1656. The newly created beds were furnished with yew topiary and box edging and the whole arrangement of geometrical plots was portrayed as reflecting the 'Tudor' scheme, even though limited archaeological excavation carried out at the time had failed to reveal evidence of the original design and planting.

Thirty years on, the shortcomings of this interpretation at such an important flagship property were painfully obvious to English Heritage, which now has responsibility for the castle's care and public presentation. Fortuitously, the advent of a major development programme for enhancing visitors' experience at the site provided the opportunity to reconsider how to display the Elizabethan garden. In order to investigate different options of interpretation fresh archaeological, architectural and historical studies were required.

A series of non-invasive evaluation techniques comprising aerial photographic interpretation, earthwork analysis, and geophysical survey helped to identify potential targets for archaeological trial excavation. In particular, the recognition that the terrace was originally shorter than its current form allowed new ideas to be tested regarding the actual size of the garden. At the same time, with improved techniques and understanding in garden archaeology, it was considered likely that Elizabethan levels could now be identified. If so, their nature and degree of survival might prove critical in determining an appropriate level of reconstruction.

In autumn 2004, archaeological trial trenches uncovered part of the foundations of the octagonal fountain that Langham had described (Figure 34.1).

It lay centrally within the perceived smaller area of the garden, where it was aligned upon the large doorway that led from the keep forebuilding onto the mid-point of the original terrace. The trenches also revealed the truncated surface of a levelling layer upon which the

Figure 34.1 Kenilworth Castle Elizabethan Garden: excavated remains of the central fountain. (© John Watkins.)

Elizabethan garden had been set out, together with possible evidence for contemporary rubble bases which might have related to architectural elements of the garden design. Furthermore, the work showed that the roots of the yew trees planted in 1975 were beginning to penetrate these archaeological horizons, with the roots of the box hedges likely to do similar damage in the near future.

In addition to being historically misleading, the modern garden was clearly threatening the survival of evidence relating to its predecessor. It was decided therefore to remove the existing scheme and carry out more thorough archaeological investigation in order to increase understanding of the original layout. By clarifying the dimensions and geometry, a more accurate representation of the Elizabethan garden could be created within the authentic footprint. At the same time its precise boundaries could be re-established, particularly on the northern side where the adjacent curtain wall had been demolished and replaced by a garden wall, further away.

Subsequent total area excavation in 2005–6 clarified the original shape and size of the Elizabethan garden. The results also added to the later history of the site during the Civil War (1642–51) and show how the area was afterwards cultivated and used right up until the late twentieth century. After recording, the remains of the Elizabethan garden were preserved and protected by a permeable and root-resistant geotextile membrane laid beneath a covering of topsoil.

The dimensions and eight-sided form of the central foundation as fully revealed following previous evaluation corresponded exactly to Langham's description of the shape and measurements of the fountain in the middle of the original garden. A rectangular scar marked the position of the column that once rose from the centre of the basin and related fragments of white marble were subsequently identified as Carrara marble, further confirming the accuracy of the historical description. However, the absence of larger pieces suggests that the superstructure was probably dismantled for re-use rather than broken up.

A series of small pits packed with broken tile or filled with sandstone rubble indicated the possible location of other architectural elements. It is not clear, however, if their differences represent separate episodes of construction or alternative purpose but their distribution suggests that the individual quarters were rectangular in shape. They lay entirely within the smaller area denoted by the original extent of the terrace and were absent where the ends of the garden had been enlarged. The rediscovery of remains of the former curtain wall beneath a recently planted beech hedge along the north side showed that the garden space had occupied almost an acre, corresponding closely to what Langham says.

Since the excavation results clearly validate important details in Langham's letter, it should be expected that the other facts he gives are equally reliable. The contents have therefore been used as the basis for reconstructing the configuration of architectural features within the historical outline indicated by the archaeological evidence.

Langham's description deals mainly with the different structures in the garden, providing important details concerning their dimensions and particular form. He is much less specific about how the garden was planted and notes only in broadest terms the range of trees, flowers and herbs that it contained. In the absence of archaeological or other direct evidence for planting, the reintroduction of individual arrangements remains wholly conjectural and relies upon knowledge of contemporary horticultural practice derived from historical gardening books and visual sources. Accordingly, the reconstruction of railed enclosures around various patterns of raised beds or knots is based partly upon concurrent written directions together with the evidence of illustrations, such as the engraved designs by Jan Vredeman de Vries (1527–c.1607). The flowers they have been planted with are all varieties that were known at the time, as depicted in books and paintings.

Likewise, information from other contemporary sources was adapted to create the new fountain which has been constructed on the original site but raised on a suspended foundation over the historical remains. Its central column features two athlants supporting a ball, or sphere, rather than a bowl which Langham's phonetic spelling could equally suggest. The carving of decorative panels around the sides of the reconstructed basin

Figure 34.2 Kenilworth Castle Elizabethan Garden: reconstructed fountain and aviary. (© John Watkins.)

extends the range of sculptured marine scenes that Langham saw and described but is similarly inspired by printed sources which survive from the period. They have been created adopting an appropriate Elizabethan style (Figure 34.2).

No evidence was found for the aviary mentioned in the letter. It seems to have been located against the tower which lay along the north curtain wall directly opposite the entrance leading to the terrace. Langham's description provides sufficient information concerning its dimensions and architectural details to enable a convincing reconstruction. Its windows and some of the other decoration are modelled on elements of a frontispiece that was re-used as a porch on Leicester's Gatehouse elsewhere in the castle.

The lack of firm foundations for other features, such as the arbours and terrace balustrade (Figure 34.3), suggests that they were of light construction and presumably made of wood that could be painted to look like stone. The tall, pierced, porphyry obelisks in the centre of each quarter were probably similarly fashioned, although the series of pits packed with hard materials could have formed solid bases to support the heavier weight of stone pedestals or other ornaments.

It may be significant that not long afterwards the only garden items of any quality to be listed in a valuation of the castle were 'the Queenes seat of freestone' and the marble fountain. This suggests that the other architectural elements either no longer existed or had become so degraded as to be worthless.

Wooden structures would quickly deteriorate without proper maintenance, especially if unseasoned timber was used as might be the case were the garden hurriedly put together and dressed up largely for the queen's visit. Its theatrical atmosphere of elaborate architecture and sensual planting, perhaps including false fruits out of season as well as other artifice, may therefore have had as much permanence as a stage-set. Indeed, the features of the garden may have been wondered at as much for their ephemerality as for their ingenuity.

The major re-creation of such a short-lived, lost garden is bound to attract controversy, particularly when it is undertaken by the country's leading heritage conservation body and government's statutory adviser on the historic environment. A television programme broadcast around the time that the new garden was completed, for example, questioned its cost, especially in view of some of the uncertainties of interpretation. Because the project is based largely upon a description provided by a contemporary letter that was never intended to answer the needs of modern enquiry – and consequently has major omissions as well as ambiguity – aspects of the reconstruction will always be open to criticism and re-interpretation. Yet, through painstaking archaeological investigation and comparative

Figure 34.3 Kenilworth Castle Elizabethan Garden: garden terrace with reconstructed balustrade, steps and arbours. (© John Watkins.)

Figure 34.4 Kenilworth Castle Elizabethan Garden: the reconstructed garden. (© John Watkins.)

historical research by leading scholars working within an interdisciplinary team, we can be confident that the re-created garden is significantly more accurate than that which was made in 1975.

It is important to explain which elements are based on archaeological research; which on parallels from other sites and sources; and which on guesswork. With these provisos, the project is designed to open visitors' eyes to how things were in the past, not only providing something real and three-dimensional to look at but also enabling them to experience those same sensations that Langham so richly described: 'the pleasant whisking wind above, or delectable coolness of the fountainspring beneath, to taste of delicious strawberries, cherries, and other fruits, even from their stalks, to smell such fragrancy of sweet odours, breathing from the plants, herbs, and flowers, to hear such natural melodious music and tunes of birds . . .' (Figure 34.4).

At the same time, the new work has been designed to be reversible and avoid further archaeological damage. It is accepted that it may need to be redone, perhaps differently, at some time in the future. Meanwhile, the current reconstruction serves as a stimulus for debate and affords a unique glimpse into a bygone world.

Further reading

Martyn, T. (2008) *Elizabeth in the Garden*, Faber and Faber, London.
Langham's letter.
Kuin, R.J. (ed.) (1983) *Robert Langham: A Letter*, E.J. Brill, Leiden.
'Elizabethan Garden' Project.
Keay, A. and Watkins, J. (eds) (2013) *The Elizabethan Garden at Kenilworth Castle*, English Heritage, Swindon.

35 Paradise restored – a case study exploring the restoration of three of Hestercombe's period gardens

Philip White
Chief Executive, Hestercombe Gardens Trust, Taunton, Somerset, UK

Introduction

Hestercombe is an ancient settlement situated on the southern slopes of the Quantock Hills overlooking the Vale of Taunton Deane in Somerset. Named after an early Anglo-Saxon owner, the estate was occupied following the Norman Conquest by a succession of Norman families one of whom created 'the garden of the Lord of Hestercombe' recorded in a perambulation of 1249. In 1391 the medieval manor house and estate (estimated at that time to be between five and six hundred acres) was acquired by Sir John Warre, whose descendants continued to live at Hestercombe for nearly 500 years.

In 1750 the estate was inherited by Coplestone Warre Bampfylde (1720–91), grandson of Sir Francis Warre, and creator of the 35 acre (14 ha) eighteenth-century landscape garden. Most garden lovers today are probably more familiar with the world-famous Formal Garden designed by Edwin Lutyens (1869–1944) and Gertrude Jekyll (1843–1932) but in the eighteenth century it was the landscape garden which was celebrated. The Warre family continued to live at Hestercombe until 1872 when, following the death of Bampfylde's great niece, Elizabeth Tyndale Warre, the estate was bought at auction by the 1st Viscount Portman (1799–1888). A prominent Somerset family, the Portmans had made a considerable fortune from property development in London and were looking for a house that would become the focus of their rapidly expanding Somerset estates and a seat for the eldest grandson, the Hon E.W.B. (Teddy) Portman.

After undertaking considerable remodelling of the house, including the creation of a terraced parterre from 1873–77, the house appears to have been shut up until Teddy, following his marriage to the Hon Constance Vesey in 1892, took up residence in 1894. In 1903, after making considerable improvements to the estate, he and his wife turned their attention to the creation of a new garden beyond the existing Victorian terrace. They were encouraged by Edward Hudson (1854–1936), the influential editor of *Country Life* magazine, to commission the young up-and-coming architect Edwin Lutyens who, in turn, called upon his frequent collaborator, the already famous Gertrude Jekyll, to create the planting design.

The early death of Teddy Portman in 1911 and the devastating effects of the 1914–18 war signalled the beginning of a long decline for Hestercombe and its gardens. The Crown Estate, a quasi-government agency bought the estate in 1944 and in 1953, following the death of Mrs Portman in 1951, Somerset County Council took a tenancy of the house and Formal Gardens. The Council installed the newly formed Somerset Fire Brigade in the building and it became their headquarters for the next 63 years. Before 1914 the gardens had been maintained by 17 garden staff; now they were managed by just two groundsmen.

In 1972, the County Council agreed to the tarmacking of the Great Plat, the centrepiece of the Lutyens garden, in order to convert it to a drill yard for the Somerset Fire Cadets. It was only after a determined intervention by the County Architect, Bernard Adams, that this decision was overturned by the full Council; shockingly, by only one vote.

Restoration of the Great Plat and Victorian Terrace

This political activity led to the County Council's decision in 1973 to restore the Formal Garden which was immeasurably and famously helped by the discovery, in a drawer in the potting shed, of the original Gertrude Jekyll planting plans. This remarkable survival has enabled the garden to be replanted as closely as possible to Jekyll's original intention. The restoration was further informed by a series of *Country Life* photographs, originally published in 1908, and a second set of plans saved by the American garden designer Beatrix Farrand (1872–1959), whose library and archive is deposited as the Reef Point Garden collection in the University of California at Berkeley.

Largely restored between 1973 and 1978, the Formal Garden is thought to be only the second period garden in the country to have been restored, and the first by a local authority. The restoration was awarded a European Heritage award by the Civic Trust in 1975. Until 2004 the garden remained under the enlightened control of the Somerset Fire Brigade who continued to manage and maintain it, supported by the County Council, whilst allowing informal access to the public.

In the early 1990s the County Council initiated the restoration of the Victorian Terrace by setting out the original shape of the beds and restoring the tiered fountain. This process was refined and completed by the Hestercombe Gardens Trust, which had taken over responsibility for the Terrace, together with the Formal Garden, in 2004. Based on contemporary photographs and press reports of the time, the trust reintroduced summer and winter bedding schemes on the Terrace based on those published in the gardening press in the 1880s and 90s, the garden's heyday.

After taking responsibility for the Formal Garden, the trust undertook a complete review of the planting scheme, which led to a major replanting programme to restore it closer to Jekyll's original design. A major Heritage Lottery Fund grant awarded in 2003 enabled the trust to replace much of the statuary that had been sold off by the Crown Estate in the 1950s.

Restoration of the Victorian shrubbery

An area immediately adjoining the house to the north had been a shrubbery in the nineteenth century but this had been completely lost over time, apart from an overgrown yew tunnel. In 1999 I decided, in conjunction with the County Council, to restore this area to decorative shrubbery based on the designs and published planting advice of William Robinson (1838–1935) whose seminal book *The English Flower Garden* (1883) was contemporary with the renovation of the house.

Research revealed that no nineteenth-century Victorian shrubberies still survived in their original designed form as change had become inevitable following the dramatic reduction in garden staffing brought about by World War I.[1] This re-creation provides the trust with a unique opportunity to interpret and explain this period of garden design to interested visitors. Eventually the Shrubbery will be extended into an adjoining area of woodland which, in turn, will be developed in line with Robinson's ideas as described in his book *The Wild Garden* (1870). The planting design will concentrate on providing horticultural interest between September and April when the seasonal displays in the Formal Garden, timed by Jekyll to coincide with the regular pattern of Portman family visits, are over.

The lost eighteenth-century garden

In 1992, when Bampfylde's all-but-lost eighteenth-century landscape garden was discovered, it posed very different challenges. The garden had gradually become overgrown in the nineteenth century although it regularly opened to the public, as it had in the eighteenth century. In 1872, after the death of Miss Elizabeth Warre, the Reverend Thomas Hugo, a noted antiquary, described the neglected state of the landscape garden:

> dark, deep silent woods . . . solemn avenues and winding walks by ponds, a dashing cascade and shady arbours . . . a shadowy thing of the past rather than a reality of the living and breathing present. For more than half a century little has been done even to preserve what was once so regularly ordered and exactly arranged. The woods have about them a primeval aspect. The lawns are overgrown with varied vegetation, the paths, where a hundred years ago the feet of fair ladies wandered amid a very paradise of delights, are now in some places all but obliterated, while those which are tended the best have entirely lost that courtly care which was once so lavishly and lovingly expended on them. The visitor has oftentimes to gaze on landscape beauties through an umbrageous screen which all but hides them from his view and to investigate the works of its old possessors, where his foot is impeded at every step and the air is dense with sylvan odours and heavy with the atmosphere of the forest and its verdure.

When the Portmans acquired the estate in 1872 they closed the garden to the public and diverted the public road which passed through the park. They appear to have systematically removed some of the garden buildings – probably those that had become dilapidated through neglect – in some cases almost to the base of their foundations. The Witch House was reported to have disappeared sometime in the 1920s after Mrs Portman is reputed to have said that 'it held no charms for her'. Otherwise, Mr and Mrs Portman did not appear to pay particular attention to the landscape garden as their interest was directed towards the country sports of hunting, shooting and fishing. They were more interested in new and fashionable pursuits; the creation of a model farm, the electrification of the house, the acquisition of new-fangled motor cars and, of course, their modern Formal Garden.

The nadir of this sleeping landscape occurred long after the Portman's stewardship had ended when, in 1963, the Crown Estate clear-felled all the eighteenth-century trees for their timber value. They dropped trees across buildings, ripped up water features and dug through dam walls. A few lone voices objected strongly to the destruction at the time and Lawrence Fricker (1963) wrote pithily in *The Landscape Journal*:

> Recently [Hestercombe] has been remodelled by a hand not unaware of at least one aspect of twentieth century art, for the taste of the Crown commissioners has clearly been formed by a close study of Paul Nash's work as official artist to the '14–18' War. By sacking the temples, felling and burning most of the timber and so exposing the vertical outcrops of rock, they have created a convincing evocation of Passchendaele Ridge.

The once magnificent valley garden, created over 40 years by Coplestone Warre Bampfylde between 1750 and his death in 1791, lay in ruins and, in a final ignominy, it was planted up as commercial forestry. Sadly, this kind of barbarous approach to historic landscape was not restricted to the Crown Estate at Hestercombe but was commonly replicated during this period by public bodies and individual owners.

In 1992 the dense woodland gave no clue as to what had once existed. The only access was a forestry track through the centre of the valley which occasionally provided glimpses of the dam walls, long silted up lakes and dry cascades. The remaining ruined buildings were, to all intents and purposes, completely lost within the impenetrable thickets.

Having discovered that no one else seemed to have the least interest in restoring this derelict and forgotten landscape, I resolved to do it myself and over the following three years managed to negotiate a lease with the Crown Estate, signed in February 1995. In the initial stages of the restoration I teamed up with the head gardener of the Formal Gardens, David Usher, and together we developed the first restoration plan. The work was funded by the Government's Countryside Stewardship scheme which would allow us to claim grants for coppicing trees, creating paths and restoring the dry stone walls. It eventually dawned on me that, by adding these elements together, sufficient grant income could be generated to employ a full-time project officer. Graham Burton started working at Hestercombe in June 1995 and continued for the next 12 years.

Five lakes formed the backbone of the valley garden and their re-instatement was key to understanding the layout of the garden. The first priority was to clear the willow carr from the silted up Pear Pond, the largest water feature in the landscape, prior to it being dredged at the end of July 1995 (Figure 35.1 shows a Bampfylde watercolour of the Pear Pond, and Figures 35.2 and 35.3 stages of its restoration). In all, some 17,000 tons of silt were removed

Figure 35.1 *The Pear Pond*, A watercolour by C.W. Bampfylde c.1775. (Whitworth Art Gallery, University of Manchester.)

Figure 35.2 The Pear Pond before restoration 1995.

Figure 35.3 The Pear Pond after restoration 2013.

from four of the five lakes and hundreds of trees were cleared from the banks in order to reveal the original design.

Archaeology and archives

View lines between buildings and features both within and beyond the garden are fundamental to the design of any garden, but this is particularly true of a landscape garden. The key to identifying these sight lines would determine the original layout of the trees within the valley and this could be achieved by surveying the tree stumps of the original planting cut down in the 1960s. It was fortunate that the majority of the stumps appeared to have survived and this provided an opportunity to digitally map their position and tag those that remained with individual identification numbers.

A dendro-archaeological survey of the whole of the wooded landscape garden site was carried out which identified the stumps to species level and, wherever possible, aged them by making tree-ring counts. Once mapped it became apparent how and where the original sight lines had been and how Bampfylde had grouped trees in order to achieve different effects.

Oak and ash had often been placed together and in areas with exposed rock outcrops beech and Scots pine had been established. Plane trees were positioned close to water features and lime trees sited along the eastern boundary where the leaves could filter the morning light. Coppicing revealed the extensive cherry laurel understorey originally planted in the eighteenth century.

Many of Hestercombe's original paths survive and those that do not were often in areas, particularly the valley floors, where the greatest damage was done by forestry operations. The value of experience in being able to 'read' the landscape was exemplified by our landscape consultant, Johnny Phibbs, who walked the valley, setting out where he believed a path should be, so that essential missing links could be created. Excavations revealed a beautifully constructed, cambered, pitched stone path which could be traced up the valley following the suggested route. The original path was covered with a protective layer of geotextile and a new path was laid over the top; thereby preserving the original for future examination.

Over the last 18 years a considerable archive has been compiled. This is an important element of the continuing restoration process and we have managed, often against the odds, to maintain a permanent part-time archivist since 1999. The earliest map of the site is a relatively late tithe map of 1839 which has only limited detail of garden features and paths; the 1st edition of the Ordnance Survey of 1886 gives more information although much had already changed following the arrival of the Portmans in 1872.

Unfortunately, the estate accounts for Coplestone Warre Bampfylde are missing, although detailed accounts for his father and grandfather exist. There are several good contemporary descriptions of the eighteenth-century garden but no financial records relating to the creation of the designed landscape or relevant bank records (often a good source of information) have yet been discovered.

Faced with a paucity of written records, archaeology has been the most important tool at our disposal. Garden archaeology is a relatively new discipline and this has meant that, together with our archaeologist, we have had to learn to interpret features as we gained experience. Occasionally we have re-excavated a site when it became apparent that our initial interpretation was not fully informed and we have discovered that archaeology can pose more questions than answers. In the last 18 years, more than 30 excavations of the site have been carried out, ranging from complete buildings to those determining the original edge or line of a path.

The buildings

One of the many roles of a landscape garden was as a living gallery of composed views designed to be seen from within the various buildings, or 'seats' ranged around the garden; these in turn, framed 'landskip paintings'. Henry Hawkins Tremayne (1741–1829) of Heligan in Cornwall visited in 1785 and in his journal described the estate and its owner:

> to Hestercombe, Mr Bampfyldes which is a very small place but planted & laid out wth uncommon taste. Mr Bampfylde himself being supposed to have the finest taste for laying out Ground of any Man in England, his Skill and taste in painting gives him an advantage as it enables him to seize every object and opportunity to set off the different points of view to advantage.

The majority of these buildings had been lost but over the last few years new buildings have been devised so that visitors might view the landscape as it was originally envisaged or, at least, how we believe it to have been from our inevitably limited twenty-first century perspective.

The designs for the reinstated garden seats were developed from evidence gathered from archaeological and topographical surveys, and historical research. This provided the basis for interpretation in the following areas:

- Landscape context, location and orientation
- Construction lines
- Water features
- Sight lines, views in/out
- Approach
- Analysis of form
- Building and landscape character
- Analysis of similar buildings and designs
- Construction materials and techniques.

Analysis was undertaken by a small team comprising architect, historic landscape consultant, academics and staff using drawings and models as vehicles for discussion. This process has led to the creation of six new buildings on the site; five are on their original foundations and the sixth is a tent. Each building is different because the evidence varied in quantity

Figure 35.4 Construction of the Gothic Alcove, first evocation 2000.

and quality so, on occasion, objective judgement gave way to subjective interpretation. These structures are perhaps best described as evocations.

In 2000, and by way of a trial of this process, the Gothic Alcove, a building first mentioned in 1761, was rebuilt (Figure 35.4).

Using the information available at the time we recreated the building only to discover a drawing in the British Museum, by Bampfylde, six months later that suggested the likely original form (Figure 35.5 is a model based on the original drawing).

Eight years after the re-creation was completed, the roof of the building was altered and two buttresses were added to better reflect the newly discovered model. Although we could not be certain that this was the original scheme, it is an eighteenth-century Bampfylde design that met the original criteria of the building's first reincarnation and which also bore an uncanny resemblance to the trial building (Figure 35.6).

The Rustic Seat was a more difficult building to resolve as there were many designs by Bampfylde and his great friend, the artist Richard Phelps (c.1718–85), that could fit the tripartite floor plan identified from the excavated foundations. Archaeological investigation revealed an absence of roof tiles, slates or nails although pieces of plaster with the imprint of lathes on one side and a rough caste finish on the other were discovered. Using this evidence we concluded that the design as built was rough timber with a thatched roof and walls of lime plaster over chestnut lathes with a rough caste finish obtained by using sieved gravel from the adjacent stream.

Figure 35.5 Model based on original drawing by C.W. Bampfylde, British Museum ref: 1918,0608.1-257. (Courtesy of Robert Battersby, Architecton.)

Figure 35.6 Gothic Alcove adapted to reflect C.W. Bampfylde's design 2008.

The position of the Chinese Seat depicted in a Bampfylde watercolour, albeit at a distance, was determined following the discovery of its incomplete foundations. Apart from evidence of a slate roof, little further information was revealed by excavation. However, the scale of the building was gleaned from close examination of Bampfylde's drawing and by analysis of the building's relationship with the associated Mausoleum and Octagon Summerhouse. When recreating buildings, the simplest possible design that will give the desired effect has been adopted. In this case the building was inspired by the Chinese Seat at Honington Hall in Warwickshire, thought to have been designed by Sanderson Miller (1716–80), who was very likely known to Bampfylde. The seat is recorded in a 1758 painting by Thomas Robins the Elder (1716–70).

The original Octagon Summerhouse was a substantial, fair-faced, red brick building built with contrasting white lime mortar which, although still extant in 1872 when its furniture was sold, had completely disappeared by 1886. Using Bampfylde's proposed design for the Bowling Green House at Dunster Castle, Somerset, as a model we deliberately avoided rebuilding it in matching red brick on the basis that if the evocation too closely resembled the original there was a danger that it could be considered a pastiche. Instead, it was built in soft grey-brown brick that toned with the soil colour.

Two of the original eighteenth-century garden buildings, the Temple Arbour and Mausoleum, had survived and the Witch House was known from a photograph of 1906. The positions of a further two missing buildings have now been identified and it is hoped that these will be replaced in due course.

Funding and future security

The majority of funding for the restoration of the gardens and the creation of the visitor centre has come from the Heritage section of the National Lottery Fund. But all the early high-risk funding, without which the project would never have got off the ground, came from independent charities and foundations together with an unsecured loan from a sympathetic and enlightened bank manager.

Garden visitors alone rarely produce sufficient income to cover the cost of maintaining a garden like Hestercombe and, even in the past, most of these great landscapes were subsidised by income derived from property, manufacturing or mining beyond the estate boundary. Additional revenue is now generated by hosting weddings, conferences and a variety of events from book fairs to ice skating. The income derived from catering is considerably greater than that generated by the gardens' ticket office.

Hestercombe is managed by a charitable trust initially set up in 1997, a few months before the landscape garden opened to the public. When first established it acted mainly as a collecting charity able to accept grants from other charitable bodies. However, between September 2003 and March 2004, and following the offer of a very generous grant from the Heritage Lottery Fund, all the land and buildings which comprised the gardens and related areas were vested in the trust on the basis of 99-year leases from the Crown Estate and Somerset County Council. This enabled the trust to reunite the gardens for the first time in 60 years and give them a secure future. Trustees, who are invited to join the Board, represent many facets of professional life and their responsibilities are to advise and guide the executive, set policy and ensure the long-term protection and viability of the historic landscape.

Constraints

As a Grade 1 listed garden on the English Heritage Register of Parks and Gardens of Special Historic Interest, a Site of Special Scientific Interest (SSSI), a European designated Special Area of Conservation (SAC) and a Regionally Important Geological Site (RIGS), not to mention being in the centre of its own Hestercombe Conservation Area, the landscape and its flora and fauna are well protected. These designations can sometimes conspire, together with the interests of the local planning officer, the listed buildings officer, the tree officer, the local bat group and the protected species officer of Natural England together with occasional visits from the Forestry Commission, the Government Department for the Environment, Food and Rural Affairs (DEFRA), and the County Archaeologist, not only to make the restoration process overly bureaucratic but even, on occasion, the victim of individual prejudices.

Restoring the gardens, although personally satisfying, has always been about opening them for the benefit and enjoyment of the public as they were in the eighteenth, nineteenth and twentieth centuries. This can, of course, be a mixed blessing. It is immensely rewarding to overhear visitors saying that they have enjoyed their visit or even better, would like to return. On the other hand, once open, the public are inclined to take ownership and, occasionally, seek to impose their own views and preferences on the management of the gardens. We have been told that: we must not open up original designed views as it would mean 'murdering my trees'; there are not enough seats in the garden; there are not enough flowers in the landscape garden or, best of all, and surprisingly common, 'there is no way Gertrude Jekyll would ever have planted *that*', even when 'that' appears on her own meticulously drawn plans.

The development of social media and the proliferation of comment sites mean that our efforts are constantly monitored and remarked upon. It is therefore essential that we continually manage and, wherever possible, raise our standards and improve communication with all our visitors.

We should remember that there is no collective memory of where we have come from or what we have achieved, as we are always judged by our visitors on what we have delivered on the day of their visit. A recent visitor reported that she was appalled and disgusted and would never visit again because the quiet of the gardens had been ruined by the sound of gardeners mowing the lawns.

The future

The fragmentation of estates through multiple ownership is a common problem and much of the work undertaken in the last 20 years at Hestercombe has been aimed at reuniting as many parts of the site as possible.

Sadly, Hestercombe's walled kitchen garden was sold off by the Crown Estate in the 1980s. The original two and a half acre eighteenth-century garden, furnished in the 1890s with a magnificent Boulton and Paul greenhouse, was almost doubled in size by Lutyens in the early 1900s. It was later turned over to pigs and ploughed for potatoes, the greenhouses collapsed and the picturesque gardeners' bothy was subsumed into a characterless modern house.

On a happier note, Somerset County Council has agreed that the trust assumes ownership of Hestercombe House which sits at the centre of the historic landscape. The trust's objective will be to find a long-term solution for the house which will allow public access while ensuring that, at a minimum, the building generates sufficient income to cover its future maintenance costs.

The park, which was first licensed in 1319–20, still survives and contains within it a remarkable water feature thought to have been an Elizabethan, i.e. late sixteenth century, water garden. Plans to investigate and eventually restore this rare survival are currently being developed.

What experience has taught me

Over the course of the restoration, field survey has been an invaluable method of determining the position of paths, fence lines and other lost features. A reflective walk in winter, at the beginning or end of the day when the light is low, will often reveal evidence of features not otherwise discernible.

Changes of texture in the landscape garden were used to indicate that a change of emotional response was called for; for example, smoothness to suggest beauty, and roughness to imply the sublime. The opportunity to experience these 'sensibilities' was an essential component of the design of an eighteenth-century landscape garden and identifying and restoring this element of the garden has been an important outcome of the project.

Many heritage assets are presented to the public without adequate reference to, and perhaps understanding of, the context in which they were made. Hestercombe's garden, like other great landscape gardens, lay at the heart of a thriving estate which itself was part of a larger, often 'borrowed' landscape. The management of grassland by grazing and haymaking was essential to the efficient running of the property and the activity and sounds of animals, the watermill and forge all animated the landscape. It is important to remember that these were indispensable components of an idealised Arcadian landscape.

The restoration must have integrity. Attention to detail should never be compromised and lost features in the landscape should only be recreated or replaced when proposals are supported by primary evidence or when they can assist in the interpretation of the heritage asset. The restoration process should always be capable of being audited; it must be recorded in detail and, wherever possible, be reversible.

Many people find it difficult to envisage what something will look like in the future and, even when fully explained, still might find the thought of change discomforting and even frightening. It inevitably requires considerable effort and patience to carry the majority through this essential process. Others, sadly, may never be reconciled and will always be ready to tell you that the object of your endeavours was better when it was an impenetrable wilderness or precarious ruin.

Regulations and policies are often designed to protect closely defined sectional interests and it can be difficult, in a wide-ranging landscape restoration programme, to encourage officials to understand the wider objectives necessary for effective conservation of heritage assets. On the other hand, where officials share the overall vision, they can be of great assistance.

In my experience, capital for restoration is easier to raise than revenue for maintenance. This conveys a false sense of security that only becomes apparent when the maintenance costs start to roll in.

Conclusion

Someone once said that it would take as long to restore Hestercombe's landscape garden as the 40 years it had taken Coplestone Warre Bampfylde to create it. That was 20 years ago and there is still some way to go.

When working over a long time frame, two things are required; the first is a 'project champion', someone with the ability to carry a vision and the determination to see it through. At the beginning of a project there are often more detractors than supporters and you have to be able to hold your nerve and remain focused on the task in hand. The second essential requirement is patience. Distrust instant restorations. More often than not, what was once considered 'finished' must be revisited and reviewed, revised or even rebuilt with the benefit of new information, greater knowledge and more experience. You must always remain flexible and be open to new ideas and interpretations.

Circumstances differ with each project and every restoration is unique but detailed research, coupled with attention to period detail, is essential. If the goal is improved interpretation then in my view it is better to do something, even if it means getting it wrong and changing it, than not doing anything in the first place.

References/Further reading

Fricker, L.J. (1963) 'Gardens at Hestercombe House, Somerset', *Journal of the Institute of Landscape Architects* (February 1963).

Hugo, Rev. T. (1872) 'Hestercombe', *Somersetshire Archaeological and Natural History Society's Proceedings*, Vol. 18 (1874), 136–68 (pp. 137–138).

Diary/Notebook of a journey of Henry Hawkins Tremayne, Squire of Heligan, from Heligan to Exeter, Taunton, Wells, Swindon, Oxford, Bicester, Stow, Warwick, Birmingham, Monmouth, Chepstow, Gloucester, Newport, Bridgewater, Taunton, etc. to Bodmin, April–July 1785 (Cornwall Record Office ref DD 1341/1).

Endnotes

1   Brent Elliot, personal communication.

36 Strawberry Hill, Twickenham

Marion Harney

Director of Studies, MSc Conservation of Historic Gardens and
Cultural Landscapes, University of Bath, UK

The villa of Horace Walpole (1717–97) at Strawberry Hill, Twickenham, Middlesex, which he leased in 1745 and acquired in 1747, started life in 1698 as a 'shapeless little box', Chopped Straw Hall, which he renamed Strawberry Hill. Walpole's innovative asymmetrical scheme for his house and naturalistic landscape setting, when complete, was one of the earliest designed picturesque ensembles in England.[1]

Traditions of husbandry, garden making and landscape design have always held a poignant place in the English psyche and garden visiting, as now, was an important cultural pursuit. Strawberry Hill received many visitors in Walpole's time but, if the house and garden were famous in their day, they are relatively little known or visited now, with comparatively little written on them.[2] It is no longer possible to experience this garden in its original conception because much has been altered or developed. The house was listed in 2002 by the World Monuments Fund as one of the 100 most endangered buildings in the world, after which the Strawberry Hill Trust was set up. The trust commissioned project architects Inskip and Jenkins Architects and the Landscape Agency to prepare a Conservation Plan to restore the house and what remains of the garden immediately surrounding the house, reinstating a context for Walpole's Gothic villa.

This chapter interprets the original Strawberry Hill garden and suggests that the restoration of the landscape, although well-intentioned, represents a missed opportunity to recreate a scheme based on Walpole's correspondence and commissioned paintings to evoke some of his primary design intentions.

However, before this is discussed further, the reader will be led through a virtual tour by means of contemporary illustrations, demonstrating along the way how the 'sister arts – poetry, painting and gardening, or the science of landscape' combine to make a building and landscape setting that was sublime, painterly and picturesque.

Horace Walpole, youngest son of Sir Robert Walpole (1676–1745), the first British Prime Minister, was historian, antiquary, Member of Parliament, collector, connoisseur, social and political commentator, prolific writer and author of the first Gothic novel.[3] Walpole's *History of the Modern Taste in Gardening* (1780) was the first book to attempt to chronicle the evolution of gardens and it played a significant role in the development of landscape aesthetics.[4] In the essay Walpole claims credit for the 'natural style' of garden as indisputably English, a claim that has distorted perceptions of garden history down the centuries.[5] He attributes the beginning of the naturalistic style to John Milton's (1608–74) description of

Gardens & Landscapes in Historic Building Conservation, First Edition. Edited by Marion Harney.
© 2014 John Wiley & Sons, Ltd. Published 2014 by John Wiley & Sons, Ltd.

the Garden of Eden in *Paradise Lost* (1667) as the first garden laid out in the English Landscape style, and he heaps praise on William Kent (1685–1748) as Milton's successor in his ability to envision the pictorial qualities in landscape, declaring, in what is now the most famous quotation in garden history, 'He leaped the fence, and saw that all nature was a garden'.[6] Walpole's influential essay, based on the theories of Joseph Addison (1672–1719) and Alexander Pope (1688–1744), was largely written during the period 1750–60 and is contemporaneous with the construction and expansion of Strawberry Hill.[7] Walpole, though not a significant Enlightenment thinker, was a man of taste and letters; a polymath whose knowledge and interests crossed cultural fields: architecture, literature, and the sister arts of poetry, painting and gardening. Notably his *Anecdotes of Painting* (1762–71), the first history of English painting and artists, led to his theories of composition and pictorial qualities in landscape.

Many of our perceptions stem from eighteenth-century theory and practice and aesthetics were the subject of much debate, particularly regarding the appreciation of beauty in natural forms and landscape and their associative potential. The pursuit of nature and the rejection of formality became the essential tenets of English garden style. The theory and practice of landscape painting played a significant role in the development of garden aesthetics. Theories, expressed in Addison's *Spectator* essays, including 'The Pleasures of the Imagination' (1712) and Pope's *Epistle IV, To Richard Boyle, Earl of Burlington: Of the Use of Riches* (1731), endorsed 'the simplicity of unadorned nature'.[8] Pope, in his *Guardian* essay (1713), severely criticised Baroque layouts as stylised, uniform and geometrical with planting severely manicured into architectural forms and with elaborate fountains, water features and very formal statuary.[9] Promoting irregular beauty through his poetry, Pope became one of the main proponents of respecting 'the Genius of the place', advocating a more natural landscape style in garden design that worked with nature rather than imposing geometrical patterns upon it.[10] Sir John Vanbrugh (1664–1726) was an early promoter of informal landscape and the associative quality of ruins through their link to history, connections with painting and their picturesque appeal to the senses.[11] At Blenheim, Vanbrugh prefigured the picturesque in the fusion of landscape, architecture and the appeal of ruins. For the composition of a particular scene (towards Woodstock Manor) he advocated principles of landscape painting – the use of light and shade, perspective and the appropriate disposition of objects – as a focal point sympathetic to the natural contours. In an oft-quoted memorandum to the Duke and Duchess of Marlborough he petitioned for the retention of the old ruined manor: 'So that all the Buildings left, (which is only the Habitable Part and the Chapell) might Appear in two Risings amongst 'em, it wou'd make One of the Most Agreable Objects that the best of the Landskip Painters can invent'.[12]

Pope and Kent did much to promote the new taste for informal landscape, often introducing eye-catcher buildings with scenographic qualities and iconographic meaning. The transition from Baroque to informal, naturalistic landscape was complete by mid-century, parallel to a similar progression in architecture with classical Palladian replacing Baroque. However, the progression was not linear, and both large and small irregular landscape parks and gardens existed side-by-side with formal gardens throughout much of the period.

Not everyone followed prevailing fashion and Horace Walpole flouted current taste, creating a Gothic villa in a complementary landscape setting: 'As my castle is so diminutive, I give myself a Burlington-air, and say, that as Chiswick is a model of Grecian architecture, Strawberry Hill is to be so of Gothic'.[13] It is misplaced to seek archaeological precedents at Strawberry Hill, just as it is to perceive it as a forerunner of archaeologically correct nineteenth-century Gothic Revival. Rather, Walpole chose Gothic for its associative connotations. The villa and landscape are not merely a structure in the linear progression of architectural style but an early and innovative essay in aesthetics.

Representations of landscape in literature and gardening variously express individual, national and cultural identity and many designed landscapes at this time were means of self-expression and related the autobiographies of their creators. Strawberry Hill is a prime example of an associative, autobiographical site, where the man, the 'little Gothic castle' and the landscape, laid out on poetic painting principles, are inextricably linked. Strawberry Hill expresses views, ideas and opinions of the self-styled arbiter of taste on landscape aesthetics, taste and culture – for while Walpole formed a 'committee' to advise on the conversion and remodelling of the Gothic villa, the landscape is a personal story. His statement in the *History*, with its implied criticism of contemporary professional landscape designers, sets out his ethos:

> In general it is probably true, that the possessor, if he has any taste, must be the designer of his own improvements. He sees the situation in all seasons of the year, at all times of the day. He knows where beauty will not clash with convenience, and observes in his silent walks and accidental rides a thousand hints that might escape a person who in a few days sketches out a pretty picture, but had not the leisure to examine the details and relations of every part.[14]

Walpole's designed landscape would be in contrast to the building and would enhance 'the gay variety of scene' which he had singled out for praise in Pope's garden. He exclaims in a letter to Mann:

> "You suppose my garden is to be Gothic too!" That can't be; Gothic is merely architecture; and as one has a satisfaction in imprinting the gloomth of abbeys and cathedrals on one's house, so one's garden, on the contrary, is to be nothing but *riant*, and the gaiety of nature.[15]

It is first necessary to understand the cultural significance of the suburban villa in relation to Walpole's occupancy for part of the year. Far from a dynastic seat of ostentatious display the villa was essentially a pleasurable retreat from the city and a place of retirement from public life and of enjoyment and relaxation for the owner and his circle; at Twickenham, Walpole, like Pope before him, was at leisure to indulge his theories on garden design at his semi-rural retreat on the banks of the Thames.

Walpole's own words best describe his delight on acquiring the small house at Strawberry Hill and it is interesting to note that, from the outset, he enhanced the pastoral scene of his 'little new farm' by purchasing sheep of a particular hue and describes the picture in art historical terms as a 'study' – and that the prospect, not the building, is the most important feature.

> The house is so small, that I can send it to you in a letter to look at: the prospect is as delightful as possible, commanding the river, the town and Richmond Park; and being situated on a hill that descends to the Thames through two or three little meadows, where I have some Turkish sheep and two cows, all studied in their colours for becoming the view.[16]

Documentary evidence points to elements of the landscape being designed by Walpole as soon as he acquired the site of about five acres, and his concept for the relationship of the house to its landscape took advantage of the natural topography and exploited its borrowed prospects. The location was chosen because of its proximity to the River Thames and its potential: 'an open country is but a canvas on which the landscape might be designed'. By 1753 Walpole had acquired more than 14 acres, begun to Gothicise the house and to introduce structural planting to frame the villa: 'the living landscape was chastened or polished, not transformed' by screening unwanted views and concealing buildings and prospects that interfered with the larger picture and creating new vistas and borrowed views where desirable (Figure 36.1).[17]

Walpole wrote to Mann again in 1753 enclosing a plan of the site (now lost) drawn by his friend Richard Bentley (1708–82) when he had expanded the house and most of the designed landscape was in place. The later estate plan (c.1793) illustrates the completed garden with features that Walpole mentions in the letter and is useful for reconstructing what would have been a delightful picturesque fusion of the new taste for naturalistic gardening and the informality associated with Gothic architecture (see Figure 36.2).

The only significant work to the topography of the site was the construction of a natural terrace to take full advantage of the borrowed prospect into the surrounding countryside:

> The enclosed enchanted little landscape, then is Strawberry Hill . . . This view of the castle is what I have just finished, and is the only side that will be regular.[18] Directly before it is an open grove through

Figure 36.1 East view of Strawberry Hill, Capn Grose, 1787. (lwlpr15063. Courtesy of The Lewis Walpole Library, Yale University.)

which you see a field which is bounded by a serpentine wood of all kind of trees and flowering shrubs and flowers. The lawn before the house is situated on the top of a small hill, from whence to the left you see the town and church of Twickenham encircling a turn of the river, that looks exactly like a seaport in miniature. The opposite shore is a most delicious meadow, bounded by Richmond Hill which loses itself in the noble woods of the park to the end of the prospect on the right, where is another turn of the river and the suburbs of Kingston as luckily placed as Twickenham is on the left; and a natural terrace on the brow of my hill, with meadows of my own down to the river, commands both extremities. Is this not a tolerable prospect? You must figure that all this is perpetually enlivened by a navigation of boats and barges, and by a road below my terrace, with coaches, post-chaises, wagons, and horsemen constantly in motion, and the fields speckled with cows, horses, and sheep. Now you shall walk into the house . . .[19]

When Walpole insists in the *History* that the 'chief beauty of all gardens [is] prospect and fortunate points of view', and, 'animated prospect, is the theatre that will always be the most frequented', he obviously had Strawberry Hill in mind. All the ingredients of Pope and Addison's theories are here; irregularity of natural landscape, borrowed views, spontaneity, movement and constant variety in the scene.

The eighteenth-century visitor would have first viewed the picturesque Gothic castle from the road: 'the approach to the house through lofty trees, the embattled walls overgrown with ivy, the spiry pinnacles, the grave air of the building, give it all the appearance of an old abbey'.[20] Monastic and religious medieval associations increased as the visitor approached the Oratory and the Abbot's or Prior's garden seen through a Gothic screen. For privacy and security Walpole screened the house from the Teddington Road with an embattled wall, in keeping with the Gothic character of the building. The wall also enclosed and sheltered the Prior's Garden, taking the form of a *Hortus Conclusus*, an enclosed medieval garden with deep historical and biblical associations (Figure 36.3).

Imaginatively, references to the 'Prior's' garden would have set the scene for the Gothic interior. They also fulfilled Walpole's stated preference for an 'old fashioned' formal garden near to the house for reasons of convenience, a methodology later adopted by the 'father

Figure 36.2 Slight sketch of the general ground plot of the Gothic Mansion. (lwlpr16005. Courtesy of The Lewis Walpole Library, Yale University.)

of modern gardening' Humphry Repton (1752–1818).[21] Walpole believed isolating the house was a 'defect':

> Sheltered and even close walks in so very uncertain climate as ours, are comforts ill exchanged for the few picturesque days that we enjoy: and whenever a family can purloin a warm and even something of an old fashioned garden from the landscape designed for them by the undertaker in fashion, without interfering with the bigger picture, they will find satisfaction on those days that do not invite strangers to come and see their improvements.[22]

Visitors would have then participated in a guided tour by the housekeeper (or Walpole himself if they were important enough) of the antiquarian contents of the interior, eventually

Figure 36.3 View of the Prior's Garden at Strawberry Hill, G. Pars. (lwlpr16054. Courtesy of The Lewis Walpole Library, Yale University.)

emerging, after experiencing a series of Gothic spaces, from the 'gloomth' of the monastic interior with an increasing sense of history, into the 'greenth' of the garden. Exiting through the Great Cloister, an open, arched outdoor room which functioned as the connection between the interior and exterior, the viewer would meet the expansive views of the sweeping Great Lawn, Open Grove, and Serpentine Wood (Figure 36.4).

Walpole created a series of character areas linking discrete but interrelated features by a sinuous path that wended its way around the southern and western extremities of the site connecting the buildings to the furthermost features in the landscape. He frequently refers to walking his 'circuit', suggesting that it was designed to be experienced in a particular sequence. Dense planting concealed each episode from the next and added the essential components of intricacy, variety and surprise. The loosely configured serpentine path gave opportunities for framed pictorial compositions as well as giving the illusion of an unending journey, while the poetic incidents gave, at the same time, the opposite impression of small scale, seclusion and intimacy and possibilities for reflection and contemplation. Walpole also used associative, emblematic and iconographic elements to create pictorial effects that were carefully contrived to evoke 'moods' in landscape. The interior of Walpole's villa juxtaposed classical artefacts with Gothic and he used the same approach in the garden, using elements which he appreciated for their poetical, metaphorical and philosophical associations. The visitor would have glimpses and alternating views of landscape outside the garden and various architectural elements, structures and variety of planting. The Gothic gate was the first medieval incident encountered on the circuit. The chapel came next in the sequence and sat sombrely in woods in the south section of the circuit surrounded by weeping willows and other melancholic planting. Classical artefacts encountered on the circuit included a

Figure 36.4 East view of Strawberry Hill, P. Sandby c.1769. (lwlpr16659. Courtesy of The Lewis Walpole Library, Yale University.)

'large antique sarcophagus in marble, with bas-reliefs', and 'two ossuary' recalling, through associative meaning, episodes from the classics and Arcadian landscapes.[23]

The next episode was the oak Shell bench designed by Bentley and based on Botticelli's *Birth of Venus*, which was oriented to the River Thames and surrounding landscape (Figure 36.5).[24] Walpole makes a direct link in his correspondence, which the erudite observer would have recognised through its associative qualities, when he relates: 'Strawberry Hill is grown a perfect Paphos, it is the land of beauties. On Wednesday the Duchesses of Hamilton and Richmond, and Lady Ailesbury dined there, the two latter stayed all night. There never was so pretty a sight as to see them all three sitting in the shell . . .'.[25]

The visitor finally emerged, after experiencing a series of contrasting scenes, moods and episodes, associative incidents and character areas, with an increasing sense of theatre, into the dramatic expanse of the spacious Open Grove where the walk terminated and where perspective views of the villa provided the closing sequence.

The creation of moods was particularly essential for evoking emotional response and Walpole employed visual effects and used spatial devices to give a series of differently framed views and picturesque episodes. As visitors made the winding walk they continually had parallactic visions of the Gothic castle, experiencing oblique glimpses and encountering multiple perspectives of the southern and eastern facades through sparsely planted trees and clumps, grouped in the manner of Kent, to add interest and break up the wide expanse of lawn. Walpole singles out the invention of the ha-ha for particular praise as the 'capital stroke' which enabled the garden designer to carry out Pope's poetical vision of 'calling in the country', and this device was employed on the southern perimeter boundary to separate unobtrusively the designed landscape from the fields and woods beyond.[26] Wherever Walpole had to erect fencing for practical purposes he used simple rustic materials and screened them with planting.

The selection of planting for evoking moods and areas of varying character was an essential tool of eighteenth-century gardeners and Walpole would have used poetic principles to make transitions from 'gloomth', with enclosed, dense evergreen planting, emerging into open spaces of contrasting light and shade. Spence records Pope elucidating

Figure 36.5 View of the Shell Seat and bridge at Strawberry Hill, J.H. Müntz, 1755. (lwlpr16430. Courtesy of The Lewis Walpole Library, Yale University.)

the use of different species of plants to obtain a painterly effect: 'The light and shades in gardening are managed by disposing the thick grove-work, the thin, and the openings, in a proper manner'.[27] He recalls Pope on how the use of perspective in planting could be achieved by borrowing the principles of painting: 'You may distance things by darkening them, and by narrowing the plantation more and more towards the end, in the same manner as they do in painting'.[28] In a letter to Montagu in November 1755, Walpole describes how planting could be picturesque:

> above all cypresses which, I think, are my chief passion: there is nothing so picturesque when they stand two or three in a clump upon a little hillock or rising above low shrubs, and particularly near buildings. There is another bit of picture of which I am fond, and that is, a larch or a spruce fir planted behind a weeping willow, and shooting upwards as the willow depends. I think for courts about a house or winter gardens, almond trees mixed with evergreens, particularly with Scots firs have a pretty effect, before anything else comes out; whereas almond trees, being generally planted among other trees, and being in bloom before other trees have leaves, have no ground to show the beauty of their blossoms.[29]

Walpole evocatively describes the feeling engendered by experiencing colour, inhaling scents and their capacity for triggering his imagination:

> I am just come from the garden in the most oriental of all evenings, and from breathing odours beyond those of Araby. The acacias, which the Arabians have the sense to worship, are covered with blossoms, the honeysuckles dangle from every tree in festoons, the syringas are thickets of sweets, and the newcut hay of the field in the garden tempers the balmy gales with simple freshness while a thousand sky-rockets launched into the air at Ranelagh or Marylebone illuminate the scene and give it an air of Haroun Alraschid's paradise.[30]

Walpole frequently mentions the 'pleasure of lilac, jonquil and hyacinth season' and lilacs are one of the most frequently mentioned species in his correspondence as one of his chief passions: 'I came hither yesterday, and am transported, like you, with the beauty of the country; ay, and with its perfumed air too. The *lilac-tide* scents even the insides of the rooms'.[31]

Walpole was influential in the Picturesque movement, believing that 'Every journey is made through a succession of pictures' and that this applied to natural scenery and landscaped gardens alike.[32] At Strawberry Hill he articulated the earlier theories of Vanbrugh, Addison and Pope, adhering to Pope's statement that 'all gardening is landscape painting', composing picturesque scenes and episodes and applying painting techniques to naturalistic landscape design. The *History* influenced gardening internationally and the concept of designing for a particular place, mindful of topographical qualities, borrowed views, and the inherent character of a site remains an important consideration in landscape architecture today.

The restoration

Restoration of the garden, now listed Grade II*, commenced in October 2010. The Landscape Agency's Conservation Management Plan (CMP) stipulated that, wherever possible, the intention was to recreate the layout of the eighteenth century as indicated by archival and field evidence and would have some regard to precedent. This philosophical approach meant that the original landscape design would be preserved, where it remained, and some important features would be restored or recreated using historically accurate planting and materials where appropriate.

Sadly, however, little is left of the broader landscape elements with the all-important connection to the river destroyed by an affluent 1930s housing development. The essential character of the Winding Walk and its incidents were also largely lost under a plethora of buildings associated with St Mary's University College, which moved to Strawberry Hill in 1923 and now occupies most of the site.

Although the wider landscape lost its quality of pastoral simplicity, there is an opportunity to recreate some key characteristics of the Pleasure Grounds which, along with the Gothic villa, remain intact. There is good detailed evidence, gleaned largely through paintings commissioned by Walpole, combined with plans, extensive written records, and accounts to reinstate designed vistas and recreate the structure and planting of the Grove, Wilderness, the intensity and intimacy of a section of the Serpentine Walk and to restore certain important character areas such as the Prior's Garden.

Yet, despite the objectives set out in the Landscape Agency's CMP to redefine the structure of the garden to Walpole's vision they were unfortunately not retained to implement the plan and as a consequence compromises were made.

Although the project is well intentioned and elements of the physical entity of the place have been restored, due to a fundamental lack of understanding of what it *meant*, its *Genius Loci* – the essential spirit of the place – has not been captured by the conservation project. Currently, Walpole's beloved landscape does not reflect the overall unity of his design or capture the sense of mood, variety, intricacy or surprise that was such a part of his original concept; there is no sense of what it would have been like to walk through and experience his 'enchanted little landscape'.

Interpretation panels have been installed at strategic points in the garden which give visual and textual interpretation, and there is more comprehensive coverage in a display inside the villa; however, on the ground, the restoration scheme implemented has been modified to such an extent that the overall coherence of the original design and the expression of different moods and character areas are not apparent. The garden, while still a work in progress, does not currently evoke the 'riant and gaiety of nature' or the important

Figure 36.6 The house currently stands isolated on York stone paving.

connection between the house and its landscape that were essential precepts of Walpole's garden.

The house currently stands isolated on a plinth of period-incorrect York stone paving to accommodate visitors and catering requirements (Figure 36.6). The garden's present condition is devoid of the vital orange trees, syringas and other perfumed plants that produced the evocative and intoxicating 'lilac-tide' of scents that inextricably linked the villa to its landscape setting. This could easily be remedied by replacing these in pots and tubs, close to the house, just as Walpole had done.

One mid-eighteenth-century oak remains of Walpole's planting scheme and this was supplemented by some nineteenth-century trees and shrubs. Extensive tree and shrub replanting has taken place and the grove of limes to recreate the Open Grove has been restored, although this is wrongly positioned and configured so that when it matures it will prevent the reciprocal views and connections between the landscape and the villa as experienced in the eighteenth century. The structure and density of the grove should be reconsidered to ensure that the visual link between house and landscape are not lost.

The theatrical border comprises a backdrop of hornbeam trees behind a row of evergreen plants with a further staged arrangement of plants in front to provide colour and scent. This is planted with brightly coloured annuals but it resembles a shrubbery that could be found in any large suburban villa garden rather than representing the riot of colour and scent evident in illustrative material and first-hand accounts. When the trees are more mature, every endeavour should be made to restore more acacias 'covered with blossoms' and reinstate the honeysuckles which Walpole records 'dangle from every tree in festoons', and to create a more evocative atmosphere with the 'pleasure of lilac, jonquil and hyacinth season' and 'syringas . . . thickets of sweets' and so forth; just as Walpole had done.

The extraordinary Shell Seat, one of the earliest features in the garden has been recreated but, at the time of writing, it is meaningless in its context (Figure 36.7). Originally it was placed within dense planting so that it appeared to emerge out of the undergrowth. It was situated to enjoy views *out* of the garden over the animated footpath and road to

Figure 36.7 The reconstructed Shell Seat.

the wider landscape and the River Thames beyond. It is now situated inappropriately in an isolated setting, looking *inward* across the lawn so that, when the lime grove matures, its occupants will see little through the trees. However, while it is appreciated that the garden is much reduced in size from Walpole's day; and even of what is left, the SH Trust leases only the part nearest the house so the siting of the seat is now something of a *fait accompli*, every endeavour should be made to integrate the seat more sensitively into the garden.

A path that leads away from the house to the housing estate is a remaining section of the Serpentine Walk and, if this were replanted with historically appropriate tree and shrub species, an evocation of the original walk could be recreated. This would achieve some semblance of the original layout and allow the lawn to be once again 'bounded by a serpentine wood of all kind of trees and flowering shrubs and flowers'. In addition, dense over- and understorey planting would screen out the unwanted views of suburban housing. Walpole did just this to conceal unwanted features in the original planting scheme.

The Prior's Garden is an altogether more successful enterprise. This is probably because the confined space remained intact and there was good evidence for the layout and plant material from contemporary illustrations and written accounts and this has been authentically recreated.

In 2013 the Strawberry Hill Trust was awarded a laureate in the Conservation category of the Europa Nostra Awards for its achievement in the 2007–2010 restoration of the Grade I Strawberry Hill villa. The villa has indeed been beautifully and painstakingly restored though, as with the landscape, the interior fails to capture the sense of contrasting moods and different spaces that was an essential part of the visitor's experience. This may come in time with improved lighting, the introduction of furnishings and artifacts, and if a better link between the outside and inside can be established.

The important landscape setting of Walpole's Pleasure Ground and its reintegration with the Gothic villa will be ongoing, together with further consideration to enhancing the interpretation of the site and restoring its cultural significance as 'one the earliest designed picturesque ensembles in England'.

Endnotes

1. See Harney, M. *Place-making for the Imagination: Horace Walpole and Strawberry Hill*, Ashgate Publishing, 2013.
2. 'my house is full of people and has been so from the instant I breakfasted, and more are coming—in short I keep an inn: the sign; 'the Gothic Castle.' Since my gallery was finished I have not been in it a quarter of an hour together; my whole time is passed in giving tickets for seeing it and hiding myself while it is seen.' The *Correspondence of Horace Walpole* (London and New York, various dates), HW to Montagu, 03/09/1763, Vol. 10, p.98. All *Correspondence* quotations are from the Yale edition.
3. *The Castle of Otranto*, London (1764).
4. In some respects Walpole's book distorted perceptions of garden history through his insistence that the English garden style had reached its epitome at the time he was writing and that it was a purely English phenomenon, with no foreign influences – a perception that garden historians are still attempting to rectify.
5. His polemic linked the development of the 'English Taste in Gardening' with the British constitution and the notion of political liberty enshrined within that constitution. Walpole's patriotism is politically motivated and he discounts foreign influences, disparages the notion of antecedents and classical precedents, insisting on English national Whig credentials.
6. Kent was the most prolific and well known garden designer of the early eighteenth century.
7. Walpole does not develop his own theory; instead he expands and reinterprets these earlier theories and is responsible for disseminating them to a wider audience. As with *Anecdotes of Painting*, his *History* relies on research carried out by George Vertue (1684–1756), whose notebooks Walpole had purchased from his widow in 1759.
8. Addison's essays made the subject of taste a fundamental concern of the modern citizen in eighteenth century society. Those who had taste had the capacity for discriminating beauty in the arts. The term was used as a metaphor for the senses and was a way of behaviour that demonstrated appropriate values and virtues to all areas of life – the now deeply unfashionable concept of 'propriety'.
9. Johannes Kip's birds-eye view of the garden at Dyrham (1710), the seat of William Blathwayt (?1649–1717), which is less than ten miles north of Bath, vividly illustrates the Baroque garden style at this time that Addison and Pope found an anathema. Blathwayt was advised by George London, who was also working at Longleat, Wiltshire which was also laid out in this severe geometric form. It is interesting to note that Dyrham would have been reaching maturity as Strawberry Hill was being laid out and demonstrates how formal and informal gardens existed alongside one another in the early part of the eighteenth century.
10. Pope's *Epistle to Burlington* (1731) sets out his concise theory of landscape aesthetics, incorporating painting principles and advocating irregular, naturalistic design. The *Epistle* contains most of the essential elements that were later to become components of the picturesque landscape. See Harney, M. 'Alexander Pope and Prior Park: An essay in Landscape and Literature', in *Studies in the History of Gardens & Designed Landscapes*, Vol. 27, No. 3 (2007), relating how Pope's theories were applied to the landscape at Prior Park, Bath, and Pope's influence on the work of William Kent.
11. For a full explanation of Vanbrugh's interest in association in landscape see Hart, V. *Sir John Vanbrugh: Storyteller in Stone*, Yale University Press, 2008.
12. 'REASONS OFFER'D FOR PRESERVING SOME PART OF THE OLD MANOUR' of 11 JUNE 1709' sent to the Duchess of Marlborough. Accurately transcribed from British Library Additional MS 61353, nos 62–63, Appendix 1, p. 252, Hart, V. *Sir John Vanbrugh: Storyteller in Stone* (2008).
13. Walpole consistently used the term Grecian to denote classical architecture.
14. Walpole, *History of the Modern Taste in Gardening* (1780), p. 58 (hereafter *History*).
15. *Correspondence*, HW to Mann 27/04/1753, Vol. 20, p. 372.
16. *Correspondence*, HW to Mann 05/06/1747, Vol. 19, p. 414.
17. *History*, p. 45.
18. The view, also lost, was of the south side towards the north-east with the picturesque villa and the River Thames juxtaposed to demonstrate their proximity.
19. *Correspondence*, HW to Mann, 12/06/1753, Vol. 20, p. 380.
20. Ferrar, J. *Tour from Dublin to London in 1795 through the Isle of Anglsea, Bangor, Conway . . . and Kensington*, Dublin, 1796.
21. Humphry Repton was delighted by Strawberry Hill and admired Walpole's *The History of the Modern Taste in Gardening*, remarking that although Walpole claimed to be writing a history, 'in his lively and ingenious manner', Walpole had given, 'both the history and the rules of art better than any other theorists'. *Observations on the Theory and Practice of Landscape Gardening*, London, 1803, p.160. Repton also advocated 'specialised gardens' which he referred to as 'episodes' in the landscape garden.
22. *History*, p. 50.
23. *A description of the Villa of Mr Horace Walpole*, 1784, p. 84.

24. Aphrodite in Greek mythology, linked to the themes in Ovid's *Metamorphoses* for she too was similarly 'transformed' on the shore at Paphos, Cyprus.
25. *Correspondence*, HW to Montagu, 02/061759, Vol. 9, p. 237.
26. *History*, p 42. The ha-ha is a sunken ditch used to make an invisible boundary so as not to interrupt the view. Despite Walpole claims in the *History* that it was an English innovation it originated in France and the technical aspects were described in Dezallier d'Argenville's *La theorie et la pratique du jardinage* (1709).
27. Spence, J. *Anecdotes, Observations, and Characters of Books and Men Collected from the Conversation of Mr Pope, and other Eminent Persons of this Time* (1734–6), 2nd edition, London (1858) p. 109.
28. *Anecdotes*, p. 158.
29. *Correspondence*, HW to Montagu 08/11/1755, Vol. 9, pp. 177–178.
30. *Correspondence*, HW to Montagu 10/06/1765, Vol. 10, p. 156.
31. *Correspondence*, HW to Conway 21/05/1784, Vol. 39, p. 411.
32. *History*, p. 56.

37 Stourhead – the conservation and management of a 'Living work of art'

Alan Power
Garden and Estate Manager, Stourhead, Wiltshire, UK

'All is grand, or simple, or a beautiful mixture of both'[1]

Stourhead was presented to the National Trust by Henry Hoare the 6th Baronet in 1946. This decision followed many difficult years for the country and the Hoare family. The management of the gardens and the wider estate became the responsibility of the Trust's Regional Agent, Architectural Adviser and the Regional Forestry Adviser. When it was given to the Trust, Stourhead was not in the condition we see today or in the pictures we admire from the eighteenth and nineteenth centuries (Figure 37.1). The most accurate representation of the garden at that time is recorded in photographs taken for *Country Life* magazine in 1937 (Figure 37.2). They capture a point in the story of the garden when it required a new level of care and attention.

The years following the handover saw much essential work take place within the grounds; dangerous trees were felled, many areas were tidied and overgrown shrubs were reduced and in some places removed. Essential repairs were carried out to the garden and buildings, including entirely re-roofing the Temple of Apollo. In 1953 a gale blew through the estate which resulted in the loss of many trees and shrubs in the garden and on the wooded hillsides. This event created a sense of space in the garden for the first time in many years that enabled a new generation of trees and shrubs to be planted. However, the opportunity to replant sparked a debate around the choice of plants and the best way of ensuring that an appropriate approach to the restoration and future management of the garden was agreed. In 1955 Graham Stuart Thomas (1909–2003) was appointed Gardens Adviser to the National Trust and began to develop plans for the garden and replanting the collection, which included introducing many flowering shrubs and rhododendrons. He also created new grass pathways around the lake. Focus then turned to re-establishing some of the historic vistas within the garden and some views out of the garden to the wider landscape. The two main dams were also secured and repaired and in 1968 all the garden buildings received care and attention following a grant secured from the Historic Buildings Council. However, questions and debates continued over the most appropriate way to present Stourhead which was seen by many, including Hymans, as one of the most important gardens in the country. He commented in 1964 that: 'The garden at Stourhead is regarded as the one total and authoritative masterwork of English Landscape gardening still in existence'.

By 1973 it was becoming increasingly apparent that the replanting and restoration of the garden at Stourhead needed careful consideration and additional expert advice. The Wessex

Gardens & Landscapes in Historic Building Conservation, First Edition. Edited by Marion Harney.
© 2014 John Wiley & Sons, Ltd. Published 2014 by John Wiley & Sons, Ltd.

Figure 37.1 View of the bridge, Temple of Apollo and Pantheon, 1758 C.W. Bamfylde watercolour. (Permission of National Trust.)

Figure 37.2 The Temple of Apollo, Stourhead 1937, *Country Life*. (Permission of National Trust.)

Regional Committee of the National Trust began to discuss future maintenance, planting policy and proposed presentation of the garden. They decided that all future planting and maintenance would be based on a long-term policy with a set of management principles underpinned by research into the history of the Hoare family and the estate. The exact brief was, 'To prepare a policy and plan aimed at the long-term preservation of the original 18th C. conception and design, taking into account subsequent developments'. It was acknowledged that recommendations made would take many years to implement.

The committee included: Lord Head, Chairman; Mr R.R. Fedden, Deputy Director General; Mr D.J. Sales, Gardens Adviser; Mr K. Woodbridge, Historian; Mr J. Workman, Forestry Adviser and Mr J. Cripwell, Regional Agent. The work of the committee over the next 2–3 years was detailed and at times controversial; however, the outcome of their deliberations produced one of the first conservation plans for a garden in the country, *The Conservation of the Garden at Stourhead* (1978).[2]

As with many gardens, different character areas can be identified and managed separately; however, it is essential that the whole of Stourhead is considered prior to any restorative work, whether this is simple planting, the rearrangement of plants or full-scale restoration of an area. Stourhead is a masterpiece of the English Landscape style and the details within other areas of the garden support the whole, merging seamlessly to create one living work of art.

It is generally acknowledged that the present Stourhead landscape is not wholly representative of the original eighteenth-century concept laid out and developed by Henry Hoare II as subsequent owners made alterations and additions within the landscape. It is essential that where later changes have taken place these too are considered when planning any alterations or adjustments to the garden design.

The recommendations and principles outlined in the Conservation Management Plan (CMP) are an important consideration in the preservation and presentation of Stourhead. In general, the guidelines within the plan are well considered and provide a secure basis for maintaining the visitor experience which has been admired for almost three centuries. The plan encourages the restoration to reveal the landscape, the buildings and the views in order to preserve and enhance the spirit in which the garden was created. Any planting undertaken will have regard for precedent, the management of those areas between the garden and parklands and the garden and wider estate and will embrace a natural transition between discrete areas. Planting should remain simple and functional in places where structure and shelter is required. However, any work undertaken needs to reflect insights gained from research into the appreciation and aspirations of previous owners. As custodians of the garden, we are fortunate to have some detailed records, anecdotal and artistic accounts, fulsome responses, descriptions, and artistic depictions of Stourhead's development. The artists' accounts vary in purpose but some accurately record the garden throughout the late eighteenth and early nineteenth century, not only giving a picture of the garden but also reflecting the owners' taste in the presentation and recording of the garden. Some of the most informative are those by C.W. Bampfylde c.1772 and Francis Nicholson (1753–1844) painted c.1812. Close attention to the detail of these illustrations informs the application of the principles outlined in the 1978 CMP. The distribution of plants in an area, the style in which the lawns were presented, the pruning methods used on the trees and shrubs and most importantly the views that were admired at the time through the eyes of the visitor and by the owner can be gleaned from studying the illustrations. Other artists visited and overlooked the horticultural and architectural detail but captured the essential spirit of the place in their work. J.M.W. Turner's (1775–1851) paintings of Stourhead c.1800 capture many of the elements close to the heart of Henry Hoare II; the atmosphere, the contrasts of light and shade and the mood he wished to portray in the creation of his garden, and these need to be understood in conjunction with the overall concept envisaged in the CMP. It is fundamental to understand that Henry Hoare II wanted to evoke an emotional response to the landscape at Stourhead. He wanted to create a garden that went beyond the visual aesthetic to an experience that penetrated the hearts and minds of those who visited. As evidenced in contemporary accounts, it had this effect in the eighteenth century and it still retains the same power today.

In 1791 Baron Van Spaen van Biljoen (1746–1827) visited Stourhead with a party, commenting 'we were in such ecstasy that we had the utmost difficulty in tearing ourselves away from this charming spot'.[3] Richard Fenton's (1746–1821) account of Stourhead in 1807 provides an insight into the pleasure, wonder and excitement of the visitors' experience:

> there is such a happy union of elegance and comfort, such a provision against the season, that leaves most fine places for five months dreary and cheerless, as little of nature as possible sacrificed to ostentation, and such an air of tranquillity over the whole, and so many happy human faces everywhere and even the un-reclaimed tenants of the wild mixing in your path, fearless and tame, as in Eden ere sin had entered; there is no satiety, and you fancy yourself in a better world.[4]

Henry Hoare II and his grandson Richard Colt Hoare (1758–1838) exerted considerable influence in their ambition for perfection in design and taste and much delight from the garden they created, and understanding their design intentions are critical to understanding how to manage and maintain Stourhead. Henry Hoare II had travelled in Italy and much admired the landscapes he was exposed to. He was also captured by the works of the great landscape painter Claude Lorraine (1600–82). In 1734 he purchased Wilbury House from his uncle, William Benson, and become neighbour to the Duchess of Queensbury at nearby Amesbury. Henry would have witnessed the improvements made to his neighbour's estate by Charles Bridgeman (1690–1738), a prominent landscape architect and Royal Gardener. The poet Alexander Pope (1688–1744) also visited the Amesbury Estate and, even if Henry Hoare never met Pope, he would surely have read Pope's *Epistle to Lord Burlington* and applied some of Pope's theories on landscape when making alterations at Stourhead.[5] Hoare commissioned the architect Henry Flitcroft (1697–1769) to realise his plans. He was a protégé of the arbiter of taste and promoter of Palladian style, Richard Boyle, 3rd Earl of Burlington (1694–1753). Thirty years of association and correspondence with Flitcroft ensued, during which time they developed and created the scene around the lake and the wider designed landscape. It is evident that full advantage was taken of the literary, artistic and social influences guiding Henry Hoare in the creation of his idyll, expressed in Pope's lines:

> Consult the Genius of the Place in all;
> That tells the Waters to rise or fall;
> Or helps th'ambitious hill the heav'n to scale,
> Or scoops encircling theatres the vale.[6]

Henry Hoare II rarely commented on the planting plan for Stourhead but a contemporary account by the literary scholar and anecdotist Joseph Spence (1699–1768) states, 'the greens should be arranged in large masses as the shades are in painting, to contrast the dark masses with the light ones, and to relieve each dark mass with little sprinklings of lighter greens here and there'.[7] Following the death of Henry Hoare II in 1785 Richard Colt Hoare inherited the estate and assumed its management. He began a major planting programme in 1791/2 and removed some of the lesser buildings in the garden. Some of the planting characteristics we see today date from this period and from subsequent members of the family after Richard Colt Hoare, who followed his fashion and the social trend of introducing 'new' plants into their garden.

Understanding the significance of these historical layers of information and inspiration is the only way the current Head Gardener at Stourhead can comprehend the multitude of reasons for the inclusion and exclusion of various features, horticultural and architectural, within the garden. As this comprehension and knowledge develops, it informs the decision-making process for improvements.

A specific example of how this conservation philosophy is applied can be seen in the reconnection of the Temple of Apollo to its landscape below. The work undertaken involved consideration of all aspects of the garden, the architectural design, the planting policy, the woodland management plans and the spirit of the place. The Temple of Apollo had faded into the very edge of the perceived garden and, as a consequence, its presence within the landscape was compromised. The 1937 *Country Life* picture records its receded position within the designed landscape, and despite improvements to the temple structure and changes in the planting scheme the required effect was never achieved. Apollo's dominance in his mythological role as God of the Sun, giving life to everything below him, was no longer visually apparent, even to the informed eye. Apollo was, for many years, hidden behind a natural curtain created by two majestic copper beech trees. These trees were eventually removed to reveal the iconic view to and from Apollo's Mount. The woodland had also encroached, with the under-planted laurel overpowering the entire area, and the grassed areas were shaded out by trees and shrubs, giving the effect of a muddy plain. The temple itself was damp because of a leaking roof and the interior was bland and uninteresting.

Informed by the plans and policies in the CMP and guided by conversations with internal advisers and curators an analysis of various descriptions, pictures and paintings gave visual direction for the improvements that followed. Timing was critical. It was important that the thinning of the woodland compartment around the temple fitted with the Woodland

Management Plan for the area. Consideration was also given to visitors to the garden, as the work would impact on visitor experience. Improvements to the immediate area were completed and the lawns seeded. The view to the area was improved from many aspects in and around the garden through the reduction of shrubs and lifting the canopy of various trees. Sections of the lake edge were exposed and laid to grass to reveal hidden architectural lines and once exposed, subliminally guided the admirer's eye to the focal point of the Temple of Apollo (Figure 37.3). Funding for the restoration project was successfully applied

Figure 37.3 The Temple of Apollo at Stourhead following some planting improvements and before the restoration of the roof (2009). (Permission of National Trust.)

Figure 37.4 The Temple of Apollo, roof restored and warmed by the sun once again (2011). (Permission of National Trust.)

for during the process and permission sought to re-roof the temple and redress and redecorate the interior.

The improvements to the Temple of Apollo and its setting are hailed a success and are now celebrated by all-comers – from the quiet admirer, to the couple who choose it as a marriage venue, to exquisite Hoare family evenings with the voices of choirs floating over the landscape from Apollo. The Temple once again sits in its exalted position overlooking the landscape at Stourhead (Figure 37.4).

> Here we ought to contemplate not only what delights, but what does not shock. In this delicious abode are no Chinese works, no monsters of imagination; no deviations from nature, under the fond notions of fashion or taste: all is grand, or simple, or a beautiful mixture of both.[8]

The conservation of this garden is due to the careful and considered management of change. Any work undertaken has to reveal the significance of the place; to understand, share and honour its past, in order to protect it now and to secure Stourhead's future.

Endnotes

1. *London Chronicle* (1757).
2. *The Conservation of the Garden at Stourhead, Report and Recommendations* (1978).
3. Heimerick Tromp and Evelyn Newby, 'A Dutchman's Visits to Some English Gardens in 1791', *Journal of Garden History* (1982), p. 50.
4. *Richard Fenton's account of his visit to Stourhead*, November 1807.
5. Alexander Pope, Moral essays *Epistle IV*, 'Of the use of Riches', To Richard Boyle, Earl of Burlington (1731).
6. Alexander Pope, Moral essays *Epistle IV*, 'Of the use of Riches' To Richard Boyle, Earl of Burlington (1731).
7. Joseph Spence, *Observations, anecdotes, and characters of books and men* (1820).
8. *The London Chronicle*, June 16–18 (1757).

38 Hackfall, Yorkshire

Patrick James
Managing Director, the Landscape Agency, York, UK

Hackfall comprises an area of about 150 acres of woodland on the steep south and western sides of a bend in the River Ure near Masham in North Yorkshire. It was this woodland that John Aislabie (1670–1742) of neighbouring Studley Royal acquired for £906 in 1731. John Aislabie was Secretary to the Navy (1716) and Chancellor of the Exchequer 1717–21; however, in 1721 he took a bribe worth £20 million in today's money to persuade the UK Government to sell the national debt to the South Sea Company. When the bubble burst he destroyed evidence of what he had done and he was imprisoned in the Tower of London for a short time. He subsequently returned to Yorkshire in disgrace and lived there until he died in 1742.

John Aislabie created the grounds and gardens at Studley Royal, but it was his son William (1700–81) who, in 1750, set about transforming Hackfall as an ornamental landscape and his work continued there until around 1768. His layout had four main components: trees, water, buildings and seats, and paths. In addition to the natural features or larger features – the steepness of the gorge, the river, distant views of Masham church – there were views to and from buildings, seats, a waterfall, cascades and pools. The frame for these inter-linking views and routes was the wood. Trees were cleared to open up views, and the more subtle in intent the more it was admired. People were encouraged to visit Hackfall to experience a 'natural' landscape in contrast to the formality of the grounds at Studley Royal. Arthur Young (1741–1820) on his visit to Hackfall in 1769 noted, 'Nothing can exceed the taste, variety and beauty of this landscape'. Thomas Pennant (1726–98) referred in 1773 to 'The celebrated Hackfall, one of the most picturesque scenes in the north of England' and John Byng, Lord Torrington (1743–1813), recorded in his journal of 1792, 'There is so much to admire, so much to celebrate, that I know not how to proceed in description or speak half in praise due to Hackfall'.

During the 15 or so years that Aislabie worked on Hackfall he transformed his wood. He built follies, including Mowbray Point, Mowbray Castle, Fisher's Hall and Rustic Temple; he created a series of named walks and a fountain set within a rounded pond in an open plain. Other named sites included Weeping Rock, Rock Walk, Forty Foot Fall, Lover's Leap and Sandbed Hut from where J.M.W. Turner (1775–1851) sat to paint one of a series of watercolours of the wood. Aislabie's work at Hackfall largely ceased in 1768, the year that he acquired Fountains Abbey, and he then set about incorporating the setting of the Abbey as part of the Studley Royal Gardens. (As a combination, Studley Royal and

Fountains Abbey form a World Heritage Site belonging to the National Trust only seven miles from Hackfall.)

Hackfall was hardly altered during the nineteenth century but it continued to be visited by large numbers of people. It was not until the early twentieth century that a series of destructive changes resulted in its decline and neglect. The principal change occurred when Hackfall was sold to a timber merchant in the 1920s. Many of the trees were felled and extracted, the follies and other structures were abandoned, and the drainage and hydrology of the site destroyed. It remained in this increasingly neglected and abandoned state until it was acquired by the Woodland Trust and Hackfall Trust in 1989.

Hackfall is unusual, therefore, in the sense that once it had been created in the mid-eighteenth century its subsequent owners added very little that contributed to its interest. It is a rare and outstanding example of the Picturesque garden style and, now restored, it continues to reflect the taste and intentions of its creator William Aislabie. Hackfall's inspiring design helps to explain why English Heritage considered Hackfall worthy of a rare Grade I listing on its Register of Parks and Gardens of Special Historic Interest in England. In addition, Hackfall is situated in an Area of Outstanding Natural Beauty (AONB), is an Ancient Semi-Natural Woodland (ASNW) and a Site of Special Scientific Interest (SSSI) with an interesting and unusual flora and woodland that dates back at least 500 years. It is the combination of these designations and the full statutory protection that SSSI status brings, that made the restoration of Aislabie's wood so challenging.

The Woodland Trust and Hackfall Trust's joint vision for Hackfall was to secure the long-term conservation of this remarkable woodland garden, keep it open to the public free of charge every day of the year and introduce a programme of educational activities in order to ensure that anyone could learn about, have access to and enjoy the genius of this place.

The practical elements of the project had to achieve an optimum balance between the restoration of the historic landscape, protection and enhancement of its natural history as well as operating as a place to be enjoyed by a visiting public. The objectives were:

- To use as a basis for restoration, a philosophy that respects the achievements and conserves the work of the Aislabie family, redefining the essential structure and retaining original features and components where possible
- To conserve and maintain Hackfall as a historic landscape in which the flora and fauna, water features, walks, paths, vistas, built features and structures remain of merit in their own right, as well as integrating to form a unified woodland landscape garden
- To maintain and enhance the ancient woodland and its significant ecological interest in keeping with its national significance as an SSSI
- To develop interpretation, information and an education programme to attract people to enjoy Hackfall and help them to appreciate the value of the built, cultural and natural heritage
- To improve ease of access around the site to increase the number and diversity of people who can visit Hackfall.

In 2001 the Landscape Agency was commissioned to coordinate and prepare a Conservation Management Plan (CMP) funded by English Heritage with assistance from English Nature (now Natural England), Woodland Trust, Hackfall Trust, Landmark Trust, Harrogate Borough Council and North Yorkshire County Council. This document identified the various elements that comprise Hackfall's landscape character and historic landscape design, and assessed these against the competing needs of natural history and public access. Most importantly, it brought all of these parties together and succeeded in enabling them all to agree how Hackfall should be restored and managed. (The Landmark Trust was involved because it had previously leased and expertly restored Mowbray Point, one of the key follies that overlooks Hackfall from the top of the gorge.)

With an agreed approach settled, the next challenge was to raise the funds to translate the wording of a well-intentioned CMP into action on the ground. This was not straightforward. In 2003 the Landscape Agency helped the Hackfall Trust and Woodland Trust to apply successfully for a Heritage Lottery Fund (HLF) Project Planning Grant which funded more detailed assessments of hydrology, ecology, views and vistas, and footpath condition; an essential resource to inform the development of detailed design proposals.

The detailed designs were accompanied by a report assessing the technical and financial feasibility of restoring the fountain, and the potential ecological impacts, benefits and mitigation measures relating to all the proposed restoration works.

Further funding was required. In March 2005, a Stage 1 Heritage Lottery Fund Grant Application submitted by the Hackfall Trust and Woodland Trust was approved. This allowed a team of consultants to be appointed, with the Landscape Agency as lead consultant, to develop detailed design proposals for the partial restoration of Hackfall's buildings, footpaths, water features, views and the provision of a 12-space car park as well as submission of a Stage 2 HLF application for funds approaching £1 million.

In December 2006, the HLF Stage 2 bid was approved. This grant provided the much-needed funds that would enable the implementation of capital works, as well as the development of plans to encourage more visitors and the preparation of a ten-year Management and Maintenance Plan, all of which were subsequently implemented from 2007 to 2010.

The project employed an innovative and pioneering approach to conservation, championed by English Heritage, that pursued the partial restoration of the Aislabie design within set ecological management objectives. This approach allowed potentially conflicting issues to be balanced, demonstrating that actions relating to the conservation of the historic landscape, including restoration of built features, could be compatible with policies and proposals relating to the statutorily protected natural history of the site.

Individual aspects of the wood and the various design features were assigned priorities within agreed ecological objectives and decisions were made on the basis of relative importance, cost, impact on natural history, public access considerations and how features such as seats and buildings were viewed from each other.

Almost 30 separate permissions, licences and consents were required from various statutory bodies before any works could take place on site. This took up much time, administration and patience. The permissions included:

- Approval of all proposals by English Heritage, given that Hackfall is a Grade I registered garden
- Planning permission and Listed Building consents from Harrogate Borough Council
- Highways licence from North Yorkshire County Council
- Felling licences from the Forestry Commission
- SSSI consents and Bat licences from Natural England
- Works in Rivers consent from the Environment Agency
- Endorsement by HLF project monitors and case officers.

Some of the restoration proposals had to be restricted in extent due to ecological considerations. For example, the width of some views was restricted to a narrow 'keyhole', and although weirs on Grewelthorpe Beck were restored, the water level was set lower than the original level so as not to recreate ponds behind the weirs, which would have meant an increased loss of woodland canopy and ground flora.

Throughout the project there had to be an overriding requirement to minimise impacts on the species and habitats of the SSSI. This informed a series of methodologies relating to the different works as well as the timing of the works. For instance, all vehicle and equipment access routes were carefully chosen to have the minimum effect on the site and narrow tracked vehicles were used to reduce ground compaction and minimise the width of access routes. But there were several other categories of works.

Building restoration

The major problem with the building repairs was the condition of the stonework. It was often badly eroded with little mortar in the joints or wall cores. Care had to be taken to

Figure 38.1 The Grotto at Hackfall was completed by 1760. These images (clockwise from top left) illustrate how it looked in the early twentieth century, its condition in the early twenty-first century, during restoration works, and completion in 2010. (Reproduced by permission of the Landscape Agency.)

ensure that wall cores were well consolidated without losing the picturesque qualities of the stonework (Figure 38.1).

Water features

The Top Pond (Figure 38.2) and weirs on Grewelthorpe Beck presented particular access problems and these had to be overcome by temporarily removing the topsoil, with the dormant plants and seeds, to create an access track.

Further downstream, access was only possible over the weirs themselves, and protective tracks were laid to bridge over the vulnerable stonework. Machines then worked back, upstream, leaving the stream banks untouched. All stone used on the weirs was recovered from the site to cut down on transportation.

The Fountain Pond (Figure 38.3) was also cleared to protect the valuable environment, with a deposit area for the silt being carefully chosen to avoid covering important species. The silt was retained by a brushwood barrier to avoid importing material from outside the SSSI.

The re-establishment of the Fountain also presented access problems in terms of how it would affect the natural history and the extreme steepness of the slopes. The new fountain feed pipe was therefore laid entirely by hand digging, and held in place by iron hooks to avoid movement on the steep slope. The lack of flow to the reservoir meant that a switching device was needed to control the length and interval for the fountain display. A novel system of tipping buckets was designed to carry out this function; the housing for the controls was located mainly underground to avoid an unsightly building.

Figure 38.2 Four views of the 'Top Pond' at Hackfall: top left: an early twentieth-century photograph; bottom left, how it looked in c.2005; top right: during works in 2008 and bottom right: completion in 2010. (Reproduced by permission of the Landscape Agency.)

Figure 38.3 Top left: the Fountain and Fountain Pond with views of Mowbray Point and the Rustic Temple in a drawing by Anthony Devis c.1815; bottom left: the Fountain Pond in c.2005; top right: during works in 2008, and bottom right: completion including the gravity-fed fountain working once again for the first time in almost 200 years. (Reproduced by permission of the Landscape Agency.)

Car parking

Several potential sites for the parking area were investigated, but only one had the necessary sightlines to create a safe entrance. This was situated on a hilltop, visible from the road in either direction and from Low Burton village. The detailed design of the car park to minimise visual impact in the AONB was therefore crucial in order to gain planning permission and to provide a high quality, attractive facility for visitors. Remodelling ground levels, native hedging and building a vernacular dry-stone wall (evoking a pin-fold) using reclaimed local materials, allowed the car park to fit unobtrusively into the landscape.

Paths and materials

Throughout the project, materials were sourced almost entirely from the site itself, often including recovered fabric of the original features. This included dressed stone from the original follies, weirs and cascades and other stone and tufa found on the site. Traditional lime mortars were used for building repairs, using sand, aggregates and charcoal mixed to match the original. Footpaths were resurfaced only where reinforcement was necessary, using timber chippings from cleared trees or gravel recovered from de-silted ponds.

By May 2010, the key buildings and water features had been consolidated or restored and the views, vistas and paths which link these features were reopened. Aislabie's inspiring creation had been carefully revealed, while respecting the sensitive natural history.

In addition, interpretation boards were erected at the main entrances, and oak signposts erected at key path junctions to aid navigation around the site. Leaflets were made available at the car park and from local village outlets and a website continues to offer detailed information on the history of the site. The Woodland Trust's Hackfall Officer – a position funded by HLF – organises volunteers, guided walks and educational activities.

Visitor numbers for 2012 were estimated to be 8,000–10,000. Hackfall is a fragile site, which is not easily accessible, and it does not naturally lend itself to large numbers of visitors each year, so this is an excellent result.

The Hackfall Trust and Woodland Trust have committed jointly to funding future management and maintenance as long as the Hackfall Trust remains the lessee. The Hackfall Trust is responsible for site management and the Woodland Trust manages the car park as well as all publicity, interpretation and education activities. All of this work has been set out in a Management and Maintenance Plan that had to be endorsed by the Hackfall Trust, Woodland Trust, Harrogate Borough Council, English Heritage, Natural England, Nidderdale Area of Outstanding Natural Beauty and the Heritage Lottery Fund; a time-consuming task.

The recently appointed Hackfall Officer has successfully promoted the site, encouraging school group visits and the involvement of local communities through a volunteer group that participates in site management, a variety of arts and nature activities, and seasonal events. The Parish Council was involved and consulted at all stages of planning and implementation of the project, and the local community enthusiastically and patiently supported the restoration of Hackfall throughout.

The project has allowed a relatively early example of a Picturesque-style landscape garden, of international importance, to be revealed, conserved and secured for future generations to visit, free of charge. This remarkable and inspirational site is now physically more accessible and information and educational activities are available in various media to encourage a wide variety of people to learn about, have access to, and enjoy an outstanding example of Britain's designed landscapes. The restoration work has been completed with minimal disturbance to the natural heritage and delicate ecosystems within the woodland. Indeed, removal of sycamore and re-establishment of ponds has improved the conservation value of a woodland SSSI.

The project required time, generous financial support, careful planning and, as already implied, patience, given that most of the major works were completed in 2009 and 2010, almost nine years after the completion of the initial Conservation Management Plan. The following year, in 2011, the entire project team was delighted when Hackfall itself secured a 'Grand Prix' Europa Nostra Award in the Conservation category at a ceremony in Amsterdam – recognition of the enormous team effort that helped to ensure a sensitive and successful restoration of this remarkable site.

39 Yorkshire Sculpture Park, Wakefield

Patrick James
Managing Director, the Landscape Agency, York, UK

Yorkshire Sculpture Park (YSP), established in 1977, is more than 200 hectares of unexpectedly fine landscape lying a few miles south of Wakefield in South Yorkshire. A registered charity and accredited museum, it attracts more than 250,000 visitors and 40,000 school and education visits each year. Hugely popular, it sits within most of what was the Bretton Estate with Bretton Hall at its core. The origins of the designed landscape at YSP can be traced back to the fourteenth century, and Bretton Hall is evident on a map of Yorkshire dated 1577. Since then, an inspiring, extensive and under-appreciated designed landscape has evolved and continues to serve as the setting for the hall as well as host to a deservedly acclaimed sculpture collection. All this has happened despite a series of disruptive ownerships and land use changes, particularly during the past 50 years.

Between the 1960s and 2010 most of the changes to the landscape that occurred across the site were detrimental. The management of what now makes up the designed landscape, park and pleasure grounds at Yorkshire Sculpture Park became particularly disjointed owing to a number of different land holding interests. This led to physical and visual dissection of the place and for visitors it was difficult to appreciate its extent or scale.

However this changed when, in 2010, the inspired Yorkshire Sculpture Park management team took responsibility for looking after the entire designed landscape. The team was supported by a generous grant from Natural England, informed by a management plan and detailed proposals, and given an early boost by a large team of contractors including engineers, builders, foresters and volunteers. The result is a rejuvenated landscape that can once again be appreciated as one of the finest parks and pleasure grounds in the north of England.

The more recent history of the landscape development at YSP starts in the early eighteenth century when Sir William Wentworth (1686–1763), whose family had owned the Bretton Estate since 1407, designed a new hall, completed in 1730, replacing a mostly wooden structure that had fallen into disrepair. The new hall was surrounded by new pleasure grounds with an old park, associated with the earlier house, retained and left largely unaltered. Sir Thomas Wentworth (1725–92) inherited Bretton Hall in 1763 and an additional inheritance in 1777 gave him the wealth to carry out major landscaping works. These included creating the Upper Lake (by 1767) designed by Richard Woods (1716–93), as well as a vast Lower Lake, Lower Cascade and the Cut (1774–75), a canal that ran along

Gardens & Landscapes in Historic Building Conservation, First Edition. Edited by Marion Harney.
© 2014 John Wiley & Sons, Ltd. Published 2014 by John Wiley & Sons, Ltd.

the side of both lakes which was probably designed by the canal engineer Luke Holt (1723–1804). A huge area of ground to the south of the hall, Longside (also known as the Great Pasture) was landscaped in the 1760s, and in the 1770s pleasure grounds and a series of garden structures including a menagerie and a temple were laid out to enhance the new lakes. An extension to the park to the east of the hall, completed in the 1780s, took in land between the hall and a fine chapel which had been completed in 1744.

Sir Thomas' daughter, Diana Beaumont (1765–1831), inherited the Bretton Estate in 1792 and she, too, immediately set about her own ambitious series of works to the gardens and grounds. This included erecting two large conservatories and the establishment of a botanical garden. Some of this work took place under the direction of Robert Marnock (1800–89), who served as head gardener at Bretton Hall between 1829 and 1834 (Robert Marnock would become one of the leading landscape gardeners and writers of the nineteenth century whose work included the Sheffield Botanical Garden). His work beyond the gardens included significant additional tree planting in the park, particularly along Oxley Bank adjacent to Longside. This tree planting, now fully mature, still provides wonderful distant views of the far reaches of Longside looking across the site from the new visitor centre.

Soon after the death of his mother in 1831, Diana Beaumont's son, Thomas Wentworth Beaumont (1792–1848), owing to a family dispute, set about demolishing much of what she had built. This included an unusual domed conservatory as well as her botanical and fruit houses. But he continued the tradition of landscaping beyond the immediate grounds and successfully linked up a number of areas of the park. His son William (1829–1907) further extended the park but added little else.

The onset of the twentieth century, however, heralded the beginning of at least 80 years of decline. In the first half of the twentieth century many more eye-catching garden and landscape features were demolished or became ruinous. This included, in particular, the beautiful eighteenth-century Menagerie to the south of Lower Lake. In 1947, having been occupied by the army during World War II, the hall and the estate were sold to Wakefield Metropolitan Borough Council and the hall became a teacher training college. Understandably, from this point on, the management of the site by the local authority, and latterly by the University of Leeds, was primarily concerned with a land use associated with education and managing students rather than as a site of landscape importance. The division of responsibility between the College and University campus, the local authority and, from 1977, Yorkshire Sculpture Park, as well as a tenant farmer and Yorkshire Wildlife Trust, led to much detrimental impact; for example, the planting of incongruous shelter belts and the introduction of a whole range of inappropriate ornamental species. The effect of a divided landscape made it all but impossible to appreciate it as originally intended.

In 2007, the Bretton Hall campus of the University of Leeds closed. This left the future of Bretton Hall uncertain, with the management of the grounds still divided and increasingly neglected. Andy Wimble, English Heritage's influential landscape architect, whose remit included reviewing the condition of protected landscapes covering the whole of the north of England, placed the landscape at Yorkshire Sculpture Park and the Bretton Estate on English Heritage's 'At Risk' Register (landscapes had only recently been included on this register, alongside buildings). The Register entry described the park as having a condition which was 'generally unsatisfactory with major localized problems', its vulnerability as 'medium' and the trend 'deteriorating'.

This declaration, stressing that the landscape was in urgent need of attention, became the turning point in its fortunes. It spurred a number of interested parties into action and ultimately resulted in a unified management regime and a far greater appreciation of the landscape by the visiting public. It is now, once again, so much more than an open space that happens to be suited to the display of sculpture.

The first step towards revitalising the landscape was the preparation and funding of a Historic Landscape Management Plan. English Heritage had no funds to support the production of this plan, but Natural England, via its Environmental Stewardship Scheme, came to the rescue.

A brief, approved by English Heritage, was quickly drawn up based on the standard briefs used by Natural England (NE) for parkland management plans in its Environmental Stewardship Scheme. (Quietly and without too much fanfare, NE's grant scheme has helped to rejuvenate scores of parks and designed landscapes across England during the past 20 years. Its contribution towards the protection and enhancement of the nation's parks and gardens deserves far greater recognition.) In September 2009, with the brief approved by all parties, Yorkshire Sculpture Park and Natural England commissioned the Landscape Agency to produce a management plan with the specific aim of providing the following:

- An understanding of the historic development of the estate
- A review of its current condition to include a number of built structures, lakes, trees, woodland, ecology, views lost or obscured, and other designed features
- Preparation of a list of management policies and a programmed schedule of proposals to enable a radical improvement in the condition of the landscape and the consequent removal from the 'At Risk' Register.

In writing this brief and preparing the plan, it was imperative that the successful and influential activities of Yorkshire Sculpture Park would continue to be respected and incorporated into a future vision for the site. As a registered charity and accredited museum YSP successfully sets out to be 'a centre of international, national and regional importance for the production, exhibition and appreciation of modern and contemporary sculpture' and aims to:

- Offer artists from Britain and overseas the opportunity and resources to work in the galleries and historic landscape of YSP
- Make art and the landscape accessible to the whole community and to offer opportunities for people to engage with sculpture in a creative and meaningful way
- Protect and enhance the historic landscape of Bretton Estate as a space in which artists and visitors can explore, be inspired and enjoy art and nature
- Make a positive contribution to the artistic, economic, social and overall quality of life of the whole community.

The production of a successful plan, which had to be completed within a few months, needed to cover a number of areas that urgently required careful attention and thought. Key areas included a requirement to provide public access to areas that had previously been restricted, including the Upper and Lower Lakes; repair of the remaining eighteenth- and nineteenth-century pleasure ground features, notably bridges and cascades and restoration of the water infrastructure to ensure public safety.

In order to begin to understand how this could be achieved, extensive archival research was started. Aerial photographs, archives, maps and plans were examined, sometimes for the first time, in order to develop an understanding of the original designs and to start the process of informing future proposals and policies.

Due to a number of deadlines relating to the availability of Natural England's allocated funds, the management plan had to be complete within four months so that the capital works programme could be approved and the funds set aside. At the meeting to present the plan and make the request that a series of projects deserved an overall grant approaching £1 million, tension was high. However Margaret Neike, Historic Environment Adviser at Natural England, and her team had clearly read the document carefully and fully appreciated the importance and inherent quality of the site. Margaret and her team received regular updates during the report's preparation and had visited the site on several occasions. Without hesitation, Margaret offered a 90% grant towards the major capital works that had been put forward in Phase I. Furthermore, thanks to Margaret Neike's practical nature and quietly determined attitude, formal approval of the grant took weeks rather than months and a full programme of repair work was soon contracted and underway. If ever a case study is required to demonstrate that public grants can be distributed efficiently, quickly and without fuss, Yorkshire Sculpture Park must surely be a leading example. For this to have happened is entirely thanks to the proactive, well informed and fully supportive attitude of the leading case officer. The frustration is that this case study is very much the exception rather than the rule.

A number of projects had been identified. For example, through a programme of selective thinning and felling, large areas of unmanaged woodland growth was removed and the intended design of the landscape revealed for the first time in decades.

As trees were felled from the lake edges, the visual boundaries expanded and visitors began to enjoy views of the distant landscape in the way that had been originally intended but had been obscured for more than 50 years. More subtle felling and pruning refined the views and vistas and re-integrated the historic structures and features (Figure 39.1).

A number of bridges and many other structures were sensitively repaired; the significance of each feature became clearer and a greater understanding was obtained of how they interacted. By restoring individual elements and reconnecting the views and vistas, the vitality of the landscape was brought back to life and it can now be understood in a way that should ensure future generations can enjoy and appreciate the impact of good landscape design on a vast and impressive scale (Figures 39.2 and 39.3).

As with many historic landscapes, it is often the lack of understanding of connectivity between features that leads to the unintentional loss of the intended layout and design.

The landscape is a living and changing place that requires constant care and attention in order to maintain what are often quite subtle designs. During the process of restoration, detailed photographic records were made in order to provide a reference point for longer-term management.

Of equal importance, the restored and enhanced landscape has created many further opportunities to display sculpture, and continue to enable artists such as photographer and sculptor Andy Goldsworthy and sculptor David Nash to create significant works inspired by the park at Bretton.

The restored landscape now provides visitors with the opportunity to explore and appreciate the setting as originally intended. A greater variety of landscape character has been created and the opportunity to apply new uses, notably through sculpture, can now be achieved. This continued evolution of the valued landscape will ensure its long-term survival as well as adding another important layer to its long history.

Figure 39.1 Left: obscured view of Bretton Hall from Menagerie Wood in 2010; right: the intended view restored and the house and its landscape reconnected by 2011. (Reproduced by permission of the Landscape Agency.)

Figure 39.2 Left: the cascade at Yorkshire Sculpture Park in 2010, overgrown and visually disconnected from the landscape; right: the cascade in 2011 shortly after completion of works. It is now redefined within its broader setting. (Reproduced by permission of the Landscape Agency.)

Figure 39.3 Left: by 2010, following more than a century of woodland growth the designed views across the Upper Lake towards the Greek Temple had been lost and forgotten; right: by 2011 selective tree removal had successfully revealed the intended view of the temple across the lake. (Reproduced by permission of the Landscape Agency.)

40 The Roof Gardens, Kensington, London

Lynne Bridge
Garden designer and historian of cultural landscapes, Bath, UK

Visitors walking through fashionable Kensington High Street in west London are mostly unaware of the historic and mature roof gardens lushly growing six storeys above. When they were constructed in 1938 their one-and-a-half acre roof surface was the largest of its kind in Europe. Since they were created they have been variously known as Derry & Toms, Barkers, Biba, Babylon, Kensington Roof Gardens and now the Roof Gardens. Listed by English Heritage on the Register of Parks and Gardens of Special Historic Interest in England they have been recently restored. Their inception was due to the genius and commitment of two men in the 1930s who collaborated in creating a full-scale garden, complete with specimen trees and flowing streams on the rooftop of a popular London department store, 'one of the wonders of horticultural England'.[1]

Kensington: a rich history

The Royal Boroughs of Kensington and Chelsea were absorbed into the modern metropolis of western London during phases of property development dating from the seventeenth century. The succeeding two centuries in the development of the area now known simply as Kensington High Street is chequered with fortunes and misadventures, battles of words and correspondence between residents of London squares and burgeoning department stores: residential covenants versus retail expansion. There still exists today a variety of architecture that survived the Blitz of World War II and demolition. Properties dating from the 1680s built on squares, Flemish-inspired terracotta family homes set in gardens and stucco-fronted terraces lining leafy streets, churches and chapels. Later additions of residential mansion blocks and commercial and retail buildings complete this fashionable London shopping and dining area; with its good transport links, and access to nearby Kensington Gardens and Hyde Park, it is a popular destination for residents and visitors alike.

From 1689 when King William III (1650–1702) and Queen Mary II (1662–94) purchased what was then known as Nottingham House, set in the village of Kensington, the first improvements to transform the area into a successful locale of property development were made. Following extensive renovations and rebuilding, the Royal Court was established at the re-named Kensington Palace. Sir Christopher Wren (1632–1723) and Sir Nicholas Hawksmoor (1662–1736) made significant architectural alterations to the building to enable

Gardens & Landscapes in Historic Building Conservation, First Edition. Edited by Marion Harney.
© 2014 John Wiley & Sons, Ltd. Published 2014 by John Wiley & Sons, Ltd.

the royal couple to take up residence. The subsequent succession of King George I (1660–1727) and further development of Kensington Palace utilised the services of William Benson (1682–1754), who replaced Wren as Surveyor. King George II (1683–1760) also favoured the palace, making Kensington one of his principal residences with little expansion or alteration other than new stable blocks. After the death of his wife Queen Caroline (1683–1737) parts of the building fell into disuse and by the 1750s Kensington Palace was in a state of disrepair.

The development of Kensington Square to the south of Kensington High Street began in 1685 to accommodate an expected influx of peripheral court residents. At times the site caused considerable financial complications for its ambitious developers working outside of the tried and tested areas of Chelsea and Hammersmith with their proximity to the River Thames. Narrowly escaping the fate of many of London's other similar garden squares marred by later development, the square retains many original features and an air of continued residential occupation. Following the withdrawal of the Court, some houses on Kensington Square were converted to genteel schools for day pupils and boarders and, by the 1830s, some eight academies were located around the gardens.

During the 1890s, residents of Kensington Square were forced to take on the ambitious John Barker and Company to prevent this local shop from swallowing large sections of their square. The owners of Barkers intended to integrate parts of Kensington Square within their expanding department store, which had grown in popularity from a humble convenience shop in 1836 to a large commercial concern spanning seven shops on the High Street. Barkers' first foray into Kensington Square was in 1890 when their horses and vehicles were stabled using the facilities of some of the houses in the square. Before long their trade vehicles surrounded the gardens, a situation that continued until the end of World War I (1918). Barkers merged with Derry & Toms, their former rival, on Kensington High Street in 1920. Residents found themselves pressed into making collaborative objections as the merged department stores pursued concerted plans for expansion into Kensington Square with proposals to redevelop the north side for loading bays. Their plans were met with vigorous protest from residents. *The Times* newspaper took up the struggle and by 1923 a brief reprieve was agreed and Barkers altered their plans for the loading bays.[2] As a consequence, a number of private house owners committed to signing covenants that restricted the use of their houses for residential purposes in perpetuity. Following extensive negotiations with the Crown and Local Authorities, by 1929 Barkers undertook to rebuild a new seven-storey department store, designed by Bernard George, their in-house architect, on the Derry & Toms site. Construction was completed in 1933. The new building loomed above the north side of Kensington Square from Ball Street. Barkers continued to acquire properties on the Square until 1939, by which time they owned more than 60% of the houses.[3]

Barkers' intention was to rival the best department stores in the United States where they had adopted their own 'horizontal system' interior style which made better use of space and improved the retail experience. Barkers also employed C.A. Wheeler of Chicago to specifically design the floor space, with lifts relegated to the outer boundaries and opening the space within the retail floors. The new store was designed in English Art Deco style throughout – a design much admired in the inter-war period. Materials and finishes used include onyx, black marble, polished stone, granite, Egyptian and themed motifs, brass finishes to staircases and grills, gold and blue carpets and modern lighting; extravagant retail design fittings as yet unseen on this scale in Britain. The fifth floor housed the elegant Rainbow Room restaurant and a fashion hall complete with runway, emulating those in New York stores.

Strict London County Council regulations prevented construction of the seventh floor; apparently the design had to be altered because the length of London Fire Brigade ladders could not extend that far. This decision inadvertently provided the later opportunity to construct a roof garden; since the building was designed with an additional floor there was sufficient load-bearing capacity.[4] The success of this type of garden installation was already proven in New York, and in London the rival Selfridges department store had already attempted the concept with their popular tea garden. Barkers' chairman, Trevor Bowen, had visited New York and seen for himself the Rockefeller Center's Gardens of the Nations, situated 11 floors above the roaring urban traffic. These full-scale designed and planted gardens were built on the concrete roof of a skyscraper, exposed to the vagaries of the North American weather, and represented an innovative and successful approach to modern urban roof gardening.[5]

Hancock and the Garden of the Nations

The British landscape designer Ralph Hancock (1893–1950) was credited with the installation and planting of the Rockefeller Center. Hancock had first travelled to America in 1930 following success in England designing gardens for the royal family and other prominent clients. He formed English Gardens Inc; published a brochure titled *English Gardens in America*, and designed and built Gardens of the Nations at the Rockefeller Center (1933–35).

Materials for the construction of the Gardens of the Nations included 3,000 tons of earth, 500 tons of bricks, 100 tons of natural stone from the Lake District, 20,000 bulbs, turf specially imported from England, and 2,000 trees and shrubs. Material loads were delivered by the service elevator or man-hauled using block and tackle systems via the exterior of the building. Ninety-six thousand gallons of water supplied the running brook, waterfall and water features that were lifted to the roof garden by electric pump.[6] Ralph Hancock was quoted as saying:

> The days of penthouse gardening are over and miles and miles of roof space in every metropolis in this country remain to be reclaimed by landscape gardening.

Within the first year 87,000 visitors were admitted to the Gardens of the Nations. The following year a further 50,000 bulbs were planted. They were closed to the public in 1938 and today little remains of the original gardens. During his working life in New York Ralph Hancock created gardens on the roof of the British Empire Building and La Maison Française on Fifth Avenue, New York, and planting plans for Rockefeller Plaza and Ground Level Plaza.

Following his New York success he proposed designs to Trevor Bowen for the roof at Derry & Toms. His designs incorporated three distinct gardens, which would provide simultaneous entertainment alternatives for visitors as well as facilities for private functions. Two of the designed garden areas that had been successful in his Gardens of the Nations were to be included in the London roof gardens. Bernard George is credited with designing the Tea Pavilion and terrace in Art Deco style, providing a stylish and modern outlook over the gardens for visitors and shoppers (Figure 40.1).

Building the gardens

The busy street location, combined with the number of men, and scale of equipment and materials required, meant that considerable effort and planning were involved to move materials up and down through staircase and service lift openings. This was a herculean task, as it had been in New York, and it was complicated by Derry & Toms remaining open as a busy trading department store when work commenced in 1936. The entire roof garden was surrounded by a 2.5 m-high wall which acted as a windbreak and safety barrier. A space between this wall and the perimeter wall of the building was used to accommodate drainage and pipe works.

In preparation for garden drainage, the roof was laid to falls of approximately 1:100. The system specified for the building was installed to the exterior of the walls, allowing rainwater to pass through the perimeter walls to conventional drainage gulleys through cast iron grids which connected to the building's general drainage system.

Figure 40.1 Postcard showing the tea (sun) pavilion, Derry gardens at Kensington, designed by Bernard George in 1938. (Reproduced by permission of Robin Hull.)

It was essential to install a watertight surface on the building's flat roof, comprising a thick bitumastic layer which was laid across the one-and-a-half-acre site. This black pitch (asphalt), sourced from Le Brea in Tobago, provided an impermeable surface on which to build the gardens and provide the vital sealant against water to the floors below. The drainage for the plants and garden features was specified to rest directly on the bitumastic layer utilising house bricks laid in fan-like patterns with clinker infill and topped with a layer of breeze to a total depth of 225 mm.[7] To provide a flattened and fibrous base to the soil a layer of upturned grass turfs was positioned over the breeze. This was finally topped-off with topsoil enriched with peat and manure giving the soil good structure and depth which ranged from 600 mm to 1000 mm. Where paths, terraces and steps were incorporated, paving stones and brick were systematically laid by skilled craftsmen, creating neat lawns and borders for flowerbeds, shrubs and trees (Figure 40.2).

Hancock's Spanish Garden, which had been a great success in Gardens of the Nations took inspiration from the glorious, medieval palace of the Alhambra in Andalucía, Spain, which had experienced a considerable revival in popularity through travel and literature. Its reincarnation in the Roof Gardens was an interpretation of The Court of the Fountains at the Alhambra and included a campanile and structures in the Moorish architectural fashion, which were almost direct replicas of those in New York. The courtyard had a string of fountains and a brightly tiled octagonal water feature, surrounded by four large planted beds in a southern Mediterranean style, wrought iron balconies and gates. A small restaurant for visitors to relax and enjoy the Spanish experience was located within the space. The far end led to the Cloister Walk and to painted views of a Spanish village. After 1969 they were opened-out to stunning views across Kensington.

T.H. Everett visited in the early 1950s and his description of the gardens was appreciative:

> The sub-tropical character was imparted by noble specimens of fan-leaved palms, healthy yuccas, figs and grapes. Borders of mixed flowers – heleniums, hydrangeas, dahlias, anchusas, gladioluses,

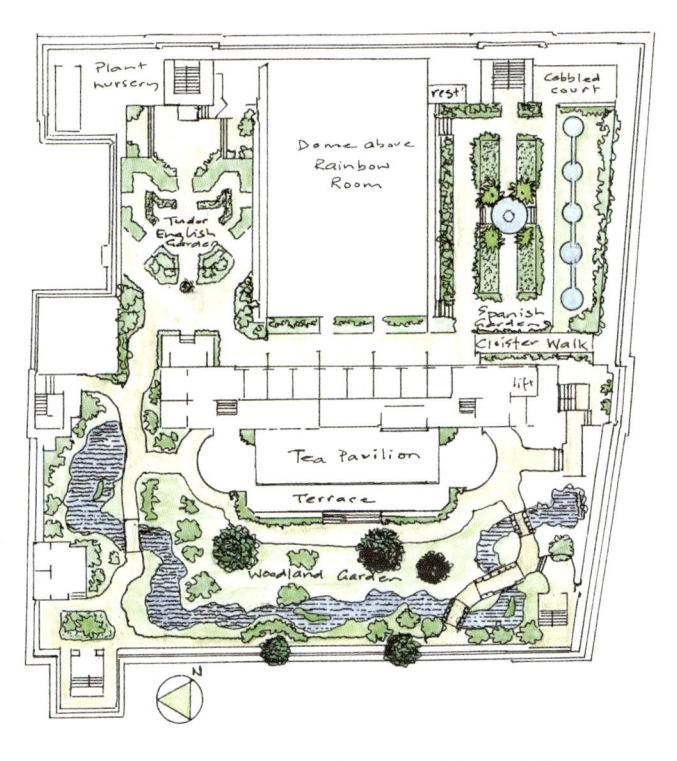

Figure 40.2 Sketch of Derry & Toms roof gardens as built in 1938 (Lynne Bridge)

Figure 40.3 Photograph of view south through English Tudor garden showing arches and planting. (Reproduced by permission of Robin Hull.)

roses, stocks, violas and false dragonhead . . . comfortable wicker chairs appropriately located were well patronised.[8]

The Tudor Courts were another example of tried and tested design from New York and repeated at Derry & Toms (Figure 40.3). The formality of the stone arches and paving, brick walls and enclosed spaces provided additional wind breaks for the high-level roof garden.

Figure 40.4 Photograph of the English Woodland garden towards the waterfall showing the 'river', pathways and mature planting. (Reproduced by permission of Robin Hull.)

The source of these features and planting was closer to home than those that had been so popular at the Rockefeller Center, and is described in Everett's account:

> Broad topped arches and beds of geranium and white alyssum . . . fuchsias and rambler roses trained in tree form. Stone urns frothed over, some with fuchsias and trailing lobelias, some with pink-flowered ivy-leaved geraniums. English lavender, hollyhocks, pinks, stonecrops and rudbeckias luxuriated in raised borders, fronted by low walls of mellowed stone . . . Purple, white and pink flowered clematises and other vines decorated the courtyard walls . . . Blue lily-of-the-valley in tubs and in fat bud lent charm to the steps that led from one court to another. Conveniently located were inviting seats of weathered wood that reminded me of old church pews . . . Tall brick walls clothed in Virginia creeper and other clinging greens . . . on the left great planting of Rhododendrons and other shrubs. A high canopy of horse-chestnut screened the sky, underneath a ground cover of ferns and other woodland plants.

The English Woodland Garden (Figure 40.4) was depicted by Hancock with a 'river' that ran across the roof of the building, complete with ornamental bridges and paved pathways. The design intention was to inspire walks to panoramas over London from viewing areas with vistas rarely seen from anywhere in the city. The Tea Pavilion and terrace looked over this garden and it could be admired while taking respite from the rigours of shopping on the six floors of department store below. This is described by Everett:

> Trees thirty feet high with trunks eight inches and more in diameter were as well established as in their nature homes. 'The art of the gardener was fully concealed'. Trees included elms, white birch, chestnuts, horse chestnuts, flowering cherries, laburnum, hawthorns, apples, peaches and medlars. A one hundred year old yew tree, an unexpected find upon a city roof.

The roof gardens were completed at a cost of £25,000 and opened by the Earl of Athlone on 9 May 1938.[9] Contemporary accounts confirm that the initial planting at the 1938 opening was extensive with 500 different varieties of trees and shrubs, 15,000 bulbs and turf. One of the medlars was the only known descendant of a tree that grew in the garden of William Makepeace Thackeray (1811–63). The figs were lineal descendants of one that grew in Whitehall Gardens and under which Nell Gwyn (1650–87) consorted with King Charles II (1630–85).[10] The roof nursery provided 38,000 of the bedding plants.

The original design incorporated extensive maintenance facilities, space for staff to service the entertainment areas and numerous gardeners and their equipment for the upkeep of

**CORNER OF SPANISH GARDENS,
THE DERRY ROOF GARDENS, KENSINGTON, LONDON.**

Figure 40.5 Postcard showing the Spanish garden and fountains; the caption does not however point out the damaged campanile tower and the unexploded 1,000-pound parachute mine seen in the entrance to the building. (Reproduced by permission of Robin Hull.)

the gardens themselves. The nursery grew some 25,000 bedding plants annually on the roof to replenish the garden stock. With the limited space available this was an outstanding achievement.

There have been a series of adaptations of Hancock's original design features. Notwithstanding the Blitz of World War II, when the gardens took two direct hits: one 250-pound device exploded, damaging the Spanish Garden campanile; the other an unexploded 1,000-pound parachute mine landed on the Tea Pavilion (Figure 40.5). Repairs were made following the end of hostilities.

1973: Biba and subsequent vacancy

In 1973 House of Fraser purchased the three department stores of Derry & Toms, Barkers and Pontings. 99–101 Kensington High Street was subsequently sold to British Land – Dorothy Perkins. Barbara Hulanicki (1936–) was brought in and rebranded the department store as 'Biba'. During a rigorous five-month programme, Markwell Associates transformed the building and the roof garden became the venue for pop stars and the famous to frolic in London. Alterations were made to the original Hancock design by painting over the wall colours and colourful Spanish tiles; some plants and containers were also removed. The short trading life as Biba ended in 1975 when the store and roof gardens were closed for business and until 1978 the gardens languished above the unoccupied building, receiving minimal attention and maintenance. The London Borough imposed Tree Preservation Orders to ensure no trees were removed or damaged. However, the unchecked tree roots interfered with the waterproof layer of the roof in some areas, causing damage to the ceilings of the Rainbow Room below. This was compounded by the age of the rooftop materials which had been in place for 35 years without major repair or replacement. Without a garden in-situ the roof materials would certainly have been considered beyond their normal lifespan.

1978 adaptations

An increase in maintenance plant and services and a change of use for the rooftop level space were the primary reasons for the adaptations to the gardens in 1978. Change of ownership entailed redesigning the Art Deco Tea Pavilion into Regine's Night Club. Access was modernised and entrances were created from Derry Street, and new lifts were installed which required space within the roof footprint. As a consequence the original bridge across the river in the Woodland Garden was adapted, along with the Pennsylvania rock cascades which became the existing grotto feature opposite a new garden entrance. The long line of the covered arcade in the Spanish Garden was detrimentally sealed with new air-conditioning units. Large decorative planters and urns were removed and flowerbeds grassed over, providing more space for entertainment and reducing maintenance costs. The teams of full-time gardeners that were the horticultural success of previous eras were replaced by a single part-time gardener and temporary contract staff as and when required. This was the largest intervention in the designed landscape since their installation in 1938. As a consequence some of their original appearance and historic significance was lost, for a time.

The Virgin Group acquired the rooftop buildings in 1981 and Regine's Night Club was replaced by The Roof Gardens. The Virgin Group took conscientious responsibility for landscape maintenance and improvements on behalf of the landlord. In 1986 English Heritage listed the gardens Grade II and the Derry & Toms building, now adapted to multiple occupancy tenancies, Grade II*. The gardens were upgraded to Grade II* some years later. The building below operated as a completely separate entity to The Roof Gardens above.

1987 restoration

In 1986, under the guidance of the head gardener, Vivienne Anderson, a restoration and revision of the gardens took place which was completed in 1992. The re-opening launch took place with a grand garden party attended by many celebrities. Various head gardeners followed until Becky Burn in 2003, who maintained the gardens to a high and colourful standard for visitors, while facing increasing challenges with the deterioration of the foot-plate which affected the fabric of the building below. Meanwhile some of the trees had reached maturity and in spite of judicious pruning, roots had advanced to the point of needing urgent attention. A comprehensive plan for restoration became unavoidable for all concerned.

2008 restoration

In 2008 the landlord began seeking solutions to the increasing problems at roof level. The Rainbow Room had experienced water ingress at different locations, and the Grade II* listed dome was in need of urgent repair. Potential new tenants were sought and negotiations for its lease were underway. The landlord requested Colwyn Foulkes Architecture & Planning (CFP) to consider ways to repair leaks to the sixth floor level and CFP organised a team of specialists which included the roof garden tenants, the Virgin Group and their new head gardener David Lewis. The team also included Randle Siddeley landscape architects together with specialist consultants in historic landscapes and gardens. In order to proceed with these works speedily as essential maintenance, detailed negotiations took place with the Conservation Officer at the Royal Borough of Kensington and Chelsea and English Heritage. It was agreed that, before works could commence, the team needed to submit a garden master plan, a management and maintenance plan, building work proposals and planting schedules. This process took eight months to complete before the now urgent works could commence.

The appointment of David Lewis as head gardener by the Virgin Group brought horticultural experience and determination to the now 'live' project. Using David's skills and knowledge, repairs to drastically reinvigorate the gardens and its planting were invoked. He ensured that the restoration of this important London site would be completed to the highest standards. Many overgrown and alien plant specimens were removed and others replaced following research into Ralph Hancock's original design concept.

In addition to repairs to the extant hard landscaping a number of mature trees carrying 1976 Tree Preservation Orders were to be replaced, having reached their lifespan, and more manageable semi-mature specimens planted. CFP were appointed to carry out the logistically complex and detailed programme of multi-faceted interventions.

Initially repairs were carried out at some 40 identified locations on the roof plate. The restaurant and gardens remained in operation as a busy entertainment venue with a steady stream of visitors and diners, and private functions. The schedule of garden restoration was negotiated between the relevant agents to take place between October 2008 and March 2009, corresponding to the Virgin Group's out-of-season period. Works were carried out sequentially at localised areas around the gardens enabling them to remain open to the public throughout the programme of works.

Investigations had uncovered breaks through the original bitumastic layer which were caused by cumulative compaction on the roof with the increasing weight of maturing trees on the soil beneath, which in turn crushed the underlying brick layer laid out for drainage in 1938. This had pierced the water-resistant layer at the heaviest points allowing water ingress below. In some areas, root systems entered the apertures, forcing them apart further and compromising the original waterproofing systems.

With the fifth floor and Rainbow Room unoccupied, the decision was made to use the floor space for storage, materials and a works area. In turn, the fourth-floor ceilings were temporarily waterproofed to protect tenants and their staff below. All the original main materials from the roof gardens such as paving stones, brick paths and hard landscape items were carefully numbered and man-handled down the staircase to the fifth floor where they were laid out in the Rainbow Room following the pattern of the roof gardens above. Civil engineers regularly ensured loading spread to take the weight, particularly when soil was also taken down for storage. Waste soil and rubble were manually bagged and taken off site. Trees to be replaced were sawn and, if diseased, sealed in containers along with all material in contact with Japanese knotweed, then removed for incineration.

The cause of much of the damage was identified as slow water drainage that left water standing for long periods on the roof plate. The original and now compromised drainage system was fed from the historical fan-style laid bricks across the entire footplate but, over time and with little maintenance, full compaction had blocked downpipes intended to carry water away from the roof. These waterways were rodded through to resolve the 'wash marshland' effect that had built up over the preceding years, particularly following heavy rain.

Winter weather during the scheduled 2008–9 work-phase was catastrophic with extremely low temperatures and high rainfall, delaying the use of waterproofing materials and repairs. There was only a short period each day in the already tight schedule to avoid clashing with diners and visitors. Colwyn Foulkes undertook these specialised works under challenging circumstances and they are a good example of exacting conservation practice. Each of the 40 identified leakage areas was carefully repaired with proprietary waterproofing materials extending one metre either side of the damaged surfaces. Some of the garden structures assembled in 1938 and the 1978 adaptations were deemed unstable, and did not conform to current building regulations. Maintenance space walls measuring 3 m high and of slender construction were rebuilt using recycled period-appropriate materials and, where possible, sourced from reclamation yards across England. The Spanish Garden arcaded area was restored using specially designed props as braces which were designed not to be visible from the gardens. Broken roof tiles were replaced after new moulds were created and replicas produced. The stored and numbered materials from the fifth-floor Rainbow Room were manhandled back up to the roof garden, reinstated and repaired with period appropriate materials. Finally, appropriate trees to replace the originals were craned in from street level and have provided a sense of increased light in the gardens. Contractors returned in autumn 2009 to finalise the programme of works.

In an example of good conservation practice, David Lewis undertook extensive archival research of the original Ralph Hancock gardens, the *genius loci*, historic significance, detailing and wherever possible reinstated material and plants appropriate to the original design intention. This was an important aspect of the works with considered planting providing the essence of the original designed landscape. Images of the Spanish Garden were discovered which showed the walls painted in an unspecified Mediterranean hue. These were repainted in Flamingo Pink closely matching the Hancock designs. David replaced a liquidambar *Liquidambar styraciflua*, six lime *Tilia* and moved the Japanese maple *Acer palmatum* and, in response to tree management issues, removed two ailanthus trees.

As an expert horticultural plantsman, David was able to recreate planting plans that were evocative of Ralph Hancock's originals. Four matching Chusan palm trees, *Trachycarpus fortune*, in the Spanish Garden were replaced as one had died; five olive trees *Olea europaea* and a pomegranate *Punica granatum*, in keeping with the Mediterranean design, were introduced. The original fig tree *Ficus carica* planted by Hancock himself was faithfully replaced. Colourful planting of *Canna* lilies, *Nicotiana sylvestris* and other Mediterranean shrubs described by Everett, were interpreted for valid inclusion into the new colourful plans for the Spanish Garden. David used Barchams in Cambridgeshire for the new trees and Hall Farm Nurseries for herbaceous replacements.

In the Woodland Gardens the original stone and wooden bridges were restored under David's supervision and new lawns laid along the stream-bank edged with new clipped box hedging marking boundaries, in keeping with the 1938 visual evidence. Original pathways and materials were reinstated.

The maintenance programme proposed by the conservation consultants at the outset was carried out by David and his team with his own contributions. The gardens now have a promising future and on 29 January 2012 a Green Plaque dedicated to the life and work of Clarence Henry Ralph Hancock was unveiled on a wall of The Roof Gardens (Figure 40.6). The celebration was attended by members of the Hancock family, The Roof Gardens Gardening Club and David Lewis, head gardener. Simon Dure-Smith read a dedication on behalf of his mother Sheila (né Hancock):

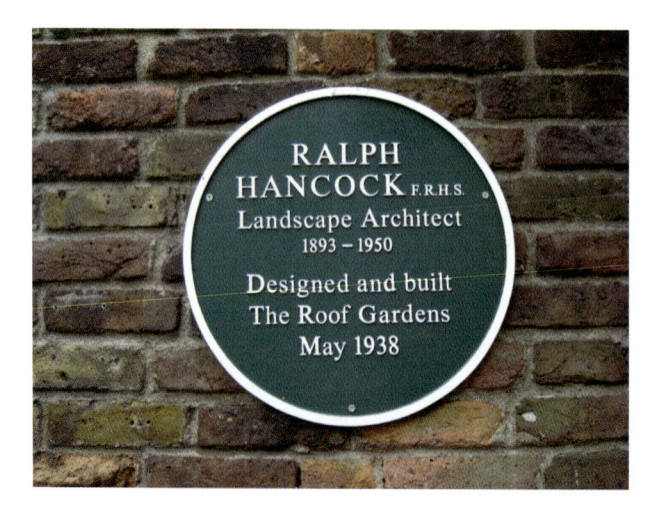

Figure 40.6 Green plaque dedicated to the life and work of Ralph Hancock on 29 January 2012.

My father's vision of using his professional knowledge to put gardens on city rooftops, providing green oases which lift the spirits of city dwellers, has even more significance today with new concerns for the health of the environment. That he did so in two of the world's largest metropolises, London and New York and met the challenges involved, is a measure of his talent and ingenuity.

The Roof Gardens, under the guardianship of David Lewis, play a large part in the horticultural life of visitors and Kensington residents. They support schools in the area for gardening, host gardening events and clubs that include Brighter Kensington and Chelsea founded in 1953, London Gardens Society, and the Woodland Trust. In celebration of the Diamond Jubilee in 2012, the owners of the Virgin Group, the Branson family, planted their Jubilee Tree. The gardens also enhance the newly designed restaurant which has triple-star rating from the Sustainable Restaurant Association. Social working is supported through participation with the Mental Health Charity MIND and the national charity THRIVE which assists the disabled through horticultural therapy and gardening experiences.

Bill and Ben, the resident pair of flamingos, have contentedly inhabited the Roof Gardens since 1978 and were recently joined by a new couple named Splosh and Becks. They are joined throughout the year at this wildlife oasis by varieties of ducks and birds.

Celebrations to commemorate their 75th year were marked by a series of garden themed events throughout 2013. They highlight the enduring Derry & Toms design and still evoke the same charm and appreciation as 'one of the horticultural wonders of England'.[11]

Acknowledgements

The Roof Gardens are, on the one hand, a hidden jewel and, on the other, a famous historic garden. During the course of my research, professionals and admirers of Ralph Hancock and the gardens have generously provided me with their time and knowledge. In particular, David Lewis, head gardener, and Peter Davies at Colwyn Foulkes Architecture and Landscape. Robin Hull was very supportive providing images and access to their archives and the Ralph Hancock website. I myself have seen many changes to the Roof Gardens over the decades, from the heady days of Biba to my own wedding party in 1985 and now, newly conserved and restored, see the gardens, once again, at their best.

References/Further reading

Bowen, T.A., *English Gardens in America*, brochure published New Jersey, USA, 1930.
Bowen, T.A., *The Kensington Story – A pictorial history of John Barker & Company Limited* complied and presented by Mr Trevor A. Bowen to Mr Hugh Fraser, 23 February 1960.
Duterloo-Morgan, F., 'Kensington's Babylon: Derry and Toms Roof Garden', *The London Gardener*, Vol. 4, 1998–99, pp. 39–45.
Everett, T.H., 'The Hanging Gardens of Kensington', *The Garden Journal of the New York Botanical Garden*, January–February 1952.
Griffiths, M., 'Take the Elevator to Horticultural Heaven', *Country Life*, 6 October 2010, pp. 89–91.
Hancock, R., *When I Make a Garden*, G.T. Foulis & Co, London, 1930.
Hobhouse, H., *Survey of London*, Vol. 42, Kensington Square to Earl's Court, Kensington High Street, south side: Kensington Court to Wright's Lane, 1986, pp. 77–98.
Irwin, R., *The Alhambra*, Harvard University Press, 2004.
Peel, D.W., *A Garden in the Sky: The Story of Barkers of Kensington*, W.H. Allen, London, 1960.
Scrivens, S. 'Derry & Toms', *Architects Journal*, 15 October 1980, pp. 759–766.
The Rockefeller Center, Guide Book, 'Gardens of the Nations', 16 April 1935.
www.british-history.ac.uk/source.aspx?pubid=366 – Survey of London.
www.british-history.ac.uk/report.aspx?compid=50310 – Section: High Street: Kensington Court to Wright's Lane.
www.ralphhancock.com
www.roofgardens.virgin.com
www.oxforddnb.com/view/article/97907, accessed 3 Jan 2013.

Endnotes

1. Everett, T.H., 1952.
2. *The Times*, 9 Feb. 1923, p. 11d; 10 Feb. 1923, pp. 9e, 12; 23 Feb. 1923, p. 15d; 18 March 1924, pp.15d – e: C.E.O. file 16684.
3. Building Act case no 19209, Greater London Council.
4. Scrivens, S., 1980.
5. Guidebook, *Gardens of the Nations*, The Rockefeller Center, April 1935.
6. www.ralphhancock.com.
7. Scrivens, S., 1980.
8. Everett, T.H., 1952.
9. Duterloo-Morgan, F., 1998.
10. Everett, T.H., 1952.
11. The Kensington Roof Gardens were purchased by the German Conley family in May 2013.

41 Lowther Castle & Gardens

Dominic Cole

Landscape architect and designer of the Eden Project in Cornwall; Chairman of the Garden History Society and Chairman of the National Trust Gardens Advisory Panel, London, UK

Lowther Castle is in the north of the Lake District National Park near Penrith, Cumbria. The 130-acre site is Grade II* on English Heritage's Register of Parks and Gardens of Special Historic Interest in England and contains at least three significant buildings. The garden is of national importance, representing 400 years of garden history with a seventeenth-century garden largely intact, but with significant Edwardian overlays (Figure 41.1).

The estate remains home to the Lowther family, although they no longer reside in the castle, which was de-roofed in the 1960s (Figure 41.2). The conservation and restoration project which is the subject of this case study addressed the castle and some 70 acres of adjacent gardens and was carried out between 2009 and 2012. The designed parkland is not part of this study, although it was incorporated into a comprehensive conservation management plan by the Landscape Agency in 2002.

The great Lowther Estate, seat of the Earls of Lonsdale, was ceded from a grant by King Edward I in 1283. It was added to over centuries to become, remarkably, the largest in England and at one time it was possible to walk from the east to the west coast without stepping off Lowther soil. Recorded in the twelfth century, the first house on the site was a simple 'pele' tower. The second burnt in 1718, only 24 years after it was built, then stood in partial ruin. The present castle of 1806 was the first commission of the architect Robert Smirke (1780–1867), who later built the British Museum.

The castle is constructed of high-quality pink ashlar and has been likened to 'an old lady with perfect skin'. The interior decoration was by Augustus Welby Pugin (1812–52) in High Victorian Gothic style, with many furnishings brought back from post-revolution France. A sculpture gallery with a vaulted plaster ceiling by Francis Bernasconi (1762–1841), was added in 1814, the final piece of executed work in the castle.

The gardens date from the late seventeenth century, and this layout predominates. They were among England's most extensive and impressive gardens; ranks of stone masons, blacksmiths, carpenters and gardeners were employed to construct the elaborate balustrades, steps, follies, and summerhouses, and tend the vast expanses of ornamental and productive lawns and gardens.

> Sixty acres of smooth green sward made up the spacious lawns and these were broken up by banks of flowering shrubs and forest and ornamental trees and gemmed with beds and borders of brilliant colour. The phlox border, 600 yards long, was filled with 15,000 phlox plants in special varieties . . . Hugh's Garden, by Jack Croft's Pond, was a sight in itself, for here were eleven acres laid out on a

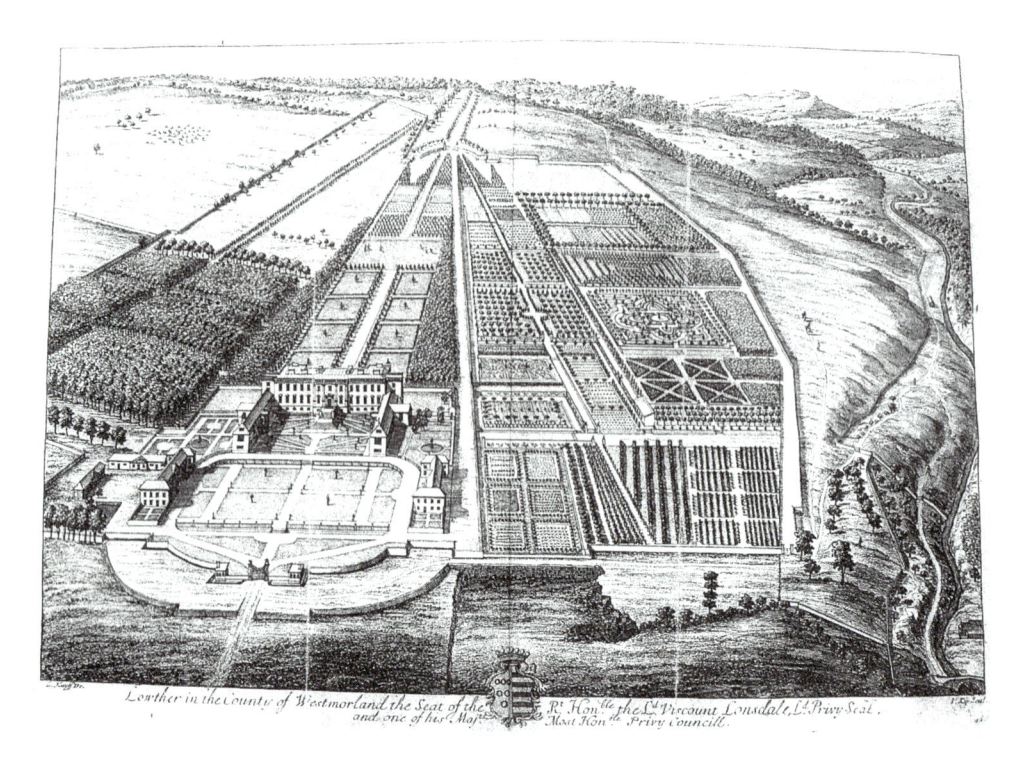

Figure 41.1 A view of Lowther by Knyff and Kip 1710. (Reproduced by permission of Lowther Castle and Gardens Trust.)

Figure 41.2 Castle pre-restoration. (Reproduced by permission of Lowther Castle and Gardens Trust.)

plan which the late Lord Lonsdale brought back from Versailles. The Rose Garden was always a great sight at Lowther, for in extent it was one acre and a third, and 20,000 roses were planted here. In the springtime daffodils made the lawns into Fields of the Cloth of Gold, for the bulbs were put in by the hundredweight year after year.[1]

The limestone escarpment on the west side extends over one kilometre and provides views across the fells to the northern mountains of the Lake District. Dating from 1680 or earlier,

Figure 41.3 The Great Terrace walk from below (author's own).

the spectacular viewing terrace (Figure 41.3) was one of the earliest of its kind in the country, and predates those at Muncaster Castle, Cumbria and Duncombe Park terrace, Yorkshire and elsewhere.

The Lonsdale family included such wild and colourful characters as the first Earl of Lonsdale, 'Wicked Jimmy'; William, 'The Bad Earl', and the flamboyant Hugh Cecil, 'The Yellow Earl' as well as William, 'The Good Earl', patron of artists and writers, including Wordsworth. More recent Earls include an industrialist, foresters, farmers and a conservationist.

The Yellow Earl (1857–1944), the longest lived of the Earls of Lonsdale, was a wayward younger son who went on to become the most famous Earl of his generation. Showman, sportsman, Arctic explorer, horse whisperer, founder of the Royal International Horse Show and the Lonsdale Belt for boxing, friend of royalty and the German Kaiser, he lived at Lowther in flamboyant style until the 1930s.

On New Year's Day in 1936, Lord and Lady Lonsdale were driven away from Lowther Castle in a yellow Daimler, leaving morning papers on the desk, clothes in the wardrobes and ironed blotting paper ready for the next guest. But Hugh, the 79-year old 'Yellow Earl' of Lonsdale, and Gracie, Lady Lonsdale, were never to return. The 1930s crash had caused the Lowther income to drop from £180,000 to just £6,000 a year and they were informed by the Lowther Trustees that they could no longer afford to maintain Lowther Castle. The castle was never again inhabited.

During World War II the estate was requisitioned by the War Office to provide a sufficiently large and secret location to develop a unique way of using tanks in warfare. The impact on Lowther was devastating; grounds scarred with secret weapons testing and the once magnificent lawns concreted over for tanks used by forces billeted in the Great Hall. Later, the challenges of restoring the fortunes of the estate were met through forestry and modern agricultural practices. These resulted in the obliteration of much of the historic gardens by overplanting. The once manicured south lawns became home to massive sheds used to rear chickens and any remaining open space was planted with Christmas trees for commercial return (Figure 41.4). The conifers were planted to strict forestry practice rules, even being planted in straight lines through Thomas Mawson's (1861–1933) delicate Edwardian flower gardens.

James Hugh, seventh Earl of Lonsdale (1922–2006), a capable engineer and industrialist who had seen war and poverty caused by the depression of the 1930s, planned to demolish the castle, stating that it 'exemplified gross imperial decadence during a period of abject

Figure 41.4 The South Lawns after clearing the chicken sheds. (Reproduced by permission of Lowther Castle and Gardens Trust.)

poverty'. Fortunately, in the 1950s he was persuaded by the townspeople of Penrith to retain the shell of the castle. The removal of the roof and its partial demolition left the facades and towers and turrets silhouetted against the skyline, resembling an eerie film set. Nothing more was done to preserve the castle and gardens, which were to lay undisturbed for a further 50 years. For over 70 years the castle and its magnificent historic gardens slept while nature crept silently through the decline.

Planning the restoration

The following years saw much hard work put into assessing, planning and funding applications for the proposed restoration. Emergency repairs were undertaken to prevent further damage. In 2009 Land Use Consultants (LUC) were commissioned to propose how the gardens should be presented and what process would be needed to achieve this. Dominic Cole, lead designer for the Eden Project and who had also worked on the restoration of the Lost Gardens of Heligan, both in Cornwall, was appointed landscape architect for the project. In 2010 the castle and gardens were leased to the new independent charity, the Lowther Castle & Gardens Trust, which includes Jim Lowther of the Lonsdale family as trustee, and £8.9 million of funds were secured from the North West Development Agency and European Regional Development Fund to develop the castle and gardens into a major visitor attraction.[2]

The first substantial task was to understand the research and other project planning that had been undertaken to date. The historical research alone filled up numerous folders and is still incomplete. The Lowther Archive is held at the Cumbria Records Office at Carlisle and is managed by an archivist funded by the estate. Although the main story of the development of the castle and gardens has been researched, there is still more detail to be revealed.

Description of the gardens

The earliest known phase of the designed gardens dates from the late seventeenth century and the general layout of these gardens around Lowther Castle has survived relatively unchanged throughout its 400-year history. This layout, which forms the underlying structure of the garden, was established by 1800, and no major changes have occurred since, apart from arrangements around the rebuilding of the castle itself. To the north of the castle and its immediate surroundings there was open parkland, with woodland to the east and south-east. To the south, along the axis of the castle, the area was open but to the south-west, between the castle and the limestone escarpment, were the formal ornamental gardens.

While the pattern of parkland and woodland areas to the north and east survived, change occurred in the South Lawn area and the adjacent eastern gardens. At different times the South Lawn would have been open lawn, or subdivided by paths. In the past this area was also functional with timber and drying yards from the mid-eighteenth to early nineteenth century, and with chicken sheds in the twentieth century.

The area immediately around the castle has changed in parallel with the changes to the castle itself. Up to 1847, around the earlier castle there were ornamental gardens and formal lawns with statues and a grid of paths. With the construction of the current castle, the palette of formal terraces and grassed area was continued, with the addition of planting beds to the south of the castle in the twentieth century.

In 2009 LUC's response to the brief was to maintain the fairytale qualities of ruins being gradually reclaimed by nature. This is a romantic ideal that requires particular consideration. To achieve a sense of discovery – the 'secret garden effect' and the feeling of 'wildness' – visitors need to have the impression that they are doing the discovering themselves. The projected increase in visitor numbers at the time of writing suggest, however, that they will potentially detract from this feeling.

LUC had previous experience of achieving this effect at Heligan, where one of the client's aims was to consider what characterises the 'lost quality' and to develop a strategy for conservation of this character. When the Lost Gardens of Heligan opened to the public it was the client's ambition for visitors to share a sense of 'discovering the sleeping beauty'; a lost garden, asleep under a shroud of rhododendron and bramble. At first the concept worked because it was a novel approach to presenting a garden. Soon, however, tiring of walking through tunnels of rhododendron and sycamore and having seen photographs of the garden in its heyday, visitors wanted more and the majority of the gardens have now been cleared of invasive scrub and 'weed' trees (mainly self-sown sycamore) and replanting has taken place based on documentary research.

To maintain a semi-permanent state of romantic ruinous decay in a garden requires as much – and possibly more – management than a 'maintained' garden. The balance between a pleasing aesthetic of decay and outright neglect requires very delicate handling. It requires brutal decisions combined with an acute awareness of the needs of managing habitats to maintain or increase biodiversity. Visiting ruins and visiting gardens are different experiences requiring diverse management approaches. Another property attempting to maintain this balance is Hackfall, North Yorkshire, created by the son of John Aislabie (1670–1742), creator of nearby Studley Royal gardens situated four miles up the River Skell from Fountains Abbey. His son William Aislabie (1700–81) created, at Hackfall, an eighteenth-century landscape garden in a magnificent natural gorge and incorporated its topographical features as part of the garden. Contemporary visitors admired the contrast between the carefully controlled man-made interventions, grass terraces, viewing platforms and follies, and their naturalistic setting.

Probably because the garden at Hackfall is not attached to a mansion, the site was never modernised and the garden went out of fashion, and through lack of maintenance it became romantic woodland with decaying follies. Eventually, acquired by the Woodland Trust, the aim was to maintain its abandoned, romantic air and the site is now open to visitors but, to ensure their safety, the follies have been stabilised, paths made safe and dead and decaying branches removed (see chapter 38 of this volume for more on Hackfall).

The unique quality of the garden at Lowther, however, is that the underlying seventeenth- and eighteenth-century structure has not been substantially altered and survives largely intact. The massive scale of the construction, with earthmoving and retaining walls, is impressive, equivalent to the monumental retaining wall at Stoke Park, Bristol. The Edwardian decorative overlay used this structure, including avenues, *allées*, and hedges to create a remarkable series of 40 enclosed gardens, each with a different character. The Edwardian gardens would have required an extraordinarily high level of attention supported by substantial wealth in order to display an opulence only possible during this period.

However, the scale of the Edwardian structures is domestic, much as you might expect to see in a large suburban garden. Each garden is themed and the experience of walking around is analogous to visiting the different garden designs on display at the Royal Horticultural Show at Chelsea. Here there was an assemblage of different styles from around the world with settings to display one or two plants in season, such as irises and roses. It has none of the subtlety of the themed garden at the National Trust's Victorian Biddulph Grange garden near Stoke-on-Trent, Staffordshire, where the transitions and 'reveals' are a key part of the experience. The Lowther Edwardian gardens are a pure ostentatious display and do not read as a coherent whole – any one of them could be transported elsewhere without loss of impact.

For the garden restoration at Lowther, the opportunity existed to reveal the unique surviving structure of the earlier gardens – the earthwork, terracing, retaining walls and banks and its remarkable landscape context. However, the vision 'to allow nature to continue to reclaim' may work as a concept for presenting the castle but it would be a false construct applied to these gardens. A tumble-down summerhouse and eighteenth-century beech trees on their last legs with rays of sunlight piercing the canopy provide occasional flashes of romantic decay, but the main sense is one of deliberate, callous destruction. The whole intricate web of the Edwardian gardens overlaid on their robust earlier foundations was later planted up with rows of conifers without regard for the several hundred years of manual labour and horticultural toil that had gone before.

A key experience in garden visiting is that gardens contain different spaces and there is usually a sequence by which visitors encounter the garden. It might be the first, explosive view from the house or the gradual reveals through doorways, arches, changes in level and textures or chasing down an elusive scent. At Lowther all these subtle elements exists as haunted ghosts, remnant steps, broken summerhouses, empty pools and outgrown hedges. But the intense conifer planting left no visual enclosure or sense of discovery; the ground, left bare, with few barriers to prevent the observer looking across several gardens where once hedges, banks and shrubberies kept the next garden secret and a surprise.

Lowther Gardens' significance and their re-presentation

The heritage asset may be summarised by the complete survival of a late seventeenth-century structure, including magnificent earthworks, massive dry stone walls, terraces, and an almost unique prospect terrace, with some veteran tree specimens, together with the topographic setting, microclimate and a dramatic quality of light and exceptional views of the surrounding Lakeland hills. Lowther also reflects the expert technology needed to garden at a grand scale as evidently understood and used in the seventeenth century.

The aim of the restoration project was to reveal the seventeenth- and eighteenth-century underlying structure of the earlier gardens including level changes, *allées*, and external views. First, it was necessary to research how the garden would have been visited and whether there was there a prescribed sequence. With so much surviving and requiring interpretation was it necessary to introduce new design, perhaps with productive but decorative gardening – fruit, flowers, and vegetables – as at the re-created renaissance garden Chateau de Villandry at Villandry, France, which is entirely planted with salads and vegetables.[3] If appropriately presented and properly understood, the place will tell its own story.

The key concepts incorporated into the masterplan of 2011 were underpinned by a thorough evaluation of the historic evolution of the gardens. The proposed layout and structure of the restoration was conceived as revealing a palimpsest of the many layers that evolved over centuries. It was not intended to peel back layers to a particular historic period, but to provide a concept that understands and respects the surviving historical footprint and fabric.

By 2012 the gardens and castle already provided different experiences that fuelled the imagination. Even in its raw state there were battlements, a sunken servants' walk, ramps, ramparts, secret gardens, mysterious woodland walks, mossy rock gardens and acres of paths, trees and shrubbery. The project aimed to enhance these existing features and reveal more of the site year on year to expand the diverse facilities, enhance the qualities of the site and include new layers representing a twentieth-century contribution. The new elements of the ongoing project are rooted in Lowther's wider cultivation context with good husbandry, silviculture and agriculture practised for practical and functional reasons to the best present-day standards. Good husbandry traditionally also recognises and understands the aesthetic opportunities of a site's natural context. A strong theme in the new garden is this combination of productivity and functionality, together with visual beauty and delight. Lord Macartney (1737–1806), the distinguished Irish-born British statesman, and the first envoy of Britain to China, 1793–4, visited Lowther around 1794 and recorded that 'if any place can be said in any respect to have similar features to the western part of Van-Shooquen, it is at Lowther Hall'.[4] The current project aims to understand and demonstrate the same qualities of light, prospects and magnificent setting that Macartney praised at Lowther and that remain today, together with the processes of best practice in horticultural diversity, propagation and soil improvement, rather than overall 'landscaping' (Figure 41.5).

Presentation of the garden

In parallel with the gardens project, the tree conservation strategy in the castle gardens and surrounding landscape was critical, as there is a strong presence of mature and ancient trees, as well as rich woodlands of younger trees, testament to the Lowther estate's tradition of managing trees and woodlands.

Trees are valued at Lowther, both as landscape elements and for historical and ecological reasons. Many trees on the estate are ancient and represent plantings by the Lonsdale family as part of its evolution. Trees were always an essential part of the gardens and are illustrated on the earliest map of 1683. Evidence from maps, plans and engravings, and from the gardens themselves, suggests that the gardens were set out with avenues of yews, many of which survive today.

Figure 41.5 South Lawns May 2012. (Reproduced by permission of Lowther Castle and Gardens Trust.)

However, since the formal gardens were abandoned in the mid-twentieth century, and the wholly inappropriate blanket planting of spruce trees across the historic garden areas occurred, more recently many self-seeded trees have established. These have no historic value, except that they illustrate the way in which nature has taken over the abandoned site. The ancient, gnarled and densely branched trees provide habitat for many species, including red squirrels, and bats, though young trees also have ecological value, providing habitats for insects and birds, as well as feeding grounds.

The underlying approach to the landscape and gardens at Lowther has been based on archival research and study of the remains of the historic gardens on the ground, both of which have informed their future. As little of the ornamental planting remains, trees, stonework and earthworks hold the key to the history of the site. The essence of the project is to respect the place that trees have in landscape and the aim is to recreate the arboriculture structure through the preservation of historic plantings and replanting where tree lines or groups have been lost. Trees that have self-seeded, or are not in keeping with the seventeenth- or eighteenth-century structure of the garden, are only be retained where they add structural, ecological or visual value to the gardens.

At Lowther, the following principles in the ongoing project are applied. The oldest trees are preserved, where it is safe to do so, with tree surgery to improve their condition where necessary. Younger, mature trees are retained where possible, with consideration of their ecological, structural and aesthetic value. Immature trees are retained where possible, particularly in shelterbelt and woodland areas. New trees will continue to be planted in appropriate places, with appropriate species, as part of the works to strengthen and re-create the historical structure of the gardens. Felling and clearance of trees within the gardens will be undertaken as appropriate to reveal the structure of the gardens and open up historic paths and sequences. Only then will decisions be made as regards removing large and historic trees.

The management strategy

The gardens are part of an entity, now managed by the Lowther Estate Trust, comprising castle, gardens and the broader Lowther Park estate which, at 3,500 acres, remains the largest home park in England. The gardens are to be managed by a head gardener, responsible to the chairman and trustees of the trust in creating and implementing current and future garden plans and, of course, to maintain traditional horticultural standards. Part of the head gardener's responsibilities will be to work closely with delivering, by 2014, an exceptional garden that will be a major new visitor attraction in this part of Cumbria. The role will also include outreach projects such as working with local schools and potential volunteers, and acting as 'ambassador' for the project.

Endnotes

1. *Cumberland and Westmorland Herald*, 14 June 1947.
2. http://www.lowthercastle.org/castle-restoration/ accessed 6/08/2012.
3. The Spaniard, Dr Joachim Carvallo (1869–1936) restored the eighteenth-century garden between 1906 and 1924. He considered the rigid design to demonstrate absolute order, in contrast to Rousseau's approach –'The principles of an absurd egalitarian contrary to nature and good sense'.
4. Burke, B. *A Visitation of the Seats and Arms of the Noblemen and Gentlemen of Great Britain and Ireland* (1854).

42 Monticello

Marion Harney
Director of Studies, MSc Conservation of Historic Gardens and Cultural Landscapes, University of Bath, UK

Monticello is a 5,000-acre plantation near Charlottesville, Virginia, and, like Strawberry Hill (see chapter 36), is an autobiographical site. The plantation house, begun 1768, was designed as a Palladian villa by Thomas Jefferson (1743–1826), America's third president and principal author of the Declaration of Independence (1776). A polymath and important Enlightenment figure, Jefferson was a farmer, spoke five languages fluently and had wide-ranging interests in new crops, soil conditions, his gardens, scientific experiment, agricultural techniques, and mechanical invention. He was also an accomplished architect. Jefferson founded the University of Virginia in 1819 and it received its first students in 1825. He was principal designer of the grounds of the university and of his home, Monticello, where he retired in 1811 following his presidency; both landscapes were based on agrarian principles. Monticello has been designated a National Historic Landmark and Monticello and the University of Virginia were together designated a UNESCO World Heritage Site in 1987.

Jefferson initially practised law and served in local government as a magistrate, county lieutenant, and member of the House of Burgesses.[1] As a member of the Continental Congress, he was chosen to draft the Declaration of Independence (1776). He left Congress that year and returned to Virginia, serving in the legislature, and was elected governor from 1779–81.

He returned to public service in 1784 after a brief private interval and was sent to France; first as trade commissioner and then as Benjamin Franklin's successor as minister plenipotentiary. While he was in Europe he indulged his passion in horticultural matters and initiated the importation of American trees and shrubs into France. He played the role of a zealous seed missionary, at times resorting to illegally secreting seeds from Italy about his person so that he could test their efficacy as alternative crop species in America. He travelled widely during this time, observing kitchen gardens and horticultural techniques in England and elsewhere. In Paris, Jefferson visited the notable *Le Jardin du Roi*, later *Jardin des Plantes* (after 1792), the main botanical garden in France, becoming a firm friend and correspondent with its director, the renowned plantsman André Thöuin, who supplied him annually with substantial shipments of plants from 1808–c.1822. His travels took in vast French gardens including Versailles and Château de Bagatelle, a *Jardin Anglais*. In 1786 he came to England and visited some 16 landscape gardens. He kept a diary to record his impressions, writing to an old friend in Virginia that, 'the gardening in that country is the article in which it surpasses all the earth. I mean their pleasure gardening'.[2] He also took the opportunity to avidly study European culture, sending books, seeds and plants, statues and architectural drawings, scientific instruments and other information back to Monticello.

He returned to America in 1789 as secretary of state under his friend, the first president of the United States, George Washington (1732–99). However, it was only with his resignation from that office in 1794 that he returned to his beloved garden at Monticello where he began remodelling the house and renewing his plantation. This new burst of activity and enthusiasm is recorded in the diary, or 'Garden Book', that Jefferson kept in which he recorded his interest in the science of gardening, meticulously recording planting and gardening activities, experiments and the organisation of planting schemes. At this time he listed a sophisticated array of more than 50 species and varieties of vegetables.

He left Monticello again in 1796 to take up office as vice-president but returned for long periods during which he continued gardening, assisted by his daughters, relatives, slaves and various hired gardeners. Four years later he became president and held the presidential office until returning to Monticello in 1809, where he remained for the rest of his life.

Jefferson was heavily in debt when he died in 1826 and his assets and the estate at Monticello were sold in a series of public auctions from 1827. Following a number of owners the property was acquired in 1834 by an admirer of Jefferson, Uriah P. Levy (1792–1862), a commodore in the United States Navy who financed the preservation of Monticello, as did his nephew, Jefferson Monroe Levy (1852–1924), who took it over in 1879. He sold it to the Thomas Jefferson Foundation in 1923, who now manage it as a house museum and educational institution.

Many, but not all, plantation homes were constructed on elevated sites with artificially constructed terraces which took advantage of the extensive panoramic views over the Virginia Piedmont. While the architecture of the villa has been much praised the significance of Jefferson's revolutionary garden at Monticello has, until recent years, received scant attention. Jefferson had a passion for plants and all things horticultural and wrote about his garden to the Philadelphia portrait painter and naturalist, Charles Wilson Peale (1741–1827):

> I have often thought that if heaven had given me choice of my position and calling, it should have been on a rich spot of earth, well watered, and near a good market for the productions of the garden. No occupation is so delightful to me as the culture of the earth, and no culture comparable to that of the garden. Such a variety of subjects, some one always coming to perfection, the failure of one thing repaired by the success of another, and instead of one harvest a continued one thro' the year. Under a total want of demand except for our family table I am still devoted to the garden. But tho' an old man, I am but a young gardener.[3]

At Monticello, Jefferson created and cultivated a 1,000-foot-long south-facing terrace vegetable garden, built into the hillside on an elevated site where he experimented in horticultural cultivation. He took full advantage of the microclimate on the site which was enhanced by the construction of a ten-foot-high paling fence above the garden and this, combined with its south-facing aspect, created a highly conducive environment for producing specialist vegetable species native to hot climates 'from South and Central America to Africa to the Middle East and the Mediterranean'.[4] He succeeded in producing a uniquely wide variety of warm- and cool-climate seasonal vegetables unrivalled in North American gardens at this time, introducing 'some 330 varieties of ninety nine species of vegetables and herbs'. Jefferson viewed his garden as a means of transforming society and he distributed rare, unusual and pioneering seeds to friends, neighbours, other plantsmen and political allies alike. In a letter of 1790 to Samuel Vaughan Junior (1762–1827) he said of his agricultural experiments, 'I have always thought that if in the experiments to introduce or to communicate new plants, one species in an hundred is found useful and succeeds, the ninety nine found otherwise are more than paid for'.[5]

Jefferson was a hands-on gardener, actively participating in planting and sowing aided by family members and slave labourers and overseers who carried out basic and necessary garden duties.

Most of his knowledge was gained from British and American literary sources and he owned three editions of the Scottish botanist Philip Miller's (1691–1771) *Gardener's Dictionary*, including the revised and extended 1768 edition. He also owned multiple copies of the *Treatise on Gardening* (1793) by his fellow Virginian, John Randolph (1727–84), which borrowed heavily and unapologetically from Miller, and the ground-breaking *American Gardener* (1804) by John Gardiner and Alexander Hepburn, which also partially relied on English sources.

Jefferson, however, formed a distinctly American terrace garden over a three-year period, moving more than 200,000 cubic feet of red clay to do so. The garden comprises two acres of kitchen garden and an additional four to five acres of fruit orchards. The vegetable terrace was supported by a 12-foot-high retaining wall of rock which extended the length of the 1,000-foot garden. He created a south orchard consisting of 400 trees surrounding two vineyards which extended below the wall and vegetable terrace with the entire complex enclosed by a 10-foot-high paling fence. A classical temple designed by Jefferson stood on top of the stone wall from which the observer had extensive views of the surrounding Virginia landscape.

The extended Jefferson family at Monticello were largely self-sufficient, eating the produce from the garden and sharing it with friends, neighbours and the streams of visitors he received following his retirement. He admitted to living 'temperately, eating little animal food', existing mainly on the fresh produce he cultivated with his own hands, but helped by others.

His garden broke with the more refined labour-intensive European tradition of tending vegetables, concentrating instead on the more agricultural aspects of planting and harvesting. Jefferson selected varieties suited to the microclimate (which extended the growing season) and that required less extensive skills or intensive use of labour (see Figure 42.1 for a view of the restored garden).

All of his gardening activities were recorded in his Garden Book; for example, in 1812, his notes provide information on how he methodically divided the vegetable terrace into 'Fruits, Roots and Leaves'. He also recorded in this horticultural diary the friendly competition among the local community to be the first to produce spring peas. Enthusiastically experimenting in cross-fertilisation and revelling in his ability to produce new varieties, shapes, colours, textures and tastes, he demonstrated his fascination with the natural world.

Figure 42.1 Restored Monticello Garden, *c.*1998. (©Thomas Jefferson Foundation at Monticello, photograph by Skip Johns.)

This is expressed in a letter to his daughter Martha in 1790 when he declares: 'There is not a sprig of grass that shoots uninteresting to me'.[6]

Jefferson kept the comprehensive and detailed book for 58 years and this unique horticultural diary has enabled an accurate and authentic restoration of his gardens at Monticello. Visitors can once again experience the garden he developed as an expression of his creative genius.

The development of the garden

It would appear from Jefferson's notes that 1774 marked a flurry of activity in the garden, which suggests that the garden layout had been partially installed at this time. A surviving scale drawing, perhaps composed as early as the early 1780s, although never fully executed, shows a proposal for a 1,000 by 80 foot garden divided into nine, 100 foot by 50 foot rectangular beds. It is similar to a later plan of 1806 that anticipates the final garden layout, but it is clear that the design went through several phases.

The terracing commenced in 1804 when he began planning his retirement garden following the death of his daughter Maria in childbirth. He outlined plans to build the terrace and walls in a memorandum entitled, 'General ideas for the improvement of Monticello'. Originally he had intended to construct four temples of different architectural styles: a specimen of Gothic, a model of the Parthenon, a model of cubic architecture, and a specimen of Chinese. These were to be sited in alcoves along the length of the terrace but he changed his mind on the basis that a productive garden was not an appropriate setting for these types of buildings. Instead, he opted for 'Bowers and trellises', concluding that the ornamental buildings were better suited to the Pleasure Grounds. However, in the end he settled for a 'cubic', i.e. classical garden pavilion, located at the centre point of the terrace.

He constructed a hawthorn hedge around the north and south orchards and this is plotted on an instructive map showing where 'everything is to be planted'. The map also helpfully identifies the location of the garden in relation to other features on the site. Jefferson produced a further detailed scaled plan in 1806, similar to the 1780 one, but this too was subject to alteration from 1808–1814 because of practical difficulties encountered during construction. The mammoth task began apace during the winter of 1807 with the first 220-foot section of the perfectly flat terrace completed by January 1808. Jefferson was forced to change his plan because of the enormous amount of earth moving required, so he pragmatically altered the original design to adapt to the contours of the site and created instead four 250-foot level terraces running the length of the garden. This subdivided the garden into two-to-four foot high platforms, which were, for expediency, reduced to three in number, and these were generally complete by 1809. The vegetable garden terrace was laid out in a geometric grid pattern of beds, walkways and squares, situated parallel to the plantation house and Mulberry Row, a strip of slave cottages, with the classical pavilion placed at the mid-point of the terrace. In addition to this basic plan he incorporated 'numerous discrete compartments – sub mural beds, circular terraces and the north-west border' (Figure 42.2).[7]

Jefferson retired from the presidency and returned to Monticello in March 1809 and began to plant the newly constructed garden. He incorporated a 'Kalender' into his Garden Book where he neatly recorded over 100 vegetable plantings in columns which described the 'what', 'where', 'sowed', 'transplanted', 'come to table', 'gone', 'seed gathered' and 'observations' of the seasonal processes taking place in the garden that year. Writing to the British neo-classical architect Benjamin Latrobe (1764–1820), Jefferson remarked that despite some evidence of failures, 'what nature has done for us is sublime, beautiful and unique'.[8] During 1810 he decided on the final layout and, in that same year, he notes his intention to construct the small garden pavilion with 'a pyramidal roof surrounded by a Chinese lattice railing', which was eventually constructed in 1812. The American lawyer and

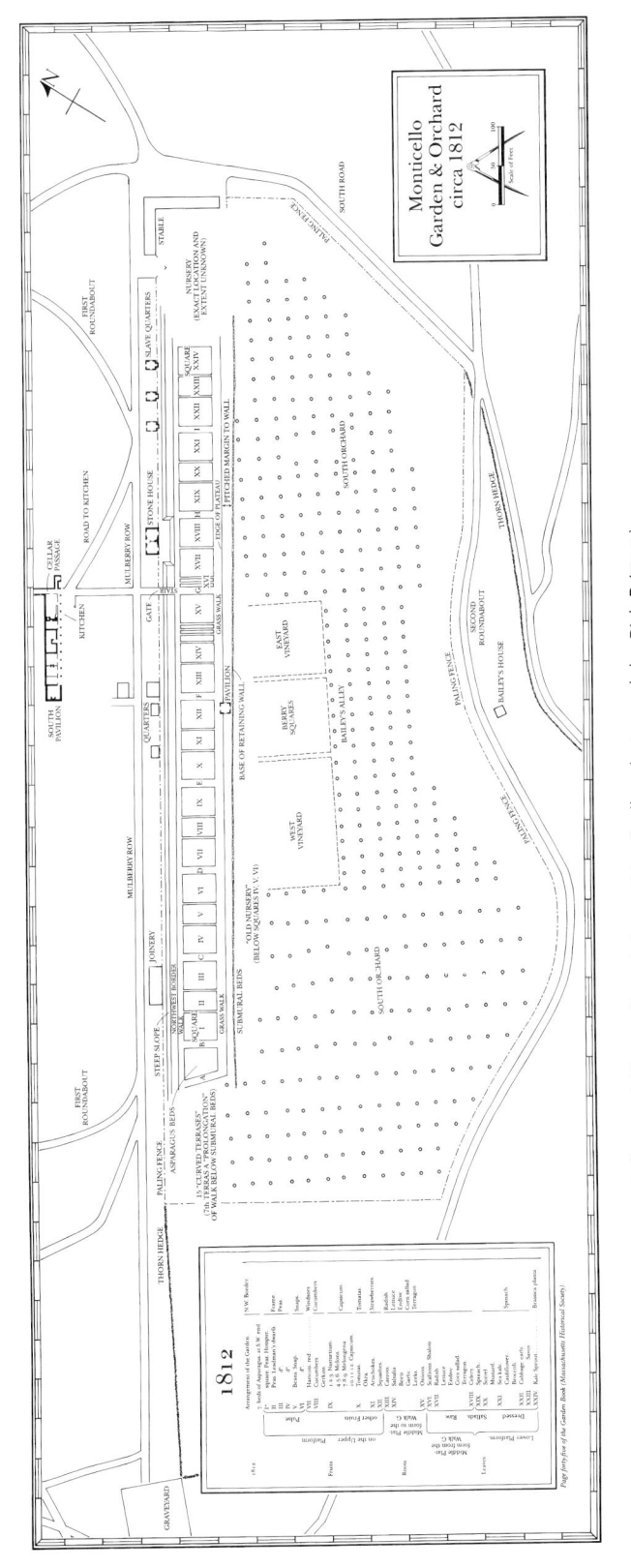

Figure 42.2 Plan of the garden c.1812. (©Thomas Jefferson Foundation at Monticello, photograph by Rick Britton.)

statesman Henry D. Gilpin (1801–60) visited Monticello in 1827 and described the site of the pavilion:

> We walked into the gardens, to see the places where the best views presented themselves, & which Mr. Jefferson had fixed on as favourite spots for walking, reading or reflection . . . on a point of the mountain . . . there is an eminence where Mr. Jefferson had erected a little Grecian temple & which was a favourite spot with him to read & sit in – we stood on the spot, but a violent storm some years ago blew down the temple & no vestiges are left.[9]

Archaeological excavations were carried out in 1958 and 1980 that revealed the foundations and confirmed the precise location of the temple.

The restoration project

Peter J. Hatch was employed at Monticello in 1977 as superintendent of grounds. At this time there was a revival of interest in historic American landscapes, which led to a reassessment of their authenticity. Williamsburg, renowned for its Colonial revival gardens, was one of the first to engage with this re-evaluation process and its foundation sponsored studies and research into colonial gardens in Virginia. As in Great Britain, garden history became a recognised academic discipline and this, in turn, fuelled new interest in garden and landscape preservation.

In 1976 the Monticello Board of Trust took a particular philosophical approach and adopted a resolution for the long-term restoration of the gardens to their c.1812 appearance when Jefferson retired to Monticello. Previously the Trust had concentrated on restoring the house, which received 500,000 visitors a year. Now attention turned to restoring Jefferson's landscape. Monticello's architectural historian, William L. Beiswanger and landscape architect, Rudy J. Favretti, developed a plan to recreate the 18-acre grove and the superintendent of grounds, Peter Hatch, would implement the replanting scheme. This needed to be carried out before work to restore the vegetable garden could begin.

An archaeological survey by William Kelso began in 1979 which defined the structure of the garden and determined the location of fence lines, paths, walkways, gates, beds, walls and so forth, in order to confirm whether Jefferson's designs had indeed been executed, as his notes and plans continually evolved and accounts sometimes conflicted. Some archaeological surveying had taken place in 1958 but this was inconclusive and many questions remained. The terrace that existed in 1978 had continued to be cultivated since Jefferson's death and was now a flower garden, but its form largely reflected the original 1806 design. However, other important elements such as the orchard and the fencing were no longer extant and building archaeology was also buried. The section of terrace under flower cultivation was terminated by an asphalt car park at the north-east end and a further two platforms had been laid out as car parking areas.

A detailed base map was compiled, supporting documentary evidence was assembled and a further archaeological exploration to determine locations, material and construction was undertaken before any restoration work took place. There was a network of paths but the archaeological investigations to ascertain their precise location proved inconclusive as many of the interior walkways were ploughed up after Jefferson's death. Archaeological exploration of the north-west border in 1980, however, revealed what appeared to be borders made of both brick and small logs. Inevitably, much of the archaeology of the central beds and paths had been destroyed due to repeated digging and ploughing, but the location of the garden gate fence posts was uncovered and this enabled the plotting and location of the garden squares and walkways using Jefferson's own survey plans. Gradually, various other features of the garden were revealed, including tree planting, structures, grid patterns, locations and original materials.

The excavations were complete by 1981. This ambitious restoration project was approved by the Monticello Board that year and Beiswanger proudly boasted that 'the evidence gleaned through archaeology studied in the light of an unparalleled wealth of documentation presents an opportunity to make the most accurate restoration of its kind in America'.[10]

The structural recreation of the garden was carried out under Beiswanger's leadership and Favretti was commissioned to oversee the reconstruction of the 1,000-foot garden wall and ha-ha based on the evidence uncovered. Some sections of the remaining garden wall were intact and provided essential clues to construction and materials, enabling restoration as faithful to the original as possible. In conjunction with this project Favretti also designed a bean arbour based on Jefferson's designs and a rustic barrier to prevent visitors inadvertently stepping off the elevated terrace. Every endeavour was made to be authentic without damaging the historic fabric, and this project was complete in 1983.

The precise location of the garden pavilion was determined by the archaeological survey and Charlottesville architect Floyd Johnson was commissioned to produce working drawings for its reconstruction. Meanwhile, Hatch researched and assembled a collection of the fruit and vegetable varieties that Jefferson had cultivated in anticipation of recreating the terrace garden. Kelso also extended the archaeological survey to include Mulberry Row and other locations. The pavilion was reconstructed between 1982 and 1984 using Jefferson's notes on its original construction but inevitably some conjectural decisions had to be made on the precise interpretation of floors, the triple-sash windows and the Chinese railing around the roof.

Hatch proceeded to lay out the garden squares and beds and turf walkways were created throughout the gardens to give a unified appearance. The newly laid garden was then planted with vegetables for the 1982 season. The turfs on the outer walkway, however, were replaced with earthen paths to reduce maintenance.

The fatal flaw in Jefferson's placement of the elevated terrace was his failure to develop an adequate watering method. It was variously watered from a well, springs, cisterns and possibly the Rivanna River located a mile and a half down the mountainside. The insufficient and sporadic water supply led him to construct four cisterns, 1808–1810, each designed to hold 3,830 gallons of water, supplying 600 gallons a day. A new and efficient irrigation system was installed as part of the project.

Because of the archaeological and practical complexities associated with the recreation of the north-west border, a narrower-width version was created which is annually sown with a diverse range of crops. Compromises were also made regarding the complete rebuilding of the 10-foot-high paling fence, so for practical and aesthetic reasons a reduced 100-foot section was re-erected in 1993 using craftsmen from Colonial Williamsburg.

The parking lots on the lower platforms were also removed and the gardens extended in 1984 to incorporate these newly restored areas. Further removal of parking areas and a roundabout above the garden had the immediate beneficial effect of enhancing the visitor experience and also allowed for the possibility of restoring Mulberry Row in the future.

The Garden Pavilion was dedicated and the restored garden formally opened at a ceremony on Jefferson's birthday, 13 April 1984.

Significant later restoration projects followed with the north-east vineyard (1984), sub mural beds (1985), berry squares (1986), south-west vineyard and paling sample (1993) and the old nursery (1994).

The literature and archaeological research undertaken, combined with Jefferson's own notes, did not furnish the complete story or provide all the answers at Monticello. Aspects of the restored landscape therefore may properly be termed an 'evocation' of Jefferson's innovative and inspirational garden. But, as discussed in previous chapters, gardens and gardening are ephemeral processes that continually change and evolve. However, the solid foundations for future landscape preservation work at Monticello have been firmly laid. Today, it thrives as a 'living exhibition' of Jefferson's scientific and aesthetic sensibility and his legacy continues with the founding in 1987 of The Thomas Jefferson Centre for Historic Plants, curated by Peggy Cornett. The centre is committed to documenting all significant historic plants at Monticello, and researches and advises on appropriate plant selections for the restored gardens and landscapes, as well as locating Jefferson-period plant varieties for Monticello gardens.

Endnotes

1. The first assembly of elected representatives of English colonists in North America.
2. Quoted in Hatch, P.J., *'A Rich Spot of Earth'*, *Thomas Jefferson's Revolutionary Garden at Monticello*, Yale University Press (2012), p. 20. I am greatly indebted to Hatch's masterly exposition of the development of the garden at Monticello and its restoration.
3. Ibid, p. 3.
4. Ibid, p. 4.
5. Ibid, p. 5.
6. Ibid, p. 13.
7. Ibid, p. 78.
8. Ibid, p. 36.
9. Ibid, p. 38.
10. Ibid, p. 104.

43 The Gardens of the Alhambra

Farhat A. Hussain
Specialist historian, archaeologist and educationalist, Birmingham, UK

The garden history of Europe is rich in periods, places and the presence of a great variety of traditions, cultures and civilisations. This is clearly evident in Spain where one thousand years ago a resplendent and industrious Moorish civilisation was present and made its mark upon the landscape of Iberia. Many books that deal with garden history and landscape or Moorish Spain neglect Moorish gardens, including the gardens of the Alhambra. Often where texts include the gardens, coverage of them is brief and includes little or no insight of Moorish approaches or the use and meaning of gardens in the Nasrid period, which provide a vital perspective on contemporary conservation issues pertaining to the gardens and relevant aspects of the wider historic landscape of the Alhambra.

Due to the widespread destruction of written sources following the capture of Granada in 1492 by Castile and Aragon and alterations to the structure, particularly during the sixteenth century, studying the history of the Alhambra is challenging. However, a range of available sources has been utilised including remaining archaeological evidence, historical material, photographs and an in-situ survey.

The Alhambra (Arabic: *Al-Hamra* – the red) was the residence and seat of rule of the last Moorish kingdom of Spain – the Sultanate of Granada, also referred to as *Dawla Nasseriya* or Nasrid State. From 1236 to 1492 the Alhambra served as the royal city of the Nasrid State. It is widely believed that Alhambra referred to the red colour of the Sabika hill where the Alhambra stands. Red was also the state colour of the Nasrids. The multifarious role of the Alhambra, which included receiving guests, minting coins, military barracks and a court of law, is evident in the character and spatial organisation as manifest in the high protective walls, military bastions, opulent palace area and serene gardens (Figure 43.1).

Following the end of Nasrid rule the Alhambra was maintained briefly by Moorish artisans, underwent varying degrees of structural changes, particularly under Charles V (King of Spain, 1516–56) and served as the local administrative centre for government in the sixteenth and seventeenth centuries. Much of the Alhambra, including the gardens, had fallen into disrepair during the eighteenth century and various conservation and modernisation efforts were undertaken in the late nineteenth and twentieth centuries.

An awareness of Moorish-Islamic approaches to sacred ecology, landscape and gardens aids the study of the gardens of the Alhambra. The Moorish-Islamic concept of the garden may be understood via a number of strands. In the Islamic faith plants, trees and flowers are considered to be manifestations of the magnificence of God. Human beings are

Gardens & Landscapes in Historic Building Conservation, First Edition. Edited by Marion Harney.
© 2014 John Wiley & Sons, Ltd. Published 2014 by John Wiley & Sons, Ltd.

Figure 43.1 The Alhambra palace (author's own).

considered as custodians of the earth, and as stewards of nature, including landscape. Gardens are also considered to evoke paradise – the afterlife that, according to Islamic tradition, comprises a continuous garden of exceptional beauty. Mosaics in some early Muslim art, as at the seventh-century Umayyad Mosque of Damascus, depicts trees and plants that are said to evoke paradise. The gardens of the Alhambra were designed and organised so that they could be viewed and interacted with in a manner reflective of the sacred ecology approach of Moorish-Islamic civilisation.

Influence upon the gardens of the Alhambra is to be found in preceding periods of Moorish Spain and other parts of the Islamic world. Ruggles (1992, p. 163) is justified in stating that the Alhambra gardens represent the culmination of a long line of gardens and garden estates that began in Cordoba in the middle of the eighth century, created by the first Umayyad ruler of al-Andalus. The pavilions and gardens of Madinat az-Zahra are smaller than the gardens of Sāmarrā (Abbasid, Iraq) and conform to two basic types from the latter: the arcaded pavilion facing a body of water and the courtyard garden (Tabbaa, 1992, p. 310). Both of these types of gardens described by Tabbaa are present at the Alhambra. The end of Moorish rule in Valencia, Cordoba, Seville and other major Moorish centres during the early thirteenth century resulted in the migration of Moors to Granada and a consequent boost for Moorish culture including architecture and gardens from the established urban centres of preceding periods of Muslim Spain.

The gardens of the Alhambra provide space and setting for recreation, contemplation upon life and the afterlife in paradise (a term introduced into the English language from the Arabic and Persian term *firdaus* which denotes garden) and reflection of order and achievement. The gardens of the Alhambra also projected the authority, prestige, custodianship and high culture of the Nasrid Sultan. Moreover, gardens provided sustenance for birds and insects in line with the sacred ecology approach of the Islamic faith and served a further practical function as a place where produce was grown.

The aim of the design of the garden for Muslim rulers in Spain including the Nasrids of Granada was to be able to enjoy the garden by surveying it in one view. Ibn Luyun, the fourteenth-century writer from Granada, emphasised that a garden should not be so large as to become problematic for the eyes but rather must be constructed in proportion so as to produce maximum delight in one view (Marcais, 1957, pp. 238–9). Appearance and modest size were therefore important features in the gardens of the Nasrid period.

Figure 43.2 The Generalife gardens (author's own).

During this period the gardens of the Alhambra were divided into four quadrants not unlike the present-day college gardens of Oxford and Cambridge and monastic herb gardens, yet there is no doubt in most people's mind that the *chahar-bagh* is quintessentially Islamic (Clark, 2004, pp. 28–9). The division of Islamic gardens into four quadrants reflects an Islamic approach to the garden and the universe, evoking aspects of cosmology and references to phenomenon such as the four seasons, four directions and four elements. The traditional division is achieved by pathways and, in some cases, the presence of water in seeking to evoke tranquillity and contemplation upon paradise. This is evident in the Court of the Lions and in the Summer Palace, though no longer present across the wider mass of the Generalife (Figure 43.2).

The gardens of the Alhambra represented the sophistication, prestige and wealth of the Nasrid State and served as a place of private contemplation and relaxation for the Nasrid Sultan and his family and visitors, and were easily accessible via the divisional pathways. On the whole the major garden spaces of the Alhambra from the Nasrid era are extant, though they have been subject to changes since 1492. The particular organisation and experience of the Alhambra gardens aided their conservation as they stood at different (lower) levels to the raised pathways of the Nasrid period and as a result were left undisturbed.

The Alhambra possessed a variety of gardens during the Moorish era ranging from the relatively large Generalife to the multi-level gardens of the major palaces and the *rauda* cemetery garden. Each garden played a particular role and held meaning and significance for the Nasrid Sultan, his family and those who experienced and maintained the gardens. The gardens arguably reflected the outlook and predicament of the Nasrid State. The major gardens in the Alhambra were private spaces only accessible to the Sultan and his family, although some spaces, such as the Court of the Myrtles, could be experienced by visitors, and those working in and maintaining the gardens.

The major garden spaces are separated from the latter by a ravine and open area containing orchards; the Generalife (Jannat al-Arif) or artist's/architect's garden is situated adjacent to the Alhambra. Established in c.1319, the Generalife is one of the oldest surviving Moorish gardens (Burton et al., 2003, p. 27). It is believed that the Generalife gardens were built upon earlier Moorish gardens from the eleventh and twelfth centuries. Following the end of Nasrid rule the Generalife Gardens were given over to private ownership and subsequently bequeathed to state ownership in the early twentieth century, by which time much dilapidation and alteration to the Moorish character had taken place. The Generalife comprises a Summer Palace or garden pavilion, terraces and a rich diversity of spaces, including terraces filled with trees, shrubs, flowers and plants in addition to oblong pools, fountains and pathways seeking to evoke a Moorish ambience. However, the present Generalife gardens are a modern twentieth-century construction and this interpretation of a former Moorish garden space has incorporated various elements of early modern Italian gardens.

Various scholars including Danby (1995, p. 77) consider that the pavilion structure in the Generalife served as a Summer Palace for the Nasrids. Comprising the Court of the Water Channel (*Patio de la Acequia*) or Water Garden Courtyard and the Courtyard of the Cypress, also referred to as the Sultana's Garden, the Summer Palace features various chambers and an oblong pool and is similar in character to other Moorish palace gardens that precede the Alhambra. The gardens of the Summer Palace comprise the largely Moorish features of flowerbeds, water features and in the case of the Court of the Water Channel, a vast palace complex that surrounds the oblong pool. Whilst the continued maintenance of the oblong pool aids in dividing the garden into four quadrants it is no longer at a higher elevation than the base level of the Moorish period gardens. Views from the pavilions of the Summer Palace are afforded into the gardens in the courtyard as during the Moorish period (Ruggles, 2008, p. 5) and the rooftop terrace of the Summer Palace continues to provide exceptional views of the gardens below, albeit somewhat different in character from those of the Nasrid period.

During the Moorish period the Generalife garden covered a larger area than remains extant in the present day. Its former size is apparent in seventeenth-century lithographs which depict the Generalife within a walled enclosure. The high walls are no longer present; security has been subordinated to tourism. The walkways, laid out in the twentieth century arguably as a facility for tourists, are paved in traditional Granadian style with a mosaic of white pebbles from the River Darro and black ones from the River Genil (Agustín, 2002). The location of many of the modern walkways may not follow that of the Nasrid period.

A fire in 1958 destroyed physical remains of the Generalife including organic material that remained deposited in the soil. However, the subsequent restoration work uncovered original garden plans that constitute a major asset for the conservation of the Generalife. The presence of jet fountains is a modern innovation which replaces the original fountains of the Summer Palace, and the distribution of water across the Generalife via fountains, pools and channels is not identical to the Nasrid period. The American writer and later Ambassador to Spain, Washington Irving (1783–1859), observed cypress trees during his stay at the Alhambra in the early nineteenth century and was of the opinion that these trees dated from the Muslim period (Irving, 1896, p. 208).

Whilst the Nasrids oversaw conservation and maintenance of the gardens of the Alhambra, the present conservation plan is not centred upon the gardens of the Nasrid era. Due in part to the return of the Generalife to State supervision in the early twentieth century, the conservation plan only came into effect at this time. Francisco Prieto-Morino was responsible for arranging the Generalife Gardens from 1931 to 1951 and is considered to have brought the Italian influence into the Generalife. This early example of conservation of a historic garden in Spain and Europe was inhibited by a lack of awareness or reference to authentic Moorish gardens. Moreover, no interventions were made in gardens elsewhere in the Alhambra. The Nasrid period walkway to the Generalife from the Alhambra is no longer extant, nor the focus of reconstruction.

With the exception of the wider space of the Generalife, the gardens of the Alhambra were largely compact during the Nasrid period and remain so in the present day, as can be seen in the gardens within the Court of the Myrtles (Figure 43.3) and the Court of the Lions. However, certain features of the compact gardens are now absent or have not been restored. The Court of the Myrtles continues to feature an oblong pool from the Moorish period though it is bereft of the scale and scope of planting of the Nasrid period.

The gardens of the Court of the Lions are no longer extant, with only a minor presence of plants and shrubbery in the corners of the Court, though the division into four quadrants remains evident (Figure 43.4).

Figure 43.3 The Court of the Myrtles (author's own).

Figure 43.4 The Court of the Lions (author's own).

The gardens of the Court of the Myrtles and Court of the Lions were some 80 cm lower at their base than at present, though the pathways remain at a similar height; hence the pathways were suspended above the level of the gardens. The nineteenth-century drawings by Washington Irving and the English architect Owen Jones (1809–74) – the latter bringing aspects of Alhambra design to the Crystal Palace exhibition in London in 1854 for which he was principal interior designer – depict a greater presence in the quantity and height of plants and foliage in both the Court of the Myrtles and Court of the Lions than are present in these spaces today.

The Generalife is considered to have contained an area dedicated to growing fruit and vegetables for the Alhambra during the Nasrid period. The large area between the Alhambra complex and the Generalife, known today as the *Heurtas de la Alhambra* (orchards of the Alhambra), was also used as a kitchen garden. During this period part of the present-day *Heurtas* area formed part of the Generalife. The absence of a kitchen garden, including Moorish produce, provides a further example of changes to the Alhambra – despite the claim in the official guide of the continuation of Moorish agriculture in the Generalife to the present day 'adding anthropological value to its historical and artistic value' (Lopez, 2011, p. 225).

The *rauda*, which denotes a form of garden, was a place of burial, located near the main palace area, where several Nasrid Sultans were buried. In the post-Nasrid period the royal graves were removed to a site several kilometres away, a change that was determined by prevailing politics. Meanwhile the original garden, which no doubt provided an atmosphere of serenity, is no longer extant although some trees remain in the *rauda*. Some gravestones from the *rauda* survive and are located in the Alhambra museum. Very little conservation work of the Nasrid era *rauda* garden is evident today.

Changes to the gardens of the Alhambra include alteration to spatial organisation, composition and place-names. The term *rauda* remains in use to denote the former cemetery garden whilst other garden names have been subject to change or modification since the Moorish period. Greater public education efforts will aid visitor and public awareness of the origin, meaning and significance of names of gardens of the Alhambra in the Nasrid period. In the present day Nasrid flags are no longer extant while Nasrid crests have been painted over so that the original red and cream/white is no longer present and is a clear indication of changes in political ownership; these factors represent a conservation challenge for this multi-period site.

Water plays a vital role in purity of body, soul and life in the Islamic faith. Clark refers to the presence of water in alluding to the Islamic character of the gardens and states that the apparently endlessly flowing water is an evocative representation of the Islamic gardens of paradise and facilitates a sense of peace (Clark, 2004, p. 28). However, the use of water has not been continuous. During the Nasrid period water was used for ablution before prayer in addition to drinking and cooking – all functions no longer present. However water is present in at least some of the same spaces in the palace areas and gardens albeit modified. The oblong pool in front of the Palace of the Partal has now been reconstructed following centuries of decay. Engineering changes are evident in the Court of the Lions, with modern engineering replacing the original water system.

Considerable changes impacted on the organisation, character and purpose of the gardens of the Alhambra following the end of Moorish rule in January 1492; however, the Alhambra gardens fared much better than other Moorish gardens captured by Castile in preceding centuries. Rojo *et al.* (2007, p. 289) state that transformation was slower (in Granada), which saved some gardens, most notably of the Alhambra palaces and the Generalife. The abandonment of the Alhambra as a local administrative centre resulted in the decline of the gardens in the eighteenth century which, together with modernisation of gardens in the nineteenth and twentieth centuries, led to changes to the Moorish character of the gardens.

The Alhambra faces further challenges in the twenty-first century. The constant sunshine and warm climate of southern Spain exposes the gardens to substantial heat that impacts

Figure 43.5 Soil and horticulture in the Generalife (author's own).

upon soil, foliage and structures. The foliage in the enclosed spaces of the Court of the Myrtles, Court of the Lions and the Court of the Summer Palace afford some physical protection from the elements, including rain. However, most of the Generalife gardens are exposed to the elements and require constant monitoring and maintenance, including watering, and a watering regime is in place as part of the conservation plan for the gardens because of the increasingly dry climate of the province of Andalusia. However, in summer months the dryness of the soils in the Generalife and in the *Las Heurtas* area between the Generalife and Alhambra is evident and modern weather monitoring systems should play a greater role in the conservation of the gardens. If greater attention were paid to the traditional Moorish approach to water provision and hydrology this could address some practical issues pertaining to water supply and conserve the Moorish heritage.

The plantings at the Alhambra are arranged in order to provide a colourful repertoire of flowers and plants for the enjoyment of visitors but often bear no relation to the history of the horticulture and botany of the gardens of the Nasrid or even post-Nasrid (pre-twentieth century) periods (Figure 43.5). Cypress, date palms, mulberry trees, myrtles *(rayhan)* and a few other plant and flower species remain but many other Moorish plants and flowers are no longer evident.

There is an opportunity to make the composition and arrangement of planting more typical of the Moorish period within respective heritage spaces of the Alhambra.

The presence of large numbers of visitors in the gardens of the Alhambra all year round constitutes a major challenge to conservation of these spaces and this is only partially mitigated by allowing a maximum daily quota of visitors. While staff monitor visitors inside the Summer Palace this is not consistent across the wider area of the Generalife. Some areas of the Generalife gardens are enclosed by borders which offer some protection from trespass but many parts are not protected from the unwitting or careless visitor. The high level of visitors means that constant maintenance of pathways and fountains is required and undertaken. There is also a need to channel visitors to prescribed routes and in the Court of the Lions this is achieved by the use of a rope-barrier which prevents visitors from walking onto the court and impacting on the plants located in its corners and which also protects the lions and fountain at the centre of the court. The fountain no longer operates and this contributes to its conservation but it requires constant monitoring and maintenance because of the impact of weather and erosion. The *rauda* garden is lacking in flora as are other former Moorish spaces across the Alhambra. Significantly visitors are largely unaware of the conservation challenges that the site faces and they are not provided with information regarding their responsibility in helping to conserve the Alhambra. This issue could be addressed through noticeboards, leaflets and presentations by guides. Major bodies such as *Legado Andalusia*, which plays an important role in providing information about the heritage of Andalusia province through various mediums, could also play a greater role in disseminating information regarding the conservation challenges facing the Alhambra.

The Heritage Law of Spain (1985) provides legal protection for historic sites; however, this law cannot reverse the damage already done to the Alhambra during preceding decades and centuries. Moreover, and ironically, the law of 1985 prevents any major structural work to the Alhambra, including the gardens, if the work carried out would change the existing character; even if the proposed work would aim to restore the original Nasrid character. It is, however, possible for the Spanish State to give consent for restoration work provided that the heritage site is conserved in an authentic manner.

While the Alhambra is a world asset and one of the best conserved Muslim palaces of the medieval era, the changes made to the gardens fall short of providing an authentic Nasrid period character and composition. A greater degree of authenticity of the heritage and character of the gardens could be achieved if the same vigour were applied to conserving these as has been applied to some of the palace structures. Very little is known about the small gardens of the other houses within the Alhambra complex that belonged to the Nasrids and other leading families such as the Abencerrages (Banu'l Serraj/the saddle makers) and officials who resided there.

While much conservation work was undertaken in the nineteenth and twentieth centuries following long periods of neglect, much of it is conjectural and is the result of redressing the impact of the regional tourism industry. The gardens have undergone a modern-day facelift including an open-air theatre for events, and their modernisation represents a challenge for the authentic conservation of these spaces. There is a lack of expertise in respect of Moorish gardens and this, combined with the alterations already made, means that much more work is needed in terms of scholarship and practice. Moreover, it is apparent that the multiple historic layers present significant challenges for those responsible for conserving the different periods of the garden: Moorish; post-Nasrid; Italianate in the Generalife and twentieth-century interventions by Prieto-Moreno.

Archaeological surveys and historical images from the sixteenth and seventeenth centuries are available to consult. In addition, references to Moorish gardens at sites across Spain, Morocco and elsewhere will help in formulating a more authentic Moorish garden so that the aims of the Council of the Alhambra and Generalife (the body chiefly responsible for the conservation of the Alhambra) are properly implemented with regard to research, maintenance and authenticity. Whilst the conservation of the gardens must be undertaken as part of the conservation of the wider landscape, the former are fragile spaces that require a specific approach and particular attention.

A greater understanding of Moorish civilisation and the conservation of other Moorish sites in North Africa and elsewhere would help to develop the conservation work required at the Alhambra. Greater integration and streamlining of administration and the various bodies and stakeholders concerned would also contribute to a more focused conservation effort, as would addressing the dilemma of balancing the needs of promoting tourism and the need for authenticity. Legislation and treaties such as the European Landscape Convention (2000) should also include greater insight into the challenges, needs and concepts of the remaining Moorish landscapes in Spain and elsewhere in Europe.

The conservation of the gardens of the Alhambra involves a great many challenges, yet there are also opportunities. A greater collaboration amongst Spain's conservation specialists who deal with Moorish sites, those in Portugal and Sicily where other Moorish sites are conserved and the conservationists of the European Union and the Muslim world could, taken together, provide an opportunity to contribute to the conservation of the Alhambra and enhance international cooperation in similar endeavours.

References/Further reading

Agustín, N.J. (ed.), *Muslim and Christian Granada*, Edilux, 2002.
Barrucand, M., Bednorz, A., *Moorish Architecture*, Taschen, Cologne, 1992.
Brett, M., Forman, W., *The Moors*, Orbis Publishing, London, 1984.
Clark, E., *The Islamic Garden*, The Crowood Press, Ramsbury, 2004.
Conan, M. (ed.), *Middle East Garden Traditions: Unity and Diversity*, Dumbarton Oaks, Washington D.C. 2007.
Danby. M., *Moorish Style*, Phaidon Press, London, 1995.
Dickie, J., 'The Islamic Garden in Spain', in *The Islamic Garden*, Dumbarton Oaks, Washington D.C. 1976, pp. 87–106.
Hunt, J.D. (ed.), *Garden History: Issues, Approaches, Methods*, Dumbarton Oaks Research Library and Collection, Washington D.C. 1992.
Irving, W., *The Alhambra*, Goodword Books, New Delhi, 1896, republished 2003.
Jones, O., *Plans, Elevations, Sections and Details of the Alhambra, Details and Ornaments from the Alhambra*, London, 1845.
Lopez, J.B., *Official Guide: The Alhambra and the Generalife*. Patronate de le Alhambra y Generalife, Tf Editores, Granada, 2011.
Prieto-Morino, F., *El Generalife y Sus*, Everest, 1976.
Rojo, J.T., Porcel, M.C., 'From the Andalusi Garden to the Andalusian Garden: Remnants and Re-creation', in Conan, M. (ed.) *Middle East Garden Traditions: Unity and Diversity*, Dumbarton Oaks, Washington D.C. 2007.
Ruggles, D.F., 'The Gardens of the Alhambra and the concept of the Garden in Islamic Spain', in Dodds, J.D. (ed.), *Al-Andalus: The Art of Islamic Spain*, The Metropolitan Museum of Art, New York, 1992.
Ruggles, D.F., *Islamic Gardens and Landscape*, University of Pennsylvania Press, Philadelphia, 2008.
Sanchez, M. (ed.), *The Alhambra and the Generalife*, Grefol, S.L. Madrid, 2001.
Tabbaa, Y., 'The Medieval Islamic Garden: Typology and Hydraulics', in Hunt, J.D. (ed.) *Garden History: Issues, Approaches, Methods*, Dumbarton Oaks Research Library and Collection, Washington D.C. 1992.
www.eui.eu/Projects/InternationalArtHeritageLaw/Documents/NationalLegislation/Spain/law16of1985.pdf accessed 12 November 2012.
www.legadoandalusi.es accessed 8 November 2012.

44 Central Park, New York City

Michael Forsyth
Director, Postgraduate Conservation of Historic Buildings programme, University of Bath, UK

The population of New York City grew from less than 100,000 in 1810 to more than half a million by 1850 and inhabitants sought refuge from the noise and bustle of the streets in the few open spaces that existed, mainly cemeteries. The Commissioners' Plan for Manhattan of 1811 which defined the city's future grid layout did not include proposals for a Central Park and the enormous 700-acre (280 ha) tract of green space spanning half a mile from Fifth Avenue to Eighth Avenue and two and a half miles from 59th Street to 110th Street, is not a part of this plan. The need for a public park was first advocated in 1844 by William Cullen Bryant (1794–1878), editor of the *Evening Post*, and Andrew Jackson Downing (1815–52), publisher of *The Horticulturist* magazine and widely regarded as the first American landscape architect, who suggested creating a tract of open land before it was swallowed up by the fast-expanding city. The vision was to create something similar to London's Hyde Park or the Bois de Boulogne in Paris, with carriage drives. But it was not until 1853 that the New York legislature selected the site and appointed a Central Park Commission which devised a design competition, held in 1857. Out of 33 entries the winning design, which became known as the *Greensward Plan*, was by Frederick Law Olmsted (1822–1903) and Calvert Vaux (1824–95), whom Downing had originally introduced to each other.

Olmsted had an unlikely career in journalism and in the 1850s was commissioned by *The New York Daily Times* (now *The New York Times*) to report on a study tour of slavery in the southern states. Earlier, an interest in landscape design took him to England where he was especially impressed by Joseph Paxton's Birkenhead Park. Vaux (the pronunciation rhymes with 'hawks') was a British architect and pupil of the Gothic revival architect Lewis Nockalls Cottingham (1787–1847). He came to Downing's attention during an exhibition of Vaux's watercolours on a visit to London seeking to recruit an assistant architect. Downing persuaded Vaux to emigrate and he became his partner before Downing's untimely death in a boiler explosion and fire on a steamer sailing on the Hudson River two years later.

Olmsted and Vaux's winning plan met the competition brief which called for pastoral, picturesque and formal landscapes to reflect the varying character of the topography. Their key concept was to separate 'crosstown' traffic from park circulation by means of sunken transverse roads heavily planted for concealment at 65th, 79th, 86th and 97th Streets. The concept became influential – one might say right down to the 1960s practice of separating

Gardens & Landscapes in Historic Building Conservation, First Edition. Edited by Marion Harney.
© 2014 John Wiley & Sons, Ltd. Published 2014 by John Wiley & Sons, Ltd.

traffic and pedestrians in 'mega-structures' of the time. To achieve this Vaux designed 56 bridges, all different, ranging from muscular granite structures to delicate spans in cast iron. On these, and many architectural landmarks in the park, Vaux was assisted by the British-born architect Jacob Wrey Mould (1825–86), who went on to a prominent career and was a founder of the American Institute of Architects.[1]

The transverse routes define the principal areas of the park, from south to north Heckscher Playground, Sheep Meadow, The Lake and The Ramble, Jacqueline Kennedy Onassis Reservoir and the North and East Meadow and Harlem Meer. Today the park has numerous restaurants, playgrounds, the Metropolitan Museum, the Central Park Zoo, and Wollman Memorial Rink.

To clear the area before work could begin about 1,600 residents were evicted, mainly poor of African American, English and Irish origin. The task of construction was enormous as the land was either rocky or swampy: rocks were blown up with gunpowder, six lakes were manually excavated and fed from the City's water supply, and 500,000 cubic feet of topsoil was imported from New Jersey by horse and cart to sustain four million trees, shrubs and plants, representing around 1,500 species. Olmsted fought many battles over the design but Andrew Haswell Green (1820–1903), who served as comptroller and treasurer of the board of commissioners and supervised construction works from 1857 to 1871, was a staunch supporter of Olmsted and ensured that much of today's Central Park is true to its original design.

The park was officially completed in 1873 but decline soon set in with a long period of neglect and lack of maintenance. The Central Park Commission was dissolved in 1870, marking the departure of Andrew Haswell Green, and Vaux died in 1895. After about 1900 walks and picnics in an Arcadian setting were overtaken by sporting and other events and automobiles, and up to the 1920s dead trees and shrubs were not replaced, grassed areas became dry and bald and there was litter and vandalism.

But in 1934 Central Park acquired powerful support when Fiorello LaGuardia (1882–1947) was elected mayor of New York. He appointed as parks commissioner Robert Moses (1888–1981), who had built Long Island's first parkways, early landscaped automobile roads, to oversee its revival. Over 25 years lawns were reseeded, drinking fountains and walkways repaired and a reservoir was infilled to create the Great Lawn, though Olmsted and Vaux's original Arcadian vision now became secondary to the provision of recreational and sports facilities. In the early 1960s cultural events on Sheep Meadow were introduced, 'Shakespeare in the Park' in 1962, the Metropolitan Opera in 1961 and the New York Philharmonic in 1965. In 1964, Central Park was declared a National Historic Landmark.

Moses left his position in 1960 and despite – and partly because of – peace rallies, protest marches and the like, the park once again in the 1970s fell into neglect and lack of maintenance and vandalism resulted in severe deterioration. Alarm at the decline was such that several volunteer and fundraising groups of philanthropists were formed, principally the Central Park Task Force and the Central Park Community Fund. These bodies approached Mayor Edward Koch (1984–2013) and Parks Commissioner Gordon Davis, which resulted in the foundation of the Central Park Conservancy in 1980, a public–private partnership charged with the task of managing and enhancing Central Park, and this was reaffirmed in 1998 and again in 2006 with a management agreement between the Conservancy and the City of New York. So began the restoration of Olmsted and Vaux's vision for Central Park together with its transformation for twenty-first century recreational needs (Figure 44.1). These include educational, recreation and volunteer programmes that serve all sections of the community. One of the first tasks of the Central Park Conservancy was to commission ten studies of the park, including its topography, hydrology, planting, architecture, circulation, drainage, and visitor usage and security. The result was a conservation master plan published in 1985, *Rebuilding Central Park: A Management and Restoration Plan*. Three principal programmes were established: the restoration of landscape and architecture, horticultural maintenance of the meadows, woodlands and gardens, and management of visitors and their security.

Figure 44.1 Central Park, New York, 1857–, designed by Olmsted and Vaux: a rural idyll in the city (author's own).

Fundraising began in earnest in 1986, with the Campaign for the Central Park Conservancy, and the following years saw the restoration of Bethesda Terrace, Grand Army Plaza, Shakespeare Garden, Cedar Hill, and the southern part of the park. During the 1980s and 1990s, the many restoration projects were jointly funded in partnership between the Conservancy, raising money from many generous individuals, corporations and foundations, and the City of New York. An early restoration, for example, was of Belvedere Castle overlooking the Great Lawn. The Castle was designed by the architects Vaux and Mould from 1865 and is a fanciful and rugged Romanesque-Gothic structure built on the prominent site of Vista Rock with views across Central Park and New York City. The Parks Department paid for the restoration of the building while the Conservancy raised money for the surrounding landscape.

In 1988–92 the Harlem Meer was restored in the north-east corner of the Park (named by Olmsted and Vaux 'meer', Dutch for 'lake' as a reference to the Harlem suburb). The land containing the Meer and its surrounding woodland was a later addition to the original park and was excavated from 1861 to Olmsted and Vaux's specifications under the direction of Andrew Haswell Green (1820–1903) from swampy, semi-tidal land that had drained into the East River. During the restoration a 1940s concrete edging was removed to reveal the 22-acre lake's naturalistic shoreline and 34,000 cubic yards (26,000 m^2) of silt was dredged. On a rocky bluff beside the lake, a small fort, Blockhouse No. 1, completed in 1814 and which Olmsted and Vaux had retained as a picturesque ruin in the landscape, was restored as the oldest historic feature in the park and a visitor facility was built on the north side of the lake, the Charles A. Dana Discovery Center, in the Victorian style of Calvert Vaux. The Conservancy has now provided five additional visitor centres in the park: Belvedere Castle, Dairy Visitor Center & Gift Shop, Chess & Checkers House, Tavern on the Green Visitor Center & Gift Shop, and at the North Meadow Recreation Center. Today fishing, skating and summer swimming take place in the area and the Harlem Meer itself is a carefully managed wildlife habitat with fish, turtles, and, on an island in the Meer, home to waterfowl. The surrounding woodland contains oak, bald cypress, beech, gingko and other tree species.

Among the many other restoration projects completed during this period were the Conservatory Garden, the Shakespeare Garden, Strawberry Fields and woodland in the Ravine. Meanwhile, the Women's Committee of the Central Park Conservancy initiated the fundraising schemes Adopt-A-Bench, Tree Trust and Playground Partners. In 1993 the Conservancy launched the three-year 'Wonder of New York Campaign', which raised nearly $77.2 million from donations by individuals, foundations and corporations, enabling the restoration of the west side landscapes, the Great Lawn and the North Meadow. In 2005, a third fundraising initiative, the 'Campaign for Central Park', enabled work to the landscapes between the Metropolitan Museum of Art and the Harlem Meer. The Conservancy public–private partnership carried out many more restoration projects in the 1990s and the first years of the twenty-first century, including landscaping around the Reservoir, the creation of an irrigation system at Sheep Meadow and the restoration of recreation areas at the Heckscher Playground, Ballfields and the West 110th Street Playground. Further –unexpected – restoration work was carried out following a colossal and unprecedented thunderstorm during the night of 18 August 2009 when some 1,500 trees were destroyed or damaged in the northern part of the park.

In landscape restoration work, as with buildings, subsequent maintenance and management is critical, and in 1995 the Conservancy divided the park into 49 zones and appointed a uniformed gardener responsible for each. Today, the Conservancy employs 90% of Central Park's field staff, managing 250 acres of lawns, 24,000 trees, 150 acres of lakes and waterways and 80 acres of woodland. The organisation carries out a vast annual programme of planting, and in addition maintains 9,000 benches, 26 playing fields for ball games, 21 playgrounds, 55 sculptures and monuments, and the 36 bridges designed by Vaux. In addition, it carries out routine day-to-day maintenance including graffiti removal and rubbish collection. The other 10% of operations are provided by the New York City Department of Parks & Recreation, which controls policy and events, and funds lighting, maintenance of the Park drives and security. In addition to securing the future of Central Park and removing the threat of renewed cycles of decline, the Conservancy has also acted as consultant to other parks in the USA and around the world.

Endnote

1. MacKay, R.B., Baker, A.K., Traynor, C.A. (1997) *Long Island Country Houses and Their Architects, 1860–1940*, Norton, p. 188.

Index

Note: Page numbers for figures are in *italics*.

Abbey Park (Leicester) 94, *94*
Abercrombie, Patrick (1879–1957) 265
Aberglasney Gardens (Carmarthenshire) 248
access and equality 301–307
   access audit/chain *303*, 303–304
   cobbles 304–305, *305*
   conservation management plan (CMP)
      and 302–303
   design principles 304
   disability, definition of 301
   Easy Access to Historic Landscapes (EA, 2005)
      302–303, 306
   health benefits 301–302
   National Trust 304
      'Conservation for Access' toolkit 19
   Sensory Trust 302
   staff and 306
   travel and transport 305–306
   visitor information 306
accuracy, historical *see* authenticity
aerial surveys 150, 163–171
   archaeology and 168
   collections 166–167
      English Heritage 166
   conservation, role in 169–170
      Elizabethan Garden (Kenilworth Castle) 340
      New Hall (Essex) *169*, 169–170
      Risby Hall (East Yorkshire) *165*, 165
      Wrest Park (Bedfordshire) *164*, 164–165
   cropmarks 164
   features 165
   function of 163–164, 170
   interpretation skills 166
   mapping archaeological features 168, 170
      National Mapping Programme (NMP) 168
   oblique 166
   soilmarks 165
   technology 167
      Airborne LiDAR (Light Detection and Ranging)
      167, 186
   vertical 166
   World War II, impact of 167
aesthetic values 175

Airborne LiDAR (Light Detection and Ranging) 167
Aislabie, William (1700–1781) 377
Alexandra Road (Camden, London), significance
   137, 137–139
   conservation philosophy 138–139
Alhambra Gardens (Spain) 421–429, *422*
   conservation 428
      archive records 428
      surveys 428
   design
      Court of the Lions 424, *425*, *426*
      Court of the Myrtles 424, *425*, *426*
      Generalife *423*, 423–424, *426*
      influences 422
      religion 421–422
      structures 424
   history 421
   plantings 427, *427*
   rauda (burial area) 426
   visitor restrictions 427
   water features 426
All Souls' Cemetery (Kensal Green, London) 104
Alpine Region 335
Amstelveen Heem Parks (Netherlands) 225–226
Ancient Monuments Act (1882) xvii
ancient trees *154*, *155*, *156*
   Ancient Tree Forum (ATF) 153
apprentice system 230–232, *231*
   Richard Review of Apprentices in England
      (Richard, 2012) 232–233
arboriculture
   ancient trees *see* ancient trees
   canopy expansion 218
   climate change 213–215, *214*
   compartmentalisation of decay in trees (CODIT)
      154
   conservation arboriculture 153–162
      Arthur Clough Oak (Oxford) 157, *158*
      Hestercombe (Somerset) 347
      Lowther Castle and Gardens (Cumbria)
      411–412
      Yorkshire Sculpture Park (YSP) (Wakefield)
      388, *389*, *391*

crown retrenchment   156, *157*
culture and   158–159
dead wood   159–160
  fungi   159–160
ecosystems   153–154
  water in   160
lifecycle stages   156, *156*
pests and diseases *see* pests and diseases
site surveys   186–187
trees, legal protection of *see* legal protection
vernacular approaches
  coppicing   158
  pollarding   158–159
veteran tree   155, 156, 160–161
archaeology   149–152
  accuracy in restoration and *see* authenticity, historical
  archaeology watching brief   250
  conservation approach (National Trust)   14, 15
  Kenilworth Castle (Warwickshire)   62–63, *63, 64*
  land use and   150
  Monticello (Virginia, USA)   418–419
  surveys
    aerial surveys *see* aerial surveys
    dendro-archaeological survey   349
    geophysical survey   151
    site surveys   187, 248
  techniques   149–150
    desk-based studies   150
    excavation   151–152
    fieldwork   151
architecture
  definition   26
  garden buildings *see* historic structures
Areas of Outstanding Natural Beauty (AONB)   277
Arnos Vale Cemetery (Bristol)   288–289
art and design *see* design
Arthur Clough Oak (Oxford)   157, *158*
ash dieback   210
Attingham Park (Shropshire)   43–46
  Cedar Grove   45
  Garden Plantation   44
  Mile Walk   *43*, 43–44
  Miller Memorial Garden   44–45
  Stables Shrubbery   44
  Walled Gardens   45–46
    Bee house   45
    Gardener's entrance   46
    Plantation   45
    Polite entrance   45
authenticity, historical   4–5, 56
  archaeology and   58
  Privy Garden, Hampton Court Palace (London)   58, *59*
  archive records and   14–15
    see also researching historic places
  Cascade at Chiswick (London)   4, 6
  Elizabethan Garden (Kenilworth Castle)   340

of labour   224
  period-correct horticulture   2, 143, 146–148
  restoration and   15
  vegetation management and   218
autobiographical site, Monticello *see* Monticello (Virginia, USA)

Bains Report (1972)   96
Bali Province (Indonesia)   327–328
Bampfylde, Copelstone Warre (1720–1791)   345, *348*
  Hestercombe *see* Hestercombe (Somerset)
bandstands   200, *200*
  Roberts Park (Bradford)   *285*
Bath Spa Conservation Area   280, *280*
Battersea Park (London)   196
battlefields, registered   276
Baxter Park (Dundee)   199
Bickling Hall (Norfolk)   15–16
Bill of Quantities   244
Birkenhead Park (Birkenhead)   198–199
blind visitors
  access to historic landscapes *see* access and equality
  visitor information for   306
Blore, Edward (1787–1879), Crom Castle *see* Crom Castle (Northern Ireland)
Bretton Estate   385–386
Bridgeman, Charles (1690–1738)   43, 52, *52*
  Stowe   69
Brookwood Cemetery (Woking)   106–107
Brown, Lancelot (1716–83)   51, 280, *281*
  Croome Park (Worcestershire) *see* Croome Park (Worcestershire)
  Stowe   69, 70
buildings *see* historic structures
Buildings at Risk Register (English Heritage) *see* English Heritage
Burial Boards *see* cemeteries
Burra Charter   xvi

CAD (computer aided design)   249
Cadw   xviii, 292, 294
  see also Register of Parks and Gardens of Special Historic Interest in England
'Capability' Brown *see* Brown, Lancelot (1716–83)
cast iron furniture   87, 87–88
Castle Drogo (Dartmoor)   33–35, *34*, 277, *277*
  rose garden   34
  setting   33–34
cemeteries   101–115
  Arnos Vale Cemetery (Bristol)   288–289
  burial reform   102
  commercial (19th Century)   102–103
    Key Hill Cemetery (Birmingham)   104
    St James' Cemetery (Liverpool)   *103*, 103–104
  commercial (London)   104–105
    All Souls' Cemetery (Kensal Green)   104
    design   105

conservation of 111–114
    anti-social behaviour 112, *112*
    monuments 112–113, *133*
    vegetation removal 112
definition 101
early English cemeteries 102
General Cemetery Company 104–105
memorialisation 111
municipal 'burial board' cemeteries 107–110
    Clutton, Henry (1819–93) 110, *110*
    Crabbe Creeke, Christopher (1820–86) 109, *109*
    design 108–110
    Paxton, Joseph (1803–65) 107
    Plymouth Road Cemetery (Tavistock, Devon) 110, *110*
    Wimborne Road Cemetery (Bournemouth) 109, *109*
private to public burial 105–107
    Brookwood Cemetery (Woking) 106–107
    Loudon, John (1783–1843) 106
rauda, Alhambra Gardens (Spain) 426
twentieth-century 110–111
War Graves Commission 111
Central Park (New York, USA) 431–434
design 431–432
    designers 431–432
    Harlem Meer 433
history 431
    Moses, Robert 432
restoration 432–434, *433*
    conservation management plan 432
    funding 433–434
    maintenance and management 434
    visitor facilities 433
Charters (international law) 336
Cheetham Hill Park (Manchester) 96, *96*
children
    gardening skills 233, *233*
    as visitors
        Castle Drogo (Dartmoor) 34
        Central Park (New York, USA) 434
Chippendale, Thomas (1718–79) 80, *81*
Chiswick House and Garden (London) 60, *61*, 287, *287*
    Cascade 4, 6
    Italian Garden 63
climate change 208–219
    England Biodiversity Strategy (Defra, 2008) 217–218, *218*
    evidence for 208
    extreme weather events *208*, 208–210
        floods, droughts and temperature extremes *208*, 208–209, 216
        holistic view of impact 211–212
        storms (Great Storm, 1987) 209, 256
    Heritage Counts (English Heritage, 2008) 216
    pests and diseases *see* pests and diseases
    planning adaptation in historic parks and gardens 210–215

conservation management plans and 212, 216
holistic view and lessons from past 211–212
lawn 214
management experts 215
water features 214
projections 208–209
trees 211–213, *214*
    composition of woodland 214
    species selection, complexity 213–214, *214*
views and vistas 215
Clutton, Henry (1819–93) 110, *110*
cobbles 304–305, *305*
communal values 175
compartmentalisation of decay in trees (CODIT) 154
computer aided design (CAD) 249
computer simulation, garden design 5
conjectural detailing xvi, 64
    landscape 130
    planting 60
conservation, historic
    acceptance of change 26, 61–62
        Environment Agency, role in 61–62
    art and design *see* design
    definition 130
    evaluation 29
    legislation 249
        see also legislation; planning control
    management 26, 29
    National Trust's approach *see* National Trust
    new work *see* new work
    philosophical approaches *see* philosophical approaches
    plan *see* Conservation Management Plan (CMP)
    principles, evolution of 55–65
        Council on Monuments and Sites (ICOMOS) 56
        historicist 55
        modernist approach 55–56
    priority 29
    site archive 64
    site/setting 25
    staffing *see* staff
    surveys *see* surveys
    terminology xvi
    types of heritage
        cemeteries *see* cemeteries
        gardens *see* gardens
        landscape *see* landscapes
        plants *see* plants
    upkeep 26
    value of 9
    visitor traffic 18–19, *19*
    see also restoration
Conservation Areas
    designation 279–280
        Milton Abbas (Dorset) 280, *281*
        Parade Gardens (Bath) 280, *280*
        planning consent and 279

legal protection 295–296
trees in 298
'Conservation for Access' toolkit (National Trust) xxi–xxii, 19
Conservation Management Plan (CMP) xvi–xvii, xix, 68
  climate change and 212, 217
  content
    access and equality 302–303
    analysis of site/surveys 188
    appendices 190–191
    gazetteer 190
    key elements 129
    management action plan 190
  definition 173, 182
  development process 173, 176, 181–191
    research *see* researching historic places
    site surveys *see* surveys
    structure of 182–183
  examples
    Hackfall (Yorkshire) 378
    Stourhead gardens (Wiltshire) 373
    Stowe (Buckinghamshire) 68–69
    Strawberry Hill (Twickenham) 365
    Yorkshire Sculpture Park 387
  functions of 182
  Heritage Lottery Fund 173
  National Planning Policy Framework (NPPF) 176–177
  National Trust 13
  Ordnance Survey based replanting 178
  planning consent (local authority) and 176–177
  policies 189–190
    'vision statement' 189
  requirement for 178–179
  scope 176, 182
    Hagley Hall (Worcestershire) 176, *177*
  significance *see* significance
  usability 178
  values *see* significance
Conservation of Habitats and Species Regulations 2010 298–299
Conservation Statement/Statement of Significance (National Trust) 13
constraints, on site 247–254
  see also project management
consultants xix
contracts/contractors *see* project management
coppicing (trees) 158
copyright libraries 127
costings, project 239–242
  see also project management
Council on Monuments and Sites (ICOMOS) 56
Courances (Essonne, France) 1–2, *2*
Covent Garden (London) 266
Crabbe Creeke, Christopher (1820–86) 109, *109*
craft skills 145–146, 148, 228–230, *229*, 253–254
  apprentice system *see* apprentice system
  children's gardening skills 233, *233*

demographics 234–235, *235*
gardening, historical approaches 142–143
head gardeners *see* head gardeners
Heritage Lottery Fund (HLF) 287
skills shortage 148, 234
stone work 253–254
Worcester College (Oxford) 235, *235–236*
Crom Castle (Northern Ireland) 31–33, *32*
  house and gardens 31–32
    old house 32
    walled garden 33
  water 32–33
Croome Park (Worcestershire) 73–78
  Dunstall Castle *74*, 74–75
    restoration approach 75
    towers 75
  ecological investigation 74
  information resources 73–74
  Panorama *76*, 76–77
    philosophy of repair 77
  Pirton Castle 75–76
cropmarks 164
crown retrenchment (trees) 156, *157*
Crystal Grotto, Painshill Park (Surrey) 288
Crystal Palace Park (London) 93, *93*, 183, *183*, 196
  Iguanodons *284*
cultural landscapes 309, 321–329
  definition 321, 324
  examples
    Bali province (Indonesia) 327–328
    Lake District 322, *323*, 323–324
    Osun-Osogbo Sacred Grove (Nigeria) 327
    Val d'Orcia (Italy) *325*, 325–326
    West Lake (Hangzhou, China) 326, *326*
  impact of Word Heritage category 328
  international law 331
  legal protection of 331–337
  religion and 324, 327–328
  types 322, 324
  value of 324
  World Heritage Convention *see* World Heritage Convention (1972)
culture
  arboriculture and 158–159
  garden creation and 1–2
    Courances (Essonne, France) 1–2, *2*
    Hestercombe (Somerset) 1
  landscapes *see* cultural landscapes
Curtis, William (1746–99) 230
customary international law 333

dead wood removal 159–160
Defined Area Survey (DAS) 257–258
Defra (Department for Environment, Food and Rural Affairs), *England Biodiversity Strategy* (2008) 217–218, *218*
demolition 293
Derby Arboretum 91, *91*, 193

derelict land, vegetation management 222
Derry and Toms gardens (Kensington) 395, *396*
design xx, 26–28
　access and equality 304
　computer simulation 5
　definition 47, 48
　'design and build' contracts 244
　'designed landscape' 47–48
　designers 10–11
　　appointment of 240
　　contracts, designer *see* project management
　historic theories 358
　international approaches 6–7
　navigation (around gardens) 3
　new work *see* new work
　objectives 142
　plants 27–28, 142
　and process 47–54
　　Bridgeman, Charles (1690–1738) 52, *52*
　　Brown, Lancelot (1716–83) 51
　　Foxley (Herefordshire) 50
　　Hackwood Park (Basingstoke) 52, *52*, 53
　　Hawkstone Park (Shropshire) 53
　　Hearne, Thomas (1774–1817) 49, 49–50, *50*
　　Heveningham Hall (Suffolk) 51
　　Île de Peupliers (Ermenonville, France) 50–51
　　Price, Robert (1653–1733) 50
designation, national 255–260, 273–280
　battlefields, registered 276
　Buildings at Risk Register (English Heritage) *see* English Heritage
　Conservation Areas *see* Conservation Areas
　Defined Area Survey (DAS) 257–258
　designed landscapes 278
　examples/specific estates
　　Hackfall (Yorkshire) 378
　　Hestercombe (Somerset) 353–354
　　Lowther Castle and Gardens (Cumbria) 405
　legislation
　　Areas of Outstanding Natural Beauty (AONB) 277
　　Heritage Protection Reform 257
　　NPPF *see* National Planning Policy Framework (NPPF) (2012)
　　Town and Country Planning Act (1974) *see* Town and Country Planning (TCP)
　　World Heritage Sites 277
　listed buildings 273, 275
　　Dairy, Endsleigh (Devon) 273, *273*
　　listed building grades (TCP Act 1974) 263
　local
　　conservation areas *see* Conservation Areas
　　Tree Preservation Order (TPO) 278, *279*
　National Heritage Protection Plan *see* National Heritage Protection Plan (NHPP)
　National Parks 277, *277*
　parks and gardens 11, 271–281

Register of Parks and Gardens *see* Register of Parks and Gardens of Special Historic Interest in England
protection of heritage *see* legal protection
scheduled ancient monuments 275, *275*
Unified Designation System (UDS) 257
'designed landscape' 47–48, 255
　see also Register of Parks and Gardens of Special Historic Interest in England
Dillistone, George (1877–1957), Castle Drogo *see* Castle Drogo (Dartmoor)
disabled people *see* access and equality
Doulton Fountain (Glasgow Green) 201, *202*
Downton on the Rock (Herefordshire) 48–49
droughts 209
Dunham Massey 20, *20*
Durlston Castle (Dorset) 278, *279*
Dutch elm disease 210, *210*

'easy access', access and equality *see* access and equality
Easy Access to Historic Landscapes (EA, 2005) xxi–xxii, 302–303, 306
Echinacea purpurea 221
ecological surveys 74, 187
ecosystems, trees as 153–154
Elizabethan Garden (Kenilworth Castle, Warwickshire) 339–344
　archive records 339
　authenticity of interpretation 340, *343*, 343–344
　Tudor garden 64, 341
　features
　　fountain 341–342, *342*
　　'Queenes seat of freestone' 342
　　terrace balustrade and arbours 342, *343*
　planting 341
　surveys
　　aerial 340
　　excavation 341
　　preservation of historic remains 341
　　trial trenches *340*, 340–341
enclosure maps 122
Endsleigh (Devon) 273, *273*
England
　England Biodiversity Strategy (Defra, 2008) 217–218, *218*
　English Heritage *see* English Heritage
　European Landscape Convention (ELC) 316
　Natural England 387
　Register of Parks and Gardens *see* Register of Parks and Gardens of Special Historic Interest in England
　Richard Review of Apprentices in England (Richard, 2012) 232–233
England Biodiversity Strategy (Defra, 2008) 217–218, *218*

English Heritage xv, xvii, 28
   aerial photographs collection 166
   Buildings at Risk Register 67
      Yorkshire Sculpture Park 386
   Conservation Principles
      adaptation decisions and 212
      values *see* significance
   Easy Access to Historic Landscapes (EA, 2005) 302–303, 306
   Elizabethan Garden *see* Elizabethan Garden (Kenilworth Castle, Warwickshire)
   establishment of 267
   Heritage Counts (English Heritage, 2008) 217
   legal protection of historic structures 294
   National Mapping Programme (NMP) 168
   primary values 60
   Register of Parks and Gardens *see* Register of Parks and Gardens of Special Historic Interest in England
   significance and values *see* significance
Environment Agency, role in conservation 61–62
environmental impact assessment 293–294
Equality Act (EA) 2010 302
   see also access and equality
estate maps 123
Europe, Grenada convention 335
European Landscape Convention (ELC) 309–320, 335–336
   adoption 313, *314*
   aims *311*, 311–312, *312*
   functions 310–313
      scope 310–311
   historic gardens and designed landscapes 318–319
   origins 309–310
   principles 312
   in UK 313, 315–318
      England 316
      implementation 315, *316*
      Northern Ireland 317
      regional/local level 317–318
      Scotland 316
      training 313, *315*
      Wales 317
evidential values xv–xvi, 175
'evocations', restoration *vs.* 15

financial considerations xxii
   Bill of Quantities 244
   conservation approach (National Trust) 19–20
   costing the project 239–242
   grant schemes 56–57
      criteria 57
      Heritage Lottery Fund *see* Heritage Lottery Fund
   Hestercombe (Somerset), funding of 353
   income generation (National Trust) 11–12
   lump sum contract 243–244

   National Trust acquisition criteria 11
   public money 56–57
floods *208*, 208–209, 214
Florence convention *see* European Landscape Convention (ELC)
flowers
   flower garden conservation (National Trust) 17–18
      National Trust Plant Propagation Centre (PPC) 17
   plant health and 17–18
      Phytopthoras 18
   in public parks *203*, 203–204
   rose garden, Castle Drogo (Dartmoor) 34
   Sissinghurst Castle (Kent) 17, *18*
   Summerfield's rose 228, *229*
'Forest Chairs' 83–84
Foxley (Herefordshire) 50
fungi, tree-related 159–160
furniture, garden 79–89
   design
      cast iron furniture *87*, 87–88
      colours 84–85, *86*
      wrought iron 87
   examples
      Hestercombe *see* Hestercombe (Somerset)
      Kenilworth Castle 342, *343*
   functions 79
   reinstated, positioning of 350
   seating *see* seating, garden

Garden City Movement xvii, 261
Garden History Society xvii, 28, 293
garden management 24, 26, 29
gardens 1–7
   components 24
   conservation xxi, 267–268
   designation, national *see* designation, national
   design of *see* design
   European Landscape Convention (ELC) 318–319
   evolution of 2
      Stowe 1, *3*, 4, *5*
   examples/specific gardens
      Aberglasney Gardens (Carmarthenshire) 248
      Alhambra Gardens (Spain) *see* Alhambra Gardens (Spain)
   features
      buildings *see* historic structures
      furniture *see* furniture, garden
      water *see* water
Garden History Society 28, 293
gardening, historical approaches 142–143
historically significant gardens
   archival records *see* researching historic places
   international significance 10
   long-term strategy 28–29
   National Trust 10
   Statement of Significance xvi, xix, xxii, 13, 29

management of *see* management, historic garden
planning adaptation for climate change *see* climate change
planning permission   292
registers   1
types of   1, 3–4, *4*, 23–24
  descriptions of   6
  roof gardens *see* Roof Gardens (Kensington, London)
  see also specific garden types and plantations
upkeep *see* maintenance/repair, garden
what to conserve?   xxi, 1–7
'Gardens of the Nations' (Rockefeller Center)   395
gazetteer (CMP)   190
General Cemetery Company   104–105
geophysical survey   151
Gilpin, William Sawrey (1762–1843) *see* Crom Castle (Northern Ireland)
Great Storm (1987)   209, 256
Grenada convention   335

Hackfall (Yorkshire)   377–383, 409
  Aislabie, William   377
  conservation
    building restoration   379–380, *380*
    funding   378–379
    management plan (CMP)   378
    objectives   378
    paths and materials   382
    permissions required   379
    water features (Top Pond, Fountain Pond)   380, *381*
  designation, national   378
  history   377
  visitor facilities   382
    car parking   382
    interpretation boards   382
  Woodland Trust, role of   378
Hackwood Park (Basingstoke)   52, *52*, *53*
Hagley Hall (Worcestershire)   176, *177*
Hampton Court Palace (London)   58, *59*
Hanbury Hall (Worcestershire)   *16*, 16–17, *17*
Hancock, Ralph (1893–1950)   395, *402*
  'Gardens of the Nations' (Rockefeller Center)   395
Handsworth Cemetery (Birmingham)   109–110
Handsworth Park (Birmingham)   97
hard landscape features   241–242
Haverfield, John (1744–1820)   134
Hawkstone Park (Shropshire)   53
head gardeners   27, 230, 232
  apprenticeship and   232
health *see* public health
health and safety (site)   249
Hearne, Thomas (1774–1817)   *49*, 49–50, *50*
Heritage Counts (English Heritage, 2008)   xxii, 216–217

Heritage Lottery Fund (HLF)   xviii, 283–289
  awards and funding   xix
  cemeteries, country parks, seaside promenades and urban squares   288–289
    Arnos Vale Cemetery (Bristol)   288–289
  changing role of   289
  conservation management plan (CMP) process   173, 286–287
  Easy Access to Historic Landscapes (EA, 2005)   302–303, 306
  funding criteria   97–98, 288
  innovative, supporting   286
  parks and gardens   97–98, 198, 283
    Crystal Grotto, Painshill Park (Surrey)   288
    Hackfall (Yorkshire)   378–379
    Handsworth Park (Birmingham)   97
    Roberts Park (Bradford)   *285*
    Urban Parks Programme *see* Urban Parks Programme
  scope   283
  staff   287
  strategic aims   285
  training, funding for   287–288
Heritage Protection Reform   257
Hestercombe (Somerset)   1, 345–356
  archive records   348
    dendro-archaeological survey   349
  buildings/'seats'   350–353
    Chinese Seat   352–353
    Gothic Alcove   351, *351*, *352*
    Octagon Summerhouse   353
    reinstated seating   350
    Rustic Seat   351
  designation, national   353–354
  Formal Garden   346
  funding   353
  future development   354–355
  history   345–346
  lost eighteenth-century garden   347–349
    Pear Pond   *348*, 348–349, *349*
    woodland   347–348
  Victorian Shrubbery   346–347
  Victorian Terrace   346
Heveningham Hall (Suffolk)   51
historicist approach   55
historic structures
  Buildings at Risk Register (English Heritage) *see* English Heritage
  conservation legislation *see* legislation
  garden buildings   25, 67–78
    Alhambra   424
    Croome Park *see* Croome Park (Worcestershire)
    evidence   68
    Hestercombe *see* Hestercombe (Somerset)
    philosophical approaches   67
    Pirton Castle (Worcestershire)   75–76
    Stowe *see* Stowe (Buckinghamshire)
    Yorkshire Sculpture Park   388, *390*, *391*

441

legal protection *see* legal protection
listed *see* designation, national
public park buildings   198–199
   Baxter Park (Dundee)   199
   bridges   198–199
   Jephson Gardens (Leamington)   199
   lodges   199
urgent repairs   296
historic value *see* significance
Hoare, Colt (1758–1838)   35–36
Hoare II, Henry   372–373
horticulture *see* plants/planting
Housing and Town Planning Acts (1909)   262
  see also Town and Country Planning (TCP)

Iford Manor (Bath)   228, *229*
Île de Peupliers (Ermenonville, France)   50–51
income generation (National Trust)   11–12
international approaches
  garden design   6–7
  Heem Parks in Netherlands   225–226
  Spain *see* Alhambra Gardens (Spain)
  USA
    Central Park *see* Central Park (New York, USA)
    Monticello *see* Monticello (Virginia, USA)
  see also cultural landscapes
international law   331–337
  Charters   336
  definitions/meanings   331–333
  ELC *see* European Landscape Convention (ELC)
  Grenada convention   335
  monuments and cultural landscapes   331–337
    legal instruments for   334–335
    protection in other legal areas   336–337
    recognition of people in   335–336
  site/landscape protection, avenues   333–334
  Stockholm Declaration on Human Environment   336
  types   332
    customary international law   333
    treaties   332–333
interpretation boards
  Hackfall (Yorkshire)   382
  Strawberry Hill (Twickenham)   365

Jefferson, Thomas (1743–1826)   413–414
  Monticello *see* Monticello (Virginia, USA)
Jekyll, Gertrude (1843–1932)
  Castle Drogo   33
  Hestercombe (Somerset)   1, 345, 346
  War Graves Commission cemetery   111
Jephson Gardens (Leamington)   199

Kelmarsh Hall (Northamptonshire)   88, *88*
Kenilworth Castle (Warwickshire)   62–63, *63*, 64, 339
  Elizabethan Garden *see* Elizabethan Garden (Kenilworth Castle, Warwickshire)
  'Tudor' Garden   64

Kensington Roof Gardens *see* Roof Gardens (Kensington, London)
Kent, William (1685–1748)   69, 358
Key Hill Cemetery (Birmingham)   104

Lake District   322, *323*, 323–324
landscapes   xviii
  access to *see* access and equality
  Alpine Region   335
  change over time   167
  conservation of   128–130
  cultural *see* cultural landscapes
  definition   48, 312
  'designed landscape'   47–48, 255
    see also Register of Parks and Gardens of Special Historic Interest in England
  hard landscape features   241–242
  legal protection   311, 333–334, 335–336, 336–337
    ELC *see* European Landscape Convention (ELC)
    planning permission   292
  and literature   358–359
  locally designated designed landscapes   278
  soft landscape features   242
  urban *see* urban landscapes
land use, archaeology and   150
Langham, Robert (c.1535–79/80) *see* Elizabethan Garden (Kenilworth Castle, Warwickshire)
lawn
  climate change   214
  foot-traffic damage   18–19, *19*
legal protection   291–300, 302
  access and equality *see* access and equality
  conservation areas   295–296
  of cultural landscapes   331–337
  demolition   293
  environmental impact assessment   293–294
  of historic structures   294–295
    curtilage of listed building   294–295
    English Heritage, role of   294
    Grenada convention   335
    listed in their own right   294
    planning permission requirement   295
  international law *see* international law
  landscape *see* landscapes
  legislation
    NPPF *see* National Planning Policy Framework (NPPF) (2012)
    see legislation
  minor works   292–293
  monuments   262, 296, 331, 333–334, 336–337
  parks and gardens   291–292
    Alhambra Gardens (Spain)   428
    Hackfall (Yorkshire)   378
  planning permission *see* planning control
  scheduled monuments   296
  trees   296–297, 296–298
    in conservation areas   298
    retention of trees during work   250–251

TCP (Trees) Regulations 2012   297–298
Tree Preservation Order (TPO)   278, *279*, 288, 401
Trees in relation to construction (BS, 2012)   250–251
urgent repairs   296
of wildlife   298–299
  Conservation of Habitats and Species Regulations 2010   298–299
  Wildlife and Countryside Act 1981   298
see also Town and Country Planning (TCP)
legislation   249, 261–270, 292
  building conservation   265–267
    Covent Garden (London)   266
    Longleat House (Wiltshire)   266, *267*
  disabled access   302
    Equality Act (EA) 2010   302
  early development controls   261, 262
  ELC *see* European Landscape Convention (ELC)
  English Heritage *see* English Heritage
  Garden City Movement   261
  garden conservation   267–268
  Housing and Town Planning Acts (1909)   262
  key figures
    Abercrombie, Patrick (1879–1957)   265
    Ruskin, John (1819–99)   263
    Williams-Ellis, Clough (1883–1978)   265
  NPPF *see* National Planning Policy Framework (NPPF) (2012)
  Planning Act (1990)   268
  Planning Policy Statement 5 (PPS 5)   268
  Town and Country Planning Act *see* Town and Country Planning (TCP)
LiDAR (Light Detection and Ranging), airborne   167, 186
literature, and landscape   358–359
Longleat House (Wiltshire)   266, *267*
Loudon, John (1783–1843)   106
Lowther Castle and Gardens (Cumbria)   405–412, *406*
  design   408–410
    Edwardian structures   410
    South Lawns   409, 411, *411*
  designation, national   405
  history   405–408
    World War II   407, *408*
  management strategy   412
  restoration   408, 410–412
    archive records   408
  trees   411–412
  viewing terrace   407, *407*

maintenance/repair
  definition   xvi, 130
  garden   26
    architecture   26
Major, Joshua (1786–1866)   92

management, historic garden   141–148
  craft skills *see* craft skills
  gardening, historical approaches   142–143
  plant cultivation *see* plants/planting
  public access   141–142
    show gardens   142
management action plan (CMP)   190
management plan *see* conservation management plan (CMP)
Manwaring, Robert   86, *86*
maps   118, 120–123, 184–185, *185*
  from aerial surveys *see* aerial surveys
  enclosure maps   122
  estate maps   123, 124, *124*
  map regression   185, *185*
    methods   185–186
  Ordnance Survey (OS) mapping   120–121, *121*
  Pitzhanger Manor and Walpole Park (Ealing)   *185*
  of public parks   123
  role of *see* researching historic places
Marnock, Robert (1800–89)   174
  Bretton Estate   386
Marot, Daniel (1661–1752)   80, *80*, *81*
materials
  choice of   251
  sourcing   250
memorialisation
  in cemeteries   111
  in parks, public *see* parks, public
  War Graves Commission   111
Milton Abbas (Dorset)   280, *281*
modernist approach   55–56
Monticello (Virginia, USA)   413–420
  archaeological survey   418–419
  design   414–415
    development of the garden   416, *417*, 418
    pavilion   416, *417*, 418, 419
  garden produce   415, *415*, 419
  Jefferson, Thomas   413–414
  restoration   418–419
monuments
  cemeteries   112–113, *133*
  legal protection   262, 296, 331, 333–334, 336–337
  scheduled ancient monuments   275, *275*
Moseley Old Hall (Wolverhampton)   16
Moses, Robert (1882–1947)   432

National Heritage Protection Plan (NHPP)   259
  activity plans   259
National Mapping Programme (NMP)   168
National Parks   277, *277*
National Planning Policy Framework (NPPF) (2012)   xviii, 176–177, 268–269, 271–272, 292
  historic conservation   268–269, *269*
  protection of heritage assets   272
  roles   xviii
  'significance'   272, 293

sustainability, definition of   271–272
World Heritage Sites   277
see also legal protection
National Trust   xvi, xx–xxi
    access and equality   304
        'Conservation for Access' toolkit   19
        Easy Access to Historic Landscapes (EA, 2005)
            302–303, 306
    acquisition criteria   11–21
        financial considerations   11
        historical significance see gardens
    conservation approach   9–21, 13, 62
        archaeology   14, 15
        Conservation Management Plan   13
        Conservation Statement/Statement of
            Significance   13
        financial implications   19–20
        innovation   20–21
        re-creation see re-creation (National Trust)
        restoration strategy   15–16
        'spirit of place'   xix, 13–14
        SSSI designation   14
        wildlife   14
    founding   xvii
    gardens   xx
        conservation approach to   9–21
        design   xx, 10–11
        role of   xx–xxi, 9
        uniqueness   xx
    history of   9–10, 28, 264
    membership   xx
    National Trust Act (1907)   264–265
    plants
        grading of collections   12–13
        Plant Conservation Centre   13
        Plant Propagation Centre (PPC)   17
    properties see National Trust properties
    staff   xx
        head gardeners   19–20
        levels   20
    visitor traffic (gardens)   xxi
        see also visitors
    volunteers   20
National Trust properties
    Attingham Park see Attingham Park
        (Shropshire)
    Bickling Hall (Norfolk)   15–16
    Castle Drogo see Castle Drogo (Dartmoor)
    Crom Castle see Crom Castle (Northern
        Ireland)
    Croome Park see Croome Park (Worcestershire)
    Dunham Massey   20, *20*
    Dunstall Castle see Croome Park (Worcestershire)
    Hanbury Hall (Worcestershire)   16, 16–17, *17*
    Moseley Old Hall (Wolverhampton)   16
    Nostell Priory (Yorkshire)   40–42
    Pirton Castle see Croome Park (Worcestershire)
    Sissinghurst see Sissinghurst Castle (Kent)
    South West Coast Path   268, *269*

Stourhead gardens see Stourhead gardens
    (Wiltshire)
Stowe see Stowe (Buckinghamshire)
Natural England   387
navigation (around gardens)   2–3
see also paths
New Hall (Essex)   169, 169–170
new work   62
    adaptation   62
Northern Ireland
    European Landscape Convention (ELC)
        317
    Northern Ireland Environment Agency, listed
        structures   294
Nostell Priory (Yorkshire)   40–42
    style of design   *41*, 41–42
    plants   42

oblique aerial photographs   166
Olmstead, Frederick Law (1822–1903)
    431–432
Olympic Park (London)   99, 223
online resources   120, 127
Orchardleigh (Somerset)   178, *178*
Orchidaceae   145
Ordnance Survey (OS)
    mapping   120–121, *121*
    replanting   178, *178*
Osun-Osogbo Sacred Grove (Nigeria)   327

Painshill Park (Surrey), Crystal Grotto   288
Parade Gardens (Bath)   280, *280*
parkland plan see conservation management plan
    (CMP)
parks, public   91–100, 193–205
    anti-social behaviour   197–198
    community groups   285–286
    design   93–94, 194–196
        Battersea Park (London)   195–196
        Crystal Palace Park (London)   195
        Victoria Park (London)   195, *195*
    designation, national see designation, national
    early examples   92, 193–194
        Derby Arboretum   91, *91*, 193
        Prince's Park (Liverpool)   91–92
    early twentieth century   196
    examples/specific parks
        Abbey Park (Leicester)   94, *94*
        Birkenhead Park (Birkenhead)   198–199
        Cheetham Hill Park (Manchester)   96, *96*
        Crystal Palace Park (London)   93, *93*
        Handsworth Park (Birmingham)   97
        Olympic Park (London)   99
        Painshill Park (Surrey)   288
        Peel Park (Salford)   202
        Philips Park (Manchester)   194, *194*
        Pulhamite waterfall (Madeira Walk, Ramsgate)
            204, *204*
        Thames Gateway Parklands   98

West Park (Wolverhampton)   203, *203*
Wicksteed Park *see* Wicksteed Park (Kettering, Northamptonshire)
features
  bandstands *see* bandstands
  buildings *see* historic structures
  plants in *see* plants
function   93
funding   96–98, *99*
  Heritage Lottery Fund *see* Heritage Lottery Fund
  Urban Parks Programme/Parks for People *see* Urban Parks Programme/Parks for People
Government initiatives   98
maintenance   197–198
Major, Joshua   92
maps of   123
memorialisation in   95, *95*, 201
  Doulton Fountain (Glasgow Green)   201, *202*
  People's Park (Halifax)   201
palm houses and winter gardens   201
  Sefton Park (Liverpool)   201
Parks and Gardens Database (PGUK)   287
Paxton, Joseph   91–92, 93, *93*, 195
planning adaptation for climate change *see* climate change
post World War II   198–204
public health and   197
reports/studies
  Bains Report (1972)   96
  Public Parks Assessment   284
  Public Walks report (SCPW, 1833)   91, 193
systems, chains and parkways   197
visitor facilities   94–95
  children, facilities for   136–137, *137*
paths
  Hackwood Park   52, *52*, *53*
  South West Coast Path   268, *269*
  see also navigation (around gardens)
Paxton, Joseph (1803–65)   91–92, 93, *93*, 107, 195, 199
Peel Park (Salford)   201
Pencarrow (Bodmin, Cornwall)   275, *275*
People's Park (Halifax)   201
pests and diseases   209–210, 211, *211*
  ash dieback   210
  Dutch elm disease   210, *210*
Philips Park (Manchester)   194, *194*
philosophical approaches   58, 60, 67, 129–139
  buildings, garden   67
  definition of terms   129
  examples/specific parks
    Alexandra Road (Camden, London)   138–139
    Chiswick House and Garden (London)   60, *61*
    Panorama, Croome Park (Worcestershire)   77
    Pitzhanger Manor and Walpole Park (Ealing)   135
    Wicksteed Park (Kettering, Northamptonshire)   137

National Planning Policy Framework (NPPF) (2012)   272
  significance and   129
Phytopthoras   18
  Nostell Priory (Yorkshire)   40
Pitzhanger Manor and Walpole Park (Ealing)   *185*
  significance   *132*, 132–135
    aesthetic and design value   134–135
    conservation philosophy   135
    Haverfield, John and   134
    Regency landscape   134
    social connections   134
    villa design   134
planning control/systems   271–281
  Ancient Monuments   275–276
  Hackfall (Yorkshire)   378
  listed buildings   273–275
  local listing   278–280
  minor works   292–293
  NPPF *see* National Planning Policy Framework (NPPF)
  Planning Act (1990)   268
  planning applications (local authority)
    Conservation Area designation and   279
    conservation management plan (CMP) and   176–177
    protection from   10
  planning permission, requirement for   292–293
    historic structures   295
    landscapes and gardens   292
  Planning Policy Statement 5 (PPS 5)   268
  registered parks and gardens   276–278
  Town and Country Planning *see* Town and Country Planning
  see also legal protection
plantations
  Monticello *see* Monticello (Virginia, USA)
  Strawberry Hill *see* Strawberry Hill (Twickenham)
Plant Conservation Centre (National Trust)   xx, 13
Plant Propagation Centre (PPC) (National Trust)   17
plants/planting   227–237
  communities *see* vegetation management
  conjectural planting   60
  conservation of   *25*, 25–26
  cultivation   143–145, 147, 227–237
    design (garden) and   142
    Plant Propagation Centre (PPC)   17
    propagation   144–145
    training and pruning   147–148
  design using   27–28
  diseases *see* pests and diseases
  expertise/knowledge   227–228
  flooding, impact of   209
  flowers *see* flowers
  gardens
    authenticity   2
    Strawberry Hill (Twickenham)   363–365
  irrigation/drainage *see* water
  management *see* vegetation management

national grading for collections   12–13
National Trust acquisition criteria   12, 12–13
necessity for conservation   xvi
period-correct   143, 146–148
Plant Conservation Centre   13
in public parks
   flowers   203, 203–204
   Madeira Walk (Ramsgate)   204, 204
   Peel Park (Salford)   201
   trees and shrubs   201–203
   West Park (Wolverhampton)   203, 203
role of   12
soil pH   143
trees see arboriculture
pollarding (trees)   158–159
Pope, Alexander (1688–1744)   358
Powis Castle (mid-Wales)   27, 27
Price, Robert (1653–1733)   50
Prince's Park (Liverpool)   91–92
Prior's Garden (Strawberry Hill, Twickenham)   360, 362, 367
Privy Garden, Hampton Court Palace (London)   58, 59
project management   239–246
  certificates, progress payment   245
  client
    brief   241
    knowledge   239
  contractors   240–241, 251–252
    team composition   244–245
    tendering   240
    termination   245–246
  contractual obligations   242–246
    Bill of Quantities   244
    continuity contracts   244
    'design and build' contracts   244
    fees (lump sum)   243–244
    key elements   243
    standard contracts   242–243, 244
  costing the project   239–242
  designer   240
  hard landscape features   241–242
  sequence of works   249–251
    archaeological watching brief   250
    legislative constraints   249
    materials see materials
    protected species   250
    public access and opening   250
    retention of trees   250–251
    seasonal factors   250
    Trees in relation to construction (BS, 2012)   250–251
  site archive   64
  site management see site
  site surveys see surveys
  soft landscape features   242
  specifications   242
propagation, plant   144–145
protection of historic sites see legal protection

pruning   147–148
public access to historic gardens   141–142
public burial see cemeteries
public engagement, parks   285–286
public health
  access to outdoors and   301–302
  recreation and   197
public parks see parks, public
Public Parks Assessment   284
public perceptions, of horticulture   234
Public Walks report (SCPW, 1833)   91, 193
Pulhamite waterfall (Madeira Walk, Ramsgate)   204, 204

reconstruction, definition   xvi, 130
re-creation (National Trust)   16–17
  Hanbury Hall (Worcestershire)   16, 16–17, 17
  Moseley Old Hall (Wolverhampton)   16
Register of Parks and Gardens of Special Historic Interest in England   xvii, 47, 255–260, 276, 292
  cemeteries   101
  first edition   255–256
  format   276
  grading   258–259
  importance   xviii
  Review Programme (1993–2000)   xvii–xviii, 256
  selection criteria   258
  upgrade programme (1996–2000)   256
  see also Cadw; *specific parks and gardens*
religion
  cultural landscapes   324, 327–328
  gardens and   421–422
repair, definition   xvi, 130
repositories see researching historic places
researching historic places   xxii, 117–128
  conservation management plan (CMP) and   176, 183–186
  images   186
  library   126, 126–127
    copyright libraries   127
    topographical images   127
  local authority records   125–126
  maps and plans see maps
  online resources   120, 127
  preliminary research   118–120
    Access to Archives (A2A)   118–119
  primary sources   68
  private estate papers   123, 123–124
    types   124
  record offices   125, 125
  repositories   118–119, 120
    catalogues   120
  secondary sources   68
  statutory information   119–120
  storage and reference system   117–118
    digital format   118
    hard copies   118

surveys *see* surveys
topics
    buildings, garden   68
    historically significant gardens   14–15, 33, 56
    written material   184
    see also specific sites
restoration   xvi
    authenticity and   15
    conservation-friendly forms   57–58
    definition   xvi, 130
    of designed landscape   51
    'evocations' *vs.*   15
    non-authentic   58
    plan *see* conservation management plan (CMP)
    Strawberry Hill *see* Strawberry Hill (Twickenham)
    see also conservation
Richard Review of Apprentices in England (Richard, 2012)   232–233
Risby Hall (East Yorkshire)   165, *165*
Roberts Park (Bradford)   *285*
Roof Gardens (Kensington, London)   393–404
    adaptations
        1978   400
        1987   400
        2008   400–401
        permissions required   400
    construction   395–399
    design   395, 396, *396*, *397*, 402
        English Woodland Garden   398, *398*, 402
        Spanish Garden   396–397, *399*
        Tudor Courts   *397*, 397–398
    'Gardens of the Nations' (Rockefeller Center) and   395
    Hancock, Ralph   395, *402*
    Kensington, history of   393–395
        Barkers   394–395
        Biba   399
        Kensington Palace   393–394
    tea (sun) pavilion (Derry and Toms gardens, Kensington)   395, *396*
    Tree Preservation Orders (TPO)   401
    water drainage   395–396, 401
rose garden, Castle Drogo (Dartmoor)   34
Ruskin, John (1819–99)   xvii, 263

Sackville-West, Vita (1892–1962)   38
St Agnes Park (Bristol)   *126*
St James' Cemetery (Liverpool)   *103*, 103–104
Sayes Court (London)   9–10
Scotland, European Landscape Convention (ELC)   316
seating, garden   79–80, 83–84
    cast iron   *87*, 87–88
    Chinese Style   84, *84*, 85–86
    designers
        Chippendale, Thomas (1718–79)   80, *81*
        Marot, Daniel (1661–1752)   80, *80*, *81*
        Yates, James   87, *87*
    'Forest Chairs'   83–84
    'Queenes seat of freestone' (Kenilworth Castle)   342
    rustic   86, *86*
    Shell Seat (Strawberry Hill)   362, *364*, *366*, 366–367
    Windsor chairs   *82*, 82–83
    Windsor seat   83
    wooden   88, *88*
Sefton Park (Liverpool)   201
Sensory Trust   302
Sherwood Forest   155, *155*
show gardens   142
significance of gardens   23–29
    assessment of   131–132, 188
        levels   131–132
    conservation management plan (CMP) and   129, 188
    definition   129, 130–131
    examples
        Alexandra Road *see* Alexandra Road (Camden, London)
        Pitzhanger Manor and Walpole Park *see* Pitzhanger Manor and Walpole Park (Ealing)
        Wicksteed Park *see* Wicksteed Park (Kettering, Northamptonshire)
    factors affecting   189
    historically significant gardens *see* gardens
    in National Planning Policy Framework (NPPF) (2012)   272, 293
    philosophical approaches and   129
    value(s)   130–131, 173–179, *175*
        aesthetic   130, 175
        communal   131, 175
        English Heritage's definition   175
        evidential   130, 175
        guidance resources   175–176
        historical   131, 175
        nature of   173–174
        of trees   250–251
Silbury Hill (Avebury)   264, *264*
Sissinghurst Castle (Kent)   17, *18*, 38–40, *39*, 221, *222*
    gardeners   39–40
    Nuttery   221, *222*
    Sackville-West, Vita   38
site (conservation)
    archive   64
    management   247–254
        protection of assets on site   252
        services, utilities and drainage   253
        soil structure   252
        subsoil disposal   253
        temporary access routes and hard-standing areas   252
    surveys *see* surveys
site surveys *see* surveys

Slaney, Robert (1791–1862)   91, 193
snow melt   209
Soane, John (1753–1837)   132–135
Society for the Protection of Ancient Buildings (SPAB)   xvii
soft landscape features   242
soil
　pH   143
　protection of assets on site   252
　subsoil, disposal of   253
soilmarks   165
South West Coast Path   268, 269
Spain, Alhambra see Alhambra Gardens (Spain)
'spirit of place' (National Trust)   xix, 13–14
sports turf usage   18–19, 19
SSSI designation   xv, 14
staff
　access and equality and   306
　authenticity of labour   224
　conservation   27
　contracts, designer see project management
　head gardeners   27, 230
　Heritage Lottery Fund (HLF)   287
　history of   146
　National Trust see National Trust
　recruitment of   234
　traditional skills see craft skills
　vegetation management expertise   225
St Agnes Park (Bristol)   126
Statement of Significance   xvi, xix, xxii, 13, 29
stewardship   xxii
St James' Cemetery (Liverpool)   103, 103–104
Stockholm Declaration on Human Environment   336
Stokes, G. F (1827–74)   199
storms (Great Storm, 1987)   209, 256
Stourhead gardens (Wiltshire)   23, 24, 35–38, 371–376, 372
　conservation management plan (CMP)   373
　Convent   37, 37
　history   371
　lower lake and cascade   37–38
　National Trust, role of   372
　Six Wells Bottom   36
　Temple of Apollo   371, 372, 374–376, 375
　Terrace   36–37
　Turner's Paddock   36
Stowe (Buckinghamshire)   xxi, 1, 3, 4, 5, 68–73
　Basilican Chapel   71
　Bridgeman, Charles   69
　Chinese House   71–72
　general plan (1739)   4, 5
　historical evidence   14–15
　Kent, William   69
　New Inn   xxi, 72–73
　　visitor facilities   73
　restoration strategy   15, 68–69
　Temple of Concord and Victory   70, 70–71
　Temple of Friendship   71, 72
　twentieth-century changes   70

Strawberry Hill (Twickenham)   357–369
　archive records   373–374
　design   359–365, 360, 361, 363
　　features   362–363
　　Prior's Garden   360, 362, 367
　　Shell Seat   362, 364, 366, 366–367
　history   358–359
　planting   363–365
　　trees   366
　restoration   365–367
　　conservation management plan (CMP)   365
　visitor information   306
Summerfield's rose   228, 229
surveys   xix–xx, 186–188, 249–254
　aerial see aerial surveys
　Alhambra Gardens (Spain)   428
　archaeological see archaeology
　covered and hidden items   248
　　trial holes   248
　drawings   249
　　CAD (computer aided design)   249
　ecological surveys   187
　health and safety (site)   249
　topographical see topographical survey
　trees   186–187
　visitor usage   187–188
　walkover   186, 186, 354–355
　Yorkshire Sculpture Park (YSP) (Wakefield)   387
sustainability
　definition   271–272
　vegetation management and   224
Sustaining the Historic Environment (1997)   xviii

temperature extremes   208–209
Temple of Concord (Stowe) see Stowe (Buckinghamshire)
temporary custodianship   xxii
tendering for contractors   240
Thames Gateway Parklands   98
topiary gardens   55
topographical survey
　library images   127
　site management   247
Town and Country Planning (TCP)
　Housing and Town Planning Acts (1909)   262
　Order (1995)   293
　(Trees) Regulations 2012   297–298
　TCP Act (1932)   262
　TCP Act (1944)   xvii
　TCP Act (1974)   263
　　listed building grades   263
　TCP Act (1990)   297
　see also legal protection
training, Heritage Lottery Fund (HLF)   287–288
treaties   332–333
trees see arboriculture

trial holes/trenches 248
  Elizabethan Garden (Kenilworth Castle) 340, 340–341
turf, sports turf usage 18–19, 19

UK, ELC see European Landscape Convention (ELC)
UK Climate Change Risk Assessment 2012 211
UNESCO see World Heritage Convention (1972)
Unified Designation System (UDS) 257
urban landscapes
  Amstelveen Heem Parks (Netherlands) 225–226
  parks in 137–138
Urban Parks Programme/Parks for People xviii, 283–286
  Public Parks Assessment 284
  Victoria Park (London) 284–285
USA
  Central Park see Central Park (New York, USA)
  Monticello see Monticello (Virginia, USA)

Val d'Orcia (Italy) 325, 325–326
value, of cultural landscapes 324
values (in heritage management) see significance
Vaux, Calvert (1824–95) 431–432
vegetation management 219–226
  authenticity and 218
  biological life 219
  derelict land 222
  design 219
  Echinacea purpurea 221
  examples
    Amstelveen Heem Parks (Netherlands) 225–226
    Olympic Park (London) 223
    Sissinghurst Castle (Kent) 221, 222
  national strategies 225
  plant
    communities 218–221
    movement 218
  principles 226
  stability 222
  staff expertise 225
  sustainability and 224
  tree canopy expansion 218
  see also plants
vertical aerial photographs 166
veteran tree 155, 156, 160–161
Victoria Park (London) 195, 195, 284–285
'vision statement' 189
visitors
  access and constraints on work 250
  demographics
    amateur gardeners as 227
    children see children
    disabled people see access and equality
  experience, 'spirit of place' (National Trust) 13–14
  foot-traffic xxi, 18–19

'Conservation for Access' toolkit 19
Easy Access to Historic Landscapes (EA, 2005) 302–303, 306
restrictions 19, 427
sports turf usage 18–19, 19
information 306
  Hackfall (Yorkshire) 382
  Strawberry Hill (Twickenham) 365
navigation (around gardens) 3
surveys of usage 187–188
visitor facilities
  Central Park (New York, USA) 433
  Hackfall (Yorkshire) 382
  in parks 94–95
  Stowe (Buckinghamshire) 73
  travel and transport 305–306
volunteers 20

Wales 299
  Cadw see Cadw
  European Landscape Convention (ELC) 317
  listed structures 294
walled gardens, Crom Castle 33
Walpole, Horace (1717–97) 357
  Strawberry Hill see Strawberry Hill (Twickenham)
Walpole Park (Ealing), significance see Pitzhanger Manor and Walpole Park (Ealing)
water
  in ecosystems 160
  features (historic parks and gardens)
    Alhambra Gardens (Spain) 426
    climate change and 214–215
    Crom Castle (Northern Ireland) 32–33
    Doulton Fountain (Glasgow Green) 201, 202
    fountain (Kenilworth Castle, Warwickshire) 341–342, 342
    Hackfall (Yorkshire) 380, 381
    lower lake and cascade (Stourhead gardens) 37–38
    Pear Pond (Hestercombe, Somerset) 348, 348–349, 349
  irrigation/drainage
    Alhambra 426–427
    Monticello 419
    Roof Gardens (Kensington, London), use in 395–396, 401
weather
  climate change see climate change
  extreme weather events see climate change
West Lake (Hangzhou, China) 326, 326
Wicksteed, Charles (1847–1931) 135–137
Wicksteed Park (Kettering, Northamptonshire), significance 135–137, 137
  conservation philosophy 137
wildlife
  Croome Park 74
  legal protection see legal protection
  protected species on site 250
  Wildlife and Countryside Act 1981 298

Williams-Ellis, Clough (1883–1978)   265
Wimborne Road Cemetery (Bournemouth)   109, *109*
Windsor chairs   *82*, 82–83
Windsor seat   83
Woodland Trust, Hackfall (Yorkshire)   378
Worcester College (Oxford)   235, *235–236*
World Heritage Convention (1972)   321
    cultural landscapes *see* cultural landscapes
    function   322–323
    World Heritage Sites   277, 334
World War II
    aerial surveys   167
    Lowther Castle and Gardens (Cumbria)   407, *408*
    public parks after   198–204

Wrest Park (Bedfordshire)   *164*, 164–165
wrought iron furniture   87

Yates, James   87, *87*
Yorkshire Sculpture Park (YSP) (Wakefield)   385–391
    conservation management plan
        aims   387
        historic structures   388, *390*, *391*
        surveys   387
        woodland   388, *389*, *391*
    history   385
        Bretton Estate   385–386
        Marnock, Robert (1800–89)   386

WILEY Blackwell

Also available from Wiley Blackwell

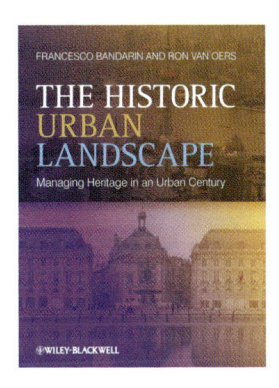

The Historic Urban Landscape
Francesco Bandarin, Ron van Oers
978-0-470-65574-0

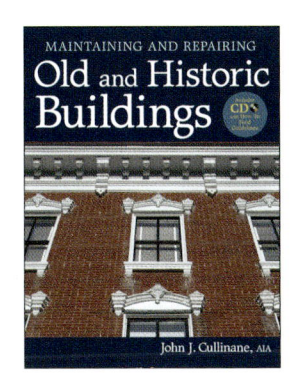

Maintaining and Repairing Old and Historic Buildings
John J. Cullinane
978-0-470-76757-3

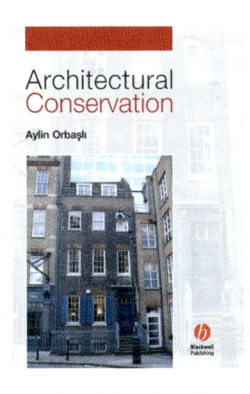

Architectural Conservation
Aylin Orbasli
978-0-632-04025-4

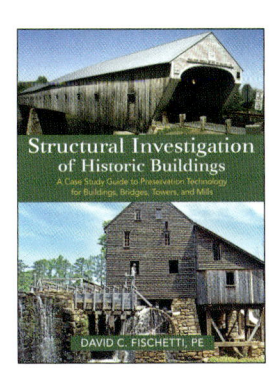

Structural Investigation of Historic Buildings
David C. Fischetti
978-0-470-18967-2

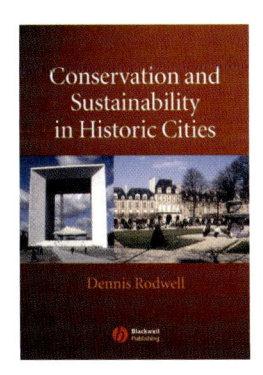

Conservation and Sustainability in Historic Cities
Dennis Rodwell
978-1-4051-2656-4

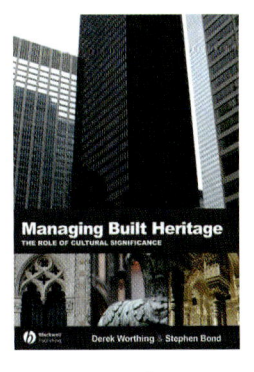

Managing Built Heritage
Derek Worthing, Stephen Bond
978-1-4051-1978-8

www.wiley.com/go/construction